Leading Successfully in Asia

Kim Cheng Patrick Low

Leading Successfully in Asia

Second Edition

 Springer

Kim Cheng Patrick Low
Kazakh Leading Academy of Architecture
& Civil Engineering (KazGASA)/Kazakh American University (KAU)
Faculty of Construction Technologies,
Infrastructure and Management
Almaty, Kazakhstan

Illustrations and cartoons are drawn by the author Kim Cheng Patrick Low

ISBN 978-3-319-71346-5   ISBN 978-3-319-71347-2   (eBook)
https://doi.org/10.1007/978-3-319-71347-2

Library of Congress Control Number: 2017959637

Printed on acid-free paper

This Springer imprint is published by Springer Nature
The registered company is Springer International Publishing AG
The registered company address is: Gewerbestrasse 11, 6330 Cham, Switzerland

To God, my family, friends and the many parties I've worked with.

Acclaims for Leading Successfully in Asia

"Here is A MUST-READ for successful leadership skills. Read on... The book contains excellent leadership tips and pointers, the Asian way."

Dr. Ali Yusob Mohd. Zain
Associate Professor
School of Business Management
Universiti Utara Malaysia

"Prof. Low has applied and injected much of the Chinese, Indian and Asian philosophies into leadership insights, discussions and applications. I really like it!"

Ang Sik Liong
MBA, M.Phil. (London University), Ph.D. (Universiti Brunei Darussalam)
Principal, Chung Ching Secondary School, Brunei.

"A HIGHLY RECOMMENDED RESOURCEFUL BOOK ON LEADERSHIP IN ASIA. For me, it is a library of leadership ideas and insights. Go ahead, read it and gain!"

Ms Makhabbat Yermekbayeva
MBA, Ph.D. Executive Candidate
Kazakh British Technical University (KBTU)
Republic of Kazakhstan

"AN INVALUABLE BOOK to help one acquire tips to be a better leader! Great thanks to Prof. Low: You can now read *Leading Successfully In Asia* to your advantage!"

Tiong Soon King
Principal Consultant and Strategist
Eagle's Wings Consultancy & Training Solutions (East Malaysia)

"My thumbs-up for *Leading Successfully In Asia*. A remarkable resource, it tackles the essence as well as cultural perspectives of leadership in Asia."

Associate Professor Dr. Habrizah Hussin
Ph.D. Entrepreneurship, Cranfield School of Management
Cranfield University (United Kingdom); Expert in Entrepreneurship
Othman Yeop Abdullah Graduate School of Business
Universiti Utara Malaysia, Sintok Kedah, Malaysia

"A good read. One needs to understand one's followers. The use of cultural understanding of their followers by the leaders is crucial for significant and sustained leadership and organizational growth and development. And once again, Patrick has put it well; *Leading Successfully in Asia* provides a compelling cultural perspective and insights on leadership, it is energizing yet practical guide on the issue."

Professor Dr. Balbir B. Bhasin
Ross Pendergraft Endowed Professor of International Business
College of Business, University of Arkansas—Fort Smith, USA
Author of *Doing Business in the ASEAN Countries, Assessing and Mitigating Business Risks in India* and *Burma:* Business and Investment Opportunities in Emerging Myanmar

"A PURE TREASURE HOUSE! An inspirational and motivational volume; readers have got much to gain from Prof. Low's book. *Leading Successfully In Asia* has USEFUL TIPS AND PRACTICAL ADVICE! I have used this as a REQUIRED TEXT in my graduate classes and students benefited immensely."

G. Saravanan
ND CH, D.Nutr, D.MLD, Ad.HRM, Reiki Master, MATMS
Trainer and Naturopathic Practitioner, Australia and Singapore.
Centre of Integrated Medicine

"*Leading Successfully In Asia*—in a capsule! Excellent read; Prof. Low's book has indeed much to offer to help you in your leadership. USEFUL TIPS!"

Selvathurai
Business Owner, Humberlincoln

"Definitely AN EXCELLENT READ. What I like best, are your checkpoints and reflection time at the end of each chapter. It is unquestionable that your responsible nurturing begins on the personal level which is very important when you're sharing something as crucial as to "how to enhance our leadership potentials", in this present fast changing world where being true to our human community as a whole is a key factor. A 'MUST READ' if you wish to enhance your leadership aptitudes."

Mohan N. Sajnani
IPMA, UK, Author/Business Owner and Small Business Consultant
Certified Professional Trainer

"Brilliant! Besides the tips and pointers, I like the simple and easy-to-understand style of writing; it's perfectly timed as Asia is also leading vibrantly!"

Alvin Tan
Networkpreneur and Business Owner,
Brunei Darussalam

"Leading is too important to leave it to chance, here is the invaluable book! It's a treasury of tips and pointers!"

Dr. Francis Or
Ph.D., M.Sc., ND, BCH, CI, CT.NLP, CM.NLP
Naturopath, Nutritionist, and Herbalist
Board Certified Hypnotherapist/Certified Instructor (NGH)
Certified NLP Trainer/DBA Supervisor, University of South Australia

"A very practical-oriented text. I like the advice. A book that helps to re-consider Asia and leadership with different eyes."

Dr. Hugo Gaggiotti
Bristol Business School (UK)

"A must-read, I have my praises for *Leading Successfully In Asia*. Prof. Low's book is a goldmine of leadership ideas and tips. Buy it, read it; and you'll gain from it."

Professor Dr. Choon Kong
Kazakh American University (KAU)
Almaty, Kazakhstan

"Sensing the significant amount of Professor Dr. Patrick Low's investment in the lives of people of Kazakhstan as well as that of several Asian countries, and understanding the core values found from his interactions with them, I find his book a precious resources yielding insights to the leadership issues not only in Kazakhstan but also within Asia and across the globe."

Dr. Sathiya Mathew
Deputy Director, Institute of Applied Data Analytics,
University of Brunei Darussalam.

"Thumbs-up! Readers will certainly gain from this scholarly work; distilled wisdom captured and now for use and applications."

Preface

Are you a leader? Do you lead as part and parcel of your day-to-day business?

If so, you probably know and do the basics, yet may somehow feel that you need to develop that little extra to give or help you grow that edge. You want to tap your potential a little further. You want to grow.

Besides, both China and India are growing politically and economically, and people want to trade and do business in these countries. Asia is rising, and the book has been written with the idea that more people will want to do business in Asia, and "Leading Successfully in Asia" would help them most. In other words, to state the aims of the book more explicitly, it is written, more so, for practitioners and business managers/people. Unlike Max Weber (1947) who distinguished between traditional, charismatic and legal-rational authority and leadership, the author does not distinguish between the different types of leadership (such as key differences between political leaders, business leaders or religious leaders) as he still believes that what's critical is to distinguish successful leaders from non-successful, Tsunami leaders (Low and Teo 2015), ineffective (or non) leaders, incompetents and even sycophants, and it is hoped that readers have these in mind when reading the book.

This author also believes that he, being born in Asia, trained in Asian thoughts, philosophies and values as well as being Western educated in post-independent Republic of Singapore, and being a practitioner-cum-academician and because of such a background and experiences, is blessed and has truly inherited much fortune! And what's more, they're to be shared.

Proverbs, countless insights exist in them, are usefully short and concise. And whether old or new, they are memorable sayings based on an important fact of experience that is considered true, hence, full of wisdom, by many people. My dear fellow readers, in this book, I have purposefully written it spiced with powerful inspirational proverbs and quotes (life's instructions and motivations) to spur us on—after all, we, harbouring much untapped potential, are all diamonds in the making.

Apart from my reliance on potent Asia and Western inspiring proverbs and sayings, I also have based my writings on my previous journal writings and publications as well as my observations, research and talking to various business people in the respective countries mentioned. On the selection of countries, it is based on the author's preference in terms of his research, observations and experiences in these countries as well as his understanding of the culture and people in the countries so selected.

Though the book *Leading Successfully in Asia*, which is easy to follow, is structured to be read from the beginning to the end, I hope readers will find it easy to dip in or refer to find the information they need most, at the time when they need it.

The chapters in the book are run in this fashion:

Chapter 1 "Leaders, Managers and Bosses" covers the differences between leaders, managers and bosses, who tells and who persuades and the process of leadership. It talks about who inspires and who motivates?

Chapter 2 "Leadership and the Importance of Example" surveys the importance of examples by leaders. In the chapter introduction, the concept of Tsunami leaders (weak or incompetent leaders) is also introduced. Overall, this chapter speaks of role modelling and examples as a key influencing factor.

Chapter 3 "Leadership and Ethics" discusses Confucian ethics and social responsibility, the Golden Rule and responsibility to the stakeholders as well as the issue of leaders, loving all and serving all.

Chapter 4 "Leadership and Motivation" looks into the Confucian philosophy (the eight tenets of self-cultivation, learning and social relationships) as sources of motivation among the Chinese. The chapter also examines Lao Tzu's three treasures, Ta Mo, self-growth and leadership, motivation the Sun Tzu (Sun Zi) way, gaining and losing influence as well as leading and managing talents.

At this point, the author wishes to highlight that the chapters (Chaps. 9–11) on Malaysia, Brunei Darussalam and Singapore have a section each on the country's context (history, culture and population), but this section has been intentionally left out in Chaps. 5–8. A compelling reason being the author's wanting to give himself and/or even readers a free-flow rather than a seriously controlled approach.

Chapter 5 "Leadership in China, Mongolia and Tibet" analyses and highlights leading the Confucius way, Lao Tzu's three treasures, leadership and organisational growth, leading the Kuan Yin way, the way of the dragon, the Bruce Lee way as well as the leadership ways of Li Ka Shing (a business leader) and Mao Zedong (a political figure). The leadership as prevailed in Mongolia and Tibet is also discussed. Interestingly, some critics have pointed out that "notwithstanding the importance of China as the second largest economy and the most populous country in the world, there is too much emphasis on Confucius and his teachings". Nonetheless, the author wishes to stress that the roots of the Chinese thinking and psyche and values have in most ways affected their present behaviour and actions; they also mould the person's leadership characteristics such as compassion, patience and humility. Truly a person's/leader's philosophical and/or religious bent and values must not be discounted and, in fact, be factored in when assessing how he or she leads or influences others.

Some critics also smartly question the author's inclusion of Bruce Lee as a leader: Is he a leader? Other critics even say that Bruce Lee's inclusion is justifiable if the book were a martial artist written for those readers interested in fighting and the arts of self-defence. To this author, such comments perhaps make us think further, food for thought? Nonetheless, it is interesting to note that Bruce Lee is still being admired and/or idolised although he died a few decades ago. And put it in another way, some may also argue that as long as a person can influence others and have a following, he or she can be identified as a leader.

Chapter 6 "Leadership in India" delves into leadership, corporate culture and the Hindu Trinity: Brahma, Vishnu and Shiva. The discussions in this chapter also include the leadership wisdom of the Bhagavad Gita, Hanuman (the Monkey God), Buddhism and that of Mahatma Gandhi. Proactivity and Hinduism is also examined. Besides, a section on Indian business leaders brings the readers to the ways of the contemporary business leaders.

Chapter 7 "Leadership in Japan" examines the leadership as exemplified by the Samurais. Also discussed include Zen and leadership, Matsushita and Nemoto's leadership principles as well as the key leadership ways of Akiro Morita and Soichiro Honda. Interesting team leadership lessons are also derived from *Shinkansen*, the Japanese bullet train.

Chapter 8 "Father Leadership in Kazakhstan" looks into the definition of father leadership and the applications and benefits of father (parental) leadership in small business management: the 5Cs, and the chapter is devoted to its discussions within the small and medium business context and Kazakhstan. Note that, however, the 5Cs can also be applied to project management. The author has basically spent some years teaching and living in Kazakhstan, he loves this Central Asian country, and hence the further reasons why Chap. 8 on Kazakhstan is included in the book.

Chapter 9 "Leadership in Malaysia" discusses the leadership of Hang Tuah (during the time of the Malaccan Sultanate in the 1400s), Islamic values and the father leadership in present-day Malaysia. The leadership ways of the Malaysian business leaders are also discussed in this chapter.

Interestingly, some critics have also questioned the author's focus on and inclusion of Hang Tuah, a legendary warrior from Malacca in the fifteenth century? What do you think? Hang Tuah is said to be held in the highest respect, even in present-day Malay culture, and he is arguably the most famous and familiar figure in Malay history/literature and Malay studies; besides, the legendary leader Hang Tuah also epitomises the concern or topic of blind obedience versus being inquisitive and questioning the authorities/those in power. So is there any other BUT(s)? Perhaps, there is now more food for further thinking (writing)?

Chapter 10 "Father Leadership in Negara Brunei Darussalam" examines National Ideology: MIB: *Melayu Islam Beraja* (Malay, Islam and Monarchy), people and culture, planning and directing as well as the leadership ways at both the national and community levels. Some Islamic values are examined. In this second edition, the author has also included the world of *silat* and its parallel with leadership.

Chapter 11 "Leadership in Singapore" looks into father leadership, the Singapore way; the leadership ways of Lee Kuan Yew, one of Singapore's founding fathers; and the leadership ways of Singapore Incorporated and that of the

Singapore business leaders. I have also added a section on "The Peranakans, Values and Leadership in Singapore". Knowing and reading this section will also enable the readers to, in most part, understand the Peranakans and leadership milieu in Malaysia.

Chapter 12 "Women and Mother Leadership" discusses the traits and characteristics of mother leadership including nurturing, caring and showing concern. The downsides and benefits of mother leadership as well as the way forward for women leaders are also examined in this chapter.

Chapter 13 "Leadership and the Twelve Chinese Zodiac Animals" highlights the traits and characteristics of leadership under each of the zodiac animals. True, some critics may even complain about the usefulness (let alone argue that the chapter be excluded; after all, this is a book on leadership and not a horoscope or zodiac book written for those readers interested in their fortunes) of this chapter, which is based on folklores or customs. However, it should be interestingly noted that this is a useful chapter in so far as much wisdom truly exists in this chapter. Leadership, life, living and doing business is about understanding the common people, their thinking and practices. And the author believes many reasons stand and speak for this chapter: First, it is a refreshing approach to the study of leadership and it reflects, in some ways, biomimicry or what man can learn from nature and, in this case, what leaders and ordinary people can learn from these animal traits. Second, some of these folklores affect business practices such as gift-giving and other customs as one would read accordingly in the chapter. Third, Chap. 13 too helps us to develop ideas and/or implicitly if not explicitly answer "what does successful leadership mean?" and "what are the traits of a successful leader?"

Chapter 14 "Leadership and Change" examines change, weak leaders and leading change and what do leaders need to do when leading change. It also discusses Tao and leading change as well as leading change the Confucius way.

Chapter 15 "Team Leadership and Teambuilding" looks into the *Shinkansen* effect on team leadership and teamwork, Tao and teambuilding.

Chapter 16 "Resilience and Leadership in Asia" discusses the ways of being resilient, the CORE qualities and ways of boosting endurance and being resilient, and these include learning from nature. Included in this chapter are also sections on "Buddha, Buddhism and Being Resilient" and "Being Resilient, the Confucian way". In this book, I have also added "The Way of the Warrior", the resilience of the Kazakhs/Kazakhstanis.

Chapter 17 "Using Soft Power" discusses what is soft power, applying soft power the Confucius way, applying soft power the Lao Tzu (the Tao) way and applying soft power the Chuang Tzu (Zhuang Zi) way.

Chapter 18 "Food for Thoughts and Actions—From Baby Steps to Bold Charges" points to the way forward—the leader's vision, mission, values, renewing the mind, the leader's action plan—enhancing, empowering, extending and expanding, as well as what leaders should be thinking about and working upon...

Chapter 19 "The Future—Going Further, Doing More, Going Stronger" further explores what successful leadership means; leaders need to move from being just a leader to being a leadership titan. The author begins the chapter by looking at complacency, what leaders should avoid. Leaders must be stronger. This chapter is also about how leaders drive, save and/or sustain their organisations, and it's also about how leaders power if not safeguard the future; leaders must cultivate a garden of greatness, building creativity and innovation in individuals and organisations as well as being entrepreneurial. The chapter too underscores that making our planet green is good—going more green and adopting earth (universe)-friendly ways can save Earth, further making a leader successful.

Happy reading!

Singapore/Kazakhstan

Kim Cheng Patrick Low

Acknowledgements

I thank several people who helped me in writing this book; they have helped along in my life journey in which I have picked up the various leadership tips and pointers. Many great thanks go to my widow mother, my wife and children as well as my brother and sister. Indeed, a great many people and many great people have provided their support and encouragement to which I am ever appreciative, thankful and grateful.

I sincerely appreciate the views and time given by several corporate leaders and many other parties I had met, worked with and interviewed earlier as well as the helpful comments made by the Editor, Reviewers and Publisher to an earlier draft of this book.

Introduction

Asia has the longest history, and it is the world's most populous continent.

Asia is situated in the northeast of the Eastern Hemisphere, east of the Eurasian landmass; it is bounded on the east by the Pacific Ocean, on the south by the Indian Ocean and on the north by the Arctic Ocean and is neighbour to Europe to its west. Asia undoubtedly has been home to various glorious cultures that have made a significant impact on our lives. It is no surprise or wonder then that the name Asia, in the old Assyrian language, means "land of the sunrise" or "the East", for the dawn of human civilisation began in Asia and spread across continents. Major world religions like Judaism, Christianity, Buddhism, Hinduism and Islam too have its roots in Asia.

Today's Asia is rising, and the world, together with the major urban, commerce and education centres, is getting to be more cosmopolitan and multiculturally diverse.

Asian leadership styles and ways prevail in Asia, and we need to identify, be aware and/or know them. Truly, Asian leadership styles and ways are certainly quite different from the Western leadership styles. For, in fact, so many years and even today, Asian universities and colleges teach Western leadership styles to Asian students, and Asian students should, on other hand, learn, if not read about, or be exposed to Asian values and Asian leadership ways; after all, they are living in Asia and when exposed to Western styles of leadership would know what these Asian styles and ways are.

From this book comes "*Leading, the Asian way*". Prof. Dr. Patrick Low wants to indicate and clarify Asian values through leadership styles and ways so that students—whether in Asia or in the West, in their respective countries—would know better and understand their own country's leadership ways, and if they (including the Western students) happen to live or work in any country within Asia, they would be aware, know, or be familiar with the respective values, leadership style(s) and/or ways.

Readers will be able to create their own mental map of the various Asian values and cultures and come to a better understanding of the Asian leadership styles and ways. Indeed, knowing these values will help them to understand the present.

Besides, it is worthy to note that today's global leader/manager should be an alchemist, blending Western and Asian ways to make leadership gold and attain success when leading and managing his or her people.

Contents

About the Author

Kim Cheng Patrick Low Currently, Prof. Dr. Patrick Low has been appointed as the Dean, Faculty of Construction Technologies, Infrastructure and Management, KazGASA: Kazakh Leading Academy of Architecture and Civil Engineering, and Director of Scientific Center and Kazakh American University/International Educational Corporation, Almaty, Kazakhstan.

Prof Dr. Low is also the Visiting Professor (Human Resource Management) in the University of the South Pacific. Prior to this, Prof. Dr. Patrick Low was teaching Managing Negotiations, Leadership, Change Management, Management and Organisational Behaviour at the graduate level and Leadership Basics, Challenging Leadership, Business and Society, Organisational Development and Change, Organisation Design and Analysis, Organisational Leadership Issues at the undergraduate level in the Universiti Brunei Darussalam. He was the Visiting Professor in the University of Malaya's Graduate Business School in January–February 2007. His most recent appointment was the Associate Dean and Full Professor of Management and Marketing in the Kazakhstan Institute of Management, Economics and Strategic Research (KIMEP)/Acting Dean Summer 2 (2006). With an International Ph.D. in Business and Management from the University of South Australia, Prof. Dr. Patrick Low also holds a Master of Business from the CURTIN University of Technology and a BA (Singapore). His other qualifications include the following:

Chartered Marketer (CIM, UK)

Chartered Consultant and an Accredited Professional Consultant (American Consultants' League)

Graduate Diploma in Marketing (UK)

Graduate Diploma in Personnel Management (SIM/SIPM)

Graduate Diploma in the Marketing of Financial Services (MIS)

Certificate in Administrative Management/Organisation and Methods

Prof. Dr. Patrick Low is also the licensed administrator, user and interpreter of MBTI personality type profiling for several years. A behavioural consultant, he is also DISC certified.

The Researcher of the Year 2004/2005 for Bang College of Business, KIMEP, Prof. Dr. Patrick Low has been a human resource professional since the late 1980s. He has work experiences in the Civil Service, electronics, trade and financial industries. He has handled HRD projects/assignments in all ASEAN countries,

Bangladesh, Hong Kong and Sri Lanka. His previous appointment was with a foreign bank as the Senior Training Manager, Management Development (Asia-Pacific Region). During 1995–2006, Patrick run his own consultancy (BusinesscrAFT™ Consultancy), undertaking consultancy work for various companies in the region, including Standard Chartered Bank, Matsushita/Panasonics and several other companies. He has also been the examiner for Ph.D. theses of several universities including Aligarh Muslim University (Marketing), Auckland University of Technology (Negotiation) and University of South Australia (Organisation Behaviour/Human Resource Management).

Multilingual and multicultural, Prof. Dr. Low's training areas include effective selling, negotiation/marketing and personal effectiveness/leadership for organisations from industries like electronics, communications, courier/transport, tourism, petroleum, financial services and trading. With many years of teaching experience and having taught in various local and overseas institutions such as the Malaysian Institute of Management (MIM), Prof. Dr. Low has also conducted exclusive fraud management courses for banks and companies. He has also taught Human Resource Management, Organisational Behaviour, Marketing and International Business at the Universities of London, Bradford (UK), Murdoch and Monash (Australia) and Ngee Ann Polytechnic (Singapore).

Awarded the MIS/Standard Chartered Gold Medal Award—1994 for being the most outstanding graduate in the Graduate Diploma in Marketing of Financial Services, Prof. Dr. Low is also the author of 14 books including the following:

1. *Strategic Customer Management: Enhancing Customer Retention and Service Recovery*, BusinesscrAFT Consultancy, Singapore, 2000 (one of Border's top ten best-selling books as featured in the *Asian Entrepreneur*).

2. *The Power of Relationships: How to Boost Your Business and Lead a Happier Life*, BusinesscrAFT™ Consultancy, Singapore, 2001. ISBN 981-04-4045-6 (used as a reading reference in one of BusinesscrAFT Training Consultants Sdn Bhd's programs, "Critical Skills in People Management" in Malaysia).

3–4. *Strategic Customer Management: Enhancing Customer Retention and Service Recovery*, BusinesscrAFT™ Consultancy, Singapore, **Revised 2002**: 2nd edition with another chapter added (one of Border's top ten best-selling books as featured in the *Asian Entrepreneur*) ISBN 981-04-1914-7 **Revised 2006**: 3rd edition for *Post-Soviet Societies' New Generations, Caspian Publishing House*, Almaty, Kazakhstan.

5. *Developing True Leadership Potential*, The Publishing Consultant/Market Asia Pte. Ltd., Singapore (co-authored with Theyagu, Daniel, Ph.D.), 2003. ISBN 981-04-7611-6.

6. *Team Success: How to Create and Manage Winning Teams*, Singapore, BusinesscrAFT™ Consultancy and Humber Lincoln Resources, Singapore, 2003. ISBN 981-04-8702-9.

7–8. *Sales Success: Up Our Sales*, Operativnaya Pechat, Kazakhstan (co-authored with Ibrayeva, Elmira, Candidate of Science), 2005/2003. **Revised 2006**: 2nd edition with **Russian** translation, "S-Print" (I.P. Lukyanova, Almaty, Kazakhstan) ISBN 9965-25-574-1 (3rd edition is on the way).

9. *Training Success: Understanding the Learning and Training Essentials*, ICFAI University Press, India (2005). ISBN 81-7881-587-7.

10. One of the co-authors: *A Handbook: (2006) Business Leadership in Central Asia*, collection of essays and papers written with other professors and students, Caspian Publishing House, Almaty, Kazakhstan.

11. Strategic Thinking and Insights (2018; forthcoming) (co-author: Dr. Teo Teck Choon), Partridge.

12. Knowledge Management (co-author: Prof NP Singh) current draft is being further researched/ revised for publications.

13. *Corporate Culture and Values: Perceptions of Corporate Leaders of Co-operatives in Singapore*. VDM-Verlag—UK/USA *ISBN-10: 3639151674/ *ISBN-13: 978-3639151671.

14. *Successfully Negotiating in Asia*, Springer, Heidelberg, Dordrecht, London, New York, published in February 2010; Refereed Publication. Website: http://www.springer.com/business/business+for+professionals/book/978-3-642-04675-9 ISBN: 978-3-642-04675-9.

His most recent publications include *Successfully Negotiating in Asia* (published by Springer, out in February 2010) and *Corporate Culture and Values— Perceptions of Corporate Leaders of Cooperatives in Singapore* (out in May, 2009).

Prof. Dr. Patrick Low can be contacted at patrick_low2003@yahoo.com

Leaders, Managers and Bosses

Introduction

> If you do not climb high to get a distant view, how can you appreciate the magnificence of the rivers flowing eastward into the sea? (Chinese proverb)

We live and thrive in a world of diversity of ideas, viewpoints and perspectives. And let us grow in a setting where our minds are not entrapped but open, finding a million flowers growing and blooming.

Many theories of leadership hail from or are anchored in Western theories of leadership. Perhaps, as it is often said that history is usually written by the victors, reflecting the fact that many Asian countries except for the Kingdom of Thailand has been conquered and colonised for several centuries by the Western powers. These Western powers include chiefly Britain, France, Germany, Holland and Spain with the latecomer United States in the Philippines though the Portuguese were the first Europeans to come to Asia, after arriving in Goa in India in the fifteenth century, and then capturing Melaka in 1511, causing the collapse of the then Malaccan Sultanate founded by Parameswara in 1401. (Parameswara took the reign name of Sultan Iskandar Shah.) Even China suffered the utter humiliation of the cutting of the Chinese melon by the European powers during the Anglo-Chinese Wars in what was dubbed as the Opium Wars, beginning in 1824 onwards.

We can also add that the West, particularly the United States of America (USA) is very good in its public relations and marketing, it markets its image, ideas and values well. And America is not just a country, but also "a brand" (Anholt 2004, p. 6).

Perhaps, our mindset has been very much cast, and stereotypes rigidly formed; hence Western concepts, ideas and values of leadership predominate, if not prevail. And this calls for a mind growth, a breakthrough, and an orientation towards greater examination of Asian ideas, concepts and theories of leadership and organisation behaviour.

© Springer International Publishing AG 2018
K.C.P. Low, *Leading Successfully in Asia*,
https://doi.org/10.1007/978-3-319-71347-2_1

Even business and leadership lessons are also derived from Western cartoons. A case in point is "Beep! Beep! Competing in the Age of the Road Runner", written by Chip R. Bell and Oren Harari in 2000.

When examining business and society, among other things, Lawrence and Weber (2008, pp. 48–50) spoke of social responsibilities and how corporate social responsibility began, but they were shown how it began in the United States and their origins were subsumed under the general charity principle and the stewardship principle. Here, to make it more complete, Confucian ethics and other Asian ethical thoughts and philosophies should have been imported or discussed here.

A key point to note is that Asia is rising. Attention needs to be paid to the Asian countries; these countries, particularly China and India, are growing. Asian markets are growing. And according to market research firm TNS, India and China have more wealthy families than European countries. And based on TNS's 'Global Affluent Investor' study, India, China and Brazil have, in fact, overtaken many European countries in the measure of consumer wealth. Each of these countries has more than three million affluent households with over $100,000 in funds for investments (Overdorf 2011).

What more, Asia too is noted to be friendly and "warmth". Asians are also said to be "authentic". "Authentic" and "warmth" are the people's qualities seen to be key factors in travellers' decision-making processes. At the recent ASEAN Tourism Ministers' conference in Brunei Darussalam in January 2010, the slogan "Southeast Asia: Feel the warmth" was adopted, intending to attract tourists in medium and long-haul markets such as the United Kingdom, Australia, India, and North America. (The Brunei Times 2010, p. 1).

"Authentic" and "warmth" qualities should be capitalised when leaders are leading and motivating the people of these countries. The people sincerely work hard. And such authenticity and warmth can be tapped to attract tourism, more tourist monies, and higher economic growth, but more importantly, better than materialistic gains, to achieve a better life and living, making, in a way, the world a better place.

Asia appears to have several noble traditional values that can be subscribed, and their practices be emulated by other countries. And some of these Asian values are, in fact, promoted by some of its leaders. Singapore—majority of its population consists of Chinese, for example, promotes some 'traditional' Confucian values, having the *Confucian Heritage* national culture (Low 2006, 2009, 2011). Service quality values are also promoted as in its national carrier, Singapore Airlines. The Chinese have a saying that goes, "Customers are jade, merchandise is grass". So to the traditional Chinese, the customers are valued, and being pragmatic (Low 2007), the Singapore Government would certainly want to promote such values to make the Republic attractive (both to investors and tourists) and economically viable.

Next, it is also worthy to note that most Asian societies are collectivistic yet when it comes to examining teambuilding and boosting team spirit, strangely enough, most authors cite Western authors and their Western perspectives. There's nothing wrong with the latter; what this author firmly believes is that there are many Asian concepts, if not ideas and/or values of teamwork that can be applied to leadership, teamwork, and organisational development and change, and the benefits reaped.

This book *Leading Successfully in Asia* is thus written with an attempt to fill this void or gap so that Asian concepts, ideas, theories and experience of leadership are explored and examined. The latter is more apt at this juncture with the opening, development and growth of what this author calls the Dragon and the Elephant, that is, the People's Republic of China and the Democratic Republic of India.

Next, it is necessary that we examine the differences between leaders, managers and bosses as it would determine the way(s) in which we, as leaders, lead—whether we are, in fact, bossing around, managing or administrating, or leading.

Differences Between Leaders, Managers and Bosses

There are differences between leaders, managers and bosses.

Who Call the Shots?

When the king makes a mistake, all the people suffer. (Chinese proverb)

Bosses are owners of the enterprises, employing the managers and leaders.

Managers are administrators, getting instructions from the bosses and administering.

Leaders direct, and implement things from the strategic perspective.

Who Want Profits and Who Pursue the Vision?

A leader has to look beyond his nose. (Konosuke Matsushita)

Bosses want profit$; they are largely concerned with profit$.

Leaders seek growth and changes while managers being administrators seek stability.

Leaders have the vision, and would like to see changes while managers prefer to have stability. The latter prefer the status quo since things would be easier to handle and deal with. Things are done based on established set of procedures or rules.

Who See Short-term? and Who See Long-term?

The fish sees the bait not the hook. (Chinese saying)

The rich man plans for the future, but the poor man for the present. (Chinese proverb)

The manager sees the short-term. The leader sees the long term. Leaders have the vision. Leaders need to have the helicopter vision or the eagle's eyes; they need to have the necessary foresight.

Who Is More Concerned with Process and People?

A leader should make it clear why his cause is a just one. (Matsushita Konosuke)

Leaders are more concerned with the process and people; they aim for, getting the results as well as ensuring that the people do their jobs happily. Leaders cherish and appreciate their people. Leaders take care of their precious, especially their talents. [Here, we need to take note that most times, as supervisors, we often take for granted the knowledge and skills of our staff—because they make their job looks easy and it's not until when they have left for greener pastures and we try to find someone with similar qualifications and/or experiences when truly appreciate what we had.]

Who Is More Concerned with Procedures and Rules?

In life, many situations and variables exist. The leader needs to have guidelines, not rigid rules to suit or meet such situation(s) accordingly. (Patrick Kim Cheng Low)

Managers are more concerned with the procedures, and the means or the way things are done. The manager focuses on systems and structures (Bennis 2003). They are more inclined to prefer the way in which things have been done. They respect the sacred cows; in most ways, they favour stability.

Leaders should know the differences between rules and guidelines. Rules are rigid; they are dead and inflexible, not catering to the needs of the organisation especially when they are obsolete and not revised to suit the changing circumstances and situations. Rules can be suffocating to the people when, as a leader, one's approach is operating with a manual after manual of rules and regulations.

People are intelligent; they know what they are doing, and as a leader, we know that they are going to make good decisions. Empower them to be creative when dealing with service excellence and/or when serving customers within general guidelines, not tough or rigid rules.

Who Inspires? Who Motivates and Who Is Feared?

If there be no faith in our words, of what use are they? (Chinese saying)

Leaders inspire. And managers motivate.

Having followers, leaders influence and persuade their people. Managers have subordinates.

Bosses have employees. And what about the bosses, how do they affect their employees? Bosses invoke fear and employees may work out of fear; more so, the bosses can (threaten to) hire or fire them. For the employees, with bosses, there's always this fear factor.

Bosses drive. Bosses tend to say, "Do as I tell you!" or "Do as I say!" [Most managers then normally say, "Do according to the procedure manual" while leaders say, "Do as I do", follow my example. I want to inspire you.]

Who Has What Power?

He is only advancing in life whose heart is getting softer, his blood warmer, his brain quicker, and his spirit entering into living peace. (John Ruskin)

Leaders have personal power while managers are appointed and have positional power. To the late Japanese corporate leader Matsushita Konosuke (cited in Low and Theyagu 2003, p. 93), "a person makes a position; if he is incompetent, his position will suffer, and if he's competent, the prestige and authority of his position will grow." This is, in fact, similar to the leaders' ways of growing personal power and enhancing influence.

Bosses are owners, and have reward and/or punishment power—to hire or fire the employees or to reward them with high salaries, bonuses and all kinds of incentives and perks.

"I have the power" or "I decide", bosses also resort to threats; bosses also like to threaten, and some, in fact, use them frequently. There can be an air of uneasiness or fear. To attend the bosses is, in fact, similar in content and meaning to the Chinese proverb, "To attend the Emperor is like sleeping with a tiger."

Who Tells? Who Persuades?

Almighty Heaven is not indifferent to those whose hearts are earnest. (Chinese proverb)

A leader must be humane in his dealings with others. (Matsushita Konosuke)

Leaders persuade. Leaders are persuasive. They establish rapport with their followers, relate, and tell stories. By and large, leaders are able to strongly influence their people.

And managers tell.

Bosses order.

Who Bark Orders? Who Are Their Own Persons?

To know one's self is to know others, for heart can understand heart. (Chinese proverb)

Leaders are their own persons; the managers are good soldiers. And the bosses are the taskmasters barking orders or giving instructions.

Who Wants Change? Who Prefers Change?

The best way to predict the future is to create it. (Peter Drucker)

Bosses may want change only if it's profitable... if it benefits his or her company.

Leaders prefer change. Change is part of realising the vision. Change is growth and the company benefits. And the people too should benefit the change. For leaders, change is good and for the better. To change is also to improve and to innovate.

Besides, a leader should endeavour to provoke the thoughts of those on the ground by raising creative, thought-provoking questions and/or questions the current systems so as to inspire and intrigue them to change, devising credible ideas as well as enduring, long-term solutions. They, in short, also tap on the strengths and energies of the people for ideas and solutions.

Managers prefer not to change. They prefer stability. Not to be inconvenienced, managers prefer routine and established procedures; after all, it is easier to get things done. Managers can be said to be the maintenance people of business.

Who Has More Egos?

At the feast of ego, everyone leaves hungry. (Chinese proverb)

It is the nature of ego to take, and the nature of the spirit to share. (Indian proverb)

The bosses—the owners of the company—are more inclined to have egos since they are owners and own the factors of production. They are inclined to say or think, "I'm the boss! I want this!"; "I want to get this to be done!" or "Don't question me!" Some bosses may even think along the line that "I can't be wrong!" or "I am right!"

Besides, remember bosses can hire and fire, and all the more, they have high ego!

(At this point, it is good and appropriate to be reminded of these: Egoistic, narcissistic bosses (persons) are attributed to portray some traits such as grandiosity, arrogance, self-absorption, entitlement, fragile self-esteem, and hostility but they have the charisma and grand vision that is vital to effective leadership (Rosenthal and Pittinsky 2006, cited in Low and Teo 2015, p. 32).

The leader tends to think objectively and function with less or little ego. They are more objective. Managers are relatively more attached to certain procedures or set ways, and thus, have some ego in that aspect.

Who Serves? Who Cares?

Leadership is the art of getting someone else to do something you want done because he wants to do it. (Dwight D. Eisenhower)

Leaders serve. They are there to serve and attend to the needs of their people or constituents.

Leaders are mindful of people. Leaders can, in fact, be more like a friend. As a Malay saying goes, "Friends to laugh with are many, friends to cry with are few." And leaders are very much like the latter.

Servant leaders listen to their followers. And people are highly motivated by listeners; listeners like you who get or understand what their needs and problems are. They find out what the people really want, and then make their goals fit inside the team's objectives. Good leaders also show the link (Fig. 1.1).

What about the bosses?

"I'm the boss!" Bosses want their needs be catered and fulfilled. Bosses want to be served! "My needs come first. I pay you. I want you to serve me. You better fulfilled my needs. So serve me!" That's ordinarily their thinking pattern.

Fig. 1.1 Leaders serve; they care and lend a helping hand

Your Choice and Selection

> When I do good, I feel good. When I do bad, I feel bad. That's my religion. (Abraham Lincoln)

Certainly, there are key differences between leaders, managers and bosses. It is more in the thinking, the way one thinks and one's attitude. One can choose and select the mind growth of a leader, preferring to pursue a dream or a vision, the mindset of a manager or that of a boss. One can choose how to connect with the people, whether with one's followers, subordinates or employees with one's thinking and actions of a leader, a manager or a boss—it's really up to us! That's one half and the other half is that you are what your people, what they say who you are.

Checkpoint: Think About It

Leaders, Managers and Bosses

Review the following key points and when you have finished the quiz, check your answers.

1. What do you think about leaders, managers and bosses?
   - Who call the shots?
   - Who want profits and who pursue the vision?
   - Who see short-term? And who see long-term?
   - Who is more concerned with process and people?
   - Who is more concerned with procedures and rules?
   - Who is more concerned with the procedures or the means to the end product or results?
   - Who inspires? Who motivates, and who is feared?
   - Who has what power?
   - Who tells? Who persuades?
   - Who bark orders? Who are their own persons?
   - Who wants change? Who prefers change?
   - Who has more egos?
   - Who serves? Who cares?
2. Reflect on how you lead in terms of:
   - Calling the shots?
   - Wanting profits?
   - Pursuing the vision?
   - Cherishing your people? Appreciating your human assets?
   - Process and people?
   - Procedures or the means to the end products or results?
   - Rules? Guidelines?
   - Inspiring you people?
   - Motivating your people? (Are you much feared by people?)

- Using power?
- Your ego?
- No ego?
- The needs of your people?
- Linking your people's needs to the team's (organisation's) objectives?
- Barking orders?
- Change?
- Hearing your people out?
- Serving people?
- Caring for your people?
3. Distinguish between bosses and managers.
4. Distinguish between bosses and leaders.
5. Distinguish between managers and leaders.
6. Identify the key characteristics of leaders.
7. As a leader, are you focusing on the fundamentals?
8. Are you focusing on the task, getting the job done?
9. Are you focusing on the team, building and growing the team spirit? Are you taking care of the relationships?
10. Are you focusing on the individual(s)?
    Are you growing, coaching and developing individual(s)?
    Reflecting on this chapter, I also wish to add other areas, including:

_____

_____

_____

References

Anholt, S. (2004). *Brand America*. London: Cyan Communications.

Bell, C. R., & Harari, O. (2000). *Beep! Beep! Competing in the age of the road runner*. New York: Warner Books.

Bennis, W. (2003). *On becoming a leader*. New York: Perseus.

Lawrence, A. T., & Weber, J. (2008). *Business and society*. New York: McGraw-Hill.

Low, K. C. P. (2006). Father leadership – The Singapore case study. *Management Decision* (Emerald Insight), *44*(2), 89–104. www.emeraldinsight.com/0262-1711.htm.

Low, K. C. P. (2007). Are Singaporeans pragmatic?. *GITAM Journal of Management*, GITAM, India, ISSN 0972-740X, *5*, 54–68. http://www.gitamcms.org.

Low, K. C. P. (2009). *Corporate culture and values: Perceptions of corporate leaders of cooperatives in Singapore*. Saarbrucken: VDM-Verlag.

Low, K. C. P. (2011). Types of Singapore corporate culture. *Business Journal for Entrepreneurs*, *2011*(2), 11–49.

Low, K. C. P., & Teo, T. C. (2015). Tsunami leaders and their style(s) and ways. *International Journal of Business and Social Science, 6*(9), 31–46.

Low, K. C. P., & Theyagu, D. (2003). *Developing true leadership potential*. Singapore: The Publishing Consultant.

Overdorf, J. (2011, October 7). India, China have more affluent families than European countries, *Global Post*.

The Brunei Times. (2010, January 26). Southeast Asia: Feel the warmth, *The Brunei Times*, 1.

Leadership and the Importance of Example

2

Introduction

Speaking pleasant words without practising them is like a fine flower without fragrance. (The Buddha)

We have discussed the differences between bosses, leaders and managers, and it is worthy to note that there are indeed vast differences between good and bad (weak) leaders. Low and Teo (2015, p. 31), through interview survey research, spoke of "Tsunami leaders"; they are weak, leaders, non-leaders and/or incompetents. Ordinarily, they are "weak leaders or what is dishonourably called 'fat cats', 'SOBs' or even 'lazy buggers' (several interviewees' inputs) exist, and they are the non-capable ones who purposely create turmoil, problems; difficulties and even commit mistakes or frauds in organizations to get personal benefits such as promotions, junket trips, bonuses and other perks. Such kind of leadership may, inevitably, put the whole organization into a black hole or in a disastrous situation. Bad leadership qualities can adversely affect potential organizational gains or benefits, not to mention the damage done to the organization's image. Furthermore, some research study has found that bad leader affects personal matters of employees such as physical health, raising the risk of heart diseases, and downgrade morale while working in office (Walton 2012, cited in Low and Teo, p. 31)".

Low and Teo (2015) pointed out the empty arrogance of these weak or bad leaders. According to their study, Tsunami leaders are really incompetent leaders; such leaders may have some traits of grandiosity ("though claiming to have great vision"; interviewees' inputs), and there are "self-preoccupation(s) with image, perks (and entitlements)", while having fragile or low self-esteem and they are better at "bullying others" (interviewees' inputs). (Here, to paraphrase Taite Adams' words, if one is worrying about one's image, reputation and perks, one is taking time away from doing leadership things that really matter). More importantly, Low and Teo (2015) underscored the fact that bad and weak leadership are "bad role models" and they set bad example to their followers.

© Springer International Publishing AG 2018
K.C.P. Low, *Leading Successfully in Asia*,
https://doi.org/10.1007/978-3-319-71347-2_2

Of interest, Low (2008) also highlighted that one of the classic leadership errors or what he terms as "sins" is that of not setting the example. When leaders do not set the right example, their credibility and integrity would be affected. Some leaders practise "do as I tell you", not "do as I do". If followers question their leaders' honesty and integrity, leaders cannot be role models. If this were so, such leaders would have difficulties in motivating, let alone inspiring their people (Low 2001, 2006). Through a series of interview, Low and Teo (2015, p. 35) added that, for weak leaders who do not set the example, 'everybody must obey (them), listening to (them) whenever (they) speak. If not, these weak leader(s) will be most unhappy and (s)he (they) will try to get rid of you'. 'Not open but narrow-minded; these weak leaders speak indirectly to their subordinates (sometimes through third person) and all the times, appear boastful and blunt'. '(The weak leader) scolds people according to his or her mood, and (s)he blames people for the mistake when a project falters'; 'I said I didn't know, he took the chance to humiliate and deride me; he did not teach or show me how to do the job'; 'he always has reasons or excuses when his project is not doing well (or delayed); he would never solve his problems' (interview data; Low and Teo 2015).

Because Tsunami leaders do not set the example or be the role model, "they never make things happen." (Low and Teo 2015, p. 35). "They divide and rule, you have locals and foreigners; things do not happen because there is no unity". 'We would never look up to him because he can never make things work'; 'Indecisive, Tsunami leaders are not achievers; they never want to get things done'; 'when things go wrong, it is good not to call him because he could never correct the situation but would blame you for the mistake instead'. 'Rather than letting everyone get up and make things work, he would start fault finding and finger pointing at the people's mistakes' (interview data; Low and Teo 2015).

There is an Asian, more specifically a Malay, saying that goes, *ketam mengajar anaknya berjalan betul* and the English equivalents are 'the blind leading the blind' or 'The devil preaching penitence'. The point here is, we learn by example. For those who are parents, they would surely notice that their children would imitate or emulate them. Most leaders forget that 'people don't listen to you speak, they watch your feet.' Their actions may not match with their words. They preach but they don't do what they say yet they expect people to do what they say! Through their non-actions, they alienate or widen their distance with their followers.

To lead successfully in Asia, a leader indeed needs to set and be the example; (s)he then sets the overall tone and cultural flavour of the organisation.

The core values of the key leaders and/or the founders would normally be adopted as the core values of the organisation too (Low 2002, 2009). It should be noted that core values are derived from the founders and leaders (Low 2009; Borromeo 1996, p. 51, Sithi-Amnuai 1996). Schein (1983) and Selznick (1957) refer founders as the principal formers of their organisation's culture.

As a matter of fact, both political and corporate leaders play a part in moulding organisation and establishing values and key beliefs (Horton 1999, p. 32; Borromeo 1996; Sithi-Amnuai 1996). Kim (1994, p. 145) likens leadership to an adage: "pure springs make for clean rivers"; like leaders' values are to culture, the upper waters determine the cleanliness of the river.

Birch (1993), for example, highlights that:

> Singapore constructs itself as modern by relying on establishing a set of shared, i.e. collective, values and ideals. Its politicians, therefore, are also its cultural managers (*leaders*) (Birch 1993, p. 76, *italics mine*).

Heavenly Mandate

> Heaven protects the good man. (Chinese proverb)

In the Confucian context, Heaven (*Tien*) selects the Emperor and it was through the Heavenly Mandate that the Emperor or the royal leader was selected (elected). It was the responsibility of the Dragon Emperor to then take care of the interests and welfare of the people. If this was not done, then the people had the right to revolt and revoke the mandate.

In the practice of Confucianism, the leader is the pillar of society and must indeed be a gentleman(lady). And (s)he should have the integrity, and practice the highest virtue.

The Public Eye

> A man's body buried in the snow will after a time come to light. (Chinese proverb)

Perhaps close to the Heavenly Mandate, the modern version, is what the late Japanese corporate leader Matsushita Konosuke called the "public eye" (Matsushita 1984, p. 80), the idea of an arbiter, a judge of right or wrong, fair or unfair, and he had faith in the judgement of the people and believed that their verdict was ultimately sound. To Matsushita, "the public eye is steadfast", and "the public or society supports anyone who conducts his business sensibly, rationally and fairly" (Matsushita 1984, p. 80).

As far as one's business practices conform to the accepted business norms, one's enterprise is on safe and solid ground. If something goes wrong, one may have veered off track and should re-examine one's own conduct before blaming one's customers, the consumers, or anyone else. If one has faith in the essential truth of popular wisdom and can accept the dictates of the people's judgement, it will be easy to amend one's mistakes and adjust when necessary. Indeed, dynamic, flexible leadership is vital for business, but it is possible only when one has broad public support behind one. For Matsushita, he was convinced that in the long run, people pass the correct judgement on what is right and what is wrong. And if we are convinced—that conviction supplies us that sense of security. "It is this fundamental optimism that allows us to make a deep commitment to our work and to the fulfilment of our ideals." (Matsushita 1984, p. 81).

In the eye of the public, a bigger leader—perhaps of a national or regional stature, the more public (s)he is, the more strongly (s)he influences the people by his actions and examples. This is perhaps tantamount to an often-quoted Chinese saying that the light of a hundred stars does not equal the light of the moon.

Doing Dharma (Duty) and Setting the Standards

> To keep the body in good health is a duty... otherwise we shall not be able to keep our mind strong and clear. (Buddha)

> Duty is the most sublime word in our language. Do your duty in all things. You cannot do more. You should never wish to do less. (Robert E. Lee)

Leadership in the Hindu or Indian context sits deep-rooted in the concept of *dharma* or virtue which is to conform to the truth of things. A leader needs to perform his duty. *Dharma* is doing one's duty. *Dharma* is the basis of order whether social or moral. In accordance to Taittiriya Upanishad, the first and most essential virtue for a good leadership is to speak the truth (*satyam vada*) and the second instruction is practice virtue (*dharma cara*). *Dharma* then basically is to act the Truth—an ultimate guide to right living and the stability of society (Muniapan 2008).

As the leader and leadership (or the king in the Bhagavad-Gita/Hindu scriptural context) is the key success factor for a nation or an organization, he plays an important role and he should set an example or be the role model. Even Sri Krishna also stressed the importance of the leaders to Arjuna in the *Bhagavad-Gita*. Sri Krishna in the *Bhagavad-Gita* 3.21 also advises these to Arjuna:

> Whatever action a great man (leader) performs, common men follow; and whatever standards he (leader) sets by exemplary acts, all (the world) pursue.

A Lovely Flower, Full of Colour and Fragrance

> Whoever puts on the saffron robe but is self-willed, speaks untruthfully, and lacks self-control is not worthy of that sacred garment. But those who have vanquished self-will, who speak the truth and have mastered themselves, are firmly established on the spiritual path and worthy of the saffron robe. (The Dhammapada)

In Asia, a person, more so, a leader has to back his or her words with actions; otherwise, such words are meaningless, and tantamount to the Chinese saying of "talk doesn't cook rice." In the business world, it is referred to as NATO, that is, Talk Only, No Action!

In Buddhism which is practised in several Asian countries such as Japan, Korea, Thailand and Vietnam, one is supposed to practice what one preaches otherwise it is akin to being "a lovely flower, full of color but lacking in fragrance". The latter are "the words of those who do not practice what they preach. Like a lovely flower, full of color and fragrance, are the words of those who practice what they preach." The Dhammapada, Chap. 4, verses 51 and 52 (Easwaran 2007, p. 118).

Normally, when one sees someone wise who sets the example and can guide or steer one in the right direction, one would follow that person. Or as the *Dhammapada*, Chap. 6, verse 76 points out, "If you see someone wise, who can steer you away from the wrong path, follow that person as you would one who can reveal hidden treasures. Only good can come out of it." The example thus set by the "one who is virtuous and wise shines forth like a blazing fire; like a bee, collecting nectar, he acquires wealth by harming none." (The Buddha, cited in Field 2007).

The Tail Trails the Head

Great men are the guide posts and landmarks. (Patrick Kim Cheng Low 2003, p. 13)

The leader should set the example, and be the role model. In Vietnam, a South East Asian country that had, in most ways, influenced by the teachings of Confucius has this saying to exemplify the fact that the leader should set the example: "The first part of the fish to rot is its head."

Low and Theyagu (2003, p. 82) when highlighting leadership in the Asian context cite the late Matsushita Konosuke:

"As an old saying goes: 'The tail trails the head. If the head moves fast, the tail will keep up the same pace. If the head is sluggish, the tail will droop.'" They also urge to the role model. "Set the example that you want your people to grow into. When you are the role model, you inspire your people. One of the greatest abilities of a leader is to show that he can also do what he expects from his employees as well. As leaders, you are forever in the limelight. Your staff are watching your every move. The way you conduct yourself, the kinds of clothes you wear and even the kind of food you eat and how many coffee breaks you have a day." (Low and Theyagu 2003, p. 78).

Everything you do count. And becoming a role model can start with little things. These include, for example, coming to office on time, dressing appropriately for the occasion, sharing success with your team members and many others.

In Asia in particular, family values and closeness are stressed, and all the more, at home, learning from examples commonly occurs. A child learns from his or her parents and/or from his or her older siblings. Boys will be boys! Boys are generally more inclined to emulate the ways of the fathers while girls tend to behave in a gentle manner, following the ways of their mothers.

Overall, a child wants to admire his or her parents; (s)he wants to imitate what parents do until (s)he sees inconsistencies or the hypocrisy of saying one thing and doing or acting another (Fig. 2.1).

Fig. 2.1 Importance of leaders in guiding and pointing or showing the way

Role Modelling and Examples Is a Key Influencing Factor

He who thinks he leads and has no one following him is only taking a walk. (Low 2003, p. 13)

Setting an example is not the main means of influencing another. It is the only means. (Albert Einstein)

Mencius's childhood life shows the importance of vicarious learning. There is a reference to Mencius' mother and that she moved house three times before finding a location that she felt was good enough or suitable for young Mencius' upbringing. This "in the spirit of Mencius's mother" in itself has become an expression in Chinese, an idiom which refers to the importance of finding the proper environment for raising children. It also clearly shows the importance of role modelling.

Mencius is also known as Master Meng—*Mengzi*, c. 372–289 B.C. and his importance, in the Confucian tradition, is second to Confucius. Mencius added much to Confucius' teachings and ideas with long arguments and his own philosophical stamp. When he was very young, his father died, and his mother Zhang raised Mencius by herself. They were very poor. And at first they lived by a cemetery, where the mother found her son imitating the paid mourners in funeral processions. The mother thus decided to move. The next house was near a market in the town; there the boy began to imitate the cries of merchants. Mencius also played games of buying and selling with his neighbours' friends. [Merchants were seen as the lowest of the social classes in early China.] So the mother moved to a house next to a school. Inspired by the scholars and students, Mencius began to study. His mother decided to remain, and Mencius became a scholar.

Confucius once said, "One phrase can sum up all the teachings of a gentleman: have no evil (*negative*) thoughts." and be the role model.

Role modelling and the examples of the leader is one of a leader's key successful influencing factors in persuading the people. Indeed so, the leader's example shines and becomes very influential, just like "the fragrant lotus, growing in the garbage by the roadside, brings joy to all who pass by" (The Dhammapada, Chap. 4, verses 58 and 59; Easwaran 2007, p. 118).

Consciously or subconsciously, the leader's examples and role modelling ways are or become very compelling for the followers to imitate. In the Confucian sense, a gentleman is bound to attract other gentlemen while a villain is bound to attract other villains. Besides, a gentleman is naturally at ease with other gentlemen, so also are villains, they are at ease with each other; birds of the same feathers flock together.

If the leader does not set the example, he lacks gravity and generally does not inspire respect. To Confucius, a gentleman-leader is like the North Polar Star, here, it keeps its position while all the other stars are attracted towards it.

The example(s) set by the leader can thus normally endorse the followers' actions. Such role modelling also motivates, and inspires confidence and support among the people whose competence and commitment depends.

Set and Be an Example of What You Want Others to Be

A good example is the best sermon. (Thomas Fuller)

Perhaps a leader needs not scold or reprimand his or her people when they make a mistake, and all in all, a good example on his (her) part plays an important role. Here, it is said that one Singapore leader, the late S.R. Nathan, the former President of the Republic of Singapore (1924–2016), one of Singapore's greatest sons was a caring leader "who led by example rather than rebuke". Yes, he "was exacting and expected excellence from his staff, but it was not his style to turn to rebuke when they fell short"; overall, "there was just something in his demeanour that made people feel comfortable"; and he inspired them (The Straits Times 2016, A8–A9).

True, generally speaking, we have expectations of others and many leaders, in fact, spend much time trying to get others to meet their standards. They demand loyalty, dependability, and enthusiasm, and want others to be 100% committed to getting the job done. These, well, are fine expectations.

But before placing these expectations upon others, ensure you live them yourself fully. You cannot ask more from others than you ask from yourself. You are the beacon, who you are always speaks much more loudly than what you say.

It is good to take a personal inventory of all the qualities you want in others. And then take a personal inventory of how you express these qualities in your own life. Pick one quality a day and work with it. Be aware of how and when you could be expressing this quality and what difference it would make, both to yourself and others.

Guard the Leader's Honour or Integrity

> Leadership to me means duty, honor and country. It means character, and it means listening from time to time. (George W. Bush)

Integrity is what you stand for. And you stand tall. This is indeed similar in spirit to an African or in particular, Senegalese proverb, "It matters not how tall you are, but how straight you grow".

Peter Scotese puts it as "integrity is not a 90% thing, not a 95% thing; either you have it or you don't." In Asia, the honour and integrity of a leader is very important, and even the leader's behaviour and examples reflect this. If a leader's behaviour and actions do not match with his integrity, (s)he loses his or her 'face' or honour.

In Japan, if such a thing occurs or a serious mistake has been made by the leader, the leader has to resign from the appointment to save his or her honour. Similar to the common Japanese saying, "Better to die than to live in shame", a Samurai would even commit suicide or do *hara-kiri* if he loses his honour.

Overall, as leader, one needs to monitor one's own behaviour and keep one's conscious clear (Matsushita 1991).

Say What You Mean and Do What You Say

> If all your life you have had a clear conscience, you need not fear a knock at the door at midnight. (Chinese proverb)

This is also called being authentic or aligned communication. When we think one thing, say another and then do something else, not only are we personally out of alignment, but the basic message we are communicating is that we cannot be trusted. We are out of balance and integrity.

When hidden agendas exist or operate and people are not living from the basic truth of who they are. Integrity is a critical quality needed in leaders. This is developed and communicated by direct, honest communication.

When one says what one means, one does not play games and manipulate others. Manipulation always backfires. Perhaps it may be exciting to be on the team but if others are manipulated, sooner or later they will feel used and recoil. A true leader inspires trust. (S)he can be trusted. This is developed when one says what one means and does what one says in a timely way. When leaders keep their promises to their people, their people will keep their promises to them.

Overall, a leader thus builds trust when a leader says what (s)he means and (s)he means what (s)he says.

Incorporate Action

It's important to know that words don't move mountains. Work, exacting work moves mountains. (Danilo Dolci)

Most leaders want to have power. Trust that most leaders know what power is. It is not for discussion or to come up with various theories of power.

The way a leader is to have power is to take it; (s)he takes power by taking action.

Be proactive.

As a leader, take it as part and parcel of you to include action, getting things done. In this way, rather than being passive, you set yourself as active role model. For example, when it comes to mentoring, you yourself should have a mentor and be a mentor.

Example is so powerful with action and examples of the leaders.

If people are often criticised, they will learn to blame others. At home and at work, if one's children and employees are not praised or commended, they will seek only routine duties. If people are often made to feel guilty, they will ordinarily avoid difficult problems. If they are allowed to make some trials and errors, they will tend to be creative. And when encouraged, their confidence will grow, their performance improved and their self-esteem boosted.

When people see their leaders are accountable, they will be more responsible. And indeed when people receive fair treatment, they decide justly too.

Rub Shoulders with Your People

Rapport leads to chemistry; chemistry leads to being part of the in-group, and being part of the in-group, 'We're all in it together'—makes people want to follow you. (Kim Cheng Patrick Low)

Remove status and other barriers. Create rapport and build bridges. Be a team player; rub shoulders with your people.

Lead by being a team player; be one of them.

Contribute, pitch in and do what is needed and when it is needed—all these make them accept and appreciate you as a leader. More importantly, as you rub shoulders with your people, they get to know you better, and your example will start to rub off on them.

Correct Mistakes and Be Self-Regulatory

Happiness is when what you think, what you say, and what you do are in harmony. (Mahatma Gandhi)

To be a role model, the leader also needs to be open to learning.

No one is perfect. Those who are willing to learn from their errors are wise. It is indeed sad to see leaders or even ordinary people still insisting that they are right even after they have been proven wrong.

Confucius said that if one finds a good man emulate his example and if one finds a bad man, search for his mistakes or fault so as to learn. To Confucius, "the gentleman broadens himself by scholarship or learning, and then regulates himself by *li* (proper conduct or moral discipline)". The Confucian believes that each of us self-regulates his or her own.

Areas in Which Leaders Can Lead By Example

By following the good, you learn to be good.

The generations of men follow each other, like the waves in a swollen river. (Chinese proverbs)

In leadership, as we have seen from the above, examples are so vital. The Malays have a saying that goes, "a year's drought (or heat) is wiped out by a day's rain". Or another Malay saying has it that, "because of one drop of indigo, a whole pot of milk is spoilt." In the same way, the longest period of good leadership or a long record of leadership merits, sad though, can be dissolved or nullified by a leader's single misdeed.

The list—the areas, in which leaders can lead by example—next to come, is by no means exhaustive; note that each of these areas may supply some ideas in which, as leaders, we can lead by example. They are meant to serve as a guide; readers can expand on these areas, which include:

- **Integrity**: How do you show or act out your integrity? In what ways can you show your integrity?
- **Work Performance**: How do you do your work? What about your job performance? How do you set the pace? Look at intensity, hours worked, and the number of rest breaks.
- **Work Performance Appraisals (Evaluations)**: Are you being fair? Do you assess your people fairly? Are you objective enough? Have you cited examples for each trait or skill assessed?
- **Company Policy**: How you do adhere to the Company's policy?
- **Health, Clothing and Overall Physical Appearance**: Are you fit? How do you dress? Do you look good? Do you look neat? Do you dress professionally?
- **Attitudes towards the Company, Co-workers, Customers and the Job**: What are your attitudes towards these people?
- **Appearance and Grooming**: How do you appear to others? Do you look good to others? Do you groom yourself well? How does your hair look? Neat? Well-combed? Do you look professional?

- **Interpersonal Communication**: How do you set the tone and style of interpersonal communication? How do you communicate? Do you appear forceful? Are you friendly? Are you courteous enough? Are you polite? Do you communicate well? Do you communicate without embarrassing or belittling others? Do you engage in insult jokes against others? Do you offend others when you joke? Are you persuasive? Are you being convincing? Do you speak in a calm, restrained manner, at most times? Do you listen well to others?
- **Team Playing**: Are you a team player? Do you lend a hand to your team members? Do you help your team members feel capable? Do you allow your people to attain success in relatively easy projects? How generous are you in giving praises (feedback) to your team members?
- **Friendliness**: How friendly are you? Do you show your friendliness readily?
- **Personal Warmth**: Do you freely express joy and personal warmth to others? Do you keep or maintain (avoid) eye contact when talking to people?
- **Energy**: Do you exude energy?
- **Enthusiasm**: Are you excited about your work (the various projects you are involved in)? Do you show your enthusiasm towards project(s) (work)?
- **Corporate Social Responsibility and Being Green**: As the title of this Chapter suggests, the key or secret of being green really lies within oneself, so as a leader, one needs to ask: Do you practice being green? In what ways can you be green? Do you show them in your actions or behaviour? What are the earth-friendly ways in which your Company or Organisation can adopt to make earth greener?
- **The Practice of Your Values**: Do you practise the values you uphold? Do you show them in your actions or behaviour?
- **Pro-active Leadership**: Do you serve as a positive model for getting things done well and on time?

Adapting the list of questions and what has been worked out in Low (2008), perhaps, as leaders, we should ask ourselves this:

- What action(s) should I be doing more of?
- Actions speak louder than words... ...and anything for me to do something (More? Positively?) about it?
- What should I be doing that I should do less of?
- What am I doing today that I should stop doing altogether?
- What am I doing that I should start doing if I want to perform at my best (setting a good example and being a role model)?

  All in all, our actions and examples represent us as leaders. So make them good.

Checkpoint: Think About It

Leadership and the Importance of Example

Role Modelling and Examples Is a Key Influencing Factor

1. Check and ask yourself, do you
   - Set and be an example of what you want others to be?
   - Guard your (the leader's) honour or integrity?
   - Say what you mean and do what you say?
   - Incorporate action?
   - Rub shoulders with your people?
   - Correct mistakes and be self-regulatory?
2. Are you in the know what actions of yours motivate or inspire your people?

Check and ask yourself what actions of yours motivate or inspire your people?

Areas in Which Leaders Can Lead By Example

Think about it... the list, serving as a guide, includes:

- Work performance
- Work performance appraisals (evaluations)
- Company policy
- Health, clothing and overall physical appearance
- Attitudes towards the company, co-workers, customers and the job
- Appearance and grooming
- Interpersonal communication
- Team-playing
- Friendliness
- Personal warmth
- Energy
- Enthusiasm
- The practice of your values
- Pro-active leadership
  I also wish to add other areas, including:
  _____
  _____
  _____

3. What area(s) which you as a leader, would like to identify as not been acting as an example and what would you be doing about it (them)?

Exercises and Activities

1. Make a list of the core values you subscribe or hold.
2. Take a personal inventory of all the qualities you want in others. And then take a personal inventory of how you express these qualities in your own life. Pick one quality a day and work with it. Be aware of how and when you could be expressing this quality and what difference it would make, both to yourself and others.

References

Birch, D. (1993). Staging crises: Media and citizenship. In G. Rodan (Ed.), *Singapore changes guard: Social, political and economic directions in the 1990s* (pp. 72–83). Melbourne: Longman Cheshire Pty.

Borromeo, H. M., Jr. (1996). Beyond strategy: The CEO as maestro. In Asian Institute of Management (Ed.), *The CEO and corporate culture* (pp. 45–55). Makati: Asian Institute of Management.

Easwaran, E. (Trans.). (2007). *The Dhammapada*. Tomales: Nilgiri Press.

Field, L. M. (2007). *Business and the Buddha*. Boston: Wisdom.

Horton, T. R. (1999). Chapter 5. In A. Vlamis (Ed.), *Smart leadership*. New York: AMA Management Briefing, American Management Association International.

Kim, W.-C. (1994). *Every street is paved with gold*. Singapore: Times Books International.

Low, K. C. P. (2001). *The power of relationships*. Singapore: BusinesscrAFT™ Consultancy.

Low, K. C. P. (2002). *Corporate culture and values: Perceptions of corporate leaders of cooperatives in Singapore*. Unpublished PhD thesis, University of South Australia, Adelaide, Australia.

Low, K. C. P. (2003). *Team success*. Singapore: BusinesscrAFT™ Consultancy and Humber Lincoln Resources Pte.

Low, K. C. P. (2006). Motivation, the Chinese leadership way in Singapore's small and medium companies. *The Icfaian Journal of Organizational Behavior, 1*, 80–90.

Low, K. C. P. (2008). Leadership thoughts to ponder – Some classic sins of leadership. *Leadership & Organizational Management Journal, 2008*(4), 65–75.

Low, K. C. P. (2009). *Corporate culture and values: Perceptions of corporate leaders of cooperatives in Singapore*. Saarbrücken: VDM-Verlag.

Low, K. C. P., & Teo, T. C. (2015). Tsunami leaders and their style(s) and ways. *International Journal of Business and Social Science, 6*(9), 31–46.

Low, K. C. P., & Theyagu, D. (2003). *Developing true leadership potential*. Singapore: The Publishing Consultant.

Matsushita, K. (1984). *Not for bread alone*. New York: PHP Institute.

Matsushita, K. (1991). *Velvet glove, iron fist*. Kyoto: PHP Institute.

Muniapan, B. (2008). Kautilyan and Confucian perspectives on leadership values. In A. Arunsimha (Ed.), *Integrating spirituality and organizational leadership* (pp. 115–127). Hyderabad: The ICFAI University Press.

Schein, E. H. (1983). The role of the founder in creating organizational culture. *Organizational Dynamics, 12*, 13–28.

Selznick, P. (1957). *Leadership in administration*. New York: Harper & Row.

Sithi-Amnuai, P. (1996). How to build corporate culture. In Asian Institute of Management (Ed.), *The CEO and corporate culture* (pp. 29–44). Makati: Asian Institute of Management.

The Straits Times. (2016, August). SR Nathan: 1924 to 2016. *The Straits Times, 25*, A8–A9.

Leadership and Ethics

3

Introduction

Leadership is responsibility. In the Asian context, leadership carries social responsibility. A leader needs to bear in mind the environment and setting in which (s)he operates. It is a gentle person's code in which (s)he carries.

From the outset, it is appropriate to stress that the external environment of business is ever changing and dynamic, and all the more the need for businesses and individuals to embrace ethics and social responsibility. First, there has been growing emphasis on ethical reasoning and actions in which the public expects business to be ethical and wants corporate managers to apply ethical principles. Second, people also increasingly expect business to be more responsible. Societal expectations of businesses' responsibilities are growing. Third, some of our natural resources such as oil, coal and gas; once used are gone forever. Human beings share a single planet and we need to ensure supplies and resources for our future generations; and the current state of our natural environment such as global warming, erratic climatic conditions powerfully impacts business-society relationship, and what more, business should do something or more with the natural environment. Managers are thus increasingly challenged to integrate ecological considerations into their decisions. Fourth, new technologies create ethical considerations. New technologies bring new equipment or gadgets, the Internet and even genetically modified, high yielding food, yet there are also threats including scams, online frauds, invasion of privacy, internet pornography. Indeed, many tough situations and ethical concerns exist.

Added to these, there is much competitive pressure to succeed, businesses must succeed. People may make their own luck by any means; worse, at times, the means may justify the ends. They would say: "Beat or be beaten!" So much so that even "Greed is good" [as proclaimed by the Michael Douglas character, Gordon Gekko, in the 1987 Hollywood movie, *Wall Street*]. Or worse, similar to what is depicted in the science fictional series *Star Trek*, through the Ferengis (To them, "Greed is eternal"). This fictional extraterrestrial race is said to have a mercantile culture,

© Springer International Publishing AG 2018
K.C.P. Low, *Leading Successfully in Asia*,
https://doi.org/10.1007/978-3-319-71347-2_3

obsessed with making profits and trade as well as their constant efforts to cheat or swindle people into bad deals in the *Star Trek* universe.

Each of us has a social responsibility. So also, each firm has a social responsibility which is the firm's recognition of how its business decision can affect society. Ethics, the yardstick, serves as the foundational stone of doing business and it should play a critical role in every business, profit or non-profit organization, society, and nation. Ethics pays. Being ethical imparts a sense of trust which promotes positive alliances among business partners and associates. Confucian ethics can supply the basis through which people do, conduct business or make business decisions. In this paper, the objectives are basically to relate to or interpret Confucian ethics in the light of the stakeholder theory and secondarily, a call for each of us to do something. Each of us (companies and businesses) also has stakeholders; we need to satisfy our stakeholders too. Similarly, a firm is to satisfy the needs and interests of its stakeholders.

To begin with, Confucius (Pinyin: *Kung Fūzi*; Wade-Giles: K'ung-fu-tzu, lit. *Master Kung*, 551 BC–479 BC) was an esteemed Chinese thinker and social philosopher, whose teachings and philosophy have deeply influenced Chinese, Japanese, Korean and Vietnamese thought and life (Wikipedia 2007; Chew 2000) and also elsewhere, even in the Western world (Yang 1993). Some of his ideas have, in fact, stood the test of time.

The Golden Rule and the Stakeholder Theory

This author is inclined to favour the Confucian's overall anchor, the Golden Rule, that is, not to do unto others what one does not want others to do unto oneself. It is also called *shu* or reciprocity as a principle of the conduct for life (Lin 1994, p. 186). Incorporating the Golden Rule, the stakeholder theory (Lawrence and Weber 2008) becomes relevant. One moves away from oneself and becomes less self-centred, and in fact, more altruistic. All businesses should recognise their responsibilities to their stakeholders and make decisions that reflect these responsibilities. Here, the business can then engage the stakeholders moving from inactive to reactive to proactive to interactive. The basic point is that one can argue that business cannot avoid but has to enter into dialogue, do something, and engage with its stakeholders—market or non-market—in an ongoing relationship.

It is axiomatic that the firm should be responsible to all its stakeholders. The stakeholder theory is very attractive in that the stakeholders can also be expanded to any party(ies) and all an individual or business ("the (*Confucian*) measure of man is man"; Lin 1994, p. 183, emphasis added) needs to do is to think of the party(ies) and be responsible to act or satisfy the needs and interests of the party(ies) involved. Besides, the normative value of the stakeholder theory should be appreciated; stakeholders are seen as possessing value regardless of their instrumental use to management. The normative view is often perceived as the moral or ethical view because "it emphasizes how stakeholders should be treated" (Buchholtz and Carroll 2009, p. 93) hence, the importance of the principle of stakeholder fairness.

It appears that many often overlooked that the essence of Confucianism is the "idea of being true to oneself in this world" (interestingly, there is an intrinsic or inside-out approach) when fulfilling obligations to family and others in society (Wang 2004, p. 51). That is the key strength of the Confucian ethics when applied to the stakeholder theory/others in society. Whatever, even very little that each of us, individuals and businesses can do for our respective universe that would be great. After all, it would contribute to the overall goodness, similar to the late Indian nationalist leader, Mohandas Gandhi's "Be the change you want to see in the world." And individuals do make a difference in ethical actions.

As Mencius said, men are inherently good (Lin 1994; Wing-Tsit 1973). Individuals have ethical attributes that can be cultivated and extends outwards. Currently, to this researcher, there is a need for ethical renewal by applying an inside-out approach. Mother Earth is sick; there should be ethical concerns, not to say, the many environmental concerns, by all. China and India are growing but "the vast majority of Asia's poor are rural", "millions more are barely getting by (*surviving*)" (Wehrfritz 2008, *italics mine*), there are problems of income gaps and other issues. As earlier said, technologies are also changing and with it, various ethical issues.

In the stakeholder theory, to its stockholders/investors, the firm and/or its managers should monitor employee decisions to ensure that they are made in the best interests of the owners and stockholders. Employee compensation may be directly tied to the firm's performance. The firm's financial reporting should also be accurate; it should give complete financial statements, those that are more understandable and more readily interpreted. Firms need to fulfil their responsibility to their creditors by providing good financial reporting. As in the case of Enron by hiding some debt, Enron was able to more easily borrow funds and ultimately, it went bankrupt because it could not cover the payments on all of its debt. Specifically Enron did not disclose some of its debt and indeed, its creditors would have been concerned about extending more credit if they had fully understood how much debt Enron already had.

To its customers, it should adopt responsible production practices and dutiful sales practices. Customers should receive fair exchange: value and quality for money spent (Lawrence and Weber 2008). In this regard, the firm, in establishing a code of responsibilities, can monitor customer complaints and make full use of customer feedback to better serve the customer (Madura 2007).

The business also needs to take care of its employees, providing stable employment, fair pay, and safety as well as the fact that employees are treated properly by other employees. Here, satisfying employees, the key issues in modern businesses include diversity, equal opportunity and the prevention of sexual harassment (Madura 2007).

The firm needs to ensure its responsibility to the community. It should be socially responsible. It needs to also take care of and protect the environment. Firms need to prevent air, water and land pollution. Automobile and steel firms have reduced air pollution by changing their production processes so that less carbon dioxide escapes into the air (Madura 2007). China, for example, has admitted that it has failed badly; the country has not made much headway in improving the environment, says its Government Report (Tschang 2007). In this aspect, present day China needs to apply the Confucian Ethics in conjunction with the stakeholder theory—particularly in terms of the firm's responsibility to the environment—to make Mother Earth a healthier and a more pleasant place for all to live. The Chinese needs to realize that in traditional Chinese or Confucian mind, men exist in harmony with nature (One with Nature), and unlike in the Western mind, traditionally, nature is to be conquered; there is a dominance orientation (Adler and Gundersen 2008). In this regard, the Chinese have to do something for the environment and Mother Earth.

Bolstering the Stakeholder Theory with the Confucian Ethical Concepts (Even at the Individual Level, One Needs to Embrace These as the Basis)

Being a Gentleperson (*Junzi*)

A person with a bad name is already half-hanged. (Chinese proverb)

Being ethical is synonymous with a gentleperson. Being a gentleman(lady), the business owner or firm must take care of the interests and needs of all the stakeholders.

Confucius impresses on us is that: To be a leader in business or in life, we need to act and behave as gentlemen (Low 2008). If we are to achieve a state of orderliness and peace, we need to return to traditional values of virtue. These values are based entirely on one concept: *jen*. Differing from the Western Biblical traditions, the fifth century Chinese sage Confucius believed that human nature is basically good. However, he also believed that this goodness needs to be nurtured and cultivated and the best way to do so is through education. According to Confucius, "unending strength, resoluteness, simplicity and reticence are close to benevolence" which is attainable through self-cultivation, education and performance of the *li* or rituals/code of behaviour (Story 2007).

Interestingly, in a capsule, just as Confucius has said, "It is man that makes truth great, and not truth that makes man great." and "the measure of man is man" (Lin 1994, p. 183).

In short, humanism and true manhood is stressed. "A gentleman understands what is moral, a base man understands what is advantageous or profitable" (Chew 2000, p. 9). Needless to say, if a gentleman were to go and live among uncivilised people, then how could these people be crude? His very character and actions will help change them for the better.

Emphasising and Practising Virtue

Virtue is the greatest happiness; vice will not go unpunished.

Govern yourself and you can govern the world. (Chinese proverbs)

Virtue is something to be desired highly. But why virtue is stressed?

When virtue is practiced, one enjoys a clear conscience. And a clear conscience is like a soft pillow, and one sleeps well. "A gentleman finds peace of mind in virtue and he covets it" (Confucius cited in Chew 2000, p. 8). Rightly too, Confucius has highlighted that "likes and dislikes should not affect our judgment. We should be on the side of what is right and against what is wrong" (Chew 2000, p. 9).

In this aspect, one's example is critical. Without example, a leader becomes "a person who lacks gravity (*and*) does not inspire respect" (Confucius cited in Chew 2000, p. 2, *italics mine*). A leader gains moral grounds and attracts his followers through his examples. His actions are louder than words.

As highlighted by Low (2006a, b, c), role models should be assessed in the light of honesty and integrity. If followers question their leaders' honesty and integrity, leaders cannot be role models. For small and medium Chinese business leaders, it is a matter of face or honour. In the case of Singapore's national values, Low (2002, 2009, 2011) speaks of the *Confucian Heritage*, here, it should be noted that Transparency International, 2002 (cited in Lim and Daft 2004) ranks Singapore as the fifth most corruption free among 102 countries. Singapore was ranked among the top ten nations in the world in governance in the 2006 World Bank's "Governance Matters" Report (The Straits Times 2006). The Singapore's People Action Party (PAP) track record and ability to fight off critics based on honesty and integrity has enabled it to stay relevant and win all election campaigns since 1959 (Lim and Daft 2004, p. 50).

Raising One's Influence by Example and Being Ethical

If you look into your own heart, you find nothing wrong there, what is there to fear? (Confucius)

The person is quiet yet ethical sound; and a silent achiever, (s)he moves on. According to Confucius, "a wise man does not readily give utterance to words in case his actions do not live up to his words" (Zhou 2005, p. 10). "One who talks too much is prone to failure" (Confucius, cited in Zhou 2005, p. 68). "A gentleman is slow to speak but prompt to act" (Confucius, cited in Chew 2000, p. 10). "When the ruler (*leader*) does what is right, he will have influence over the people without giving commands" (Lin 1994, p. 199) (Fig. 3.1).

"A good leader may be compared to the wind and the common people to the grass. Let the wind blow over the grass and the grass, under the force of the wind,

Fig. 3.1 Importance of setting an example and being consistent in one's words and one's actions

cannot but bend" (Chew 2000, p. 18). Pro-active, through his or her examples and behaviour, the business owner/firm thus builds his or her/its influence.

Here, "a gentleman is bound to attract other gentlemen. A villain is bound to attract other villains. Moreover a gentleman is naturally at ease with other gentlemen; a villain is naturally at ease with other villains" (Confucius cited in Chew 2000, p. 2).

Interestingly, one's best way to raise one's influence is to apply the Golden Rule, the gentleman's code of conduct. To reinforce, it is worth repeating this—in essence, one does onto others what one oneself likes, and "do(es) not impose to others what (one oneself) dislike" (Zhou 2005, p. 4). When doing as such, one will not incur resentment, and win others over.

The four essential virtues of an ethical leader are that in one's personal conduct, one is respectful. In one's dealings with one's staff, one is considerate; in caring for the common people's welfare, one is generously kind; and in dealing with all, one is just.

Loving All and Serving All

All the world loves a lover. (English proverb)

If you haven't any charity in your heart, you have the worst kind of heart trouble. (Bob Hope)

Love all and serve all is the Confucian message and when applied to the stakeholder theory, it becomes wholesome and without discrimination.

Discrimination at workplace is a haunting reality of the corporate world even in this millennium. Bias, prejudice and differentiation treatment rather than actual job-related basis constitute discrimination.

However, Confucianism indeed stresses on humanism. Love for mankind. And may we add, love for nature too. According to Confucius "no man is a machine. He should not behave heartlessly like one, or as if others were machines" (Chew 2000, p. 5). "A gentleman is (*also*) conscious only in the knowledge of others' comfort; the mean is conscious only of his own comfort" (Chew 2000, p. 2, *italics mine*).

As a teacher (*business owners*), Confucius further believed that to elicit good results, he must guide, teach, advise and love his pupils (*employees*) (Yang 1993, *italics mine*). This is tantamount to the Chinese saying that "If there were no fishermen to guide us, how could we ever see the great waves of the ocean". The teacher needs to know them well, understand their psychological particularities, give thought to ways and means of making easy their access to knowledge and, to that end, develop an effective methodology.

The hallmark of a teacher's virtue, in Confucius' eyes, was loving commitment through his lessons to his pupils' development. The teacher needs to look into the moral development of his pupils too, and that is an attractive way or value that a teacher may want to hold.

The Master once said: "Love makes a spot beautiful: who chooses not to dwell in love, has he got wisdom?" (Scholastic 2007). A leader needs to be compassionate too. "Few are competent to love and to hate others" (Chew 2000, p. 8). "The emotion of love in a gentleman is passionate but not sensual, and sad also, without being painful" (Chew 2000, p. 7).

To this researcher, a very good example of loving, as well as being influential and leading the Confucian way is that of the late Matsushita Konosuke (1894–1989), the founder of Japan's Matsushita Electric. The business owner/marketer should be people-centred. Putting "people before products" (PHP 1994, p. 54), the business owner should also be responsible to his employees as well as customers, serving their needs.

The late Matsushita Konosuke believed in producing people, and consulting. "Consulting is better than ordering." "He was known for broaching the topic as if seeking advice or offering a suggestion. In other words instead of simply saying, 'Would you do such and such', he would say something like, 'I've been thinking we could do such-and-such this way; what do you think' or 'Would you undertake this job?, thus making his subordinates feel free to present their own opinions and suggestions on the matter'" (PHP 1994, pp. 58–59).

A Western example of leading ethically, the Confucian way is that as practiced by billionaire Kenneth Fisher who is the founder and chief executive of money management firm, Fisher Investments. To him, loving is best shown by adopting the best way—giving back to the community by creating jobs for the people. Besides, he has willed 80% of his estate to John Hopkins for medical research rather than set up a trust (Tan 2007).

Fostering Family Closeness and Fatherly Care

There is one word which may serve as a rule of practice for all one's life—reciprocity.
(Confucius)

It is said that should the families be unstable, and if there are break-ups and quarrels in the family, the whole country is not stable. If the families are at peace, the country is stable and at peace too. Businesses are also run along the family line, creating a congenial family or small group atmosphere.

Confucius stresses on the importance of the family; and in the family unit, the father is the key figure. He should be the role model, a good example to his children. For the son, it is the son's duty to obey without questioning and honor his father, even after death. When the father dies, obedience is given to the oldest brother. Confucius states in the *Analects*, "Meng I Tzu asked about the treatment of parents. The Master said, 'Never disobey! ...While they are alive, serve them according to ritual. When they die, bury them according to ritual and sacrifice to them according to ritual.'" (*Analects* II: 5).

Showing care and concern to his followers, the benevolent Confucian leader is like a father to his followers. Besides, the family spirit is often fostered, and to quote Confucius:

A true gentleman is in harmony, and is friendly with others though he does not agree with them... (Chew 2000, p. 17).

In the small business situation, the father leader/small business-owner collaborates with his "family members" in a purposeful team fashion, "rubbing shoulders and doing something together also gives the opportunity to share. There is joint purpose, sharing the same dreams and bringing the relationship to a higher plane. There is also synergy" (Low 2001, p. 101; Low 2005). Employees' successes are celebrated and with effective team leadership, teamwork is fostered and higher performance attained (Zimmerer and Scarborough 2005).

At the core, it appears that this teamwork, or more appropriately, consensus-seeking culture may be related to loyalty, which is also considered to be a virtue by the Chinese (Bond 1987, cited in Low 2002, 2009). Chinese are taught from a young age to be loyal to their family and kin. Hsu (1984) claims, loyalty to the family will continue to play a critical role among Chinese. Family is important in any culture, but it is extraordinarily so in Chinese culture. But more importantly, "relations among family members provide the human basis for the moral virtues of the Chinese" (Nakamura 1978, cited in Low 2009, 2002). Hsu (1984) has identified some of the significant characteristics of the Chinese family that have a strong impact on Chinese organizations. The Chinese as a people are special in their relationships with others, and a strong emphasis on the importance of blood relations, parental authority, filial piety and loyalty exists. The late Kwek Hong

Png, founder and chairman of the Hong Leong (Singapore) group of companies, for instance, pointed this out when he was expanding his business:

> Mindful of the old Chinese proverb that when tackling a tiger, one needs the help of one's brothers, I invited my brothers to join my firm. (Kwek 1987, cited in Low 2009, 2002).

Embracing High Learning, Education and Utmost Integrity

A beard does not make a philosopher. (Russian proverb)

A book is like a garden carried in the pocket. (Chinese proverb)

The Confucian practitioner sets the heart right (ethical goodness, awareness and reasoning); and does personal cultivation (ethical action and leadership).
One makes mistakes but learns from it.
One learns to attain moral perfection.
Here, Low (2006b, citing Sie 1997 and Cham 1998) highlights these:

> Wu, a Chinese scholar mentioned that learning, or the Confucian concept of *keji* (one must learn and be ready to move), was important to Singapore and its future. *Keji* was also reflected in the way the Government made its education, IT and technology plans about 30 years ahead, and Singaporeans must learn to move ahead in today's world. In a true Confucian fashion, the Singapore Government has invested much to better the Singapore workers' educational status. University education is also given much emphasis; the government is seeking to make local universities world-class and best in the region; and with Singapore's ambition to be the knowledge centre of the region, it is only natural to emphasise research and development.

To Confucius, "the gentleman broadens himself by scholarship or learning, and then regulates himself by *li* (proper conduct or moral discipline)".

The Confucian leader, even in the modern day, stresses on learning, education and high integrity. Its investments on schools and education are high (Low 2002, 2005, 2009, 2011). Having the Confucian Heritage *practical thriver* culture (Low 2002), the Singapore Government relies on the Mandarinate or scholars to administer the City-state. Although appearing elitist, the efficient and honest civil service promptly attended to the needs of its citizens, and it is said that for Singapore everything was on the table with clear rules (Thurow 1996 and Schein 1996, cited in Low 2002, 2009). High integrity is maintained with the Corrupt Practices Investigations Bureau (CPIB) under the charge of the Prime Minister's Office. Indeed, as Confucius highlighted, "We are saying (*emphasising*) all the time: *Li! Li!*" (Lin 1994, 2000, *italics mine*).

Learning and improving never stops. To the Confucian gentleman, to be capable, one must study; to be intellectual, one must learn from others (Zhou 2005, p. 36), profit(ing) by good examples and avoid(ing) bad examples (Chew 2000, p. 13). To this researcher, the Confucian gentleman benchmarks, learns and improves. It's

Kaizen (continuous improvement) in the ethical sense. Continuous improvement indeed builds and grows his or her moral fiber.

Being Prudent

> Besides the noble art of getting things done, there is the noble art of leaving things undone. The wisdom of life consists in the elimination of non-essentials. (Lin Yu-tang)

Being prudent is also a virtue, another trait of the Confucian ethics. Confucius is attributed to say these:

> Tsze-chang asked Confucius, "In what way should a person in authority act in order that he may conduct government properly?" The Master replied, "Let him observe the five excellent things, and banish away the four bad things, then he may conduct government properly." And one of the five excellent things is as Confucius replied: "When the person in authority is beneficent without great expenditure." (Pay 2000).

Being prudent means one would be cautious, not extravagant or spending beyond one's means as well as 'keeping up with the Jones's'. Such ways can lead one to be corrupt, committing frauds or accepting bribes to cope to ends meet in which one would not be responsible to one's employer/customers/investors or even suppliers/community.

We should take note of the issue of being prudent or thrift commonly found among people from the East Asian societies which are highly influenced by Confucian values (Hung 1995). This can be seen in the very high household savings found in these countries as compared to the others especially the West and also the relatively higher reserve funds. In the light of the current Greek debt crisis (at the time of writing this book), being prudent can be clearly seen as something good, and perhaps Greece's austerity drive (and the Greeks must have the will and act on it!) can help the country to stable itself, the Euro Zone as well as the world.

Low's (2002, 2009) and Low's (2005, 2011) studies support that the Chinese mind, strongly influenced by Confucianism, is said to be pragmatic and devoted to seeking profit. Here, such a company culture, particularly in some Chinese small and medium companies such as in the "*mee pok* (noodle) seller corporate culture" (Low 2002, 2005, 2006a, b, c, 2009, 2011), profits are ploughed back and being frugal is a virtue. Here, thrift involves the use of limited resources—material, capital and human resources, and these results in improving productivity and overall profitability. In fact, Low's (2005) study supports that being prudent is one of the success values for the growth of Singapore companies. And Low (2006b) argues that being prudent also serves a crisis prevention, containment and management for the island-Republic of Singapore and perhaps it can also help companies and countries to better lead or manage themselves.

Conclusion

As a man thinks in his heart, so is he. (Proverbs 23, p. 7)

Confucian ethics should be done with personal convictions, and ultimately, for the stakeholders' well-being, and not for the sake of personal glory or self (firm's or business interests). Besides, the leader should be able to communicate with his or her people, mobilise them as well as persuade and convince them. In this way, the leader can also feel the pulse of the stakeholders and make appropriate decisions accordingly based on a bigger picture and from a wider view and, overall, for the sake and interests of the public at large.

In sum, the Confucian business owner (firm) grows or 'perfects' his (its) virtue. Being just to humanity, the Confucian business owner (firm) would build his (its) credibility, and has the right status so that what he (the firm) says is justifiable. When the firm/employer's words are justifiable, then what he does can be successful—he's respected and emulated by his followers (employees, customers, suppliers, investors and community).

Checkpoint: Think About It

Leadership and Ethics

Leadership, Confucian Ethics and Social Responsibility: The Golden Rule and Responsibility to the Stakeholders

1. Do you care about ethics? Do you really care about ethics? If so, why? If not, why not?
2. In line with satisfying or fulfilling the needs of your constituents, are you
   - Being a gentleman (*junzi*)?
   - Emphasising and practising virtue?
   - Raising your influence by example and being ethical?
   - Loving all and serving all?
   - Fostering family closeness and showing fatherly care?
   - Embracing high learning, education and utmost integrity?
   - Being prudent?
3. How can you put into practice or action the following?
   - Being a gentleman (*junzi*)?
   - Emphasising and practising virtue?
   - Raising your influence by example and being ethical?
   - Loving all and serving all?
   - Fostering family closeness and showing fatherly care?
   - Embracing high learning, education and utmost integrity?
   - Being prudent?
4. In what other areas can you do more for each of your stakeholders?

5. As a leader, are you prudent? How can you be more prudent or practise being thrifty?
6. How can you make your team (organisation) be more prudent?
7. Do you each time after an action has been taken, reflect on it? Think of the benefits of the action for others (your people)?

References

Adler, N. J., & Gundersen, A. (2008). *International dimensions of organizational behavior.* Mason, OH: Thomson South-Western.

Bond, M. H. (1987). Chinese values and the search for culture-free dimensions of culture. *Journal of Cross-Cultural Psychology, 18*(2), 143–164.

Buchholtz, A. K., & Carroll, A. B. (2009). *Business and society.* Boston: South-Western Cengage Learning.

Cham, T. S. (1998). Making a world class university (I). In *Commentary* (Vol. 15, pp. 35–40). Singapore: The National University of Singapore Society.

Chew, K. H. P. (2000). *A gentleman's code.* Graham Brash (Pte): Singapore.

Hsu, P. S. C. (1984, June). *The influence of structure and values on business organisations in oriental cultures: A comparison of China and Japan.* Unpublished paper, School of Management, National University of Singapore, Singapore.

Hung, C. T. P. (1995). *Measuring the economic impact of Confucianism: Empirical evidence from a survey, Confucianism and economic development.* Taipei: Chung-Hua Institution for Economic Research.

Lawrence, A. T., & Weber, J. (2008). *Business & society.* New York: McGraw-Hill/Irwin.

Lim, G. S., & Daft, R. (2004). *The leadership experience in Asia.* Singapore: Thomson Learning.

Lin, Y. (Ed.). (2000/1994). *The wisdom of Confucius.* New York: The Modern Library.

Low, K. C. P. (2001). *The power of relationships.* Singapore: BusinesscrAFT™ Consultancy.

Low, K. C. P. (2002). *Corporate culture and values: Perception of corporate leaders of co-operatives in Singapore.* Unpublished PhD thesis, the University of South Australia, Adelaide.

Low, K. C. P. (2005). Towards a framework & typologies of Singapore corporate cultures. *Management Development Journal of Singapore, 13*(1), 46–75.

Low, K. C. P. (2006a, January). Motivation, the Chinese leadership way in Singapore's small and medium companies. *The Icfaian Journal of Organizational Behavior, V*(1), 80–90. The Institute of Chartered Financial Analyst India: ICFAI University Press.

Low, K. C. P. (2006b, March). Father leadership – The Singapore case study. *Management Decision, 44*(2), 89–104. Emerald insight, www.emeraldinsight.com/0262-1711.htm.

Low, K. C. P. (2006c). Crisis management – Can core values be considered as a built-in safety net? The Singapore case. *Insights to a Changing World, 2006*(3), 133–150. http://franklinpublishing.net/insightstoachangingworld.html.

Low, K. C. P. (2008). Value-based leadership: Leading the Confucian way. *Leadership & Organizational Management Journal, 2008*(3), 32–41.

Low, K. C. P. (2009). *Corporate culture and values: Perception of corporate leaders of co-operatives in Singapore.* Saarbrücken: VDM-Verlag.

Low, K. C. P. (2011). Types of Singapore corporate culture. *Business Journal for Entrepreneurs, 2011*(2), 11–49.

Madura, J. (2007). *Introduction to business* (4th ed.). Mason: Thomson South-Western.

Nakamura, H. (1978). *Ways of thinking of Eastern peoples.* Honolulu: East–west Centre Press.

Pay, R. (2000). *Confucius.* Retrieved June 27, 2008, from http://www.humanistictexts.org/confucius.htm

PHP. (1994). *Matsushita konosuke (1894–1989): His life & his legacy.* Kyoto: PHP Institute.

Scholastic. (2007). Grolier online: Asian Pacific American Heritage: Confucius, sayings (document)' *Scholastic*. Scholastic, Inc. Retrieved June 7, 2007, from http://content.scholastic.com/browse/article.jsp?id=4985

Story, C. (2007). *Asian studies/confucianism*. Accessed June 5, 2007, from http://www.castilleja.org/faculty/christy_story/C&C/Buddhism/confucius.htm

Tan, L. (2007, September 30). Best way to give back? Create jobs, says billionaire. *The Sunday Times*, 24.

The Straits Times. (2006, September 17). Singapore scores high on governance. *The Straits Times*.

Thurow, L. (1996). Foreword. In E. H. Schein (Ed.), *Strategic pragmatism: The culture of Singapore's Economic Development Board*. Massachusetts Institute of Technology: Cambridge.

Tschang Chi-Chu. (2007, Janurary 29). Ecology: China admits it has failed badly. *The Straits Times*, 2.

Wang, G. (2004). Confucianism. In F.-J. Richter & P. C. M. Mar (Eds.), *Asia's new crisis: Renewal through total ethical management* (pp. 51–62). Singapore: Wiley (Asia).

Wehrfritz, G. (2008, September 8). The price of survival. *Newsweek*, 39.

Wikipedia. (2007). Confucius, *Wikipedia*. Retrieved June 6, 2007, from http://en.wikipedia.org/wiki/Confucius

Wing-Tsit Chan. (1973). *A source book in Chinese philosophy* (Trans and commentary). Princeton University Press: Princeton, NJ.

Yang Huanyin. (1993). Confucius (Kung Tzu) 551–479 BC. *Prospects: The quarterly review of comparative education* (Vol. XXIII, pp. 211–219). UNESCO: International Bureau of Education, No. 1/2. Retrieved June 29, 2008, from http://www.ibe.unesco.org/publications/ThinkersPdf/confucie.PDF

Zhou, K. (2005). *A basic Confucius* (1st ed.). Hong Kong: Long River Press.

Zimmerer, T. W., & Scarborough, N. M. (2005). *Essentials of entrepreneurship and small business management* (4th ed.). Upper Saddle River, NJ: Pearson-Prentice-Hall.

Leadership and Motivation

4

Introduction

> At times our own light goes out and is rekindled by a spark from another person. Each of us has cause to think with deep gratitude of those who have lighted the flame within us. (Albert Schweitzer)

> There is an enormous number of managers who have retired on the job. (Peter Drucker).

Motivation is one of the keys to successfully leading people. And as leaders, we inspire or motivate our people, and we also need to motivate ourselves. We need to enthuse ourselves. We learn. And we need to feed ourselves with the necessary fuel to boost our actions and up our performance. Here, we will examine the various sources of motivation among Asians.

More specifically, in this chapter, we will examine the following:

The Confucian Philosophy (The Eight Tenets of Self-cultivation, Learning and Social Relationships) as Sources of Motivation Among the Chinese
Motivation and Leadership According to Lao Tzu's Three Treasures
Ta Mo, Self-Growth and Leadership
Motivation, the Sun Tzu (Sun Zi) Way
Losing and Gaining Influence, Motivating and Managing Talent
Managing Talent, the Confucian Way (It's All About Leadership Development)

These teachings or thinking (key beliefs or value formation) are important in terms of enhancing the performance of business leaders and managers as they help leaders to cultivate themselves and their followers and people. Besides, these teachings would help to nurture the essential and good traits of successful leaders which, among other things, include making or cultivating the leaders to be more humane, compassionate, patient, of the listening sort, relating well with others, learning, be humble, sincere, clear-minded and focused or to be strategic and of

© Springer International Publishing AG 2018
K.C.P. Low, *Leading Successfully in Asia*,
https://doi.org/10.1007/978-3-319-71347-2_4

high integrity as well as to set the example for others to emulate them. In other words, these teachings also help us to derive the answers to the questions: what are the traits of a successful leader? And in some ways, what successful leadership means?

The Confucian Philosophy (The Eight Tenets of Self-Cultivation, Learning and Social Relationships) as Sources of Motivation Among the Chinese

Learning is treasure no thief can touch. (Chinese proverb)

Here, the Confucian philosophy or the eight tenets of self-cultivation, learning and social relationships serve as sources of motivation. One learns and self-cultivates oneself; one knows that what one knows, and knows that what one does not know. It does not matter if others do not know that one is learning and improving oneself as long as one keeps on learning, and (quietly and patiently) improving oneself, just like "orchids in remote places may look and smell beautiful, though no one sees, smells or admires them" (Zhou 2005, p. 10). What is also important is that one remains contented or happy with life and living.

Chinese, Japanese, Korean and Vietnamese ethics are strongly influenced by Confucius, as well as elsewhere in the Western world (Yang 1993). Confucius (551–479 BCE) was a thinker, political figure, educator and founder of *Ru* school of Chinese Thoughts (儒家思想). He was honoured as Exemplary Teacher of All Ages (萬世師表) and Sage of the Orient (東方聖人) by the later generations (Low and Associates 1995). According to Confucius, we cannot change the parameter of our birth, but we are responsible for our actions especially in relation to others. Under the given condition, each of us determines what each could achieve and be remembered for. Hence, in his teaching, he introduced the principle of great learning (大學) with the presumption that each of us is motivated to seek for "natural virtues given by heaven". He explained that one of the key sources of human motivation is perfect virtue (至善) and this virtue has to be made very clear so that a person's will be set to attain it. Only when a person's will is firmly set, (s)he will be calm, tranquil and focused in pursuing his or her goals. This state of mind would help him or her in deliberating and determining all matters. When (s)he can evaluate or judge all matters in all clarity, (s)he will achieve his or her goal that is the desired state of perfect virtue. And to achieve perfect virtue, Confucius set up eight hierarchical tenets of self-cultivation, learning and social relationships. These, which would enable us to further understand the concept of motivation among the Chinese, are as follows:

格物 gé wù: Observing Object(s) in Order

Every road has two directions. (Russian saying)

The first step in learning is to understand the first tenet. Literally in Chinese, 格 gé means to focus or to concentrate and 物 wu means the thing or object. One of the famous Confucius scholars in the Ming Dynasty, Wang Yang Ming (王陽明) at his early age, wanted to put it into practice. He invited two of his fellow scholars to come to his home and study the bamboos behind the window. It is said that they sat down quietly, watching the bamboos for a long time until at the end of the day, his two friends fell sick. Wang Yang Ming came to realise that knowledge is not stagnant but dynamic and that to attain knowledge such as on bamboos, it is not only to interpret or to describe the bamboos in one's own mind, but also, one has to appreciate and feel the existence and essence of the bamboo. One grasps the essence of a particular object. This would enable one's mind to be active, perceptive as well as to perfect its understanding of the subject matter. By doing this, one does not attach to the thing hence one would be more flexible in thinking and achieve the clarity of mind (清靜心). It is said that if one's mind is clear, one can then properly observe the object. The author takes the first tenet as a mean to motivate a person by actively looking for and understanding in-depth of the object or subject in question (or the target audience).

致知 zhì zhī: Perfecting the Knowledge

Do not be in a hurry to tie what you cannot untie. (English proverb)

Leaders need to study. Great leaders become what they are because they learn, they take the time to study the conditions and relationships of events and occurrences.

The second tenet is to achieve perfect knowledge. This can be done through thorough investigation of "the nature of all things".

Confucius said,
"物有本末, 事有終始, 知所先后, 則近道矣" which is translated as:

Things have their roots and branches; and human affairs have their endings and beginnings; to know what comes first and what comes after is to approach the principles of The Great Learning. (Tsai and Ng 1992)

Again to strive for ultimate knowledge, one should have a clear mind. Many Confucian scholars interpret the second tenet as a means to motivate a person by understanding the breadth of a subject matter and the author agrees with this interpretation for it enables one to understand the subject matter better. The author would also add that when one knows the subject well, (S)he would know the sequel and consequences, cause and effect and various ways of looking at the subject or topic concerned.

The applications of both the first and second tenets hand in hand would enable a person to understand better "the nature of all things" or have what is called total insight.

This is linked to motivation among the Chinese since one should know oneself well in order to know what motivates oneself. The employers or the managers need to know and understand their employees well, be empathetic enough so that they can (further) motivate their employees.

誠意 chéng yi: Being Clear in Thinking and Sincere in Intention

Goodness speaks in a whisper, evil shouts. (Tibetan proverb)

It is natural that with the perfection of knowledge, human thinking becomes clearer. The third tenet calls for the clear thinking and sincere intention (I would take it as honesty at heart) to enable a person to strive for perfect virtue.

Basically, it means that when one is clear on what one sincerely wants, it is easier for one to achieve what one wants.

Besides, it is in this clear thinking and sincerity of intention that the employers and managers can then wholeheartedly assist, encourage, support and hence motivate their employees and work well with them. The goals, in the practical sense, for the employees to achieve must be there, and be clearly stated; everyone then can work together and in a typical strong team spirit.

正心 zhèng xīn: Be One-Minded

When there is no enemy within, the enemies outside cannot hurt you. (African proverb)

Confucius once remarked, (學而時習之, 不亦說乎?) translating as "Isn't it a great joy to acquire knowledge and be able to put it to use?" (Analects of Confucius, Chap. 1:1). As one acquires knowledge through clarity of mind, one applies it with full intention. The fourth tenet calls for "one-mindedness" without hesitation. The author would agree that inspiring knowledge coupled with "one-mindedness" or focus would help a person to perform a job or the task effectively.

This is linked to the theory of motivation in terms of goals. When one is set on one's goal(s), one would be motivated and work towards achieving and realising these goals. This is similar to Locke's goal setting theory in which challenging goals are set to improve the level of performance.

修身 xiū shēn: Self-Cultivating in All Stages of One's Life

> Good leaders develop through a never-ending process of self-study, education, training, and experience. (Manual on military leadership)

After knowing and using the above tenets in acquiring and applying knowledge, the fifth tenet is then applied. The latter encourages one to cultivate and discipline oneself in all stages of life. Confucius stressed the importance of continuous learning, and he once said to his disciple, "To love cleverness without loving learning may lead to misconduct." (好知不好學，其蔽也蕩) (Analects of Confucius, Chap. 17:8).

Such a practical motivational attitude can be typically seen as coming from Dato Y.H. Tan, a Chinese Malaysian, "You can't run away from competition. You must look for ways to do better." (Khoo 2001, p. 45). One is motivated to grow one's potential, one would thus learn and practise self-cultivation. One learns and improves.

齊家 qí jiā: Building a Harmonious Family

> Charity begins at home. (English proverb)

> A lone sheep is in danger of the wolf. (Chinese proverb)

The sixth tenet depicts the importance of regulating one's family which depends on the cultivation of oneself. It is said that unless there is self-cultivation, a person will not be able to regulate his family or bring them into a state of ordered harmony (Low 2009a).

One self-actualises, and after improving on oneself, one seeks to extend help to others. This is similar to Maslow's (1954) hierarchy of needs. When one level of needs is satisfied, the next level of needs emerge and one seeks to attain and satisfy this higher level of needs. This is perhaps best expressed by Chai Beng Hwa, a Chinese Malaysian leader (cited in Khoo 2001, p. 120), "It is seeing your business grow, your employees grow, your children grow and do well, your friends doing well in their respective careers and their families growing that really gives you the sustained happiness."

The next two Confucian tenets—the seventh and the eighth—operate in the same way.

治國 zhì guó: Governing a State

> Ruling other has one advantage: you can do more good than anyone else. (Baltasar Gracián)

> There go the people. I must follow them for I am their leader. (Alexandre Ledru-Rollin)

To govern a state well, it is necessary for a person to have the capability first to regulate his family. In other words, it is not possible for one to discipline others when one is not able to discipline one's own family. Therefore, a gentleman(lady) does not need to complete his(her) learning on managing a state without his(her) knowing in regulating his(her) own family.

平天下 píng tiān xià: Striving for Peace and Harmony

Seek peace, and pursue it. (Proverb 34: 14)

This is perhaps best seen in terms of the leader-practitioner's way, as expressed by Tan Sri Datuk (Dr.) Kazumasa Suzuki President of The Japanese Chamber of Trade and Industry, Malaysia and President/CEO of Motoko Resources Sdn. Bhd., his "philosophy is very simple: harmony and humility. Inside harmony, outside humility. When I manage (*lead*) companies and the Japanese Chamber, I always bear that in mind." (Khoo 2001, p. 140, *italics author's*).

The good government of nations will help in stabilising the world, and hence providing a peaceful and harmonious environment for people to live in. Confucius propounded some good virtues such as being humble, practising filial piety, respecting the elders; upholding fraternal brotherhood; being compassionate to the lonely and weak to achieve the above-stated objective. He also proposed the principle of reciprocity (or the way of the measuring square) in which we can use ourselves as the measuring square of how we should treat others, hence regulating our behaviour constantly. For example, what we dislike such as the treatment of those we received from our superiors or those above us, we should not display the same treatment to those below us. This also applies to our friends, our neighbours and others (Fig. 4.1).

Summary

Nowadays, these Confucian values are innate or implicitly imbibed through cultural socialisation in an Asian individual, at least among the older generation. In many instances, an Asian's actions are determined by internalised values of what he or she ought to do. Since Confucianism presupposes that people are motivated to excel when they are guided by these virtues, thus lack of motivation means that the person has not learned the virtue or (s)he was not guided properly, and he needs to be aware of his or her roots and be triggered.

The 8 Tenets of Self-cultivation, Learning And Social Relationships (Confucius' Philosophy On Motivation)

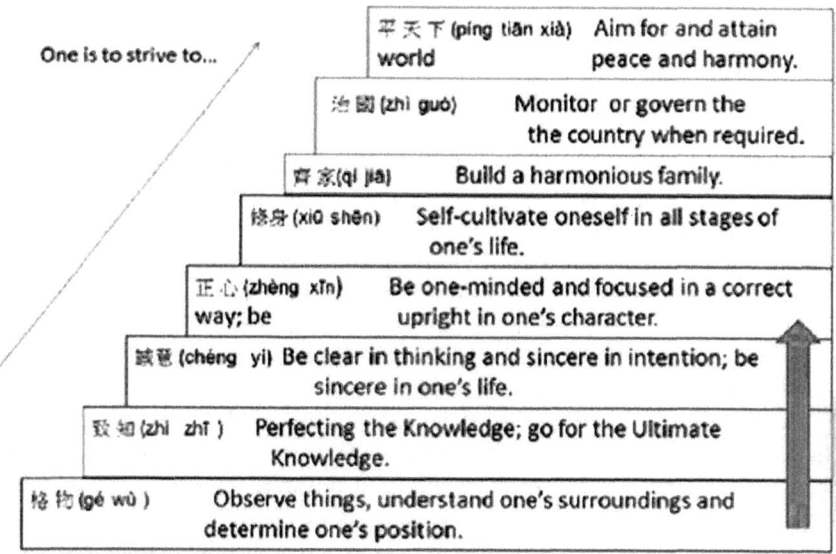

Fig. 4.1 A person should be striving to achieve the highest level. One self-actualises, and after improving on oneself, one seeks to extend help to others, ultimately aiming for and attaining world peace

Motivation and Leadership According to Lao Tzu's Three Treasures

What are the three (3) treasures of Lao Tzu? As Lao Tzu points out, these three treasures are:

> "simplicity, patience, compassion.
> These three are your greatest treasures.
> Simple in actions and in thoughts,
> you return to the source of being.
> Patient with both friends and enemies,
> you accord with the way things are.
> Compassionate toward yourself,
> you reconcile all beings in the world." (Lao 2007, Verse 67, *Tao de ching*)

Low (2009b) speaks of Lao Tzu's three treasures and relates them to organisational leadership and growth, and here in this section, the author would relate the applications of the three treasures with regard to motivation and leadership. The aim and purpose of the section is thus to apply the three treasures to motivation and leadership.

Simplicity

> The ability to simplify means to eliminate the unnecessary so that the necessary may speak. (Hans Hofmann)

> I believe that a simple and unassuming manner of life is best for everyone, best both for the body and the mind. (Albert Einstein)

Simplicity is also a characteristic feature of nature, and simplicity helps and can, in fact, motivate. The best and most simple way to motivate one's people is to follow, learn and emulate those who have motivated oneself. Learn from the great leaders one once has had. Chandler and Richardson (2009, p. 68) suggest this, "Channel them, clone them, and incorporate them into who you are all day".

As leaders, to motivate well, we need to communicate, and say in simple terms so as to promote greater understanding between ourselves and our followers. Simply, say what we mean and mean what we say.

The Chinese saying that goes, "The heart of the child is like the heart of the Buddha" is to be appreciated in the context of the leader's motivation of his(her) people. Un-trapped by ego or detached from rewards, the leader should simply serve and get the job done. (S)he does not play games, but rather be direct and concerned with the results and outputs as well as the people. Selfless, the leader, applying the language of the heart, should simply take care of the needs of their people, and this would motivate the people greatly.

When the leader listens to his or her people, (s)he appears as being humble to them. A good leader also asks and gets input from the people, and that in itself can be motivating (Chandler and Richardson 2009). (S)he is also showing that (s)he is concerned for the people, and cares for them. The heart shows the way. When the leader, and simply cares for his(her) people, (s)he is likely to be liked by the people. Ta Mo who came from India to preach or transmit Chan (Zen in Japanese) Buddhism in China (during the early fifth century), not using with even a word, he used his heart to communicate, and that is essentially good enough. It is beyond words. ["In motion, there is silence and in silence, there is motion." Some accounts speak of Ta Mo having told emperor Wudi that meditation, not good deeds, led to enlightenment. He himself was said to have meditated sitting motionless for 9 years.] From some Chinese texts and interpretation, it is said that the clarity of the mind and purity of the heart enabled him to do things, and through meditation and spiritual discipline, Ta Mo taught the *Shaolin* monks Buddhism as well as ways to keep themselves healthy; they were weak and sick due to poor blood circulation during their long meditational sessions. These monks were also taught on martial artist techniques and ways, and later, they used them to defend their faith and protected themselves against attacks on their temples.

To motivate the people well, the leader also needs to know them well. In essence, it is good for the leaders to appreciate the people's goodness and tap their strengths, and these would be motivating for the people. Collins (2001) has highlighted that companies grow from good to great when leaders really know their people's strengths so that they can help them to express or display these strengths even more. Their talents or gifts are then better used. It is really common these days, managers have spent much time trying to fix what is wrong when they can better focus on what is good and positive.

The leader simply needs to appeal to the followers' interest or passion. The leader needs to simply let or empower the individual to do what (s)he likes to do. Donald Trump once said that "without passion, you don't have energy; without energy, you have nothing. Nothing great in the world has been accomplished without passion". Passion is indeed a powerful source of energy—akin to rocket fuel. Here, it is worth-noting that jobs that make one happy or satisfied are one's own calling; and every individual has a fair turn to be as great as (s)he pleases. The person-job fit should be in place, and the individual will naturally be motivated or even perhaps inspired. It is indeed interesting when a person likes what he does and does what he likes; then, he is paid for his hobby and interest! How wonderful!

What more, a good and simple way to have people or talent on one's team be motivated is to hire self-motivated people? Yes, they are already motivated, and how wonderful! Uncover this during one's recruitment and selection interviews. Talk less, and allow the interviewees to talk. And basically one is to ask questions, and get the feel of their motivations and what makes them tick.

Another classical case of simplicity and one that is most appealing and motivating is that of the leader serving as a role model. Here, Low (2006a, p. 86) has highlighted that "role models should be assessed in the light of honesty and integrity. If followers question their leaders' honesty and integrity, leaders cannot be role models. For leaders, it is a matter of face or honor." It is very motivating and appealing for the followers after all, they simply emulate their leaders; it's more or less a situation of 'monkeys see, monkeys do' or vicarious learning.

Leaders should overall make things simple and easy for their followers.

Keeping in the dark is good for growing mushrooms. However, leaders need to share information with their people; they should not keep people in the dark (Low 2001). Martin and Schmidt (2010) has, in fact, highlighted the importance of sharing the company's future strategies with young talents and rising stars—and emphasize their role in making them real.

A basic and simple thing to do is to let the people know the purpose. Once they know the whys, it is easier to get them to do the job or task(s). Once they know the purpose, they feel right about doing the goal (job) and they get naturally motivated. After all, they know that they are doing a priority or meaningful work.

This author observes that many a corporation has a list of many values as their core values when instead they should choose and stick to three or four values as their core values. Besides, a few are easier to remember, and most people would then have no trouble keeping them in mind. Most employees would really want to work for company whose values and priorities coincide with theirs.

If a leader has a simple slogan, that slogan can be his jingle or war-cry, and it can be very motivating to not only to him or her, but also for their people.

Another simple thing the leader can do to motivate the people is just to give, give generously. It is simple to give praises, and praises are a form of giving. Praise and give more praises. And indeed praises are motivating. Praises and compliments are powerful drug; they work miracles. Praises can increase the productivity of your people.

Conversely, it should be pointed out that leaders should not simply criticise their follower(s) in public, any reprimand or disciplinary action should be done in private, period. The critical issue is—never do anything in a group meeting that would humiliate a staff.

Overall, in each of us, there lies this deepest principle in human nature, the craving to be appreciated, liked or even admired; so also our followers too have this craving to be praised. [In fact, all of us wear this sign saying, "We want to be appreciated". Lao Tzu, *Tao te ching*, verse 33, speaks of "mastering others is strength", meaning knowing men is clever.] When we praise our followers, they are pleased. Even a child who is praised for his ability and intelligence is likely to perform well in his studies; (S)he seeks very much to please the adults. And when you praise your business associates, they are likely to cooperate and work well with you. Why? Because you give them what they want. When you praise your business associate or customers, you give her confidence and make her feel secured, if not good to do business with you. She then returns you what you want: cooperation and collaboration.

Patience

Our patience will achieve more than our force. (Edmund Burke)

Patience is the key to contentment. (Prophet Mohammad)

The author here wishes to highlight that patience, a virtue is the second treasure valued by Lao Tzu. Patience is a good quality that all leaders should possess; the Chinese usually say that patience and mulberry leaves will make a silk gown.

Although at times, patience can be mistaken as sloth or laziness more so in this modern rush, rush world, this quality is very noble and can indeed be helpful in growing our followers. Patient people are not thrown off by unexpected delays or momentary difficulty(ies). They usually use idle time rather than be frustrated by the delay; they read books while queuing up or do other tasks while on a hold.

It is said that patience is a bitter plant, but it has sweet fruit. One leads better when one slows down; indeed, one needs to slow down to be motivated and win, and very interestingly, one gets more done too. When one slows down, as one reviews and reflects, one learns and understands better. Accordingly when every day one experiments with slowing down, one will understand and realise the real meaning behind the legend of the tortoise and the hare. Here, this author would also suggest another definite area in which slowing down helps is that of taking more time to talk and listen to one's people; one then makes one's relationships with one's people more relaxed, sincere and stronger.

Patience enables leaders to be good coaches, listening patiently and patiently giving feedback or input to the coachees. Leaders breed leaders. Patience is gold. Patience can build and grow great things and great people. Tiny drops of water make the mighty ocean. Heaped up earth becomes a mountain, accumulated water becomes a river. The future belongs to those who generally know how to wait, continuously learn, sharpen their saw and grow professionally. Skills, competences and expertise can be built and improved upon. Shaolin Kung Fu fighters and other martial artists, in particular, are very disciplined and patient; they persevere, growing their internal strength while practicing and developing their art forms and skills.

When one likes or loves someone, one is patient with the person; one does not judge. Calmly and without being easily annoyed, the patient leader points to the coachee his or her mistakes and allows the latter to gather lessons and learning points; the coach guides the coachee enduringly and endearingly. And in this way, the coachee picks up things faster and learns better. Perhaps, patience is love without getting tired or fed up; instead, the leader often attempts and in fact, makes continuous efforts to energize or give life to others.

It is good to be patient or simply slow down. Also teach others to be patient.

[How can we be patient? So often, one should perhaps just stay in bed until the alarm goes off. Or sit quietly in the car for a few minutes before entering the house and relax before turning on the TV set. Take a longer, more scenic route to work, walk up the stairs instead of taking the elevator and spend a few minutes greeting other members of the staff before looking at the email or tackling those voice mail messages. In other words, slow down. Do not get attached to things or routine; yes, one at times needs to change one's routines.]

Compassion

Confrontation or condemnation: I don't think it works. The only practical way is to be a genuine friend. (The Dalai Lama)

Let us next discuss the advantages and benefits of the third treasure, that is, compassion. Having a loving and compassionate nature enables leaders to pay attention to people; they, in fact, possess or display effective interpersonal skills and that's where they become more charming or charismatic. Compassion, like rainbow, has many colours and ways. Being empathetic, they smile, laugh, forgive and forget, lend an ear and get on with helping and serving others.

Compassion can also be taken as love. When one has high interest, loves one's job and has the critical passion, one does one's job smoothly and well. This is similar to the common Japanese saying, "He, who travels for love, finds a thousand miles only one mile."

And as the proverb goes, "true love never grows old." And love is wonderful, and love conquers all! Or to paraphrase the words of Rupert Brooke, love is a flame—and it beaconed the world's night. On the other hand, picture this. Imagine the very opposite of "relate well, be compassionate, love and help others": "I know a planet where there is a certain red-faced gentleman. He had never smelled a flower. He has never looked at a star. He has never loved any one. He has never done anything in his life but add up figures" (Antoine de Saint-Exupéry, *The Little Prince*). And what a sterile world a person, let alone a leader, would live as such!

Mother Teresa once said, "There is a terrible hunger for love. We all experience that in our lives—the pain, the loneliness. We must have the courage to recognize it. The poor you may have right in your own family. Find them. Love them." She added that, "(and) even the rich are hungry for love, for being cared for, for being wanted, for having someone to call their own."

Interestingly, one respondent intimated incisively to this researcher-author that "when love runs thin, whatever the other person does would be wrong or incorrect. One can then become impatient or very intolerant of the other person." Conversely, if there's love and if one lives in another's heart, one lives rent-free. We need to love and treat our other party, colleagues or all with love and love just multiplies. And grow. Yes, love them. Perhaps these are better explained with inputs gathered from several interviewees.

"Yes, I am always motivated by the compassion of my supervisor or leader. If he's compassionate, he is likely to be caring, and shows deep concern. He would also better listen to me. I'll perform better if my team leader is indeed compassionate; it's motivating to have a caring superior." intimated one interviewee to this researcher.

Other interviewees added that, "If there are any disagreements or conflicts among us, they are easily settled with empathetic concerns by my supervisor, and this is helpful." "Generally-speaking, my leader would look and focus at finding solutions, resolving the problem(s) rather than being fault-finding. Such a caring (loving) attitude helps."

Fear can cripple or immobilize us. We may not do things for various reasons but perhaps, it is the fear of making mistakes or at times, it may stem from the negative outcomes of the mind. To motivate and inspire people, a leader needs to be positive, seeing things from positive viewpoints while encouraging people to make a try, learn and/or resolve problems. And overall, as the leader shows more care and compassion, the people will dare to try, learn from their mistakes (they know that they are not punish when they make mistakes) and, in fact, when they feel psychologically safe, they learn better. The coaching and caring or loving attitude takes the power out of fear; the people then experience successes and build their confidence. Indeed this compassion attitude can be very motivating and inspiring.

Section Conclusion

The three treasures of Lao Tzu are indeed helpful, as a leader, in motivating oneself as well as our followers and those whom we lead and care for.

Ta Mo, Self-Growth and Leadership

Look within. Be still, free from fear and attachment; know the sweet joy of living in the way. (The Buddha)

In this section, the author speaks of Ta-Mo and the objective of the article is to relate some of his thoughts and/or Ch'an (Japanese term: "Zen") Buddhism in relation to leadership and its key lessons.

Ta-Mo, a Bodhidharma, is recognized as the founder of Ch'an (Japanese term: "Zen") Buddhism in China. Born into a Brahman family in southern India, Ta-Mo became a Buddhist monk, and he was totally engrossed in Mahayana Buddhism. He claimed to be the 28th generation disciple of Sakyamuni, the founder of Buddhism. Ta-Mo arrived in Guangzhou (also known as Canton), in southern China in 527 A.D.

After he crossed the Yangtze River, Ta-Mo learned from the people he met that the Northern Wei emperor, How Ming-Ti (516–527 A.D.), was also a Buddhist follower and that Shao Lum Gee, located on Ng Yu Fung, would be a suitable place for him to visit. Pui-Tai Ta-Mo arrived at Shao Sit San (the western range of Sung Mountain) and went up Ng Yu Fung (Five Nipples Peak). However, about half way up, it started to rain. Ta-Mo decided to go down, but the rain was getting heavier. Suddenly he raised his head, saw a cave in front of him and went inside. After the rain stopped a rainbow appeared. Ta-Mo went further into the cave, sat down facing the wall and began to meditate. From that day forward, Bodhidharma would remain in this cave for 9 years practicing his form of Buddhism known as Mahayana Ch'an.

Ch'an Buddhism stresses on:

1. Silent awakening
2. Wall gazing
3. Being focused, emptying all unnecessary thoughts
4. Perceiving man's nature or attaining Buddha nature.

It is said that Shaolin kung-fu has its origins in the form of Ta Mo's teachings.

In their earlier history, the Shaolin monks faced destructions of their sacred temples, and they decided to defend themselves. Inspired by observing several animals' (the monkey's, the snake's, the tiger's, the eagle's and other animals') various movements and their spiritual beliefs, the Shaolin monks developed a unique form of self-defence and martial arts called kung-fu. Here, we can learn the art of using models to inspire and motivate ourselves.

In the Shaolin mind, life is a circle. It is a series of cycles. We learn. We embrace change; we adapt to change as we learn. We also need to benchmark. Here, as Low (2000, 2006b) has argued—perhaps as leaders, we need to ask ourselves: what can we learn from others (friends and competitors)? How can we learn? And how can we apply what we have learnt?

Based on Ta Mo and his ways, we can also attribute the key idea of leadership on personal mastery, one develops and grows oneself. We would want to develop successful leadership habits, honing pour skills further. In Ch'an Buddhism, self-cultivation is encouraged. Personal mastery is attained in a disciplined manner. It's about practising or sharpening the axe. Keep going. Then there is silent awakening and growing into achieving the Buddha nature. The practice of cultivation even if it takes a long time is a sort of preparatory work, and this cultivation may be climaxed by sudden enlightenment (Fung 1948).

Motivation, the Sun Tzu (Sun Zi) Way

In this section, the author, a practitioner-academician, highlights and examines the various motivational ideas and insights in relation to the Chinese philosopher and Taoist Master strategist, Sun Tzu's (Hanyu pinyin: Sun Zi's) notion of motivation in his *Art of War* treatise. At times, the author, using examples, also imports and illustrates how a country's rulers can motivate its people. And what more, the applications of Sun Tzu's motivational ways are also shown in practice.

Introduction

As generals or leaders, motivating soldiers to fight, not to say die, for the country is an enormous task. And it is in this context that we could better appreciate Sun Tzu's concept or ideas of motivation. Although he is generally better known for crafting strategies and strategic thinking, Sun Tzu's sources of motivation or motivational ideas, when identified as examined in this section, can be both useful and strategic.

"In ancient times, skilful warriors made themselves invincible, and then watched for vulnerability in their opponents" (Sun Tzu, cited in Cleary 1991, p. 25). One can make one's organisation (also read as nation) invincible by having a highly motivated workforce (also read as citizens). Motivation among the employees (citizens) is so vital. And the leaders should motivate his troops well, and get them to be united. If there is unity within the troops, it is easier for the leaders to organize the troops, moving them to action and achieving results. Sun Tzu (Sun Zi) has highlighted that "those skilled in military operations achieve cooperation in a group so that directing (*motivating*) the group is like directing (*motivating*) a single individual with no other choice" (Cleary 1991, p. 98, *italics mine*).

Motivation can be defined as "anything that affects behavior in pursuing a certain outcome" (Lussier and Achua 2007, p. 74). This is very strategic, contributing to strategic human resources management while building the organization's strengths and invincibility. Note Sun Tzu speaks of creating "invincibility...in oneself." (Cleary 1991, p. 25), and indeed motivation can build one's invincibility, as it sustains one's pursuits of goals and determination. The organisation (nation) then can defend itself well.

At a personal level, the individual needs to know: What is the purpose for working? Why do you work? What sustains you? Are you connected or feel linked to the organisation (nation) you work for (live in)? If so, what are the ways in which you feel connected? Once one gets the answers for these questions, motivation is not what one attains from seminars or from reading a book but rather it resides deep in oneself, yes, in every cell in one's body and even perhaps in one's very soul. Then, that very purpose or answers to the above questions would compel you to work with all your heart or determination.

The Section Purpose and Objectives

Here, in this section, the purpose and objectives are to highlight and examine the various motivational ideas and insights with regard to Sun Tzu, the Chinese philosopher and Taoist Master strategist's reference to motivation in his *Art of War* treatise. In reading this paper, it is also hoped that the reader may also find out and identify his or her own key source(s) of motivation and move forward in the path towards leadership success and excellence.

Key Sources of Motivation

Here, the various sources of motivation, according to Sun Tzu, are examined and listed as follows:

Being in Unity with Tao

> When the Universe is with you, you will succeed. (Chinese saying)

When being in unity with the Tao, "halves are united and incompletes completed. In the losing of each into both and one, there is wholeness again" (Lao Tzu, cited in Grigg 1994, p. 51). [In unity with the Tao means inducing the followers to have the same aim as the leadership so that they will share death and share life, without fear of danger—or in short, motivated or energised.]

Besides, in working and living, we need to be motivated, and getting motivated starts with one's sense of purpose. A great need exists for both the commander and the army to be united and be one with the Tao ("the Way"); this, to this author, is so critical. This unity with the Tao would give leaders and followers a sense of higher purpose, and hence motivation—even inspiration—and accomplish what's to be done. It gives a sense of higher destiny.

Very spiritual too, motivation overall comes from the spirit of one's mission and the strength and trust, if not faith, of one's belief that one's purpose is morally sound.

Knowing Your People's Strengths

Do not fall before you are pushed. (English proverb)

Sun Tzu's idea here is to gain victory of the other party or the competition, yet it can be applied to the people one leads. It is really far more effective to build on their strengths than to worry too much on their weaknesses Low (2006e).

The leader really needs to know the people's strengths so that (s)he can help them to express more. The people then can capitalise on their strengths and assets. Sometimes, we just spend too much time, trying to fix what's wrong. If we build on our strengths, we can in fact not only fly but soar!

Besides, shin-kicking does not help. Attacking or make a criticism of their weaknesses does not motivate. On the other hand, when you know your people's strength(s) and praise them, it motivates them.

Creating Opportunities for Your People

If you endeavour, the fate will favour you. (Mongolian proverb)

More of serving the people and not being self-centred as well as being unduly worrying about their weaknesses, leaders can create or seize opportunities for his or her people. And these can spur them on. The people can be trained and coached.

Communicating and Connecting

Use soft words and hard arguments. (English proverb)

Communication is the process of conveying information and *meaning* (Lussier and Achua 2007, p. 172, *italics my emphasis*). Leaders should communicate effectively to their people to motivate them well. How a leader communicates affect their followers' motivation and their satisfaction with the supervisory leadership. When the leader communicates and relates well with the employees, they feel connected or engaged; good rapport must exist. And the followers should feel that they can trust their leader, their words and promises.

To Sun Tzu, communicating within and among the rank and file is critical. It is tantamount to the Chinese saying, making the clothes to fit the body. It is not a matter of making the back of the gown longer since one will bow down to meet higher officials; it is also not a matter of making the front of the gown longer because one will stand with one's chest out and head held high when meeting junior officials. It is, all in all, a matter of making the back and front of equal length; the gown is made for upright people who meet others on the same level. In short, leaders should not be a snob! To follow the Tao is to be humble or egoless. In *Tao Teh Ching*, verse 61, Lao Tzu points out that:

"When a country obtains great power,
it becomes like the sea:
all streams run downward into it.
The more powerful it grows,
the greater the need for humility.
Humility means trusting the Tao,
thus never needing to be defensive."

Indeed a leader who is humble, and one who sees the followers on the same level would likely to be more effective in communicating with them. More so, there would be little or no status barriers and distance; and as Daft (2008) has highlighted, the leader is more effective by using informal communication and management by wandering around. When the leader gets out and mingles with followers and customers, they learn more about their ideas, problems and needs. Here, the relevance of the Chinese proverb, "the tongue can paint what the eye can't see" floats out and can thus be seen. The Singapore leaders have, over the years, put into effect Ministerial walkabouts and grassroots gatherings to know and/or understand their constituents. Low's (2006a, p. 84) study has indicated that:

Corporate leaders should use more saliva than drinking tea—meaning, talking, coaching and taking personal interest in the employees' welfare. Informal talks with employees help the supervisor to listen, uncover, and find out more about the employees' needs. Such leadership also facilitates bottom up flow of information, and can be motivating too.

What more, to feel motivated, the people should feel close, and have that 'buddy-buddy' feeling with their leaders; they should not feel alienated from the leaders (Low 2001). Many leaders complain of "feel(ing) alone at the top" (Gordon 2001, p. 180). If this is so as the case of most authoritarian rulers—they normally maintain a relationship or even a communication gap with their people. Such leaders avoid getting buddy-buddy with their followers, and the latter would not be warm to them. When the leaders exercise too much control and use too much power, people feel quite hostile, if not showing less warmth to the leaders (which is one of the hidden costs of using power).

Mobilising, Rallying and Unifying

A good horse needs only one whipping, a bad horse needs a thousand. (Uighur proverb)

To Sun Tzu, there exists a clear need "to unify the people's ears and eyes to make them look and listen in concert so that they are not become confused disorderly" (Cleary 1991, p. 56). "Cymbals, drums, banners and flags are used to focus and unify the people's ears and eyes. Once the people are unified, the brave cannot proceed alone, the timid cannot retreat alone—this is the role of employing a group" (Sun Tzu cited in Cleary 1991, p. 56). While the leaders communicate to his or her people and use many signals to startle the rival's perceptions. And indeed, such ways, it can be interpreted as, giving positive energy to one's people, and in battles, read as competition in business and economy, "tak(ing) away the (rival's) energy… ….and the heart of their generals (leaders)" (Sun Tzu cited in Cleary 1991, p. 57).

This coincides with what several respondents who intimated to this researcher. "The company logo such as symbols, slogans, banners and other sources of identification put the people together". "Team efforts, team spirit and a motivated workforce make the organisation stronger." (several respondents input).

The above Sun Tzu's notion of "mobilise and unify" can also be seen in the Singapore context. A sense of unity is also created [not to mention that it is grown or nurtured into one of Singapore's national core values] by the Singapore Government (Low 2002a, b, c, 2009a, b, c). Rules for unity and religious harmony such as live and let live, exercise tolerance and restraint and other ways to share the common space are called upon so as to ensure that all groups live together in peace. Accordingly, "the public debate cannot be on whose religion is right and whose religion is wrong. It has to be in secular, rational considerations of public interest—what makes sense (*or serves as the motivational basis*) for Singapore." (Prime Minister Lee Hsien Loong cited in Hussain 2009, p. B3, *italics mine*).

Additionally, in Singapore, Harmony Day, 1 day each year is set aside for racial harmony celebrations especially in schools. Successes are also celebrated, and that is also motivating.

Setting the Example

> Young pigs grunt as as old pigs grunted before them. (Danish proverb)

Motivate by doing.

According to Sun Tzu, the leader leads more by example and not by force. Sun Tzu knew how to create conditions so that his people would want to follow him. He inspired his people by example (Baldoni 2004). And in this author's view, it is perhaps similar to personal satisfaction or gratification of a leader (person) in which Mahatma Gandhi referred to as happiness—more so when what one thinks, what one says and what one does are in harmony.

A leader's examples are critical; as a Chinese saying goes, "a tiger father begets a tiger son". A frightened captain makes a frightened crew. If the leader is courageous, so would be their people. The leader commands, and this is similar to what Chandler and Richardson (2009, p. 38) has exhorted, "Lead from the front". It motivates the people to see that the leader is out there and (s)he does it him(her) self. This matches with Low's (2006a, p. 85, *italics my additions*; 2001) research in which the findings indicated that the leaders' presence and "leaders serv(ing) as role models" were sources of motivation among the employees of Singapore's Chinese small and medium companies.

Setting the example, the leader shows the way (Low 2003; Low and Theyagu 2003). Pro-active (Low and Theyagu 2003), the leader needs to be in the forefront;

(s)he should set the example in motivating (inspiring) his or her followers. As Mahatma Gandhi once said, "You can't change people. You must be the change you wish to see in people".

Using Banners, Symbols and Signs

A good horse doesn't have to be whipped. (Uighur proverb)

Always showing them, the leader becomes not the only symbol (of examples set); and other aspiring symbols and signs are also used. Just as in wars, banners and cymbals are used to rally or unify the forces against the enemy, in daily living, symbols and signals are used to energize one to forge ahead or attain success in one's career.

The use of banners and symbols as a source of motivation can still be seen in many Chinese homes and offices. In Chinese weddings, to bring good luck, Double Happiness, a large Chinese character, on a red piece of paper or in paper cut is often put. Often, other good luck and motivating symbols such as *Fu Lu Shou*—the Chinese gods of good luck and happiness, wealth and longevity are also used to adorn the homes of the Chinese. Here, through a unity and through this trinity, they enhance each other's powers. Their statues, each hardly being sold on its own or separately, are ordinarily sold as a trio [each one of their powers depends on their unity]. The Chinese are indeed motivated by happiness or good fortune, prosperity and longevity (Low 2010a). Better seen in the Chinese Lunar New Year practices, oranges, given in pairs, are exchanged between relatives and friends; similar in colour as gold, oranges represent fortune and prosperity. Oranges being round or 'in circles', without a beginning or an end, symbolises forever happiness or joys for both the receiver and the giver.

Thinking Big, Working Small

It is better to take many small steps in the right direction than to make a great leap forward only to tumble backward. (Chinese proverb)

In their book, *Sun Tzu for Marketing Strategies*, Michaelson and Michaelson's (2004) reminds us of thinking big in terms of *what* one wants to achieve yet to work small in *how* to achieve it. And rightly so, he directs that leaders should be concerned with the individuals and groups within the organisation, and their motivation, more so, when one bears in mind that the macro organisation is a collage of the teams and individuals.

When deliberating, a wise general should consider both favourable and unfavourable factors. According to Sun Tzu, when the leader takes into account favourable factors, one is likely to succeed. If one takes into account the unfavourable, he may avoid or avert possible disasters.

Work small energises. Work small like an entrepreneur can also give much energy. There is less structures and formalities but with more creativity. Work small helps to gain strength. Work small can also be taken as working on individuals—growing them. When your people increase their skills, the leader gains strengths and leverage. Interestingly, work small can also be seen as continuous improvement. And as Lao Tzu said, "The journey of a thousand miles must begin with a single step"; and the work gets done. This, to the author, is akin to the Chinese saying "ants eat bone"; a metaphor describing a situation where people trying an overwhelmingly big task by doing bit by bit with perseverance. Personal mastery, the discipline of personal growth and learning, of mastering oneself in a way that make easy one's leadership and achieves desired results (Daft 2008; Senge 1992), is overall encouraged and practised.

"Thinking big, working small" also implies that change is actively embraced; bit by bit until it is completed. And the proactive shapers are those who are ready to change and be changed. Effective change leadership and management need strong leaders to ensure that the change process remains on track.

Hiring the Motivated and Giving Big Rewards

If you pick the right people and give them the opportunity to spread their wings—and put compensation as a carrier behind it—you almost don't have to manage them. (Jack Welch)

At the outset, it should be noted that "leaders who figure out, on their own, ways to reward their people for good performance get more good performance than leaders who run around all day putting out fires caused by their people's poor performance" (Chandler and Richardson 2009, p. 207).

Hence, a simple yet effective key source of motivation is still giving rewards. To the soldiers, "what gets the enemy's goods is reward" (Sun Tzu, cited in Cleary 1991, p. 13). If the leader rewards the people with spoils, that will make them fight on their own initiative, so that the opponent's goods can be acquired. That is why, accordingly, it is said that where there are big rewards, there are valiant men.

Then again, if the leader rewards everyone, there will not be enough to go around; so reward one or a few to encourage the many and everyone.

Note that for Singapore, foreign talent is here to stay, there are four million people in Singapore and one million of which are foreigners (Lee Kuan Yew, cited in Chong 2003). Singapore needs to "attract, welcome and make foreign talent *feel comfortable*" here for it to become a global city (Lee Kuan Yew, cited in Chong 2003; *italics author's emphasis*). According to Sun Tzu "captured soldiers should be well treated, to get them to work for you" (Cleary 1991, p. 16). In the Singapore context, "captured soldiers" can be analogous or parallel to foreign talents. In the same way, one can say that Singapore's good treatment of the foreign talents results in attracting foreign talents; they work and live in the island-Republic to boost its economy. Among other things, various schemes and policies including Deposit scheme for permanent residence and Scheme for housing foreign talent (shiFT) exist to attract the best brains to Singapore's shores (Bhasin and Low 2002). Many are given permanent resident status, and with that a stake in the City-state. And interestingly to paraphrase Sun Tzu, in business and economic growth, if one uses foreign talent to compete or reduce foreign competition while boosting the country's core competences and skills leverage, then one can or will be economically strong.

All the above sounds good but it is not all that rosy; to make a fair comment, some of these foreign workers are living in "crowded dormitories, the siting of which remains controversial. . . . . .a record 2600 living in cramped unhygienic and unapproved housing" was uncovered and reported in the local papers (He 2009, p. D1). More definitely thus need to be done to improve the living conditions of these foreign workers.

Allowing the People to Think Hungry and Always Be Prepared

If a son is uneducated, his dad is to blame. (Chinese proverb)

Not to be complacent, instead to be motivated, getting things done and acquiring rewards, the people should feel hungry. What is meant by this? Here, if one can always remember danger or crisis when one is secure and remember chaos in times of order, watch out for dangers and troubles while they are still formless and prevent or avoid them before they occur, this is best of all.

In terms of the above practice and applications to Singaporeans and Singapore as a nation, it is best put when Minister Mentor Lee Kuan Yew (cited in The Brunei Times 2010; *italics mine*) confirms these:

. . .Singaporeans know and we (*the leaders*) keep on reminding them that this is all they have, and if they don't make use of it and train (*prepare*) themselves and learn. . ., they are going to go very hungry.

Indeed, as Low (2006c) has argued, Singaporeans' need to achieve value is a good insulation against problems or crisis. Such a value with the competitive spirit is very strong among Singaporeans and Singapore companies. The Government has, in part, created Singaporeans' "crisis mentality" by expressing a "permanent sense of crisis" (Clammer 1985, p. 509); this preoccupation with survival has given rise to what Schein (1996, p. 69) calls the "island mentality" "we have to do it on our own". Singaporeans' watch out for dangers and "we must achieve" (Ong 2002; Chiew 2002, p. 14) have thus been etched or become ingrained in Singaporeans' psyche that has been moulded by the Singapore Government. Stressful as it may be; nonetheless, these make the ordinary Singaporeans tick.

Besides, the possible racial fault-lines in multi-ethnic and multi-cultural Singapore have often been highlighted; racial harmony and business growth should not be taken for granted. For example, on the 50th anniversary of the island-Republic self-government, Prime Minister Lee used the year 2009s biggest political platform to issue a rallying call for unity across different races and religions (Oon 2009, p. 1; Wong 2009, p. B1). The practical outcome and preparing for the long term is often given emphasis, and the people in Singapore have opted for political stability and economic growth with its attendant benefits. This study confirms the Singaporeans' tendency to think and feel hungry, and coincides with Low's (2002a, 2006d) studies. Singaporeans are, in most ways, highly geared—if not motivated— to prevent or avoid problems while seeking for economic growth (survival).

Applying Benevolence Yet Being Firm and Consistent

If your heart acquires strength, you will be able to remove blemishes from others without thinking evil of them. (Mahatma Gandhi)

A Taoist normally regards a relationship we call caring and loving as intrinsic to us as heat is to fire or hardness is to rock; wind is to air. Sun Tzu recommended that the leader cared for his or her soldiers. Sun Tzu says: "Look upon your soldiers (also read as employees or citizens) as you do infants, and they willingly go into deep valleys with you; look upon your soldiers as beloved children, and they willingly die with you" (Cleary 1991, p. 85; Gagliardi 1999). Conversely, if the leader is so nice to the people (employees), so kind to them that one cannot command them, so casual with them that one cannot establish order, then they are useless, tantamount to "spoiled children, useless" (Cleary 1991, p. 86). Interestingly, such motivational ways is also seen in practice in Chinese small and medium companies; In Low's (2006a, p. 85) study, the researcher speaks of "the leader is like a father; 'father-leadership' is practised. There is nothing really bad of the word 'paternalism' as the Chinese corporate leaders show much care and concern to their employees. Besides, 'employees get the all-in-the-family feeling'".

When applying Sun Tzu's way(s) to motivating citizens, governments need to direct the people to bring about economic growth and good living standards. "The people are the basis of a country, food is the heaven of the people. Those who rule over others should respect this and be sparing" (Sun Tzu cited in Cleary 1991, p. 14). Being benevolent yet firm, and looking after the people's well-being, the government facilitates economic growth by building the necessary infrastructure and amenities and giving the people law and order as well as peace and political stability (Low 2006d). Here, the author has the Governments of the island-Republic of Singapore, Japan and South Korea in mind. As Low (2006d) has argued, the Singapore government leaders act as benevolent father leaders. Sun Tzu puts it as:

...direct them through cultural arts, unify them through martial arts; this means certain victory.

Besides, "when directives are consistently carried out to edify the populace, the populace accepts. When directives are not consistently carried out to edify the populace, the populace does not accept. When directives are consistently carried out, there is mutual satisfaction between the leadership and the group." (Cleary 1991, p. 79)

Applying Relationships

With true friends... even water drunk together is sweet enough. (Chinese proverb)

Underlying the above notion, Sun Tzu's "applying benevolence yet being firm and consistent" is the fact that relationships rule.

The leaders' rapport and relationships with his or her followers help. Be warm. It motivates them. Such a leadership is more than a just contractual relationship between the employer/manager and the employee. This author would classify or term such a contractual relationship as impersonal and cold. Applying relationships, to this author, is interestingly applying leadership with a heart; it's more than getting the job done. In leadership with a heart, the tasks or the job should be accomplished yet it's done with the welfare and interests of the followers in mind and at heart. The followers' needs and interests are also looked into. Motivating, such a leadership, can perhaps be best seen in Akira Kurosawa's 1965 Toho-Kurosawa classic movie *Red Beard*; this is an original story by Shugoro Yamamoto. Fictional though, and set in the Tokugawa Shogunate era, Dr. Niichi, the head doctor of a government clinic, is portrayed here as looking into the hearts as well as the bodies of his patients. He cared very much for his poor patients. Most of the patients came from the slum areas and was infested with lice and fleas. One old patient, for example, was very sick and quiet; he had liver cancer; here, Red Beard saw that there was some great misfortune behind his silence. And when the old man was about to die, he asked his assistant doctor, Dr. Yasumoto to keep a watch, as it was the dying man's solemn moment, his last moment. In coaching Dr. Yasumoto, Dr. Niichi also wanted him to gain that people touch in creating rapport and building relationships with the hospital's patients.

Section Conclusion

A motivated workforce or people supply much force or accumulated energy as well as momentum; skilled leaders are able to allow the force of the momentum to gain victory and secure success for them without exerting their strength. Indeed, as Sun Tzu points out, "getting the people to fight by letting the force of the momentum (*motivation*) work is like rolling logs and rocks. Logs and rocks are still when in secure place, roll on an incline...when the people are skilfully led... ...the momentum is like that of round rocks rolling down a high mountain—this is force." (Cleary 1991, p. 38).

Losing and Gaining Influence, Motivating and Managing Talent

Salt away—save something (for example, money) for future use. [This originates from the days before refrigeration, when salt was widely used to preserve meat and fish for later consumption.]

People of talent resemble a musical instrument more closely than they do a musician. Without outside help, they produce not a single sound, but given even the slightest touch, and a magnificent tune emanates from them. (Franz Grillparzer)

Selfless or without much ego, leaders should be motivated to grow themselves as well as they grow their people. The Chinese saying, "dragons beget dragons, phoenixes hatch out phoenixes" is applicable here. Leaders motivate their people to grow leaders. Leaders breed leaders. Genius is the diamonds and gold in the mine; a leader is the miner who works and brings them out.

In the first place, leaders should know how to motivate their people and up their influence. Perhaps this can best be handled by asking ourselves, "How can we lose our influence of our people?" or "How can we annoy our people?" and after answering this, we ask, "How can we win or gain our influence of our people?"

How Can We Lose Our Influence of Our People? Or How Can We Annoy Our People?

A burnt child reads fire. (English proverb)

Take the assumption of McGregor's Theory X, that is, the people are lazy and are not capable of self-direction. They basically dislike work and are not responsible (McGregor 2006).
Take away or reduce your people's confidence. Make them feel small. Talk down to them.
Be impolite or rude.
Have harsh words with our people.
Take the people's credits.
Be insincere. Uphold the view that honesty is not the best policy.
Be impatient.
Don't listen.
Interrupt our people when they talk.
Act egotistically.
Be a Smart Alec, and act that we know all!
Boast or brag about ourselves.
Bulldoze your way. My needs and my way come first.
Tell the people what to do. Just make commands to our people; order them around.
Be task-oriented; don't care about the human aspects. Treat them like machines or robots—after all, they are here to do the job.
Be formal. Get your people to refer you by your titles. Demand respect.
Do not trust the people.
Be vague.

Instil fear among our people; make them afraid of us. Better still, be oppressive. Always remember, and apply the Confucian saying, "An oppressive leader is much more feared than a tiger."

Hide or hijack information from the people. Run a secret service agency. Practise lack of transparency.

Be more concerned with our needs than their (the people's) needs.

Be concerned with the tasks and results.

Do not give good reasons or evidence, based decisions on hearsays.

Be narrow-minded, be closed to ideas. Be intolerant or reject new ideas.

De-motivate and demoralise the people.

Be fault-finding. Look at the people's weaknesses.

Criticise the people.

Be passive.

Downplay the people's strengths and belittle their efforts. Don't recognise their efforts.

Be pessimistic, and apply negative thinking. People often avoid negative-thinking people. For them, things are often not right for them. Often feeling down, they mope and mow.

Don't praise the people. Be stingy with praises.

Be bad. Don't practise benevolence. Don't practise virtue, and drive people away from us.

Create obstacles to the people when they are accomplishing their goal(s).

Don't be a role model. Create differences in your speeches (words) and actions. Create confusion.

Create mismatches. There are contradictions to cause disagreements. Everything does fit well. The leader's needs and the people's needs are not matched.

How Can We Win or Gain Our Influence of Our People?

E raka te maui, e raka te katau. (Maori) or the English equivalent: *A community can use all the skills of its people.* (Maori proverb)

Much of influencing and other forms of persuasion or changing minds is based on various principles. If one understands the principles of persuasion, then as leaders, we can be creative, inventing and adapting our own ways or techniques. It makes sense to invest time to understand these principles, and they include:

Take the assumption of McGregor's Theory Y, that the people are capable of hard work and self-direction. They like work and are responsible (McGregor 2006).

Give our people confidence: "If I am confident, then you can also be confident."

Be polite and diplomatic.

Sharing a kind word with our people.

Give the people due credits.

Promote exchange. "If I do something for you, then you are obliged to do something for me." (Low 2001)

Be open and honest with the people. Be sincere.

Be patient. Take time to spend with them.

Listen well to our people.

Let them talk. Listen, listen deeply.

Be informal. Be flexible. Relate well with the people (Low 2001). Here, Confucius said, "No man is a machine. He should not behave heartless like one, or as if others were machines." (Chew 2000, p. 5)

Be humble.

Find out more about the people. Get to know and understand them better.

Trust the people; they are capable of self-direction and setting goals for themselves.

Empower the people. Leaders should empower their people to act. After all, "the history of company success is the history of staff empowerment, involvement and ownership." (Low 2000, 2002a, 2006b, p. 77)

Build the people's trust. "If I trust you, then I will accept your truth and expose my vulnerabilities."

Be specific. People fill in gaps in vague statements. When we are specific in what we say, we seek to remove ambiguity, communicating completely and precisely. Specific language utilises words that have single meaning and uses complete sentences, leaving nothing to imagination.

Practise love and compassion. Show care and concern to our people. Love is a magnet; it is the greatest of them all.

Share information. Encourage openness, different perspectives and diversity of views and ideas. Allow and encourage transparency.

Amplify. Make the most important bits bigger and other bits smaller.

Repeat. Repetition, at most times, helps to reinforce ideas and is necessary to change minds.

Show concern with the people's needs.

Be concerned not only with the tasks and results but also with the people; relate well with them.

Give evidence. People cannot deny what they see with their own eyes.

Adopt mind growth (Low 2002a, b, 2006b). Be open to ideas.

Resolve problems and be solution-centred.

Guide and give the people inputs and feedback.

Inspire the people. Excite and enthuse the people.

Energise the people with fresh ideas and perspectives, changes and projects.

Be proactive.

Be passionate. People can get excited by the leader's passion or the way (s)he speaks. Enthusiasm is catching, and can spread like wild fire.

Appreciate and cherish the people's strengths and efforts.

Be optimistic. Apply positive thinking; people usually like positive thinking people. Positive-thinking people are often happy. And as Mark Twain once remarked, "Whoever is happy will make others happy, too". Happy positive-thinking people are highly influential.

Praise or give compliments. People want to feel appreciated.

Apply humour. Have fun. People like to have fun.

Replace. Put the ideas and tell them in story form; it's more appealing.

Be good; practise benevolence as advocated by the likes of Confucius. Good people nurture virtue and inspire others.

Provide solutions, going all the way to lend a hand or help our people.

Be the role model. Set the example. To paraphrase Confucius, when the leader him(her)self does what is right, (s)he will have influence over the people without giving commands, and when the leader him(her)self does not do what is right, all his commands will be of no avail. Besides, in the Confucian sense, a gentleman (lady) is bound to attract other gentleman(lady). A gentleman(lady) is at ease with other gentlemen(ladies). The leader's actions speak louder than words, and such examples can be inspiring and motivating.

Ensure alignment. When everything lines up, there are no contradictions to cause disagreement. Everything fits well. The leader's needs and the people's needs are well-matched.

Bond with the people; one ordinarily does what one's close friends ask of one, without much fuss (Low 2001).

One more critical point—overall, it's good to have new blood but it should not be at expense of the existing talent pool. Leaders should be aware and not engaging in what this author calls the Dracula syndrome, often just interested in taking in new talents or fresh blood but often neglect to grow the existing talents in-house. Yes, we can take in foreign talents but what about our existing or local talents. It is no point in jumping to reach the stars when we trample upon the very flowers, beautiful flowers at our feet.

Talents need to be grown. Leaders grow their followers' confidence and self-esteem. The talented followers also score a high level of self-efficacy. Leaders adopt Theory Y assumptions of their people, that is, they are capable of self-direction and growth. They like work and are indeed responsible.

Leaders motivate their followers so that they strife to achieve and grow. Leaders engage, enthuse, energise, and empower their followers. They make use of any opportunities to allow their followers to build their self-esteem as well as putting their skills and/or strengths to use.

To inspire and motivate their people, good leaders get their people's involvement and input; these are essential if the leaders want to get their people to buy into their plans.

Additionally, leaders need to give their talents psychological safety—that when they make mistakes, they are able to learn from them and yet keep their jobs; they would not be penalised.

Contrariwise, some organisations and leaders may impose heavy penalties, and apply massive punishments to deal with mistakes or rule violations. These may suffocate many or everyone because of one person's mistakes, missteps or an isolated incident. Over-reacting and using mass punishments can indeed stifle the

Company's talents, demoralise the people and destroy the very inspiration that takes so much hard work to create.

Trusting the leaders, the people are ordinarily comfortable working with them. Leaders should also engage their people assets to give them that valuable psychological ownership so that organisations can nurture and retain the talented individuals. These individuals are happily absorbed in their work, being passionate in what they do as well as becoming highly skilled professionals. What more, they have personal mastery of what they do and enjoy a high level of high job satisfaction.

Rather than dwelling on their weaknesses (if any), leaders, being positive and tapping on their followers' strengths, make their followers soar. Rather than robbing them of credits, they give credits to their followers where and when they are due. Besides, in a prosper-thy-neighbour attitude and posture, leaders reward their followers accordingly. All these would allow the followers to grow, becoming (true) leaders.

In the next section, we will define and examine talent management, the Confucian way.

Managing Talent, the Confucian Way (It's All About Leadership Development)

Introduction

The Chinese have a saying that, "An army of a thousand is easy to find but ah, how difficult it is to find a general."

People should be valued and talents respected. Confucius cared most about people. When the stables burned down, Confucius enquired if any person had been hurt but did not ask about the horses. He recognised the free will of every individual, believing that the commander of three armies could be removed, but the will of even a common person could not be taken away.

In mid-1990s, the fast growth in many Asian countries had, more or less, created a deficit of leadership. Indeed with increasing competition, better talents differentiate higher performance companies from the rest.

Talent is the primary driver of any successful company, and this is tantamount to what Jack Welch (cited in Schiemann 2009, p. 23) has highlighted, that is, "we spend all our time on people. The day we screw up the people thing, this company is over."

What Is Talent Management?

Everyone according to their talent and every talent according to its work. (Proverb)

Let us define talent. We can take talents within organisations as highly skilled people with leadership qualities. Leadership is a vital skill in inspiring and motivating a group of people towards a common goal; the people get things done as well as they happily do the job. It is taken that leaders with talents and skills drive the business to success. Talent management is also about companies motivating and retaining these productive talents within their organisations.

To most business owners and executive teams, it is becoming increasingly obvious that rather than being constrained by capital, they are typically constrained by talents. And companies realise that they need the right talents to work out their vision, execute the strategy and deal with the company issues, problems and challenges ahead. In short, effective talent management builds successful or winning organizations.

The purpose and objectives of the section is to demonstrate talent management by applying the ways of Confucius as discussed in the Analects and other Confucianism literature.

Selecting Talents: The Talent Portfolio or the Qualities of Leadership Valued

If one does not plough, there will be no harvest. (Chinese proverb)

The right and good wood or material should be derived before one sculptures an art object, so also the right talent must be selected and hired for the right appointment.

In the Confucian context, a person, more so, a leader should uphold the value of *Jen* acting and behaving as gentleman (lady). People are grown to be gentlemen (ladies), and they become better leaders.

According to Han Yu, a Tang Dynasty scholar although talented people are important to society, even more important is the person who knows how to find talented people. And in this aspect, Confucius stressed that the selector of talents should understand the person (the talented individual) throughout. For Confucius, he was not concerned about other not knowing him; his great concern is his not knowing men.

Leaders spot leaders; and they breed leaders. It takes talent to spot talent! Just as Confucius instils a leadership or more specifically an ethical mindset throughout the rank and file, so also, talent management is about instilling a talent mindset at all levels of the organisation, beginning with senior leaders (Serrat 2010). Holding a humanistic philosophical viewpoint, Confucius stressed that leaders should pay attention to these areas, and likewise, in this author's view, in managing talents, the leader should focus on:

- Being benevolent, a characteristic element of humanity, is an inseparable part of an individual's talents. A worthy person is a benevolent person, and A benevolent person gives love. Mencius added that (s)he who practises benevolence is invincible. Accordingly, to Confucius, a non-respecter of talent is not worthy to be respected (Dai and Zheng 2002). This shows the critical importance of talent management, talent should be well selected, nurtured and grown.

- Setting the example, thus receiving the Heavenly Mandate (authority) to lead. The Old Master was reputed to say, "Go before the people with your example, and be laborious in their affairs." Through leading by example, the company or the leader should be the magnet that attracts the best talents. For Confucius, a good leader—with the example (s)he sets—is just like the wind and the people are like the grass. Let the wind blow over the grass and the grass, under the force of the wind, cannot but bend. The talent or the leader is inspiring, and others emulate them.
- Being analytical. The talented individual selected is also analytical, (s)he "can see a question from all sides without bias." (Confucius, cited in Chew 2000, p. 6)
- Learning. Note that "the mind of a gentleman (lady) progresses upwards" (Chew 2000, p. 22). "If a man improves himself, is he not indirectly improving his family, his country and ultimately the world?" (Chew 2000, p. 20). A person studies for the sake of self-improvement. Confucius said, "Isn't it a great pleasure to learn and relearn again?" (Lin 1994, p. 202).
- Being self-motivated. The talented individual should also be self-directed, being intrinsically motivated. Confucius spoke of the measure of a person is a person, (s)he who loves to live according to the true principles without external inducements, and (s)he who dislikes all that is the opposite to the principles of true personhood without outside threats of punishments.
- Upholding integrity and honesty, making the will clear. The leader should have a high moral standing.

The Chinese saying, "If you are standing upright, don't worry if your shadow is crooked" is apt here. "If a leader's personal conduct is upright, the common people will do their duty without being ordered. But if he is not upright in his personal conduct, even though he gives order, they will not be followed" (Chew 2000, p. 20). Low (2008, p. 33) has indicated that "When virtue is practiced, one enjoys a clear conscience. And a clear conscience is like a soft pillow, and one sleeps well." Lin (1994) refers this as satisfying one's own conscience.

- Loving and being compassionate. A gentleman(lady)'s humanity extends to all. People-oriented, the benevolent leader loves others and the courteous respects others. He who loves others is loved in return. With this, what more, peace and harmony is attained. And they are precious, and this is the basic Confucian perspective in terms of human relations. Mencius, in a typical Confucian fashion, added that, "a gentleman(*lady*) has a sensitive heart which cannot bear to see suffering in others." (Chew 2000, p. 36; *italics mine*).
- Winning the people's trust. The leader should take care of the people's interests; hence the people can trust the leader. "Without the trust of the people, there can be no government (leaders)." (Chew 2000, p. 18)

- Being pragmatic. From the Confucian angle, the leader and the talented should also be pragmatic. Pragmatic, Confucius was believed to have said—accord respect to the heavenly and earthly spirits but keep them at a distance. And he did not talk about monsters, physical exploits or ghosts.
- Being resilient. Interestingly, "the Confucian leadership style can be seen as practicing resilience too" (Low 2008, p. 38). Mencius (cited in Chew 2000, p. 43) maintained that "there is goodness out of adversity." Poverty, exhaustion, hardship, bitterness and frustration will stimulate or excite a man's mind, strengthen his character and make good his flaws.
- In the Confucian tradition, it is also said that *Yi Chou Shu* (The Remnant of the Chou Dynasty), one of the earliest history books of China devoted a whole chapter to discovering talented people (Dai and Zheng 2002). *Sincerity*, for example, is noticed by focusing on a person's personal characteristics and feelings, *evaluating words* which uncovers a person's intended meaning; *listening to tones* and *observing expressions* focus on finding personal qualities by studying facial expressions and listening to voice pitch changes. *Observing hidden sign* strips off the cover to reveal one's character traits. And *appraising virtue* assesses the whole person.

Lin Shao of the Han Dynasty (Dai and Zheng 2002) developed seven methods focusing on emotions and behaviours in identifying a talented person:

1. Decide with whom the person associates
2. Identify the person's motives
3. Observe changes in emotions to establish the person's integrity
4. Assess the person's level of expertise
5. Watch attentively the person's interaction with others
6. Confirm whether the person is modest and polite
7. Determine the person's strengths through his or her weaknesses.

During the Three Kingdoms period, Zhuge Liang, a well-known politician and strategist summarised from his experience seven principles for evaluating a person's potential, and they include:

1. Check reasoning and analytical skills by asking conflicting questions.
2. Assess the person's ability to debate an issue by repeatedly arguing with him on the same issue and observe how he views the problem.
3. Review decisiveness by letting the person make a decision and see whether (s)he is capable in his(her) analysis of the situation.
4. Check the person's commitment level by handling him(her) over a difficult task and by clearly indicating to him(her) of a danger or difficulty, then see how bold (s)he is and how willing (s)he is to make self-sacrifice.
5. Assess the level of the person's self-control by making him(her) drink alcohol and examine his exercise of self-control.

6. Provide him(her) with access to something of worth, and see whether (s)he acts with integrity.
7. Assign an important task to measure and check the person's dependability. These Zhuge Liang's principles reflect the Confucian standard for judging a person's potential and character. (Complete Works of Zhuge Lian 1986, cited in Dai and Zheng 2002.)

Selecting Talents Who Are Holding the Same Values as the Company's

Motivation will almost always beat mere talent. (Unknown)

It is critical to note that people who are most attracted to us are the people who are most like us. Here, the "like" that I wish to stress is that of the likeness of values. There is a need to ensure that the organisation gets and hires the people who share the same values as the organisation. The person's values and the organisation's values must match. Stahl (2007) points out that furniture retailer IKEA selects employees on grounds of their attitudes, values and cultural fit with the company as much as for their qualifications; this is because, in certain professions at least, job-related skills are not always the best performance predictor and can easily be changed, while values and personalities do not.

This author would also want to argue that better still if the leader's values match with that of the talented professional hired too since Mariotti (1996, pp. 121–122) has pointed out that "when the leader's values are strong, the people can sense it like an aura around him or her".

Indeed unity is strength, and values too bind the people within the organisation together; Confucius did exhort to "work together with one heart..." and that one heart are matching of values between the Company's and the talented as well as that of the leaders and the people.

Empowering Your Talents

If you're poor, change and you'll succeed. (Chinese proverb)

The organisation needs to empower its talents; they are capable of self-direction and growth, both for the organisation and themselves. For Confucius, "a gentleman demands much of himself", and as such, the organisation should its people feel more confident, allowing them to set the goals and standards. When there is empowerment, there is much involvement, engagement and ownership on the part of the organisation's talents (people). The best performance comes when everyone understands what the standard for good performance is for the organisation.

Being Persuasive with Your Talents

I have no particular talent. I am merely inquisitive. (Albert Einstein)

Anyone can simply lead or manage by instructing, telling or commanding but that is not smart leadership or management.

An important element of talent management is not to adopt a command and tell approach; instead, be persuasive with your talented people. Mana Lohatepanont, the Hay Group's managing director for Thailand and regional director for Southeast Asia is quoted to say that in Asia, leaders emphasise on harmonious relationships and they "are supposed to guide and give emphasis to teamwork rather than pointing their fingers" (Management by bungapos 2010).

"One can never win the allegiance of others by trying to dominate them. One can only succeed by caring for their welfare" (Mencius, cited in Chew 2000, p. 41). If indeed one bonds with one's people and 'command' wisely, one will be obeyed cheerfully.

Showing Care and Concern for Your Talents

Nice words won't come from a bad source. (Chinese proverb)

When leaders recognise their people's strengths, they further show that they really care for their people. The people also feel that their talents are well harnessed, and that they are able to use their potentials.

We care and you matter. You can shout from the roof top that you care but you got to be sincere. And act. The company has to honestly say and live it. And that is critical. Accordingly, Mencius spoke of feed(ing) a man without showing him love is to treat him like a pig; to love him without showing respect is to keep him like a domestic animal. For Mencius, love and respect are gifts for the giving. But without sincerity, they are empty show (Chew 2000).

Likewise, when senior leaders genuinely care for their people, the people would feel connected, motivated, recharged and energised. By practicing father leadership (Low 2007, 2006a, d), benevolence and showing good care of the people, they would feel motivated. And people, though they like to think that they are rational, are really emotional beings. And because they feel good they are likely to remain with the Company.

Recognising Talents and Appreciating the Strengths of Your Talents

I believe that I often bring out the best in somebody's talents. (David Bowie)

There is an old Chinese proverb that goes, "When one drinks the water, one should not forget but appreciate the people who helped to dig the well". The company should recognise talents within its organisation, and this coincides with what Aliakbar (2004) has highlighted, that is, recognise talent: "Notice what do employees do in their free time and find out their interests. Try to discover their strengths and interests. See all possibilities. Look deeply and listen deeply and soon, the leader can uncover the strengths of their people (Chandler and Richardson 2009). It is indeed very Confucian for the nobler sort of person or gentleman(lady)-leader to stress on the nobler qualities of their people, and does not accentuate the bad; the inferior person (leader) does.

Also, leaders are to encourage their people to discover their own latent talents. "For instance, if an employee in the operations department convincingly explains why he thinks he's right even when he's wrong, consider moving him to sales!" Here, the Confucian or Chinese saying is apt—"He who knows others is good, but he who knows and conquers himself is better (more superior)."

In the Confucian context, a good leader also helps the people to realize what is good in them. And this is very positive; the Confucian leader appreciates and builds up his people's strengths and indeed, based on these strengths, allows them to soar.

Identifying Those with the Highest Leadership Potential Early in their Careers

Hide not your talents. They for use were made. What's a sundial in the shade? (Benjamin Franklin)

In talent management, there is a strong need to identify those individuals with the highest leadership potential across the organisation early in their careers.

It can be argued that this can be seen, as Confucianism, in the way in which Mencius was brought up. His mother shifted their home three times in order to ensure that Mencius was being brought up in a good setting, and that examples are critical. [When Mencius was living near the cemetery, he emulated the actions of the paid mourners, and when staying near a marketplace, he followed the ways of the merchants. Finally, when Mencius' mother brought him to live near a school, he learnt well and followed the ways of a scholar.] Here, the first vital point underscores the importance that talent management starts early and when one begins one's career in the organisation. And the second key point is that the examples of the leaders are critical in grooming and growing the talented individuals with the company. The third key point is that it is critical that the talented within the organisation are imbued with the organisational core values, being soaked or immersed in the organisation from their early career days.

Being Friendly, Approachable and Communicable

The tongue is but three inches long, yet it can kill a man six feet high. (Japanese proverb)

To retain talents, the leadership approach needs to be people-oriented. And in this aspect, Low (2006a, 2007) speaks of the Chinese leadership approach as being personable and more people-oriented, rather than task or performance-oriented. Low (2002b, 2009c) speaks of *киm cheng*, relationship-based, rather than just hiring and firing or based on results; loyalty is emphasised. Low (2006a) elaborates what he has uncovered in his study:

In Confucius' teachings, *jen* means humanity (love to all men. . .) and a wise leader practises *jen*. He pays attention to the people around him. The analogy used here is water. A leader should be just as responsive as water is, to its surroundings. He needs to listen, and show care and concern to the people around him. After all, there's a Chinese saying that goes, "a person's success is dependent not on the number of servants he has, but on the number of people the leader serves". "We admire such a leader; his behaviour is very motivating" (an interviewee's input).

Interestingly as this author was talking to several Chinese leaders they revealed that, "when the leader is friendly, approachable and communicable plus caring, he becomes a teapot, serving the many cups around him. Somehow, the Confucian leader just wants to do good; and believes it would benefit others." And to them, such ways, which can be motivating, can help to retain the talents within the company.

Knowing Oneself Is Vital, Coaching Is Necessary

"Thirty years the east bank, thirty years the west bank". (Meaning, one's luck and one's destiny will change over time) (Chinese proverb)

For Mencius, it is necessary that one rectifies the mistakes in others by first rectifying them in oneself. Knowing is critical and it is the starting point. Each person should know what (s)he knows and what (s)he does not know. For Confucius, each person should also know what is right and what is wrong, and that is wisdom. (S)he should also know what is his(her) strengths and weaknesses, then the leader coaches and guides the talents that (s)he has. The leader "enlightens others by being learned and wise. You cannot help others if you remain in benighted ignorance." (Chew 2000, p. 45).

Confucius was willing to teach and learn with anyone who came to him. So the good (Confucian) leader coaches the talented. And the talented are being coached, mentored and guided. Jack Welch (cited in Serrat 2010, p. 3) once said that, "My main job was developing talent. I was a gardener providing water and other nourishment to our top 750 people. Of course, I had to pull out some weeds, too."

Training Your Talents, Investing in Your People

If you think in terms of a year, plant a seed; if in terms of 10 years, plant trees; if in terms of 100 years, teach the people. (Confucius)

Confucius stressed on learning, education and training, and in fact, he was the first man in Chinese history to end the ruling class monopoly on education by opening the first private school where his human-centred philosophy was developed and lectured (Dai and Zheng 2002).

In today's global economy, companies must continually invest in human capital. Training and development is inclusively applied to all within the organisation. A more 'inclusive' whole workforce approach is necessary, some authors argue, because '... an inclusive talent management strategy is a competitive necessity' (Chris Bones cited in Warren 2006, p. 25).

In his paper, *Applying Strategic Leadership, the Way of the Dragon*, Low (2010b) has highlighted these:

> Get better, or get beaten! Training 'little dragons' or soldiers for battle are essential. Likewise, training, coaching and mentoring employees in today's ever-changing world is critical. Untrained troops, like untrained employees, will only yield casualties, and allow the competition to take advantage of the company's situation.

He further indicated that these are "tantamount to one of Jack Welch's key leadership secrets, that is, more specifically, leadership secret number seventeen. Leaders should 'provide an atmosphere where people (*talents*) can have the resources to grow, the educational tools are available and they can expand their horizons' (Jack Welch in Slater 1994, quoted in Low 2010b, *italics mine*) as well as capitalising opportunities for both individual and organisational growth". In this regard, one can argue that Confucian ways and methods are as fresh and relevant today as in the days of the old.

Conclusion

In the Confucian sense, people are grown to be gentlemen (ladies), and they become better leaders. By growing better leaders at all levels, from the first line onwards, good talent management can be effected within the organisation.

Chapter Conclusion

Successful leaders are, among other things, often growing their people. They are inclined to be more humane, compassionate, patient, of the listening sort, relating well with people, learning, humble, sincere, clear-minded and focused. They are also strategic and of high integrity as well as being an example for their people to emulate them.

All in all, people click with those they like or able to relate to. People like people who are very much like them; they are motivated when they are connected to their leaders. People are motivated by leaders who are humble, simple, friendly, caring, listening and showing compassion as well as being patient. Ordinarily, people feel cared for, they feel that they can learn and grow, and that their talents are used (these successful leaders effectuate and realise good talent management of their people); thus, they are motivated, if not inspired by such leaders. Besides, we can also surmised that **the 4As** as propounded by Low, Islam and Ang (2013, p. 520) are very much applicable in today's context; here, they indicated in their findings that people are motivated by:

Being **Acknowledged**: "To be acknowledged is to be given recognition."; "it is an ego-booster."; "to be acknowledged is a "good basic source of motivation"";"I feel that I am part of the team if I am being recognized for the job."; "I am motivated if I am being acknowledged the work I am asked to do"; "it is important that I understand and clarify the work before starting to do it"; "before accepting the job, I need to have known that I have the potential and skill to do it"; "we are not treated as PNG: persona non grata, this means that we have to acknowledge our capability and role before we start our work"; "there is no point of asking us to participate without acknowledging our contributions to that piece of work afterward".

Being **Accepted**: "When I accept the job, I'm committed to doing it"; "I would make sure that I appreciate the work before I accept it"; "I do not like it when it is so impersonal", "we want to feel part of the family"; "one feels good to be accepted"; "being accepted is a positive stroke"; "to be accepted is to be given a role (and I feel good)"; "I feel happy to be accepted"; "there's this ingroup feeling"; "being a cautious manager, I must have good preparation and great confidence in my team before I accept the new contract or challenges"; "I feel good to be accepted"; "in being accepted, we feel connected"; "I dislike impersonality" and "we want to have that familial feeling."

Being **Appreciated**: "I would appreciate the work in order to complete it"; "if you don't appreciate the work, then it is better not to accept it". "I normally appreciate my work. If I don't appreciate my work what for I do it"; "I feel good when other especially my bosses show their appreciation of me"; "believe in us shows the leaders or managers' trust of us, it also shows their appreciation"; "money is valued; giving monetary rewards is one way of showing appreciation."; "it's like getting a hug or a kiss"; "of course like anybody else, I always expect an appreciation of words/token from my boss when I have done well with my work" "I feel good when others especially my bosses show their appreciation of me." "I feel happy or satisfied when my work is praised."

Having **Achieved**: "I'll go all the way to achieve it when I accept it"; "I normally... ...accomplishing things... completing a project successfully makes me feel great"; "I want to achieve, achievements energize me."; "achievements are energizing"; "I enjoy working and achieving things and goals". "I like taking actions"; "I always feel great when I've delivered my products/services on time and on budget"; "achievements are energizing."

Checkpoint: Think About It

Leadership and Motivation

Review the following key points and when you have finished the quiz, check your answers.

The Confucian Philosophy (The Eight Tenets of Self-cultivation, Learning and Social Relationships)

1. What are the eight tenets of self-cultivation, learning and social relationships?
2. When leading your people, how and in what ways can each of these ways motivate or help them?
3. How do you motivate yourself?
4. What are the ways in which you, as a leader, can improve yourself?

Motivation and Leadership According to Lao Tzu's Three Treasures

1. As a leader, what are the things you can simplify? And how can you make things simple to motivate your people?
2. How and in what ways can you simplify the paperwork within your organisation?
3. As a leader, what are the ways in which you can be patient to motivate your people?
4. As a leader, what are the ways in which you can show compassion so as to motivate your people.

Ta Mo, Self-Growth and Leadership

1. State the key points in relation to your understanding of Ta Mo?
2. What habits do you wish to cultivate and make it a part of you?
3. Do you benchmark? What can you benchmark?
4. What can you learn from others?

Motivation, the Sun Tzu (Sun Zi) Way

1. What are the ways to motivate your people?
2. When motivating your people, are you
   - Being in unity with Tao (being aware of your higher purpose)?
   - Knowing your people's strengths
   - Creating opportunities for your people
   - Communicating and connecting with your people?
   - Mobilising, rallying and unifying your people?
   - Setting the example?
   - Using banners, symbols and signs?
   - Thinking big, working small?
   - Hiring the motivated and giving big rewards?
   - Allowing the people to think hungry and always be prepared?
   - Applying benevolence yet being firm and consistent?
   - Applying relationships?

Losing and Gaining Influence, Motivating and Managing Talent

Reflect on what you have read in this section and list out your key learning points.

Activities and Exercises

1. What do you really want out of life? Decide what you want out of your life. What really motivates you?
2. Ask yourself: What do your key people really want out of life? Find out more and check: What really motivates them?
3. Do you want to differentiate yourself? If so, how would you differentiate yourself? Think of ways in which you can differentiate yourself and stand out.
4. Motivate yourself. Fire yourself. Think of what would you do should you start anew. What would you do differently? What changes would you effect? If we are too entrenched (or rigid), it is difficult for us to see further. Re-energise ourselves for the challenges ahead.
5. What are the vision, mission and values/goals of your organisation?
6. Do the values of your people/talents match with the values of the organisation?
7. Motivate your people. Fire-up your people. Find out more and check: What are your people's core values? What they value most? What really spurs them?
8. Do the goals of your people/talents match with the goals of the organisation?
9. What are the gaps in leadership/skills that exist in the organisation?
10. What are your ways in identifying your talents?
11. How do you recruit and select your talents?
12. How much attention do you give to the talents you have?
13. How much action do you give to the talents you have?
14. What actions do you take for the talents you have?
15. What sort of training is being implemented for your talents?
16. What procedural support or documentation do you intend on providing to ensure the skills of staff are maintained? Do you have an appropriate allocation of responsibilities? How will the new responsibilities be documented and communicated to staff? What internal processes will you do to regularly check that the current skills of your staff members are still appropriate for the business/unit?
17. What training programmes will you be organising for possible/potential successors? [Are these conducted in-house or by external providers?]
18. Have you also considered change management training for the organisation in preparation for the succession?

Managing Talent, the Confucian Way (It's All About Leadership Development)

1. How do you select your talents?
2. Do you do the following
   - Selecting talents who are holding the same values as the company's
   - Empowering your talents
   - Being persuasive with your talents
   - Showing care and concern for your talents
   - Recognising talents and appreciating the strengths of your talents
   - Identifying those with the highest leadership potential early in their careers
   - Being friendly, approachable and communicable
   - Knowing oneself is vital, coaching is necessary
   - Training your talents, investing in your people

References

Aliakbar, S. (2004, July 28). Talent management. *The Hindu*. Retrieved Apr 28, 2010, from http://www.hinduonnet.com/jobs/0407/2004072800100100.htm.

Baldoni, J. (2004). *Great motivation secrets of great leaders*. New York: McGraw-Hill.

Bhasin, B. B., & Low, K. C. P. (2002). The fight for global talent: New directions, new competitors. *Career Development International* (Published by the MCB University Press, UK in association with the University of Strathclyde, Scotland), *7*(2), 109–114.

CC Low & Associates. (Edited and translated in 1995). *Confucius – Sage of orient*. Singapore: Canfonian Pte.

Chandler, S., & Richardson, S. (2009). *100 ways to motivate others*. Singapore: McGraw-Hill/MDIS Membership Publications.

Chew, K. H. P. (2000). *A gentleman's code*. Singapore: Graham Brash (Pte) Ltd.

Chiew, S.-K. (2002). Chinese Singaporeans: Three decades of progress and changes. In L. Suryadinata (Ed.), *Ethnic Chinese in Singapore and Malaysia* (pp. 11–44). Singapore: Times Academic Press.

Chong, V. (2003, February 19). Foreign talent policy here to stay: Lee Kuan Yew. *The Business Times*. Yale Global Online. Retrieved August 14, 2009, from http://yaleglobal.yale.edu/display.article?id=999.

Clammer, J. (1985). *Singapore: Ideology, society and culture*. Singapore: Chopmen.

Cleary, T., (Trans.). (1991). *Sun Tzu – The art of war*. China: Shambala.

Collins, J. (2001). *Good to great: Why some companies make the leap. . . and others don't*. New York: HarperCollins.

Daft, R. L. (2008). *The leadership experience*. Boston: South-Western Cengage Learning.

Dai, C., & Zheng, Z.-g. (2002). Chapter 11: Managing talents in China: Confucian origins. In C. Brooklyn Derr, S. Roussillon, & F. Bournois (Eds.), *Cross-cultural approaches to leadership development*. Westport: Quorum Books.

Fung, Y. L. (1948). *A short history of Chinese philosophy*. New York: The Free Press.

Gagliardi, G. (1999). *Sun Tzu's art of war plus the ancient Chinese secret revealed*. Seattle: Clearbridge.

Gordon, T. (2001). *Leadership effectiveness training*. New York: The Berkley Publishing Group.

Grigg, R. (1994). *Tao of relationships*. Singapore: SS Mubaruk & Brothers Pte.

He, S. (2009, April 18). Home away from home. *The Straits Times*, D1–D4.

Hussain, Z. (2009, August 17). PM's 4 basic rules for religious harmony. *The Straits Times*, B3.

Khoo, C. (Ed.). (2001). *Malaysia savvy*. Petaling Jaya: PHP International Singapore Pte. Ltd. and Malaysia Institute of Management.

Lao, T. (2007). *Tao te Ching* from a translation by S. Mitchell. Retrieved May 22, 2007, from http://acc6.its.brooklyn.cuny.edu/~phalsall/texts/taote-v3.html.

Lin, Y. (1994). *The wisdom of Confucius*. New York: The Modern Library.

Low, K. C. P. (2000). *Strategic customer management*. Singapore: BusinesscrAFT™ Consultancy.

Low, K. C. P. (2001). *The power of relationships*. Singapore: BusinesscrAFT™ Consultancy.

Low, K. C. P. (2002a, 2009). *Corporate culture and values: Perception of corporate leaders of co-operatives in Singapore*. Unpublished PhD thesis, the University of South Australia/Published. VDM-Verlag, USA/UK.

Low, K. C. P. (2002b). *Strategic customer management* (2nd ed.). Singapore: BusinesscrAFT™ Consultancy.

Low, K. C. P. (2002c). *Corporate culture and values: Perception of corporate leaders of co-operatives in Singapore*. Unpublished PhD thesis, the University of South Australia, Adelaide.

Low, K. C. P. (2003). *Team success*. Singapore: BusinesscrAFT™ Consultancy and Humber Lincoln Resources Pte.

Low, K. C. P. (2006a). Motivation, the Chinese leadership way in Singapore's small and medium companies. *The Icfaian Journal of Organizational Behavior, V*(1), 80–90.

Low, K. C. P. (2006b). *Strategic customer management* (3rd ed.). Almaty: Caspian Publishing House.

Low, K. C. P. (2006c). Crisis management – Can core values be considered as a built-in safety net? The Singapore case. *Insights to a Changing World Journal, 2006*(3), 133–150. Retrieved Oct 31, 2006, from http://franklinpublishing.net/insightstoachangingworld.html.

Low, K. C. P. (2006d). Father leadership – The Singapore case study. *Management Decision, 44* (2), 89–104. Emerald Insight, www.emeraldinsight.com/0262-1711.htm.

Low, KCP. (2006e, December). Sun Tzu's art of war – Planning in negotiation & persuasion. *Effective Executive* (pp. 22–26). Institute of Chartered Financial Analyst India: ICFAI.

Low, K. C. P. (2007). Father leadership and small business management: The Singapore case study. i-manager's. *Journal on Management*, December 2006–February 2007, 5–13.

Low, K. C. P. (2008). Value-based leadership: Leading, the Confucian way. *Leadership and Organizational Management Journal, 2008*(3), 32–41.

Low, K. C. P. (2009a). The way of the dragon – Some strategic leadership ways. *Leadership and Organizational Management Journal, 2009*(2), 40–59.

Low, K. C. P. (2009b). Lao Tzu's 3 treasures, leadership & organizational growth. *Leadership and Organizational Management Journal, 2009*(3), 27–36.

Low, K. C. P. (2009c). *Corporate culture and values: Perception of corporate leaders of co-operatives in Singapore*. Saarbrücken: VDM-Verlag.

Low, K. C. P. (2010a). *Successfully negotiating in Asia*. Berlin: Springer.

Low, KCP. (2010b, January 4–6). Applying strategic leadership, the way of the dragon. *e-Leader conference*. Chinese American Scholars' Association: CASA, Singapore.

Low, K. C. P., Islam, Z., & Ang, S. L. (2013). Acknowledging, accepting, appreciating and achieving, are these really motivating?, *Educational Research, 4*(7), 517–524, ISSN: 2141-5161.

Low, K. C. P., & Theyagu, D. (2003). *Developing true leadership potential*. Singapore: The Publishing Consultant.

Lussier, R. N., & Achua, C. F. (2007). *Effective leadership* (3rd ed.). Mason: Thomson South-Western.

Management by bungapos. (2010). Leadership traits of the East and West. *Management*. Published on 6 Jan 2010. Management by bungapos is licensed under a creative commons attribution-noncommercial-share alike 3.0 Thailand license. Accessed May 6, 2010, from http://bungapos-management.blogspot.com/2010/01/leadership-traits-of-east-and-west.html.

Mariotti, J. L. (1996). *The power of partnerships*. Cambridge, MA: Blackwell Business.

Martin, J., & Schmidt, C. (2010). How to keep your top talent. *Harvard Business Review, 2010*, 53–61.

Maslow, A. H. (1954). *Motivation and personality*. New York: Harper and Row.

McGregor, D. (2006). *The human side of enterprise*. New York: The McGraw-Hill Companies.

Michaelson, G. A., & Michaelson, S. W. (2004). *Sun Tzu for marketing strategies*. New York: McGraw-Hill.

Ong, C. B. H. (2002). *The Singaporean achiever*. Third year academic project, Degree of Bachelor of Science Honours (Business Management) (Intake: 99/06), The University of Bradford.

Oon, C. (2009, August 17). PM warns of religious fault lines. *The Straits Times*, 1.

Schein, E. H. (1996). *Strategic pragmatism, the culture of Singapore's Economic Development Board*. Cambridge, MA: Massachusetts Institute of Technology.

Schiemann, W. A. (2009). *Reinventing talent management*. New York: Wiley.

Senge, P. (1992). *The fifth discipline: The art and practice of the learning organisation*. New York: Random House.

Serrat, O. (2010). *A primer on talent management*. Mandaluyong: Asian Development Bank (ADB). Retrieved Apr 28, 2010, from http://www.adb.org/documents/information/knowledge-solutions/primer-on-talent-management.pdf.

Slater, R. (1994). *Get better or get beaten*. Burr Ridge: Irwin Professional Publishing.

Stahl, G. (2007). Talent management: Building and sustaining a strong talent pipeline. INSEAD. Retrieved Apr 28, 2010, from http://knowledge.insead.edu/contents/stahl.cfm.

The Brunei Times. (2010). Lee Kuan Yew on Brunei's next level of growth. *The Brunei Times*, 15 Jan 2008. Retrieved Feb 1, 2010, from http://www.bt.com.bn/en/home_news/2008/01/15/lee_kuan_yew_on_bruneis_next_level_of_growth.

Tsai, C. C., & Ng, E. T. (1992). *Da Xue, the great learning*. Singapore: Market Point Design Pte.

Warren, C. (2006). Curtain call. *People Management, 12*(6), 24–29.

Wong, K. H. (2009, August 17). Twin threats of race and religion. *The Straits Times*, B1.

Yang, H. (1993). Confucius (Kung Tzu) 551–479 BC. *Prospects: The Quarterly Review of Comparative Education*. UNESCO: International Bureau of Education, XXIII(1/2), 211–219. Retrieved June 29, 2008, from http://www.ibe.unesco.org/publications/ThinkersPdf/confucie.PDF.

Zhou, K. (2005). *A basic Confucius*. San Francisco: Long River Press.

Leadership in China, Mongolia and Tibet

5

China

Leading, The Confucian Way

There is a well-known Chinese saying that goes, "consider the past and you will know the future." Here, in this section, leadership is seen through the Confucian visor and it is also applicable in Asian countries where the overseas Chinese live and where the *Confucian Heritage* exists or prevails in these countries' national culture such as, for example, Singapore. With quotations from Confucius and the Confucian texts, this section attempts to explain and illustrate leading, the Confucian style. This section intends to also examine and show the ways in a leader can raise his influence through the Confucian tenets and principles. Among other things, humanism and loving is stressed, and some lessons in teaching can also be derived. Several benefits and minuses of the Confucian leadership and its traits are also discussed.

Introduction

Leadership as the driving force of organisations has played an important role in every profit or non-profit organisation, society, and nation. In this section, the objectives are first, to identify or interpret what is leadership according to the Confucian tenets and principles and second, show the importance and benefits of such a value-based leadership style and ways.

To begin with, Confucius (Pinyin: *Kǒng Fūzǐ*, Wade-Giles: K'ung-fu-tzu, lit. *Master Kung*, 551–479 BC) was an esteemed Chinese thinker and social philosopher, whose teachings and philosophy have deeply influenced Chinese, Japanese, Korean and Vietnamese thought and life (Wikipedia 2007) and also elsewhere, even in the Western world (Yang 1993). Some of his ideas have, in fact, stood the test of time.

© Springer International Publishing AG 2018
K.C.P. Low, *Leading Successfully in Asia*,
https://doi.org/10.1007/978-3-319-71347-2_5

A worthy point to note is that, as what one respondent opined to this author, that all Chinese schools, that is, schools teaching Chinese language and culture agree that Confucius is 萬世師表 *Hanyu Pinyin: Wan Xe Se Piau* which means:

Wan means 10,000 (expressed as millions)
Xe means generations
Se means teacher
Piau means example.

The whole sentence is interpreted to mean that Confucius is a role model, a teacher for millions, millions of generations to come.

The Confucian Leadership and Its Ways

Being a Gentleman (*Junzi*)

> The gentleman is learned in right; the small man is learned in gain. (Chinese proverb)

The leadership message Confucius impresses on us is that: As leaders, we need to act and behave as gentlemen.

If we are to achieve a state of orderliness and peace, we need to return to traditional values of virtue. These values are based entirely on one concept: *ren*. Differing form the Western Biblical traditions, the fifth century Chinese sage Confucius believed that human nature is basically good. However, he also believed that this goodness needs to be nurtured and cultivated and the best way to do so is through education. According to Confucius, "unending strength, resoluteness, simplicity and reticence are close to benevolence" which is attainable through self-cultivation, education and performance of the *li* or rituals/code of behaviour (Story 2007). Low (2010a, p. 39) has, in fact, argued that being a gentleman(lady) (being benevolent or virtuous) can raise the leader's soft power.

Interestingly, in a capsule, just as Confucius has said, "It is man that makes truth great, and not truth that makes man great." and "the measure of man is man." (Lin 1994, p. 183)

In short, humanism and true manhood is stressed. "A gentleman understands what is moral, a base man understands what is advantageous or profitable" (Chew 2000, p. 9). Needless to say, if a gentleman were to go and live among uncivilised peoples, then how could these peoples be crude? His very character and actions will help change them for the better.

Stressing on and Practising Virtue

> Virtue never dwells alone, it always has neighbours. (Chinese saying)

Virtue is something to be desired highly. But why virtue is stressed?

When virtue is practised, one enjoys a clear conscience. And a clear conscience is like a soft pillow, and one sleeps well. "A gentleman finds peace of mind in virtue and he covets it" (Confucius cited in Chew 2000, p. 8). Rightly too, Confucius has highlighted that "likes and dislikes should not affect our judgment. We should be on the side of what is right and against what is wrong" (Chew 2000, p. 9).

In this aspect, the leader's example is critical. Without example, a leader becomes "a person who lacks gravity (*and*) does not inspire respect" (Confucius cited in Chew 2000, p. 2, *italics mine*). A leader gains moral grounds and attracts his followers through his examples. His actions are louder than words.

As Low (2006a) has highlighted, role models should be assessed in the light of honesty and integrity. If followers question their leaders' honesty and integrity, leaders cannot be role models. For small and medium Chinese business leaders, it is a matter of face or honour. In the case of Singapore's national values, Low (2002) speaks of the *Confucian Heritage*, here, it should be noted that Transparency International, 2002 (cited in Lim and Daft 2004) ranks Singapore as the fifth most corruption free among 102 countries. The Singapore's People Action Party (PAP) track record and ability to fight off critics based on honesty and integrity has enabled it to stay relevant and win all election campaigns since 1959 (Lim and Daft 2004, p. 50). True, though some critics may perhaps highlight that there is nothing Chinese or non-Chinese leadership way; perhaps, it is just the spill-over effect or influence of the national leadership on the island-Republic's small and medium companies (Low 2007a). Then again, one can safely say that if "honesty and integrity simply form the unshakeable foundation of effective leadership', then virtue and gentleman-ness (*jen*) synonymously form the foundation of the Confucian leadership style.

Boosting One's Influence

A man must do something worthy of mention when he has reached manhood. Merely to live on, getting older and older year by year, without having accomplished anything or getting wiser, is to be a good-for-nothing. (Confucius)

According to Confucius, "a wise man does not readily give utterance to words in case his actions do not live up to his words" (Zhou 2005a, p. 10). "One who talks too much is prone to failure." (Confucius, cited in Zhou 2005a, p. 68). "A gentleman is slow to speak but prompt to act" (Confucius, cited in Chew 2000, p. 10). "When the ruler (*leader*) does what is right, he will have influence over the people without giving commands" (Lin 1994, p. 199).

"A good leader may be compared to the wind and the common people to the grass. Let the wind blow over the grass and the grass, under the force of the wind, cannot but bend" (Chew 2000, p. 18). Pro-active, through his examples and behaviour, a leader thus builds his influence.

Here, "a gentleman is bound to attract other gentlemen. A villain is bound to attract other villains. Moreover a gentleman is naturally at ease with other gentlemen; a villain is naturally at ease with other villains" (Confucius cited in Chew 2000, p. 2).

Interestingly, your best way to raise your influence is to apply the Golden Rule, the gentleman's code of conduct. In essence, you does onto others what you yourself like, and "do not impose to others what you yourself dislike" (Zhou

2005a, p. 4). By applying the Golden Rule, you will not incur resentment, and in fact, win others over.

The four essential virtues of a leader are that in his personal conduct, he is respectful. In his dealings with his staff, he is considerate; in caring for the common people's welfare, he is generously kind; and in dealing with all, he is just.

Being Humble

> Use your light, but dim your brightness. (Lao Tzu)

It has been said that, "The arrogant army will lose the battle for sure." In battle, leadership and living, humility is regarded as a virtue and strength; it is to be treasured (Fig. 5.1).

Confucius specifically said, "A man who brags without shame will find great difficulty in living up to his bragging" (Lin 1994, p. 179). The superior person or leader is dignified, but not proud or arrogant. The inferior person is proud but not dignified.

Humble, the leader blames him(her)self, while a lesser or common person blames others. Besides, a good leader does not criticise other people's faults, instead (s)he criticise his(her) own or examine him(her)self. Because a leader is humble, (s)he learns. Not to learn from one's mistakes would be to commit a double mistake.

The Confucian leader is unassuming and humble. And because of this and the lack of egoism, (s)he becomes a good team-player and even a likeable team leader.

According to Confucius, "a wise man does not readily give utterance to words in case his actions do not live up to his words" and "one who talks too much is prone to failure.".

Fig. 5.1 For Confucius, one should not boast; a wise man does not readily talk or say things in case his actions do not live up to his words

The relationships among the team members are good and harmonious; with the team leader, the team members get along well with each other.

Loving

> A man without love; what is courtesy to him? A man without love; what is music to him? (Chinese proverb)

Confucianism indeed stresses on humanism; and a successful leader should be more humane or compassionate.

A benevolent person gives love, and is indeed an admirable person. He who is kind or munificent is supreme,

According to Confucius "no man is a machine. He should not behave heartlessly like one, or as if others were machines" (Chew 2000, p. 5). "A gentleman is (also) conscious only in the knowledge of others' comfort; the mean is conscious only of his own comfort" (Chew 2000, p. 2, *italics mine*).

As a teacher (course leader), Confucius further believed that to elicit good results, he must love his pupils (Yang 1993). He needs to know them well, understand their psychological particularities, give thought to ways and means of making easy their access to knowledge and, to that end, develop an effective methodology.

The hallmark of a teacher's virtue, in Confucius' eyes, was loving commitment through his lessons to his pupils' development. The teacher needs to look into the moral development of his pupils too, and that is an attractive way or value that a teacher may want to hold.

The Master once said: "Love makes a spot beautiful: who chooses not to dwell in love, has he got wisdom?" (Scholastic 2007). A leader needs to be compassionate too. "Few are competent to love and to hate others" (Chew 2000, p. 8). "The emotion of love in a gentleman is passionate but not sensual, and sad also, without being painful" (Chew 2000, p. 7).

To this researcher, a very good example of loving, as well as being influential and leading the Confucian way is that of the late Matsushita Konosuke (1894–1989), the founder of Japan's Matsushita Electric. Putting "people before products" (PHP Institute, Inc. 1994, p. 54), Matsushita Konosuke believed in producing people, and consulting. "Consulting is better than ordering." "He was known for broaching the topic as if seeking advice or offering a suggestion. In other words instead of simply saying, 'Would you do such and such', he would say something like, 'I've been thinking we could do such-and-such this way; what do you think' or 'Would you undertake this job?, thus making his subordinates feel free to present their own opinions and suggestions on the matter'" (PHP Institute, Inc. 1994, pp. 58–59).

A Western example of leading the Confucian way is that as practised by billionaire Kenneth Fisher who is the founder and chief executive of money management firm, Fisher Investments. To him, loving is best shown by adopting the best way—giving back to the community by creating jobs for the people.

Besides, he has willed 80% of his estate to John Hopkins for medical research rather than set up a trust (Tan 2007).

Fostering Father Leadership

The beginning of wisdom is to call things by their correct names. (Chinese proverb)

Confucius stresses on the importance of the family; and in the family unit, the father is the key figure. He must be the role model, a good example to his children. For the son, it is the son's duty to obey without questioning and honour his father, even after death. When the father dies, obedience is given to the oldest brother. Confucius states in the *Analects*, "Meng I Tzu asked about the treatment of parents. The Master said, 'Never disobey! ...While they are alive, serve them according to ritual. When they die, bury them according to ritual and sacrifice to them according to ritual.'" (*Analects* II: 5) Analects of Confucius (1992).

Showing care and concern to his followers, the benevolent Confucian leader is like a father and an example to his followers, a useful characteristic that a leader should possess. Besides, the family spirit is often fostered, and to quote Confucius:

A true gentleman is in harmony, and is friendly with others though he does not agree with them... (Chew 2000, p. 17).

In the small business situation, the father leader/small business-owner collaborates with his "family members" in a purposeful team fashion, "rubbing shoulders and doing something together also gives the opportunity to share. There is joint purpose, sharing the same dreams and bringing the relationship to a higher plane. There is also synergy" (Low 2001, p. 101; 2005a, 2007a). Employees' successes are celebrated and with effective team leadership, teamwork is fostered and higher performance attained (Zimmerer and Scarborough 2006; cited in Low 2007a).

At the core, it appears that this teamwork, or more appropriately, consensus-seeking culture may be related to loyalty, which is also considered to be a virtue by the Chinese (Bond 1987; cited in Low 2002). Chinese are taught from a young age to be loyal to their family and kin. Hsu (1984) claims, loyalty to the family will continue to play a critical role among Chinese. Family is important in any culture, but it is extraordinarily so in Chinese culture. But more importantly, "relations among family members provide the human basis for the moral virtues of the Chinese" (Nakamura 1978; cited in Low 2002). Hsu (1984) has identified some of the significant characteristics of the Chinese family that have a strong impact on Chinese organisations. The Chinese as a people are special in their relationships with others, and a strong emphasis on the importance of blood relations, parental authority, filial piety and loyalty exists. The late Kwek Hong Png, founder and chairman of the Hong Leong (Singapore) group of companies, for instance, pointed this out when he was expanding his business:

Mindful of the old Chinese proverb that when tackling a tiger, one needs the help of one's brothers, I invited my brothers to join my firm. (Kwek 1987; cited in Low 2002)

Emphasising Learning, Education and High Integrity

Learning is a treasure that will follow its owner everywhere. (Chinese saying)

In this aspect, Low (2006c, citing Sie 1997; Cham 1998) highlights these:

Wu, a Chinese scholar mentioned that learning, or the Confucian concept of *keji* (one must learn and be ready to move), was important to Singapore and its future. *Keji* was also reflected in the way the Government made its education, IT and technology plans about 30 years ahead, and Singaporeans must learn to move ahead in today's world. In a true Confucian fashion, the Singapore Government has invested much to better the Singapore workers' educational status. University education is also given much emphasis; the government is seeking to make local universities world-class and best in the region; and with Singapore's ambition to be the knowledge centre of the region, it is only natural to emphasise research and development.

To Confucius, "the gentleman broadens himself by scholarship or learning, and then regulates himself by *li* (proper conduct or moral discipline)".

The Confucian leader, even in the modern day, stresses on learning, education and high integrity. Its investments on schools and education are high (Low 2002). Having the Confucian Heritage *practical thriver* culture (Low 2002), the Singapore Government relies on the Mandarinate or scholars to administer the City-state. Although appearing elitist, the efficient and honest civil service promptly attended to the needs of its citizens, and it is said that for Singapore everything was on the table with clear rules (Thurow 1996; Schein 1996; cited in Low 2002). High integrity is maintained with the Corrupt Practices Investigations Bureau (CPIB) under the charge of the Prime Minister's Office. Indeed, as Confucius highlighted, "We are saying (*emphasising*) all the time: *Li! Li!*" (Lin 1994, p. 200, *italics mine*).

Being Prudent

The prudent embark when the sea is calm—the rash when the sea is stormy. (Chinese proverb)

Being prudent is also another trait of the Confucian leadership. Confucius is attributed to say these:

Tsze-chang asked Confucius, 'In what way should a person in authority act in order that he may conduct government properly?' The Master replied, 'Let him observe the five excellent things, and banish away the four bad things, then he may conduct government properly.' And one of the five excellent things is as Confucius replied: 'When the person in authority is beneficent without great expenditure.' (Pay 2000).

Low's (2002, 2005a) studies support that strongly influenced by Confucianism, the Chinese mind is said to be pragmatic and devoted to seeking profit. Such a company culture, particularly in some Chinese small and medium companies such as in the "*mee pok* (noodle) seller corporate culture" (Low 2005a), profits are ploughed back and being frugal is a virtue. Here, thrift involves the use of limited resources—material, capital and human resources, and these results in improving productivity and overall profitability. In fact, Low's (2005b) study supports that being prudent is one of the success values for the growth of Singapore companies. And Low (2006c) argues that being prudent also serves a crisis prevention, containment and management for the island-Republic of Singapore.

Growing Resilience

> Adversity is the foundation of virtue. (Japanese proverb)

PRC study (cited in Low 2002) has found that a relationship exists between certain Confucian values (such as perseverance) and firm performance. Perseverance and industriousness lead logically to focus, working towards the company goals that enhance company profitability, adding to corporate success. Indeed, resilience can be considered as the people's or followers' vitality and their drive and, indeed, the latter has made countries such as Germany, Japan and South Korea economically successful.

At this point, we can also assert that the Confucian leadership style can be seen as practicing resilience too. This is also another successful leadership trait which is good to have. Prudence also adds to the resilience of the leaders and Singapore's economic strengths (Low 2006c). The Confucian leader is bold. "Act resolutely, and both heaven and hell will respect you" (Matsushita, cited in PHP Institute, Inc. 1991, p. 39). As a leader, when you make up your mind to do something, you must have the determination to carry it out.

Additionally, as Confucius puts it, "One who has his arms broken three times may become a good doctor" (Zhou 2005a, p. 170). Confucius has further pointed out that:

> ...a king can't become a real ruler without encountering difficulties; and soldiers can't become crack troops without suffering setbacks. (Zhou 2005a, p. 171)

To cite a practical example, this researcher would highlight these: With the *Confucian Heritage* culture (Low 2002, 2005a, 2006b), Singapore's ejection from Malaysia in 1965, its caesarean national birth and the influence of other factors as highlighted by Low (2007b), Singapore/Singaporeans are said to possess resilience. Most or older workers, who have lost their jobs, persevere in finding jobs, and being flexible being open to options in their job search. In times of recession and unemployment, they search for opportunities to keep afloat. Perhaps, this could be interpreted as Confucian leadership of the ordinary people in their everyday lives. They, in fact, subscribe very much to the Chinese saying of "not be afraid of going slow, but be very much afraid of standing still." (Low 2007b, p. 142)

Interestingly, the resilient leader also learns; hence he is able to correct himself, strengthens and grows. In the *Analects*, Confucius presents himself as a "transmitter who invented nothing" (Wikipedia 2007). He put the greatest emphasis on the importance of study or learning, highlighting that:

> Not to correct the mistake one made is to err indeed. (Zhou 2005a, p. 79)

> Never be afraid of correcting mistakes one has made. (Zhou 2005a, p. 80)

Confucius has also spoken of:

> "To be capable, one must study; to be intellectual, one must learn from others" (Zhou 2005a, p. 36), "profit(ing) by good examples and avoid(ing) bad examples." (Chew 2000, p. 13)

To this researcher, this means that the leader benchmarks, learns and improves. Hence, we can also add the touch of *Kaizen* (continuous improvement). Continuous improvement indeed builds and grows the resilience in a leader.

Assessing the Downsides

True, the Confucian leader can be benevolent with proper conduct, being prudent, helping to bring about higher company profits and triggering economic success, but he can be a strict, disciplining or domineering leader. "Firm control and, at times, explicit direction (*telling or even giving a good scolding*)" may be applied by the father-leader (Low 2006b, *italics mine*, Low 2002; Scarborough 1998). Like a father, he may claim to be always right, and demands obedience. "The father knows best" is enforced, and the leader may not want to listen to his children (followers).

He, however, needs to be open to feedback as much as followers should not only be open but also not just sing only music to the Confucian leaders' ears.

Another downside is that "Confucius would undoubtedly have been a High Churchman in temperament... He loved the rituals of worship... ceremonial acts" (Lin 1994, p. 15). A leader should realise that he should not stress too much on rituals lest (s)he becomes more managerial and administrative. However, to understand Confucius better, we need to factor in that such ceremonial acts are not without meaning as rituals do bring about in the worshipper a respectful or God-fearing state of mind. If that is so, national leaders can apply ceremonial acts such as National Day parades as one of the tools to boost the spirit of patriotism and nationalism among the citizens. Rituals too teach people to observe form and order, drink well or behave generally well in their festivities, bringing about a sense of general order and courtesy among the general masses.

Overall, the Confucian leader should subscribe to the Confucian concept of "beneficial pursuits", these will help to overcome such downsides. Among other things, these "beneficial pursuits" are not "to be arrogant about one's position", "(*listen, study and*) praise (take delight in advertising) other people's (*followers'*) merits" (Zhou 2005a, p. 102, 103, *italics mine*), and "spot their shortcomings for reference to overcome... (one's) own shortcomings" (Zhou 2005a, p. 33). The

Confucian leader should "never be afraid of correcting mistakes one has made" (Zhou 2005a, p. 80).

United States President the late Kennedy once said, "If I walked out on stage and fell flat on my face, father would say I fell better than anyone else." Good fathers (leaders) look for opportunities to encourage their children (followers), not with false praise, but with honest appraisal. This means being alert to your child's (follower's) talent or gift, being quick to affirm it, and providing opportunities to exercise it. It's simple, yet not many of us, as working adults and citizens, often get this from our leaders. This is, in fact, similar to Blanchard and Johnson's (1983) leaders' "catch(ing) their followers doing something right".

Section Concluding Remarks

All in all, the Confucian leader grows or 'perfects' his virtue. Being just to humanity, the leader would build his credibility, and has the right status so that what he says is justifiable. When his words are justifiable, then what he does can be successful—he's respected and emulated by his followers.

Lao Tzu's Three Treasures, Leadership and Organisational Growth

Introduction

There is no simple definition of the term—leadership. A close one would be that of leadership as "the ability to influence a group toward the achievement of goals" (Robbins 2005). However, simply put, leadership gets things done, and organisations (also read as nations) need strong leadership and strong management for optimal effectiveness. Leaders make a difference. And in these recent decades—with political scandals, troubled economies, frauds and well-publicised corporate failure such as Enron and WorldCom, there's certainly a great need for leaders and leadership excellence (Low 2009a; Lussier and Achua 2007a) plus the earnest applications of Lao Tzu's three treasures. Accordingly, leaders need to:

- Be simple, without ego.
- Exercise patience.
- Have compassion.

The aim and objectives of this section are to illustrate that when leaders apply and practice the three treasures, they grow themselves and perform effectively, and the organisations they lead also benefit and grow (Fig. 5.2).

The Three Treasures

Let us see what the three treasures are. Lao Tzu points out:

> I have just three things to teach:
> simplicity, patience, compassion.
> These three are your greatest treasures.

Lao Tzu: "I have just three things to teach: **simplicity, patience, compassion.** These three are your greatest treasures."

Fig. 5.2 The 3 (three) things taught by Lao Tzu: simplicity, patience and compassion

Simple in actions and in thoughts,
you return to the source of being.
Patient with both friends and enemies,
you accord with the way things are.
Compassionate toward yourself,
you reconcile all beings in the world. (Verse 67, Tao de Ching)

The First Treasure

A truly great man never puts away the simplicity of a child. (Chinese proverb)

The first treasure notes that when one needs to be simple. Simplicity is treasured. Lao Tzu's contemporary, Confucius, is reputed to say these: "Life is really simple, but we insist on making it complicated."

When one is simple, one is or becomes frugal. One has less or fewer desires. One lives simply, and that helps a lot. One spends less. Likewise, "don't spend a $1.00's worth of time on a $0.10 decision" (Maxwell 1994, p. 36). One saves when relying on simplicity. Simplicity makes one prosper.

Simplicity means without ego. When there is no ego, one simply gets things done. There is no attachment; one serves and remains detached. Servant leadership is practiced.

The wisdom of the *Tao* has it that:

All streams flow to the sea
because it is lower than they are.

Humility gives it its power.
If you want to govern the people,
you must place yourself below them
If you want to lead the people,
you must learn how to follow them. (Lao Tzu, verse 66)

"The best athlete wants his opponent at his best. The best general enters the mind of his enemy. The best businessman serves the communal good. The best leader follows the will of the people." (Lao Tzu, verse 68). The *Tao* practitioner serves the people and, accordingly, practices servant leadership. The *Tao* practitioner acts without self-interest and is giving. (Lao Tzu, verse 7).

The leader operates without pride or ego. Lao Tzu, verse 11 asserts:

We join spokes together in a wheel,
but it is the centre hole
that makes the wagon move.
We shape clay into a pot,
but it is the emptiness inside
that holds whatever we want.
We hammer wood for a house,
but it is the inner space
that makes it livable.

The wise leader does not boast; the leader achieves results, but do not glory in them or is proud of his or her victories, and does not boast (boasting is not natural). When ego gets into the way, the leader simply does not think or feel straight—(s)he goes against the natural way, and will fail in his or her endeavour.

Heider (1995, p. 65) indicates: "If I am content with what I have, I can live simply and enjoy both prosperity and free time." One should learn to un-clutter one's mind. Simplicity also brings about clear goals, and if my goals are clear, I know what I want and can (easily) achieve them. Organisations need clear goals and vision to know where it's heading to.

One can easily deal with matters using understanding. It is as easy as using sunlight to melt ice. Simplicity is wonderful and in fact, Occam's Razor basically says that all things being equal, the simplest solution is the best. The principle has implications in virtually every field of science, not to mention philosophy, aesthetics, marketing, economics, and yes, leadership. If for some reason one does not buy the word of a fourteenth century Franciscan monk, it would be of interest to know that Albert Einstein also believed the universe loves simplicity (Tobak 2009).

Some leaders are simply good at making things complicated than they need to be simply to prove that they are right. They make wrong assumptions and get intertwined in an endless but futile effort to prove themselves right.

Most times the more we talk, the more we muddy the water. In communication, simplicity means one saves on words—one is not long-winded—yet one is clear and communicates well. If we simply need ten cents to make a phone call, why then do we use (waste) 40 or 50 cents? A leader needs to communicate clearly and well, and be understood by his or her audience.

If we look at Zen Buddhism, it is also revealed that we should—when sleeping, sleep, when eating, eat and when cutting vegetables, just cut. It teaches us to be more focused and concentrated on what we are doing lest we get distracted and harm ourselves. The lessons are also applied to strategic thinking, as we simply need to be focused and not spread all over, and become weak. Here, the power of concentration should be applied.

Simplicity is to be better appreciated in this age of consumerism. We can cut down waste and diminish our wants and consumerism as a practice and a lifestyle. We can have a way of life as such that we do not buy, use things and throw them away. Overall, simplicity is to minimise our wants and desires; we recycle or reuse things, and we would also desire less. Besides, we can appreciate the fact less is good. And smartly use and cherish the available resources given to us. Note the problem of waste is one of two halves: one, creating less waste, and two, then disposing of it in a safe and sustainable way. More importantly, when we should decrease our wants, we reduce our waste—resorting to the ever familiar English proverb, "want not, waste not".

Next, when it comes to organisational structures, it is critical to get things done; and results and people matter. The means should not be make complicated by bureaucratic procedures or committees. This is similar to what H. Ross Perot has indicated: "If you see a snake, just kill it. Don't appoint a committee on snakes." (Maxwell 1994, p. 152)

It has been highlighted that Google's founders had great difficulty getting the company off the ground because nobody—not even them—thought search could be a large enough business on its own. Ironically, Yahoo-founder David Filo encouraged them to start a search-engine company. Who thought something so simple could generate so much money? (Tobak 2009).

One of Jack Welch's leadership secrets, that is, number 31 is "aim(ing) for speed, simplicity and self-confidence" (Jack Welch, cited in Slater 1994, p. 140). Indeed, small groups or teams are also simple, they are better agents of change and organisational growth particularly when the organisation has gone too big. Teams can be more creative and productive, with much learning, and individual growth and development (Low 2003). Teams are the anti-dote to organisational bigness, layers or fatness; clumsiness, slow decision-making and organisational decline. When the organisation has gone too big, it becomes more administrative-oriented—more procedures installed and more paperwork made routine. The organisation then becomes less entrepreneurial, more of a machine and can be more bureaucratic than creative (Farrell 1993; Cummings and Worley 2001, 2009). The way to rejuvenate a big organisation is to introduce simple teams and "small company bodies" within it. Teams, for one, communicate better and can be both creative and entrepreneurial. Besides, small companies move faster—as Jack Welch puts it:" What we are trying relentlessly to is to get that small-company soul—and small-company soul and small-company speed—inside our big company body." (Welch, cited in Slater 1994, p. 73)

Corporate leaders these days really need to restore or increase simplicity. Simplify, simplify, simplify! Here, they can apply the tools of 5Cs:

Working out and effecting Common goal(s)
Getting Cooperation
Increasing Collaboration
Ensuring Coordination
Increasing Communication, are needed. Silos, the enemy of simplicity, are bad; and they results in lack of cooperation, coordination and communications. While getting rid of unnecessary complexity, more communications and increased collaborations arc needed to improve organisations and departments. Corporate leaders need to communicate simply and simply explain. Common goal(s), coordination and communications can put the various parts of the organisation and people to function together, smoothly and attain the bottom-line.

The Second Treasure

> If you are patient in one moment of anger, you will escape a hundred days of sorrow. (Chinese proverb)

When the flower is ready to be picked, then one picks it. Patience is beautiful; it pays. If one is not promoted or has been bypassed, one should be patient. Instead, one should train oneself, upgrading one's knowledge and skills. One should not pull the shoot to grow the plant. Patience can be seemingly bitter yet its fruits can be sweet; once one becomes an expert and a professional, and when one has the necessary skills and competences, one would then be better able to do one's job as well as better perform one's role(s) and duties, contributing further to one's community.

Even Confucius has these to say, that is, in planning and decision making, "never make haste, nor covet small gains. (*There is a need to be patient and not*) eager for quick success, (a) one may not reach his goals; covetous of small gains, one cannot make great achievements." (Zhou 2005b, p. 191, *italics mine*)

When we are impatient, we rush and gloss things over. We can do a lower quality work. Besides, when we want quick results, we only stress ourselves unnecessarily. We may perhaps also not pay attention to people and may hurt their feelings. When we are impatient, we even get angry easily. We may even say certain words to loved ones that we may later regret saying it, as expressed in the common Chinese saying, "Not the fastest horse can catch a word spoken in anger."

Patience, the second treasure, is good and in fact, great. It can be taken that patience is soft and gentle, and it can be powerful. A quiet, lull or gestation period can suddenly lead to an emergence of a great idea. Patience can thus lead to ingenuity, brilliant cleverness or inventiveness, as Sir Isaac Newton once said, "If I have made any valuable discoveries, it has been owing more to patient attention than to any other talent."

Lao Tzu expresses it as:

The gentlest thing in the world
overcomes the hardest thing in the world.
That which has no substance
enters where there is no space.
This shows the value of non-action.
Teaching without words,
performing without actions:
that is the Master's way. (Verse 43, Tao de Ching)

Patience also helps to build our relationships with others. As the Indian proverb goes, "For the friendship of two, the patience of one is required."

When we are patient, we do not rush. We are not easily provoked or get angry. We, in fact, become more being than becoming.

Low (2008b) asks: "Must all things be manufactured and be made it fast? Instant noodle style? To borrow Chu (1998, p. 9) words, 'let the water boil'". He cited Chu (1998, p. 9) in the context of *Doing Less, Achieve More*:

in order to boil water, you pour it into a kettle and place the kettle over a fire. These actions all involve expending energy. When you close the lid of the kettle, you let the water boil. If you become too anxious about the result and keep opening the lid, you hinder the process of heating up the water, and you delay its boiling.

Lao Tzu (verse 29) points out:

There is a time for being ahead,
a time for being behind;
a time for being in motion,
a time for being at rest;
a time for being vigorous,
a time for being exhausted;
a time for being safe,
a time for being in danger.

So being patient is a virtue, and something to be appreciated—a good leadership trait to possess. Besides, when you are patient, your eyes are wide open... You sharpen your human perception for all things beautiful too. Interestingly, Low (2008b) has pointed out that Singaporeans (for that matter, everybody) need to sharpen their perception for all things beautiful. Indeed so, many people are so caught up in everyday matters that they simply don't see the beautiful things in life and in the world around them. No wonder many people only feel happy when something really unusual happens. But it is so easy to feel happy or contented—at least for a short while or just a little. We simply have to train our eyes to view the beautiful things around us and look for the little pleasures in life. We simply have to count our blessings.

You need to pay attention to details. For example, when you next look out at the home or office window, perhaps you may discover something you have not noticed so far—a new ad, new window lighting or decorations in your neighbour's home. You and your child or loved ones can also get pleasure from watching insects and the raindrops that splash against the window. In this way, one can sharpen one's perception for the little things that make life worth living.

Also, while at work—working, gaze or look at different things now and again. Look out at the window and get the pleasure out of "little things" such as birds flying by, palms or nice trees. Once you begin looking for the little things, you will soon notice more and more, for example, a blooming rose; a pretty caterpillar on top of a leaf, and many beautiful sunrises or sunsets (Low 2008b).

Be patient enough; decorate your office with some items that you enjoy. When you've to do an inane task, look at them occasionally to brighten up your mood. When decorating your office, it's good to add your own personal touch; it's refreshing.

Patience is indeed a valued commodity—remember the simple English proverb: 'Rome is not built in a single day'. Personally, we need to sharpen our axes, and increase our skills. Large bureaucracies or mechanistic organisations are slow to change, with too many controls and too much review of decisions. There is much rigidity in handling people and problems (DuBrin 2007).

Organisational growth can, on the other hand, be attained through a natural acceptance of change ("It is part of life and living"), learning as well as continuous improvement; bit by bit, and it becomes a cinch. And when the concept of learning organisation is applied, the organisation becomes organic, there is greater cooperation among the units and the organisation grows.

Learning, training and cultural change, appreciation of the learning value, needs patience. Training will bear fruits and it takes time. Organisational members learn surely and steadily, and learning needs patience too. Systemic thinking is promoted, and team learning is also reinforced and put into practice. Organic organisations grow; please see Table 5.1: A summary of differences between mechanistic organisations and organic organisations.

The Third Treasure

How beautiful! And "it is indeed propitious that the halfness of man and the halfness of woman should each be completed by the halfness of the other. Halves are united and incompletes completed. In losing of each into both and one, there is wholeness again". (Ray Grigg)

Weapons of war augur evil. Even things seem to hate them.

Lao Tzu, in verse 31, highlights that:

Weapons are the tools of violence;
all decent men detest them.
Weapons are the tools of fear;
a decent man will avoid them
except in the direst necessity.

Table 5.1 Mechanistic organisations versus organic organisations

Mechanistic organisation	Organic organisation
(What makes an organisation be machine-like?)	(What makes an organisation organic?)
The organisation is *not* flexible or adaptable to change	The organisation is both flexible and adaptable
Many rules exist which may lead to RIGIDITY	Fewer rules and procedures prevail in such an organisation
Machine organisations are often bureaucratic, with lots of paperwork to be done	Bureaucratic procedures and paperwork are minimised
In a machine organisation, separate tasks are done by different people and departments	Here, work teams, Quality Control Circles: QCCs. are implemented which help to promote team learning and growing of new ideas
Many levels prevail, with a hierarchy of authority	Hierarchies are discouraged and/or reduced. Team culture is in practice. A performing culture is also put in place, and creative. The people are also entrepreneurial and forward looking
The existing bureaucratic culture may stifle staff creativity and initiative	Horizontal communication is promoted
Vertical (top down) communication prevails	Decentralisation and empowerment prevails. Staff creativity and initiative are also encouraged
A strong tendency towards centralisation prevails	

Sources: Low (2009c), Cummings and Worley (2001, 2009) and Daft (1998)

The third treasure is compassion. 'A bit of fragrance always clings to the hand that gives you flowers', goes a Chinese saying. Compassion and love is a powerful influencing tool, and helps win many a heart. Another Chinese saying speaks of: "to attract good fortune, spend a new coin on an old friend, share an old pleasure with a new friend, and lift up the heart of a true friend by writing his name on the wings of a dragon."

To achieve more for others, enlarge your heart. Be loving, magnanimous and as the Chinese proverb goes—"Keep a green tree in your heart, and perhaps a singing bird will come." "The Buddha said to his monks, walk over the earth for the blessing of many, for the happiness of many, out if compassion for the world, for the welfare and blessing and the happiness of gods and men" (Vinaya Pitaka, translated by Parrinder, cited in Kornfield and Fronsdal 1991, p. 126).

When we give compassion to others, we become happy. Leaders make others better and take others up with them (Mason 2003). Come to think about it, indeed, making others better is a boomerang. In the organisational context, as leaders, when we coach and grow our people, enriching their jobs and empowering them, we make them happy. When others show us their love and compassion, we become happy too. But to get, we need to give. To be happy. . . to win or gain one's life, one needs to lose one's life. And life is about giving, and sharing, and that creates happiness.

When one is without any ego, one loves and gives much to others. Heider (1995, p. 59) speaks of: "group members will challenge the ego of one who leads egocentrically. But one who leads selflessly and harmoniously will grow and endure." Compassionate, the leader shows care and concern for his or her followers.

When viewing it from the Buddhistic perspective, "compassion includes qualities of sharing, readiness to give comfort, sympathy, concern, caring. In Buddhism, we can really understand others, when we can really understand ourselves, through wisdom." (Buddha Dharma Education Association: BDEA/ BuddhaNet 2008). Help yourself, and then help others. These speak volumes when applied to leadership. We can define compassion or caring as a deep or profound feeling or emotions prompted and moved by the pain of others and those around oneself. With such emotions or feelings, servant leadership may be embraced to serve, help and take care of others. In many professions for example, in the medical, when compassion is injected to cure, much value is added, and leadership excellence is attained. Here, perhaps not all cases can be cured, but all should be cared for through lending an ear, patient listening and good bedside manners.

When the leader is selfless, (s)he is compassionate; (s)he relates well with the people. (S)he shows care and concern for the people; the people would feel appreciated. They would be happy, in fact, their morale would be high. "Success to me means being able to contribute to society. When we talk about society that means people" (Ms Khunying Suriyasat, Chairwoman, Toshiba Thailand Co. Ltd., cited in Low and Theyagu 2003, p. 81). Achievements are made, yes, but made for the people. Caring for the people is of paramount importance.

When we put a premium on compassion, we value relationships. We cultivate interpersonal relationships, applying the power of relationships (Low 2001). We advise, coach and train everyone to realise his or her potential, growing them to be leaders (Zenger and Folkman 2004; Low and Theyagu 2003). True, we value our family members and friends. Yet there should not be a distinction between us and them, and the love and compassion is extended. Indeed, historically, leadership "that goes beyond the nation-state and seeks to address all human beings "has been the most important, but rarest and most elusive, variety of leadership" (Former United States Secretary of State Madeleine Albright, cited in Alder and Gundersen 2008, p. 170). Relating to the Confucian concept of ethics, Low (2008c, p. 50) has, among other things, indicated that "lov(ing) all and serv(ing) all is the Confucian message, and when applied to the stakeholder theory, it becomes wholesome and without discrimination". And Low (2009b, p. 48) adds, "As leaders, we treat all more justly and with love and compassion, and perhaps the world will become a better peaceful place. There'll also be more joint work, strategic alliances and cooperation with outside organisations and agencies, both within and cross borders."

Concluding Remarks

The three treasures are age-old wisdom, and should be practised by leaders who would want to show much care to their people. To this author, his overall key learning from the TAO in this regard, its great success secret is non-attachment to outcome; doing your best now, and letting go, allowing the outcome to take care of themselves. Through the three treasures, leaders work on good or effective strategies and based on the three treasures; they get results or outcome and build relationships with their people, as well as excellence for their organisations. Additionally, in using the three treasures as self-growth tools, the leaders are also building themselves and their organisations on solid foundations.

The next section deals with applying strategic leadership, the way of the dragon, an iconic Chinese symbol.

Applying Strategic Leadership, The Way of the Dragon

Introduction

Low (2008d) has indicated that one of the most common mistakes of the leaders is that of not thinking strategically. Employees surely like to know that there is an organisational vision or master plan in which they are playing a part. If leaders are unable to communicate that vision, plan or goals to followers, or if followers do not recognise the significance of their contributions, individual motivation can be diminished if not lost.

Interestingly, weak leaders (tend to) practise "the mushroom principle", keeping their people in the dark even in their day-to-day leading (Low 2001). Besides, to be successful, a strategy must involve people in how the strategy is formed, and this involvement should be at various stages in the exercise from start to finish. Most successful strategies use cross-departmental/divisional teams and specifically include vertical integration of those teams to ensure input from the top to the bottom of the organisation (Robertson and Low 2006). Leaders should indeed be sensitive and seek their followers' input. Here, drawing the wisdom from various corporate experiences, it is noted that a serious leadership sin is that of lack of followers' buy-in, and with that, there can be no followers' ownership, motivation or a sense of commitment and follow through. This is, in fact, linked to a key pointer, another common leadership mistake, that is, being callousness or insensitive to their followers' needs when formulating and effecting strategic plans (Low 2008d).

Having said these, we next ask, why refers to the Chinese or oriental dragon? The Chinese dragon, a celestial mythical creature, is one of the world's most recognised symbols. Many take it that the Chinese dragon originated with the 'Yellow Emperor' Huang Ti who is said to reign from 2696 to 2598 B.C.; the dragon is considered the ancestor of all Chinese. Chinese around the world, proudly proclaim themselves the Descendents of the Dragon (*lung tik chuan ren*; CDOT 2009 or "*long de chuan ren*"—in *hanyu pinyin*; Chen 2005). Traditionally, Chinese emperors took the dragon as their representation.

Better known as a creature of good than evil, the Chinese dragon is also traditionally the embodiment of the concept of *yang* (male) and is associated with the weather as the bearer of rain and water in an agriculturally water-driven nation such as China. The *yin* (female) counterpart is the *Fenghuang* (phoenix). Symbolizing power, strength, vigour, vitality, wisdom, resilience and growth, the dragon thus reflects positive values, and the values of independence, perseverance and dedication (Low 2009b, p. 42).

The Definition

Defined as supplying "the vision, direction, the purpose for growth, and context for the success of the organisation, strategic leadership also initiates 'outside-the-box' thinking to generate future growth" (Kotelnikov 2001). Strategic leaders usually adopt a big picture perspective, choosing to see the global, regional or national perspective rather than the narrow 'inside-the-box' (although they may, in fact, function in an uncertain environment on highly complex problems that affect and are affected by events and organisations outside their own.) (U.S. Army Field Manual 22–100, cited in TMCG: The Milum Communications Group 2008).

Having a long-range view of things, strategic leaders often do not see their ideas come to fruition during their watch and their initiatives may take years to plan, prepare, and implement. In-process reviews (IPRs) might not even begin until after the leader has left the job. This has important implications for long-term planning. On the other hand, some strategic decisions may become a front-page headline of the next morning's newspapers.

Perhaps of vital importance—because they exert influence primarily through subordinates—strategic leaders must develop strong skills in picking and developing good second-tier leaders. They must also replace themselves. Magnanimous in growing their followers to be even 'bigger', smarter and perhaps better skilled than them; organisations grow and benefit.

The Objectives

Much wisdom exists in the ways of the old and that of Imperial China. Wisdom is a prerequisite for leadership and organisation's (nation's) success. And there is much to learn from the Chinese civilisation with its long history.

This section is intended to examine the ways, uncover the gems of wisdom (though we are not saying that there had been no errors or wrong doings) in which the ancient Chinese emperors led and administered the country, the advocacy of steadfast character, goodness, virtue, humaneness and harmony with the world at large. The essay also carries several leadership relevance and lessons.

Strategic Leadership Relevance and Lessons

Water far away cannot help put out a fire nearby. Water far away cannot quench one's immediate thirst. So also, a simple meal before one is good enough to quench thirst and fill one's stomach, and this is not to say we ignore what lies ahead. The ability to plan long term while maximising performance in the short term is a must for leaders. The strategic leadership significance and lessons are as follows:

Know Thyself, Know Thy Other Party

Raise your sail one foot and you get ten feet of wind. (Chinese proverb)

Knowing (and appreciating) one's place in society and others' worth, one should capitalise one's strengths, and eliminate one's weaknesses to be successful in life.

As pointed out by Low (2010b), to be a strategic leader, one should know one's people and stakeholders well, and this means preparation, planning, and assessments. By knowing oneself and the other parties, one can seek to better influence and win them over. To paraphrase Sun Tzu (traditional Chinese) (Sun Zi—*Hanyu Pinyin*), knowing and understanding the enemy and oneself, one can engage in a thousand battles without ever being in danger and/or in fact, win.

If one understands oneself without understanding the other party(ies), one's chances of influencing and winning are limited, if not simply, on the average. If one does understand neither the other party(ies) nor oneself, then one will lose. Simply put, one should understand oneself and the other party(ies) as well as better assess the strengths, weaknesses; opportunities and threats (SWOT analysis) of both oneself and the other party(ies).

Set the Example, Act and Realise the Power of Example

Better to light a candle than to curse the darkness.

If you don't want anyone to know, don't do it. (Chinese proverbs)

Idle talks should *not* be encouraged, and actions promoted. One should not fear having faults or shortcomings, but what's critical is that one should know of one's faults and be sure or determined to do something about them.

The dragon, as highlighted earlier, is a powerful symbol. The strategic leader's example(s) can also be powerful. And the strategic leader is much needed. As the Chinese saying goes, 'when there's a strong general, there will be no weak soldiers'. The strategic leader sets himself as the standard. With "sageliness within and kingliness without" (Fung 1948, p. 8) as well as accomplishing spiritual cultivation, the leader functions well in society. (S)he gets things done. Doing things in the right spirit, such a leader's actions and examples, speaking louder than words, become very influential.

As argued by Low (2008a), in the Confucian context, "a wise man does not readily give utterance to words in case his actions do not live wise up to his words" (Zhou 2005a, p. 10). "One who talks too much is prone to failure" (Confucius, cited in Zhou 2005a, p. 68). Yet on the downside, most leaders may under-sell, under-promote or market themselves. As such, what is then advocated is that leaders should pro-actively set the example, and at that, lead the way. Moreover, they learn from the wisdom and even mistakes of others.

Better Be a Silent Achiever and Up-Keep One's Integrity

If the stick is crooked, the shadow cannot be straight. (Unknown source, cited in Low 2000, p. 139, 2006b)

Tao follows the natural order; the human mind is originally quiet but is normally clouded by thoughts and desires. Once such mental obstacles are eliminated, then clear mind or perhaps heart will naturally manifest itself, and that is integrity.

Ancient Chinese scriptures have it that:
The false Master is quite ferocious,
But possesses no real power.
The Master does not make such a show,
But his touch is as heavy as a mountain (Chueh Yuan, cited in Lerner 1976: 119)

Low (2009b, p. 45) speaks of "the turtle cries while laying hundreds of eggs; the cock crows while the hen lays an egg. A great general needs not blow his trumpet. As a leader and a man of true worth, it's better to be a quiet achiever while up-keeping one's integrity.

Work things out; achieve the goals first. The former is better than talking and without fleshing things out and getting results. Talking without working would, in fact, affect one's integrity and that would make it difficult for a leader to persuade or influence his or her people.

Confucius pointed out that "a gentleman is slow to speak but prompt to act" (Chew 2000, p. 10). "When the ruler (*leader*) does what is right, he will have influence over the people without giving commands" (Lin 1994, p. 199).

"A good leader may be compared to the wind and the common people to the grass. Let the wind blow over the grass and the grass, under the force of the wind, cannot but bend" (Chew 2000, p. 18). 'Talk doesn't cook rice' (or to present its meaning in a positive way, action gets results) but pro-active, through his examples and behaviour, a leader thus builds his influence.

Integrity is the purity and clarity of both the mind and heart. "What is planted cannot be uprooted. What is embraced cannot slip away. Your descendants will carry on the ancestral sacrifice for generations without end" (Verse 54, Lao-Tzu 1990). Integrity's so critical, and as the Chinese saying goes, 'Heaven protects the good person.' This can be taken as bearing long-term gains and benefits both for the leader and his people. And even benefits his descendants. A heart of supreme kindness and goodness is the root of one's descendants. If one does not commit an evil at the root, then the branches and leaves will be good. If one is absolutely good, then one's descendants will benefit abundantly too.

In maintaining one's integrity, Confucius once said that, "the superior man does not, even for the space of a single meal, act contrary to virtue." Integrity is seen as "the uncontaminated heart"—there is no greed but integrity, "when the heart has no desires, everywhere is paradise. When leading a life of simplicity (*integrity and without attachment*), one knows true joy and beauty of things" (Hong Yingming, cited in Tsai 1991, p. 77; *italics mine*)".

In essence, the strategic leader's best way to increase his influence is to apply the Golden Rule, the gentleman's code of conduct. In essence, you do onto others what you yourself like, and "do not impose to others what you yourself dislike" (Zhou

2005a, p. 4). When one follows this tenet, one will not incur resentment of others, and in fact, win others over.

Practice Humaneness, the Tao of the Ancient Emperors (Read as Strategic Leaders)

Believe in relationships, partnerships, teamwork. Good things occur in pairs; it's double happiness. (Patrick Kim Cheng Low)

Behave toward everyone as if receiving a guest. (Chinese saying)

The benevolence of the dragon signifies "greatness, goodness and blessings" (CDOT 2009). Humane (Cleary 1991, p. 4), the emperor rules justly and with compassion—after all, he is given the Heavenly Mandate. Positive relationships and harmony are stressed. The country and its citizens are considered as one big happy family; this has its roots in Confucianism.

Relationships rule. Confucius stresses on the importance of the family; and in the family unit, the father is the key figure. A role model, a father is a good example to his children. For the son, it is the son's duty to obey without questioning and honour his father, even after death. When the father dies, obedience is given to the oldest brother. Confucius states in the *Analects*, "Meng I Tzu asked about the treatment of parents. The Master said, 'Never disobey! ...While they are alive, serve them according to ritual. When they die, bury them according to ritual and sacrifice to them according to ritual.'" (*Analects* II: 5)

Low (2005a, 2006b, 2007a) found that the Confucian notion of *Wu Lun* (especially the father–son relationship) has been as deeply implanted in the father leadership practices both at the organisational and national levels in Singapore. This is beneficial as the strategic leader is indeed caring; Lao Tzu, verse 59 (Mitchell) has pointed out that:

Nothing is impossible for him.
Because he has let go,
he can care for the people's welfare
as a mother cares for her child.

And "the best masters are servants." Grigg (1994a, p. 157). "Gold in the heart is better than gold in one's purse." as a Chinese saying goes. Showing care and concern to his followers, the benevolent Confucian leader is thus like a father to his followers. Besides, the family spirit is often fostered, and to quote Confucius:

A true gentleman is in harmony, and is friendly with others though he does not agree with them... (Chew 2000, p. 17)

Overall, only when all contribute their firewood can they build up a strong fire. Team work or more appropriately, consensus-seeking culture may be related to loyalty, which is also considered to be a virtue by the Chinese (Bond 1987; cited in Low 2002, 2009d). Chinese are taught from a young age to be loyal to their family and kin. Hsu (1984) claims, loyalty to the family will continue to play a critical role among Chinese. Family is important in any culture, but it is extraordinarily so in Chinese culture. But more importantly, "relations among family members provide the human basis for the moral virtues of the Chinese" (Nakamura 1978; cited in Low 2002, 2009d). Hsu (1984) has identified some of the significant characteristics of the Chinese family that have a strong impact on Chinese organisations. The Chinese as a people are special in their relationships with others, and a strong emphasis on the importance of blood relations, parental authority, filial piety and loyalty exists. The late Kwek Hong Png, founder and chairman of the Hong Leong (Singapore) group of companies, for instance, pointed this out when he was expanding his business: Mindful of the old Chinese proverb that when tackling a tiger, one needs the help of one's brothers, I invited my brothers to join my firm (Kwek 1987, cited in Low 2002, 2009d).

It should be stressed that on one hand, attachment to one's in-grouping as well as too much inward thinking and perspective can lead to much ethnocentrism, bias and discrimination. Yet on the other hand, one can also argue that the bigger picture angle here and what this author is emphasising that of extending out the love, we look at all others—even those outside our racial, ethnic or religious groupings—as our brothers or sisters. In a big-hearted fashion, not keeping in mind the services he has rendered nor should he forget the troubles he has caused, but not forgetting the favours others have done for him, such a leader harbours not feelings against his 'enemy', but promotes peace and love.

As leaders, we treat all more justly and with love and compassion, and perhaps the world will become a better peaceful place. There'll also be more joint work, collaborations, strategic alliances and cooperation with outside organizations and agencies, both within and cross borders.

Respect Talents and Inspire Followers

> One can easily deal with matters using understanding. It's as simple as using sunlight to melt ice (Wang 1993, p. 24).

Strategic leaders have several good, loyal followers or teams. They grow their people and achieve success through the strengths and gifts of their own teams, co-workers and employees. "When recruiting always pay respect to talent, That is the way to make a country (*also read as company or business*) strong and its citizens prosperous. Only the foolish do otherwise" (Wang 1993, p. 11, *italics mine*). Strategic leaders appreciate the human capital. Look at Bhasin and Low (2002, p. 110), Singapore recruits and selects the best in the world. "Singapore leaders have long realized the need to augment from abroad the limited local talent available at home, especially... technical and managerial expertise."

Besides, setting the example and being humane and compassionate makes the strategic leaders inspiring to their people. Such leaders (similar to Jack Welch's leaders who "energize"; Krames 2005, p. 49) normally keep their troops highly spirited, motivated and more importantly, their people enthusiastically carry out their orders. And strategic leaders lead their organisations in attaining high level performance. Even punishments and decorations or rewards are carried in strict manner (Chu 1994, p. 291). Wang (1993, p. 152) cites one of Feng Menglong, the famous Ming scholar's masterpiece, that "only with clear commands and strict discipline can an army be trained and ready for war (*competition in the present day context*). Killing one to teach a hundred is a necessary thing to do" (*italics mine*).

Employ 'Big Picture' Thinking, Be Objective and Love

> Be board-minded, avoid strategies that lack foresight... the tree trunk should always be stronger than the branches. This is true in leading an organisation or a country.

Low (2008a) has highlighted that even in this millennium, one haunting reality of the corporate world is discrimination at workplace. Bias, prejudice and differentiation treatment rather than actual job-related basis constitute discrimination.

In a Zen (*Tao*) parable, it is highlighted that one needs to have an overall view of a problem before solving it. The strategic leader should be global in outlook, objective and loving. And here, a return to the old fashioned Confucianism would indeed stress on humanism, and universal love for mankind. "A compassionate nature is inherent in sentient beings. All good deeds spring from compassion. One who does not have compassion is no better than an empty shell of a body." (Hong Yingming, cited in Tsai 1991)

The strategic leader should also value talent in whatever forms. According to Confucius, "no man is a machine. He should not behave heartlessly like one, or as if others were machines" (Chew 2000, p. 5). Besides, detached and un-trapped by power, position and wealth, the strategic leader steadfastly serves. "A gentleman is (*also*) conscious only in the knowledge of others' comfort; the mean is conscious only of his own comfort" (Chew 2000, p. 2, *italics mine*).

The strategic leader is also sensitive to his people's needs—as real as the flowers in spring; those made of silk pales in comparison; the latter, artificial, lacks natural beauty. Those who are sincere, loving and wise are naturally faster than the ordinary people in solving the problems.

With the leader's love, there should be 'Big Peace', and...

'Prosper Thy Neighbour': When There Is 'Big Peace', There Is 'Big Prosperity'

> Men in the game are blind, men outside see clearly. (Chinese proverb)

True, ancient China often had many wars and internal strife. But the wise Chinese emperor very much avoided wars and violence. Normally non-violence was embraced, and war or violence was deemed necessary as the last resort. To win without fighting is better than winning with losses. "In war, the victorious strategist only seeks battle after victory has been won, where as who is destined to defeat first fights and afterwards looks for victory" (Sun Tzu, *The Art of War*, third century, cited in de Smedt 1995).

Taoism also influences China very much. The strategic leader should uphold the idea of non-contention. Lao Tzu pointed out that violence and conflict, no matter how tightly controlled, could not help but cause negative side effects. The *Tao* ideal is to solve problems through peaceful means. Those who win using force alone lacked strategies. Those who mastered human psychology and moral values, and are able to use them against the enemy or the other party are truly wise.

Causing harms, war and aggression is indeed bad and should, in fact, be avoided at all costs. Strategies are preferred to the use of force or violence. Sun Tzu once said that 'complete victory is when the army does not fight' (Cleary 1991, p. 20). To win without fighting is best; win with wisdom is the surest form of victory. Even in the present-day, peace should indeed be favoured as it brings economic growth and prosperity. Look at the Malayan emergency period and the fight against communism in Malaysia and Singapore in the 1970s and 1980s, they were won by giving the people employment and economic advancement. The governments were improving the living standards of their peoples and sought to eliminate or reduce poverty.

Another good example is that of Singapore's (the City-state Singapore has a Confucian heritage cultural model—Low 2002, 2005d, 2009b, d) and Malaysia leaders' adoption of a realistic approach, that is, a good neighbour is better than a friend, a few thousand miles away. Like it or not, Malaysia and Singapore are stuck with each other for better or worse, thus it's more realistic to work together and adopt a prosper-thy-neighbour way as in the Iskandar Development Region (IDR) (Wong 2007) and other projects. [Both countries' prime ministers agreed to set aside 'legacy' problems or take steps to resolve them (Oon 2009, p. 1)] In another case, the close security/police cooperation between Singapore and Malaysia has also led to the recent arrest of the fugitive Mas Selamat who escaped in February 2008 (Goh 2009, p. 1).

Unite Your Troops

You can't clap with one hand. (Chinese proverb)

According to Sun Tzu (cited in Cleary 1991, p. 17), "The general rule for use of the military is that it is better to keep a nation intact than to destroy it. It is better to keep an army intact than to destroy it, better to keep a division intact than to destroy it, better to keep a battalion intact than to destroy it, better to keep a unit intact than to destroy it."

Leaders should ensure that the units or divisions within the organisation do not operate in silos; coordination and cooperation must exist so that the plans and strategy(ies) work, and that everyone within the team works in unison. Unity binds the troops together, and makes it stronger. Unity is strength. To be united also makes the organisation (nation) resilient.

The trick is to put the sticks together; sticks in a bundle cannot be broken. Good strategic leaders are good team leaders. Cooperation or teamwork is the art of working in unison toward a common purpose, knowing well that together the team can achieve even more than alone. Teamwork, cooperation and communication build possible bridges and connections; it needs that all within the organisation to put shared goals and dreams above differences of opinion about how and who.

Successful cooperation demands that members embrace their differences and put them to creative use, because differences are what creates the synergy, the whole greater than the parts. Synergy can overcome a big obstacle and attain victory, very much like the Chinese saying, "spiders when united can tie up even a lion".

Toughen Up and Embrace Resilience

You think you lost your horse? Who knows, he may bring a whole herd back to you someday. (Chinese Proverb)

Foster (2003) notes that suffering has its purpose. It can perhaps produce tough or more vital people.

The Chinese saying, "out of the ashes rises the phoenix" signifies the emergence of something good out of a difficult and perhaps painful process, and it is akin to the purification of gold using intense heat. Here, the dragon is also said to be resilient, overcoming obstacles until success is his. Hence, such a leadership is a resilient leadership, one that overcomes obstacles to attain success and excellence. Such a leader is "energetic, decisive, optimistic, intelligent and ambitious" (Chinese Culture.Org 2003).

'Failure is not falling down but refusing to get up', goes a Chinese saying. One should embrace the spirit of 'a fall into a ditch makes one wiser'; the strategic leader takes the hit as something positive. Low (2005e) speaks of any unexpected misfortune; any sudden hit produces significant physiological and psychological effects. One's blood pressure rises; the muscles in one's body tense up, and one's breathing gets shallow. Adrenaline is pumped in to meet the 'challenge'; the hit say, a serious obstacles faced, is considered as a gift or a challenge.

Here, take the growing of the lotus for an example; the dirty mud supplies the nutrients for the healthy growth and blossoming of the lotus. 'He who tasted the bitterest of the bitterness can be a man above men', goes a Chinese saying; failures and obstacles, the pain have their value. They add to the leader's growth and develop their character. The strategic leader presses on, he should act with resolve and determination, and not because of a moment's comfort slacken in one's efforts; only then will he make progress.

In short, going through muddy waters, like the gentle, delicate lotus, the various handicaps, obstacles, trials and conflicts should not stop the dragon leaders from blossoming or growing.

Be Creative and Inject Resourcefulness

A closed mind is like a closed book, just a block of wood. (Chinese proverb)

The ways in which the wise chooses to solve life's problems are impeccable. They are like lotus—elegant and beautiful though it emerge from the mud. The strategic leader needs to tackle all situations in different but clever sort of ways to avoid hardships and disasters and to attain happiness for the local populace.

In life, there are ups and down; there're always cycles. *Tai Chi* (there is no beginning or end) prevails, with interplay of *yang* and *yin*; neither an absolute 'good' nor an absolute 'evil' exists, but instead harmony through balance and the flowing change of the opposite polarities. There is a unity of opposites (for example, "being" versus "non-being"). Or that great fortune has the seed and concealment of misery. And crisis or misfortune has the seed of greatness, resilience, growth and fortune.

Understanding this and reversing the ideas or concepts, the strategic leader can be truly creative, developing various alternative creative solutions as well as coming up with various new products. Ordinarily, people only see one aspect, either *Yin* or *Yang*. One can indeed learn and apply creativity by looking at one side, we are reminded of the other side. What done during the day can creatively be applied and thought through of what can be done for the night. Singapore's Night Safari was born when the former Prime Minister Lee Kuan Yew thought that the Mandai Zoo should be fully made use of during the night to attract tourists (Low 2005c, p. 48, 2005d). Interestingly, Lao-Tzu indeed reminds us that if out there is Being, there is also Non-being. For example, if you see a baby, you will remember there must be a mother. If you see a son, there must be a father. They always come together and depend on one part or idea that produces each other.

Embrace Long-Term Thinking, Being Patient and Apply Foresight

Tranquil moments: "In a valley of pines, I walk alone with staff in hand..." (Hong Yingming, cited in Tsai 1991, p. 82).

When this dragon analogy is applied to strategic leadership, it is linked to longevity and success. And one can construe such a leadership as having vision, long-term thinking and planning which grows the organisation's (nation's) strengths and success. This is also coupled with patience which becomes another virtue in the way of the dragon.

Creating a sense of urgency within the organisation (nation) is good but not generate too many restructuring, 'workouts', and helter-skelter and cause fatigue to one's people. It's better to capitalize or consolidate your people's strengths than to tire them out unnecessarily. As a strategic leader, the Chinese Emperor would also prepare or work out his generals gearing them for wars and victories. However, he should not tire out his generals, making them fatigued.

For longevity to happen, a definite need prevails for pauses, meditative breaks or silences. Such is the nature of things so that one can think forward and plan. Such breathing spaces or respites supply quietude and relaxation to add clarity of mind and peaceful thinking. Crooked thinking is avoided; "if there is silence of the mind, nothing can unsettle it" (Hong Yingming, cited in Tsai 1991, p. 96). Seriously note that peace comes from within. This is all the more relevant in this age of rapid changes and happenings, otherwise, "the mind is not quiet (and) when the wind blows, the grass moves; one becomes agitated" (Hong Yingming, cited in Tsai 1991, p. 96). Low (2009e) speaks of the attendant patience:

a virtue, and something to be appreciated. Besides, when you are patient, your eyes are wide open. . . You sharpen your human perception for all things beautiful too.

A pertinent point here is that human beings are inclined to be easily excitable. As the common saying goes, 'men trip not on mountains, they trip on molehills'. In handling affairs too, the strategic leader is watchful and mindful. (S)he observes the situation comprehensively and calmly; and when acting thus with reason, (s)he keeps his(her) cool, not falling into error.

Seize Opportunities, Learn and Apply Training and Overall Growth

If you are planning for a year, sow rice; if you are planning for a decade, plant trees; if you are planning for a lifetime, educate people.

A chicken is hatched even from such a well-sealed thing as an egg. (Chinese proverbs)

Strategic leaders also adopt, as a rule, taking advantage of the situation to render the competition ineffective. Opportunists are those who know how to capitalize situations and with this, come the positive element. Even a crisis (this is related to the saying earlier mentioned: 'a fall into a ditch makes one wiser') is seen as (a growth) opportunity(ies). And whenever the competition faces an adverse situation, one should seize the opportunity to strike or fight back. Whenever favourable conditions exist, one should seize the opportunity to strengthen. Generals are warriors, and soldiers are courageous. Soldiers fight well when they have high morale; in the same way, company executives should find ways to boost the employees' morale. When the employees' morale and fighting spirit is strong, they should advance to fight the competition (Low 2010b).

Get better, or get beaten! Training 'little dragons' or soldiers for battle are essential. Likewise, training, coaching and mentoring employees in today's ever-changing world is critical. Untrained troops, like untrained employees, will only yield casualties, and allow the competition to take advantage of the company's situation.

The above is tantamount to one of Jack Welch's key leadership secrets, that is, more specifically, leadership secret number 17. Leaders should "provide an atmosphere where people can have the resources to grow, the educational tools are available and they can expand their horizons" (Welch, cited in Slater 1994, p. 50) as well as capitalizing opportunities for both individual and organizational growth.

Apply Flexibility and Agility

To know when to be generous and when firm—that is wisdom. (Elbert Hubbard)

The wise adapt themselves to circumstances, as water moulds itself to the pitcher

Of all the stratagems, to know when to quit is the best. (Chinese proverbs)

The Chinese dragon is said to be flexible, applying appropriate strategy depending on the situation and circumstances. When the competition attacks its head, the Chinese dragon uses its tail to strike. When its tail is attacked, it uses its head to strike the enemy. When the enemy attacks its centre portion, both its head and tail will strike the enemy (Low 2009b, p. 55, 2010b).

There's wisdom in quick-wittedness, and mental agility is often valued. First gets the oyster, and last gets the shell. Good generals often act or move their troops with lightning speed as those who delay will be on the defensive. It's also like putting a bottle of good wine at the finishing line, those who arrive first enjoy the drinks, and get drunk while those who come later could not even wet their lips. There's much cleverness in Singapore's hosting of Asia's first night Grand Prix, reaping the publicity and benefits of the first mover (Low 2008e).

Besides, in wars, the generals often use frontal attack methods of waging battle with the enemy yet they adapt to changing circumstance of the war and apply surprise attacks to gain victory. The commander, who knows how to employ surprise attacks is flexible, or as what Sun Tzu would say, is like heaven and earth—infinite in transformation and like rivers and streams, flowing endlessly. According to Sun Tzu, the principle in deploying manpower and resources is to emulate water flowing from higher ground to lower ground. Just like water changes its course depending on the terrain, so also in military deployment, one wants to change one's course towards victory according to the competition's changing circumstances, confronting him and defeating him (Low 2009b, p. 55, 2010b).

Of paramount importance is that of realising that advantages and disadvantages exist for any or every course of action. One makes good assessments of them and should cleverly apply flexibility and maneuverability; here, one turns all types of one's disadvantages to advantages and the enemy's advantages into disadvantages.

Low (2009b, p. 56) speaks of the People's Republic of China (PRC) Chinese brand of communism's survival and in fact it's doing well. It's tempered or made hybrid with capitalism very much as what Deng, the late Chairman once said to the effect that it did not matter whether the cat is black or white as long as it catches the mice. In the 1980s, PRC attempted to combine central planning with market-oriented reforms to increase productivity, living standards, and technological quality without exacerbating inflation, unemployment, and budget deficits (TDS 2009). PRC has an economy in which the commanding heights are publicly owned, private sector companies dominate small and medium sized enterprises and foreign owned companies hold significant investments (Anderlini 2008). Here, flexibility is applied.

A strategic leader thus needs to review the organisation's sacred cows. Good traditions should be upheld but bad ones that are unproductive should be discarded.

Section Conclusion
In the final analysis, we should act, bearing in mind that people generally don't change and human beings are creatures of comfort. As the Chinese saying goes, "I dreamed a thousand new paths. . . I woke and walked my old one." Indeed people normally find it difficult to change and here, I would suggest that we work out and

have an action plan detailing a step-by-step approach so that we can change incrementally and gradually—and change we will.

Two pointers should then be adhered and followed through. One, you must have the passion to be a strategic leader, and you need to be earnest, really interested to change... get absorbed, absorb in the change. The secret is losing your life in it, in becoming a strategic leader. It's only when you lose your life that you gain your life, and become a strategic leader.

Two, emulating the dragon in leading and inspiring one's people, the strategic leader should also tap his or hers, and the people's strengths and potential. (S)he needs to let his or her heart go, feel and love; the potential can indeed be great. As the saying: *wo hu chang long*, or "crouching tiger, hidden dragon" goes and for which the hit movie was named, it reminds us not to underestimate individuals who may have hidden talents and so, all of us need to develop our true leadership potential.

Tao and Tough Leadership: Having the Power to Prevail

A pessimist sees the difficulty in every opportunity; an optimist sees the opportunity in every difficulty. (Winston Churchill)

This section shows the workings and applications of the Chinese philosopher Lao Tzu's *Tao Teh Ching* (the "Book of Meaning and Life"), indicating the critical importance of understanding and practicing the *Taoism* principles. We will discuss the belief in *Tao* and its influence on leadership, and that leadership, to the *Tao* practitioner, can be tough leadership. In embracing and understanding *Tao*, the leader, being detached, learns well and becomes tough and resilient.

Introduction

Tao

Tao can be talked about, but not the Eternal Tao.
Names can be named, but not the Eternal Name.
As the origin of heaven and earth, It is nameless.
As 'the Mother' of all things, it is nameable.
So, as ever hidden, we should look at its inner essence.
As always manifest, we should look at its outer aspects.
These two flow from the same source, though differently named;
And both are called mysteries.
The Mystery of mysteries is the Door of all essence. (Verse 1, Lao Tzu's *Tao Teh Ching*, cited in Wu 1990, p. 1)

Tao is ever pervasive.

Tao is ineffable, it cannot be described. In fact, to describe Tao Itself is un-Tao, words are outside Tao and therefore things outside Tao cannot describe or be attributed to what's inside Tao.

Tao is to be experienced, we create our own universe. We create the Tao, that is, the resilience that we create and build upon. "He who knows men is clever; he who knows himself has insight." (Verse 33, *Tao Teh Ching*, Lao Tzu cited in Wu 1990, p. 51)

The Tai-chi way, the Great Way is so interesting; whenever there is yin (female), there is yang (male), and when there is yang, there is yin. In this respect, whenever there is a downfall, there is an upward movement. Whenever there is turbulence, there is bound to be a forward movement.

Section Purpose and Objectives

The purpose and objectives of the section are to illustrate the critical importance of the practice of Tao, and show its influence on leadership, and that leadership, to the Tao practitioner, is tough leadership. Through Tao, one becomes strong and resilient. Facing adversities, the Tao leader is a climber and a peak conqueror.

The *Tao* Way to Be Tough and Resilient

> Some people change their ways when they see the light, others when they feel the heat. (Caroline Schroeder)

A person normally has all kinds of experiences. There is a Chinese saying that goes, "the source of wealth widely entering from all directions of oceans." (財源廣進達三江) and in life, it is indeed better to start with hard work when you are young and then be more relaxing towards old age. (Begin with the sour and taste the sweetness later) (先苦後 *tien*).

But more critically, note that when one fails, one does not become a failure. One becomes a failure only when one stays down, and refuses to get up. The Chinese have a saying that—"Be not afraid of going rather slowly, but be afraid of not moving at all".

When one fails, one learns, and overcomes that failure. One then becomes a tough leader. Setbacks thus interestingly pave the way for comebacks. In subscribing to and understanding the Tao, the leader becomes tough and resilient. These are ways in which the leader should be aware, know and practice...

Therein Lies the Seed...

Perhaps we may feel we miss something or feel a little 'hungry', and in actuality, there is more satisfaction in releasing rather than eating the fish.

Several interviewees intimated to this researcher that "some struggles and troubles in life are good" and in fact, "struggling gives meaning to our lives". "Whenever there is beauty, there is ugliness to define beauty. Whenever there is good, there is evil to define good... ...Low arises from high, work from play, difficult from easy, uncertainty from confidence, not enough from too much." (Grigg 1994a, p. 3)

The seed of downturn lies in a great boom, and the seed of a great boom lies in a great depression. Therein lies a strength in every difficulty, and there's a weakness in every strength.

Lao Tzu highlighted that:

"Welcome disgrace as a pleasant surprise. Prize calamities as your own body." Why should we "welcome disgrace as a pleasant surprise"? Because a lowly state is a boon: Getting it is a pleasant surprise, and so is losing it! That is why we should "welcome disgrace as a pleasant surprise." Why should we "prize calamities as our own body"? Because our body is the very source of our calamities. If we have no body, what calamities can we have? (Wu 1990, p. 17).

As such, what is critical is the spiritual strength and vigour. Tao thus strengthens and empowers, making the Tao practitioner resilient and seemingly, as in the Christian sense, walking on water.

Drawing Strengths From Adversities

Those who dare to fail miserably can achieve greatly. (John F. Kennedy)

We indeed learn wisdom from failure much more than from success.

When it is dark enough, then and only then, one sees the stars. Not knowing the depths of the valley, how can one appreciate the majestic heights of the mountain peaks? Some of the best lessons in life are, in fact, learned from mistakes and failures.

Overcoming difficulties is like the way of the lotus. The lotus floats and grows, with the plant turning and taking nutrients from the mud. It transforms the dirty mud into its good nutrients for its growth. Just like the lotus that floats on the water, we are on top of the situation or event.

Low (2009b, p. 52) speaks of:

'He who tasted the bitterest of the bitterness can be a man above men', goes a Chinese saying; failures and obstacles, the pain have their value. They add to the leader's growth and develop their character. The strategic leader presses on, he should act with resolve and determination, and not because of a moment's comfort slacken in one's efforts; only then will he make progress.

Drawing Strengths from Collaboration

The function of wisdom is to discriminate between good and evil. (Cicero)

All in one and one in all, when one is in unity with the *Tao* or the Universe, we are all ONE, melting into the Universe; there is no ego. We should collaborate and synergize.

The Tao practitioners are team-players and when synergizing, they become strong, and are hence resilient. A good and tangible example of reaping the benefits of good teamwork and collaboration is that of the Japanese bullet train *Shinkansen*. Interestingly, it was the Japanese who invented the famous bullet train that stunned the world with its unmatched speed. And its vital secret lies in that each car has its own small engine, and the total force (teamwork) of these motors produces a final speed that is faster, more efficient, and nearly instantaneous.

Learning's Vital and Is the Key

Each of us has our own inner resources. "To know how other people behave takes intelligence but to know myself takes wisdom" (Heider 1994, p. 65). We learn and manage ourselves.

A vital point to note is that in all uncertainty, there's certainty. In all certainty, there is uncertainty. Accept uncertainty.

In life and as a leader, the moment we give up certainty; learning begins. Be absolutely sure and certain, we'll never learn. When we are raw, we are in the process of ripening—we learn but when we think we are ripe, we rot! We think we are ripe, we stop learning, we don't learn!

Be silent, be very silent. Take the time to reflect. We reflect. . . we ponder, we learn. We translate the experience. . .

Be the pond in the valley. When we are open, we learn. It is yin, the feminine, the valley. One needs to be open and receptive (Heider 1994).

The Opposite of Negative Is. . .

"In negative (yin) situation, leaders should be positive (yang)" (Low 2009g, p. 126). Low (2009f, g) argues that: "being positive helps people to weather the storm, building resilience in both leadership and organization. In spite of the economic downturn, . . .(the) alphas need to be positive; they seek to create a positive future ("tough times will come to an end"), and in fact, a positive future must exist. The rainbow appears after the rain."

When we are positive, we are not cowed by the event, instead we also learn. We learn from the obstacles, trials, conflicts, troubles and problems in life and convert them into lessons in our lives. We are not cowed by such events, instead we prevail. And grow.

Be Supple

> It is not the strongest of the species that survive, nor the most intelligent, but the one most responsive to change. (Charles Darwin)

Low (2009g) indicates that we can learn well from nature, as from the bamboo. It is better to be the slender bamboo than the mighty oak tree. The massive oak tree may snap comes the high winds of the Monsoons. The bamboo, on the other hand, is well-grounded and flexible. The bamboo—keeping its vitality in summer, flourishes through the fall, and blooming in late autumn or early winter—represents endurance, and the ability to cope with adversity.

Also, "be supple like the new born child" (Grigg 1994b, p. 19). When we are flexible, we are alive. We live. Interestingly when negotiating, when the successful negotiator cleverly adopts style flexibility while taking cognizance of the needs of the other party and his or her needs as well as the negotiation climate; (s)he then becomes more negotiation savvy and resilient (Low 2010c).

Once we are rigid, we become the disciple of death. In death, the body develops rigis mortis. From this we learn the virtue of adaptability through flexibility.

The secret of resilience is to be flexible, adapt and adjust to any given situation and. . .

Not to Be Affected by Adversities

Another interesting way of looking at adversities from the Taoism perspective is that of detachment or stoic about the event(s), and one is thus not affected by such difficulties or adversities.

When we let go of what we are, we become what we might be. When we let go of what we are, we receive what we need. Heider (1994, p. 43) specifically speaks of the paradox of letting go, citing the yin paradoxes which include:

By yielding, I endure
The empty space is filled.
When I give of myself, I become more.
When I feel most destroyed, I am about to grow.
When I desire nothing, a great deal comes to me.

Here, the Master Lao Tzu spoke of:

The practice of Tao consists in daily diminishing. Keep on diminishing and diminishing, until you reach the state of No-Ado. No-Ado, and yet nothing is left undone. To win the world, one must renounce all. If one still has private ends to serve, one will never be able to win the world. (Wu 1990, p. 71)

When one faces an adverse situation or a difficulty, one is not affected by it; just like water, water reflects things, and things are not part of it. "The water forms a perfect mirror". One is thus not affected or disturbed by the event that occurs.

Nurturing the Greatness

What one should appreciate here is the caveat against violence and that of meeting the challenge.

Low (2005e) highlights that any unexpected misfortune; any sudden hit produces significant physiological and psychological effects. One's blood pressure rises; the muscles in one's body tense up, and one's breathing gets shallow. Adrenaline is pumped in to meet the 'challenge'; the hit say, a serious obstacles faced, is considered as a gift or a challenge.

Interestingly, like potatoes, the swollen roots, of a potato plant, one stores—take in nutrients—to grow. It also shows the leader's perseverance—very much like the Chinese proverb that goes: "Ants eat bone", here, the metaphor is used to describe a situation where people attempting a huge perhaps an overwhelmingly big task by doing bit by bit and with perseverance.

Besides, as a leader, one has to learn how to see problems as challenges. "Leaders are moulded their ability to take charge of the situation and turning them around. When the going gets tough, the leaders get going. They show that they can take on challenges and attain the ultimate goal. As a leader, you can achieve this if you have a clear vision of what you seek and the purpose for it." (Low and Theyagu 2003, pp. 57–58)

The event or adversity is also seen in the right context. After the event or an adverse situation, one nurtures and develops one's restored energy to make it even greater, more indestructible and incorruptible. One's strength is stilled while on this journey so that it can be nurtured and grow. This is a journey without force or non-violence but with gentleness; and greatness, so to speak, results in great development.

Section Concluding Remarks

Remember we can choose and make the most of any given situation. We can see the positive out of every negative that comes in our way. And we then learn and grow, and we have the power to prevail; it's really up to us. So may the Tao be with you!

Leading, the Guan Yin Way

Commonly known in the West by the name of the Goddess of Mercy, Guan Yin (literally means, "One who hears the cries of the world") was originally Avalokitesvara Bodhisattva in Indian Mahayana Buddhism; she is the female reincarnation of the Buddha. Guan Yin is the Bodhisattva of compassion.

Here, with regard to leadership, Guan Yin is chosen because it is commonly accepted by the ordinary people in traditional China and by Overseas Chinese as a kind of patron saint. Besides, Guan Yin is a prominent deity in Chinese mythology. Interestingly, Guan Yin's immense appeal transcends national and religious borders. She is revered and worshipped by followers in Taiwan and even in India, Indonesia, Japan and Korea. Guan Yin is the patron saint of women, sailors, merchants, craftsmen, and those who are under criminal prosecutions.

Most times, paintings of the Goddess appear in the form of lotus-carrying Guan Yin and statues of the Goddess are normally that of Sprinkling water Guan Yin, blessing the people. Guan Yin is also interestingly depicted as having a thousand hands, and how is this so or possible? It is perhaps because of the Goddess's basic love, her ardent wish to reach out to help human beings. It is believed that she once said that, "As long as one is kind, and there's love in one's heart, a thousand hands will reach, coming to one's aid." Each of Guan Yin's thousand hands is believed to make gestures associated with awakening or meditational postures.

Also commonly featured is the White-robed Guan Yin—in Buddhism, white is the symbol for the mind of enlightenment. She is sometimes depicted as holding a branch of a weeping Willow tree, symbolising the tears that she shed for the sufferings of the world.

Whatever it is, it is often said that one look at any statues and paintings of Guan Yin, the observer would immediately notice the Goddess's obvious softness, gentle gaze and compassionate features. She is filled with compassion for all beings.

Guan Yin is considered as merciful and has the heart of compassion. It is, to this author, the Buddhism's equivalent of the Catholics' Virgin Mother Mary.

Here, leading the Guan Yin way is that of showing love and compassion. It is said that Guan Yin's vows of compassion are like the clouds which provide shade for living beings under the hot sun and which keeps the world cool. "Her wonderful dharma metaphorically resembles the raindrops from the sky which nourishes the Earth and which puts out the fire of affliction in the minds of beings, giving rise to the mind of enlightenment" (Koh 2004, p. 54). Guan Yin is overall seen as a source of unconditional love and more importantly as a saviour. Guan Yin, in her bodhisattva vows, promises to answer the cries and pleas of all beings and to free all beings from their own karmic woes. Based upon the Lotus Sutra and the Shurangama sutra, Avalokitesvara Bodhisattva is generally seen as a saviour, both spiritually and physically.

To emulate the Goddess Guan Yin's ways, indeed leaders should abolish any feelings of greed (Note that there's no fire greater than the fire of greed.), unnecessary wants and extravagance. Needless to say, similar to the Catholics' Virgin Mother Mary, regardless of one's gender, one can take Goddess Guan Yin as the role model to emulate.

Leaders need to love their people, attending to their needs and cares; they selflessly need to help the needy while avoiding the greedy. This is all the more important at this time of the world history so that sufferings are banished or reduced, and mankind can then experience greater peace and live harmoniously.

Leading, the Bruce Lee Way

Introduction

Who Is Bruce Lee?

The late Bruce Lee was born on 27 Nov 1940. A Chinese-American martial artist, philosopher, instructor, and martial arts actor, he is widely regarded as the most influential martial artist of the twentieth century. Iconic for his presentation of Chinese martial arts to the non-Chinese world, Bruce Lee's films, especially the Hollywood-produced *Enter the Dragon*, raised the traditional Hong Kong martial arts film to a new level of popularity and praise. In fact, it sparked the first major surge of interest (in the 1970s) in Chinese martial arts in the West. Bruce died on 20 July 1973.

Even to this day, an iconic Chinese Kung-Fu martial artist, Bruce Lee remains very popular among Asian audience and in particular among the Chinese, as he portrayed Chinese nationalism through his films (Bowman 2010; Dennis 1974). In Asia, "the appeal of Lee integrally includes an indelible and active reference to a certain 'Chinese nationalism', which 'cannot be easily dismissed if one wishes to appreciate fully his appeal to Chinese audiences'... (there is) 'an emotional wish among Chinese people living outside China to identify with China and things Chinese, even though they may not have been born there or speak its national language or dialects'" Thus, Lee's films emphasized themes of pride and anti-racism (Bowman 2010, p. 123).

Section's Objectives

Here, the author seeks to uncover, demonstrate and reveal the various leadership ways and key lessons that can be garnered from the late martial artist, Bruce Lee through examination and inference of the various quotes from book, *Tao of Jeet Kune Do*. The late Bruce Lee, the founder of his own-styled *Jeet Kune Do* martial arts, can be said to be more or less influenced by Confucianism, Taoism and Buddhism/Zen, and these can be seen, inferred and implied from the writings in the said book and other literature.

What Is Leadership? The Emphasis on Action

For the purpose of this section, leadership is again emphasised as getting results or things done through people. It is about taking action, and accomplishing things through others by way of influencing them; leadership is action and not mere position or appointment. When linked to martial arts (with 'quick hands and legs'), leadership should be clearly seen as action-orientated.

Having a Health Body with a Healthy Mind

> Put your heart at rest. (Chinese proverb)

Many people saw in the 70s and speaking with several respondents who are fans of Bruce Lee's movies they agreed that even now Lee is still an example to get a strong and efficient body and to master the martial arts skills in combat without weapons (Low 2010d). The late Bruce Lee was renowned for his physical fitness and vigorous, dedicated fitness regime to become as strong as he possibly could. He later concluded that in order to attain a high-performance body, one could not fuel it with a diet of junk food, and with "the wrong fuel", one's body would achieve or move lethargically or sloppily (Little 1998).

Leaders should think strategically and think smart. They should undeniably strive to develop healthy bodies and grow themselves mentally and spiritually what the author calls developing the clarity of mind and the purity of heart.

Look into yourself, and ask: Are you leading and living healthily? Are you thinking smart? Are you thinking strategically? Are you practising good leadership ways? Are you leading ethically? Are you growing yourself spiritually?

Being Different, Standing Out Because of One's Integrity (*Lien*)

> If virtue fails, honour decreases with it. (Telugu proverb)

One Chinese proverb goes as such, "Virtue travels uphill, vice travels downhill." And as a leader, because one is selfless and caring, one is honoured and stands tall; one's reputation grows.

One respondent, who was familiar with Bruce Lee and his martial arts way, expressed these:

The martial artist sets a good example of what (s)he can perform. In order to do so, (s)he needs to master his or her art before (s)he can talk about his or her art and style. (S)he can then show the art when (s)he has mastered it. Through personal mastery and self-growth [act on what (s)he talks about and (s)he does what he says (s)he can do], the martial artist wins the respect of his followers.

Here, the leader needs to, more specifically, ask: How do I stand? How do I fare ethically in my profession? Does I fulfil my role(s) and responsibility(ies) or my *dharma*?

Meditating, Learning and Practising

A clear conscience is the greatest armour. (Chinese proverb)

According to Bruce Lee, some people are born with good physique, a sense of speed and much stamina. That is fine, however in martial arts; everything one learns is an acquired skill. And when applied to leadership, it simply means that the leader needs to keep learning and practice. For Bruce Lee, "life itself is your teacher, and you are in a state of constant learning" (Little 2000, p. 5).

One can take that, it in itself, is very Chinese or that Bruce Lee was very much influenced by Confucianism. The leader should plan well; it is often expected for the leader to, beforehand, cleverly plan and prepare, and in doing these, he learns.

And when the Confucian leader meditates, he keeps learning to reach the truth (*The Analects*, Chap. XIX: 7), improving his (Confucius') ways. In an attempt to meditate, I (Confucius) once spent a whole day without food and a whole night without sleep: it was no use. It would have been better for me to have spent the time in learning (Analects XV: 31). Indeed, studying the situation, having a good analysis, knowing the needs of the followers and having preparatory plans are so essential when it comes to dealing or handling them.

Bruce strongly believed that martial artists should train diligently to defend themselves (Lee and Uyehara 1976a). "Like the martial artist, the leader too needs to constantly practice his art or skills, practicing them everyday." (Several respondents' input). This coincides with Low's (2005d) observation and emphasis that in growing ourselves as leaders, we need to practice and keep on training ourselves. Like young and flexible bamboos, it is, in fact, good for leaders to start from young, get early training and keep on practising (Low and Theyagu 2003).

Questions a leader should ask include: Do I take periodic stock? What are the areas which I need to practise more?

Affecting and Involving Simplicity

Man is an over-complicated organism. If he is doomed to extinction he will die out for want of simplicity. (Ezra Pound)

Lao-Tzu advocates simplicity in life and living and this is very much applicable in martial arts as well as in leadership ways. The steps are simple yet potent and powerful. Simplicity is to be appreciated as it leads to be easily remembered to be put into practice. Because Lee believed that the best defence is the most simple and effective, his no-nonsense counters include eye gouges, groin kicks, heads stomps and other techniques (Lee and Uyehara 1976a) are indeed remarkable.

In *Jeet Kune Do*, the fighter, keeping his cool, has to relax his body and with the lightness of the legs, he can move easily and smoothly and effect good blows against the opponent (Lee and Uyehara 1976b). Simplicity adds to this smooth flow of movements and striking power.

Leaders should also subscribe to simplicity just as a truly great man never puts away the simplicity of a child. They communicate in simple and clear words; they are easily understood or their words misconstrued. Leaders also need to be cool and calm so that they can think well, be responsive—not reactive to the situation that they are in, and be overall, dynamic.

Questions as a leader, one needs to ask: Am I communicating simply? Am I communicating clearly? Am I showing to my people the tasks to be done in a simple manner?

Applying Soft Power

> One who seeks beauty with a pure heart with a pure heart finds what one is searching for. (Chinese proverb)

Leaders, using soft power, are more charming. Like Sun Tzu's preferred victory is victory without fighting, *Jeet Kune Do* is the art of fighting without fighting. It is good for leaders to use *Jeet Kune Do* Tao-like soft power. *Jeet Kune Do* leaders exude soft power. Lee once explained: "Be formless... shapeless, like water. Now you put water into a cup, it becomes the cup. You pour water into a bottle; it becomes the bottle. You put water into a teapot; it becomes the teapot. Now water can flow, or creep or drip or crash! Be water, my friend" (Little 1997).

When one walks the talk, one sets a good example, being role model for the followers to copy and emulate (Low 2005d, 2008c; Low and Theyagu 2003). The followers would certainly want to follow, imitate and emulate the ways of the example-setting leader. And being a role model is one of the most persuasive ways of a successful leader.

A virtuous leader is influential. Friendly, calm and non-confrontational, the *Jeet Kune Do* leader is also kind and gentle, and wants to help others and his (her) followers. Collaborative and adopting a win-win mind growth, the leader seeks to gain cooperation from others. And that makes the leader charming and appealing.

Questions one needs to ask include: Am I applying soft power? What are my sources of soft power? And how can I apply them?

Being Selfless

> A great general need not blow his own trumpet. (Chinese proverb)

A leader has to be humble, and this is similar in spirit to the popular Confucian-based Chinese saying, "The superior man does not think himself so. His humility is what sets him apart." For Bruce Lee, one should not be conscious of oneself—"establish nothing in regard to oneself" (Lee 1975, p. 8). This is important; otherwise, the self becomes a hindrance to physical movements. And in the case of leadership, it is not leading without caring for others, and seeking benefits not for others, but more for oneself. The opposite is true.

The *Jeet Kune Do* leader, with no sense of self-importance, should be selfless; (s)he has no ego. For Bruce Lee, in affecting the martial artist's punches and blows, one needs to "turn into a doll made of wood: it has no ego, it thinks nothing, it is not grasping or sticky. Let the body and limbs work themselves out in accordance with discipline they have undergone." (Lee 1975, p. 7)

Like *Jeet Kune Do* or for that matter, any martial arts, when one is devoid of the self, and there is no conscious of the self, the art of leadership reaches its peak. Here, it can be taken that servant leadership is to be practiced. This matches with Low's (2005d, p. 14) Taoism explanations of *Yin-Yang*, that is:

> When you are *nobody* (perhaps through service or serving others) you can be *somebody* (others may like according to you their liking and you become *somebody* or a leader). But being somebody (a leader, author's words), one must continue the process (continue to be service-minded, help serve others). Otherwise, we forget to grow or learn and then we become nobody (leaders need to continue to serve and be of service)!

Interestingly, this is similar to what Zig Ziglar has once said, that is, one can get everything one wants in life if one just help enough other people get what they want, and this is very true of leadership in the *Jeet Kune Do* way; the leader serves and his people willingly help and attain the results for the leader. A concomitant issue related to being a leader selfless is that a leader needs to be genuinely accessible to their people. In the army, the soldier who writes to the Congress or Parliament points to the fact that he has been denied access or has difficulties in accessing his commander; he is off on his own without benefit of counsel and fouls up with some unsound action. Interestingly, commanders who adopt an open door policy for their men should not have their men blocked by their officers lest commanders will be cut off from dealing with the ground people with real problems or issues. Whatever it is, in essence, there is a need for a leader to truly be in touch with the people while looking at one's 'command' and people from the bottom-up. And really be hands-on and connected with the people.

Here is the question as a leader, one needs to ask and answer daily: What can I do to increase the value of my service to my people (and citizens/customers) today? And also, look for the ways to add value to what one does and to the people who depend on the leader every each day.

Preferring Harmony

> One who is happiest finds peace and harmony at home. (Chinese proverb)

Bruce Lee once said, "One should be in harmony with, not in opposition to, the strength and force of the opposition" (Little 2000, p. 20). He certainly favoured peace and harmony. To win without fighting, without even a punch or a blow is the best fight one can have.

Peace is wonderful—as in the Chinese saying, as always, "under the heavens there is but one family".

Like the martial artists, excellent leaders are, a Chinese proverb goes, "those who seek harmony (and they) know how to find it". Good leaders, people-centred, are collaborators or good team-players, and they secure peace and harmony among their followers and with others.

Questions one needs to ask include: Am I affecting (promoting) peace and harmony within my people? What are the ways I do to resolve conflicts and promote peace and harmony among my people?

Adapting as Well as Being Flexible and Agile

> When the wind is great, bow before it; when the rain is heavy, yield to it. (Chinese proverb)

Bruce Lee was believed to have said these: "Life is wide, limitless. There is no border, no frontier" (Little 2000, p. 2). "The meaning of life is that it is to be *lived*, and it is not to be traded and conceptualized and squeezed into a pattern of systems" (Little 2000, p. 3). In other words, life is not to be fixed or rigidly patterned; life lives and in the living flow.

The leader, in leading the Bruce Lee way, should also be flexible. Being creative also contributes to being flexible; one is not rigidly fixed or attached to a single form, ritual, pattern or routine. For Bruce Lee, the softest thing cannot be snapped, and moving, the martial artist leader acts like water. Lee once said, "Running water never grows stale. So you just have to 'keep on flowing.'" (Bruce Lee, cited in http://en.wikiquote.org/wiki/Bruce_Lee)

In *The Analects*, II: 12, "The Master said, 'The gentleman is no vessel'" (Lau 1979). Here, it is taken that negotiator should not be like a utensil. (S)he should have broad knowledge, broadening his (her) learning and not be confined to merely one use. And indeed, the effective leader should be flexible, adapting his ways or styles to meet the various situations (s)he is thrown into. Interestingly, there is no fixed teaching. To borrow Lee's (1975) words, like real combat, real leading, is not fixed; it is very much "alive". "When you're talking about fighting, as it is, with no rules, well then, baby you'd better train every part of your body!" (Lee 1971).

To interestingly add further, Bruce's style of fighting cleverly drew on several martial arts traditions—even Western boxing. Bruce Lee once said that "(he learnt from this experience) soon my fists began to swell from hitting his hard head. Right then I realized Wing Chun was not too practical and began to alter my way of fighting." (Bruce Lee 1976, cited in http://en.wikiquote.org/wiki/Bruce_Lee). And this author reckons that this learning from the various martial arts, to some extent, contributes to the flexibility of the *Jeet Kune Do* fighter. And because this style of fighting drew on various martial arts traditions, it outraged purists. But Lee didn't care; he creatively danced upon the parapets of orthodoxy, laughing at those below who were too slow to share his vision of a multi-disciplinary approach to fighting.

What more, as a leader in his field, Lee was also very much creative as well as ahead of his game.

Questions as a leader, one should ask include: Am I being flexible and agile? What are ways that can help me be more flexible and agile when leading my people?

Being Detached

> Do not run away, let go. Do not seek, for it will come when least expected. (Bruce Lee)

> Get over with it and move on. (Kim Cheng Patrick Low)

Lee's *Jeet Kune Do* treats life and death indifferently. The martial artist leader is detached. One just does without regard to the results and in doing so, one attains and achieves. Thinking or desiring, being so attached to the results can in fact be a hindrance. Why?

In martial arts, when one is free from mechanical conditioning, there is freedom. And when there is freedom, there is simplicity. To gain freedom, the past is also let go and one must die and renew, be born and live again, with the old making way for the new. One rejuvenates and lives. Spiritually, one must die to save oneself, so one becomes detached without much desire, and in that sense, there are elements of influence of Taoism and Buddhism in *Jeet Kune Do*. A leader may not want to have fixed or narrow ways of doing things as this can be stifling not only to the leader's creativity but also that of his or her people.

Questions as a leader, one should ask include: Am I being detached when leading? What are ways that can help me be more detached or less fixed when leading my people, or when asking them to do things?

Coordinating and Ensuring a Smooth Flow of Actions (Results)

> A single tree cannot make a forest. A single beam cannot support a great house. (Chinese proverb)

To any martial artist, good coordination of the arms and legs and the entire body lead to smooth flow of attacks and defences against the opponent. A fighter whose movements are awkward or uncoordinated would not be able to fight well. And (s) he would ultimately lose out to his (her) opponent.

"A well-coordinated fighter does everything smoothly and gracefully" (Lee 1975, p. 43), gliding in and out with a minimum of effort and a maximum of deception; there is a good timing, appropriate blows at the right time. And the movements have a flow, rhythm, purpose and bears merits against the opponent.

Likewise, the *Jeet Kune Do* leader ensures smooth coordination, and integrates all the resources, power and strengths of the organization into an effective doing/executing organism. Like a good coordinated muscle work of the fighter, the effectiveness of teamwork/spirit brought about the leader is one of the factors that determine speed, power, endurance, agility and performance of the organization. Just as the Chinese proverb goes that "if there is a good general, there will be no weak soldiers", similarly, if there is a good (team) leader, there will be no weak team members (Low 2010d, p. 132).

The key questions a leader should ask include: Am I coordinating my unit/ department well? How can I better coordinate my people?

Being Self-Disciplined

With oars, a boat drifts. (Chinese proverb)

Self-discipline leads to mastery and expertise in one's field. The *Jeet Kune Do* fighter is very self-disciplined. Self-discipline is the power or ability to make yourself do what you should do. You have your own vision and long-term goal, and self-discipline requires your self-direction and control, self-mastery and overall self-responsibility.

The *Jeet Kune Do* leader is self-disciplined, learns; practices and works hard. This is in same spirit as what a leader would usually be and do; the harder (s)he works, the luckier (s)he gets.

As a leader, your action point here is identify one area in you life where lack of discipline is interfering with your success; then decide to develop discipline in that area, and work hard at it. Several respondents spoke of "being self-disciplined helps us much and in fact gets us determined to move towards our goals, and we pursue our dreams. Discipline makes leaders be better focused and also build up their patience and endurance while training, upgrading and polishing their skills".

Note that the lack of self-discipline can sometimes really cause us trouble or interferes with our success. One thus needs to ask: Whether there is any lack of discipline in an area in our lives so that we can do something to overcome this weakness and develop discipline in that area, and in deciding to do so, we could really change our lives.

Enduring

Adversity is a mirror that reveals one's true self. (Chinese proverb)

For Bruce Lee, the fighter should be fearless, never fear failure and in fact, is enduring. Bruce urged leaders not to *fear failure*; to him, "Not failure, but low aim, is the crime. In great attempts it is glorious even to fail." (Little 2000, p. 121)

The tough fighter trains, exercises and practices to have endurance (Low 2010d). This, when applied to leadership, simply means that the leader should have the valued quality of endurance as well as resilience. Or we should simply say that endurance contributes to building a resilient leadership. Such leaders do not lose their hearts because of setbacks, instead they learn from mistakes and setbacks. And they improve on their ways, becoming better leaders. What more, they also expect adversity and learn to live with it. In the face of adversity, leaders simply need to learn to keep their cool yet keep doing the best, keep charging and keep going. And yes, keep accomplishing.

In the martial arts of *Jeet Kune Do*, endurance is lost rapidly if one stops to work at its maintenance (Lee 1975). And it means practice makes perfect. Like martial artists, leaders should not, for one moment, blink or get complacent. (When the martial artist blinks, he may miss or lose out certain movements of the opponent and weaken his defence, and hence, a chance prevails for his opponent to hit him.) And there is a need for all leaders to adopt a *kaizen* mind growth—keep on going and keep on improving.

The key questions here that leaders should ask include: Am I being tough? How motivated and prepared am I to climb or scale to scale the peak? How can I keep on improving? What values do I hold that will spur me on?

Being Strategic

One who gains mastery will create his own opportunities. (Chinese proverb)

Like any other martial arts, *Jeet Kune Do* fighter applies strategy for long-term advantage and tactics for short-term gains. In the same way, the *Jeet Kune Do* leader does the same. The martial artists must seize any opportunity or chance to advance and in the same vein, leaders should be strategic and bring growth to the organization(s) and people they are leading.

Strategic-minded with long-termism in approach, *Jeet Kune Do* leaders are "not being tense but ready, not thinking yet not dreaming, not being set but flexible—it is being wholly and quietly alive, aware and alert, ready for whatever may come."

A key question that a leader should ask is: How can I lead more strategically?

Being Action-Oriented

Maintain soldiers a thousand days, use them for the moment. (Chinese proverb)

For Lee (1975, p. 8), "an assertion is Zen only when it is itself an act and does not refer to anything that is asserted in it."

Besides, seemingly the proponents of Taoism, with *wu wei* (or non-action) appear to be passive yet it is on the contrary. According to Taoism, the *Yin* and the *Yang* must take place, with the flow of things. Days and nights alternate; there is the going and coming, the to-ing and the fro-ing; and the ups and downs. There are beginnings, and there are endings, and there are always the seasons and actions.

In Taoism, though 'being' is more valued than 'doing', there should not be any bottlenecks; instead, movements should be effected. Sharpening the saw, often practicing or even perfecting, the *Jeet Kune Do* leader is action-oriented. Bruce Lee speaks of "Action is a high road to self-confidence and esteem. Where it is open, all energies flow toward it." (Lee 1975, p. 206)

Action is, besides, power in each blow or strike. Each punch or blow is packed with power; inside his weaponry of strikes, Bruce Lee had the 1 in. punch and the 3-in. punch (Demile 1994). The whole body should participate in the thrust or strike, and that force and impetus can become very powerful.

Similarly if the leader is passionate and carries out a particular action enthusiastically, there's little inertia and instead, the forward motion and accomplishments become potent and significant. Great leadership is as much about preparation and training as it is about action. Leaders are also change agents (Low and Theyagu 2003) and they should also lead change effectively. As a matter of fact, true leaders in leading change effectively can rejuvenate the organizations, giving them a new lease of life.

The key questions a leader should ask include: Am I being proactive? How can I be more proactive? How can I make or spur my people to be more proactive? How can I be more effective when leading change?

Section Conclusion

Clearly, there is much to learn, and many wise leadership ways that can, in fact, be gleaned from Bruce Lee's philosophies and thoughts behind his martial arts and sports. As leaders, it is worthy to note what Bruce Lee himself has indicated, that is, it is one's courage and one's striking thoughts that will create a brighter future for all of us.

Mao Zedong and His Leadership Ways

Introduction

Mao Zedong himself was one of only three peasants to gain control of his country throughout its long history—the others were the founders of the Han and Ming dynasties. The aim of this paper is to examine the leadership ways of Mao Zedong (1893–1976), the Chinese political leader, poet and statesman, founder of People's Republic of China (PRC).

Mao Zedong's chief leader ways include:

Knowing the People Well and Connecting with Them

Great leaders know their people well, and they stay connected with them.

Born in the village of Shaoshan in the Hunan province of China, Mao's father was a peasant while his mother was a devout Buddhist. Encouraged by his father, Mao Zedong had a great interest in the political system. And in addition to his limited formal education, Mao spent 6 months studying independently. Mao, first introduced to communism while working at Peking University, co-founded the Communist Party of China (CPC) in 1921. Such a background helped Mao to be seen as a realist, a leader and in touch, well grounded, with the common people.

In doing business, one needs to know but also establish good relationships with not only our people, but also with our fellow customers.

Uniting China and Making Good Strategies

China is such a huge country and unlike the Kuomintang (Nationalist government forces) and without alienating the masses, he was able to connect with the people. His strategies were well-thought and appropriate. He understood the Chinese people, and indeed, in spite of drawbacks and hardships, knew the right strategy to assume control of the country. To Mao, "the people are like water and the army is like fish" (Mao wrote in *Aspects of China's Anti-Japanese Struggle* in 1948). Mao perceptively saw the revolutionary potential of the peasantry.

Unlike Marx and Lenin who had viewed in their urban doctrine the working class as the leading revolutionary force, Mao recognized the revolutionary potential of the peasantry (though when first articulated, Mao's views were rejected by the Party in favor of orthodox policy). Coming from a peasant family, Mao cultivated his reputation among the farmers, and introduced them to Marxism.

Strategic, Mao Zedong very much applied Sun Tzu's dictum "Know yourself, know your enemy; a thousand battles, a thousand victories." It can also be assessed that Mao Zedong adopted and adapted many of Sun Tzu's strategies including "luring the enemy in deep—avoiding the enemy's main force and striking at his weak spots" and "conserving energy—carving up and destroying the exhausted enemy" (Liu 1993; cited in Low 2010e) when dealing with the larger Nationalist (Kuomintang) forces (Low 2010e).

Doing business is about thinking ahead, strategizing and growing the business. As a business leader, one should think, in fact, better still, think out-of-the-box and plan ahead; one needs to strategize to expand one's market and business.

Being Powerful and for Mao, that Power Comes from the Barrel of the Gun
Mao believed that might make right, and that political power comes from the barrel of the gun. In 1934, the Kuomintang government destroyed the Jiangxi Soviet, and the Communist forces started the legendary retreat and the Long March, a military expedition of 6000 miles, said to be similar to the march of Alexander the Great. In

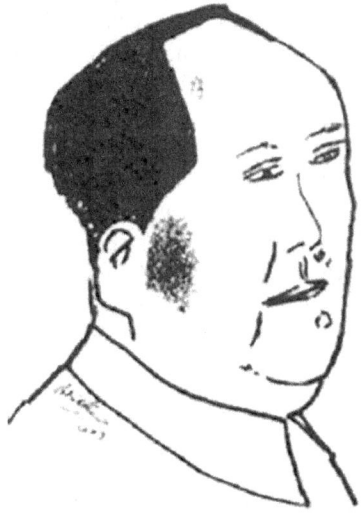

China has seen the rise of charismatic Mao Zedong and the greatest peasant revolution in the world history.

Mao believed in hard power and to him, power comes out from the barrel of the gun. To Mao, might indeed make right.

Fig. 5.3 Mao Zedong, as drawn by the author

1935, Mao's political power increased when he was elected Chairman of the Politburo. Mao's rural based guerrilla warfare led to the fall of the government. In 1949, the new People's Republic of China (PRC) was proclaimed (Fig. 5.3).

In 1965, Mao Zedong set in motion a series of events that were to unleash the turmoil now known as the Cultural Revolution. Having socialized industry and agriculture, Mao called on the people to transform society itself—all distinctions between manual and intellectual works were to be abolished and class distinction disappeared. In 1967, the revolution reached its violent peak, with the Red Guards spreading social unrest; Mao appealed to students to form the Red Guard, in whom he entrusted the fate of the revolution. The People's Liberation Army (PLA) finally restored order, but the ensuing years were characterized by fear, violence, and mistrust.

Mao believed in hard power and to him, power comes out from the barrel of the gun. To Mao, might indeed make right.

If we were to apply this to business, it is equal to liking competition. Competition can spur us to attain greater heights. Yet while competition is good, one pertinent criticism against it is that when pursued to the extreme, competition can be tough and very severe. And this can create a cold, harsh world with peace and harmony being hampered; little cooperation and harmony exist. In business, one needs to build and foster relationships, cooperate, collaborate and synergise to achieve greater goals and better results (Low 2001). In business, one should have friends; one needs partners and strategic alliances as well as networks, support and networking (Low 2003). Interestingly, co-opetition—a buzzword termed to describe a business strategy of co-operative competition—occurs when companies team up for parts of their business where they deem that they have no competitive advantage and where they consider they can share common costs. For example, the arrangement between PSA Peugeot Citroën and Toyota to share parts for a new city car simultaneously sold as the Peugeot 107, the Toyota Aygo, and the Citroën C1— qualifies as co-opetition. In this case, companies save money on shared costs while remaining fiercely competitive in other areas

Being in the Constant State of Revolution

Mao believed that such a way of life would be keeping people on their toes as well as getting rid of complacency. Besides, communist cause and ideas would then be entrenched in the people's mind. Hence, he had his 'Let a thousand flowers bloom', the Great Leap Forward and the Cultural Revolution in the 1980s.

Here, one becomes or is a revolutionary, one keeps on learning and improving; one betters oneself. And when applied to running a business, this means continuous learning and improvement to the benefit of the organisation.

Section Conclusion

Overall, the Father of Modern Communist China, Mao Zedong's strategic reliance on the rural rather than the urban proletariat to instigate violent revolution distinguished Mao from his predecessors and contemporaries. His rapport and close relationships with the masses can be likened to the common touch of a leader which is critical in running any organisation; indeed the leader should know how the common people think and what motivates them. Besides, his ways of constant revolution also means continuous learning and improvement, and that from the business angle is good, and continuous learning and upgrading makes it tough for rivals to compete with the Company, which in essence becomes a hard-to-hit moving target.

Li Ka Shing

Introduction

Li Ka Shing is a wealthy businessman from Hong Kong. The richest person of East Asian descent in the world and the eleventh richest person in the world with an estimated wealth of US$26.0 billion on 10 March 2011, Li is a well-known philanthropist and Li's foundation had donated over HK$10 billion ($1.28 billion) in the past 30 years, 80 % of which was sent to China. In the past 3 years, HK$5.2 billion to HK$5.3 billion has been donated, including cash for five mainland hospital projects. Li pledged a third of his assets to his charity foundation, days after 40 American billionaires signed a pledge to give away over half of their fortunes. (International Business Times 2010)

Li Ka Shing has these traits or qualities:

A Sense of Purpose

> I would like to devote my energies to make more money for my shareholders as well as for myself. Then, I will use my money for my shareholders as well as for myself. Then, I will use my money, my position, energy and experience to benefit the community. (Li, cited in Low and Theyagu 2003, p. 91)

"Life offered him a single purpose when he was poor—to become rich." "You need to have an objective." (Low and Theyagu 2003, p. 91) And the key to his success is his logical mind and his self-control. With that, he pursues what he sees as his idea of happiness. Indeed, he is now fabulously rich, the territory's richest leader.

Simple but Effective

Simon Murray, a one-time managing director of Hutchison Whampoa indicates that Li is a "great man (who) has used nothing more than 'simple sales techniques'" (Cragg 1995, p. 147).

Being Prudent

Known to avoid excessive debts, this Chinese Taipan, "the man with the golden touch", ensures that his monies are well invested in well-managed companies rather buying into ailing ones.

Honesty Is Power

Wilson, in *Hong Kong, Hong Kong*, speaks of Li as being "of several grades higher than most of his rivals . . . His integrity is recognised and welcomed in a city which does not see much of that commodity, and he himself says that 'honesty is power'".

Alliances

Li always tries to forge his business alliances by being a "little bit more than fair" (Cragg 1995, p. 147).

Admitting Mistakes and Not Afraid to Take Risks

Li Ka-shing is not afraid of admitting mistakes. He once said this: "Nobody is God. People are not gods; they are human beings, and human beings make mistakes. Me too." Unafraid to fail, Li goes on to take risks, preferring to take risks in exploring rather than not trying at all. (Cragg 1995, pp. 148–149)

Mongolia

Ten Leadership Lessons Learnt from the Warrior-Conqueror, Genghis Khan

Introduction

Again, leadership here is taken as "the ability to influence a group toward the achievement of goals" (Robbins 2005). However, simply put, leadership gets things done, and organisations (read as nations too) need strong leadership and strong management for optimal effectiveness. Leaders make a difference. And in these recent decades—with political scandals, troubled economies, frauds and well-publicised corporate failure such as Enron and WorldCom, there's a great need for leaders (Lussier and Achua 2007a). In the past, we have seen great leaders such as Genghis Khan and several others, and in this section, it is hoped to draw some lessons of leadership in which we can apply in today's dynamic world.

Genghis Khan (more properly known as Chinggis Khan), his reign name, was originally called Temujin. Living from 1167 to 1227, the Mongol conqueror, succeeded his father, Yekusai, as chieftain of a Mongol tribe and then fought to become ruler of a Mongol confederacy. After subjugating many tribes of Mongolia and establishing his capital at Karakorum, Temujin held (1206) a great meeting, the *khuriltai*, at which he accepted leadership of the Mongols and assumed his title. He welded his group of ill-disciplined warriors into a united fighting force (Low and Theyagu 2003, p. 3). He promulgated a code of conduct and reorganized his armies and indeed, as a leader, "you've got to want to be in charge" (Roberts 1990; cited by Low and Theyagu 2003, p. 2).

Leadership Lesson 1: Having a Vision and a Set of Values

> If mind is clean, fate is good. (Mongolian saying)

Poor leadership leads to failure and good leadership leads to success. "Start living. Start visioning." (Low and Theyagu 2003, p. 52)

The invincible Mongolian hordes, under the leadership and tutelary power of Genghis Khan, overran most of the Asian and Eurasian land, and in their heyday, the Mongols never met an army they could not beat. They were incomparably superior, man for man, to what their formidable military opponents in China, Russia, Persia and Western Europe could muster (Oestmoen 2007). This is attributed to Genghis' vision of one nation as well as his promotion of (the value of) Mongols' solidarity and teamwork (Low 2009h).

Accordingly, on a five-point scale survey conducted by a *Training* magazine and The Center for Creative Leadership, the ability to construct and articulate a clear vision was identified as critical, scoring a 4.89 point (Schettler 2000; cited in Robbins 2005). In this regard, Bill Gates was a true visionary leader of his time, and he still is. When mainframe computers were still the focus of computing and the personal computer was in its infancy, Gates envisioned the future of today with a computer in every office desktop and in every home (Lussier and Achua 2007b).

The point here, the key leadership lesson is that of having a vision, mission and values and that of perpetuating a corporate culture that sustains and lives. In terms of values and leadership, one needs to decide what one stands for—leading and living with the highest values one knows and holds dearly, close to one's heart, and these values are plucked from or linked with the vision and mission.

Having vision, mission and values, leaders build clocks and build organizations that last—even after they are long gone. A common sense of purpose helps a lot. Here, the leaders would be able to engage and involve the hearts and souls of their followers. Ordinarily, most people share a yearning to a part of something bigger than their selves. Something they can be excited about, feel good about, and that will challenge them to do something important and perform or do what that is "above and beyond." Vision fulfils that yearning (Pellowe 2000).

Leadership Lesson 2: Having Goal(s), Desire and Passion

The second leadership lesson is that of having goals, desire and passion. Genghis Khan had his goal of growing his empire, and his desire and passion translate his goals into reality. All these appear even greater when one bears in mind that the Mongolians were illiterate, religiously shamanistic plus the fact then they were sparsely populated (perhaps no more than around 700,000 in number) (Smitha 2004).

"Truly successful leaders know that the key to their success lies in creating a passionate desire for the development of that potential... in themselves and in members of their team (*their followers*) (Meyer 1998, p. 111; *italics mine*). Even after Genghis Khan died in 1227, the Mongol armies dominated the battlefield until the empire stretched from the Pacific Ocean to the Adriatic Sea (May 2001). Desire and passion—the inner essence of the leaders—serve as catalysts and developers of talents of the leaders and their followers. They also energise leaders, turning them from average to becoming outstanding.

Desire and passion create actions and lead the leaders to accomplish greater things. And such leaders leave behind their legacies (Low and Theyagu 2003).

Leadership Lesson 3: Energising and Taking Actions

If you endeavour, the fate will favour you. (Mongolian proverb)

Passivity does not bring one anywhere. "Leaders do not wait around", and Low and Theyagu (2003, p. 44) put it in the form of an old adage: "You have to crack a few eggs to make an omelette". The third leadership lesson is that action is good and has its results and benefits.

Enthusiasm and high energy helps. Leadership "all begins with energy" (Jack Welch, cited in Krames 2005, p. 25). Leaders energise, they energise with the vision, and people respond to them. Genghis Khan was pro-active; he led his people and fought well to gain new territories. He had energy, similar to what Jack Welch calls by the same term. Genghis Khan has "a strong penchant for action", and a love, "the thrill of the game" (Welch, cited in Krames 2005, p. 25). An effective leader spreads confidence like gardeners spread fertiliser, and instil confidence into the soul of their people and organization (Krames 2005).

Leadership Lesson 4: Effecting Teamwork and Solidarity

Union is source of success. (Mongolian proverb)

Teamwork is a way of life and a critical component of work-life in modern organisations. And team leadership is critical for organisational growth. Successful leaders develop and use their effective teams to achieve organisational goals (Lussier and Achua 2007a; Low 2003). The present-day example can be seen in Bill Gates—the chairman and chief software architect of Microsoft, the worldwide leader in software services, and Internet technologies for personal and business computing. Gates actively participates in and "coordinates the business units, and holds Microsoft together" while he delegates authority to his managers to run their independent departments (Lussier and Achua 2007b, p. 59).

The fourth leadership lesson is that unity and teamwork is good and has its benefits. To Genghis Khan, a single tribe is like a single arrow, but many tribes combined become powerful; they become like a quiver of arrows. The latter is stronger. Teamwork and solidarity, as the Mongolian saying—"Union is source of success (*Evlevel butne*)" goes, was thus favoured.

Indeed, Genghis Khan's non-military achievements include tribal unity among the Mongols. Without Genghis, there would not be a Mongolia, and through the great Khan a nation was born.

Organisations can learn and instil in their organisational citizens this sense of common purpose ("We're all in it together.") and destiny; their people would be united and committed. Mongols today venerate him as the country's founding father (May 2001). Teamwork in the modern sense serves to supply one of the mechanisms for team learning through collective problem solving. As team members solve problems jointly, they continue to learn, and bring about organizational improvement (DuBrin 2007; Low 2003).

Leadership Lesson 5: Applying Common Sense

> While horse is strong, travel to see places. (Mongolian proverb)

One of the classic sins of the leaders is that they do not think strategically (Low 2008d, p. 69). Worse, common-sense may not be commonly applied. So the fifth leadership lesson is the need to apply common sense; common sense matters a lot. And keeping it simple helps overall understanding especially when communicating.

Clearly most perceptive about politics in rival tribes and cities, the Great Khan understood what drove individuals. Usually his strategies involved finding psychological ways to undermine his enemies, based on these perceptions (Yates 2007).

Applying simple commonsensical ways, a strategic genius Genghis Khan overcame the Great Wall of China by getting around it. And from there, reinforced by mercenary troops, he was able to take China, defeating the Chinese who were then more civilized than the Mongols.

It is good to apply common sense, and keep things easy and simple. Easy and effective communications are made when we keep things simple. Simplicity promotes greater understanding while encouraging better interactions between or among team members. Besides, teams need information to get things done, and accomplish their objectives.

Leadership Lesson 6: Practicing Meritocracy

The sixth leadership lesson is that of employing quality people.

Genghis Khan obtained able and fierce warriors. He was good in employing his people; he practiced the principle of promotion based on capability alone (Oestmoen 1998). By rewarding skill, commitment and allegiance, and punishing those who opposed him, Genghis Khan established a vast empire and the most powerful empire to ever exist.

By the same token, Bill Gates and Microsoft get the best talented people and be a premier software organisation. The meritocratic Singapore civil service is also another example; much efficiency, good corporate governance and effective leadership has been attained through this principle of meritocracy (Neo and Chen 2007; Low 2002).

Leadership Lesson 7: Being the Role Model

The seventh leadership lesson is that a leader should set an example and be seen as a role model. On one level, explicitly seen, it's like 'monkey see, monkey do' (Low and Theyagu 2003). Leaders need to bear in mind that "if the stick is crooked, the shadow cannot be straight" (Low 2006d, p. 139). [When leaders don't set the right example, their credibility and integrity would be affected. Yet some leaders practice "do as I tell you", not "do as I do". If followers question their leaders' honesty and integrity, leaders then lose their authority let alone be role models (Low 2008d)].

However, on another level, "winning is a matter of how you keep the score" (Chu 1992, p. 133) and to this researcher, it can be unseen and matters most to the individual leaders, and that can be based on his values and self-cultivation. The leader sticks to his values and core beliefs. His core beliefs endure and resilient, he endures by enduring values.

Genghis Khan totally shared his people's core beliefs in the nomadic way of life, recognizing that, in war as in the hunt, booty is the main aim. . . and winning was what counted. However, amassing material wealth did not matter much to him, as he shared everything with his loyal supporters. He was seen as a generous leader. This also built his followers' trust and admiration of him as their great leader.

Leadership Lesson 8: Applying Tolerance to the Belief of Others

Being open-minded is one of the priced qualities of leadership. This is the eighth leadership lesson derived, that is, applying being tolerant to the belief of others. This is the legacy he left for his people—the idea of religious tolerance to the country.

Genghis Khan showed a rather liberal and tolerant attitude to the beliefs of others, and never persecuted people on religious grounds (Yates 2007; May 2001). This proved to be good military core strategy, as when he was at war with Sultan Muhammad of Khwarazm, other Islamic leaders did not join the fight against Genghis—it was instead seen as a non-holy war between two individuals.

Being tolerant to the beliefs or ideas of others also leads leaders to learn. . .

Leadership Lesson 9: Subscribing to the Power of Learning

Learning never stops. "Learning brings out the best in people and their competencies" (Low 2003, p. 90). A good leader learns, and applying the power of learning is the ninth leadership lesson.

A Mongolian saying has it that, "Supreme treasure—knowledge" (*Erhem bayan—erdem*). Genghis Khan's descendants, the Kazakhs have many sayings on learning and education. Low (2005f, p. 9) has cited two of these proverbs, and they are: "A sixty-old person should welcome a young educated person returned from schooling abroad."

> To be educated is like digging a well with a needle.

The first one demonstrates the value of learning and education (how society respects the educated person) while the second one reflects that of educating oneself, one needs efforts, energy, time and patience to think, reflect, discover and grow.

Genghis Khan himself valued knowledge and learning. While Genghis Khan was himself illiterate, he understood the power of spreading ideas through the written word, and used it to administer his empire. Not only was he responsible for the introduction and spread of the Uighur's script as the common Mongolian alphabet, Genghis Khan was also relentless in learning new things, and absorbing ideas from other cultures as often as he could (Yates 2007). Many of the Chinese characters and written ideas were borrowed to improve the lives of the Mongolians.

Leadership Lesson 10: Having Courage, Enduring and Being Persistent

Do not start if afraid, once begun do not be afraid. (Mongolian proverb)

Genghis Khan and the Mongols were tough people. Mongolian wisdom has it that, "misfortune and destruction are not final. When the grass has been burnt by the fire of the steppe, it will grow anew in Summer".

The tenth leadership lesson derived from the Great Khan is that of having courage, enduring and being persistent as a leader. This involves self-confidence and the courage to be bold to take risks as well as having the iron-willed commitment to a cause or crusade (Meyers 1998, p. 159). The successful leader is both persistent and resilient. Having and projecting self-confidence is particularly crucial when leading an organisation or a group of people out of a crisis—more so, because most of the followers need to rely on a strong person when faced with turmoil (DuBrin 2007).

After his father died, Temujin returned to his family, still a boy. According to *The Secret History of the Mongols*, the primary source of information on Temujin's life, the later-to- become-the-Great Khan endured many hardships, including the kidnapping of his wife Borte, but he slowly but surely recruited supporters and assumed a mantle of leadership among the Mongols (May 2001). It is also said that after rising to power in 1185, Temujin experienced numerous setbacks and, eventually, victories.

Chu (1992, p. 146) speaks of "let(ting) the dark night pass". Leaders are not immobilized. Determined and strong, successful leaders translate their negative setbacks into positive experiences, and unless we possess the power of endurance to live through the dark of the night, we'll not see the glory and beauty of daybreak.

Conclusion

Though dwindled or weakened, his empire continued by his dynasties established, even after his death, in Central Asia, Russia and India. The Golden Horde, the name given to the Mongol kingdom set up in Russia by Batu, Genghis Khan's grandson; it endured until the sixteenth century and the Khanate in Crimea lasted until 1783. Genghis' great-great-great grandson through Tamerlane's line, Baber invaded India and there, found the Mogul (Mongol dynasty) whose rulers eventually conquered the whole of India and remained in power until the mid-eighteenth century. The Great Khan can indeed be given a huge credit as one of the few leaders who controlled a large territory and population with such an enormous influence.

Overall, many lessons can be gleaned from Genghis Khan, but the key issue here is that as a leader, one definitely has tremendous power to influence and motivate one's followers—one creates actions and becomes the role model, the inspiration and the rallying point.

Tibet

The Dalai Lama, Tenzin Gyatso, and His Leadership Ways

Introduction

Educated in Tibet, Tenzin Gyatso is the present Dalai Lama, the 14 Dalai Lama, and he lives and leads in exile outside Tibet. The present Dalai Lama is referred to as His Holiness by Westerners. Dalai is the Mongolian word, meaning "ocean" (Tibet was once under the control of the Mongols in the days of the Great Khan, Kublai Khan). Lama is the Tibetan equivalent of the Sanskrit word, "guru"; Lama is, in fact, a general term referring to Tibetan Buddhist teachers.

During 1959, after the initial Chinese occupation of Tibet sought refuge in India, Jawaharlal Nehru, the then Indian Prime Minister, was instrumental in granting safe refuge to the Dalai Lama and his fellow Tibetans. The Dalai Lama has since lived in exile in Dharamsala, in the state of Himachal Pradesh in northern India where the Central Tibetan Administration (the Tibetan government-in-exile) is also established. Tibetan refugees have constructed and opened many schools and Buddhist temples in Dharamsala.

On 8 August 2011, Lobsang Sangay, a 43-year-old Harvard scholar, was sworn in as head of the Tibetan government-in-exile, replacing the Dalai Lama as the movement's political leader. In a historic shift from the dominance of Tibetan politics by religious figures, the new prime minister, who has never set foot in Tibet, assumes the temporal duties relinquished by the Dalai Lama in May 2011. The Dalai Lama still continues as the spiritual leader (Sino Daily 2011).

The Thoughts and Ways of the Dalai Lama

> All major religious traditions carry basically the same message, that is love, compassion and forgiveness the important thing is they should be part of our daily lives. (The Dalai Lama)

Fundamentally, the thoughts and ways of the Dalai Lama follow that of the Buddha and the Tibetan Buddhist tradition and practices. In today's world dominated by yearnings for material comfort, the Dalai Lama, a man of peace, inspires people to go in search of the spiritual realm outside their physical domains. People become more aware of their surroundings and the people around them to help and assist them. His messages to the world have always been that of peace, non-violence, inter-religious understanding, universal responsibility and compassion. The Dalai Lama has, in fact, won world wide acclaim and the Nobel Peace Prize 1989 for the role in promoting a non violent response the problems faced by the Tibetans. Time 100 (Time's fifth annual list of the world's most influential people) spoke of the Dalai Lama as "Tibet's beacon of peace maintains a calm compassion-even as Beijing cracks down on his people" (Time 2008, p. 29). He wisely applied Buddhist principles of non-violence in both action and thought.

Love and Happiness

Be kind whenever possible. It is always possible. (The Dalai Lama)

To the Dalai Lama, the purpose of life is to be happy. And on achieving happiness, the Dalai Lama advises, "the greatest degree of inner tranquility comes from the development of love and compassion" (The Office of His Holiness The Dalai Lama 2010b). It is not a zero sum game, in fact, the more we care and love for the happiness of others, the greater our own sense of well-being becomes.

The Dalai Lama's message to all is that there is a need to contribute, and give to the world; the leader should be compassionate. For all, the Dalai Lama proposes, a simple religion to have, there is no need for temples; no need for complicated philosophy for "our own brain, our own heart is our temple; the philosophy is kindness" (Thinkexist 2008; cited in Low 2010f).

The Dalai Lama (1999, p. 287) spoke of humans, being social animals, depend for their survival on the cooperation and assistance of others. He highlighted that it is better not to have a companion at all than to have one who is very aggressive and harmful. And also, he added that one can never rely on such a person but always have to be suspicious and apprehensive about him or her. On the other hand, if one's own character and personality is such that all people avoid the person, that is very sad. What the Dalai Lama is stressing on is that everyone, perhaps more so for leaders, to have a kind heart and compassion as they are the real sources of peace and happiness.

The Dalai Lama's Three Key Commitments

My religion is very simple. My religion is kindness. (The Dalai Lama)

The Dalai Lama has three key commitments. First of the three commitments is that of promoting human values such as compassion, forgiveness, tolerance, contentment and self-discipline. The second commitment, as a religious practitioner, is that of promoting religious harmony and understanding among the world's major religious traditions. And the third is that of promoting the Tibetan cause which "will cease to exist once a mutually beneficial solution is reached between the Tibetans and Chinese" (The Office of His Holiness The Dalai Lama 2010a).

Low (2010f) speaks of leadership the Buddha way as being sensitive to the needs of the people around them. In that sense, the Dalai Lama is also sensitive to the needs of his fellow Tibetans as well as that of his fellow human beings—the world at large, wanting the people to gain happiness, and specifically, their spiritual well-being.

Resilience

In the practice of tolerance, one's enemy is the best teacher. (Dalai Lama)

The Dalai Lama once said that, "Remember that not getting what you want is sometimes a wonderful stroke of luck." To this author, the struggle or upholding the Tibetans' cause has, in fact, strengthened the Dalai Lama, making him a stronger leader. Interestingly, to use his words:

> As long as we live in this world we are bound to encounter problems. If, at such times, we lose hope and become discouraged, we diminish our ability to face difficulties. If, on the other hand, we remember that it is not just ourselves but every one who has to undergo suffering, this more realistic perspective will increase our determination and capacity to overcome troubles. Indeed, with this attitude, each new obstacle can be seen as yet another valuable opportunity to improve our mind! (The Office of His Holiness The Dalai Lama 2010b).

Concluding Remarks

"It is my belief that the lack of understanding of the true cause of happiness is the principal reason why people inflict suffering on others." (The Dalai Lama 1997; cited in Thurman 1999, p. 54). Indeed the Dalai Lama believes in happiness for one and all, and makes the world a happy and peaceful place. And indeed leaders must believe, do something about it and put in all efforts to realize this.

Checkpoint: Think About It

Leadership in China, Mongolia and Tibet

After reading the chapter, ask yourself:

1. What does successful leadership (in China/ Mongolia/ Tibet) mean?
2. What are the traits of a successful leader (in the respective countries)?

Review the following key points and when you have finished the quiz, check your answers.

China

Leading, The Confucian Way
1. How can I lead the Confucian way?
2. Check, if as a leader, you can subscribe to these key ways of the Master
   - Being a gentleman (*Junzi*)
   - Stressing on and practising virtue
   - Boosting one's influence
   - Being humble
   - Loving
   - Fostering father leadership

- Emphasising learning, education and high integrity
- Being prudent
- Growing resilience
3. How can I lead by example?
4. What are the other pointers from this section that I can apply to improve my leadership ways?

Lao Tzu's Three Treasures, Leadership and Organisational Growth
1. What are your views in terms of Lao Tzu's three treasures: simplicity, patience and compassion?
2. How do you apply simplicity in your ways as a leader?
3. How do you exercise patience?
4. How do you exercise love? What ways you could do to show love in your lead 5. What other ways can apply Lao Tzu's Three Treasures to my leadership?

Applying Strategic Leadership, The Way of the Dragon
1. How can I apply strategic leadership, the way of the Dragon?
2. How can I apply the following strategic leadership ways?
   - Know thyself, know thy other party
   - Set the example, act and realise the power of example
   - Better be a silent achiever and up-keep one's integrity
   - Practice humaneness, the Tao of the ancient emperors (read as strategic leaders).
   - Respect talents and inspire followers
   - Employ 'big picture' thinking, be objective and love.
   - 'Prosper thy neighbour'– When there is 'big peace', there is 'big prosperity'
   - Unite your troops
   - Toughen up and embrace resilience
   - Be creative and inject resourcefulness
   - Embrace long-term thinking, being patient and apply foresight
   - Seize opportunities, learn and apply training and overall growth
   - Apply flexibility and agility

Tao and Tough Leadership: Having the Power to Prevail
1. How can I be tough and resilient?
2. How can I apply the Way of the Tao and tough leadership?
3. How can I draw strengths from adversities?
4. How can I draw strengths from collaboration?
5. How can I be supple in my leadership ways?
6. How can I not be affected by adversities?
7. How can I nurture the greatness, the Way of the Tao?

Leading, The Guan Yin Way

1. What are the pointers that I have gathered here that I can apply to improve my leadership ways?
2. What are the ways that I can follow or emulate from the leadership ways of Guan Yin?

Leading, The Bruce Lee Way

1. How are you leading?
2. How can I emulate leading, the Bruce Lee way? In what ways can I emulate lead the late martial artist?
3. Check if, as a leader, you have been paying attention to these:
   - Having a healthy body with a healthy mind
   - Being different, standing out because Of one's integrity (*lien*)
   - Meditating, learning and practising
   - Affecting and involving simplicity
   - Applying soft power
   - Being selfless
   - Preferring harmony
   - Adapting as well as being flexible and agile
   - Being detached
   - Coordinating and ensuring a smooth flow of actions (results)
   - Being self-disciplined
   - Enduring
   - Being strategic
   - Being action-oriented

Mao Zedong and His Leadership Ways

1. Knowing the people well and connecting with them
   - Do you know your people well?
   - What are the ways in which you can better your rapport with your people?
   - Uniting China and making good strategies
   - Suggest the ways in which you can raise the sense of unity of your people?
   - Being powerful and for Mao, that power comes from the barrel of the gun
   - How and in what ways can you better compete with the competition?
   - Being In The Constant State of Revolution
   - Suggest the various ways in which you (your Company) can keep on learning and ne in a state of constant revolution?

Li Ka Shing

Let us review the leadership qualities of Li Ka Shing and ask ourselves what we can learn from him in terms of:

- A sense of purpose
- Simple but effective
- Prudence
- Honesty is power
- Alliances
- Admitting mistakes and not afraid to take risks

Mongolia

Ten Leadership Lessons Learnt from the Warrior-Conqueror, Genghis Khan

1. Let us review the leadership lessons derived from the Warrior-Conqueror, Genghis Khan

   Leadership Lesson 1: Having a vision and a set of values
   Leadership Lesson 2: Having goal(s), desire and passion
   Leadership Lesson 3: Energising and taking actions
   Leadership Lesson 4: Effecting teamwork and solidarity
   Leadership Lesson 5: Applying common sense
   Leadership Lesson 6: Practicing meritocracy
   Leadership Lesson 7: Being the role model
   Leadership Lesson 8: Applying tolerance to the belief of others
   Leadership Lesson 9: Subscribing to the power of learning
   Leadership Lesson 10: Having courage, enduring and being persistent
2. Think on the various ways in which you can apply them to your leadership ways? What are your action plans to attain (some/all of) them?

Tibet

The Dalai Lama, Tenzin Gyatso, and His Leadership Ways

1. Let's review the thoughts and ways of the Dalai Lama. What about:
   - Love and happiness?
   - The Dalai Lama's three key commitments?
   - Resilience?
2. Ask: Am I sensitive to the needs of my people?
3. How and in what ways can I give happiness to my people?
4. How and in what ways I can emulate the Dalai Lama?

References

Alder, N. J., & Gundersen, A. (2008). *International dimensions of organizational behavior* (5th ed.). Cincinnati, OH: Thomson South-Western.
Analects of Confucius. (1992). (A. Waley, Trans.). New York, NY: Harper Collins.

Anderlini, J. (2008, December 26). *China's state sector urged to boost economy.* Accessed May 18, 2009, from http://www.ft.com/cms/s/3c301096-d37b-11dd-989e-000077b07658, Authorised=false.html?_i_location=http%3A%2F%2Fwww.ft.com%2Fcms%2Fs%2F0%2F2F3c301096-d37b-11dd-989e000077b07658.html%3Fnclick_check%3D1&_i_referer=http%3A%2F%2Fen.wikip-dia.org%2Fwiki%2FEconomy_   of_the_People%2527s_Republic_of_China&nclick_check=1

Bhasin, B. B., & Low, K. C. P. (2002). The fight for global talent: New directions, new competitors. *Career Development International, 7*(2), 109–114.

Blanchard, K., & Johnson, S. (1983). *The one-minute manager.* Glasgow: William Collins Sons & Co.

Bond, H. (1987). Chinese values and the search for culture-free dimensions of culture. *Journal of Cross-Cultural Psychology, 18*(2), 143–164.

Bowman, P. (2010). *Theorizing Bruce Lee: Film-fantasy-fighting-philosophy.* The Netherlands: Rodopi.

Bruce Lee. (1971). *Bruce Lee: The lost interview.* Accessed November 6, 2010, from http://www.maniacworld.com/bruce_lee_8.htm#

Bruce Lee. (1975). *Tao of Jeet Kune Do.* Dallas, TX: Ohara.

Bruce Lee., & Uyehara, M. (1976a). *Bruce Lee's fighting method, volume 1: Self-defense techniques.* Dallas, TX: Ohara.

Bruce Lee., & Uyehara, M. (1976b). *Bruce Lee's fighting method, volume 2: Basic training.* Dallas, TX: Ohara.

Buddha Dharma Education Association: BDEA/BuddhaNet. (2008). *A five minute introduction, Buddhist studies.* Buddha Dharma Education Association & BuddhaNet. Accessed November 13, 2008, from http://www.buddhanet.net/e-learning/5minbud.htm

CDOT: Crystal Dragon of Taiwan. (2009). *Dragon articles—'Celestial Chinese dragon'.* Crystal Dragon of Taiwan. Accessed March 4, 2009, from http://www.cdot.org/history/dragon_articles.htm

Cham, T. S. (1998). Making a World Class University (I). In *Commentary* (Vol. 15, pp. 35–40). Singapore: The National University of Singapore Society.

Chen, M. (2005). The dragon's trail in Chinese culture. *Pearl River.* Accessed March 5, 2009, from http://pearlriver.com/v2/newsletter/dragon/dragon_newsletter.htm

Chew, K. H. P. (2000). *A gentleman's code.* Singapore: Graham Brash.

Chinese Culture.Org. (2003). *The almighty dragon.* Chinese Culture.Org. Accessed March 4, 2009, from http://www.chinaculture.org/gb/en_chinaway/2004-02/25/content_45896.htm

Chu, C.-N. (1992). *Thick face, black heart.* New York, NY: Warner Books.

Chu, C.-N. (1994). *Thick face, black heart.* New York, NY: Business Plus.

Chu, C.-N. (1998). *Do less, achieve more.* New York, NY: HarperCollins.

Cleary, T. (1991). *The art of war—Sun Tzu (translated).* China: Shambala.

Cragg, C. (1995). *The new Taipans.* London: Century.

Cummings, T. G., & Worley, C. G. (2001). *Organization development and change* (7th ed.). Cincinnati, OH: South-Western College.

Cummings, T. G., & Worley, C. G. (2009). *Organization development and change* (8th ed.). Cincinnati, OH: Thomson South-Western.

Daft, R. (1998). *Organization theory and design* (6th ed.). Cincinnati, OH: International Thomson.

de Smedt, M. (Ed.). (1995). *Sun Tzu, The art of war.* Hong Kong: Abbeville Press.

Demile, J. W. (1994). *Bruce Lee's 1 and 3 inch power punch.* Seattle, WA: Tao of Wing Chun Do.

Dennis, F. (1974). *Bruce Lee, King of Kung-Fu.* London: Wildwood House.

DuBrin, A. J. (2007). *Fundamentals of organizational behavior.* Canada: Thomson South-Western.

Farrell, L. C. (1993). *Searching for the spirit of enterprise.* New York, NY: Dutton.

Foster, D. (2003). *The power to prevail.* New York, NY: Warner Books.

Fung, Y.-L. (1948). *A short history of Chinese philosophy.* New York, NY: The MacMillan Company.

Goh, C. L. (2009, May 10). Why secrecy over Mas Selamat's arrest: PM Lee. *The Straits Times*, p. 1.

Grigg, R. (1994a). *Tao of being*. Singapore: S.S. Mubaruk & Brothers.

Grigg, R. (1994b). *The Tao of relationships*. Singapore: S.S. Mubaruk & Brothers.

Heider, J. (1994). *The Tao of leadership*. Singapore: S.S. Mubaruk & Brothers.

Heider, J. (1995). *The Tao of leadership*. London: Wildwood.

Hsu, P. S. C. (1984). *The influence of structure and values on business organisations in oriental cultures: A comparison of China and Japan*. Unpublished paper, School of Management, National University of Singapore, Singapore.

International Business Times. (2010). *Li Ka-shing to donate 1/3 of wealth to charity*. Accessed August 8, 2010, from http://hken.ibtimes.com/articles/41684/20100807/li-ka-shing-donate-charity.htm

Koh, K. K. (2004). *Guan Yin, heart of compassion*. Singapore: Asiapac Books.

Kornfield, J., & Fronsdal, G. (1991). *Teachings of Buddha*. Singapore: Shambala.

Kotelnikov, V. (2001). Strategic leadership. *Business e-coaching*. Accessed February 26, 2009, from http://www.1000ventures.com/business_guide/crosscuttings/leadership_strategic.html

Krames, J. A. (2005). *Jack Welch and the 4Es of leadership*. Singapore: McGraw-Hill.

Lao-Tzu. (1990). *Tao Teh Ching* (J. C. H. Wu, Trans.). Massachusetts: Shambala.

Lau, D. C. (1979). *Confucius, the Analects*. London: Penguin Books.

Lerner, I. (1976). *Diary of the way*. New York, NY: A Ridge Press Library.

Lim, G. S., & Daft, R. (2004). *The leadership experience in Asia*. Singapore: Thomson Learning.

Lin, Y. (Ed.). (1994). *The wisdom of Confucius*. New York, NY: The Modern Library.

Little, J. (1997). *The Tao of Gung Fu: A study in the way of Chinese martial art*. North Clarendon, VT: Tuttle.

Little, J. (Ed.). (1998). *Bruce Lee: The art of expressing the human body*. North Clarendon, VT: Tuttle.

Little, J. (Ed.). (2000). *Striking thoughts: Bruce Lee's wisdom for daily living*. North Clarendon, VT: Tuttle.

Low, K. C. P. (2000). *Strategic customer management*. Singapore: BusinesscrAFT™ Consultancy.

Low, K. C. P. (2001). *The power of relationships*. Singapore: BusinesscrAFT™ Consultancy.

Low, K. C. P. (2002). *Corporate culture and values: Perceptions of corporate leaders of co-operatives in Singapore*. Unpublished PhD thesis, University of South Australia, Adelaide, Australia.

Low, K. C. P. (2003). *Team success*. Singapore: BusinesscrAFT™ Consultancy & Humber Lincoln Resources.

Low, K. C. P. (2005a). Towards a framework & typologies of Singapore corporate cultures. *Management Development Journal of Singapore, 13*(1), 46–75.

Low, K. C. P. (2005b). Values that contribute to companies' success—Perceptions of Singapore corporate leaders. In *Effective executive* (pp. 45–55). The Institute of Chartered Financial Analyst India: ICFAI University Press. http://www.icfaipress.org/effective.asp.

Low, K. C. P. (2005c, October). Putting learning and creative thinking into practice—The Tao Way. *Today's Manager*, April–May 2005, 48–49.

Low, K. C. P. (2005d). *Training success*. India: The ICFAI University Press.

Low, K. C. P. (2005e). Tao & negotiation: Excelling in harmonising with others. *The Icfaian Journal of Management Research, IV*(10), 7–18.

Low, K. C. P. (2005f). Culture, education and Kazakhstan: Kazakhstan riding high on learning and earning. *The Icfaian Journal of Organizational Behavior*, 7–15.

Low, K. C. P. (2006a). Motivation, the Chinese leadership way in Singapore's small and medium companies. *The Icfaian Journal of Organizational Behavior, V*(1), 80–90.

Low, K. C. P. (2006b). Father leadership—The Singapore case study. *Management Decision, 44*(2), 89–104. Emerald Insight: www.emeraldinsight.com/0262-1711.htm

Low, K. C. P. (2006c). Crisis management—Can core values be considered as a built-in safety net? The Singapore case. *Insights to a Changing World, 2006*(3), 133–150. Franklin Publishing House: http://franklinpublishing.net/insightstoachangingworld.html

Low, K. C. P. (2006d). *Strategic customer management*. Kazakhstan: Caspian Publishing House.

Low, K. C. P. (2007a). Father leadership and small business management: The Singapore case study. i-Manager's. *Journal on Management*, December 2006–February 2007, 5–13.

Low, K. C. P. (2007b). The cultural value of resilience—The Singapore case study. *Cross-Cultural Management: An International Journal, 14*(2), 136–149. Emerald Insight (www.emeraldinsight.com/ccm.htm).

Low, K. C. P. (2008a). Value-based leadership: Leading, the Confucian way. *Leadership and Organizational Management Journal, 2008*(3), 32–41.

Low, K. C. P. (2008b). Not just Singapore—A city of excellence and world class but. . . People with heads cool, hearts calm. *Insights to a Changing World Journal, 2008*(4), 66–77.

Low, K. C. P. (2008c). Confucian ethics and social responsibility—The golden rule and responsibility to the stakeholders. *Ethics and Critical Thinking Journal, 2008*(4), 46–54.

Low, K. C. P. (2008d). Leadership thoughts to ponder—Some classic sins of leadership. *Leadership and Organizational Management Journal, 2008*(4), 65–75.

Low, K. C. P. (2008e). How to win big in place marketing battlefield—Formula one night race, the Singapore perspective. *Business Journal for Entrepreneurs, 2008*(4), 115–125.

Low, K. C. P. (2009a). How to lead in today's context? What leadership skills set do we need? *Leadership and Organizational Management Journal, 1*, 48–56.

Low, K. C. P. (2009b). The way of the dragon: Some strategic leadership ways. *Leadership and Organizational Management Journal, 2009*(2), 40–59.

Low, K. C. P. (2009c). Lao Tzu's three treasures, leadership and organizational growth. *Leadership and Organizational Management, 2009*(3), 27–36.

Low, K. C. P. (2009d). *Corporate culture and values: Perception of corporate leaders of co-operatives in Singapore*. Germany: VDM-Verlag.

Low, K. C. P. (2009e). Lao Tzu's three treasures, leadership and organizational growth. In *Leadership and organizational management book*. Arlington, TX: Franklin Publishing House.

Low, K. C. P. (2009f). Tao & tough leadership—Having the power to prevail. *Leadership and Organizational Management Journal, 20-09*(4), 124–128.

Low, K. C. P. (2009g). Leading globally—What makes a successful global leader in today's turbulent times?. In *e-Leader conference*. CASA: Chinese American Scholars Association, Tallinn, Estonia, 8–10 June 2009. Accessed October 16, 2009, from http://www.g-casa.com/conferences/tallinn/pdf%20papers/Low.pdf

Low, K. C. P. (2009h). 10 leadership lessons learnt from the warrior-conqueror, Genghis Khan. *Leadership and Organizational Management Journal, 2009*(2), 75–86.

Low, K. C. P. (2010a). Applying soft power, the Confucian way. *Conflict Resolution and Negotiation Journal, 2010*(4), 37–46.

Low, K. C. P. (2010b). Applying strategic leadership, the way of the dragon. In *Chinese American Scholars' Association: CASA e-Leader conference*, 4–6 Jan 2010, Singapore.

Low, K. C. P. (2010c). *Negotiation success in Asia*. New York, NY: Springer.

Low, K. C. P. (2010d). Leading, the Bruce Lee way. *Business Journal for Entrepreneurs, 2010*(4), 127–135.

Low, K. C. P. (2010e). Strategic leadership, the Sun Tzu (Sun Zi) way. *Leadership & Organizational Management Journal, 2010*(2), 118–126.

Low, K. C. P. (2010f). Leading, the Buddha way. *Insights to a Changing World, 2010*(1), 23–33.

Low, K. C. P., & Theyagu, D. (2003). *Developing true leadership potential*. Singapore: Booksmith Consultants.

Lussier, R. N., & Achua, C. F. (2007a). *Effective leadership* (3rd ed.). Canada: Thomson South-Western.

Lussier, R. N., & Achua, C. F. (2007b). *Case: Bill Gates—Microsoft, effective leadership* (3rd ed., pp. 59–60). Canada: Thomson South-Western.

Mason, J. L. (2003). *An enemy called average*. Malaysia: Advantage Quest.

Maxwell, J. C. (1994). *Leadership 101*. Oklahoma: Honor Books.

May, T. (2001). Genghis Khan (1165–1227). Accessed June 19, 2008, from http://www.accd.edu/sac/history/keller/Mongols/empsub1.html

Meyer, P. J. (1998). *Bridging the leadership gap*. Arlington, TX: The Summit Publishing Group.

Nakamura, H. (1978). *Ways of thinking of Eastern peoples*. Honolulu: East-West Centre Press.

Neo, B. S., & Chen, G. (2007). *Dynamic governance*. Singapore: World Scientific.

Oestmoen, P. I. (1998). *Chinghis the King*. Accessed September 6, 2007, from http://www.coldsiberia.org/chingis.htm

Oestmoen, P. I. (2007). *The Mongolian message*. Accessed August 6, 2007, from http://www.coldsiberia.org/

Oon, C. (2009, May 23). PMs pledge to take bilateral ties forward. *The Straits Times*, p. 1.

Pay, R. (2000). *Confucius*. Accessed June 27, 2008, from http://www.humanistictexts.org/confucius.htm

Pellowe, J. (2000). The motivating power of vision. *Leader values*. Accessed September 7, 2007, from http://www.leader-values.com/Content/detail.asp?ContentDetailID=283

PHP Institute, Inc. (1991). *Velvet glove, iron fist*. Japan: PHP Institute.

PHP Institute, Inc. (1994). *Matsushita Konosuke (1894–1989): His life & his legacy*. Japan: PHP Institute.

Robbins, S. P. (2005). *Organizational behavior*. Upper Saddle River, NJ: Pearson-Prentice Hall.

Robertson, R. W., & Low, K. C. P. (2006, March). Six deadly sins of strategic management. *Caspian Business News Digest, 9*.

Scarborough, J. (1998). Comparing Chinese and Western cultural roots: Why 'East is East and...'. *Business Horizons, 41*(6), 15–24.

Schein, E. H. (1996). *Strategic pragmatism, the culture of Singapore's Economic Development Board*. Cambridge, MA: Massachusetts Institute of Technology.

Scholastic. (2007). *Grolier online: Asian Pacific American Heritage: Confucius, sayings (document) Scholastic*. Scholastic, Inc. Accessed June 7, 2007, from http://content.scholastic.com/browse/article.jsp?id=4985

Sino Daily. (2011). Dalai Lama's political successor to be sworn in. *Sino Daily*. Accessed August 18, 2011, from http://www.sinodaily.com/reports/Dalai_Lamas_political_successor_to_be_sworn_in_999.html

Slater, R. (1994). *Get better or get beaten! 31 leadership secrets from GE's Jack Welch*. Huntersville, NC: Irwin.

Smitha, F. E. (2004). *Genghis Khan and the Mongols*. Macrohistory and World Report. Accessed March 26, 2009, from http://www.fsmitha.com/h3/h11mon.htm

Story, C. (2007). *Asian studies/Confucianism*. Accessed June 5, 2007, from http://www.castilleja.org/faculty/christy_story/C&C/Buddhism/confucius.htm

Tan, L. (2007, September 30). Best way to give back? Create jobs, says billionaire. *The Sunday Times*, p. 24.

TDS. (2009). *'China economy': China Asia*. TDS: Travel Document Systems. Accessed May 18, 2009, from http://www.traveldocs.com/cn/economy.htm

The Dalai Lama. (1999). *The path to tranquility*. New York, NY: Viking/Arkana.

The Office of His Holiness The Dalai Lama. (2010a). *Three main commitments. His Holiness the 14th Dalai Lama*. Accessed March 16, 2010, from http://www.dalailama.com/biography/three-main-committments

The Office of His Holiness The Dalai Lama. (2010b). *Compassion and the individual. His Holiness the 14th Dalai Lama*. Accessed March 16, 2010, from http://www.dalailama.com/messages/compassion

Thurman, R. A. F. (1999, August 23–30). Dalai Lama. *Time 100*, pp. 106–108.

Thurow, L. (1996). Foreword. In E. H. Schein (Ed.), *Strategic pragmatism, the culture of Singapore's Economic Development Board*. Massachusetts Institute of Technology: Cambridge.

Time. (2008, May 12). The Dalai Lama. *Time 100—Time's Fifth Annual List of the World's Most Influential People*, p. 29.

TMCG: The Milum Communications Group. (2008). *Leadership levels*. The Milum Communications Group. Accessed February 26, 2009, from http://www.milum.net/strategic_leadership.htm

Tobak, S. (2009, April 16). In management, keep it simple. *BNET Insight*. Accessed May 6, 2009, from http://blogs.bnet.com/ceo/?p=2109&tag=nl.e713

Tsai, C. C. (Ed.). (1991). *Roots of wisdom*. Singapore: Asiapac Books.

Wang, X. (1993). *Mastering the art of leadership—Gems of Chinese wisdom* (L. Weng Kam, Trans.). Singapore: Asiapac.

Wikipedia. (2007). *Confucius*. Wikipedia. Accessed June 6, 2007, from http://en.wikipedia.org/wiki/Confucius

Wong, C. W. (2007, May 20). Prosper thy neighbour. *The Sunday Star*. Accessed March 9, 2009, from http://www.malaysianbar.org.my/index2.php?option=com_content&do_pdf=1&id=8998

Wu, J. C. H. (1990). *Lao Tzu: Tao Teh Ching*. Boston & London: Shambala.

Yang, H. (1993). Confucius (Kung Tzu) 551–479 BC. *Prospects: The Quarterly Review of Comparative Education, XXIII(½)*, 211–219. UNESCO: International Bureau of Education. Accessed June 29, 2008, from http://www.ibe.unesco.org/publications/ThinkersPdf/confucie.PDF

Yates, M. (2007). Genghis Khan. *Leader values*. Accessed September 7, 2007, from http://www.leader-values.com/Content/detail.asp?ContentDetailID=799

Zenger, J. H., & Folkman, J. (2004). *The handbook for leaders*. New York, NY: McGraw-Hill.

Zhou, K. (2005a). *A basic Confucius* (1st ed.). China: Long River Press.

Zhou, K. (2005b). *A basic Confucius*. South San Francisco, CA: Long River Press.

Website

Accessed November 7, 2010, from http://en.wikiquote.org/wiki/Bruce_Lee

Leadership in India

6

Leadership, Corporate Culture and the Hindu Trinity: Brahma, Vishnu and Shiva

Introduction

The purpose and objectives of the paper is to relate leadership and corporate culture with organisational growth vis. the Hindu trinity—Brahma, Vishnu and Shiva. Lord Brahma is the first member of the Brahmanical triad, Vishnu being the second and Shiva, the third. An organisation's corporate culture—a set of values, what is held dearly, close to our hearts (Low 2002b, 2005a, 2009b)—can contribute and lead to a firm's start-up, stability and/or growth.

The use of metaphors by researchers when depicting corporate culture is not uncommon. Metaphors can indeed be used to illustrate such a pattern or theme, and Gannon (cited in Low 2002b, 2009b) has used them to describe cultures. Metaphors are usually situations, events or circumstances that occur in a culture that capture and clarify its essential elements. One such example is the symphony orchestra as the cultural metaphor for Germany. Germany is a musical nation with many orchestras, and operates like one. In a symphony orchestra, conformity is valued, rules are established and each person is expected to work for the overall goodness and efficiency. Several other examples given of national cultural metaphors include the Italian opera, French wine, Russian ballet, Japanese garden, Spanish bullfight, American football, and Turkish coffee-house. The use of metaphors to understand cultures has therefore much potential, and they create new understanding about the original objects (cultures) (cited in Low 2002b, 2009b).

The Hindu Trinity

The Hindu trinity consists of Brahma, Vishnu and Shiva. Brahma is the creator, the Creator God, Vishnu the preserver and presiding deity of peace; and Shiva, Shiva

© Springer International Publishing AG 2018
K.C.P. Low, *Leading Successfully in Asia*,
https://doi.org/10.1007/978-3-319-71347-2_6

the God of destruction. [In Low's (2010a, pp. 136–140) study, he even speaks of the Brahman Negotiator; the Vishnu Negotiator and the Shiva Negotiator, and applies the various negotiation ways to each of these Hindu Godly metaphors.]

This religious metaphor is aptly chosen because at the end of the day, certain values have to be religiously or ritualistically perpetuated; and at that, in fact, be strongly adhered. That certain values, the author is referring to, are the company's success values (Low 2005c) as well as ethical values. However, of the values that make up an organisation's culture, ethical values are now considered among the most important (Daft 2004). Widespread corporate scandals, missing or embezzled funds and charges of insider trading have blanketed the newspapers and the media in recent years. Chief Executive Officers (CEOs) are also under scrutiny from the public as never before. Corporations, even some small companies are putting emphasis on ethics to restore that vital trust among their stakeholders, particularly customers and the communities. Ethical values set standards of what is good or bad in conduct and decision-making (Daft 2004).

How Corporate Culture Begins

The Brahmanic Act is critical for organisational growth.

Good visioning, mission and values need to be created and practiced. A leader can uncover a compelling vision with its attendant values and he articulates this vision that is appealing and motivating to employees. In every organisation, leadership needs renewal, and successors must come to replace the present leaders.

Good corporate leaders visualise well, have good visions and they also plan well. Planning includes anticipating potential problems or opportunities the organisation may face. Here, we can perhaps apply what McDaniel and Gitman (2008, pp. 237–241) have advocated, that is:

• Strategic planning, creating a long-range (1–5 years) broad goals for the organisation and determining what resources will be needed to achieve these goals.
• Tactical planning (normally less than a year), this begins with implementing the strategic plans.
• Operational planning, creating specific standards, methods, policies and procedures that is used in specific areas of the organisation.
• Contingency planning, identifying alternative courses of actions for very unusual crisis situations.

In Hinduism, it is said, an individual's subtle body is made up of his mind and intellect, that is, his entire thoughts. A person's subtle body is responsible for the creation of his gross body and also the world that he experiences. The individual's thoughts determine the type of physical body he possesses. The same thoughts are also responsible for the kind of world and universe that the individual experiences around him. As the thoughts merge, so is the world. If a person possesses good thoughts, he sees a good world. If an individual's thoughts are bad, he sees a bad world (Rudra Centre 2007).

From the start, the company's code of conduct should be initiated and created; and training courses in ethics are taught. Strict ethical standards and ethical values need to be prioritized.

Citing Dubrin (2007) and Low (2008c), organisational members learn the corporate culture and core success/ethical values to some extent by observing what leaders pay attention to, measure and control (DuBrin 2007). Monkeys see, monkeys do; organisational members follow the river (the leader) and it will lead to the sea (the leaders' key values and the corporate values). More specifically, they look up to their leaders and imitate their examples; the corporate leaders become their role models in line with what Low (2002b, p. 139, 2006a, 2009b) has highlighted: "if the stick is crooked, the shadow cannot be straight".

An organisation's leaders, its founders, the Chief Executive Officers (CEOs) and their philosophies, values, examples and stories are strong influences on the formation and conditioning of corporate culture (Low 2002b, 2009b; Weiss 1996). It is said that the core values—"long lasting beliefs about what is worthwhile and desirable" (Nahavandi 2009, p. 117) of the company's founders have been responsible for the organisational growth. Similar to the Brahmanic drift: 'as the thoughts merge, so is the world', these core values acts as a compass in growing companies and businesses. They also account for the success as well as the higher performance of organisations and nations (Low 2005c, 2006a). A company—with its core values in place ("intensely held" and "widely shared")—has a strong corporate culture, and a strong corporate culture like Walmart's gives the company direction (Robbins 2005, p. 488).

It is also important to recruit like-minded people, hiring people whose personal ideologies (values) are congruent with that of the organization (Zachary and Kuzuhara 2005). In Low's (2005b) study (citing Dessler 2005), he has highlighted that the simplest way, ethically speaking, to improve an organisation is to select carefully and hire more ethical people. Here, proper selection and screening of employees is critical, as these are good human resources management practices. The applicants' references need to be thoroughly checked. Yet another critical but practical guideline in creating corporate culture entails the corporate leaders and managers to creatively identify specific types of cultural elements such as symbols, stories and rituals that communicate and reinforce the company's culture in a compelling way (Zachary and Kuzuhara 2005).

Leaders should also inspire, bring about invention and create or trigger growth. Innovation, new product development and new markets are thus needed for organisational growth. At times, some companies can also "empower their managers to go out and recruit, hire and develop other people who will buy-in to the culture and act to support it" (Zachary and Kuzuhara 2005, p. 244).

Sustaining and Keeping the Culture Alive

The core values of the company's founders when permeated through, being practiced and adopted, as the corporate values need to be preserved. Here, the Vishnu principle is to be applied. Vishnu is the God of maintenance. The company's core values need to be preserved. Values and practices that promote high performance and integrity are promoted; an excellent corporate culture is attained through hiring, training and promoting people who endorse the corporate values. The Vishnu principle must come into being; institutionalisation must take place.

The core values, once taken roots, serve to supply and encourage some form of stability. For example, in Thailand, several Buddhist factions are calling for Buddhism to be enshrined as the state religion. They want some form of stability, "claim(ing) that such a move is necessary to preserve Thailand's character and prevent the encroachment of foreign mores. 'The Thai people just copy Western culture,' says university professor and Buddhist activist Dhirawit Pinyonatthagarn. 'Our values are under threat'" (Caryl 2008, p. 21).

Also as seen in the Singapore Civil Service, among other key values, the value of integrity is up-kept, and that value is responsible for Singapore's good corporate governance climate. The economically prosperous island-republic of Singapore enjoys an "efficient and honest civil service that promptly attended to the needs of its citizens" (Ganesan 2002, p. 53); in Singapore, everything was on the table with clear rules (cited in Low 2002b; Schein 1996, p. 169).

Further, there is a feeling of stability in the sense of organisational identity provided by these core values or corporate culture. Interestingly, Walt Disney is able to attract, develop and retain top quality employees because of the firm's stability and the pride of identity that go with being part of the Disney team (Ivancevich and Matteson 2008).

Just like the peace-loving God Vishnu, the Preserver or Sustainer of life with his steadfast principles of order, righteousness and truth (About.com: Hinduism 2008a), so also is the way in which the corporate culture, its core values are to be preserved. When the preservation of these values is good for the company's organisational growth and progress, it is critical that the corporate leaders work proactively, up-keeping parts of the past, and respecting the past yet relevantly adapt to the present. Focusing on the core elements (*ethical values*) that should not change over time, they adapt the existing values and ideologies to meet current challenges and crises (Zachary and Kuzuhara 2005; *italics mine*).

Vishnu is often shown as reclining on a *Sheshanaga*—the coiled, many-headed snake floating on cosmic waters that depicts the peaceful Universe. This pose represents the calm and patience in the face of fear and worries that the poisonous snake depicts (About.com: Hinduism 2008b). The message here is that corporate leaders should not let fear overpower them and disturb their peace. Organisations, more critically, need to let go gracefully; Zachary and Kuzuhara (2005, p. 244) speak of company founders and CEOs, as the keepers of the culture, ensure that the culture lives on after they have long been gone. They should plan, engaging in succession planning in order to have the time needed to identify and groom replacement(s) who will support or upkeep the culture in future.

For employees, they go through the socialization process, and part of the socialisation process consists of the rites of passage, ceremonies that reinforce the organisation's core values (Zachary and Kuzuhara 2005; Weiss 1996). These rites include:

- The "Passage" rites which assist transition employees into new roles and statuses. For example, Induction and basic training in the United States of America Army or the Republic of Singapore's basic military training, National Service.
- The "Enhancement" rites which strengthen the employees' bond by acknowledging status—such as Mary Kay awards ceremonies, and the company-held annual meetings or dinners honouring their high performers.
- The "Renewal" rites such as training, retreats and award trips help to revitalise and maintain the employees' identity with the company.
- The "Integration" rites—including promotion ceremonies, Christmas parties and other ongoing programs and activities—continue the process of cementing the employees' loyalty to the company.

Mentoring can also take place. In most companies, mentoring is used as a means to grow and groom leaders (Ivancevich and Matteson 2008). New employees can obtain valuable career and psychosocial influences from a variety of individuals—managers, peers, trainers, coaches and contacts.

Eliminating or Minimising Bad Corporate Practices

As the Hindi proverb goes *mare bina swarg nahi milta*, meaning, "without death, there can be no heaven". By eliminating bad practices, new values and practices can be put into place and be nurtured.

Shiva is the God of destruction. The Shiva Principle—that of destroying or eliminating bad practices within the firm must be applied and come into the picture. Bad practices such as absenteeism, turnover and low job satisfaction that may weaken the organisation (vis-à-vis the competition) need to be weeded out. Work flows are studied, and bureaucratic obstacles or paperwork blocks are eliminated or reduced. Service recovery audits with checklists are put in place to eliminate bad customer service practices while promoting values of service excellence (Low 2002a, 2006a).

Certain knowledge management strategies and techniques too may be deployed. The corporate culture, know-how and experiences of the company is systematically documented, applied and transmitted to the employees. To promote information and value sharing, dialogue among the corporate members is fostered; and shared facilities and informal learning encouraged. Much information and value sharing is likely to occur in a snack lounge, corporate information resource centre or in the company's intranet communication systems.

Additionally, corporate leaders do not hire those who do not endorse the company's values or if the latter are employed, are not promoted so that after some time, they leave the company.

One of the key strategic ways is "to structure to influence sub-cultural formation" (Zachary and Kuzuhara 2005, p. 244). The aim here is to reduce the emergence and influence of sub-cultures in the organisation as they may weaken the culture of the overall organisation. A subculture is an ideology that exists in one part of the organisation that is somewhat different from the organisation's culture. For example, a company's sales division may be more collaborative, quality conscious and willing to take risks than the overall culture of the company which is collaborative and quality conscious but averse to risks.

Next, cross-training can also be deployed to eliminate or minimize sub-cultures within the organisation; members are cross-trained so that everyone can perform a wide range of jobs across different functional units. Besides, "alignment" is made by emphasising managers of specific units to ensure that their goals, strategies and cultures are consistent or aligned with those of the overall company (Zachary and Kuzuhara 2005, p. 244).

Corporate leaders and managers also need to conduct culture audits. Such an audit is a systematic and formal process in which elements of the company's culture are assessed through surveys and interviews with managers and individual contributors with the purpose to locate and reduce cultural disparities (Zachary and Kuzuhara 2005). This process indeed helps management identify potential inconsistencies in its culture that need to be addressed. A case in point, one of the company's core values may emphasise on teamwork and collaboration, but the compensation system and job design may show an emphasis on individual contributions and performance.

It is critical at this point to highlight that the Shiva Principle—that of destroying or eliminating bad practices within the firm must be applied and come into the picture. Corporate culture can indeed be seen as the key tool against corporate fraud. True, internal controls may provide the structural hardware, but corporate culture and the leader's influence can serve as the employees' personal "heartware". Low (2005b) study shows that a substantial proportion of corporate leaders (48% of his study's sampling) perceived the importance of leadership and corporate culture as the way to make their companies ethical or fraud-free.

Section Conclusion

Companies can basically go through the cycle of life and death, but by applying the Hindu Trinity way, corporate leaders lead changes, eliminating or getting rid of bad practices while nurturing (religiously practise) good (success and ethical) values and practices to grow the Company. Therein lies the benefits of the understanding corporate change and growth by way of the Hindu Gods and its analogies presented.

The Essential Leadership Wisdom of the *Bhagavad Gita*

The *Bhagavad Gita*, the sacred song of God composed about 200 BC, is really ancient truths for our modern world, and these will be related to the art and wisdom of essential leadership. This section examines the various tenets of the *Bhagavad Gita* and applies them and their relevance to leadership and our lives. Some of these teachings can indeed inspire us.

Introduction

Love everyone. Serve mankind. (Key teachings of most religions)

Learn to love Divinity in everything—everything—you do. Little by little, convert your entire earthly existence into an inner mood of constant worship. (The *Bhagavad Gita*, Hawley 2006a, p. 64)

The *Bhagavad Gita*, one of the sacred books in Hinduism, is basically appealing on the account of the contents of the book; it contains the tried-and-true methods of gradually and carefully reaching these higher planes of consciousness; it is not about religions but more on rising above our worldly miseries and afflictions; it's about being greater than our mundane problems or (leadership) troubles.

The *Bhagavad Gita* is a small part of the Mahabharata. On the eve of what promised to be a great battle, Krishna of the Bhagavad Gita was driving the chariot of Arjuna, the warrior-hero. The two armies were ready to engage; Arjuna seemed confident of victory but all the same was troubled. He foresaw that in the battle he would kill members of his own extended family who were fighting on the other side. He was very reluctant to do this, and one way to avoid it would be to refuse to fight. Luckily, there was someone he can ask for advice, his charioteer, the god Krishna. The Bhagavad Gita was Krishna's reply.

Section Aim and Objectives

The *Bhagavad Gita* is really ancient truths for our modern world and these will be related to the art and wisdom of essential leadership. In this section, the various tenets of the *Bhagavad Gita* will be examined, and they or their relevance floated out and applied to the leadership basics.

The ethical principles of the *Bhagavad Gita* begin from what is good: specifically the moral issue of whether it is right for Arjuna, the archer to fight and to kill his kinsmen. The story is widened out to considering the kind of life that would be most fulfilling for Arjuna and in fact, for anyone. The issues here are not what we would usually think of as moral but rather ones of value (axiology). Discussing what the most desirable kinds of life are is closely linked to the world picture, the metaphysics, of the *Bhagavad Gita*. In this aspect, when applying the *Bhagavad Gita* to our leadership ways, when we lead, we would want to ask ourselves are we leading in a way that is morally good or ethical as well as with the peace of mind and for total goodness for the greatest number of people; in short, the author would also want to make lessons of the *Bhagavad Gita* handy and utilitarian. And besides, to stimulate us into thinking more on our leadership ways as well as, if need be, improve on these ways.

Love and Be Loving

As you progress in this, you will in effect become a more godly person of wisdom, united with the supreme. This high state should be achieved while you are fully active and effective in the world. (The *Bhagavad Gita*, Hawley 2006a, p. 64)

The essential lesson in the *Bhagavad Gita* is to find oneself in love, triggering that seed and quenching the thirst. "Essential things... love, joy, cheerfulness, a sense of humor, peace that passeth understanding, an inward journey to find yourself... these are the essential things which you cannot do, which you have to learn to allow to happen." (Osho 1996 cited in Low 2011, p. 92)

The master (read as leader) loves, his presence is love. His very presence is magnetic. Without saying a word...just be close to him, you will feel a certain pull, a certain love, a trust (Osho 1996 cited in Low 2011, p. 92).

One Hindu respondent expressed these: "Hinduism is centered on the concept of Love for God. God is Love and Love is God. God exists in all living things and every atom; it is thus only natural for a true practitioner of the Hindu faith or for that matter any human, to love and be loving". And a famous Hindu, Mahatma Gandhi once said, "I am a Hindu because it is Hinduism which makes the world worth living. I am a Hindu hence I Love not only human beings, but all living beings." (Low 2011, p. 93)

Love is light. Very much like the Bible's (Galatians 5: 13) "by love serve one another", one key tenet of the *Bhagavad Gita* is about unconditional love. As a leader, one should love and be loving. First of all, it should be highlighted that in the *Gita*'s teachings, much prominence is given to the principle of love and this is entirely intentional. The sages realized eons ago that love is not a mere emotion but a genuine force with the power to guide, teach, and relieve, to move the immovable and change people's lives. How true too, true happiness consists in making others happy. Love is a wonderful force, and focusing always on love moves leaders to care for their people. Shakespeare's "love comforteth like sunshine after rain" is so true, and is much welcomed; leaders should also adopt listening to their people as love's first duty. And to be loved, leaders indeed should love—similar to Ovid's "to be loved, be lovable". As Low and Theyagu (2003, p. 80) has highlighted, there is a need to "make your people part of the planning and problem-solving process. Teach your people and coach them. This motivates your staff This also inspires your staff as you are willing to share. Because you share, you show that you care."

Not many people would follow a leader who is quiet and reticent, and who likes to remain silent or reserved all the time. (S)he appears not communicable as well as unapproachable. The leader should really establish rapport with his or her people while taking the initiatives and caring for their well-being (Several Hindu respondents' input).

Follow Your *Dharma,* and Lead Well

Whatever you have in your mind—forget it; Whatever you have in your hand—give it; Whatever is to be your fate—face it! (Sufi Quote)

If it is your life purpose to be a leader, then lead well. Follow your *Dharma.* Follow your call. Do your duty well.

When we do our *Dharma* wholeheartedly and passionately, we will succeed. We live with intensity and totality, whatever the moment allows us and we feel like doing, we do it. Live the day and live the night too, we don't miss anything! Instead, we become everything!

Here, it is appropriate to quote the *Bhagavad Gita* (Hawley 2006a, p. 30): "Your purpose in life—the very purpose of all humanity—is to gradually achieve spiritual perfection, which is your own Divinity. Being devoted to your duties helps you eventually find this perfection; detesting or avoiding your duties helps you lose it."

Know Your Vision

All the flowers of all of the tomorrows are in the seeds of today. (Chinese proverb)

To know the Godhead in the *Gita* can be taken in leadership terms as to know one's vision. The highest Godhead or the Absolute is both being and nonbeing, both manifested and un-manifested, both formed and formless. It exists throughout all creation, in all hands and feet. It appears to be many but is one, undivided.

True leaders provide vision and values; they are also passionate about their visions (Low and Theyagu 2003). Leaders have vision and strategize; they 'visualize' the roadmap to achieve the goals. Having the vision (knowing the Godhead) enables the leader to go beyond the smoke of the organisation's day-to-day operations and the daily grind and to see clearly its strategic path.

Move from Ego to Divinity; Move from Self to Other-Centeredness

Self-sacrifice, giving, and self-discipline should not be renounced, for they purify the thoughtful. Yet even these, Arjuna, should be performed without desire for selfish rewards. This is essential. (Bhagavad Gita 18:3–6)

As a wave, seething and foaming, is only water. So all creation, streaming out of the Self, is only the Self. Consider a piece of cloth, it is only threads! So all creation, When you look closely, is only the Self (Ashtavakra Gita 2:4–5).

The surrender must take place, and the ego needs to be obliterated. This Hindu proverb goes "Nobody can enter the gates of heaven without one's own death" is applicable.

And here there is nothing passive or negative, in fact, it is totally positive. It's moving away from the narrowness of the self, surrender here means total acceptance of love as well as the extension and expansion to others, and more supremely, to the Universe. A leader normally aspires, seeks and works towards extreme greatness and something supremely magnificent, wanting to achieve universal excellence.

The *Gita* urges every human being to move from ego to divinity. Each of us needs to transcend the narrow notion that one has any existence separate from God or the Universe. Also go all-out to continually or often focus one's mind on the absolute oneness of Divinity and on one's own real unity with that oneness.

Endeavor to make selfless (egoless) action one's path. One seeks to abandon all selfish desires, cravings, and torments or distress of the heart. One tries to grow to want nothing, *nothing* outside of the true self, the soul within! And so, as a leader, one moves from self-interest to care for others and to become community-centered and others-based. Servant leadership is practised.

These coincide with what several Hindu respondents had expressed, "If a leader only thinks of him(her)self in whatever things (s)he is doing then (s)he would not be able to help others and care for others. One would fail in one's *Dharma* or duty, simply spending time and efforts doing one's own thing; the aim and purpose of a leader is to serve or assist others. In this regard, one has to behave selfless." "The Hindus believe that even Lord Shiva himself is the servant of all servants."

The leader harbors no ill will toward any being and in fact, returns love for hate; indeed (s)he is forgiving and contented. (S)he should also see him(her)self as a team leader; after all, (s)he needs to relate and collaborate with others (Low 2003, 2001). Teams maximise the organisation's human resources. And team members coach, help and support each other, and enlightened leaders grow and serve their teams well. Good leaders in fact serve others and the welfare of the world.

Foster Team Leadership and Team Building

> Remember upon the conduct of each depends the fate of all. (Alexander the Great)

The (spiritual) leader who is connected to the Universe would also see a bigger picture and would also work well to connect to the others and the human community. Such a leader would also promote team leadership, working together and synergizing well with others. While (s)he coaches, mentors, loves and cares for others, and that flame of love has to be taught too. (S)he also builds and promotes trust between him(her)self and others and among members of the team.

"'Like the body that is made up of different limbs and organs, all mortal creatures exist depending upon one another' (a Hindu proverb). Similarly, a leader needs the support of his/her followers and the followers need their leader to lead and work well with them. To have many loyal followers, (s)he should love and care for others as well as foster togetherness, team spirit and harmony" (Several respondents' input).

Henry Ford once said that, "If everyone is moving forward together, then success takes care of itself." And indeed how true this is; the work unit/organisation when well-synergised would be well oiled, efficient, co-ordinated and work well. And more importantly, the people are happy.

Grow Resilience

Dig the well everyday to drink water everyday. (Hindu proverb)

Good leaders recognise that never was good work done without much trouble or problems.

Persistent, leaders are tough or die-hard; they are climbers (Stoltz 1997), they persist. They keep on climbing in spite of obstacles.

In the *Gita*, it is said that one should learn to be neither an agitator in nor agitated by the world and to accept the knocks of life as blessings in disguise. One strengthens oneself.

When one learns to take shelter in the Beyond or the Universe, one experiences great peace of mind, which displaces all negativity and pain. Those who do not learn to do this keep on bringing suffering, agitation and a stressful life upon themselves or even violence onto others. They become losers. And note that leaders are winners, they want to win, if not, at least they survive!

Be Disciplined

By working faithfully 8 h a day, you may eventually get to be boss and work 12 h a day. (Anonymous)

It is worthy to note that the devoted and disciplined person who controls his mind will achieve tranquility and oneness, so also is the leader who is disciplined, (s)he is likely to attain calmness, composure and is capable of clarity of mind when strategizing and/or leading his or her people.

Through discipline, the leader also builds up his or her patience. In the *Gita* (Hinduism) a particular emphasis on meditation exists and aspects of this lead to a natural state of mindfulness that is conducive to patient, effective and well-organized thought as well as clarity of mind.

Have Spiritual Ballast

Everything has beauty, but not everyone sees it. (Chinese proverb)

All spiritual disciplined are done with a view to still the mind. The perfectly still mind is universal spirit. (Swami Ramdas)

Ballast is anything that serves as a source of stability or steadiness.

Over the past two or three decades, there have been, separately occurred, many natural disasters, global warming, political disorders, terrorist attacks as well as scams, business and financial troubles in several parts of the world (Low 2010b). Turbulent times are indeed presently upon us (Low 2009a, 2010b); life is and can be topsy-turvy, and more so, many people are experiencing a terrible emotional nausea as our life boats toss to and fro. So, what we need is faith, hope and something immensely positive; perhaps, spiritual ballast would enable or keep us level, cool and composed—it would buoy us up and to give us a sense of stability as we sail through rough and choppy waters.

A leader should also have spiritual ballast, and this spiritual counterweight or even a spring well could greatly assist one in overcoming obstacles in the course of doing one's daily work or duty (*Dharma*). With adequate ballast, rock and roll is reduced, and the danger or menace of capsizing and getting drowned is greatly reduced. Believers thus strongly believe that only the Divine could inspire something so powerful and cavernously deep! And that they face the Absolute for direction and answers. The *Bhagavad Gita* also grounds or anchors us with some critical values, and it also supplies us with much wisdom, ethical codes and moral courage in our daily lives.

One respondent intimated these to the researcher-author; these were what he opined, that is, "spirituality or spiritualism is a way of life. It cannot be separated from one's daily life". He added that "Sri Krishna says in Mahabharata, 'Do all that you do truthfully and in my name, when you do I will bear your consequences. Thus when a leader lives a spiritual life, he will be an embodiment of common sense, morality and living values. A true spiritual leader has only to follow two ideals, Soulful compassion and Dharma (Selfless service).'"

Needless to say, spirituality and spiritual practices often lead to an experience of connectedness with a larger reality, yielding a more comprehensive self; with other individuals or the human community; with nature; or with the Divine realm. And that can be very self-fulfilling or satisfying for the individual leaders (humans). Spirituality after all helps or leads to finding greater purpose and meaning in our lives. We see fresh perspectives and spirituality overall supplies fresh or added meanings to our work and daily tasks.

(Don't Just Do; at Most Times) Reflect and Take Stock!

> Meditation brings wisdom; lack of mediation leaves ignorance. Know well what leads you forward and what hold you back, and choose the path that leads to wisdom. (Buddha)

A Persian saying has it that one should "seek truth in meditation, and not in moldy books. Look in the sky to find the moon, not in the pond."

Meditation is any actions done with awareness; meditation is the art of staying in this present moment and it is also about knowing oneself as one is. Through reflection, the Higher Self is seen.

So also in our leadership actions, it is indeed good to reflect and take stock so as to be aware of oneself as one is, see the big picture and be aware where one is bringing one's people and organization to.

In taking stock, we ask ourselves: Are we leading well? How can we improve the ways we lead our people? When leading, are we seeing the bigger picture? How can we lead with a sense of humility? Are we attaining the greatest goodness for the greatest number of people? How can we attain the greatest goodness for the greatest number of people in our organisation? How can we be more people-centered? How can we lead in a servant leadership way? Are we bringing in togetherness, love, cooperation and team spirit? How can we bring in more harmony to the workplace?

Also, leaders know where they stand and they stand tall; with moral courage, they persist.

We take stock at regular intervals and each time, we take corrective actions, minimize the gaps, and we improve our ways of leading.

Conclusion

> By the accident of fortune, a man may rule the world for a time, but by virtue of love and kindness he may rule the world forever. (Lao Tzu)

One leads and loves. One learns and takes from whatever resources to update and upgrade. And good leaders develop through a continuous, never ending process of learning, education, training, and experience as well as mindfulness of what has been learnt. And they learn and apply well.

Hanuman, the Monkey Deity: Leadership Lessons Learnt

Hanuman, the mighty monkey deity is among the most popular gods in the Hindu pantheon.

According to Indian mythology—in the Ramayana (Way of Rama) epics—going back more than 2000 years, Hanuman, chief of the monkeys, plays an important role. Lord Rama, the deity worshiped as the seventh incarnation of Vishnu, is assisted by Hanuman in his great battle for the rescue of his wife Sita. Hanuman's association with Rama brought recognition to him who thus acquired divine rank. The monkey deity is renowned for his boldness, courage, power, faithful and selfless service (Marchand 2009) and is taken to be as an able and effective negotiator (Low 2010a).

Besides his heroism in defeating the demon Ravana, Hanuman is credited with bridging the strait between Sri Lanka and the mainland of India. This he achieved with the assistance of his monkeys, who carried rocks and boulders from the Himalayas for the purpose. Many temples, especially in southern India, were erected in Hanuman's honor.

The aim and objectives of this section are to examine Hanuman as well as happenings and events in his life so as to glean leadership lessons and tips.

Leadership Lessons Learnt

Situational Leadership

It is always good when a man has two irons in the fire. Francis Beaumont and John Fletcher—The Faithful Friends (Act 1, Scene 2)

The monkey deity has many powers—one of which is becoming big. He only became available again when Jambavant, King of the bears, reminded Hanuman that he has that power. And that power was really great. Hanuman could easily fight an elephant for example, since he could, at will, become much bigger than the elephant.

One of the key leadership lessons learnt here is that as leaders, we need to be flexible in the use of our powers and also depending on the situation. This reminds me of the use of situational leadership in which the leader applies the different leadership styles depending on the follower's ability and willingness; the follower's needs are assessed before applying any style.

Servant Leadership

No act of kindness, no matter how small, is ever wasted. (Aesop)

The next lesson is that of servant leadership. Hanuman is famous for his heroism in helping Lord Rama in rescuing his wife Sita from the demon Ravana. Some effective leaders believe that their primary mission is to serve their constituents' needs. They measure their effectiveness in terms of their ability to help others.

How true, leaders should not expect to be served! They should serve; in fact, they should have the service heart, helping people or their constituents to achieve their goals.

Symbols and Icons

One man with courage is a majority. (Andrew Jackson)

Symbols are useful aids for leaders. Psychology has it that people and even animals respond well to symbols. As in Pavlov's experiments, the dogs salivated they heard the sounds of the bell which they associated with food, even if there was no food.

Bearing in mind that leadership is "the ability to inspire confidence and support among people on whose competence and commitment performance depends on" (DuBrin 2007, p. 231), it is necessary for leaders to create symbols and icons to persuade the people and get their support. Additionally, such symbols can be placed in the workplaces to motivate the people.

In this aspect, the Hanuman symbol is said to inspire a person to use their power in the service of the greater good. A highly respected character in Indian, Chinese, and Thai legend, Hanuman serves as a guard and a soldier of God. Here, another leadership lesson is that leaders (should) create symbols and icons, and these can inspire their followers and others to emulate them.

Interestingly, in Thailand, among Muay Thai boxers, the Hanuman tattoo represents strength, stamina and agility, all attributes of a champion fighter (Tattoo Design Directory 2009).

Humility

> Be humble for you are made of earth. Be noble for you are made of stars. (Serbian proverb)

I am sure that many of us would have encountered some business people who are proud or arrogant. And certainly they are not pleasant, if not difficult, to deal with. Surely you wish that you never come face-to-face with the person again! One vital leadership lesson and/or principle I gathered from Hanuman and the story of his rescuing Lord Rama's wife Sita is that humility is a good quality, and ought to be generally fostered by leaders.

Being humble, the leader listens. He understands the people and their needs. He does not tell them what to do. If he simply tells his people what to do without even listening to them or asking for their input or suggestions, then that's arrogance! Then again, by simply telling his people what to do does not mean that the job gets done.

Indeed we can learn more on leadership and its parallels from the Indian scriptures.

Other Successful Leadership Principles and Lessons Gleaned

Take a further example, the verses in *Sundar Kand*. Hanuman's mission was to locate Sita and give her Ram's message. Several other key principles and lessons of successful leadership include:

- Preparing oneself mentally to execute the job (This raises the leader's confidence and self-efficacy. The latter can lead to the successful execution of the job.)
- Adopting a positive attitude (This also normally increases the leader's confidence.)
- Analysing the key strength(s) of competitors/the other parties (OPs) (This enables the leader to better know his or her competitors, come up counter-strategies, measures or tactics and better deal with the competition.)
- Embarking (Going into action. Getting the results).

Accordingly, Hanuman made his own strategy to know the strengths and weaknesses of the Lankans. There is certainly a need to analyse the OP's strengths, weaknesses, opportunities, and threats (SWOT). Using core competency of an individual or an organization should be the strategic leadership mantra.

The Buddha and Leadership Lessons and Relevance

Buddhism originates from India, and in this section of the chapter, the Buddha and leadership lessons and modern day relevance are discussed. The Buddha—"The Awakened One" or "He who knows" whose original name was Prince Siddhartha; he was the founder of Buddhism, one of the world's great religion, and listed within the 100, a ranking of the most influential persons in history (Hart 1992). Here, several Buddhistic principles and insights are identified and examined, and they are then applied to key leadership principles and practices.

The Teachings of Buddha and Becoming Leaders

Leadership can be simply put as "getting people to do things willingly" (Mullins 1995, p. 228). The reason is rather simple—If there's trust, then leaders can get their people or others to follow them and get things done; and today, more than ever, we see organizational leadership requires trust. Events of recent years have certainly brought the issue of protecting the people and trust into the headlines—for example, WorldCom faked nearly US$4 million in operating cash flow. Enron executives manipulated their financial statements (Robbins 2005). Before the Bank of America's 2008 takeover, Merrill Lynch paid US$100 million in fines for misleading investors.

Besides, more commonly, the classic sins of leaders include "being callous to the needs of others", if not, not taking care of the needs of their people; they are not empathetic (Low 2008a, p. 67).

Protecting the People, Bringing Peace and Harmony

The general who advances without craving fame and retreats without fearing dishonour, whose only thought is to protect his country and do good service for his sovereign, is the jewel of the kingdom. (Sun Tzu)

On the other hand, in leadership the Buddha way, it's being sensitive to the needs of the people around them. Of paramount importance, leaders achieve their plans through their people, and hence all the more, they need to care and motivate their people so that their people would achieve things for them (the leaders).

Leaders need to be empathetic (Low 2008a). The people are there to be loved and helped. Love-kindness (*metta*) is one of the boundless states that are developed by practising Buddhist; the practice of loving-kindness involves developing the attitude that 'may all beings be free from enmity, free from affliction... and live happily. They also practice compassion, sympathetic joy and equanimity (Gruzalski 2000).

"(With the need to) free oneself from materialistic obsession and desire" (an interviewee's input) compassion and loving-kindness, such leaders protect their people, practicing love while showing care and concern. "Just as a mother would protect her only child at the risk of her own life, even so, let one cultivate a boundless heart towards all beings. Let thoughts of boundless love pervade the whole world... without any enmity. Whether one stands, walks, sits or lies down, (and) as long as one is awake, one should develop this mindfulness" (Sutta Nipata 146–151, cited in Conway 2008).

Such a leadership idea is so essential so more in today's context. The world has seen many wars including the recent (December 2008/January 2009) Israeli attacks on Gaza. The world have also seen the recent (September/October 2008) People's Republic of China milk scare as serious (The Brunei Times, 2008a; The Brunei Times, 2008b). Melamine was added to milk powder and animal feed to boost the protein content (Even eggs were affected and said to contain melamine, the hens were affected by the melamine content in the chicken feed). Several babies had died because of the melamine-laced milk. This is indeed sad, and businesses should not be thinking of mere profits; the people need to be cared for and protected. And the recent Indian case involving Satyam, India's fourth largest software exporter, is also shocking... The Indian software boss, Mr. Ramalinga Raju quitted, admitting faking US$1 billion in profits, and the "Satyam scandal raises questions about corporate governance" (Velloor 2009, p. 1).

The Sutra in Section 42 says, 'When people give in to their desires, they become enchanted with excess and showing off. They become like a stick of incense that burns itself out; though others may admire its fragrance, the incense itself pays for the spell it casts by destroying itself.' (Hsing Yun 2001, p. 58)

Greed is the cause of suffering. The Commentary on the Sutra of Golden Light says, "Greed is like an ocean current that flows without ceasing." Excessive desire is managed and minimized by its opposite—balanced awareness. The sutra says: "Have few desires, be receptive, and you will be content in body and mind." (Hsing Yun 2001, pp. 57–59). Greed needs to be abolished; there is no need to be greedy. Be content in body and mind. Businesses need to instead help the needy.

"The wise control themselves" (Chin Kung 2002) for if one is greedy, then it is like drinking seawater, the more one drinks, the more one gets thirsty. Instead, one should need to strive to...

Being Altruistic and Other-Centred

> To stop suffering, stop greediness. Greediness is a source of suffering. (The Buddha)

Instead of robbing or taking credits of the subordinates, betraying individual trust which are other classic sins of leaders (Low 2008a) and being self-centred, leaders should be altruistic.

Buddha, the *Pali* canon preaches that the human being is without self (*anatman*) (Easwaran 2007). One interviewee expressed that, "If all the staff embraces this principle, they would be considering the well-being and happiness of others first, the selfish attitude of an individual will be of non-existence in an organisation. This means that everybody will be considerate and working together in an effective and efficient way. Here, the benefit would be that the leader will find it easier to run his department/division or even the organization as a whole. . . . . .In an organisation where altruism prevails. . . kindness and forgiveness are practiced, conflict management and resolution will not be required. Other-centred, the employees will be helping amongst each other to make the organisation run smoothly. The older generation will be teaching the younger generation and vice versa."

In essence, leaders need to strive to be. . .

> One who is virtuous and wise
>   shines forth like a blazing fire;
>   like a bee collecting nectar
>   he acquires wealth by harming none. *The Buddha*, cited in Field (2007).

Being Compassionate and Contributing to the Society

> If you want others to be happy, practise compassion. If you want to be happy, practise compassion. (Dalai Lama)

The author prefers not to talk on *karma* (for every cause there is an effect; man reaps what he sows) and punishments, but rather on love, the positive aspects of Buddhism and applies it to leadership. Love and leadership is indeed intertwined. The leader is compassionate. The Dalai Lama points out: "This is my simple religion. There is no need for temples; no need for complicated philosophy. Our own brain, our own heart is our temple; the philosophy is kindness." (Thinkexist 2008)

"Compassion includes qualities of sharing, readiness to give comfort, sympathy, concern, caring. In Buddhism, we can really understand others, when we can really understand ourselves, through wisdom." (Buddha Dharma Education Association: BDEA/BuddhaNet 2008). Help yourself, and then help others. These speak volumes when applied to leadership.

In Buddhism, of transient beings, we all are living in the world of "anicca" (a transient world). One of the main teachings of Buddha is that "all formations are transient; all formations are subject to sufferings; all things are without a self" (Kornfield 1993, p. 53). Some critics may however level the arguments that in Buddhism, one can be less achieving yet when applying to leadership lessons and practices, such a principle is indeed beautiful. The leader is selfless, showing care and concern for others and his people. "Success to me means being able to contribute to society. When we talk about society that means people." (Ms Khunying Suriyasat, Chairwoman, Toshiba Thailand Co. Ltd., cited in Low and Theyagu 2003, p. 81) (Fig. 6.1).

Instead of robbing or taking credits of the subordinates, betraying individual trust which are other classic sins of leaders (Low, 2008) and being self-centred, leaders should be altruistic.

Fig. 6.1 Speaks of, among Buddha's main teachings, the need to show love and compassion to one's subordinates by building their confidence and trust

Achievements are still attained but made for the people. Caring for the people is of paramount importance. Indeed, historically, leadership "that goes beyond the nation-state and seeks to address all human beings" "has been the most important, but rarest and most elusive, variety of leadership" (Former United States Secretary of State Madeleine Albright).

Loving the Absolute Reality by loving others is a leadership perspective that can be referred to as mastery in servitude. It is perhaps the highest form of service. Mastery in servitude can be better understood when one speaks in the form of the elephant metaphor. The elephant is referred to in the Indian scripture and folklore which puts it as ranking first among all animals in importance. Elephants have been trained to do hard work, lift and transport burdens and overall to serve men. A trained elephant, carrying the king, bears the arrows on the battlefield. With its strength, endurance, gentleness and remarkable restraint, the elephant has long symbolised to the Indian mind the enormous power locked within every human being. Through this analogy of the trained elephant, whose immense power has transformed into loving human service, it is accordingly said that the Buddha also conveys to his Indian audience the importance of spiritual discipline.

Arguably, it does not matter whether the Absolute Reality can be proved or otherwise, what matters most, however, is that the Absolute Reality is a subjective experience, and that experience energises or empowers the leader to do more for others and his people. Look, for example, at the work of the Dalai Lama.

Being Humble, Humility Has Advantages

The more noble, the more humble (German proverb)

Cultivate peace first in the garden of your heart by removing the weeds of selfishness and jealousy, greed and anger, pride and ego. Then all will benefit from your peace and harmony. (Chin Kung 2002)

When subscribing to Buddhism, leaders also need to be humble. One interviewee highlighted that that as a Buddhist leader, he subscribes to being humble; he opined that:

A humble, ethical leader will increase one's own good qualities and wisdom (the intelligence to distinguish between good and bad) as he'll be easy to interact and speak to... he learns from others. If a leader is proud, one will become jealous of others and angry with others, and also... looking down on others. Because of that, there would be (less) unhappiness in the organisation.

There is, in fact, nothing to be proud of. Humility makes one approachable, and it opens the door to building relationships (Zenger and Folkman 2004). As mentioned earlier, the world is transient and impermanent. Interestingly, the leader should well understand this, and this helps the leader to accept change—change is the only constant; he leads his people to also accepting and managing change. One of the universal truths of Buddhism propagates that "everything is continuously changing. Life is like a river flowing on and on, ever-changing. Sometimes it flows slowly and sometimes swiftly. It is smooth and gentle in some places, but later on snags and rocks crop up out of nowhere. As soon as we think we are safe, something unexpected happens." (Instilling Goodness School 2008)

Collaborating and Being Positive

We make a living by what we get, but we make a life by what we give. (Winston Churchill)

Being a Buddhist, a leader is also patient and tolerant. "As a leader, I am compassionate, understanding, I talk to my staff nicely and allow fair tolerance for mistakes." "In times of difficulties, a tolerant leader would find ways to overcome problems or difficulties. If a leader has little tolerance or without it, the smallest mistake made by a follower would irritate him; and sometimes, he may over react. The purpose of practising patience is to become 'stronger' in the mind and the heart. Through calmness, one learns wisdom. If you lose patience, you lose power... you're not calm enough to analyse." "When you tolerate, you're patient and get along with others" (Interviewees' input).

When one collaborates, one becomes a team player (Low 2003). Great leaders "look to collaborate rather than compete" (Zenger and Folkman 2004, p. 9). They see others through the positive visor. Ordinarily speaking, leaders take it that others have good intentions rather than bad.

The Buddha once told a story of a man being shot by a poisonous arrow and when being attended by the physician, he said, "I will not allow you to remove the arrow until I learn the caste, the age, the birthplace and the motivations of the one who wounded me." Indeed, the man would die before having learned all these. By the same token, there are enough problems on earth; we should not give stress on problem(s), witch-hunting and seeking to blame when a problem occurs. But rather, we need to collaborate with others, working on the solutions, curing and making the world a better place for all.

That's in itself is being positive. Besides, when reading these sentences from the Dhammapada:

> The kind of seed sown
> will produce that kind of fruit.
> Those who do good will reap good results.
> Those who do evil will reap evil results.
> If you carefully plant a good seed,
> You will joyfully gather good fruit. (The Dhammapada, cited in Instilling Goodness School 2008),

we also get the intuitive idea of creating positive actions. "Our thoughts and actions determine the kind of life we can have" (Instilling Goodness School 2008). We reap what we sow. So our leaders should be positive, create their own niche and play to their strengths as well as grow their followers and their entire teams.

To this author, bringing about positive thinking and discipline within one's mind is the essence of the Buddha's teaching. We thus need to train or discipline our mind for happiness. The systematic training of the mind is critical; cultivating happiness and positive thinking can lead to the real inner change; our inner change begins with learning (new input) and involves the discipline of gradually replacing our negative conditioning with positive conditioning (forming new neural circuits).

Being Objective

> Better to shave the heart than to shave the head. (Japanese Buddhist proverb)

If leaders are not objective, they are inclined to bear grudges, be attached to the wrong doings of their staff or even practise favouritism, the various other common leadership mistakes. Lingering grudges, these negative thoughts if they are not addressed or dismissed in a timely way ordinarily destroy the delicate fabric of leadership. Why? "Followers are fearful that their mistakes and shortcomings, even those committed years before, are never really forgiven and definitely not forgotten." (Low 2008a, p. 71)

This brings to mind the next important tenet—among the many others—of leadership, that is of, up-keeping objectivity. A leader should be fair and objective (detached), and not have any favourites among his followers. Favouritism can bring about much unhappiness, causing lower staff morale and decreasing productivity.

In this aspect, one respondent this author spoke to has these to say:

> A Buddhist person, not a monk or a nun, in a business organisation may have a bird-eye-view on ups and downs of a business, because (detached) he or she understands that everything is finite in this world. He or she may show compassion to the colleague, employees, bosses and even a competitor. The detached perspective may help to make decisions based on merits and welfare, rather than emotions such as fear, greed, hatred or individuals needs (for power, affiliation and achievements). He or she may be more socially responsible not to cause harm.

Another respondent highlighted these:

> As leaders we should view things as in life in a detached way. It is very much like the saying, "Life is like a bridge, cross over it, but build no house on it." We live well when we are detached. We view things based on the white hat thinking, look at the facts and figures.

Achieving Mastery

> Fear is only as deep as the mind allows. (Japanese proverb)

To paraphrase Richard Bach, learning is finding out what we already know while doing is showing that you know it; and teaching is reminding others that they know just as well as you. You are all learners, doers and teachers. And to that, whether learners, doers and teachers, in order to be happy, we should feel that we are continuing to grow (Robbins 1994).

Buddhism encourages meditation, learning and self-growth. In the deep inner silence, we understand, and are aware. A leader meditates, contemplates and is never lonely, loneliness is quite a disease. It is "monophobia". Every thinker, every great leader and a number of good men and women have in some ways gone off alone... be still and listened spiritually.

"Meditate. Live quietly. Be quiet. Do your work, with mastery" (The Dhammapada, cited in Kornfield 1993, p. 78). As a leader, one learns and attains personal mastery. "Little by little a person becomes good (*or develop leadership mastery*), as a pot is filled by drops of water." (The Dhammapada, Chapter 9, verse 122, cited in Easwaran 2007, p. 142, *italics mine*). One improves one's ability, achieving mastery of core competences; and guides others. One betters oneself and coaches others.

Leaders cultivate awareness, having the vision and steadily gearing towards turning that vision into reality. In this regard, as leaders, we learn, and should learn well and update continuously. This can contribute to our mindfulness. Mindful leaders are broad and open-minded, looking for new ideas and mind expansion, and integrating things learnt with existing information to come up with new solutions and practical ways of doing things. So, mindfulness can thus be seen as continuously reassessing previously learned ways of doing things in the light of evolving information and changing circumstances. Ordinarily, mindfulness is the opposite of mindlessness as the former is alert and active. Mindfulness thus leads to leadership mastery and excellence. Mindlessness is passive, doing without thinking, following rules, letting others do the thinking, accepting others' answers or learning new things without integrating them with previously learned ways of doing things; there can also be no or little applications.

Removing Ego, Listening Well and Being More Creative

All lust is grief. (Japanese Buddhist proverb)

A leader who listens well makes a better leader. Learn it from the Buddha, remove one's ego and pride, and listen. Much pain is caused to others through one's ego. Diminish one's ego, and creates more happiness for others.

The Buddha says, "The abolition of the conceit 'I am'– that is, truly the supreme bliss." (Buddha, in the Udane Sutra, ii.1, cited in Conway 2008). Listen well to one's people. When one listens well, one gets much feedback from one's people. One also caters to the needs of one's people.

One can also argue that leaders can be more creative when they remove or diminish their egos. When a leader stubbornly sticks to "my way is the only way", (s)he is edging greatness out. When (s)he, in fact, realises that "my way is *not* the only way", (s)he would be willing to listen to others' solutions, views and perspectives. (S)he thus broadens her(his) perspectives, and be more open while being more creative.

Avoiding Pain and Sufferings (Creating Happiness in Our Own Setting)

Life is suffering. (The Buddha)

In leadership, the Buddhist way, it is the Noble Eightfold Path, the way that leads to the extinction of suffering, namely: (1) Right Understanding, (2) Right Thought, (3) Right Speech (4) Right Action, (5) Right Livelihood, (6) Right Effort, (7) Right Mindfulness; and (8) Right Concentration. This is the Middle Path that the Buddha has uncovered, which makes one both see and know which leads to peace, to discernment, to enlightenment. One avoids craving, hence, be detached and avoids suffering. One also learns to be contented.

"A Buddhist practitioner is generous and equal minded toward both friend and foe. He does not dwell on old wrongs, or make new enemies". Besides, contentment is the source of happiness and wisdom is a Buddhist practitioner's concern (Hsing Yun 2001).

These, to all of the respondents, are "great, one learns and practices for self-growth and cultivation" and as individuals, "we learn, cooperate... collaborate", and "grow our leadership and human potential" (interviewees' input).

One can also add that a leader is born in times of crisis and more likely, avoiding pain and sufferings results in the making of leaders. One interviewee expressed these:

> Look at our past Buddhist stories. When you look at them, it is evident that when the country is booming the people are happy and the leader (the King) can follow the righteous acts to rule the country. So my view is that a true Buddhist leader cannot be born or exist, but be forged in a time like this.

Being the Salt of the World or Being the Beacon

(Be) salt of the earth, the best of people, especially the most dependable. (Matthew, 5: 13)

"Not setting the right example" is yet another common leadership sin (Low 2008a). Some leaders practise "do as I tell you", not "do as I do". If followers question their leaders' honesty and integrity, leaders cannot be role models. If this were so, such leaders would have difficulties in motivating, let alone inspiring their people (Low 2001, 2006b).

Akin to Christianity, in Buddhism, everyone should strive to be "a light. Pure, shining, free" (Kornfield 1993, p. 47). The Bible speaks of the salt of the earth; salt not only flavours the food but also acts as a preservative in preserving the food. The Buddhists, on the other hand, speak of flowers: "(Being) a lovely flower, full of colour but lacking in fragrance, are the words of those who do not practice what they preach. Like a lovely flower, full of colour and fragrance, are the words of those who practice what they preach" (The Dhammapada, Chap. 4, v. 51, cited in Easwaran 2007, p. 118). All in all, the leader should set the example and be the role model. After all, "true leaders stand out. People observe a leader's actions" (Low and Theyagu 2003, p. 35).

To be exemplary, the leader himself must take the actions. "To straighten the crooked, you must first do a harder thing—straighten yourself" (The Dammapada, cited in Kornfield 1993, p. 65). "An individual will help himself to achieve inner peace with good personality characteristics (being humble, compassionate and non-violent) through self-cultivation. ...this would enable him to set an example for others to follow..." (an interviewee's input).

One clear benefit of this 'leading the Buddha way' is that actions speak louder than words. The leader becomes an exemplar, a model of behaviour for members of the group, setting an example of what is expected. And indeed, the leader's examples secure the followers' trust of the leader.

In setting the example, the leader also inspires his followers. "To inspire followers to do the right thing, a forgiving leader will attempt......strive; showing the ways and coaching those who make mistakes. If a leader cannot forgive, but keeps on blaming and scolding the follower, then this may hurt the latter's feelings and instead de-motivate him" (an interviewee's input). Overall, when the leader is inspiring, the inspiration can grow the followers' trust of the leader.

Section Conclusion

When we lead, we grow our potential. We also care for, attend to the needs of others and grow them. And all in all, in conclusion, it should be noted that "Buddha's teachings are more of a philosophy, a way of life rather than a religion. . . .it can, in fact, be accepted and practised in Christian, Islamic context or for that matter, any religious context" (interviewees' input).

Pro-Activity and Hinduism

Introduction

The Buddha once said that, "An idea that is developed and put into action is more important than an idea that exists only as an idea". Indeed, in leadership, "nothing is ever gained by dreaming about a goal and not doing anything concrete towards attaining it" (Low and Theyagu 2003, p. 55).

Think BIG and ACT BIG! Actions flesh things out!

The core of leadership is pro-activity and not being reactive. Leaders should be planners, planning, preparing and preventing bad things from happening to the organisation. And as leaders, we get things done or results through people; we should be proactive to achieve results and enjoy good relationships while having motivated, productive work teams. Even as an ordinary human being, one should not be like a jelly fish, floating passively with the tide; one should not be waiting passively or aimlessly; one needs to be directing oneself while applying one's initiative and resourcefulness.

The aim and objectives of this section are to examine pro-activity in relation to Hinduism and what is the leadership learning. There is a common saying that, "God helps those who help themselves". And more so in Hinduism, pro-activity is important. In one's life, one has to fulfil one's *dharma* or duty. One actively acts on one's duty. In the same way, as a leader, one should evidently be proactive, and fulfils one's role and responsibility.

What is then the leadership lessons gleaned from the *Bhagavad Gita*?

The *Bhagavad Gita* starts with an imminent war. So sad at the possibility of battling armies of teachers, relatives, and friends, the warrior Arjuna refuses to fight. The God Vishnu, incarnated as the charioteer Krishna, tells Arjuna he must fulfil his destiny as a warrior; the soul is indestructible and Arjuna should fight without attachment, aversion or dislike to an outcome.

By the same token, Krishna's advice is to be adhered; people should not renounce the world. Let me explain, people frequently get mixed up and think that the spiritual life is necessarily a non-active existence. This is not right or proper, but the misconception causes much sadness and agony, particularly among those who incorrectly seek to withdraw from worldly activities. As Hawley (2006b, p. 29) has pointed out, one cannot attain the highest goal—which is self-realization—through merely shirking one's worldly duties and deluding oneself that one is renouncing the world. One must indeed live, face and cope with the world. One needs to practice...

Taking Charge

> Perform one's obligatory duty for action is better than inaction. (The Bhagavad Gita)

Every one is gifted—but some never open up their package. And that package is being in charge. We should take charge of our lives.

Are we awakened or still sleeping? Do we know of our life's purpose?

Yes, we are often hungry to find life's purpose, and perceive and understand why we are here in this world. We recognise that we're not here to merely be born, to drift along like a leaf in a river, just doing-doing doing, and then, worn, washed-out, and water-soaked, to sink.

Most of us often think of *dharma* or duty too narrowly, as our life's work or professional role. If we see duty instead from a loftier perspective, as our duty to our highest self, the *Atma*, then we think of it as our duty to the Divinity that dwells within us. And we'll take charge!

In the *Bhagavad Gita*, Krishna advises us to be proactive. There, according to Krishna, are four basic reasons:

One, we are to benefit mankind.

Two, we are here to gradually achieve the perfection of our divinity.

Three, we're to achieve our uncommon path to become the one to know the Supreme Divine.

And four, we are to attain the peak of all spiritual pursuits, to actually merge into the supreme universal soul and never again to come back to our worldly sufferings. Similar to the Celtic proverb, a leader should "listen to the sound of the river and (s)he'll get a trout", leaders should always be in charge. Only then would the leader be able to get results and be respected. One respondent spoke to this author on these: "Nowadays, most of us know that business constantly changes over a short period of time. It is very important that business leaders need to be proactive to be competitive against one other. If a leader is not proactive but passive, (s)he could resembles a captain who is sailing a ship (that is his/her small business) round and round aimlessly and would eventually run out of power or aground. From time to time, business leaders should think of expanding their businesses into a wider horizon to ensure their business growth and sustainability into the future." Besides, when things happen, a leader should be in the know, and be able to explain things. His ears must be on the ground, being sensitive to the needs and requirements of the people. (S)he should not and cannot callously say "I am not in charge" or "I don't know." (S)he should able to supply the reasons, explain things, assure his or her constituents, be accountable and be on top of the situation. And his or her constituents would then take comfort or feel secured in the leadership and its ways.

In short, in leadership, as Low (2011, p. 94) puts it, "If it is your life purpose to be a leader, then lead well. Follow your *Dharma*. Do your duty well."

Believing in One's Potential. . .

Know thyself. (Socrates)

A word informs the wise at once. A hundred lashes teach the dunce. (Indian proverb)

And applying pro-activity.

If one believes in one's potential, one naturally and logically has the courage to do and be proactive.

And one also applies pro-activity in learning. And when one believes in one's potential, one also applies pro-activity in learning. One would keep alive one's quest for knowledge.

One learns and reflects, turning inwards. As Confucius once said, "Be ashamed of mistakes and thus make them crimes"; one would avoid as well as learn from mistakes, and learn well to improve one's self. One would commit oneself to making one's life better and not bitter; one continuously improves oneself. And one achieves.

We must indeed believe in our potential. As the *Bhagavad Gita* has pointed out, the power of the Supreme Being is with you at all times; through the activities of mind, senses, breathing, and emotions; and is constantly doing all the work using you as a mere tool. One then just does. The wise see knowledge and action as one, they see truth. One can still do good while one lives.

Becoming Role Models

On a green tree are many parrots. (Guajarati saying)

Talk is cheap. A Chinese proverb has it that, "The chat is the scum of the water; the action is a drop of gold."

We must act. And to apply pro-activity, we act it out.

We become role models so that others may follow or emulate us. And to be role models, it carries heavy responsibilities with the vital need to show the example. In this connection, this author likes to cite what Confucius once said, "The nobler man first practices what he preaches and afterward, preaches according to his practice."

Becoming a role model is really one of the most effective ways in which a leader can encourage one's followers to achieve the goals of the organisation. Leaders' examples serve as a driving force or a sort of template to pursue the organisation's goals and carry out its activities well (Low and Theyagu 2003).

Being Passionate

When work, commitment, and pleasure all become one and you reach that deep well where passion lives, nothing is impossible. (Unknown)

When we are one with the Universe, we merge and nothing is impossible.

We should not be just average. If we are just average, we are perhaps without the right elements. We are missing certain ingredients.

If one is passive, not bothered much by things around oneself and one, in fact, does not want to do anything active, then one would just take life away slowly with no challenges or effort. And as time goes on, one's life would become unproductive, stagnant and reactive or even wasted. One can also then become very much lonely and dull; one's life then lacks the necessary active ingredient—PASSION. Passion fulfils things.

Anthony Robbins once said that, "Passion is the genesis of genius". Indeed we should be passionate in what we are doing. And passion cannot be faked as others can see through us. We need to be convinced, believing in what we do and doing what we believe in. When we are passionate, when we do and act based on our values or convictions.

Anyone who wants to be an effective leader needs to have passion first. Passionate leaders are not afraid to express their feelings. You can only expect to move others when you have moved yourself (Low and Theyagu 2003, p. 54).

Where so ever one goes, go with all one's heart! Be passionate; give life!

As leaders too, we are change agents. And if we are not passionate in our wanting to change, how could we lead change or help others to embrace change within the organisations?

Low and Theyagu (2003, p. 55) also speak of, "When you do things with a passion, others will notice you." And at a practical level, this is good for one's image and career development.

Investing Time and Effort in People and Relationships

The road to a friend's house is never long. (Danish proverb)

Homer once said, "labour conquers all things"; leaders should indeed invest in people. Well-informed and well-trained human resources are undoubted asset in every field of work. Leaders should not cut costs on training and development of their people; it is in their interests in keeping the people well-trained and duly informed. Top leaders would do well to groom their staff accordingly.

Human beings also need to put in time and effort to relate with each other. As an Indian saying goes, "Don't let grass grow on the path of friendship", a leader needs to be pro-active in relating with one's people, the very people who gives them the position.

A leader connects. One needs to create the rapport and build relationships with the people; one needs to meet and talk with them. One needs to actively invest time and effort; and relate. One may also want to invest time and effort to...

Being Practical

I hear and I forget. I see and I remember. I do and I understand. (Confucius)

The author loves the Gita's stress on application, its insistence that one puts the teachings of the *Gita* into practice in one's daily life. The *Gita* insists that "theory and make-believe have no place in true spirituality".

In the leadership sense, it is like sharpening the saw, making it a habit as well as part and parcel of our lives. And we grow or 'perfect' it! To paraphrase Confucius, man's nature are alike, it's the habits that carry leaders far apart from non-leaders.

Doing Good and Caring for Others Actively

Do not make promises—make good (Unknown)

A Cherokee expression highlights this: "When you were born, you cried and the world rejoiced. Live your life so that when you die, the world cries and you rejoice."

Do good. Care for others. And serve others.

Even a minute, the smallest, a teeny, mini, bitsy good deed is better than the biggest or grandest intention. Intention or plan is not good enough; actions count.

One respondent intimated to this author that he really liked the Gita, he spoke of "(the Gita) pushes me beyond merely trying to be a good person, putting effort toward becoming my own Divinity within. And I love it. . . . . .page after page of the means to call forth that supreme goodness in me"

When one is pro-active, one also does good, actively caring for and loving others.

One listens to others; one gathers one's people input, hears them out. One really listens to them; one shows deep concern and love to others.

Perhaps at this juncture, it is appropriate and good to ask these questions: Can you think or reflect of the times when you have helped others in need without asking for anything in return. Did you receive some special inner feeling? Did you find that while helping your own needs were met with even less focus or effort? Can you think of the times when your actions were dictated by your conscience and not fear of financial or social retribution? Did things ultimately work out for you better than imagined?

Acting Selflessly and Making Sacrifices

When you give, forget it. When you take, remember (Unknown)

As long as we live, we are to help each other; we are to live, moving from self to other-centredness (Low 2011, p. 94, 95).

To get more than to give is tantamount to stealing. You need "to balance your life by giving more than you receive... The whole scheme of nature is not centered on grabbing but on offering loving, selfless service, which is sacrifice" (Hawley 2006b, p. 77). Such a leader is helpful and works in the interest of the community.

Sacrifice is not self-neglect or abuse; sacrifice is sharing. The *Gita* highlights that it is the spirit of giving that pervades all of creation. We'll be wasting our lives away if we turn our backs to others, ignoring their needs, and if that is so, we are only living uselessly, and in the same way, if leaders are not serving their constituents, then that only defeat the very purpose of leadership; leaders exist to serve their people; each selfless act is an important contribution to the whole or the community.

Being Open

A closed mind is like a closed book. (Chinese proverb)

A closed mind, a psychic prison, is a good thing to lose. (Patrick Kim Cheng Low)

Chopra speaks of wealth consciousness in the field of possibilities. A truly wealthy person's attention is never focused on money alone. If one keeps on thinking of money, about getting more, about losing it though one has enough or is rich, one is basically poor. For the poor think more about money than the rich, and in fact, the poor think of nothing else.

When one reads the *Bhagavad Gita*, one would ask oneself these questions: "Who am I?"; "Why am I here?" "And what is my relationship with the Universe or God?" "Is it possible to live a spiritual life?" As a leader, the *Gita*'s messages would also be resurrected, and one would also ask, "Who am I?", "Am I a good leader?"; "Why am I here in this place (organisation/society or community)?"; "How can I contribute or value-add to the organisation?" and "Is it possible for me to lead well?"

Next, as a leader, one should not discriminate or treat one's people unfairly. One should be open, broad-minded enough to treat people fairly and justly.

To be open is also to be broad-minded enough to accept suggestions and ideas from people. One's mind should be as open as a parachute so it that it works well. To be open also serves as the foundation of creativity; one does not impose self-censure or immediately block ideas. One is willing to accept and bounce ideas, and finally review the applications of the various ideas received.

Interestingly, when our mind is open, we accept——whatever that comes, good or bad, akin to the Christian's "Thy will be done!" And this author loves the *Gita*'s teachings on acceptance—not mere compliance or conformity, but acceptance as a state of mind and way of being—a reception so elevated that one's life forever soars when touched by the magic of it. Most times, this state of mind can lead or lift us to positive thinking which in turn can be beneficial to our well-being and others around us.

Being Positive

Let the waters settle you will see stars and moon mirrored in your Being. (Rumi)

Some of the respondents whom this author spoke to have these to say:

When one is negative, one tends to withdraw from any activity. I think it is obvious that negative thinking and Attention-Deficit Hyperactivity Disorder (ADHD) have something to do with one another or that they are inter-linked; many humans with such disorder develop negative thinking patterns because they easily become frustrated by the challenges and frequent feelings of being overwhelmed. Such a negative outlook makes it even harder for them to manage those challenges and move forward.

That being the case, we humans must instead be proactive so that we don't fall into the psychological trap of being passive and not moving forward or becoming too dependent on others.

Instead of thinking of karma which is source of negative energy, each of us should think and act positively in terms of dharma or duty, and leads a proactive life and leadership. Adopting a proactive life is one way of fighting negative thoughts or fears especially that of rejection or loneliness that all of us, in some ways or the other, are experiencing. So, by practicing positive thinking, humans are able to focus on strengths and accomplishments, which enable them to increase happiness and motivation. This, in turn, allows them to spend more time making progress, and less time feeling down and stuck.

Section Conclusion

So, from Hinduism, one learns pro-activity ("It's my life! I'm in charge!"). One is proactive, one improves and achieves. The leadership lessons include learning that one needs to be in charge of one's life, believing in one's potential, being proactive, becoming a role model and having the passion in one what does. One also cares and loves others.

Mahatma Gandhi and His Leadership Ways

Mohandas Karamchand Gandhi (1869–1948) was born into a Hindu Modh family in Porbandar, Gujarat, India in 1869. The title "Mahatma" (Sanskrit for 'great soul') was given to him by his followers to denote Gandhi's spirituality.

Mahatma Gandhi is also seen as the master strategist and an exemplary leader as well as someone whose ideas and tactics corporate India can emulate (Ganapati 2003). The aim of this paper is to thus analyse the key leadership qualities of the Father of India, the spiritual and political leader of India who led the struggle for Indian independence from the British; Gandhi was indeed admired and empowered by tens of millions of Indians.

The son of Karamchand Gandhi, the *diwan* (Chief Minister) of Porbandar, and Putlibai, Karamchand's fourth wife, a Hindu of the Vaishnava sect, Gandhi grew up with a devout Vaishnava mother and surrounded by Gujarat's Jain influences. From an early age, Gandhi learnt the tenets of non-injury to living beings, vegetarianism, fasting for self-purification, and mutual tolerance between members of various creeds and sects.

Key Leadership Qualities

Albert Einstein once said of Mahatma Gandhi, "Generations to come will scarcely believe that such a one as this, ever in flesh and blood, walked upon this earth." He was a great leader. And the following are the key leadership qualities (with vital leadership lessons extracted) of Mohandas K. Gandhi, the Father of India:

Changing the Rules of the Game
The lesson here is 'differentiate or die' or 'be different and grow'!

Leaders need to stand out!

Making a paradigm shift, Gandhi reinvented the rules of the game to deal with a situation where all the available existing methods had failed. Leaders must accept change, and change accordingly.

A transformational leader, Gandhi broke tradition; in most ways, he was being different. He understood that you cannot fight the British with force. Although resource constraint, this did not bother him. Gandhi decided to change the game in a basically different way. As leader, when leading and accomplishing goals, being different or adopting a different approach is indeed an excellent, if not strategic, move.

A good resistance fighter, he planned resisting the British, asking for a free India. He led a peaceful march, marching some 240 miles with the people to the sea to make salt. To Gandhi, the Indians, the civil resistance were in control; his strategic role was to elicit or provoke a response and continued to do so until the British responded changing the law (the salt tax).

The simple lesson here is that leaders should learn to act in a contrarian way to stand out. Interestingly, one of the greatest compliments that anyone can give to you is to say, "You're so different!" We should talk differently, act differently and perform differently. As a leader, there should be something different about you. We must stand out! (If there is not something unique or different in your leadership or life, you should perhaps re-assess yourself.)

Of interest, DuBrin (1993) speaks of cultivating lower-ranking people as a way to impress in order to stand out. Here, we can say that Mahatma Gandhi developed the common people's touch, cultivating their trust in him, and in this sense, they were impressed as well as connected to him, and clearly, he stood out.

Moreover, Gandhi's unassuming and humble posture together with his simplicity becomes his unique selling proposition (USP) or positioning. Differentiation can be applied by leaders as a way or a process of building personal branding. Differentiation, with Gandhi's simplicity and single-mindedness of purpose, is a winning formula and even applicable in business; leaders should emulate and pursue such differentiation strategy or approach.

Realising the Power of the Common People

Where there is love, there is life. (Mahatma Gandhi)

Unleashing the power of ordinary people and inspiring women and men in India to fight under a unifying goal, he aimed at a common agenda: Freedom or *Poorna Swaraj*, and that were the motivation. Here, the lessons learnt can be that India needs to basically change the way it can grow. The Indians have to learn a new way; perhaps corporate India has learnt from Gandhi the clarity of goal(s) or the need to make the paradigm shift.

Gandhi was able to establish the rapport with his people. Bearing in mind at that time over 80% of India lived in her villages and they were poor, illiterate, diseased and discouraged. Distances in India are great and communication poor. Tagore puts it that in the 'correct grammatical whine' would freedom be won. 'No paper contributions will ever give us self-government', Tagore told an illustrious assemblage of notables and students at the opening of the Hindu University Central College in Benares in Feb 1916. 'No amount of speeches will make us fit for self-government. It is only our conduct that will fit us for it.' Many maharajas and rajas were in the audience giving an exhibition of jewelry.

Village uplift was Gandhi's first freedom and peasant liberation from poverty and destitution could not be the achievement of the small upper class or a gift of the foreign power. The peasants really had to win it. For Gandhi, he got rid of western clothing; he was himself naked except for a lion-cloth, the clothes of a peasant and established his rapport with them. Gandhi was the padi-field, the working arm, in the marketplace and not in the ivory tower! He spoke the lingo and identified himself with the masses.

Besides, in understanding the masses and the prevailing local conditions, Gandhi took it that happiness (for the people) did not come with things, even twentieth century things but rather it can come from work and pride in what one does. He strongly believed that poverty, India's scourge and the worst form of violence—can be eradicated when the local skills of the villagers were revived.

Inspiring and Motivating the Followers

Leaders don't create followers, they create more leaders. (Tom Peters)

Gandhiji really knew how to inspire and motivate the masses.

Gandhi's well-known leadership secret is that of—to paraphrase Rudyard Kipling's *If* poem, he walked with the crowd and kept his virtue. The Mahatma walked with the kings and did not lose the common touch. Believing passionately in freedom and the right of self-determination for the Indians as well as being in touch with the common people, Mahatma Gandhi could inspire and move them. Establishing a clear relationship with the people, Gandhi toured across India, leading all the major movements personally and by holding various public meetings; and listening and talking to the people repeatedly. In this way, Gandhi always managed to be accessible, and stay connected to the common people. These coincide with what Low's (2006b, p. 84) study has affirmed, that is, indeed when leaders are "personable, friendly and communicable", they motivate their people.

Of great significance, the Mahatma showed that every individual Indian matters, and even (s)he can make a difference and bring the British Empire to its knees. Gandhi's leadership ways factor in the followers and more importantly, the local conditions involved. Follower-centric, the Mahatma touched the ordinary people, and his leadership style, when applied, can be said to make even the lowest people in the organisation believe in the organisation's cause (or goals) and the significance of their contributions towards it (them). In business, empowerment is all about making sure everyone is connected to the organisation's goals, and Gandhi has a way of doing that. His ways ensure that everyone in the cause is connected to the goal.

Embracing and Practising Non-Violence

Non-violence is a weapon of the strong. (Mahatma Gandhi).

Gandhi held the view that the principle of non-violence (*ahimsa*) should be adhered. He also practised (*satyagraha*). "In *satyagraha*, the cause has to be just and clear as well as the means. The ideal of *satyagraha* is not meant for the select few—the saint and the seer only, it is meant for all." (Gandhi, cited in Merton 1996, p. 79). He believed that non-violence is impossible without humility. If one has pride and egoism, there is no non-violence. Besides, non-violent action, to Gandhi, is "the vindication of truth not by infliction of suffering on the opponent but on one's self" (Fischer 1954, p. 35).

Gandhi firmly believed that non-violence was actually more natural to man than violence. His doctrine is anchored on the confidence in man's natural disposition to love.

"In the empire of non-violence, every true thoughts count, every true voice has its full value" (Gandhi, cited in Merton 1996, p. 78). If one just takes the name of non-violence yet carries a sword in one's heart, then such an act is not only hypocritical and dishonest, but also, cowardly. Indeed, one should truly think, feel and practise non-violence.

Gandhi highlighted that "an eye for eye only ends up making the whole world blind." Violence, to the Mahatma, is accordingly the expression of weakness and confusion. A weak person, inclined to violence, acts justly only by accident. It is the non-violent person and by expression, the non-violent society which is commonly fair and just. Therefore, a truly free and just society should be constructed on a foundation of non-violence.

Interestingly enough, he fasted not against the British since one cannot fast against a tyrant; to Gandhi, a fast had to be unselfish. Gandhi fasted for his people for a bond and a chord of sympathy and close relationships existed between the Indians and him. (Gandhiji fasted because the Hindus closed the temples to the untouchables and treated them badly.) Since a fast was not for personal gain, it was for public benefit, and the public would thus see and be affected (Fischer 1954).

One can assess that basically Mahatma Gandhi's philosophy of non-violence and the practice of non-violent action are anchored in compassion as he said, "Whenever you are confronted with an opponent. Conquer him with love." This is absolutely beautiful as a leadership principle and practice, more so, when assessed in the light of today's world of frequent terrorist attacks—New York's 911 terrorist attack in 2001, the Bali bombings in 2002, the London bombings in 2005, the Mumbai's bombings in 2006, and other recent ugly terrorist incidents (Low 2008b).

Interestingly, Gandhi's principle of non-violence (*ahimsa*) and the practice of non-violence action (*satyagraha*) can be said to be echoed in the words of General George C. Marshall's (the then American Secretary of State at the time of Gandhi's death in 1948), "Mahatma Gandhi has become the spokesman for the conscience of all mankind. He was a man who made humility and simple truth more powerful than Empires".

Being Empathetic, Understanding the Needs of the People

Your suffering is my suffering and your happiness is my happiness. (The Buddha)

The ordinary people touch enables leaders to connect with the masses. And the people trust such a leader. The ordinary Indians—farmers and workers can identify with him.

Leaders should emulate Gandhi's leadership ways in terms of being empathetic and understanding the needs of their people. Such a leadership quality and soft skill seem to be particularly important in today's collaborative organisations. The days are over when a hard-driving manager, without listening, can run through or bulldoze over others to get results and output. Today's successful leaders are not the rough and tough men and women of the past, but those men and women who know how to get people to like and trust them. (Daft 2008).

A people's leader, Mahatma Gandhi also led by example which brings us to the next point. As the late Richard Nixon, the American President once mentioned, "theorists like to treat power as if it were an abstraction. Leaders know better: Power anchors them in reality... Those with power have to keep an eye firmly on the results, the impact, the effects. Leaders deal with the concrete" (Nixon 1982, p. 340). And what better is there than can be more influential than to be...

Leading by Example

If you actions inspire others to dream more, learn more, do more and become more, you are a leader. (John Quincy Adams)

There exists leaders who lived for their own selfish reasons, and they may also not do what they preach, living in comfort and luxury, or even worse, pampering themselves at the expense of the vast (citizen) majority or followers.

Gandhi, on the other hand, lived in voluntary poverty, even making his own clothes and marching along side his fellow Indian citizens. He urged all Indians to wear *khadi* (home-spun cloth) as part of a boycott of foreign made products, so he made his own clothes to wear. A people's leader, Mahatma Gandhi led by example. For the Mahatma, to lead and understand the masses, he felt that he needed to live and be like one of them, hence, he dressed like the common man, and just with a lion-cloth.

Gandhi opposed the British Salt Tax which he knew was wrong, and in spite of fears of being arrested, he marched along with the protesting Indians nearly 250 miles to Dandi.

As a practitioner of non-violence (*ahimsa*), he swore to speak the truth and advocated that others do the same. Eating simple vegetarian food, Gandhi undertook long fasts as a means of self-purification as well as a social protest.

Gandhi did not approve violent actions, and indeed he expressed against violent British rule and the violent Indian reactions. And when he thought that his non-violent campaign might become violent, he called off all activities to help stop any violence in spite of opposition from the Congress. What more, Gandhi never used violence himself.

A critical leadership lesson here is that leading by example gives high credibility and supreme legitimacy to leaders. With the initial credibility established through his work and movements in South Africa, Gandhi's followers already had great honour with high confident desires for him because of what he could achieve in South Africa. And his non-violent methods were also very well respected within India. Besides, Gandhi gained high credibility by leading through example; overall, he was immensely recognised and thrived as a servant of the Indian society, empowering the general public.

Modern leadership lessons and relevance here include the abolition of and fight against terrorism and love for the environment. There exists a strong need for humankind to show compassion, preserve the bio-diversity and promote the care for nature. The fauna and flora species need to be preserved for future generations, with the love for plants and animals nurtured, and our earth's eco-system up-kept.

Being Pro-Active

Wisdom is knowing what to do next; Skill is knowing how not do it, and Virtue is doing it. (David Starr Jordan)

A man is the sum of his actions, of what he has done, of what he can do, nothing else. (Mahatma Gandhi)

Although this Gandhi's key quality appears obvious and seemingly needless to say, it is worth stressing it here. Gandhi once said, "Be the change you want to see in the world." He also said that "whatever you do may seem insignificant, but it is most important that you do it." Besides, "you may never know what results come of your action, but if you do nothing there will be no result." (Gandhi).

Rather than being passive, leaders, in fact, should serve, and in that aspect, Gandhi's way of leadership can be said to be both proactive "There was nothing passive about (Gandhi's) motivation or actions," he was "driven by fierce desire to create a just environment, not only for (his) people, but for all humankind" (Times 1999, cited in Low and Theyagu 2003).

What then are the leadership lessons? Here, leadership is action. Leaders get things done. And it should also be noted that confidence and assurance indeed generates action. To this author, Gandhi held that the view that once we are confident and assured, we become capable and achieving. Confidence is thinking one can do or accomplish something, and that serves as a springboard, generating action (Fig. 6.2).

Gandhi once said, "Men often become what they believe themselves to be. If I believe I cannot do something, it makes me incapable of doing it. But when I believe I can, then I acquire the ability to do it even if I didn't have it in the beginning." Such an approach can be seen as positive as one can do anything if one believes one can. One's self-efficacy is also built up; "I think, I can, therefore I can, and I accomplish!" For Gandhi, "nothing is impossible", and this keynote, rang with faith in self, people and God (Gandhi cited in Fischer 1954, p. 64).

Avoiding Ego, Thinking Not of Himself but More of the Audience, and Inspiring People with a Clear, Compelling Message

When communicating, Gandhi avoided displaying ego and thought more of his audience; his message was "clear, simple and precise" (Maier and Kourdi 2010). Ensuring that his audience was motivated, simplicity was important to him. He wanted the British to leave yet he did not want violence although much hatred existed among the Indian populace against the British rule.

Mahatma ('Great Soul') Gandhi, the founding father of free India. The Mahatma led 350 million Indians to freedom from 300 years of British rule. And the Indian fakir managed to do this by means of non-violence

Fig. 6.2 Mahatma Gandhi in loin cloth, as drawn by the author

Most of Gandhi's speeches can, overall, be considered as motivational, inspirational and persuasive; they were normally distinguished by "eloquence, power and humanity... with excellent use of language and imagery" (Maier and Kourdi 2010, p. 100).

Being Service-Orientated

Trust movement. Life happens at the level of events, not of words. Trust movement. (Alfred Adler)

The best way to find yourself is to lose yourself in the service of others. (Mahatma Gandhi)

Gandhi's pro-active ways are also service-orientated. ("The best way to find yourself is to lose yourself in the service of others." Gandhi)

Leaders serve and not to be served. And leaders attend to the needs of the followers.

Being Magnanimous, Big-Hearted and Compassionate

Mahatma Gandhi was magnanimous. This author once read from somewhere this anecdote, showing such a leadership quality of the Mahatma; it goes like this: A mother and her son once visited Gandhi. And believing her son's health was at risk due to high sugar intake, and not being able to persuade her son to reduce his sugar intake, the mother hoped that Gandhi could convince the child to do so. However, Gandhi asked that the woman and son return the following week. Upon their return, Gandhi simply said, "Don't eat sugar. It's not good for you." The puzzled mother asked why he had not given this advice earlier. Gandhi smiled, saying, "Last week, I too was eating sugar."

The point here is that Gandhi lived up to a trustworthy model; indeed leaders may not be perfect people, but more critically, they big-heartedly acknowledge their mistakes, vulnerabilities or just plain humanity; and even if they make mistakes, they pick themselves up, forge on and move forward.

Gandhi "never sought to humiliate or defeat the whites in South Africa or the British in India. He wanted to convert them" (Fischer 1954, p. 35). To him, "power is of two kinds. One is obtained by the fear of punishment and the other by acts of love. Power based on love is a thousand times more effective and permanent then the one derived from fear of punishment" (Patel 2010). Although fighting against the British colonialists, he did not hate them. An interesting case in point is indicated in (May 1921) Lord Reading's, the then Viceroy of India's writing to Edwin Montague, the Secretary of State for India in London:

> Gandhi came to visit me in a white dhoti and cap, woven on a spinning wheel, with bare feet and legs, and my first impression was that I should have passed him by in the street without a second look at him. When he talks, the impression is different. He is direct and expressed himself well in excellent English, with a fine appreciation of the value of the words he uses. His religious views are, I believe, genuinely held, and he is convinced to the point almost bordering on fanaticism that non-violence and love will give India its independence and enable it to withstand the British Government. His religious and moral views are admirable. Our conversations were of the frankest; he was supremely courteous with manners of distinction. He held in every way to his word in the various discussions we had... Altogether you will judge that I liked him, and I believe there are possibilities in the future...

A key leadership lesson from the Gandhi model, with a need to practice and grow, is the need to empathize with others and one's followers. To the author, this is the first step towards compassion. Start by imagining the sufferings of a loved one. Understand their experiences, their pain, the feelings and what they go through, and why they would react the way they would. By doing this several times, one then can develop a skill that can be applied to others. For every person one sees, one can attempt to understand what he or she is going through. Once this skill has been developed, one can then grow the other half of compassion. One then acts on one's understanding to help others, relieving their pain, giving comfort, acting with kindness and making the world a better and happier place to live.

Section Concluding Remarks

All in all, in leading and inspiring, the Mahatma showed that non-violence, gentleness, love and compassion would triumph—as always.

And he was indeed a truly great leader who led India's struggle for freedom. Although an assassin's bullet ended Mahatma Gandhi's life prematurely in 1948, his life, thinking and exemplary acts remain a brilliant example today. His example and teachings have helped to reshape a country while enriching the lives of millions.

N. D. Modi

Narendra Damodardas Modi has been the Prime Minister of India since 26 May 2014.

The Prime Minister of India is the head of government and leader of the executive branch of the Government of India. The Prime Minister is also the chief advisor to the President of India and head of the Council of Ministers. They can be a member of any of the two houses of Parliament (the Lok Sabha or the Rajya Sabha), but has to be the leader of the political party, having a majority in the Lok Sabha.

Indian Business Leaders

In general, Indian corporate leaders can be said to possess these characteristics:

Resilient and Adaptive Indian Business Leaders

Indian business leaders can be said to be preoccupied with internal management, flexibility and organizational culture and long-term strategic vision, more so, being in a family ownership structure and competitive, entrepreneurship/risk-taking culture. The leaders do realise that the strict regulatory climate and challenging infrastructure environment in India necessitate businesses and leaders the capacity to be resilient, adaptive and moving forward in the face of adversities.

Doing Business in a Limited Resources and Volatile Environment

In a complex, often-volatile environment with few resources and much red tape, Indian business leaders have learned to rely on their wits to circumvent the innumerable hurdles they recurrently confront. Take, for example, they would improvise and adapt outdated equipment nursed along a generation past its expected lifetime with retrofitted spare parts and jerry-rigged solutions. Indian business leaders think broadly and act pragmatically, setting grand agendas and then repeatedly testing through trial and error what works and what does not. Emphasising improvisation and adaptability, they stress sideways movements into areas with promising prospects, building a model of what should work by witnessing what does work (http://www.europeanbusinessreview.com/?p=1951). Most CEOs are said to believe that their firms' competitive advantage lay in their high-performance culture, customer focus, innovation and entrepreneurship, and low cost.

Caring and Motivating Indian Workforce as Top Priority in Business

Indian business leaders see their firms as organic enterprises where sustaining employee morale and building company culture are treated as critical obligations and foundations of their success (Useem et al. 2010). They care more about motivating their employees and setting an example. Indian business leaders put people as their centre of the thought process. They think about the people's welfare; their future and their opportunities for self-realisation. This is because India can grow, prosper, flourish only if their people grow, prosper, flourish. People are viewed as assets to be developed, not costs to be reduced; as sources of creative ideas and pragmatic solutions; and as bringing leadership to their own place in the company. Creating ever-stronger capabilities in the workforce is a driving objective. One can thus see that their purchasing power, economic strength and their marketplace all depends on the prosperity of the people.

Section Conclusion

Overall, to do business with the Indians/Indian business leaders, there is a need to get to know them first and relate with them.

And it is good to note that these days in India, more and more women leaders are in the business and corporate scene. Whether in rural or in urban areas, women also have empowered themselves (Ramani 2005). At times, through micro-credits, they get together, organise themselves and run home-based cooperatives and businesses, working cooperatively and earning incomes as well as helping the community.

Checkpoint

Leadership in India

Let us reflect and think about it.

Leadership, Corporate Culture and the Hindu Trinity: Brahma, Vishnu and Shiva

1. Ask what are the role(s) am I playing in terms of:
   - Starting the corporate culture of the company
   - Sustaining and Keeping the corporate culture Alive
   - Eliminating or minimising bad corporate practices

The Essential Leadership Wisdom of the Bhagavad Gita

1. How can I improve my leadership ways in terms of
   - Loving
   - Following your *Dharma*, and leading well
   - Knowing your vision
   - Moving from ego to divinity; moving from self to other-centeredness
   - Fostering team leadership and team building
   - Growing resilience
   - Being disciplined
   - Having spiritual ballast
   - (Not just doing but at most times) reflecting and taking stock!
2. What are the other pointers that I have gathered here that I can apply to improve my leadership ways?

Hanuman, the Monkey Deity: Leadership Lessons Learnt

1. What are the pointers that I have gathered here that I can apply to improve my leadership ways?

The Buddha and Leadership Lessons and Relevance

What can I do to better myself in terms of these qualities?

- Protecting the people (followers), bringing peace and harmony
- Being altruistic
- Being compassionate and contributing to the society
- Being humble
- Collaborating and being positive
- Being objective
- Achieving mastery
- Being (adopting) mindfulness
- Removing ego, listening well and being more creative
- Avoiding pain and sufferings (creating happiness in our own setting)
- Being the salt of the world

Proactivity and Hinduism

Anthony Robbins once said that "quality questions create a quality life. Successful people ask better questions, and as a result, they get better answers." And in applying the Section's lessons: Pro-activity And Hinduism, one should ask oneself the following questions. Are you:

- Taking charge?
- Believing in your potential?
- Becoming a role model?
- Being passionate?
- Investing time and effort in people and relationships?
- Being practical?
- Practicing enough?
- Doing good?
- Doing good enough?
- Caring others enough?
- Caring for others actively?
- Acting selflessly and making sacrifices

Mahatma Gandhi and His Leadership Ways

1. What have I learnt about Mahatma Gandhi and his leadership ways?
2. As leader, do you stand out? Are you being different?
3. In what ways and how can you be different?
4. How can I improve my leadership ways in terms of:
   - Changing the rules of the game
   - Realising the power of the common people
   - Inspiring and motivating the followers
   - Embracing and practising non-violence
   - Leading by example
   - Being pro-active
   - Being service-orientated
   - Being magnanimous, big-hearted and compassionate

Self-esteem Booster Activities/Exercises

1. Each morning the minute when you get up, repeat to yourself at least three times: "I am a unique and wonderful person."

Also, write it down and tape it to the mirror. Read it while you brush your teeth!

Indian Business Leaders

Let us review the section on Indian Business Leaders and ask: what we can learn from them in terms of:

- Being resilient and adaptive Indian business?
- Doing business in a limited resources and volatile environment?
- Caring and motivating the workforce as top priority in business?

References

About.com: Hinduism. (2008a). *Vishnu the Godhead*. About.com: Hinduism. Accessed July 8, 2008, from http://hinduism.about.com/
About.com: Hinduism. (2008b). *The presiding deity of peace*. About.com: Hinduism. Accessed July 9, 2008, from http://hinduism.about.com/od/godsgoddesses/p/vishnu.htm
Buddha Dharma Education Association: BDEA/BuddhaNet. (2008). *A five minute introduction*. Buddhist Studies, Buddha Dharma Education Association & BuddhaNet. Accessed November 13, 2008, from http://www.buddhanet.net/e-learning/5minbud.htm
Caryl, C. (2008, March 10). Armies of enlightened. *Newsweek*, pp. 18–21.
Chin Kung, Master. (2002). *Heart of a Buddha*. Singapore.
Conway, T. (2008) *Inspiring quotes on spiritual realization, leadership, excellence, character, virtue, service, work-ethic, and more*. Rare Leadership.Com. Accessed October 11, 2008, from http://www.rare-leadership.org/leadership_quotes.html
Daft, R. L. (2004). *Organizational theory and design*. Mason, OH: Thomson South-Western.
Daft, R. L. (2008). *The leadership experience*. Mason, OH: South-Western Cengage Learning.
DuBrin, A. J. (1993). *Stand out!* Englewood Cliffs, NJ: Prentice-Hall.
DuBrin, A. J. (2007). *Fundamentals of organizational behavior*. Canada: Thomson South-Western.
Easwaran, E. (2007). *The Dhammapada* (2nd ed.). Canada: Nilgiri Press. Translator.
Field, L. M. (2007). *Business and the Buddha*. Boston, MA: Wisdom.
Fischer, L. (1954). *Gandhi, his life and message for the world. A mentor book*. New York, NY: Penguin Group.
Ganapati, P. (2003, April 11). *India Inc. rediscovers Mahatma Gandhi, Business*. Rediff India Abroad. Accessed January 13, 2010, from http://www.rediff.com/money/2003/apr/11spec2.htm
Ganesan, N. (2002). Governance: Its complexity and evolution. In D. da Cunha (Ed.), *Singapore in the new millennium* (pp. 1–25). Singapore: Institute of Southeast Asian Studies.
Gruzalski, B. (2000). *On the Buddha*. Boston, MA: Thomson Learning.
Hart, M. (1992). *The 100*. London: Simon & Schuster.
Hawley, J. (2006a). *Essential wisdom of the Bhagavad Gita*. Canada: New World Library.
Hawley, J. (2006b). *Essential wisdom of the Bhagavad Gita*. Novato, CA: New World Library.
Hsing Yun, Master. (2001). *Buddhism pure and simple*. West Linn, CA: Weatherhill.
Instilling Goodness School. (2008). *Basic teachings of Buddha, following the Buddha's footsteps*. Ukiah, CA: Instilling Goodness School. Accessed November 3, 2008, from http://online.sfsu.edu/~rone/Buddhism/footsteps.htm
Ivancevich, K., & Matteson, M. T. (2008). *Organizational behavior and management*. New York, NY: McGraw-Hill Irwin.
Kornfield, J. (1993). *Teachings of Buddha*. Boston, MA/London: Shambala.
Low, K. C. P. (2001). *The power of relationships*. Singapore: BusinesscrAFT™ Consultancy.

Low, K. C. P. (2002a). *Strategic customer management*. Singapore: BusinesscrAFT™ Consultancy.

Low, K. C. P. (2002b). *Corporate culture and values: Perceptions of corporate leaders of co-operatives in Singapore*. Unpublished PhD thesis, International Graduate School of Management, University of South Australia.

Low, K. C. P. (2003). *Team success*. Singapore: BusinesscrAFT™ Consultancy and Humber Lincoln Resources.

Low, K. C. P. (2005a). Towards a framework & typologies of Singapore corporate cultures. *Management Development Journal of Singapore, 13*(1), 46–75.

Low, K. C. P. (2005b). Fraud prevention, the corporate cultural way—A Singapore case study. *Journal of Contemporary Business Issues, 13*(1), 31–39.

Low, Kim Cheng P. (2005c). Values that contribute to companies' success—Perceptions of Singapore corporate leaders. In: *Effective executive* (pp. 45–55). The Institute of Chartered Financial Analyst India: ICFAI University Press.

Low, K. C. P. (2006a). Crisis management—Can core values be considered as a built-in safety net? The Singapore case. *Insights to a Changing World, 2006*(3), 133–150.

Low, K. C. P. (2006b). Motivation, the Chinese leadership way in Singapore's small and medium companies. *The Icfaian Journal of Organizational Behavior, 1*, 80–90.

Low, K. C. P. (2008a). Leadership thoughts to ponder—Some classic sins of leadership. *Leadership and Organizational Management Journal, 2008*(4), 65–75.

Low, K. C. P. (2008b). Counter-terrorism and the theory of influential leadership—It's the people who should be swayed. *Leadership and Organizational Management Journal, 2008*(2), 117–140.

Low, K. C. P. (2008c). Leadership, corporate culture and the Hindu Trinity—Brahma, Vishnu & Shiva. *Business Journal for Entrepreneurs, 2008*(4), 37–45.

Low, K. C. P. (2009a). How to lead in today's context? What leadership skills set do we need? *Leadership and Organizational Management Journal, 2009*(1), 48–56.

Low, K. C. P. (2009b). *Corporate culture and values: Perceptions of corporate leaders of co-operatives in Singapore*. London/Buchanan, NY: VDM-Verlag.

Low, K. C. P. (2010a). *Successfully negotiating in Asia*. Heidelberg: Springer.

Low, K. C. P. (2010b). Leading globally—What makes a successful global leader in today's turbulent world?. In *E-Leader, Chinese American Scholars Association: CASA Conference*, Tallinn, Estonia 8–10 June 2010. Accessed June 30, 2009, from http://www.g-casa.com/conferences/tallinn/pdf%20papers/Low.pdf

Low, K. C. P. (2011). The fundamental leadership wisdom of the *Bhagavad Gita*. *Business Journal for Entrepreneurs, 2011*(1), 90–100.

Low, K. C. P., & Theyagu, D. (2003). *Developing true leadership potential*. Singapore: The Publishing Consultant.

Maier, S., & Kourdi, J. (2010). *The 100*. London: Marshall Cavendish Business.

Marchand, P. (2009). *The life of Hanuman*. Sanatansociety.com. Accessed April 6, 2009, from http://www.sanatansociety.org/indian_epics_and_stories/the_life_of_hanuman.htm

McDaniel, C., & Gitman, L. J. (2008). *The future of business*. China: Thomson South-Western.

Merton, T. (1996). *Gandhi on non-violence*. New York, NY: Shambala Pocket Classics.

Mullins, L. J. (1995). *Management and organizational behaviour*. Singapore: Pitman Publishing.

Nahavandi, A. (2009). *The art and science of leadership*. New York, NY: Pearson Education International.

Nixon, R. (1982). *Leaders*. New York, NY: A Warner Communications Company.

Osho. (1996). *The master is a mirror*. Delhi: Diamond Pocket Books.

Patel, S. (2010). Mahatma Gandhi's 5 teachings to bring about world Peace. *Zen habits, simple productivity*. Accessed January 16, 2010, from http://zenhabits.net/2008/09/mahatma-gandhis-5-teachings-to-bring-about-world-peace/

Ramani, V. V. (Ed.). (2005). *Women empowerment*. India: The ICFAI University Press.

Robbins, A. (1994). *Giant steps*. New York, NY: Simon and Schuster.

Robbins, S. P. (2005). *Organizational behavior* (11th ed.). Upper Saddle River, NJ: Pearson Prentice-Hall.

Rudra Centre. (2007). *Lord Brahma*. Rudra Centre. Accessed July 5, 2008, from http://www. rudraksha-ratna.com/hindu_trinity.php

Schein, E. H. (1996). *Strategic pragmatism, the culture of Singapore's economic development board*. Cambridge, MA: Massachusetts Institute of Technology.

Stoltz, P. G. (1997). *Adversity quotient: Turning obstacles into opportunities*. Hoboken, NJ: Wiley.

Tattoo Design Directory. (2009). Hanuman the monkey god. *Tattoo designs and symbols*. Accessed April 6, 2009, from http://www.vanishingtattoo.com/tattoos_designs_symbols_hanuman.htm

The Brunei Times. (2008a, September 18). Ministry recalls food products of 3 brands. *The Brunei Times*, p. 2.

The Brunei Times. (2008b, September 21). Ban on China's milk products. *The Brunei Times*, p. 1, 9, 10.

Thinkexist. (2008). *Dalai Lama quotes*. thinkexist.com. Accessed November 17, 2008, from http:// thinkexist.com/quotes/dalai_lama/

Useem, M., Capelli, P., Singh, H., & Singh, J. (2010). *The India way: How India's top business leaders are revolutionizing management*. Boston, MA: Harvard Business Press.

Velloor, R. (2009, January 8). Indian software boss quits, admits faking US$1 billion in profits. *The Straits Times*, p. 1.

Weiss, J. W. (1996). *Organizational behavior and change*. New York, NY: West Publishing Company.

Zachary, W. B., & Kuzuhara, L. W. (2005). *Organizational behavior*. Mason, OH: Thomson South-Western.

Zenger, J. H., & Folkman, J. (2004). *The handbook of leaders*. New York, NY: McGraw-Hill.

Websites

Hanuman, Microsoft® Encarta® Online Encyclopedia. (2008). Accessed April 7, 2009, from http://encarta.msn.com ©1997–2008 Microsoft Corporation.

Thinkexist.com. Accessed January 14, 2010, from http://thinkexist.com/quotes/mahatma_gandhi/ 4.html

Accessed August 24, 2011, from http://www.europeanbusinessreview.com/?p=1951

Leadership in Japan

7

Introduction

This chapter presents and examines the leadership wisdom of Japan. The chapter intends to offer key leadership pointers for effective strategies for succeeding in business/corporate world, conflict, and life. The sections that follow will examine:

Leading, the Samurai Way

Zen and Leadership

Nemoto's Key Principles of Leadership

Leading, the Matsushita Way

Akio Morita and His Leadership Ways (Sony)

Soichiro Honda and His Leadership Ways

Team Leadership Lessons from Shinkansin, the Japanese Bullet Train

Leading, the Samurai Way

> The flower of flowers is the Sakura – Cherry Blossom. The Samurai is the man among men.
> (Japanese proverb)

The Samurai is a term for the military nobility of pre-industrial and agrarian Japan. From the Samurais, the warrior class (known as "bushi", hence "bushido"), one learns the art of being disciplined in growing or perfecting oneself. One learns to outthink, outmanoeuvre and out-win one's enemies or rivals. Low (2010a, p. 121) speaks of the Samurai negotiators, attributing these characteristics to them:

> Strongly Confucian in nature, bushido stressed concepts such as loyalty to one's master, self-discipline and respectful and ethical behaviour. So, a samurai negotiator will negotiate, getting the job done with much equanimity while achieving the goals. Besides, there will be mutual gains for both parties.

© Springer International Publishing AG 2018
K.C.P. Low, *Leading Successfully in Asia*,
https://doi.org/10.1007/978-3-319-71347-2_7

In the past, as skilled martial artists, the Samurais used bows and arrows and swords, and they could kill with bare hands too. They usually fought alone, one on one.

As mentioned by Low (2010a), the Samurais follow the code of Bushido, a set of written rules which, in most ways, builds their discipline. Interestingly, Samurai teachings can still be found today in modern day Japanese society with Kendo (meaning the way of the sword), a form of martial arts.

In the Japanese sense, the Samurais do not have to look good or be physically strong in appearance; he does not have to be tall or heavily muscled to be strong. In fact, he can be barely five feet tall, seemingly weak and even handicapped; and females too can be Samurais. In the Japanese context, being big size or physically powerful is not equated with power and strength.

Samurais are expected to behave properly regardless of his personal circumstances, hence the common Japanese saying "Even though he has not eaten, he wields his toothpick (like a lord)" arises. What more, Samurais ensure that they carry their honour and dignity through their everyday living and example. That is more persuasive. Examples are better than mere words and speeches. A Samurai is said to be very careful, and that everything that comes from the mouth of the Samurai should be considered and guarded. To him, right or wrong are nothing but good and evil, there is a need to refrain from wrong and cleave to what is essentially right. A Samurai upholds justice and would not act in a bullying manner to on who is weaker than him or her, that is, an act that a brave Samurai never does. Though the Samurai can be deadly in combat yet he is gentle and compassionate to the weak, the aged and the children.

Samurais also adopt the practices of Zen Buddhism which is discussed in the next section. To be more specific and detailed, the virtues and values of Samurais are derived in part from Confucianism (A gentleman's code), in part from Zen Buddhism, and in part, Shintoism; and they include:

Rectitude—integrity (*Gi*) [Here, it is taken that a person who lacks gravity or integrity does not inspire respect.]
Courage—bravery (*Yu*)
Benevolence—compassion (*Jin*)
Respect—reverence (*Rei*)
Honesty—sincerity (*Makoto*)
Honour—nobility (*Meiyo*)
Loyalty—faithfulness; devotion (*Chugi*)

And here is the Samurai Creed:

I have no parents; I make the Heavens and the Earth my parents.
I have no home; I make the *Tan T'ien* my home.
I have no divine power; I make honesty my Divine Power.
I have no means; I make Docility my means.
I have no magic power; I make personality my Magic Power.
I have neither life nor death; I make A Um my Life and Death.

I have no body; I make Stoicism my Body.

I have no eyes; I make The Flash of Lightning my eyes.

I have no ears; I make Sensibility my Ears.

I have no limbs; I make Promptitude my Limbs.

I have no laws; I make Self-Protection my Laws.

I have no strategy; I make the Right to Kill and the Right to Restore Life my Strategy.

I have no designs; I make Seizing the Opportunity by the Forelock my Designs.

I have no miracles; I make Righteous Laws my Miracle.

I have no principles; I make Adaptability to all circumstances my Principle.

I have no tactics; I make Emptiness and Fullness my Tactics.

I have no talent; I make Ready Wit my Talent.

I have no friends; I make my Mind my Friend.

I have no enemy; I make Incautiousness my Enemy.

I have no armour; I make Benevolence my Armour.

I have no castle; I make Immovable Mind my Castle.

I have no sword; I make No Mind my Sword. (http://victorian.fortunecity.com/duchamp/410/bsamurai.html)

It is the duty of the Samurai to be vigilant and careful at all times. Samurais are bold and courageous, and this is reinforced by the spirit of detachment, and indeed, they attach no importance to leaving this life. They are ever always in the state of preparation; never for a moment would they be without a short sword. In the past when out, leaving the gate, they took it and acted as if the enemy was in sight.

Samurais learn a lot, and they are diligent to learn and study whenever they have any spare time, striving to gain a thorough knowledge. In this aspect, it is good to follow the Samurai way. And as Rohn (1996) points out that all leaders are readers, we need to learn from others:

- Through published literature such as books and audio tapes or video tapes/CDs/DVDs.
- By listening to the wisdom and folly of others.
- Through observations of winners and losers.

More importantly, a leader's conduct is very critical since it plays an important role in the destiny of the daimyos (counties), countries and determines the fortunes of so many lives. A Samurai must resolve to avoid mistakes by regular and rigorous examination of his conscience. If as a leader one should adopt the Samurai way, one needs to constantly ask oneself whether one's policies are correct, and whether one has judged one's capabilities correctly. This day to day examination is something one should never neglect. This is akin to what Konosuke Matsushita referred to as "self-interrogation" (Matsushita 1991, p. 71).

However, Matsushita did indicate that not everything can be clarified by soul-searching alone, and when in doubt ask for second opinion. Explain your viewpoint, then ask for the other person's opinion. By listening to what the other person says and thinking it over one should be able to keep mistakes to a minimum. To this author, that is the application of Confucian wisdom when one is aware of what one knows, to maintain that one knows it; and when one does not know, to acknowledge one's ignorance.

Zen and Leadership

All things share the same breath - the beast, the tree, the man… the air shares its spirit with all the life it supports. (Attributed to Chief Seattle but actually written in 1972 by screenwriter Ted Perry)

Silence is an empty space, space is the home of the awakened mind. (The Buddha)

Zen (Chan in China, Seon in Korea and Thien in Vietnam) is one of the several forms of Buddhism. Zen is actually a form of the Mahayana Buddhism. Interestingly, the name *Zen* is Japanese, deriving from the Chinese Cha'an-na which is a corruption from the Buddhist Dhyana, meaning "meditation".

In China, the teachings of Lao Tzu, the founder of Taoism and best known as the author of the *Tao Teh Ching*, influenced the mystic experience of the Buddha's enlightenment. So while the seed of Zen came from India, it grew in China, being transformed there. However, it did not reach full blossoming until it came, with Chinese (Mahayana) Buddhism, to Japan. Here, Zen was crystallized into a system, although its adherents insisted that it could not be taught, and argued that there could be no dependence on explanations, sermonizing, and on any formal creed or rituals (Gunes 2010).

Zen practitioners prefer relying on the spirit and meaning of the teachings, not on the words. They also prefer relying on the teachings, not on the personality of the teacher and relying on real wisdom, not superficial interpretation, and overall, relying on the essence of one's pure Wisdom Mind, and not on judgmental perceptions.

Zen is becoming popular and this popularity particularly outside of Asia can perhaps be better explained by the universality of its tenet that humbly emptying oneself leads one to go beyond oneself to be aware that all are interconnected, by its rejection of intellectualism that is refreshing in Western culture which makes high demands on the intellect at every moment.

Zen is also appealing in terms of its simple and natural aesthetic.

The air we breathe is very important; all of us breathe from the same air, the very oxygen that gives us life, and this air connects all of us, big or small, humans or animals. We should always be grateful and appreciative of the air we breathe, so also should we learn to appreciate everything in the universe. Through breathing and meditation Zen practitioners and leaders become part of the infinite universe in which all things are united—that Oneness. Every one is connected through the *ki* of the universe.

To this author, with Zen practices and ways, one can better or grow one's leadership skills and ways.

The following, though not in order of priorities, are what the author believes to be the key applications of Zen to leadership mastery and excellence.

Being Pro-Active

Fools wait for a lucky day but every day is a lucky day for an industrious man. (The Buddha)

Everyday is a good day.

The Buddha once said, "Each morning, we are born again". What we do today is what matters most." Several practitioner-interviewees also intimated these to the author, "Seize the day!"; "Burn the candles, use the nice sheets; don't save it for a special occasion. Celebrate life now! Today is special."

Looking at the above quotation and views, and linking leadership to Zen, this author takes it that when leading and practising Zen, one leads in a proactive fashion. We seek to achieve 'what we do today is what matters most.' This can indeed gear or even mould one's proactive leadership stance. Pro-activity connects the leaders with others and the people around them; it is also necessary for leadership excellence—after all, proactive leaders get things done, keep their people informed as well as care and show concern for their people. "There has never been a leader who has been able to move his team without action. Action is the quality that sets the leader apart from followers." (Low and Theyagu 2003, p. 83). Besides, as a leader, "once you take action, even if it's only a single, small step, you've set things in motion." Fuhrman (2004, p. 22). And indeed, proactive leaders leave behind their legacy.

To subscribe and follow Zen is to be in one with the Universe. One connects with and cares for others while seeking greater understanding, and overall, acts to attain unity or oneness with the Universe.

Similar to Jesus' "take therefore no thought for the morrow for the morrow shall take thought for the things of itself" (Mathew 6, p. 34), Zen is about capturing the moment. Life is a moment, seize the moment (Carpe diem!), and make it burn with the hardest flame! And whatever that can be done is done by the leader.

Zen training emphasises daily practice, along with intensive periods of meditation. Practising with others is considered a critical part of Zen practice. D. T. Suzuki wrote that aspects of this life are: a life of humility, a life of labour, a life of service; a life of prayer and gratitude and a life of meditation.

One needs to put into practice, and practice makes perfect.

In short, just as many garlands can be made from a heap of flowers, so also, the many good deeds of a proactive leader can be done in his or her life.

Accepting and Leading Change

Everything changes. Nothing remains without change. (The Buddha)

Change is part of life. Each day is a new day. And each new time brings renewed optimism for change. Accepting changes, seasons and cycles, the Zen leader also leads and manages change well. Not afraid to change, the Zen leader is also a risk taker.

The practice here is to approach each day creatively. Try something new at least once a day. More so, it really does not have to be anything major. Bear in mind that it is wonderful to always have fresh start each day, new things to do. It is because this fresh start, each new day gives us a chance to reinvent our lives and ourselves. It allows us to reinvigorate ourselves, and with such a frame of mind, the Zen leader can sweep away the baggage of the previous period (day/week/month/year), and do anything. And anything is possible!

Growing, Learning and Doing What Matters Most

The Master observes the world but trusts his inner vision. He allows things to come and go. His heart is open as the sky. (Lao Tzu, verse 12)

There's a Zen saying that goes, "Everyday is a good day".

Each time, our cells die and new cells grow. Every day, one is reborn. So, the Zen leader learns and reinvents him(her)self and his(her) life, every day.

The Zen leader does what matters most, that day.

Finding Happiness Now

Happiness never decreases by being shared. (The Buddha)

In the Dhammapada, Chap. 3, verse 35, it said that "hard it is to train the mind, which goes where it likes and does what it wants. But a trained mind brings health and happiness." (Easwaran 2007, p. 115).

The Zen leader understands well what is happiness; (s)he doesn't look at happiness as something that will come when one is done with this goal, or when one has attained a certain achievement or certain amount of wealth or material goods. Don't look at happiness as a destination, something that one will get later.

Zen is now!

The Zen leader knows that happiness is possible right now. (S)he always remember that. When one pushes it back until later, it will never come. When one learns to be happy now, it will always be here.

When one is doing whatever one is passionate about, whatever matters most, whatever one decides is worthy of one's time and heart and focus . . . be happy! One is doing what one loves. And that is truly a blessing.

More so, one just does what one wants to do, one does so without any expectation. When one does something with expectations, one gets disappointed if it fails to achieve according to what one expects. When it is done without expectations, one is not disappointed. And that is the beauty of just doing and. . .

Following the Natural Order

> Open yourself to the Tao, then trust your natural responses; and everything will fall into place. (Lao Tzu, verse 23)
> No snowflake never falls in the wrong place. (Zen saying)

A Zen saying has it that, "Sitting quietly... doing nothing. Spring comes and grass grows by itself." Zen follows the natural order.

The Buddha said, "Compassion and wisdom are qualities of the true nature."

A leader connects and should identify with his or her followers. The Zen leader cares for his followers.

A parent acts with affection, and a child acts with filial piety. As such, a leader leads, serves and cares for his or her followers. (S)he seeks to understand his or her followers; selfless, (s)he acts in the interests of his(her) followers. [Allow the followers to do their part. The followers would, in most ways, be obligated and hence, reciprocate; they would also be engaged, energised, motivated or inspired by such a leader. They would then assist and contribute to bring about results, achieving the leader's goals.] Indeed so, this is, all the more, enhanced by the leader practising the language of the heart. That's simplicity too.

Simplicity is also a characteristic feature of nature, and simplicity helps and can, in fact, motivate. This author observes that many a corporation has a list of many values as their core values when instead they should choose and stick to three or four values as their core values. Besides, a few are easier to remember, and most people would then have no trouble keeping them in mind. Most employees would really want to work for company whose values and priorities coincide with theirs.

Practising the Language of the Heart

> He who receives kindness should never forget it; but he who performs it should never remember it. (The Buddha)

The Zen leader practises the language of the heart. The Buddha said, "Serenity and generosity are the qualities of the heart."

On language and words, there is a Zen story, the Fragrance of the Rose, which goes:

The disciples were absorbed in a discussion of Lao-tzu's dictum:

> Those who know, do not say;
> Those who say, do not know.
> When the master entered,
> they asked him what the words meant.
> Said the master, "Which of you knows the fragrance of a rose?"
> All of them indicated that they knew.
> Then he said, "Put it into words."
> All of them were silent (Anthony DeMello, cited in Pearls of Wisdom 2007).

One should indeed not be attached to words; whatever one does, one just does it. So a Zen leader just loves and gets things done. (S)he serves. When egoless enters the heart of things, doing things and leading, it is speaking the language of the heart.

Leaders can lead the countries (companies) effectively. In Zen and leadership, love or compassion has to start from the top for society to feel its effects. Indeed so, a king or a leader can attend to his royal (state) duties and lead a spiritual live. The key point here is that regardless of one's duties, one, capable of loving, can always seek spiritual truths.

There is no Buddha in the mountains or in the caves, but the Buddha is in one's mind. If one is awakened to the mind that is calm and has understanding, that is, Buddha. One needs not look elsewhere.

Being Focused ("One Heart, One Intention")

Irrigators guide the water to their fields. Fletchers shape the arrow shaft. Carpenters shape the wood. The wise shape their lives. (The Buddha)

Focus like a camera.

The Buddha said, "Insight and concentration are qualities of the mind." "(Just) as an archer aims an arrow, the wise aim their restless thoughts, hard to aim, hard to restrain." The Dhammapada, Chap. 3, verse 33 (Easwaran 2007, p. 115).

Peace comes from within. Do not seek without. (The Buddha)

The Zen leader is not distracted and focused. In fact, the Zen leader shuts off him (her)self for awhile, meditating to find focus.

Readers—whatever profession that you are in—can practise this: Everyday, even if only for 15 or 20 min at first, but preferably for 30–60 min, one can take a break (pause) and check one's email or do the chores after one has focused. One focuses on the thing that matters most.

Fellow readers, remember to take your pauses and clear away your distractions. You can clear away all the little nagging work, chores and errands that pull at your attention, sweep away the clutter that surrounds you (brush it off to the side to deal with later). In fact, if you can, shut off the Internet for a while. You can come back to it when you take a break.

Yes, you feel free to take a pause, but always return to your focus.

When you're done, focus on the next thing that matters most, and so on.

Developing Patience

I have just three things to teach: simplicity, patience, compassion. These three are your greatest treasures. (Lao Tzu *Tao te Ching*, verse 67)

The Dhammapada, Chap. 23, verse 320 speaks of, "patiently I shall bear harsh words as the elephant bears arrows on the battlefield." The leader is patient and listening. He attends to the needs of the followers.

Impatience creates anxieties, and patience creates assurance and confidence. To develop patience is to exercise restraint. Such a virtue allows a person to feel good, to be calm, cool and composed to do, and live successfully no matter the circumstance.

When one is not attached to one's ambitions, wealth or anything; one lets go; one too grows or develops one's patience. Also not attached to any forms of ego, one develops a sense of patience. Many times we are held back by the tangled web of previous failures, commitments, emotions, barriers. We cannot change careers because we are used to what we are doing and it is too hard to change.

Detaching and Letting Go

A flower falls even though we love it. Weed grows even though we do not love it. (Zen saying)

He who experiences the unity of life sees himself in all beings, and all beings in himself.
  He looks on everything with an impartial eye. (The Buddha)

Linked to the previous pointer on developing patience is the fact that the Zen practitioner let attachments go. As Aitken Roshi once said, "Renunciation is not getting rid of the things of this world, but accepting that they pass away." There is a strong need to allow everything from the past go, and one cultivates inner peace.

The Zen leader cultivates the inner peace. (S)he grows his patience. When one cultivates the inner peace (and the focus), the passing of time becomes matters of small concern. All time can be realised as perceived temporal space for the manifestation of intent.

A farmer knows that if his interference is minimal, the seeds will sprout. He will release worry. He will release fear. Once he has planted and watered the seeds, he will know that the seeds can grow on their own.

Applying Objectivity and Having No Favourites

If you over-esteem great men, people become powerless. If you overvalue possessions, people begin to steal. (Lao Tzu, verse 3)

Having a calm and tranquil mind, the Zen leader is objective, and has no favourites. Conversely, when the mind is not objective, it is unsettling, not calm or disturbed (Low 2009).

The Zen practitioners, in most ways, are inclined to make good decisions, with their minds trained. In the Zen way, being detached, our minds are like the water reflecting the moon, and no image is retained. That way the leader will take changes as they are; and this also helps the leader when coping with change. (S)he will be free of worries and cares. When the mind is empty and non-attached, then it will forget both the self and the outside world (Low 2009).

Having Stillness

Express yourself completely, then keep quiet. Be like the forces of nature: when it blows, there is only wind; when it rains, there is only rain; when the clouds pass, the sun shines through. (Lao Tzu, verse 23)

There's a Chan (or Chinese Zen) Buddhism saying that goes, "No wisdom like silence". Akin to the meaning in the Japanese Buddhist proverb, "The flower goes back to its roots", Zen stresses the practice of meditation as the key to enlightenment.

Activity or getting things done suggests or leads us to think of a life filled with purpose. In the fast pace of today's modern world, meditation helps us to capture the now, the present. This is stillness that is so essential in the hurly-burly and rush-rush of today's world. Stillness can be purposeful, not to mention it can be restorative or curative, getting to know or understand ourselves—at the core—better. It is good to be in touch with our inner self, intuition and higher intelligence.

Interestingly, that stillness, even for a brief period, all thoughts, many words in our heads and the feelings of fears, anxieties and regrets they all can simply be let go. For that 'here and now', there's no worrying of the past or tomorrow. Fears and anxieties can be eradicated.

Stillness or reflecting—further thinking on the subject—can also be refreshing; it can generate further creativity; in fact, leading to emerging, new ideas.

Being Inspired and Inspiring Others Through the Use of the Koans

It is good to live in virtue, good to have faith, good to attain the highest wisdom, good to be pure in heart and mind. Joy will be yours always. (The Dhammapada)

Koans are parables, stories or dialogues related by the Zen Master to their followers. They can also be in the form of questions. A popular and widely known koan is "Two hands clap, and there is a sound; but what is the sound of one hand?" Another popular koan is that of "not thinking of good, not thinking of evil tell me what was your original face before your mother and father were born?"

One koan relates a parable of some men, wanting to pluck some sweet fruits from a tall big fruit tree, chop down the tall fruit tree to get the fruits. Lesson (s) learnt?

What then are the uses and applications of these koans? Koans can be used to test a disciple's ability. They are normally used to stimulate reflection, and they serve as meditation aids. As positive affirmations, Zen practitioners concentrate on koans during meditation. Teachers may also probe such disciples about their koan practice using 'checking questions' to validate an experience of insight or awakening. Responses by disciples have included actions or gestures, and verses inspired by the koan.

Identifying Talents, Coaching and Growing Others

> Pity arises when we are sorry for someone. Compassion is when we understand and help wisely. (The Buddha)

The Dhammapada, Chap. 6 verse 77 and 78, highlights these "letting them (*true or exemplary leaders*) admonish or instructs or restrain you from what is wrong... ...make friends with those who are good and true" (Easwaran 2007, p. 126, *italics mine*).

Selfless, Zen leaders grow leaders. And it is good that each of us have mentors to learn from and grow.

In the organisational context, it is normally good to survey or see the potentials and talents available within one's company or business concern. And to aid the growth of the business, there is certainly a need to identify talents and grow them.

The whole idea of assessing, grooming and growing talents, leaders or successors is a good idea. Succession planning and preparations as well as staff training are good human resource management policies and practices to pursue.

Being Humble, Giving and Serving

> We join spokes together in a wheel,
>   but it is the center hole
>   that makes the wagon move.
>   We shape clay into a pot,
>   but it is the emptiness inside
>   that holds whatever we want.
>   We hammer wood for a house,
>   but it is the inner space
>   that makes it livable.
>   We work with being,
>   but non-being is what we use. (Lao Tzu, verse 11)

"It is a mistake to believe that a great leader is above others." (Heider 1995, p. 121). On the contrary, greatness comes from knowing how to be lowly, empty; receptive and be of service. An old Japanese saying has it that, "the heaviest ears of rice bow the lowest." And the Chinese speaks of, "If you bow at all, bow low."

Humility is one of the key characteristics that leaders should, in fact, possess. To this author, humility grows the person, if not leader, from ground zero to becoming a hero. The Buddha himself was called the Great Elephant (Throughout Indian scripture and folklore, the mighty, fiercely loyal, serving and enduring elephant is revered and ranks first among all animals in importance. For many centuries, the Indian people had trained elephants to transport logs or burdens much heavier than the human being can manage. From the time of the Buddha onwards, the elephants, playing a decisive role on the battlefield, were considered the most important division of the Indian army.) By taking the analogy of the trained elephant, whose great power has been transformed into loving human service, he manages to tell his followers both the difficulty and the rewards of discipline.

Without ego, the Zen leader practices humility and serves.

The wisdom of the *Tao* says:

All streams flow to the sea
  because it is lower than they are.
  Humility gives it its power.
  If you want to govern the people,
  you must place yourself below them.
  If you want to lead the people,
  you must learn how to follow them. (Lao Tzu, verse 66)

"The best athlete wants his opponent at his best. The best general enters the mind of his enemy. The best businessman serves the communal good. The best leader follows the will of the people." (Lao Tzu, verse 68). The Zen leader serves the people and, accordingly, practices servant leadership. Acting without self-interest, the Zen leader is giving (Lao Tzu, verse 7) and this coincides with what has been highlighted by Low 2009, 2007a, p. 58, "the leader practises servant leadership". "The Master has no possessions. The more he does for others, the happier he is. The more he gives to others, the wealthier he is." (Lao Tzu, verse 81). Indeed "the leader (thus) demonstrates the power of selflessness and the unity of all creation." (Heider 1995, p. 143). The Dhammapada, Chap. 13, verse 177 indicates that "misers do not go to the world of the gods; they do not want to give. The wise are generous, and go to a happier world."

Collaborating and Team-Playing

… we all want the same things (to be happy and be loved) and we are all connected to one another. Spend 5 min breathing in, cherishing yourself; and, breathing out cherishing others. If you think about people you have difficulty cherishing, extend your cherishing to them anyway. (Dalai Lama, Practice for the New Millennium)

Interestingly, related to the point on being detached and the fact that the Zen leader has no favourites, (s)he leads the team well. And effective teamwork is based on the common Japanese saying that "none of us is as smart as all of us".

Should there be favourites within the team, effective teamwork would be absent; and the morale of the team members would be affected, if not, dented. Indeed, the wise leader is a good collaborator, and brings harmony to the team (Low 2009).

As a Zen saying goes, "The moon shows in every pool; in every pool the one moon. The moon shows in every pool; in every pool the one moon", we are all in it together.

Disciplining and Thinking Positively

All that we are arises with our thoughts. With our thoughts, we make the world. (The Buddha)

The first duty of a leader is optimism. How does your subordinate feel after meeting with you? Does he feel uplifted? If not, you are not a leader. (Field Marshall Montgomery)

All in all, bringing about discipline within one's mind is the essence of the Buddha's teaching, Zen or in any form of Buddhism. We thus need to train or discipline our mind for happiness. The systematic training of the mind is critical; cultivating happiness and positive thinking can lead to "the genuine inner transformation" (Dalai Lama and Cutler 1998, p. 31).

We need to purposefully focus on positive mental states, and to put it simply, it is scientifically argued that our brains are genetically hardwired with certain instinctual behaviour patterns. Our brains are adaptable, predisposing ourselves mentally, emotionally and physically to respond to our environment in ways that enable us to survive. Our inner transformation starts with learning (new input) and involves the discipline of gradually replacing our negative conditioning with positive conditioning (forming new neural circuits). "We are what we think", as the Buddha said, and disciplining and thinking positively will lead to our (ultimate) happiness.

Section Conclusion

There is no point in worrying about past or about future. A smart and intelligent person thinks and works only about present. (Sanskrit proverb)

Overall, water cleans and refreshes as mentioned in *Tao Teh Ching*, such are the qualities that Zen leaders bring to their people. Sincere, soft and bringing about positive influence to those around them, the *Tao* leaders express simply and honestly, and intervene to give fresh and insightful perspectives, shed light and create harmony. They contribute or make the world a better place for all to live.

Basically, leading the Zen or the *Tao* way is about developing wise and insightful leadership. People understand how to read books that have sentences and words. Yet they may not be able to understand how to read those that lack them. Zen leadership is concerned with the essence of things; to the person of wisdom, there is the unwritten book of nature, mountains, skies and rivers, bamboo; and the book of the moon and the universe as a whole. And in leading, the journey itself is enjoyed, and becomes the reward.

Nemoto's Principles of Leadership

Here are the Nemoto Principles of leadership as practised in the Toyota car-making workplaces, and they are as follows:

1. Get Improvement After Improvement
   Managers should look continually for ways to improve the work of their employees. Indeed Kaizen is embraced and subscribed to. Growth must start from within, a company cannot grow without growth of its leaders from within.
2. Coordinate Between Divisions
   Good coordination is necessary within any organisation, big or small. Managers should ensure good coordination.
3. Let Everyone Speak
   This rule guides supervisors of Quality Circles (QCs) of Toyota and it helps to ensure participation and learning by all members.
4. Do Not Scold
   In Toyota, the policy is for supervisors to avoid giving criticism and threatening punitive measures when mistakes are made. This ensures that mistakes are reported and root causes identified and amended.
5. Make Sure Others Understand Your Work
   This stresses on the importance of teaching and presentation skills because of the need to collaborate.
6. Send the Best Employees Out For Rotation
   Toyota has a rotation policy to train employees. There is a strong tendency among managers to keep their employees from rotation. But company benefits most in the long run by training its best employees.
7. Issue A Command With A Deadline
   A command without a deadline is not a command; deadlines should be included. This rule is used so that managers always give a deadline.
8. Rehearsal Is An ideal Occasion For Training
   Managers give frequent progress reports. In QCs, there are many reports. Rehearsal times are used to teach presentation skills to members as well as to explore problems or check the level of members' understanding of the topic.
9. Inspection Is A Failure Unless Top Management Takes Action
   The idea behind this is that management should prescribe specific remedies whenever a problem is observed or reported. Delegating, saying "to shape up" is ineffective; so is failing to take any action once a problem is identified. That problem, needless to say, has to be resolved.

10. Ask Subordinates, "What Can I Do For You?"
    This is what is called "creating opportunity" to be heard at the top. It allows the top management to get feedback from the grassroots.

Leading, the Matsushita Way

In this section, we examine the key thoughts and leadership ways of the late Matsushita Konosuke, one of pioneering leaders of Japanese and world industry as well as Japan's most accomplished business leaders. Matsushita's thoughtful approach and ways to leading a business, the blueprint for his unparalleled success, have moulded and shaped the corporate culture of the Panasonic Corporation [formerly known as Matsushita Electric Industrial Company Limited].

Introduction

From one of the pioneering leaders of Japanese and world industry and Japan's most accomplished business leaders comes a unique and thoughtful approach to leading a business. Matsushita Konosuke's thoughts, the blueprint for his success, have also moulded and shaped the corporate culture and values of the Panasonic Corporation.

Here, the key thoughts and leadership ways of the late Matsushita Konosuke, the founder of the Matsushita Group of Companies/Panasonic Corporation, are assessed.

Matsushita Konosuke's Key Thoughts and Leadership Ways

Having a Vision

Leaders in any field should always have a clear vision of what they want to do. (Matsushita Konosuke)

For Matsushita, simply acting on the advice of others without thinking or having ideas of one's own or vision is not leadership. A leader should have a vision. Seeking the input of others is very critical, but only if the leader maintains a firm sense of authority and ultimate control. "A leader who serves as a firmly fixed axis can most effectively mobilize others and maximise the results of what they do." (Matsushita 1994, p. 49)

Believing in and Tapping the People's Potential

Everyone is an asset. (Matsushita Konosuke)

People are diamonds in the rough. (Matsushita Konosuke)

Believing that one's humility will allow one to appreciate the merits of one's employees better, Matsushita believed in the people's potential (Matsushita 1984), urging his managers not to assume that their employees because they are subordinates, are less skilled or talented than them. True, not all one's employees are superior workers, but he believed that, being humble, leaders can better understand how to capitalise on their people and tap their ideas well.

With "people before product" in mind, the supervisors or leaders should continually encourage their people, helping them to overcome their shortcomings and weaknesses. Besides, a leader should have a deep sense of gratitude for all things. And for Matsushita, gratitude was an excellent quality to cultivate, with a focus on the people's strengths. A strong sense of appreciation will help person finds something good in everything, making him(her) light-hearted and at peace with others (Matsushita 1991). Otherwise, if one has little capacity to appreciate, then one may develop a jaundiced eye, becoming resentful and discontented for no good reason.

Here, at this juncture, readers should perhaps take a reflective pause, and ask themselves these questions: Do I appreciate my people (employees)? How do I show to my people (employees) that I appreciate them? Do, all in all, I count my blessings or think my blessings don't count?

Using the Umbrella When It Rains [or Guided by the Laws of Nature]

Don't call in the doctor after the funeral. (Japanese proverb)

Here, relying more on common sense, Matsushita believed that a good leader is guided by the laws of nature. Subscribing to Lao Tzu's tenet, "if a ruler keeps to the path, matters will take care of themselves", Matsushita took it that if one should do commonsensical things at all times, then one would then make fewer mistakes; and one would well be on one's way to achieve success and growth. "To run a good business, you must develop a good product, sell it at reasonable price... and collect payments punctually." (Matsushita 1991, p. 137). He claimed that in practice, usually this was not easy because people got carried away by their own desires and selfish feelings, and forgot to apply common sense. In any case, overall, if there is a formula for business success, he felt that it was critical to operate in this straight-forward, down-to-earth way as simply and sensibly as opening an umbrella in the rain.

In his applications of this tenet, one can see its operations in the fact Matsushita stressed on the importance of the customers, and looking after the employees. "Put people first"; a leader must be humane in his dealings with others (Matsushita 1991, p. 152). It is also taken as axiomatic for leaders to "look after those who serve you"

(Matsushita 1991, 78). Because leaders treat their people with kindness, their people and their spheres prosper.

Being Customer-Driven

When it rains, you put up an umbrella. This is the secret of success in business and management. (Matsushita Konosuke)

A smile a day. (Japanese proverb)

"Good business needs good products, but more good service." "Service comes first" and after-sales, to Matsushita, is the key to keeping one's customers (Matsushita 1991, 70). A product from your store is like a married daughter; and the business needs to think about the customer, who has after buying its product, becoming something like a relative. So, one has to "check up from time to time by giving 'hello' service" (Matsushita 1991, p. 72) and also grow the relationships.
Being Humble

Hidden virtues ring like a soft bell. (Japanese saying)

Get your ego out of the way and move on. (Ken Blanchard)

"The higher a leader's position, the more humble he should be." (Matsushita 1991, p. 42). And indeed a leader must not lose a sense of humility. To Matsushita, a humble person extracts genuine respect from those (s)he meets. A humble leader also listens to what people say, and so is able to gather information from many sources. Besides, such a leader is ordinarily "agreeable", being able to get along with others and in most ways, being good-natured, cooperative, warm and approachable (Daft 2008, p. 99).

Being Service-Oriented and Serving the Community

Be generous with your smiles. (Japanese proverb)

Matsushita's chief philosophy is that of providing a large supply of consumer goods at the lowest possible prices—without compromising quality and service. For him, the corporate exists for society, is of society and remains with the society. The mission of manufacturing is to overcome poverty, bringing products and goods, relieving the society from misery as well as generating wealth to it.

Matsushita held the view that a corporate should create wealth for society and for shareholders and should always work to alleviate poverty. Leading in a fatherly way, employees are seen as being part of a family and are assured of lifetime employment. Of great importance, the employees are assured of training and growth, and hence assured of lifetime employment.

Leading by Example

Don't tell others to do what you cannot do. (Japanese proverb)

"As a leader, you must convey your principles to people, but you yourself must set the example." (Matsushita 1991, p. 111). Matsushita also believed that the employer should inject "the human quality into personnel education" (Matsushita 1984, p. 42), and through the dedication to work and unfailing loyalty to the company, the top person must set the example. Like anybody else, the top person is not expected to be perfect yet this gives the top person a common ground with those working with him or her. They know that he will make mistakes too, but one area where (s)he cannot fail, where (s)he must be exemplary, is his(her) commitment to his(her) work.

Drawing from the analogy of "the tail trails the head": "if the head moves fast, the tail will keep up the same pace. If the head is sluggish, the tail will droop", Matsushita (1984, p. 43) highlighted that, "from a hard working proprietor, employees learn the virtue of diligence". Employees will look up to their leaders for a model worker or committed leader. The work team emulates the commitment and the loyalty of the leader. And the pace of the leader is also the pace of the work team.

Being Pro-Active and Passionate

Be generous with your energy. (Japanese saying)

Of high energy and youthfulness, it can be said that Matsushita ensured pro-activeness when leading. A leader should also be productive as a dead cherry tree will not blossom.

"You have to like your job." (Matsushita 1994, p. 49). To him, the difference between a good businessman and a poor one is that the former loves the work of business management and the latter does not. Indeed what one enjoys, one would do well.

Additionally to Matsushita, youth is a state of mind. One should be young at heart. While one does one's best, full of faith, hope and courage, in one's ever-changing daily activities, youthfulness will be owned forever. Embedded in such a positive viewpoint, it can be assessed that as a leader, Matsushita embraced change and responded to change pro-actively or positively.

Passionate, Matsushita Konosuke believed that in whatever a person does, (s)he should do it well. One must indeed work with conviction (Matsushita 1994).

Being Persuasive, Having the Power of Persuasion

Employees need dreams. (Matsushita Konosuke)

Building and growing on one's charisma, a leader has to be persuasive. When the employees are persuaded, they then operate as in the Japanese proverb, "I like you, I like work, I love your smile."

For Matsushita Konosuke, the power to persuade and motivate others is "born of strong inner convictions". How does one arrive at such convictions? Matsushita expressed, "Simply by working hard at your job every day. If you don't put your heart and soul in to your work, you don't develop confidence in your performance. Without confidence, you fall into the habit of glossing over your weaknesses. By glossing over your weaknesses, you lose credibility. And without credibility, you grow even less inclined to give your utmost to the job. That is the vicious circle you must take care not to get sucked into." (Matsushita 1994, p. 64).

For him, persuasion pays off. Consulting with the employees is better than ordering. Dreams should be shared. As president of Matsushita Electric, Matsushita Konosuke took every opportunity to inform employees of his plans and dreams for the company's future.

Without forcing and letting people see eye to eye with one's idea or proposal, "a good leader knows how to win people to his cause." (Matsushita 1991, pp. 100–101) and overall, one's ethos and approach should be correct.

A leader needs to know how to convince, especially, the company's customers (Matsushita 1984, pp. 72–73). (S)he is expected to comply with the highly diverse, specific needs of consumers and the confidence in the quality of the products and services one is selling as well as in their value to consumers. Matsushita's philosophy is simple, if you cannot sway your customers, then you are not cut for business.

"All fired up" (Matsushita 1991, p. 156), the leader is more persuasive and effective. "Enthusiasm is magnetic." (Matsushita 1994, p. 67). Enthusiasm is half the battle in pursuing any matter. To him, half-heartedness would not get the person anywhere. Others or even one's followers may be more intelligent but if one is more enthusiastic than others, the intelligent people will contribute their ideas and insights. A leader needs "never worry because he lacks a particular talent; what he should worry about is lack of enthusiasm." (Matsushita 1991, p. 157).

To be persuasive, a leader should also be able to present the same issue in different ways to different people, appealing to them to his(her) sense of honour, desire for profit, emotions or his(her) reason. In other words, one needs to cleverly tailor one's approach to suit the individual. And a leader should continually try out new techniques of persuasion and should always attempt to learn more about human nature.

Winning Trust

A leader must examine his behaviour daily. (Matsushita Konosuke)

Eggs and promises are easily broken. (Japanese proverb)

When one begins and leads an enterprise, trust is very important. It would be much easier when one has people's trust. "Trust can be thought of as an invisible force or an intangible asset." (Matsushita 1991, p. 87). A leader, a person of his (her) words, should win trust; people will shy away from someone they do not trust, whereas they will pledge their allegiance to or support someone they do.

Believing that Trouble Is Good and It Makes Us Strong

Adversity is the foundation of virtue. (Japanese proverb)

Matsushita Konosuke believed that trouble was good, helping a business to grow. Kotter (1997, pp. 35–47) spoke of Matsushita's belief in growth through hardship; for Matsushita the years around puberty turned out to be bother severe and a source of learning as well as growth as he worked as an apprentice. Hardship became the driving force behind his subsequent successes.

As a leader, Matsushita managed to keep the company together during economic trouble times and the occupation after World War II. Matsushita Electric, in fact, supplied three essentials or "three treasures": a washing machine, a refrigerator and a black-and-white television to the then recovering Japanese households. Believing that trouble, "a good teacher" (Matsushita 1984, p. 92), helps us, as leaders, to grow our resilience; it makes us tough.

Complaints, for instance, can be troublesome, but in business, having to attend to each of them ensures that the customers emerged satisfied. For Matsushita, complaints are treasured as "they give an opportunity to establish direct contact with customers" (Matsushita 1984, p. 76) and attend to them. Those who do not complain, probably come to the decision never to buy that company's products again. Those who complain might think the same thing initially, however, if the Company takes the trouble and care to resolve the complaint, they appreciate the Company's sincerity, and they may end up being a fan instead of a critic.

Thus, overall, as leaders, through failure, we acquire wisdom and defeat gives us a valuable fund of experience to draw from later on. Failure also gives us useful insights into ourselves and our circumstances, from it, we can grow and progress.

Doing What One Knows to be Right

A leader must never let personal considerations cloud his judgment. (Matsushita Konosuke)

Matsushita Konosuke believed that a leader needs the courage of his convictions (Matsushita 1991). This would definitely up the leader's integrity. Integrity is essentially people know what you stand for, and this can indeed win the hearts and minds of your people—it can be very persuasive.

Military power or even whatever power one has counts for something when backed up by firm convictions. Without convictions, strength does not always prevail. Here, it is critical for a leader to have the courage or boldness of his convictions if he is to be successful.

Being Bold and Determined

Depend on your walking stick, not on other people. (Japanese proverb)

For Matsushita Konosuke, leaders should be bold and determined. This reflects the resilient nature that leaders should possess. Leaders need "the drive to act decisively" (Matsushita 1991, p. 38). It is critical for the leader to have a definite goal in mind and achieve it by the only means possible, resolute determination to pursue that goal.

A leader needs to maintain his determination, constantly spurring oneself on and keeping one's resolve fresh. ("A leader must constantly renew his determination to succeed"; Matsushita 1991, p. 36). A leader never gives up.

Surging Ahead

Great men are they who see that thought is stronger than any material force, that thoughts rule the world. (Ralph Waldo Emerson)

Another interesting key leadership idea and thinking of Matsushita is that of "the untrapped mind" (Matsushita 1994; Low and Theyagu 2003a). To him, human beings can get "pre-occupied (easily) with a single pattern of thought or behaviour". Here, one can take it that if one applies this concept and keeps one's mind open, then one can, in fact, be entrepreneurial (don't assume that something is impossible) and be creative, and besides, see many possibilities of learning from others as well as improving oneself. Thus, using the untrapped mind, we learn abundantly, grow and surge ahead (Fig. 7.1).

Being Adaptable and Flexible

A person with "the untrapped mind" (the author refers this as "mind growth"), open to new ideas and approaches, is flexible and adaptable. Conversely, a person with a trapped mind would say, "But I've always done it this way," and when (s)he says it as such, (s)he is a stumbling block, closing his or her mind to possibilities and new ways, and thus gets left behind.

Fig. 7.1 Matsushita
Konosuke, as drawn by the
author

Matsushita Konosuke believed that a leader should possess "the untrapped mind". Having "the untrapped mind", one would develop the quality of "ready adaptability"; here, Matsushita chose the legendary confrontational example between the twelfth century warlord, Minamoto no Yoshitsune and the formidable Benkei, who afterwards became Yoshitsune's faithful servant (Matsushita 1994, p. 62). To him, possessing "the untrapped mind" would make one think, nothing is impossible, and be more flexible, creative and entrepreneurial.

Section Conclusion

It is indeed worth studying Matsushita's thoughts, his works and leadership ways. Cherishing and valuing people while believing in and tapping their potential, his people-oriented approach gives new meaning to the words "success" and "leadership excellence". His ideas, in most ways, also supply a philosophical grounding for an individual's success and personal achievement.

Akio Morita and His Leadership Ways (Sony)

In this section, we look into the co-founder of Sony, Akio Morita's leadership ways.

Introduction

While people leaves behind their footprints, leaders leave behind their achievements; leaders inspire others. Their followers and others, in fact, get energized, and many want to emulate them. In true entrepreneurial fashion, Japanese businessman Akio Morita took a small radio repair shop of bombed-out Tokyo building, and converted it into the powerhouse electronics company, the Sony (sonus is Latin for sound, and Sonny-boys is Japanese slang for "whiz kids") Corporation.. Here, in this section, the key leadership ways of Japanese corporate leader, Akio Morita, are examined.

In December 1998, *Time* magazine featured him as "a man who created one of the first global corporations". Over the next 50 years after the post war period, Sony was to go on to become the Number 1 consumer brand name in the world; he was responsible for this amazing feat of making "Sony a trusted name everywhere" (Time 1998). Akio Morita also typifies or personifies Japan's post-war technological ascendancy.

Akio Morita suffered a stroke in 1993, during a game of tennis, and on October 3, 1999, Morita died of pneumonia at the age of 78.

This section seeks to examine the key leadership ways and lessons of the Japanese corporate leader, Akio Morita. Here then are the ten key leadership lessons learnt from his ways. It would be good that the reader would customize to suit to him(her)self, ultimately relating them to the ways in which (s)he would act. And benefit.

Creating and Growing the Competitive Edge

The key to success is to control what you think about, for you always get what you keep telling your mind you want. (Walter D. Staples)

Born in Nagoya, Japan, in 1921, Akio Morita was the son of sake brewers. Instead of staying in the family company, in true entrepreneurial spirit, Akio Morita in 1946 helped start Tokyo Tsushin Kogyo KK (the Tokyo Telecommunications Engineering Corporation) with Ibuka Masaru. Still hard hit by the war, the Japanese could not really afford expensive electronics, so Ibuka set his sights on the overseas US market with a brand new idea—a small pocket-size transistorized radio. Then a US company built such a radio, but more as a gimmick than an actual product. When Morita's company then renamed Sony, came out with their radio, it quickly took the market.

Things Sony, over the years, became associated with innovations, more specifically, of miniature electronics—even for miniature Walkmans and televisions. [Watching his children and their friends listening to music from morning until night, Akio Morita was inspired to develop the Walkman, after observing people listening to music in their cars and carrying large stereos to beaches and parks. The engineering department at Sony opposed the concept of a tape player without a recording function (this was added later), thinking that it would not sell, but Morita declared that if 30,000 of these machines could not be sold, he would resign as company president. Morita wanted a high quality product that was easily portable, and allowed the user to listen while doing something else; the new device was named "Walkman". The Walkman was indeed successful, and Sony sold, by the year 2000, 200 millions Walkmans.] Becoming the top of the mind awareness among its customers, Sony's association with things small or miniature electronics grows into its positioning edge as well as its competitive advantage. Sony also produces its own CD players and in 1989, Sony bought Columbia Pictures, and it enters Hollywood, music production and global media.

O yes, there's no excuse to not being good or even great. Decide now; decide to be great. And also, know what you want to grow. Ask, "What is your positioning? What is your positioning edge? And what is your competitive edge? And how can you build your competitive edge?"

Having Clarity of Goals and Taking Responsibility

> You must be single-minded. Drive for one thing on which you have decided. (George S. Patton)

> Great souls have wills; feeble ones have only wishes. (Chinese proverb)

Much as a loud voice cannot challenge or compete with a clear voice, even if it's a whisper, leaders, who does not have clear vision and goals, cannot compete with those who have.

Business is about winning, and leaders often do something that differentiate them and have an edge. Akio Morita's stand and advice reflecting his leadership thinking is always to "be clear on what you have decided to do and what you ask others to do and take responsibility".

Sony was the first Japanese company to build a manufacturing plant in the United States. Akio Morita, over time, set up many other manufacturing, research and development and design centres in North America, Europe and Asia. He believed that Sony should play a part to the economies of the countries where their biggest markets were located.

Ask, "Are your clear on your vision? And goals?"

Finding the Need and Filling It: Satisfying the Market

> Choose your inn before dark, get back on the road before dawn. (Japanese proverb)

Akio Morita once said, "Our plan is to lead the public with new products rather than ask them what kind of products they want. The public does not know what is possible, but we do."

A master at finding a need and filling it, Morita smartly observed that Americans loved music and would listen to it in their cars and even carry large stereos to the beach and the park. He came up with an idea for a product that offered high-quality sound yet was portable enough to allow the user to listen while doing something else. Thus, one of Sony's most popular and profitable products was born: the miniature Walkman.

A Sony's big windfall, the Walkman, its technology was difficult to duplicate, and it was more than 2 years before other companies could introduce similar or competing models. By that time, Sony had sold 20 million units, and the company's reputation and brand recognition soared worldwide.

Indeed it is Akio Morita who pioneered the marketing concept of brand-name recognition at a time when most companies in Japan were producing goods under somebody else's name.

Ask specifically, "Have you found the vital needs of your customers? What are they? Are you satisfying them? Are you really satisfying your customers? If not, what else can you do to better satisfy your customers?"

Learning from Mistakes, Learning from Failures

Individuals with edge have competitive spirit and know the value of speed. They're confident; they know when to green-light or red-light a project or acquisition. They don't get paralyzed by paradox. (Jack Welch)

Akio Morita once said, "Don't be afraid to make a mistake. But make sure you don't make the same mistake twice"; these very words in fact become part of the treasury of modern Japanese wise sayings. For Morita, to ensure that one did not make the same mistakes twice, one should learn from mistakes. From here, this author can safely conclude that for Akio Morita, this is one best way to change. One dares to take risks, to create, adopt and accept change as well as to make progress for one's company as well as for oneself.

On the reader's part, I urge you to introspect, look into your life, and next ask, "What are these mistakes that you've made and what are their learning points? What really are their lessons for you?"

Coping with the Speed of Change

The ability to learn faster than your competitors may be only sustainable competitive advantage. (Arie de Geus)

Akio Morita, the gadget guru and an engineer by training, was determined to change the image of Japanese goods to one of quality in foreign markets, especially in the U.S. where he established a subsidiary, he was thankful that Sony products were soon copied by global competitors. Yet, committed and dedicated to be ahead of the competition, he strived to make Sony leader of the pack and led Sony to produce or boast of the industry's firsts including the first pocket-sized transistor radio and the first all-transistor television set. [It should be noted that the situation and the world has now changed; at that time, in the 1980s, Morita considered Japan and US to be the only tech powers and business leaders.] Needless to say, Akio Morita, an inspirational icon, epitomizes the struggle and success of that generation of post-war business leaders who turned the image of Japanese goods from a second rate or low quality to that of a cutting edge, if not, high quality products in demand.

In any case, for Morita, "we . . .are challenged to create things that will be new and intriguing enough to bring customers to us . . . we can never expect to survive in business if we do not keep improving what we offer to the public, and that takes new technology." (Akio Morita, cited in Low and Theyagu 2003, p. 94). He often urged his people to look at ways to improve, improvise and innovate to meet the speed of change. On your part, within your own context, "Do you, as a leader, do that?"

Making Full Use of People's Potential

Every place on Earth, every human person is a centre of the world. (Japanese saying)

Leadership is basically about making full use of what one has, whatever the available resources are, and in terms of human capital, it's about getting out by triggering the people's creativity and potential.

Akio Morita sees things from a management and leadership viewpoint, it is critical to know how to unleash people's inborn creativity. Interestingly, his concept is that "anybody has creative ability, but very few people know how to use it"; he highlighted that "curiosity is the key to creativity." For Akio Morita, his "solution to the problem of unleashing creativity is always to set up a target." He gave the example of the Apollo project in the United States; indeed much collective efforts were made with NASA as a focal point, and finally Apollo landed on moon in 1969.

What are the key lessons here? As a leader, you should know your people as well as their strengths. Ask yourself then: "Are you making full use of your people's potential? Are you getting the best of your people?"

Motivating and Energizing People

A good Jack makes a good Jill. (Japanese saying)

An apprentice near a temple will recite the scriptures untaught. Meaning, the environment makes our characters. (Japanese proverb)

It is critical to know how great leaders motivate their people to produce great results. But more often, more importantly, one should act or apply what one has learnt.

Often a spokesman for Japanese management and in expressing his own ideas, Morita stressed on the value of teamwork and of motivating people by providing challenging work in a family-like environment.

For Akio Morita, "what we in industry learned in dealing with people is that people do not work just for money and that if you are trying to motivate, money is not the most effective tool."

"The investor and the employee are in the same position, but sometimes the employee is more important, because he will be there a long time whereas an investor will often get in and out on a whim in order to make a profit."

He believed that Sony wanted to keep the company healthy and its employees happy, and Sony wanted to keep them on the job and productive. He believed that one of the reasons Sony went through such a remarkable growth period was that it had this atmosphere of free discussion.

Morita had always made it a point to know his employees, to visit every facility of the company, and to try to meet and know every single employee. He stayed connected to the people. The lesson here is that, as a leader, ask yourself, "Do you act in this way? Are you connected to your people? Do you hear your people out?" There is really one very fast way; we would ask the people who follow you; they know. And what they say is true; you are who they say you are.

Fostering the Good Family-Like Relationships Within the Company

Affinity is a mysterious thing, but it is spicy! (Japanese proverb)

In touch with the people, he always fostered good working relationships with his people. For Morita, as he once said: "the most important mission for a Japanese manager is to develop a healthy relationship with his employees, to create a family-like feeling within the corporation, a feeling that employees and managers share the same fate" (Morita 1987, p. 130).

Interestingly, for Akio Morita, and it is still valid today especially in Asia, it is important that the Company tries to create conditions where persons could come together in a spirit of teamwork (enjoying good family-like relationships), and exercise to their heart's desire their technological capacity. This very much sparks, builds; grows or enhances the innovative spirit of the employees.

Also, showing much care and concern and helping his people to grow, Akio Morita believed in educating and training his people.

He also networked with others. Morita's association was not narrowed to businessmen. Every United States ambassador to Japan during the 1970s and 1980s left the country with fond memories of evenings at the Morita's home in Tokyo and an indefinable but certain sense of loyalty to Sony (*Time* 1999).

Perhaps, you should ask yourself, "Are you fostering the good family-like relationships within your department/team? How do you get your team involved in the success of your department/shop/company?"

Taking Market Research to the Streets

People are not what they appear to be. (Japanese saying)

Although he was the Chairman of Sony Corporation, but that did not mean he stayed cooped up in his office or ivory tower all day long, removed from the daily action. A practical businessperson, Morita enjoyed tinkering with electronics as a child, and nothing had changed in the years since. He took a constant and keen interest in the research and development branch of his company. In fact, in the early years, there was one product that particularly caught Morita's attention.

Akio Morita, an optimist, "believe(s) that there will be a glorious future for human beings. Respectful advances in technology are promised for the future and (he) believes that it will enrich people's lives all over the world." (http://www. akiomorita.net/en/contents/word/018.html). He believed that any problem can be solved with human technology, for example, that of starvation or energy, these are not unsolvable problems, considering from the experiences of human beings. In Morita's mind, such problems are problems because one takes those problems negatively; that is the problem. If one makes positive efforts, one can solve any problem, even difficult ones. Perhaps here you need to ask yourself, "How do you approach problems? Are you being optimistic in solving them?"

Combining the Best of the Western and Asian Culture

Western knowledge with Japanese spirit. (Japanese proverb) [The Japanese still use this saying not to lose the Japanese Spirit. This Japanese proverb was born in nineteenth century when Europe was leading the world and the samurai era was coming to an end. The Japanese Meiji government decided to adopt European style to catch up with Europe and America. However, we did not want to lose our identity; hence this proverb was created.]

Use one eye for knowledge and the other one for love. Together they will give you untold happiness. (Japanese saying)

For Akio Morita, there is no secret ingredient or hidden formula responsible for the success of the best Japanese companies (Morita 1987). To him, all of us learn by imitating, as children, as students, as novices in the world of business. And then all of us grow up and learn to blend our innate abilities with the rules or principles we have learned.

Akio Morita told American business students in 1995, "We thought if we run our company the Japanese way, always we cannot be successful. So that's why Sony's management concept is mixture Japanese and Western concept." With his expertise

(Morita's ability to study both Western and Asian cultures and smartly combining the best parts of each), he was often consulted about the American-Japanese trade issues.

Ask, "Are you combining, using the best of your values, training and skills to achieve the best? And how can you tap further?"

Section Conclusion

Virtue is not knowing but doing. (Japanese proverb)

Thanks to Akio Morita; "from the rubble of post-war Japan, Sony's charismatic (*people-centred*) co-founder built his electronics firm into a trusted and a truly global company" (Time 1999, cited in Low and Theyagu 2003 *italics mine*). He became one of the twentieth century's most influential industrialists.

From Akio Morita, we can also indeed learn the power of passion; his passion was that of innovation. One's passion, excitement or eager interest on a particular subject can often lead to many successes; Akio's passion also fuelled innovations, product successes and Sony's growth as well as Japan's successful image. Finally, this author leaves you with one question, find out or uncover one vital passion you hold; know what motivates you. Then attempt to work things out based on that passion; see next how it propels you to greater heights.

Soichiro Honda and His Leadership Ways

One may excel oneself in any trade. (Chinese proverb)

For Soichiro Honda, It is easy to lead by telling or giving instructions, leadership skills are much more than the use of force. Leaders not only get results accomplished but also raised the satisfaction level of the people they lead.

Having the Passion, Energy and Enthusiasm

Nothing worthwhile is ever achieved without great enthusiasm. Leaders know this, and great leaders have the ability to put passion, energy and much enthusiasm into everything they touch. One such leader, Soichiro Honda (November 17, 1906–August 5, 1991), with a passion for motorcycle and automobile racing, injected much enthusiasm and energy into the people around him, and they assisted him achieve great things. He ensured close relationship between the managers and the employees.

Indeed, Honda had the vision and passion.

Being a Risk-Taker, Learning and Learning from Failure

Success is 99 percent failure.

Man has the right to fail, but failure is accompanied with the duty to reflect upon the failure. (Soichiro Honda)

A risk taker, Honda believed in learning especially from mistakes or failures.

In a typical Honda workplace, education and training is stressed and is indeed another key part of the Honda Way. A Honda training facility offers many, perhaps more than 300 classes, most of which are taught by Honda associates. Outside instructors' are brought in to teach engineering, English, and Japanese. It is also said that Honda production associates spend approximately 35 h a year in classroom education, and in the United States, Honda routinely sends associates to Japanese plants to further their practical education. All of this training is part of Honda's strategy to promote from within.

For Soichiro Honda, learning from failure is part of success. People who often play it safe seldom succeed as leaders. Honda believed that courage was not being fearless in one's endeavours. True courage is, in fact, having fear, but still being willing to learn and take the risks.

Being Determined to Succeed

During his employment at the auto shop, Soichiro Honda built his own racing car using an old aircraft engine and handmade parts; he then participated in racing. His racing career was short lived when he suffered serious injuries in a 1936 crash.

It is obvious that Soichiro Honda was a business leader who was not easily discouraged by any difficulties. By 1937, after recovering from his injuries, Soichiro Honda established his own company, manufacturing piston rings, but he found that he lacked a basic knowledge of casting. Interestingly, though enrolled in a technical high school, applying theories as he learned in the classrooms to his own factory, Honda did not bother to take examinations. And when informed that he would not be graduated, he commented that a diploma was "worth less than a movie theater ticket. A ticket guarantees that you can get into the theater. But a diploma doesn't guarantee that you can make a living." (Honda, cited in Motorcycle Hall of Fame 2010)

Team Leadership Lessons from *Shinkansen*, the Japanese Bullet Train

Introduction

Talent wins games, but teamwork and intelligence wins championships. (Michael Jordan).

Section Purpose and Objectives

One flower makes no garland. (George Herbert, 1593–1632)

The purpose and objectives of the section are to draw team leadership cum team lessons and insights from *Shinkansen* or even the *Harmony Express*, the Chinese equivalent, and assess what is relevant to organisations and businesses.

It was the Japanese who invented the famous bullet train that stunned the world with its unmatched speed. Indeed the Japanese bullet train system has been long credited with being the world's first purpose-built high-speed railway, and the model and inspiration for all other similar type systems running today. The reputation it has earned for safety, speed and punctuality is unsurpassed. [Wholly Chinese-built, though using technology from Siemens and Kawasaki, the Harmony Express is faster than Japan's *Shinkansen* bullet trains and France's TGVs (Train à Grande Vitesse, meaning high-speed train)—The Telegraph 2010.]

In terms of safety, it is said that there has never been a death on the bullet train system since it's inception in 1964, other than that caused by deliberate passenger misadventure. There has never been a serious accident, let alone a fatality, to any of the 3 billion passengers who have so far used the *Shinkansen* lines (Semmens 1995).

As for speed, the *Shinkansen* holds the present world records for the fastest average speed between two station stops—261.8 km per hour (km/h) between Hiroshima and Kokura (192.0 km in 44 min), and the fastest average speed between starting and terminating stations—242.5 km/h between Shin-Osaka and Hakata (553.7 km in 2 h 17 min). These records are from the 500 series "Nozomi" trains running at a maximum speed of 300 km/h between Shin-Osaka and Hakata, which commenced in March 1997. A magnetic levitation test vehicle has also clocked the fastest manned run at 531 km/h.

With regard to punctuality, the Japanese bullet trains arrive at their destination punctually One record shows that in 1 year, the total time that ALL bullets trains were late by was 12 s! (http://www.geocities.com/Tokyo/island/2589/nmt/bullet.html)

The bullet train's secret lies in that each car has its own small engine, and the total force of these motors produces a final speed that is faster, more efficient, and nearly instantaneous. The synergized effect of these engines all moving the train in unison is called the *Shinkansen* effect. Imagine or picture an organization as a huge train, with its motors and cars. Each unit of an organization is to ensure that all or the entire organization attains *Shinkansen*, the sense of smart teamwork that creates better service. *Shinkansen*—becomes the feeling of all for one and one for all. *Shinkansen* or team success as what the author would attribute to—this effort that lends value to our work and imagination to our service. Basically, if we can apply the *Shinkansen* effect which is so much needed, the future of an organization would most certainly be better.

The Shinkansen Effect on Team Leadership and Teamwork

Coming together is a beginning, staying together is progress, and working together is success. (Henry Ford).

Using the *Shinkansen* metaphor and applications (Low 2011), the author is putting up the case of the effects and benefits of effective team leadership cum teamwork. Accordingly, the future is team leadership cum smart teamwork. The world is becoming increasingly diversified, and smart teamwork, despite their individual differences, capitalise on their common goal and common ground that supply the thread that defines and enables them to work as a team, and at that, even more so successfully.

To demonstrate the fundamentals of teamwork, this author would like to indicate what Low (2003, p. 1) has highlighted; he uses an analogy on organisational structures when there is essentially little or no collaboration and teamwork. Such organisational structure precisely happen when there is wedge between an organization's lead and the led and when little or no team spirit. To quote:

An organisation is like a tree full of monkeys – all on different levels, some climbing up. The monkeys at the top look down and see a tree full of smiling faces.
The monkeys at the bottom look up and see nothing but 'ass holes'.

All the while, the monkeys at the top will get the fruits first, and most of the time, they will eventually produce SHIT for all the monkeys below. And all the time, that is what the monkeys below will get.

Low (2003, p. 2) further indicates that when such thing happens, there is much lack of trust. On one hand, the managers get all the credits for the work done. On the other hand, the organization's employees feel exploited and de-motivated. The managers also do not communicate much with their subordinates.

It is commonly said that Japan has also, over the past few hundred years, been strongly influenced by Confucianism. And here, to add, we can also apply Confucian ideas and values to Adair's (2006, 1998, 1990) Action-centred (team) (ACL) leadership. Yes, one can dream, but one needs to ACT. Note that in Confucianism, it is often about taking actions and doing rather than mere talking about it or sheer publicity. In *The Analects (Lun Yu)*, "Tzu-kung asked about the gentleman. The Master said, 'He puts his words into action before allowing his words to follow his action.'" (*The Analects*, II verse 13; Lau 1979, p. 64). And ACL gives us that framework and ways to move into action.

Firstly, in terms of task actions or what is needed to do the job. Goals and actions need to be defined and clarified as well as things that are to be done. "The Master is good at leading one on step by step." (*The Analects*, Chap. IX verse 11; Lau 1979, p. 97).

When two dragons or leaders combine, it has what is called the *double dragon* effect and all parties gain. Confucius encouraged teamwork, and the work needed to be divided, with all chipping in and contributing to the common goodness. "The

Master said, 'In composing the text of a treaty, P'i Ch'en would write the draft, Shih Shu would make comments, Tzu-yii, the master of protocol, would touch it up and Tzu-ch'an of Tung Li would make embellishments" (*The Analects*, Chap. XIV verse 8; Lau 1979, p. 125). Team leaders need to plan, organise while attending to the staffing needs, direct and monitor or control. Team leaders need to ask: What will be the team's goals and directions? What the resources, people, processes, systems and tools (including the financials, communications, information technology) are to be deployed? What is the plan to achieve the task—deliverables, measures, time-scales, strategy and tactics? Who is to do what? How the work is to be distributed?

Secondly, in terms of team actions, getting together, being organised and being up-kept, concrete ways should be in place to upkeep harmony and help each other within the team. Relationships among the team members need to be built and fostered. Peace and harmony is emphasised; shameful actions are to be avoided by one and all with the group. "The Master said, 'Cunning words, an ingratiating face and utter servility, these things Tso-ch'iu Ming found shameful. I, too, find them shameful. To be friendly towards someone while concealing one's hostility, this Tso-ch'iu Ming found shameful I, too, find it shameful;'" (*The Analects*, V verse 25; Lau 1979, p. 80).

One Confucian proponent gave these input, "Confucius explained clearly how each person's potential and capability in team work can contribute or boost the team spirit, leading to the success of a team. Therefore, team dynamics and harmonious relationships are important. If a team consists of players who are too opinionated in their views, and team would not be able to reach an agreement in its decision-making, and members have to spend much energy in convincing each other, even to the extent, at times, to no avail. So teamwork and harmonious relationships are both key factors in team success."

In a team or in the small business situation, the team leader or small business-owner really collaborates with his "family members" in a purposeful team fashion, "rubbing shoulders and doing something together also gives the opportunity to share. There is joint purpose, sharing the same dreams and bringing the relationship to a higher plane. There is also synergy" (Low 2008, p. 36, 2007b, 2005, 2001, p. 101).

Confucian collectivistic values are to be applied; the greater good is often being subscribed, and things are done for the majority. Here, team leaders need to ask: What standards of performance and behaviour are to set, agree and communicate to one and all within the team? The team leaders too should anticipate and resolve group conflict, struggles or disagreements. Also, overall, they need to motivate the team and provide a collective sense of purpose.

And thirdly, in terms of individual actions, team leaders need to issue or give challenges to the team members. Low (2010c, p. 44) has argued that leadership success is in serving and caring too, and that is a variant of soft power; he cited that, "The Master said, '. . .do your best for others.'" (*The Analects*, IX verse 25). Growing individual team members, team leaders need coach and guide members. They can show concern and care as well as praise and guide members individually.

Indeed team leaders should challenge the team to pursue team (organisational) goals. Team spirit normally thrives in a setting filled with short term assignments, medium term goals and long term missions linked directly to the organisation's health, survival and progress.

Tseng Tzu said, 'The way of the Master consists in doing one's best and in using oneself as a measure to gauge others. That is all.' (*The Analects*, IV, verse 15; Lau 1979, p. 74). Leaders should set the example for the team members to emulate and grow. Another Confucius' quote to support the self-cultivation and growth of the individual is this: "Tseng Tzu said, 'A gentleman makes mends through being cultivated, but looks to mends for support in benevolence.'" (*The Analects*, XII verse 24; Lau 1979, p. 117). Learning from one's mistakes, self-cultivation and personal growth of the individual is stressed and practiced; and the individual learns and grows while working harmoniously with the other team members; everyone's (job, self and other-centred) needs are being looked into and attempts made to fulfil these needs. Team leaders need to identify, develop and use each individual's capabilities and strengths as well as look into ways and means to help and support individual members.

Team leaders are indeed committed to grow individual members with the team. "The Master said, 'There are, are there not, young plants that fail to produce blossoms, and blossoms that fail to produce fruit?'" (*The Analects*, IX, p. 22; Lau 1979, p. 99). What Confucius indicated here is that there were individuals who can be groomed to do specific tasks satisfactorily and there were people who cannot. Therefore, in order to ensure good leadership succession planning for the future, leaders are committed to grow individuals. Confucius was also aware and positive of the fact that young people can be groomed to be future leaders and he remarked, "It is fitting that we should hold the young in awe. How do we know that the generations to come will not be the equal of the present? Only when a man reaches the age of forty or fifty without distinguishing himself in any way can one say, I suppose, that he does not deserve to be held ill awe." (*The Analects*, IX, p. 23; Lau 1979, p. 99).

Next, we will explore why the team spirit is really needed in any organization. Teams are needed for:

Moving from Goodness to Greatness

> If two men unite, their money will buy gold. (Chinese proverb)

TEAM: Together Even Achieves More; after all—as a Zen Japanese saying goes, "The moon shows in every pool; in every pool the one moon." (Low 2010b, p. 8).

A Chinese proverb goes as follows, "a single tree makes no forest; one string makes no music." It's really teamwork for the greater good. Interestingly, Wells et al. (2010) speak of the ant colonies operating through organized co-operation and task-sharing. Work together marvellously, ants even capture prey that is bigger than they are, and they can call up extra workers when an abundant food source is discovered; and they can defend a colony by fending off invaders.

Practical case evidence also suggests that teams typically outperform individuals when the tasks being done require multiple skills, judgment and experience (Macmillan 2001). There's a clear need to use strengths in numbers—"Spices are nice. Spiced rice is thrice nice." And like a maestro, team leader will play to their strengths to create a melodious symphony (Low 2003, p. 21).

Like *Shinkansen* in which each car has its own small engine (also read as its own strengths), winning teams can be powerful or cutting edge with superior outputs and high relationships when their team leaders know and play up to their people's strengths. It's the basic business insight that inspired Collins' (2001) *Good to Great* book, and this idea also applies to team success and the way team leaders lead. It is far more effective to build on one's people strengths than to worry too much about their weaknesses. Such an idea and insight can also be very motivating to the people one motivates. Of course, the leader really needs to know his (her) people's strengths so that (s)he can help them to express even more. [Note that Clifton and Nelson (1992) also argued that time and energy spent trying to improve a weakness could far more productively be focused on maximising a strength. Each of us needs to "manage" weakness, not try to "overcome" them, because it is our strengths which we can best contribute to the world, and that will bring us our greatest satisfaction.]

Interestingly, Fisher et al. (1995) offered this useful pointer—team leaders should assume the best about people for team success. When team leaders assume that the people they work with are lazy, mean or stupid, it becomes very counter-productive. This is because, among other things, such assumptions cause people to want to defend their viewpoints and fight to win for their side of the argument. This makes it difficult to sit down and work things out or improve things together. As team leaders, we thus need to change the way we think about work and about others. In other words, as opposed to McGregor's (1960, 2006) theory X, the latter's Y is embraced—akin to one of Matsushita's leadership tenets, that is, a leader must trust his staff to get the best out of them (Matsushita 1991). And what more, effective team leaders need to assume that problem(s) is caused by good people who are trying their best they could with the information, systems and skills they had at the time. Then, team leaders work to better information, systems and skills. More specifically, they need to focus on creating good real-time information systems; without them, teams can't make good decisions.

Boosting the 1 + 1 = 5 (Synergy)

> To beat a tiger, one must have a brother's help. (Chinese proverb)

In the same way as the Chinese saying goes, "one cannot clap with one hand", none of us is as smart as all of us; and without teamwork, there is no synergy.

Henry Ford's quote is ever relevant; he said, "Coming together is a beginning. Keeping together is progress. Working together is success." Through team success, superior outputs and high productivity are attained. As Low (2003, p. 10) has argued, teams and allow its members to "get a better perspective on the whole task and a better understanding of ways to make improvement." And because of synergy, the team can and will outperform a group of individuals. Interestingly, teamwork thus divides the task, with different team members having different tea roles, and doubles the success.

What more, with team and "action-centred leadership", the job or task gets done, the relationships get going—team members are happy, and the individuals grow and develop themselves, being coached and trained by the team leader. Adair (1998) sees "action-centred leadership" as a process of meeting all three of these essential needs: the task (the needs relating to achieving the goal), the team (the needs relating to building and maintaining the group) and the individual (the needs of the follower(s)).

Enhancing Successful Leadership, Team Roles and Shared Leadership

> Help your brother's boat across, and your own will reach the shore. (Hindu proverb)

Leaders are fundamental to teams since they set the vision and bring the team together. Strong leaders also protect their teams.

It is almost impossible to reach one's goals alone. We need people, roles and relationships. And we need teams. Team members, when given their respective roles and responsibilities, do and execute their tasks can produce wonderful output or get good results. And when a team goal is achieved, there is a payoff for all the team members. Achievement is shared, rewards are distributed, every one wins.

Michael Jordan once said that "talent wins games, but teamwork and intelligence wins championships." Teamwork is so essential. "Usually personal motives would be pushed aside to allow the team motives to succeed. With teamwork, there is increased ability and desire to improve" (Low 2003, p. 12). Now and in the future, team effectiveness is the key to successful leadership as well as management.

Shared leadership should also be encouraged and practiced. Like each powered *Shinkansen* carriage, each team member holds the potential or seed for greatness, and into that greatness they will become when empowered or allowed to. Be a team leader, not a boss. There is also a need to rotate team leadership among team members.

Effecting Increased Communications

> The more high-tech the world gets, the more 'cold' it is and, the more we need the soft human touch. Low (2001, p. 13)

Team members get comfortable and relate well with each other. Status within the team is removed, if not minimised, akin to the Russian proverb, "after the game, the king and the pawn are kept in the same box". And other barriers are also removed. There is better coordination, and team(s) result(s) in increased communications within the organisation, with the left hand now knowing what the right hand is doing.

Hallam and Campbell's (1992) research indicated that high levels of communications were often associated with effective teams. The authors believed this level of communication helped team members to stay focused on the mission and to take advantage of the skills, knowledge and resources available to the team. High levels of communication too helped to reduce or minimise interpersonal conflicts on the team which often drained energy needed for team success and effectiveness. The current authors believe that high levels of communication lead to high-touch and better relationships.

Increased communications indeed promote better relationships among the team members. Many people who are involved in teams intimated these to this author, "they like working in teams, and enjoy the relationships with team members. The nice or sweet thing about teamwork is that you always have others on your side"; "we support each other, and all of us feel good and we can overcome whatever obstacles". (interviewees' input).

Growing Holistic Thinking

Limited or narrow thinking can be myopic and stuffy, it can, in fact, lead to bad decisions being made; it should thus be avoided.

On the other hand, holistic or big picture thinking results in better decision-making; not just a portion, part of the picture or a tree, but the whole picture—the entire forest—is seen.

Being Organic

Teams are organic (not mechanistic), and being organic has its advantages and benefits. Flexible, "teams learn and grow. They are dynamic. They lead to continuous improvement. No one knows the job, tasks and goals better than a team" (Low 2003, p. 12).

There is also a shift from individually-led mindset to a participative mind growth. Empowering leadership involves the continual process of creating expanded competence and giving away responsibility. With this, it means leadership exists at every level of the organisation (Low 2003, p. 62).

With much open-mindedness that prevails, team culture is very much in practice in organic organisations. In such organisations, hierarchies are also discouraged while horizontal communication is promoted and paperwork minimized. In contrast with mechanistic organisations which stresses on centralisation and bureaucratic

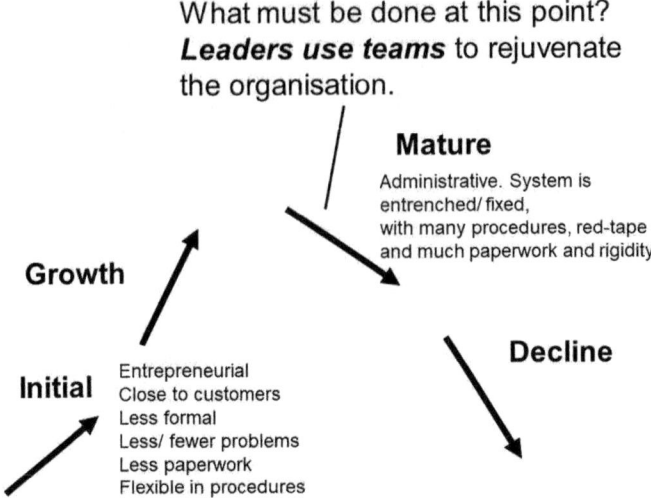

What must be done at this point?
Leaders use teams to rejuvenate
the organisation.

Mature

Administrative. System is
entrenched/ fixed,
with many procedures, red-tape
and much paperwork and rigidity.

Growth

Decline

Initial Entrepreneurial
Close to customers
Less formal
Less/ fewer problems
Less paperwork
Flexible in procedures

Fig. 7.2 The organisational life cycle (OLC) and when team(s) is(are) applied to rejuvenate the organization or spur organisational growth

procedures, organic organisations emphasise decentralisation and empowerment. Besides, staff creativity, initiative and team learning are also encouraged, and the people tend to be entrepreneurial and forward-looking (Daft 1998; Cummings and Worley 2001, 2009). In rejuvenating organisations (Organisational Life Cycle: OLC—see Fig. 7.2), teams can also be used to introduce much creativity, life and growth; self-directing teams can serve as a tool to rejuvenate organisations especially when they get old, with too much administration, bureaucratic procedures, paperwork and red-tape as well as slower decisions made. Many prevailing hierarchies and rigidity as well as mechanistic ways of the mature organisation can be got rid of; and smart team "small is beautiful" and simple ways can then replace them.

Having Improved Morale and Greater Job Satisfaction

"The history of company success is the history of staff empowerment, involvement and ownership." (Low 2000, 2006, p. 77). And self-directing or empowered teams allow for greater involvement, learning, personal growth and ownership.

Team members learn and grow and team learning is encouraged. As a leader, one lets one's people see one is learning. One also lets the people know that one is a work in progress (Chandler 2009). All these make the team members happy, enjoying an improved morale (Low 2003). Team members ordinarily also enjoy higher self-esteem and increased job satisfaction. Teams, when self-directed or empowered like the powered engine of each *Shinkansen* carriage, thus own their success, and overall, team members are motivated and have a strong sense of fulfilment.

Having a Higher Level of Creativity and Better Problem Resolutions

Two heads are better than one. (English saying)

Teams can be creative, and new product development (NPD) reaped. By bringing together people with a variety of experiences and backgrounds, cross-functional teams increase the creative capacity of an organisation. Studies (for example, Maggin 2004; Parker 2003; Low 2003) have repeatedly shown that the quality of ideas/decisions and the level of creativity emerging from teams are substantially better than from average individuals working alone. A great team, in fact, produces fast, creative, smart, decisive, consistent results. The point is no one can go it alone. People really need to get together to share ideas to achieve a common goal.

Teams such as Quality Circles (QCs) can be tapped to solve problems. Through empowered teams, employees are creatively involved in brainstorming, streamlining work processes and coming out with good or wise solutions as well as product and/or service ideas to work on. Teams can even be innovative, coming out with new and improved products and services for the company's customers.

Creating Greater Customer Satisfaction, Higher Sales and Increased Market Share

Empowered teams can focus their resources and better satisfy their customers (Low 2006, 2002, 2000; Parker 2003). Units and departments operating in silos, separated from one another, are no good for customer excellence and service recovery (Low 2006, 2002, 2000). Yes, staff in one department may say, "It's not my department! Please refer to the Marketing side"; however, as far as the customer is concerned it doesn't matter which department is responsible, the buck must stop at the Company. And (s)he is indeed dealing with the Company. In many companies such as 3Ms, teamwork should be carried out to attend to the customers, satisfying their needs and requirements. For example, when a new product is to be out, employees in all the local branches are team-briefed so that there is much coordination, and everyone within the team/company is in the know so as to better attend to the customers should there be any enquiries.

Organisations that develop strategies, organisations and human resources based on teambuilding and teamwork will reap countless benefits. In the first instance, it is easier for organisation to implement or carry out the strategies since everyone within the organisation sings the same tune, and from the same song sheet; they understand one another (Low 2003).

Triggering Greater Business Success

If brothers disagree, the bystander takes advantage. (Chinese proverb).

Low (2003) speaks of the world is changing, companies aplenty and competition goes intense. There are now increasingly strong global competitors. Predators would try to seize the most attractive opportunities. Technology is changing. New products and services are produced and sold. In such a challenging environment, we will find ourselves working with our colleagues, looking at new ways to cooperate, work together and finding the competitive edge. We can also add that a successful team beats with one heart; they are of one mind, sharing the same core values and getting things done in winning ways. Teams are the path to business success and excellence. Only those organisations that have skilful leaders committed to teamwork can look into the future with more confidence.

Overall, while the business part is being fulfilled, that is only one part of the equation and the other part, a critical part too is the relationships—as Anthony Robbins puts it, "The quality of your life is the quality of your relationships".

This author also feels that teams are often referred to in his working life. In fact, in our personal lives, we are all part of one or more teams that is, families, friends, communities, associations, clans, and others. So, we want to improve ourselves professionally and personally. Don't we? We should always bear in mind that the support, people joys, connections and relationships that are so vital to life and human spirit, and that keep us going. Relationships and teams add purpose and meaning to our lives, sharing key moments of our lives with people who matter. And that, whatever it takes employers and team leaders need to build teams into, growing teams as "families", being supportive to one another as well as life-giving and harmonious living.

Section Conclusion

Go to the people
    Learn from them
    Love them
    Start with what they know
    Build on what they have
    But of the best leaders
    When their task is accomplished
    Their work is done
    The people will say:
    'We have done it ourselves. (Old Chinese proverb – of Taoist origin)
    Teamwork is the fuel that allows common people to attain uncommon results.
(Unknown)

It is appropriate to conclude with a quote from Vince Lombardi, a football coach (1913–1970) who once said that, "Individual commitment to a group effort—that is

what makes a team work, a company work, a society work, a civilisation work."
The future is in the team, teams can be flexible. The future is organisational growth,
and that future lies in teams.

Believe in teams. Believe in the wisdom of teams. Be team-wise. Certainly there
is no better way to address a lack of conviction about teams than by seeing teams in
action.

Checkpoint: Think About It

Leadership in Japan

Review these key points and when you have finished the quiz, check your answers.

Leading, the Samurai Way
1. What is a Samurai?
2. How are you leading?
3. How can I emulate leading, the Samurai way? In what ways can I emulate
   leading the Samurai way?
4. What (successful) Samurai leadership characteristics that I would like to identify
   and cultivate? And why?

Zen and Leadership
1. Do I lead
   - A life of humility?
   - A life of labour?
   - A life of service?
   - A life of prayer and gratitude?
   - A life of meditation?
2. Do I care and uphold the interests of my followers? Fulfil their needs?
3. Are you
   - Being pro-active?
   - Accepting and leading change?
   - Growing and doing? What matters most?
   - Finding happiness now?
   - Following the natural order?
   - Practising the language of the heart?
   - Being focused?
   - Developing patience?
   - Detaching and letting go?
   - Applying objectivity and having no favourites?
   - Having stillness?
   - Being inspired?
   - Inspiring others through the use of the koans?
   - Identifying talents, coaching and growing others?

- Being humble and serving?
- Collaborating and team-playing?
- Disciplining and thinking positively?

4. Find a Zen quote. Check or search one that really means something to you. Copy it or cut it out and hang it on your wall where you can see it everyday. Such a quote can take you a thousand miles and it can energize you.
5. What things could you, as a leader, do to improve things?

Think about people in your life. Take an honest look at the people around you. How can you help them? In what ways can help them?

Nemoto's Key Principles of Leadership
Using the Nemoto Principles of leadership as practised in the Toyota car-making workplaces, and ask—Are you subscribing to:

- Get Improvement After Improvement?
- Coordinate Between Divisions?
- Let Everyone Speak?
- Do Not Scold?
- Make Sure Others Understand Your Work?
- Send the Best Employees Out For Rotation?
- Issue A Command With A Deadline?
- Rehearsal Is An ideal Occasion For Training?
- Inspection Is A Failure Unless Top Management Takes Action?
- Ask Subordinates, "What Can I Do For You?"

Leading, the Matsushita Way
1. Please check and review these leadership qualities – Are you
   - Having ideas of your own? Do you have a vision?
   - Believing in and tapping the people's potential?
   - Using the umbrella when it rains [or guided by the laws of nature]?
   - Being customer-driven?
   - Being humble?
   - Being service-oriented and serving your community?
   - Leading by example?
   - Being pro-active and passionate?
   - Being persuasive, having the power of persuasion?
   - Winning trust of your people?
   - Believing that trouble is good and it makes us strong?
   - Making hardship as a source of your driving force for success?
   - Doing what you know to be right?
   - Being bold and determined?
   - Applying the untrapped mind?
   - Surging ahead?
   - Being adaptable and flexible?

Akio Morita and His Leadership Ways (Sony)

1. Think about it. Ask yourself what about yourself in terms of
   - Creating and growing the competitive edge?
   - Having clarity of goals and taking responsibility?
   - Finding the need and filling it—satisfying the market?
   - Learning from mistakes, learning from failures?
   - Coping with the speed of change?
   - Making full use of people's potential?
   - Motivating and energizing people?
   - Fostering the good family-like relationships within the company?
   - Taking market research to the streets?
   - Combining the best of the Western and Asian culture?
2. What strategic leadership lessons you can gather from Akio Morita's ways?

Soichiro Honda and His Leadership Ways

1. Think about the leadership of Soichiro Honda, the Honda founder. And ask yourself what about yourself in terms of:
   - Having the passion, energy and enthusiasm?
   - Being a risk-taker, learning and learning from failure?
   - Being determined to succeed?
2. What key leadership lessons you can gather from Soichiro Honda's ways?

Team Leadership Lessons from Shinkansen, the Japanese Bullet Train

1. Think about it, and ask how your team is doing in terms of:
   - The job or the various task? What job's to be done, and allocated; and how is it to be done?
     - Planning of the job? What standards are to be adopted?
     - Organising it?
     - Staffing? Who's who to do the job? Who's to do what task(s)?
     - Directing the job?
     - Controlling the job?
   - The relationships among the members and between the members and team leader? Is team operating harmoniously?
   - What conflicts exist in your team? What can you do to resolve these conflicts?
   - What are the ways in which you, as a leader, can help promote the harmony of the team?
   - Are the self-growth and development needs of each individual team members being attended to? Is your individual team member being trained? Is (s)he growing? Is (s)he being coached and guided?
   - Are setting an example in terms of learning and self-cultivation (the value of integrity)?
2. Reflect, ask if your team is
   - Moving from goodness to greatness
   - Boosting the $1 + 1 = 5$ (synergy)

- Enhancing successful leadership, team roles and shared leadership
- Effecting increased communications
- Growing holistic thinking
- Being organic
- Having improved morale and greater job satisfaction
- Having a higher level of creativity and better problem resolutions
- Creating greater customer satisfaction, higher sales and increased market share
- Triggering greater business success

References

Adair, J. (1998). *Action-centred leadership*. London: Ashgate.
Adair, J. (2006, 1990). *Leadership and motivation*. London: Kogan Page Limited.
Chandler, S. (2009). *100 ways to motivate others*. Singapore: McGraw-Hill.
Clifton, D. O., & Nelson, P. (1992). *Soar with your strengths*. New York: Dell Publishing.
Collins, J. (2001). *Good to great*. New York: HarperBusiness.
Cummings, T. G., & Worley, C. G. (2001). *Organization development & change* (7th ed.). Nashville, TN: South-Western College Publishing.
Cummings, T. G., & Worley, C. G. (2009). *Organization development & change* (8th ed.). Mason, OH: Thomson South-Western Publishing.
Daft, R. (1998). *Organization theory and design* (6th ed.). Mason, OH: International Thomson Publishing.
Daft, R. L. (2008). *The leadership experience*. Boston, MA: South-Western Cengage Learning.
Dalai Lama, H. H., & Cutler, H. C. (1998). *The art of happiness*. London: Hodder & Stroughton.
Easwaran, E. (trans.) (2007). *The Dhammapada*. Canada: Nilgiri Press.
Fisher, K., Rayner, S., Belgard, W., & Belgrad-Fisher-Rayner Team. (1995). *Tips for teams*. New York: McGraw-Hill.
Fuhrman, J. (2004). *Leading leaders to leadership*. Austin, TX: Possibility Press.
Gunes, M. (2010). *Zen philosophy*. http://goto.bilkent.edu.tr/gunes/ZEN/zenphilosophy.htm. Accessed 9 Jan 2010.
Hallam, G. I., & Campbell, D. P. (1992). *Selecting team members? Start with a theory of team effectiveness*. In Seventh Annual Meeting of the Society of Industrial Organizational Psychologists, May 1992, Montreal, Canada.
Heider, J. (1995). *The Tao of leadership*. London: Wildwood.
Kotter, J. P. (1997). *Matsushita leadership*. New York: The Free Press.
Lao Tzu *Tao te Ching*. From a translation by S. Mitchell. http://acc6.its.brooklyn.cuny.edu/~phalsall/texts/taote-v3.html. Accessed 10 Jan 2010.
Lau, D. C. (1979). *The analects (Lun Yu)*. London: The Penguin Group.
Low, K. C. P. (2001). *The power of relationships*. Singapore: BusinesscrAFT™ Consultancy.
Low, KCP. (2002, 2000). *Strategic customer management*. Singapore: BusinesscrAFT™ Consultancy.
Low, K. C. P. (2003). *Team success*. Singapore: BusinesscrAFT™ Consultancy and Humber Lincoln Resources.
Low, K. C. P. (2005). Towards a framework & typologies of Singapore corporate cultures. *Management Development Journal of Singapore, 13*(1), 46–75.
Low, K. C. P. (2006). *Strategic customer management* (3rd ed.). Almaty: Caspian Publishing House.
Low, K. C. P. (2007a). Ten leadership lessons learnt. *Global CEO, 2007*, 55–59.

Low, K. C. P. (2007b). Father leadership and small business management: The Singapore case study. December 2006–February 2007, i-manager's *Journal on Management*, www. imanagerindia.com, pp. 5–13.

Low, K. C. P. (2008). Value-based leadership: leading, the Confucian way. *Leadership & organizational management Journal, 2008*(3), 32–41.

Low, K. C. P. (2009). What art *Tao*? A study of leadership, the *Tao* way. *Leadership & Organizational Management Journal, 2009*(4), 83–92.

Low, K. C. P. (2010a). *Successfully negotiating in Asia*. Heidelberg: Springer.

Low, K. C. P. (2010b). Zen and leadership – growing one's leadership excellence. *Insights to a Changing World, 2010*(1), 1–10.

Low, K. C. P. (2010c). Applying soft power, the Confucian way. *Conflict Resolution & Negotiation Journal, 2010*(4), 37–46.

Low, K. C. P. (2011). Leadership and team lessons from *Shinkansen*, the Japanese bullet train. *Global Education Journal, 2011*(2), 181–195.

Low, K. C. P., & Theyagu, D. (2003). *Developing true leadership potential*. Singapore: The Publishing Consultant.

Macmillan, P. (2001). *The performance factor: Unlocking the secrets of teamwork*. Nashville: Broadman & Holman.

Maggin, M. (2004). *Making teams work*. New York: The McGraw-Hill.

Matsushita, K. (1984). *Not for bread alone*. New York: PHP Institute.

Matsushita, K. (1991). *Velvet glove, iron fist*. Japan: PHP Institute.

Matsushita, K. (1994). *Matsushita Konosuke (1894–1989): His life and his legacy*. Japan: PHP Institute.

McGregor, D. (1960, 2006). *The human side of enterprise*. New York: McGraw-Hill.

Morita, A. (1987). *Made in Japan*. New York: Plume.

Motorcycle Hall of Fame. (2010). *Soichiro Honda*, AMA Motorcycle Hall of Fame. http://www. motorcyclemuseum.org/halloffame/hofbiopage.asp?id = 199. Accessed 30 Jan 2010.

Parker, G. M. (2003). *Cross-functional teams*. Hoboken, NJ: Jossey-Bass.

Pearls of Wisdom. (2007). Buddhist wisdom quotes. http://www.sapphyr.net/buddhist/buddhist-quotes.htm. Accessed 9 Jan 2010.

Rohn, J. (1996). *7 Strategies for wealth & happiness*. Northbrook, IL: Prime Publishing.

Semmens, P. (1995). Shinkansen practice and performance. *Japan Railway and Transport Review, 1995*, 38–39.

The Telegraph. (2010). China steams ahead with world's fastest train. *The Telegraph*. http://www. telegraph.co.uk/news/worldnews/asia/china/7230137/China-steams-ahead-with-worlds-fastest-train.html. Accessed 7 Dec 2010.

Time. (1998). Akio Morita. *Time*. http://www.yachtingnet.com/time/time100/builder/profile/ morita.html. Accessed 30 Jan 2010.

Time. (1999). Akio Morita. *Time 100*, Aug 23–30, 1999. Vol. 154 No. 7/8. http://www.time.com/ time/asia/asia/magazine/1999/990823/morita1.html. Accessed 22 Jan 2011.

Wells, S., Bailey, E., Keller, L., Low, Kim Cheng P., & Ang, Sik-Liong. (2010). *What animals can teach us about leadership*, 30 Oct 2010. http://guamanimalsinneed.blogspot.com/2010/10/ what-animals-can-teach-us-about.html. Accessed 16 Dec 2010.

Web-Sites

http://www.geocities.com/Tokyo/island/2589/nmt/bullet.html. Accessed 17 Nov 2008.

http://www.akiomorita.net/en/contents/word/018.html. Accessed 23 Jan 2011.

http://victorian.fortunecity.com/duchamp/410/bsamurai.html. Accessed 30 Sep 2011.

Father Leadership in Kazakhstan

8

Introduction

Business and projects, like sports, are always looking for an edge over the rest of the competitors; more so, in this age of hyper-competition. In small business management that edge comes not only from investments in technology or efficient resource allocation, but also from father leadership with its attendant or valued people-rapport and building/nurturing skills.

The business owners/project leaders or entrepreneurs are to extend their personal influence so that there can be positive effects with results attained for the organisations. In fact, there have been very few studies on leadership in small businesses in the Republic of Kazakhstan; hence the need for such study. "Leadership involves the influencing of others through the personality or actions of the individual" (Maylor 2003, p. 248). Leadership is the positive influence of the individual on the people.

Father Leadership Defined

As small as a sparrow, it still protects its nest. (Kazakh saying)

Father leadership can be defined as a paternal style of leadership, one that is normally telling yet it shows care and concern for the people; the followers' welfare is being looked into. The people or relationships side of leadership is stressed here, and the leaders are in constant touch with their people, talking and relating well with them (Low 2004a, 2006).

In this section, the soft skills and attributes of a good small business leader: the 5Cs of father leadership and its benefits are being examined. Business leaders can be fatherly in their leadership approach to their employees, and such practices, to this researcher, appears to have a cultural fit and relevance in Kazakhstan. Indeed, leadership is one of the most essential ingredients for entrepreneurial success yet it

© Springer International Publishing AG 2018
K.C.P. Low, *Leading Successfully in Asia*,
https://doi.org/10.1007/978-3-319-71347-2_8

is said to be conceptually elusive (Wickham 2001, p. 369); however, when defined in a father leadership manner, it is easier to understand how such leadership skills can be used to enhance the small business organisational performance.

From the outset, it should be asserted that within the Kazakhstani culture, there is respect to the elders and seniors (Akshalova 2002) and hence, all the more, father leadership should be encouraged and practised in small business management. After all, it is a benevolent leadership style that benefits all parties concerned— the leaders, the people and the organisations.

To paraphrase President Nursultan Nazarbayev's 1991 speech, as cited by George (2001), Kazakhstan is in fact rich in patriarchal traditions; it has been through 300 years of tsarism and 75 years of Soviet government; besides oriental autocracy has a long tradition in the region (George 2001, p. 12). To this, one may argue that there is nothing wrong with autocracy as long as it is "father leadership", in line with benevolence, and bring benefits to the followers. Here, The Economist (2006, p. 13) reports of "soft paternalism" and the government appeals to the citizenry, nudging them to do things that are best in their interests. This can also be applied to small businesses employees with the owners running the businesses along the same line.

During Soviet times too, the head of the family was the person responsible for the whole family (Odgaard and Simonen 1999). One can argue that such "father leadership" practices have been reinforced by "Asian values in Kazakhstan … understood as a block, in which hierarchy, discipline and obedience form an entire horizontal line coming down from the state to the subject. Therefore, obedience of son to father, wife to husband, younger brother to elder one can be found in overall obedience to the state" (www.cvi.kz/text/Journal/N1/AsianValues.html accessed 23 February 2004). Here, it can be said that "father leadership" is in place, quite akin to that as in Japan and Singapore (Low 2002, 2004a, 2006).

True, the laissez-faire style of management is not prevalent. Indeed, when this is mentioned, it appears that father leadership has no place here. Besides, Low's (2004a, b, 2005, 2006) studies view that as the country develops, people will acquire more skills and further education, and with adequate numbers of skilled business executives, more will be exposed to individualism and the laissez-faire style; leaders will be more willing to practise such a style. Nonetheless, one can also argue that father leadership, coupled with concern for the staff's welfare, can in a way, be seen as a laissez-faire style, a benevolent form of leadership; and that is gaining currency especially among the more educated Kazakhstanis. Collectivism as well as family orientations are still relatively practised in the country (www.cvi. kz/text/Journal/N1/AsianValues.html accessed: 23 February 2004; Akshalova 2002) and support father leadership.

Besides, leadership and motivation are intrinsically linked. Being fatherly, means one shows care and concern. When the father shows care and concern to his children, it helps; the children feel motivated and happy. The father leader looks after the welfare and well-being of the employees. More so, it can be said that Kazakhstani people tend to expect that employers provide transportation and this is a standard practice in many banks and most manufacturing companies. The people do look for such benefits as incentives, and that keep them motivated (Low and Ahsan 2004; Low 2004a).

Next, based on Low's (2007) study, the 5Cs of father leadership and small business management in Kazakhstan are examined.

Applications and Benefits of Father Leadership in Small Business (Project) Management: The 5Cs

A father is a banker provided by nature. (French proverb)

The word "father leadership" sounds ominous and has authoritarian overtones; however in the context of entrepreneurial venture, the notion corresponds more to the positive qualities of leadership. Leadership normally offers people a direction forward (Wickham 2001); and father leadership aptly supplies this.

The Kazakhstani employers are to be very much like fathers; they are akin to the Japanese companies in their father *oyabun* leadership *kacho* (the employers/management takes care of their employees with reciprocal relationships) (Keeley 2001, pp. 45–46; Hanada and Yoshikawa 1991, pp. 39–40). There is mutual commitment and loyalty; this fosters the *wa* or harmony spirit, thus ensuring industrial peace. Both the manager and his staff behave like a father and his children in one happy family situation (Low 2006).

"Leadership involves followers as much as leaders and that leadership takes place in a social setting" (Wickham 2001, p. 369); indeed, father leadership recognises these, rather than looking at "great men" to supply examples of how to behave. Father leadership can also be analysed as similar to "the networkers" as identified by Lee and Chan (1998, p. 137); such business owners display a certain level of people awareness in their business dealings. They believe in the importance and influence of relationships and fought actively to build meaningful and strong ones that could indeed give a boon to their business. Figure 8.1 shows the 5Cs of father leadership in small businesses/project management.

The First C: Communicating

The way we communicate with others and with ourselves ultimately determines the quality of our lives. (Anthony Robbins)

A leader can use words to accomplish much (Baldoni 2003, p. xiv). Leaders have dialogues with their people; the gathering together of individuals with the aim of making them a cohesive whole and getting the maximum results for the business and its stakeholders is a basic role of most business leaders. When running the business, the tasks to be done and planning normally involve "small group" situations—"we are in it together"; "father leadership" can close ranks, bringing about an "all-in-the-family" situation (Low 2001, 2002, 2004a, 2005; Dessler 2001).

Fig. 8.1 The applications of the 5Cs can lead to high task completion and high relationship attainments. There are both formal and informal talks, with much teamwork and spirit fostered

Frank discussions can also ensue, and open communications take on even greater importance when a company, especially in its early stages, faces a difficult or uncertain future (Zimmerer and Scarborough 2005).

Benefits Informal communications foster teamwork and such teamwork, "we are in it together" and the "all-in-the-family" situation ensures good communications (Low 2001, 2004a) that is indeed vital in a small business management situation. Indeed so, "routine sessions are at times turned into rousing debating sessions where key issues of the small business are discussed" (focus groups' input, cited and referred to ten times), that created high involvement among the "family members". Besides, when the employer-employee communications and relationships are good, the employees then develop strong feelings of personal loyalty to their employer (Longenecker et al. 1998).

The Second C: Collaborating

> Get the work done, get the relationships right; everyone's happy. (Kim Cheng Patrick Low)

The father leader also collaborates with his "family members" in a purposeful team fashion. "Rubbing shoulders and doing something together also gives you the opportunity to share. There is a joint purpose, sharing the same dreams and bringing the relationship to a higher plane. There is also a synergy" (Low 2001, p. 101; Dessler 2001). Employees' successes are celebrated and with effective team leadership, teamwork is fostered and higher performance attained (Zimmerer and Scarborough 2005; Low 2005).

"Children and employees can be afraid to be frank or open to their parents and employers respectively"; however, "these can be overcome if the father leader shows sincerity in wanting to help or showing care and concern" (Focus groups' input). Leaders need to build their followers' trust in them. "In families, children trust parents... Trust can help us build bonds with people" (Low 2001). "The top leaders need to be sincere" (Focus groups' input) and these seem to coincide with Low's (2001) views that business leaders need to be sincere, keeping their promises and be committed to them.

Benefits With father leadership, much teamwork can ensue; such high-task and high relationships setting bring about many benefits such as realising the goals as well as bonding. The people feel energised, creating a high-energy setting (Low 2003, 2004a).

The Third C: Coaching

Any man can be a father. It takes someone special to be a dad. (Anonymous)

Credibility is critical for leadership, that is, it attracts followers (Wickham 2001) and builds their trust of the leaders. And when the father leadership framework is applied, the small business leaders can also be role models and coaches; they set the standards and the example (Low 2001). "Coaching is the art of improving the performance of others" (Eaton and Johnson 2001, p. 6).

Past researchers agree that entrepreneurial activity rarely takes place in isolation, but through social interaction and the acquisition of knowledge needed (Gaskill 2001; Carsrud et al. 1987). "Teaching is fundamental to coaching; providing information and ensuring that learning occurs is what coaches do." (Baldoni 2003, p. 148). Many entrepreneurs reported having benefited from the existence of a role model in their workplace, business, social context or the family (Gaskill 2001; Carsrud et al. 1987).

Besides, as their guide and mentor, the business leaders set the example, and it seems that the leader leads like a coach, not a cop (Low and Robertson 2006).

Benefits Learning takes place; the small companies' employees then emulate the father leaders as they advise, coach and transfer their knowledge and skills to them where possible. Besides, there is team learning and good relationships, and this can bring out the best in people and their competencies (Low and Yunak 2006; Low 2003; Petersen and Hillkirk 1991).

The Fourth C: Caring

A hug is a great gift—one size fits all, and it's easy to exchange. (Anonymous)

A kind word is a like a spring day. (Russian proverb)

Good coaches are inspiring, they are also masters of motivation; they prod their teams to win (Baldoni 2003). If people are to deliver, they require support (Wickham 2001; Dessler 2001). The father (business owner/leader) can be strict (task-oriented) and may discipline yet he is caring (relationship-based); he looks after the well-being of his off-springs (employees).

Evaluating the Singapore's Confucian heritage cultural model, Low (2002) has argued that the corporate leaders or managers, like benevolent fathers, "use more saliva than drinking tea"—meaning talking, listening, coaching and taking personal interest in the employees' welfare. Informality and intimacy exists—with everyone undertaking a variety of activities to meet daily performance demands (Lasserre and Schutte 1995, p. 105; Low 2001, pp. 98–99, 2002). Telling stories (and experience sharing) offers a vital route to the people's hearts, and it is one of the most effective tools leaders can use (Denning 2004, italics mine).

Motivating employees to their potential is critical; indeed, employees without motivation can sap any business (Caplan 2001). "As a child, you sought to impress or seek your parents' approval. People have the desire to do the job well; therefore, there is a need to give your employees the necessary challenge and they will do their jobs well. Like a father (to the employees), the need to be encouraging is apt ... and real" (focus groups' input and these were referred to nine times).

Benefits Moreover, such air of informality and intimacy can be very morale-lifting and motivating to the company employees, within a high task and a high relationship setting. While tasks are achieved, the relationships between and among each project members are also nurtured. "A little warmth energises both the receiver and the giver" (Low 2001, p. 106, 2003).

Great leaders know their success is determined by the success of their followers; they create a climate that enables others to achieve maximum performance (Zimmerer and Scarborough 2005). When such a supportive climate is applied, the employees will have greater satisfaction, working and enjoying the relationships (Low and Tabyldy 2005a, b; Low 2004a, 2007). Employees will also be looking up to their company leaders, their good conduct is stressed; and leaders and members are also expected to be showing care and concern to each other. They should both be respectful, reliable and trustworthy to one another. Indeed, "a family" that does business together stays together and grows the business.

The Fifth C: Controlling

If you command wisely, you'll be obeyed cheerfully. (Thomas Fuller)

The entrepreneur (project leader) is in a special position with regard to the information on which the business (project) is founded; he will control over what information is regarded as vital and should be invested in. At every stage of the business development, it is the entrepreneur who has the unique position of looking at the venture strategically (Wickham 2001, p. 373; Low 2005).

While not dismissing or denying the formal business controlling process such as Gantt charts, critical path analysis (CPA) or the various reports, the more informal ways (the "soft skills" aspects) of controlling through "father leadership" can also be instituted (Low and Tabyldy 2005a, b; Low 2004a). The father leader can encourage openness that can be fostered by allowing employees to voice goal-achieving ideas and concerns; with such openness, "the father leaders' ears are on the ground" (These were referred 19 times by the focus groups, and seven times by the interviewees in Low's (2007) study). And in fact, there would be no ugly surprises. Things are learnt, and errors if any, rectified. Good communications and collaborations ensure good monitoring and tracking of projects (Low 2004a, 2005).

Benefits At home, the father will normally talk with the family members during breakfasts, lunches or dinners, and by the same token, the business leaders, adopting "the father style" will gain input and feedback during such informal sessions. Indeed, this researcher likens this to that of "a Singapore Bank Chief Executive who relies on his regular breakfast gatherings with his general managers to get feedback and other vital information on the work projects he delegated to them" (Low and Tabyldy 2005a, b; Low 2004a, 2005).

Chapter Summary

A good man will appear when talked about. (Turkish proverb)

It is noteworthy to highlight that understanding and applying father leadership in the small business (project management) context in Kazakhstan can also help to build or grow the core competences of family businesses, the pop's and mom's businesses. These small and medium businesses can, in fact, provide strong support to and service the multinational companies operating here.

Why is it relevant to modern leadership or management? With father leadership, the 5Cs ensure high task completion and high relationship attainments. Besides, the "father" business leader informally talks; listen and flexibly upkeep close links with his or her team members. Work gets done, and objectives met, with a high camaraderie feeling among the team members. There is "an all-in-the-family feeling" too.

Such informality also fits well into both the small and medium company (project management context) as well as the big company context. With such informality, it also means much de-layering, faster information flow, good communications and high motivation that benefits everyone in the company in achieving the company's goals and objectives.

Most experts' lists of excellent companies included them as having used or encouraged informal communications, hence all the more this research has brought out the relevance of father leadership to modern management as well as to small businesses in Kazakhstan. "Excellent companies are a vast network of informal, open communications. The patterns and intensity [of informal communications] cultivate the right people into contact with each other, regularly, and chaotic/ anarchic properties of a system are kept well under control simply because of the regularity of contact and its nature" (Peters and Waterman, cited in Dessler 2001, pp. 376–377).

In analysing the relevance of father leadership in Kazakhstan, it can also be said that such a leadership style is especially needed in the early years of a company's development (Zimmerer and Scarborough 2005, p. 488). Indeed in emerging economies, explicit direction is also needed. This is more so and this researcher agrees with Low (2004a) and Low and Tabyldy (2005a). Arguing in terms of applying the Hersey and Blanchard's Situational Theory of Leadership model (Daft 2000, p. 515) or father leadership, Low (2006), indicates that in the early years of a country's development—with the populace's prevailing low level of education and/or low skills level/skill shortage (presumably, the followers' readiness can be taken as not able and not willing), a strong, telling leadership ("provide specific instructions and closely supervise performance") is necessary to lay the foundations for economic development and growth. Again, a strong, telling leadership is necessary to lay the foundations for the small business' development and growth in the Republic. There is indeed merit in this argument, and this author is also optimistic that with more experienced and skilled workforce and in time to come, with the country's further growth, selling or even participatory style of leadership may be practiced. Perhaps then, more delegation and empowerment may also take place. Until then, meanwhile, father leadership is the right approach in getting projects, large and small, and small businesses to move forward.

Checkpoint: Think About It

Father Leadership in Kazakhstan

Review the following key points and when you have finished the quiz, check your answers.

Applications and Benefits of Father Leadership in Small Business (Project) Management: The 5Cs

1. Define father leadership.
2. What are these 5Cs? State them.
3. How would you want to practise the 5Cs as mentioned in the chapter?
4. What are the benefits of each of these 5Cs?
5. I would also like to add these points:

_____

_____

_____

_____

6. Can you also apply 'Father Leadership in Small Business (Project) Management: The 5Cs' to teamwork or teambuilding? If so, how?
7. Can you also apply 'Father Leadership in Small Business (Project) Management: The 5Cs' to project management? If so, how?
8. Can one also argue and add the 6th C to father leadership to small business (project) management in terms of "commandeering"? If so, why? If not, why not?

   To add, please note that in a small business or project management, the business owner or project leader needs to tell the team members of his goals, expectations, and the details of which will have to come from or worked upon by the team members. Hence, after the basics have been settled, there is buy-in and ownership by the team members. At the beginning of the business (project), the telling style is applied as elaborated by Hersey and Blanchard's Situational Leadership Theory (Hersey and Blanchard, 2001; Robbins, 2005). The 'telling' is also done particularly at the start of the business (project) when people are not too sure of the hard details—project deadlines, targets, expectations and the roles each team member plays.
9. Read also Chap. 11 "Leadership in Singapore", refer on the issues as they would apply to the Republic of Kazakhstan, and think of the problems and prospects of father leadership in Kazakhstan.

References

Akshalova, B. (2002). *Kazakh traditions and ways*. Almaty: Dyke Press. translated version.

Baldoni, J. (2003). *Great communication secrets of great leaders*. New York: McGraw-Hill.

Caplan, S. (2001). *Small business success kit*. Avon, MA: Adams Media Corporation.

Carsrud, A. L., Gaglie, C. M., & Olm, K. W. (1987). Entrepreneurs–mentors, networks and successful new venture development: An exploratory study. *American Journal of Small Business, 12*(2), 13–18.

Daft, R. (2000). *Management* (5th ed.). Hillsdale, IL: The Dryden Press.

Denning, S. (2004). Telling tales. *Harvard Business Review, 82*(5), 122–129.

Dessler, G. (2001). *Management*. Englewood Cliffs, NJ: Prentice-Hall.

Eaton, J., & Johnson, R. (2001). *Coaching successfully*. New York: Dorling Kindersley.

(The) Economist. (2006, April 8). The state is looking after you. *The Economist*, p. 13.

Gaskill, L. (2001). A qualitative investigation into developmental relationships for small business apparel retailers: Networks, mentors role models. *The Qualitative Report, 6*(3.) Available at: www.nova.edu/sss/QR/QR6-3/gaskill.html.

George, A. (2001). *Journey into Kazakhstan: The true face of the Nazarbayev regime*. Lanham, MD: University Press of America.

Hanada, M., & Yoshikawa, A. (1991). Shop-floor approach to management in Japan. In J. Putti (Ed.), *Management: Asian context* (pp. 36–60). Singapore: McGraw-Hill.

Hersey, P., & Bianchard, K. H. (2001). *Management of organizational behavior: Leading human resources*. NJ: Prentice Hall.

Keeley, T. D. (2001). *International human resource management in Japanese firms*. London: Palgrave.

Lasserre, P., & Schutte, H. (1995). *Strategies for Asia Pacific*. London: Macmillan Press.

Lee, J., & Chan, J. (1998). Chinese entrepreneurship: A study in Singapore. *The Journal of Management Development, 17*(2), 131–141.

Longenecker, J. G., Moore, C. W., Petty, J. W., & Donlevy, L. B. (1998). *Small business management*. Canada: International Thomson Publishing.

Low, K. C. P. (2001). *The power of relationships*. Singapore: BusinesscrAFT Consultancy.

Low, K. C. P. (2002). *Strategic customer management* (2nd ed.). Singapore, BusinesscrAFT™ Consultancy.

Low, K. C. P. (2003). *Team success*. Singapore: BusinesscrAFT™ Consultancy/Humber Lincoln Resources.

Low, K. C. P. (2004a). *Father leadership and project management in Kazakhstan*. Presented at the 3rd International Symposium Project Management, , Almaty, Kazakhstan, 27–29 October (in English and Russian).

Low, K. C. P. (2004b). The value of diversity – The Kazakhstan perspective. *Journal of Management Development, 26*(7), 683–699.

Low, K. C. P. (2005). Father leadership and project management in Kazakhstan. *The Icfaian Journal of Organizational Behavior*. submitted.

Low, K. C. P. (2006). Father leadership – The Singapore case study. *Management Decision, 44*(2), 89–104.

Low, K. C. P. (2007). Father leadership and small business management: The Kazakhstan perspective. *The Journal of Management Development, 26*(8), 723–736. Emerald Insight, ISSN: 0262–1711.

Low, K. C. P., & Ahsan, K. (2004, June–July). Impressions of business culture of Kazakhstan. *Today's Manager*, pp. 39–41. Available at www.sim.edu.sg/sim/pub/mag/sim_pub_mag_list. cfm?ID¼41501 (Singapore Institute of Management web site).

Low, K. C. P., & Robertson, R. W. (2006). Not for bread alone: Motivation among hospital employees in Singapore. *Public Organization Review, 6*(2), 155–166.

Low, K. C. P., & Tabyldy, I. (2005a). *Father leadership and project management in Kazakshtan*. Presented at the 5th KIMEP International Research Conference, Almaty, 6–8 October.

Low, K. C. P., & Tabyldy, I. (2005b, November). Leadership and project management in Kazakhstan. *Caspian Business News Digest*, pp. 14–15.

Low, K. C. P., & Yunak, O. (2006). Small family businesses in Kazakhstan – Its key problems and prospects. *Journal of Business in Developing Nations*. submitted.

Maylor, H. (2003). *Project management*. London: Pearson Education.

Odgaard, K., & Simonen, J. (1999). The new Kazak elite. In I. Svanberg (Ed.), *Contemporary Kazaks*. London: Curzon Press.

Petersen, D., & Hillkirk, J. (1991). *Teamwork*. London: Victor Gollancz.

Robbins, S. (2005). *Organizational behavior* (11th ed.). USA: Pearson Prentice Hall.

Wickham, P. A. (2001). *Strategic entrepreneurship*. London: Prentice-Hall.

Zimmerer, T. W., & Scarborough, N. M. (2005). *Essentials of entrepreneurship and small business management* (4th ed.). Upper Saddle River, NJ: Pearson-Prentice-Hall.

Leadership in Malaysia

9

Hang Tuah: Leadership Lessons from a Malay Warrior

In this section, through the story of Hang Tuah, the legendary Malay hero of the Malacca Sultanate, several universal leadership lessons learnt are uncovered.

Introduction

> Leave your mark where others can only dream on going. (Unknown)

Leaders live on! Their names and actions are never forgotten. A Malay saying goes: *Harimau mati meninggalkan belang, manusia mati meninggalkan nama.* Meaning, tigers die leaving their stripes (their hide), but humans die leaving their names and reputations. A person dies, but his deeds live on.

In the Malay world, Hang Tuah was a legendary hero who lived during the reign of Sultan Mansur Shah (1456–1477) of the Malacca Sultanate in the fifteenth century. The origin and history of Malaysia could, in fact, be traced back to this Sultanate. The greatest of all the *laksamana* or sultan's admirals, Hang Tuah, was known to be a fierce warrior. Held in the highest regard, even in present-day Malay culture, Hang Tuah is arguably the most well-known and illustrious figure in Malay history and literature.

Ever since his early days, Hang Tuah and his four friends embodied comradeship and stood by each other through thick and thin. They even dug a well in their village known as the Hang Tuah Well which still stands today. Hang Tuah and his close-knit group of friends eventually became the Malay equivalent of the Three Musketeers. As they grew older, Hang Tuah and his buddies learnt the Malay art of self-defence (or *silat*) from a renowned guru named Adiputra in a cave somewhere in a remote part of Melaka. All five friends, with their courage and mettle, coupled with their expertise in martial arts, helped in keeping the peace in Melaka.

© Springer International Publishing AG 2018
K.C.P. Low, *Leading Successfully in Asia*,
https://doi.org/10.1007/978-3-319-71347-2_9

Bendahara (Prime Minister) Saved

> Kalah jadi abu menang jadi arang: Most conflicts are not a zero-sum game. The vanquished
> will be reduced to ashes and the victor to charcoal. (Malay proverb)

The turning point in Hang Tuah's life came when he saved the Bendahara (Prime
Minister) from falling victim to a man who ran amok in town. Other accounts have
it that (e.g. Wikipedia 2007a):

> ...Hang Tuah was first noticed by the *Bendahara* (the Prime Minister) of Malacca, Tun
> Perak. A band of pirates ran amok, causing havoc in a village, and Tun Perak and his
> guards' attempts to quell the unrest resulted in further attacks on the Bendahara. The
> Bendahara's guards fled, but when Hang Tuah and his friends saw the commotion, they
> were reported to have killed the group of pirates, thus saving the Bendahara.

The boys' courage impressed Tun Perak, and when Sultan Mansor Shah heard
about Hang Tuah's bravery, he made the latter the Laksamana-(admiral)-cum
Syahbandar (harbour master). The five youths were recruited to work in the palace,
rose in the ranks, to eventually become the Sultan's fearless knights.

The Malays Will Never Vanish...

> Hilang bahasa lenyap bangsa: Lose your language, lose your race (that is, if one doesn't
> preserve one's language, it will cause the downfall of one's race). (Malay proverb)

This saying: *Takkan Melayu Hilang di Dunia* (The Malays will never vanish
from the face of this earth) attributed to Hang Tuah shows that he was proud to be a
Malay, and the quote has become a famous rallying cry for Malay nationalism.

Hang Tuah remains an extremely popular Malay legend, embodying the values
of Malay culture at a time when allegiance and loyalty were paramount above all
else. The Hang Tuah and Hang Jebat story, whether completely true or not,
represents a paradox in the Malay psyche about loyalty and justice, and remains a
point of debate among students of Malay history and literature.

Turning Point in the Relationship Between Hang Tuah and Hang Jebat

> Laut yang dalam dapat diduga, hati orang siapa tahu: The deep sea can be fathomed, but
> who knows the hearts of men. (Malay proverb)

Perhaps, the most famous event in Hang Tuah's life was when he was involved is
a fight with his closest childhood companion, Hang Jebat. Hang Tuah's deep loyalty
to, and popularity with, the Sultan led to rumours being circulated that Hang Tuah
was having an illicit affair with one of the Sultan's concubines (Wikipedia 2007a).
The Sultan sentenced Hang Tuah to death without trial for the alleged offence.

However, the execution was never carried out because Hang Tuah's executioner, the Bendahara, went against the Sultan's orders and hid Hang Tuah in Melaka's remote region.

Believing that Hang Tuah was dead, murdered unjustly by the Sultan he served, Hang Jebat acts to avenge his friend's death. To Hang Jebat, *Raja adil raja disembah, raja zalim raja disanggah.* (A fair king is a king to obey; a cruel king is a king to fight against.) Hang Jebat's revenge allegedly became a palace killing spree or furious rebellion against the Sultan (sources differ as to what actually occurred).

It remains consistent, however, that Hang Jebat wreaked havoc on the royal court, and the Sultan was unable to stop him, as none of the Sultan's warriors dared to challenge the more ferocious and skilled Hang Jebat. The Bendahara then informed the Sultan that the only man able to stop Hang Jebat, Hang Tuah, was still alive. The Bendahara recalled Hang Tuah from his hiding place and the warrior was given full amnesty by the Sultan and instructed to kill Hang Jebat. After seven gruelling days of fighting, Hang Tuah was able to kill Hang Jebat.

It is notable that the two main sources of Hang Tuah's life differ yet again on the details. According the *Hikayat Hang Tuah*, it was Hang Jebat who avenged his friend's death, only to be killed by the same friend, but according to *Sejarah Melayu*, it was Hang Kasturi. The *Sejarah Melayu* is the more historical account, but the Hang Jebat story, as the more romantic tale, remains popular (Wikipedia 2007a).

To date, the Hang Tuah-Hang Jebat dichotomy continues to draw intense attention and interest remains a mark of the enduring experience of divided loyalties in the Malay mind or perhaps that of leadership and follower loyalty. Perceptions of the heroism afforded by both protagonists have shifted according to the value-based exigencies of age and epoch. Though some critics also point out that Hang Tuah "was a little more than a running dog of the establishment" (The Other Malaysia 2007), the romance of Hang Tuah's loyalty to the Sultan was extolled for centuries as a paradigm of Malay character, worthy of all emulation. But then again, the rise of a political consciousness brought about by leftist sensibilities, forced a reassessment of these characters, and the 'truth' they represented for the Malay psyche. The fact that Kassim Ahmad's and Usman Awang's works hint at the Hang Jebat character as a radical warrior pitted against the forces of corruption and tyranny continue to be intensely debated and is a testament to the moral questions regarding power and authority. And the latter continues to beset the modern Malay mind (Khoo 1999). Or, dare I say, provoke such issues and concerns in the minds of leaders and leaders-to-be or in the minds of the followers.

Lessons Learnt

You have the power to change. (Les Brown)

The key lessons or pointers to be extracted here include:

Lesson 1: Embrace Value-Based Leadership

Sincerity and innocence will in the end triumph. (Vietnamese proverb)

Clarify and know your values well. As a leader, what do you value? Be steadfast in your values. Appreciate and be steadfast in your values since these set your (the leader's) standards.

Your values will direct your work without distractions. They keep you focused. They keep you alive to your vision and mission. This is similar to lessons learned from 'Matsushita Konosuke: Be Steadfast in Your Principles' (PHP 1994).

Lesson 2: Practise Team Leadership

Ênggang sama ênggang dan pipit sama pipit juga: Hornbills will with hornbills sport; Sparrows with their kind consort—The English equivalent: Birds of a feather flock together. (Malay proverb)

Teamwork is of utmost importance; stand by each other through thick and thin—One for all, and all for one! As a team, Hang Tuah and his comrades defeated the pirates, and saved the *Bendahara*. They worked as a team, becoming feared members of the Sultan's royal guard. 'Give everyone on the team a way to contribute.' Here, a Malay adage has put it aptly, *berat sama dipikul, ringan sama dijinjing* (a heavy load should be borne together as well as a light load). Compare also another English saying: *A trouble shared is a trouble halved*—and how true!

Team members need to develop openness in their ways, building rapport and understanding one another. Another Malay saying goes, *Terbakar rumah nampak asap, terbakar hati siapa yang tahu* (if a house is on fire, we can see smoke, but if the heart is broken, no one can tell). Team members need to be frank with each other. They should learn to trust each other and allow their relationships to flourish.

Besides, easy-going team members *gotong-royong* (work together). This is particularly practised in the *kampungs* (villages); indeed so, the communal spirit (*gotong-royong*) is so important in the national culture of Malaysia. But what's more important, as Lim points out, is "this sense of continuity brought on by *gotong-royong* that is priceless", bridging the gap between the old and the young as well as giving back to the community so that leaders can instil a sense of unity among their people.

Lesson 3: Be Courageous, Showing Care and Concern for Others

Where there's a will, there's a way. (English proverb)

The Hang Tuah leadership style can be said to be resilient too; Hang Tuah was bold. As a leader, when one makes up one's mind to do something, one must have the determination to carry it out. He serves the Sultan well. The leader is selfless, rendering help when it is needed.

In today's corporate world, leaders need to act with courage. In the everyday rush of business, moral courage is often overlooked. Moral courage is the willingness to stand firm on your values, principles and convictions even under duress. Courage also involves speaking up to the higher-ups if need be. Some of the signs or symptoms of fear in an organization include: A widespread reluctance to speak of the 'unmentionables' (and every organization knows what they are—simply ask privately) or make decisions that are known to be politically charged.

The right thing to do may not only be unpopular, but dangerous as well. Situations of that sort reveal the true character of a leader.

Even service leaders must have the courage to listen to the complaints and objections of the customers. The latter should be seen in the right perspective. After all, they express dissatisfaction even to the point of going elsewhere to satisfy their needs. They can still be interested as long as the service leaders are sincere and interested, treating their complaints with respect and root out the cause of the problem. In the end it is the good faith that customers will remember.

Whatever the controversies or debates as to who was right: Hang Tuah or Hang Jebat (Some Malays hero-worship Hang Tuah for his loyalty to the sultan and country, while some lionise Hang Jebat for sacrificing his life in the name of friendship and justice), the other leadership lessons learnt include:

Lesson 4: Be Patriotic and Loyal to Country (Company)

> Hujan emas di negeri orang, hujan batu di negeri sendiri, Lebih baik negeri sendiri: It may rain gold in a foreign land and stones in your country, but your own country is always better. Loyalty and patriotism should lie in your own country. (Malay proverb)

Loyalty must indeed be practised, not preached by the leaders. As said by Brigadier-General SLA Marshall, *in Men Against Fire,* "Loyalty is the big thing, the greatest battle asset of all. But no man ever wins the loyalty of troops by preaching loyalty. It is given to him as he proves his possession of the other virtues."

Opposing views and stands aside, a positive way and valuable leadership lessons gained when looking at the Hang Tuah/Hang Jebat characters is that: True, we extol Hang Tuah's loyalty to the Sultan, and by the same token one needs to just do the job, be loyal to service and to the people, and ensure service quality.

Lesson 5: The Leader Practises Servant Leadership

> Seperti bumi dengan langit: The earth compared to the sky, that is, very distinctive or unique. (Malay proverb)

This author likes Hang Jebat's assertion: *Raja adil raja disembah, raja zalim raja disanggah.* A fair king is a king to obey, a cruel king is a king to fight against.

As a member of the public and/or an employee, perhaps, one may prefer to take the proactive stand of the Jebat character, a direct warrior pitted against the forces of corruption and tyranny. He is courageous enough to openly question and act when things appear not to be appropriate. Here, some check and balance is put into place.

Lesson 6: Fallibility of a Leader

> Where there is a sea, there are pirates. (Malay proverb)

The key point to note here is that leaders should realize that they are fallible too. And often they should set or be the example.

There is a Malay saying that goes, *seperti ketam menyuruh anaknya berjalan betul*—like a crab instructing its offspring to walk properly, refers to the fact that there is no use in advising others, when one, oneself, does not follow what is being advised (by oneself). What this proverb shows is that, it is impossible to teach or require others to set a good example when the leader him(her)self performs badly, and as a leader, they must practice what they preach prior to asking the followers to do the same thing (Fig. 9.1).

Interestingly, at this point, the public and the people overseas are basically observing a key issue that is now prevailing in the Malaysian setting. And this is the case of 1Malaysia Development Berhad (1MDB) which is a strategic development company, wholly owned by the Government of Malaysia. 1MDB was set up to push strategic initiatives for the country's long-term economic development by forging global partnerships and promoting foreign direct investment. 1MDB is currently involved several high-profile projects such as the Tun Razak Exchange.

In terms of corporate governance, 1MDB has a three-tier check-and-balance system consisting of a Board of Advisors, a Board of Directors and a senior management team. The Board of Advisors is chaired by the Prime Minister of Malaysia, Najib Razak. However, back in 2015, claims or allegations were made in several newspapers, including the Wall Street Journal that the organisation had

Fig. 9.1 Illustration of the Malay saying, a crab instructing its offspring to walk properly or in a straight manner

been used to draw off state funds into the accounts of Prime Minister Najib Razak, and people associated with him. The corruption scandal is said to have caused a political crisis in a key U.S. ally in Asia and threatens to upend years of one-party rule in the country (The Wall Street Journal 2016).

Conceivably so, whatever may have happened, the Prime Minister Najib "denied wrongdoing or taking money for personal gain"; "the 1MDB fund denies wrongdoing and says it's cooperating with probes" (The Wall Street Journal 2016). Prime Minister Najib Razak is currently doing some damage control, upping the Public Relations (PR) machinery and is certainly building the credibility and good image of his government.

Lesson 7: Promote Loyalty Among Your People

Clapping with only one hand will not make a noise. (Malay proverb)

This also promotes unity among them. However, avoid having yes-men among your people—don't accept blind loyalty.

Lesson 8: Encourage Your People Even to Question or Challenge You

If you plant grass, you won't get rice. (Malay proverb)

As leaders, we certainly do not like being questioned or challenged. However, as leaders we may also make mistake(s). One Malay proverb goes as such, *Setinggitinggi tupai melompat, akhirnya jatuh ketanah juga* (No matter how high the squirrel jumps, it will eventually fall onto the ground). Even smart leaders do make mistakes at times. So, note that when followers or people care enough to ask leaders tough questions, it gives leaders an opportunity to provide honest feedback. And that's good. Leaders too can come to realise if mistakes are unwittingly made.

As leaders, ask your followers questions. Ask them about their understanding of the topic being discussed or key issues affecting them. For example, a leader might ask an employee, "What happens if we do change? And, what will happen if we do not change?" Leaders who dislike being challenged are leaders who lack confidence in their ability to do the job. Leaders who enjoy challenges from followers/ employees recognise that working through the difficulties and questions presents opportunities to develop followers/employees who are even more loyal than followers or employees who never question anything.

Lesson 9: Be Determined, Honest, Sincere and Embrace the Spirit of Competitiveness

Success is not final, failure is not fatal: it is the courage to continue that counts. (Winston Churchill)

Overall, emulate the positive qualities of Hang Tuah. We must grow and we need to be leaders. To paraphrase the Raja Muda of Perak Raja Nazrin Shah, the fate of the people is dependent on their determination, honesty, sincerity and spirit of competitiveness. He was urging the Malays to strengthen their mind-set to face the challenges of globalisation. The Raja said they should emulate the positive qualities of the legendary Malay warrior Hang Tuah (*New Straits Times* 2004).

Lesson 10: Leaders Must Have the Passion

> A great leader's courage to fulfil his vision comes from passion, not position. (John Maxwell)

Hang Tuah's saying, "The Malays will never vanish from the face of this earth." This reflects his passion or love for his country and people. In the modern-day context, the leader should care for and be passionate about his country, Mother Earth and his people. As leaders, we should not *melepaskan batuk ditangga* (perform a task without heart and soul).

> Leadership is passion. Without passion, a person will have very little influence as a leader. I believe passion provides an individual with the light of leadership and creates an undeniable drive to make a difference (Payn-Knoper 2005).

"No matter, how much talent or knowledge you may have", Matsushita Konosuke said, "They will be of no use if you lack devotion. If, on the contrary, you are not particularly brilliant or gifted, but apply yourself with unflagging zeal, all manner of things become possible. And though you may not expressly seek it, you will nonetheless earn the unspoken support of those who recognise the intensity of your efforts" (PHP 1994, p. 67). Insofar as you are passionate about what you do, you will have a positive influence on the people around you, and with their help your goals will be quickly accomplished. "Just as a magnet attracts and energises iron filings near it", Matsushita explained, "so enthusiasm attracts others and charges the atmosphere with a productive vibrancy" (PHP 1994, p. 67).

Father Leadership: The Malaysian Perspective

> A strong hand, a rule properly planned makes a prosperous land. (Unknown)

> Love and fear. Everything the father of a family says must inspire one or the other. (Joseph Joubert)

In Asia, several countries such as India, Indonesia, Singapore (Low 2002, 2006) and Brunei (Low and Mohd Zain 2008), their leaders and governments do practice a benevolent type of leadership, the father leadership style. In this section, leadership is examined through the visor of the fatherly way in the Malaysian milieu. This

Malaysian perspective seeks to answer the following questions: What are some of the father leadership qualities that Malaysian leaders display or possess? How should Malaysian managers be different from those in the West? One answer comes from these questions, and that is Malaysian leaders and government practices a disciplined yet benevolent type of leadership—the father leadership. The section also sheds some light on a genre of leadership, that is, father leadership style, fundamentally based on Islamic values and Malay/Asian culture.

Country's Background and History

> One generation plants the trees; another gets the shade. (Chinese saying)

The federation of 13 states in South-east Asia, Malaysia consists of two geographical regions divided by the South China Sea: (1) The Malay Peninsula or West Malaysia, located between Thailand in the north and the island-Republic of Singapore in the south. (2) East Malaysia occupies the northern part of the island of Borneo, bordering Indonesia and surrounding the Sultanate of Brunei. Although politically dominated by the Malays or *Bumiputera*s (sons of the soil), modern Malaysian society is heterogeneous, with substantial Chinese and Indian minorities (Wikipedia 2007a).

History has shown that the Malaysian political leadership has been practising father leadership style and ways since its independence in 1957. Tun Abdul Rahman, the first Prime Minister and Father of Malaysia who fought against the British for *Merdeka* (independence) was said to be "a classic case of the iron hand within the velvet glove" (Hamzah 2003, p. 24).

The Malaysian leadership style under its former Prime Minister, Dr. Mahathir Mohamad (also popularly known as the Father of Modern Malaysia), who was in power from 1981 to 2005, can be evaluated as practising father-leadership; Dr. Mahathir was "blunt, traditional but bold" (Hamzah 2003, p. 25), and "put (ting) on a tough act" (Hamzah 2003, p. 24). From his perspective, Asian leaders should assume and assert true leadership, seizing the initiatives in terms of ideas and thoughts and getting their people's respect. He viewed that some countries "suffer from too much democracy", with too many political parties; and even if good leaders were elected, they cannot finish their work or produce results within a short time (Today's Manager, 2004/2005, cited in Low 2006). It appears that the West or some may suspect that governments are not democratic because the government party remains in power for so long. However, he argued that if the people choose the same party and the same leader, then it is the people's democratic right to do so as long as proper elections were held. He also cited some undemocratic leaders in the past such as China's Deng Xiaoping who have dragged their countries and people kicking and screaming into the modern world (Today's Manager, 2004/2005, cited in Low 2006).

Islamic Values and Father Leadership in the Malaysian Context

What is Islam? someone asked. Muhammad said, Purity of speech and charity

It should be noted that Malaysia is "a country with Islamic institutions" and "the Muslims are given priority" (M. Manoharam, a lawyer cited in YouTube 2007).

Dr. Mahathir's successor, the then Prime Minister Dato Seri Abdullah Ahmad Badawi took over the premiership in October 2005. Minister Dato Seri Abdullah Ahmad Badawi gave a keynote speech when addressing the United Malay National Organisation (UMNO) assembly in 2005. Although during Dr. Mahathir's tenure, some form of Islamic resurgence in Malaysia had already existed (Ho and Chin 2001), Abdullah Ahmad Badawi called for the country's Malays or *Bumiputeras* (sons of the soil), mostly Muslims, to be more proactive, learning to be competitive and making the quantum leap. He asserted that this was necessary because help would not be forthcoming otherwise; the days when easy money could be made through selling licences and permits given to Bumiputeras were over (Low 2008). In that speech Islam was mentioned 49 times. Among other things, what seemed to be Abdullah's priorities (which support the idea and Islamic practice of leadership) were, they need only look at his speech and count how many times some words were used include:

- *Prinsip, integriti, moral* (principles, integrity and morals) 14 times
- *Rasuah* (corruption) 23 times
- *Upaya* (capacity) 24 times
- *Capai, pencapaian* (achieve and achievements) 32 times
- *Pembangunan* (development) 33 times

Malaysia is not an Islamic state. In the Prime Minister's keynote speech, Abdullah has indeed urged that Islam be anchored in the country's developmental model with integrity being up-kept, and a better world created. Here, the pursuit of excellence is thus seen as strongly recommended for the country's development and growth and Islamic values has moulded the country's father leadership style and ways (Low 2008). Recently, Abdullah further clarifies Malaysia's stand, that is, Malaysia, "a negara Islam", is being governed by Islamic principles [not a theocracy], but is also a parliamentary democracy (Hong 2007, p. 12).

In Islam, the faithful are asked: "what actions are most excellent? To gladden the heart of a human being, to feed the hungry... to remove the wrongs of the injured". They are then told: "God's pleasure is a father's pleasure; and God's displeasure is a father's displeasure". The leader can be seen as a father—after all, "the best of your leaders are those whom you love and they love you; you pray for them and they pray for you" (Low 2008, p. 38; Philips 2002).

"The creation is as God's family". "All God's creatures are His family; and he is the most beloved of God who doeth most good to God's creatures". In a typical Islamic fashion then, the leader, like the father, "needs to show care and concern to his followers, helping his fellow-creatures in the hour of need" (Low 2008, p. 3).

The father leader is ordinarily gentle: "Whoever hath been given gentleness hath been given a good portion, in this world and the next". "God is gentle and loveth gentleness".

Goodness begets goodness; kindness begets kindness. Followers listen to and trust their leaders as long as the leaders are good and trustworthy. "A man is bound to do good to his parents, although they may have injured him". The old or parents should be respected. "Verily, to honour an old man is showing respect to God".

The Practice and Relevance of Father Leadership

One father is more than a hundred Schoolmasters. (George Herbert, Outlandish Proverbs 1640)

Let us begin with a common Malay and Malaysian proverb: "*bapa borek anak rintik*—like father (mother), like son (daughter)". Here, this proverb is defined as the attitude and behaviour of a father (mother) will eventually reflected on the son (daughter). This, in most ways, refers to any quality possessed by a leader that would, in turn, be portrayed in the followers or employees too. For example, if the leader is meticulous, goal oriented, ambitious and high achiever, these qualities will be obviously passed on to or reflected in the follower(s) or employee(s) in one way or another; they would display the same qualities or characteristics. The follower would naturally follow the example set. Though the followers may not be aware or even notice it but from the outside, others may detect such similarities between the leaders and the followers. And one can thus argue that this then supplies us the thinking by blinking or the hunch that such a practice of father leadership indeed exists, if not thrives, in Malaysia.

Low's (2008) study shows that the majority (30 interviewees or 88.23%) cited the Malay culture or that "it is very Asian"; "We're Asians" (25 interviewees or 73.52%) and "Islamic in character" (interviewees' input; mentioned 26 times) as the reasons and practice of father-leadership. "We'll normally follow the leader when he is smart or wise; and when there's this all-in-the-family feeling and co-operation" (interviewees input; mentioned 39 times). This aptly fits into Abdullah's (1996, p. 247) research: The typical Malaysian culture has its roots in "respecting the elders and those who are more knowledgeable" and Islamic values. Besides, some of the common Malaysian values are "collectivistic", "hierarchical" and "relationship-oriented." (Abdullah 1996, pp. 104–106).

"If the leader's vision is right, then it is good. One can see father leadership as practiced by Tun Dr. Mahathir; he came up with Vision 2020, that vision has served Malaysia well" (interviewees' input). Ordinarily, father leaders supply the vision and direction, allowing the people to co-operate, and/or trust them, and the people gets (seeks) the direction of the country's growth and progress. Dr. Mahathir "has the difficult task of pointing the people in the right direction, convincing them of the need to change their attitudes to help the country become more developed." (Hamzah 2003, p. 23). Indeed, all the more important, given the prevalence of the above Malaysian values, "Malaysians *pragmatically* prefer to work for leaders who are able to provide them with a clear understanding of (organizational) goals." (Abdullah 1996, p. 109, *italics mine*).

Even with Mahathir gone, Asian authoritarianism is alive and kicking (Buruma 2003) and as Abdullah himself said, "it is still the same Barisan Nasional government in charge. There is therefore a sense of continuity in policy" (Shameen 2004, p. MF7). Given this backdrop, perhaps, the then Prime Minister (PM), Malaysia's fifth, Abdullah Badawi's style was "pretty much in keeping with the authoritarian rule of the Mahathir regime". When there were protests, there were crackdowns—a case in point is banned human rights march and anti-government protests, and Abdullah defended the arrests as "They ignored the law and still wanted to protest... of course police have to take action. This (protest) is not our culture" (Abdullah, cited in Ng 2007, p. 1). "Effective", "the father leader is very telling; just like Frank Sinatra's song, My Way'". Such a leadership style "aims at getting things done" (interviewees' input; 100% agreement and such words were mentioned 34 times; Low's 2008 study).

Nonetheless, it can be a matter of "deliver or get out" (Koh 2007, p. 11). The PM "can take tough decisions and once a decision is made, he wants his cabinet ministers and civil servants to execute and deliver" (Shameen 2004, p. MF5). Datuk Seri Hishammuddin Hussein, Education Minister (cited in Koh 2007, p. 11) once said, "I told them what I expected of them and that they had to deliver what we had promised." Here, a more effective and performing civil service can thus be seen as in the making. Rule breakers, under-performers and errant officials cannot take things for granted anymore—"unless they can expect to remain where they are in years to come as promotions are not automatic or purely based on seniority." Tan Sri Mohd. Sidek Hassan, Chief Secretary to the Government has urged civil servants to shape up or ship out. (New Sunday Times 2007, p. 1; Karim 2007, pp. 6–7).

Interestingly, even at the ministerial level, the then Prime Minister Abdullah Badawi told off the Works Minister, Samy Vellu. The Works Minister had said in Parliament House that the maintenance woes at Malaysian Government buildings, such as collapsed roof ceilings of two Government buildings at Putrajaya and burst pipe that flooded the brand new court complex, was not his responsibility. The Premier indicated to the Works Minister to "just do it". His exact words were:

It is shameful that government departments have to quarrel over their respective responsibilities. Don't wait to be told that is your responsibility.

(Datuk Seri Abdullah, criticising the Works Minister).

Furthermore, "father leadership protects the citizens' interests" and/or "national interests" (interviewees' input; mentioned 21 times). A case in point is that during the Asian economic meltdown in 1997/8, Malaysia under Dr. Mahathir disliked the International Monetary Fund's (IMF) remedies and refused its offer of help (Ho and Chin 2001). Instead, Dr. Mahathir then imposed the fixed exchange rate in

September 1998 as part of capital controls designed to stem the outflow of short-term capital in the wake of the Asian financial crisis (Feld 2005). Clearly so, capital control measures, being clear examples of the father leadership way (interviewees' input; mentioned 34 times), Malaysia has since maintained its policy of a fixed exchange rate between the ringgit and the U.S. dollar (Feld 2005).

Malaysia has transformed and stood economically resilient. Today, it is a Southeast Asian powerhouse, a key exporter of high-technology manufacturing and an influential voice among the world's developing nations. Thanks to Malaysian political leaders in particular, Mahathir's famed mega-projects, most noticeably, the gleaming new administrative capital of Putrajaya (rugged jungle until just a few years ago) and the soaring Petronas Towers in Kuala Lumpur (Havely 2003). Interestingly, under Dr. Mahathir, Malaysia turned rapidly from an agriculture base economy to an industrialised and manufacturing base, but under Abdullah's leadership, the country is "moving up to a value chain economy by developing its inherent strengths in agriculture without losing its existing manufacturing base" (Wikipedia 2007b).

The Problems and Prospects of the Father Leadership Way

Several serious "leader-dependent" problems can occur in the father leadership way. One, the followers can be "leader-dependent"; "they are yes-men. The followers become over-dependent on their leaders; they cannot grow out of the box or mould" (interviewees input; mentioned 25 times). Two, "the followers tend to be complacent with what they have (and that) they would be less adventurous in suggesting or carrying out new initiatives" (interviewees' input; mentioned 20 times). Three, "father leadership is based on connections and relationships, and in this case, it leads to the political leadership being confined to the political elite or families. Examples would include Hishamuddin Hussein and Dato Hussein Onn; and Dato' Najib and Tun Razak" (interviewees' input; mentioned 25 times). Besides, "when it comes to the allocation of government tenders and projects, companies connected to the political elites or the favourites may be awarded with these governmental projects or contracts" (interviewees input; mentioned 25 times). All these coincide with what Low (2006) has highlighted, that is, there are concerns that favouritism, nepotism, patronage and cronyism may occur (Low 2006).

"Firm control and, at times, explicit direction (*telling or even giving a good scolding*)" may be applied by the father-leader (Low 2006, *italics mine*). Like a father, he may claim to be always right, and demands obedience. "The father knows best" is enforced, and the leader may not want to listen to his children (followers). "The (father) leaders (tend to) be insistent, even adamant that they are right" (interviewees' input, mentioned 34 times). One interviewee, a Chinese Malaysian, spoke of "usually the father wants to have his way", citing the atypical phrase—

"need or should follow what "Nee peh kong" (your father says lest the father would be offended)". Another interviewee highlighted that "criticisms are a no-no". This coincides with Abdullah's (1996) study—that face is a critical issue, the leaders must not lose their 'face' ("muka" in Bahasa Malaysia).

Other than the problem of being "adamant that they are right", another related drawback is that feedback may indeed be not forthcoming. More so, when the father-leaders may not fully welcome feedback from the local populace or that they may feel offended by the frankness of their followers. One interviewee eloquently put this when he said:

> The father's face must be taken care of. He should indeed not lose his face. The children must not be seen as openly opposing him. Talk to him, yes, but it has to be in a very tactful and diplomatic way. I would add if the father makes mistakes, then he may also not openly admit so.

The father leaders thus rarely welcome challenges from their followers. To cite a chief example, the "authoritarian and impatient" Dr. Mahathir (Wain 2009) never liked being challenged—by his then deputy, Anwar Ibrahim. Here, "the speed in which Anwar was sacked and expelled from United Malays' National Organisation: UMNO astonished even the most seasoned UMNO watchers" (Ho and Chin 2001, p. 3). Of the then Prime Minister Dato' Abdullah Badawi, he was gentler, and more diplomatic (Seah 2003), expressing that bloggers can "feel free to say what they like via electronic media"—they can "do it (post comments) anonymously" (Ahmad 2007, p. 4).

Nonetheless, thus far said, the above problem is compounded by the fact that like the typical Asian father—although being kind and good hearted, father leaders can be aloof or distanced. The father-leaders need to "be more close to the people" (10 interviewees or 29.41% expressed this) "Reticent" (Hamzah 2003, p. 25) and "a difficult man to assess" (Hamzah 2003, p. 54), Dr. Mahathir is likened to be "a velvet hand within the iron glove": "Difficult to read. . . (his) mind" (Hamzah 2003, p. 24), "he puts on a tough act and so people get intimidated by that" (Hamzah 2003, p. 24). To be fair to the then Prime Minister, commonly called Pak Lah, Abdullah is said to be "gentle" (Wong 2004), "Mr. Nice" (Hamzah 2003, p. 101), and hence is more approachable. Though some political critics may say otherwise, "Abdullah. . . (has) projected himself as relaxed and accessible to the youth, especially young urban professionals, who wanted to have their views respected rather than brushed aside by elders." (Wong 2004, p. 3).

On the flip side, however, Low (2006) has highlighted that there is indeed nothing ominous of such leadership style as long as the father leader is benevolent, showing much care and is concerned with the welfare and well-being of his people. For "all his bluntness, all his emphasis on self-help and discipline", Mahathir showed that he cared for his people, provided for the Malaysian family, even to the point of "blaming national problems on the unfairness of the world" (Hamzah 2003, p. 74).

Low's (2008, p. 10, *italics mine*) study also shows that "the father-leader can (*also*) encourage openness that can be fostered by allowing citizens (*employees*) to voice goal-achieving ideas and concerns; with such openness, the father leaders' ears are on the ground". Perhaps, to add, at Malaysia's national level, more forums can then be held, and with more dialogues and communications, greater transparency's imported in.

The leadership of the present Malaysian Prime Minister Najib Razak and his administration appears to be open. Najib Razak allows people to share and express their thoughts. When they need to get consultation from anybody, they will do so. This is perceived to have resulted in, in part, a better-shaped policy, and also better support from the public. However, it has been observed that racial tensions are felt quite strongly these days (at the point of writing). This may be due to being too open in the freedom of speech and perhaps a monitoring system is required to prevent such happening. Communities need to be aware and sensitive of each other's feelings so as not to hurt each other; the various people should value racial, ethnic and religious peace and harmony.

Uniting and looking after his people, such a leader is very much in line with the Asian ways, and has a cultural fit. The Islamic values and beliefs have also brought about the need for the political leaders to be father leaders, uniting the people together like a family. After all, Muslims must be united because Islam demands unity among believers, and it is the notion of the *umma* (brotherhood) (Ho and Chin 2001). There is no conflict between Islamic values and economic prosperity, progress and developmental success—in fact, a success formula as in Abdullah Badawi's 2005 speech (Ho and Chin 2001). Note in the past, former Prime Minister Dr. Mahathir's speech was conferred the King Faisal International prize for Service to Islam. Dr. Mahathir was describing how Malaysia would continue to practise Islamic principles which are just to non-Muslims and pursue material progress even if deemed secular and condemned by other Muslims. He then indicated that political stability, good government, knowledge of science and technology, material wealth and modern sophistication are all part of the process of strengthening the Muslim *umma* for the future (cited in Ho and Chin 2001). All in all, Tun Dr. Mahathir, during his years as the Prime Minister, raised the people's living standards and won international acclaims for Malaysia. Although it seems he encouraged cronyism and failed to prevent the spread of corruption, the "abrasive and outspoken" Mahathir, in many ways, emerged as "a Third World champion and Islamic spokesperson". He criticised the West for trying to impose its liberal democracy and neo-liberal economics on developing nations (Wain 2009). In any case, it can be said that as a national leader, he did, to a great extent, contribute to a high sense of identity, pride and confidence among ethnically diverse Malaysians.

Additionally, some built-in discipline, or perhaps safeguard is also incorporated into such a leadership way. Islam dictates that "whoever is kind to His Creatures, God is kind to him; therefore be kind to man on earth". Kindness is therefore stressed, and "kindness is a mark of faith: and whoever hath not kindness hath not faith". Such care, kindness and doing good to one's fellow human beings can thus be overall seen as part and parcel of father leadership (Low 2008). Further, in so far as the father is morally upright, the followers will obey and listen; they become compliant or are generally law-abiding. The vital point here is that avoiding much disunity and drama, the father leaders can then grow and develop the country further. "Father leadership is good for developing countries. The basics need to get right first and after building the necessary infrastructure such as education, then more people then express more views" (interviewees' input; mentioned 12 times).

Take Singapore for instance, at least during its formative years under the then Prime Minister Lee Kuan Yew, the Father of Modern Singapore (Low 2002, 2006), it is fundamentally easier to build and grow a country where its citizens, valuing a sense of unity, are compliant. And the government/father leader can then focus on building the country's infrastructure while tapping the country's resources and growing its economic strengths.

By the same token, "father leadership is good for newly-formed companies". "The basics need to get right first and after building the necessary infrastructure. . . after the employees have been well trained, then more of them can be empowered" (interviewees' input; mentioned 12 times). "The father relates well in a small group or team situation, and that's good in small businesses, such a way is good. The workers are happy and motivated" (interviewees input, mentioned 16 times). These coincide with Low's (2008), Low and Or's (2004) studies: with the leader's personal orientations and informality, it also means much de-layering, faster information flow, good communication and high motivation that benefits everyone in the company in achieving the company's goals and objectives.

True, "times are changing, the younger generations may not like to be lectured by the father leaders or seniors", but "in Asia, there is *hormat* (respect), respect to the father is essential" (interviewees' input; mentioned 16 times). "Mutual obligations also exist. The leaders care for the people and the people being cared for, trained. . . Besides, the family is stressed and that's good. . . promot(ing) that 'all-in-the-family' situation or mood, even in the small company situation" (interviewees' input). This is amplified by a practical move that is currently practised—the retired employees are re-employed to coach or served as consultants to younger or inexperienced new or young employees. Abdul Ghani, Fadhal Ilahi reports:

> Old hands will teach, guide (police) officers. . . Retired police officers who will be re-hired on contract basis will not be placed in operational positions. They will be re-employed as instructors at police colleges and will also guide and train personnel in all divisions and states.

Overall, if the father leader informally connects, talks, listens and up-keeps close links with his followers, then father leadership can be very successful, ensuring high task completion and high relationship attainments (Low 2008). The father-leader's followers can also close ranks and be united.

In the following section, we will next examine Malaysian Chinese business leaders.

Malaysian Business Leaders

Blood is thicker than water. (Chinese and Malay sayings)

A single member of a family eats; the whole family will not be hungry. (Chinese saying)

As Datuk Dr. Paddy Bowie (cited in Khoo 2001, p. 110, *italics author's*) once said, "As a genuinely multicultural society, Malaysians have learnt to relate to other cultures and work with other people. Malaysia is a laboratory of race relations and cultural relations. When we go to the bigger world, Malaysians (*its leaders*) will have an advantage." Malaysian leaders thus learn to lead in a diverse setting.

This author would also take it that Malaysian corporate leaders are resilient, rising above the storms. We indeed see the likes of Dato O.K. Lee, Executive Director and General Manager, Penfabric Sdn. Bhd., Robert C.M. Tan, Dato Alfred E.L. Teh, Tan Sri Wan Azmi Wan Hamzah and Tengku Tan Sri Mahaleel bin Tengku Ariff (Khoo 2001, p. 16, 53, 55, 62, 84), just to name a few, working hard, facing pressures, taking responsibilities, building on the experience and being determined to succeed for their business and country.

Next, similar to other Asian countries, Chinese Malaysian business leaders are influenced by Confucian philosophy and values. Here, one is heavily dependent on the relationships of one's immediate surrounding or setting to do business. First of all, when one wants to start up a business, one needs the support of one's family members, relatives and/or friends for their moral support and/or even their financial support. Second, one needs the support of the Chinese contacts, basically, the clans and the Chinese community at large in order to do one's business well. This means that to the Chinese Malaysian business leaders, personal relationships with the key stakeholders and robust networking is of immense importance in their business

Fig. 9.2 Importance of relationships in Chinese Malaysian businesses

dealings. In Chinese business, opportunities for making monies are everywhere particularly so when one has good reputation, character and integrity and when other business people are confident and trust one in any business dealing. By having such attributes, one could and would draw more people to helping the business and gaining more (loyal) customers to supply constant or good support to the business. In this respect, profitability of the business is of second nature, and it would materialise when many customers are buying one's goods and services (Fig. 9.2).

When the Malaysian Chinese business leaders do well, they then return to the community in the form of company's scholarships, charities and donations, and this can help build the community's goodwill as well as better their relationships with the various key stakeholders, including the government and the various states' sultans.

Checkpoint: Think About It

Leadership in Malaysia

Review the following key points and when you have finished the quiz, check your answers.

Hang Tuah: Leadership Lessons from a Malay Warrior

1. How can you get loyalty from your people?
2. What values you uphold most? And why?
3. What is your passion when leading your people?
4. What are the ways in which you can practise team leadership?e
5. What are the ways in which you can practise servant leadership?
6. Find out more on the 1MDB case, and if you were Malaysian political leaders, what would you do to handle this?

Father Leadership: The Malaysian Perspective

1. Do you think you are a father leader?
2. What are the ways that make you one (a father-leader)? If not, suggest ways to practise father leadership?
3. What 'infra-structure' or support could you give to your people?
4. What are the ways in which you, as a leader, can give care and concern to your people?
5. Suggest ways in which you can get your people to do more of the tasks/job required of them.

Malaysian Business Leaders

1. What are the ways in which you can network in your respective community/ surrounding?
2. Suggest ways in which you can get support from your community.
3. What are the ways in which you can give to your community?
4. What is the way forward to building or growing your business?
5. For my own leadership style and ways, I would like to include these points:

_____

_____

_____

References

Abdullah, A. (1996). *Going glocal*. Malaysia: Malaysian Institute of Management.

Ahmad, R. (2007, January 29). Abdullah hits back at bloggers, websites out to 'rubbish' him. *The Straits Times*, p. 4.

Buruma, I. (2003, October 13). The last of the strongmen. *Times*. Accessed May 27, 2007, from http://www.time.com/time/magazine/article/0,9171,501031020-517783,00.html

Feld, L. (2005). *Malaysia country analysis brief*. Accessed May 24, 2007, from http://www.eia.doe.gov/emeu/cabs/malaysia.html

Hamzah, H. (2003). *Mahathir: The wake-up call*. Shah Alam: Anzagain Sdn Bhd.

Havely, J. (2003). Mahathir: Tough act to follow. *CNN*. Accessed May 26, 2007, from http://www.cnn.com/2003/WORLD/asiapcf/east/10/29/mahathir.legacy/

Hong, C. (2007, August 28). Malaysia a 'Negara Islam' but not a theocracy. *The Straits Times*, p. 12.

Karim, F. N. (2007, January 14). The good bad and ugly sides of civil servants. *New Sunday Times*, pp. 6–7.

Khoo, E. (1999). *ICT: Accidental death of an anarchist—Articles by Eddin Khoo: Warisan tukang cerita: Farce and the Malay tradition*. Accessed June 8, 2007, from http://www.artseefartsee.com/instantcafe/accidental/eddin.html

Khoo, C. (Ed.). (2001). *Malaysia savvy*. Malaysia: PHP International Singapore Pte. Ltd/Malaysia Institute of Management.

Koh, L. C. (2007, January 20). Deliver or get out, Minister tells staff. *New Straits Times*, p. 11.

Leong, H. K., & Chin, J. (Eds.). (2001). *Mahathir's administration: Performance and crisis in governance*. Singapore: Times Media Private Limited.

Low, K. C. P. (2002). *Corporate culture and values: Perceptions of corporate leaders of co-operatives in Singapore*. Unpublished PhD thesis, University of South Australia, Adelaide, Australia.

Low, K. C. P. (2006). Father leadership—The Singapore case study. *Management Decision, 44*(2), 89–104. Emerald Insight (www.emeraldinsight.com/0262-1711.htm). Accessed March 2006.

Low, K. C. P. (2008). Father leadership—The Malaysian perspective. *Leadership and Organizational Management Journal, 2008*(1), 75–95. (http://www.franklinpublishing.net/leadership.html).

Low, K. C. P., & Mohd. Zain, A. Y. (2008). *Creating the competitive edge, The father leadership way*. International Conference on Business and Management, Universiti Brunei Darussalam Brunei Darussalam, 8–9 January 2008.

Low, K. C. P., & Or, K. H. F. (2004). Are Singaporeans ready for their retirement? *Management Journal Development of Singapore, 12*(1), 39–55.

New Straits Times. (2004, December 17). Emulate positive qualities of Hang Tuah, Malays urged, Lifestyle. *New Straits Times.*

New Sunday Times. (2007, January 14). Shape up or ship out. *New Sunday Times*, p. 1.

Ng, E. (2007, December 10). M'sia crackdown. *Borneo Bulletin*, p. 1.

Payn-Knoper, M. (2005). *Passion: The light of leadership.* Cause Matter Corp. Accessed June 8, 2007, from http://www.michelepaynknoper.com/articles/passionleadership.html

Philips, A. A. B. (2002). *The best in Islam according to Qur'aan and Sunnah.* India: Islamic Book Service.

PHP. (1994). *Matsushita Konosuke (1894–1989): His life & his legacy.* Japan: PHP Institute Inc.

Seah, C. N. (2003, November 3). A gentler, kinder Malaysia? *Today.* Accessed May 28, 2007, from http://www.littlespeck.com/region/CForeign-My-031103.htm

Shameen, A. (2004). *Remaking Malaysia.* Asia Inc, pp. MF5–MF8.

The Other Malaysia. (2007). Hang Tuah sucks: Why we need to deconstruct our flawed heroes. *The Other Malaysia.* Accessed June 10, 2007, from http://www.othermalaysia.org/content/view/60/52

The Wall Street Journal. (2016). Malaysia controversy. *The Wall Street Journal.* Accessed November 25, 2016, from http://www.wsj.com/specialcoverage/malaysia-controversy

Wain, B. (2009). *The Malaysian Maverick.* China: Palgrave Macmillan.

Wikipedia. (2007a). Hang Tuah. https://en.wikipedia.org/wiki/Hang_Tuah

Wikipedia. (2007b). Economy of Malaysia. https://en.wikipedia.org/wiki/Economy_of_Malaysia

Wong, K. K. (2004). The Pak Lah factor. *Aliran Monthly*, p. 3. Accessed May 25, 2007, from http://www.aliran.com/oldsite/monthly/2004a/3f.html

YouTube. (2007). At the crossroads—Malaysia. *YouTube.* Accessed October 29, 2007, from http://www.youtube.com/watch?v=G9zmRMoDt58

Father Leadership in Negara Brunei Darussalam

10

Introduction

In this chapter, what are being examined are:

The concept and practice of father leadership. The national ideology that prevails in the Sultanate, and interestingly, the people and culture and other key factors that support the concept and practice of father leadership.

Leadership at the national level

Leadership at the community level

The world of *silat* and its parallels to leadership

Islamic values and leadership

National Ideology: MIB: *Melayu Islam Beraja*

National ideology, created to foster national identity, can also serve as a basic source of a particular country's national culture or values. Examples include the *Pancasila* (five principles) in Indonesia (Sedyawati 1996, p. 55; Clammer 1998, p. 238) and the *Rukun Negara* (Articles of Faith of the State) in Malaysia (Andaya and Andaya 2001, pp. 299–300; Clammer 1998, p. 238).

In Brunei Darussalam, MIB [*Melayu Islam Beraja* or 3M: Malay Muslim (Islamic) Monarchy] is actively promoted as a national ideology (Hussainmiya 2006; Omar 1996, pp. 13–14). With its MIB philosophy and with a small population of less than 400,000 people, Brunei with the Sultan as the Head of State and Government is able to bring about a sort of an all-in-the-family situation; the majority of the Bruneians are loyal to the people-caring Sultan (Low 2008; Low and Md Zain 2008). Much national unity exists, with the majority of Bruneians seeing the Sultan as fatherly, the provider, caring and showing concern for their welfare and wellbeing. Bruneians also enjoyed many benefits and these, among other things, include no income tax, free education and health services.

© Springer International Publishing AG 2018
K.C.P. Low, *Leading Successfully in Asia*,
https://doi.org/10.1007/978-3-319-71347-2_10

Besides, one can argue that Islam subscribes to father or parental leadership. Take for example, in Islam, the followers are asked: "what actions are most excellent? To gladden the heart of a human being, to feed the hungry... to remove the wrongs of the injured" (Al-Suhrawardy et al. 1992, p. 89). They are then told: "God's pleasure is a father's pleasure; and God's displeasure is a father's displeasure" (Al-Suhrawardy et al. 1992, p. 103). The leader can be seen as a father—after all, "the best of your leaders are those whom you love and they love you; you pray for them and they pray for you" (Low 2007, p. 38; Philips 2002).

"The creation is as God's family" (Al-Suhrawardy et al. 1992, p. 75). "All God's creatures are His family; and he is the most beloved of God who doeth most good to God's creatures" (Al-Suhrawardy et al. 1992, cited in Low 2007). The leader, like the father, "needs to show care and concern to his followers, helping his fellow-creatures in the hour of need" (Low 2007, p. 38; Al-Suhrawardy et al. 1992).

"Whoever is kind to His Creatures, God is kind to him; therefore be kind to man on earth" (Al-Suhrawardy et al. 1992, cited in Low 2007). Kindness is therefore stressed, and "kindness is a mark of faith: and whoever hath not kindness hath not faith" (Al-Suhrawardy et al. 1992, cited in Low 2007). Such care, kindness and doing good to one's fellow human beings can thus be overall seen as father leadership.

The father leader is normally gentle—after all, it is said that, "whoever hath been given gentleness hath been given a good portion, in this world and the next". "God is gentle and loveth gentleness" (Al-Suhrawardy et al. 1992, cited in Low 2007). During the 2002 Brunei Independence Day celebrations (Borneo 2002), His Majesty in his *titah* (official speech and directive) stressed the importance of God-fearing citizens and pointed out that a citizen with strong faith in Allah the Almighty would not steal nor kill others.

As a devout Muslim and a leader of religion in the country, His Majesty has always emphasised that success in this life and hereafter could only be realised if one upholds the Holy Quran as a guiding light. His Majesty pursues a rigorous policy of propagating Islam in the nation; he has introduced Islamic principles and ideas in his government. In order to achieve this, His Majesty has built many religious schools, and centres of Islamic religious teachings/studies and mosques nation-wide to ensure that citizens and residents are able to continue to learn, enriching their Islamic knowledge and performing piety towards Allah with more humility.

We will next see that the people and culture appears to also support the concept and practice of father leadership in the Sultanate.

People and Culture

When speaking to several people, the author perceives that generally it seems that the psychological insights and inclinations towards father leadership lie in a person's perspective. Or it "boils down to how individual sees the individual's father. Individuals have different views of his (her) father. Some fathers are good, caring and listen to their children, some are not" (one interviewee's input). Be it as it may be, "in reality, there is no such thing as a perfect father", but it can also be argued that national ideology, religion and culture may mould or induce people to accepting the practice of father leadership.

Much admired, the Sultan is close to his people. He gives a personal touch (The Brunei Times 2007, p. 1). "Father leadership is indeed practised in Brunei, and it's also reinforced by the Malay culture in Brunei Darussalam" [as expressed by 100% or all of the interviewees]. The Bruneian Malays are also well known for their values such as respecting one's elders, obedience to one's parents, being loyal and obeying one's leaders, as well as showing empathy and being considerate to others (Haji Abdul Aziz 1992). Such cultural values, along with the national MIB national philosophy, thus reinforce the practice of Father Leadership in the country.

Interestingly, one youth, in her 20s, intimated these [*italics mine*] to the researcher:

> The younger generation may not view father leadership as the answer or being effective since they tend to be more rebellious (*an adolescent or growing up issue?*) against the father, just in the family situation. 'Westernisation' and even lack of religious knowledge or training may have brought about this phenomenon.

However, this youth added that, "as a Muslim, she would subscribe to father leadership", besides, it brings about "much togetherness, family closeness among the people as well as unity." The same youth also expressed her further agreement, indicating that there was a strong link between such the leadership style, respecting one's elders and the Malay culture. She then cited the Malay saying, *Orang tua lebih banyak makan garam*, meaning the elders have more experiences, and they are respected; the saying also implies, "with age comes wisdom".

Traditionally in Bruneian Malay families, key decisions made are normally vested on the father as the head of the family, and he is the sole authority regarding family matters. If the father has made a decision, the children do not question the decision(s) made; it is more of a one way communication. Nonetheless, nowadays, since the children are more exposed to external influences such as knowledge and exposure gained from formal education, children tend to seek, request and/or demand the rationale and justifications for the decision(s) made to ensure or take the comfort that the right decisions are made. Yet at the same time, they still obey while respecting the father as the head of the family.

Planning and Directing

Under the reign of the Sultan, the nation has "enjoyed uninterrupted peace and much prosperity for almost four decades" (Asia Inc. 2006, p. 60). The people are happy. Oil and gas export revenues and government income has also made possible for Bruneians to enjoy a standard of living that is among the highest in the world

(Asia Inc. 2006). Policies of economic diversification are also currently effected to generate higher economic growth.

Generally-speaking and in the Asian context, the father leader knows best, and he gives direction to his people. His vision guides his followers. In his *Titah*, the Sultan gives direction to his people. The Deputy Sultan and Crown Prince Haji Al-Mutadee Billah, for example, has urged the people to adopt a healthy lifestyle to avoid a risky lifestyle prone to chronic diseases when he launched the scheme to mark the hundred years of health services in the Sultanate (Han 2007, p. 1).

True, some critics may argue that there has been too much planning and directing on the part of the government. Anecdotal evidence suggests that some may even point out that Bruneians may be too scared to talk back or give feedback to their leader. However, proponents' view that what is critical is that the father leadership ways get things done, and that gives the competitive edge. What's more, things get done in a fatherly manner—with care and concern in their heart.

Providing and Showing Fatherly Care and Concern

> Raja sebagai payung negara (The King is the nation's umbrella, protector).

A parent of the father leader is ordinarily gentle, and nurturing. In Islam, it is said: "Whoever hath been given gentleness hath been given a good portion, in this world and the next". "God is gentle and loveth gentleness" (Al-Suhrawardy et al. 1992, cited in Low and Md Zain 2008).

On many occasions, His Majesty visits his subjects to lend a hand, showing care and concern for them. Concerned when several houses in Kampong Ayer were affected by the storms in July 2007, His Majesty—"the Caring Monarch" (Wani Abdul 2007, p. 1) made visits to give a sense of presence while ensuring that repair works and relief to the residents were duly made. "The second visit surprised most villagers, even though some had expected the return of His Majesty to see the progress made." (The Brunei Times 2007, p. 1).

A further example includes the recent 15 February 2008 incident when His Majesty the Sultan and Yang Di-Pertuan of Brunei Darussalam paid house calls to some badly affected homes by flood in Temburong (Waleed 2008). He stopped by just long enough to ask villagers and their families the extent of the damage suffered by the floods, taking the time to offer some advice and caring words to several as well as sharing some laughter during light-hearted moments. At one particular house, His Majesty came across an elderly lady, who came forward to greet the monarch. His Majesty enquired, *Is there anything I can help you with?* The old woman simply replied by gesturing with her thumb and fingers to indicate the universal sign of money. His Majesty laughed and mimicked the woman with his own hand and said to her *Bah, nanti tah mencarikan.* (Yes, let me go find some for you.) (Waleed 2008). This little episode thus captures the very essence of the caring leader and the close family-like bond between the monarch and his loyal subjects.

His Majesty's birthday celebrations also usually see His Majesty working since the Monarch every year graces with his district visits and presence in the *Bercemar Duli* in which people of various races, cultures and ethnic backgrounds have the opportunity to meet and greet His Majesty. "His compassion and sincerity for his subjects extends beyond such visits and onto a national level" (Wani Abdul 2007, p. 1).

Caring and nurturing, the "father figure to the nation" (Wong 2008, p. 16) also encourages dialogues from his followers or *anak buah*. Low's (2007, p. 10, *italics mine*) study also shows that "the father-leader can (*also*) encourage openness that can be fostered by allowing citizens (*employees*) to voice goal-achieving ideas and concerns; with such openness, the father leaders' ears are on the ground".

The leaders' benevolent ways and people-centred ways are usually appealing; such ways are ordinarily much appreciated by the people, and the father-leaders are thus able to bring about unity among their people.

Giving Presence

Appreciate again and again, freshly and naively, the basic goods of life, with awe, pleasure, wonder and even ecstasy, however stale these experiences may have become to others. (Abraham Maslow)

Quintessentially critical, leaders give their presence to the people, and that presence can be assuring and comforting to the people.

His Majesty, Sultan Haji Hassanal Bolkiah Mu'izzaddin Waddaulah and the Yang di Pertuan of Brunei Darussalam and in fact, members of the royal family serve as role models. Even His Royal Highness Haji Al-Muhtadee Billah, the Crown Prince and Senior Minister at the Prime Minister's Office, gives his presence to the citizens. And among the many examples of his working and industry visits include that of the Water Works Department under the Public Works Department, and the Town and Country, Land Planning Department, the Housing Development Department and several other departments at the Ministry of Development (Abu Bakar 2007; Ong 2007).

The key benefits here are that the leader is indeed there for the people, and the leader, humble, serves the people. Akin to servant leadership, the father leaders also "focus on helping people to develop. . . The humanistic approach. . . also helps build community or a sense of togetherness among the stakeholders" (DuBrin 2007, p. 243). Moreover, as in the Fish! Philosophy, the presence of the leader—"be there" can be very motivating for the followers (*stakeholders*) (Pike Place Fish Market 2007, *italics mine*).

Role Modelling, Guiding and Growing

The leaders set the example, advise and guide; and the followers learn and grow. His Majesty Sultan Haji Hassanal Bolkiah demonstrated this in his inspiring advice to Bruneian students in the United Kingdom and Ireland. His Majesty called on students to succeed by being single-minded in their academic pursuits and help Brunei become a generation of intellectuals and to turn the country into a great and prosperous nation (The Brunei Times (2007), cited in Low and Md Zain 2008).

Senior civil servants, the village heads (in Malay: "Penghulus") and chiefs, taking the cue from the Sultan, must also be the role model in guiding and growing the people. They can develop the community, raising the living standards of the villages as well as improving the local economy and the nation as a whole. They can also enhance the villagers' skills, education and the use of information-technology throughout the villages (Abu Bakar and Lakshmi 2009, p. 5).

Apart from His Majesty Sultan Haji Hassanal Bolkiah Mu'izzaddin Waddaulah, Her Majesty Raja Isteri Pengiran Anak Hajah Saleha, through officiating ceremonies, also guides the people of Brunei Darussalam. For example, she has stressed the need for a clean and healthy environment (Abu Bakar 2007, p. 1). Here, she speaks of the environment influencing and designing the level of human life and simultaneously, the human lifestyle needs to influence and take care of its surroundings. If an area is clean and beautiful, then ultimately, the entire surrounding area, *kampung* or *mukim* as well as nation will also be organised, clean and beautiful.

Next the author will also discuss Malay leadership at both the national level and the community level (Fig. 10.1).

Low, K. C. P. (2008a). 'Father Leadership with special reference to Negara Brunei Darussalam', *E-Leader, Chinese American Scholars Association: CASA conference*, Krakow, Poland. 9 – 11 June 2008.

Fig. 10.1 Characteristics of father leadership in the Bruneian context

Leadership at the National Level

Groomed and trained in the Executive Development Programme (EDP), Senior Development Programme (SDP) and other training programmes run by the Institute of Public Administration, the Brunei civil servants administers the Sultanate well.

The leaders are there traditionally to protect the people. *Ibarat kayu besar ditengah padang, tempat bernaung kepanasan, tempat berlindung kehujanan* (translated, meaning 'like a big tree in a middle of the field, a place for shades in a hot day, a place for shelter on rainy days'). This Malay proverb indicates that a good leader is someone who will look after the well-being of his followers by ensuring their safety and security. A Malay leader would always be seen by his followers as their patron or protector. Thus he will have to be sensitive to the needs of his followers, and the environments. He must have the following values; caring (*pemedulian*) towards his followers, strive for the welfare (*kebajikan*) of his followers, shows mercy (*belas kasihan*) towards them but being fair and firm to them. This can also be seen in the next proverb that highlights the importance of being fair and upholding justice. *Matahari itu, gunung dan lembah sama diterangi* (The sun brightens not only the mountains but the valleys too) meaning, 'a leader will ensure justice for all'.

The leadership in the government ministries and departments can be said to be based on the traditional role of a leader, his authority, and accordingly, there is the deference of the followers to the leader's position and authority. There are ordinarily few people in the top positions which usually consist of the Minister, Deputy Minister, Permanent Secretaries, Deputy Permanent Secretaries, Director-Generals, Directors of Departments under the ministries. The Ministry's leadership usually issues directives from the top to the bottom within the organisation. Thus, the traditional role of the leader is to take unilateral and decisive actions. These are, in most ways, aligned to a directive style, mostly task-oriented and production-centred. However, in the present the twenty-first century, with changes in communication-technology, knowledge and expertise as well as improving skills at the departmental levels, the leadership at the directors' level also involves other levels of authority within the organisations. The various Assistant Directors, Senior Special Duties Officers and the Head of Units also lend a hand in leading the organisation by facilitating, communicating and solving problems; they serve as team leaders, change agents, coaches and mentors to the employees.

Leadership at the Community Level

At district, *mukim* and *kampung* (village) level, the District Officers oversee the management and running of the district with cooperation and collaboration with other government departments in the district as well as with the *Penghulu*s or Village-heads (*Ketua Kampung*). The leadership styles of the District Officer, *Penghulu*s and *Ketua Kampung*s are not restricted to a particular style. Here, in the District Department and government departments, the leaders of these departments normally have to get their respective Ministry's and Department's Approval when dealing with the affairs of district concerned. However, for the *Penghulu*s and *Ketua Kampung*s to work effectively with their respective communities, they have to switch or change their leadership styles accordingly, moving from participative style to situational style. The *Penghulu*s work together with the Ketua *Kampong*s in the *Majlis Perundingan Mukim* (MPM: Mukim Consultative Council) and the *Ketua Kampung*s normally work together with members of the community in the *Majlis Perundingan Kampung* (MPK: Village Consultative Council). The members come from various backgrounds and education, and by involving them, the *Penghulu*s and *Ketua Kampung*s could get the community to work and make decisions in the interests of the districts and villages as well as getting them run smoothly.

The World of Silat and Its Parallels to Leadership

The Potato grows in silence, the iron corrodes in silence. (*Diam-diam ubi berisi, diam-diam besi berkarat*, Malay proverb)

Silat (the Malay martial art) can be said to be a collective word for a group of native martial arts from a geo-cultural area of Southeast Asia covering the majority of the Nusantara, the Indonesian Archipelago, the Malay Archipelago (counting Borneo including the Brunei Sultanate) and the entirety of the Malay Peninsula. Indeed besides the Sultanate of Brunei Darussalam, any parallels of the two: silat and leadership can thus be said to be also applicable to the other South-East Asian countries of Malaysia, Indonesia and Southern Phillippines.

Here, the questions posed are: What it takes to be a *silat* practitioner? And to add this, what it takes to be a good or successful leader?

Similar to all other forms of martial arts, *silat*'s origins and roots has to do with self-defence, and the *silat* practitioner learns to defend him(her)self as well as the weak. And in leadership, one thinks of service, serving and helping the people.

One of the most important parallels or similar principles of *silat* and leadership is that of upholding one's integrity and protecting one's people. There's always a need "(to battle) injustice"; in the old days, "(there were) warriors, princes and princesses battling injustice" (Talib 2009: Introduction). Just as the *silat* practitioner upholds the honour and integrity as well as defends and/or protects the weak, a leader too is to protect and defend his or her people. (S)he upholds integrity and ensures no misuse or abuse of his (her) powers and skills; (s)he must always hold the high moral ground.

One can keep one's stick (staff), *keris* (an asymmetrical, wavy dagger), *parang* (Malay for a long knife) or gun, but never have to use it unless it is absolutely necessary. And indeed one is never angry. It should be noted that one of the most important principles or pillars of *silat* and leadership is humility or humbleness. Humility is always valued; although skilful, one should not boast or appear loud, talking carelessly or senselessly. One's words are measured, careful and sensible.

Lying low while not indulging in loose talks, one cultivates one's self-growth. One also goes about doing one's business and affairs but one truly rises to the occasion when the need arises.

Just like the silat practitioner—no matter how skillful one is or that one knows many techniques, tactics and styles, the leader is thus also humble; and (s)he is not arrogant or boastful. Sensible and careful with words, (s)he does not talk big or is loud.

The next parallel principle of *silat* to leadership is that of upholding peace. To be seen as gentle and peaceful is not a weakness; it is, in fact, one's strength. And one must have peace residing in one's heart and mind; the seed of wanting or even desiring peace must be there, perhaps similar to the Malay proverb, "*tanam lalang tak akan tumbuh padi*" (meaning in English, "If you plant grass, you won't get rice.").

Trading and doing business is certainly better than wars and battles. Peace is of paramount goodness, and it promotes trade and business as well as the prosperity of lands, countries and their peoples. The Malays are peaceful people (Several people spoke to this author, expressing, "Kita mahu dan cinta keamanan"; translated to English: "We want and love peace." "Keamanan dan kemakmuran adalah kembar"; translated to English: "The 2Ps: Peace and Prosperity are twins: they go hand in hand."). And peace is always valued. In the old days, the village headmen or leaders worked for, if not, ensuring the peace, harmony, well-being as well as the prosperity of their villages or kampongs. Just as the *silat* practitioner avoids conflicts and goes about life in a peaceful way, so also should the leader; the latter should not be a war-monger, disturbing peace and triggering or causing conflicts and disorders. (Not many people like a person let alone a leader who is overly competitive and aggressive. Just imagine the quarrelsome person in one's office or workplace, the combative student at school or the critical person in a voluntary organisation or in a temple—picture now that person with political ability on a global scale who loves war.) War is bad; it is a scourge and a tormentor to all people. And a leader who divides and rules, promoting conflicts and wars, is concerned with his(her) own agenda; that leader has little or no concern for his(her) people's welfare and well-being—and in essence, to this author, (s)he is a non-leader.

Another critical parallel of the Malay art of combat and leadership is that of (*jaga*) guarding—staying alert and (*pasang dan buat persiapan*) matching, adapting and making preparations; it can be used for advancing or retreating and between a change in directions. This *Jaga/ Pasang* is "the 'mother' stance/ position from which all attacks and defenses are executed" (Talib 2009, p. 5).

Fascinatingly, a leader "never sit(s) still" (Jack Welch cited in Crainer 2002, Chap. 3). Maintaining high energy, a leader too certainly needs to be (well-) prepared, knowing the situation or sensing the environment, having a SWOT Analysis and gearing, tackling the situation while averting an unfortunate event or crisis as well as listening to and caring for his(her) people. (S)he needs to get the necessary information, vital input and feedback while sensing the environment, factoring or reasoning these in, marshalling them (the key factors or reasons) and deciding while gaining support and moving forward ('sideways' or even 'backward').

Another noteworthy point is that what more, whether armed or unarmed, the *silat* warrior has an array of skills and techniques as well as movements; and (s)he is adept and flexible, deploying various styles, using empty hands, striking punches, spraying, thrusting, kicking and/ or using poles while blocking or parrying (Talib 2009). (Note that for the *silat* warriors, the *keris* was particularly useful for fighting in limited or enclosed spaces, such as inside a building or in the jungle, where longer weapons would be most unwieldy.) The *silat* warrior is thus practised and supple, and this gives to the next important parallel. So too, a leader needs to be adept, supple and flexible in capitalising one's competences (One indeed has to know oneself too) and deploying one's skills to attain one's leadership goals or objectives and truly work things out.

Another interesting parallel value of *silat* when compared to leadership is that of ensuring good health and happiness (psychologically and spiritually); most people want to be happy and healthy. It is said that the basis of all happiness is good health. (The Buddha once said that "To keep the body in good health is a duty, otherwise we shall not be able to keep our mind strong and clear."). And indeed both silat practitioners and leaders would want to be healthily and happily doing things in their daily lives (Jim Rohn spoke of "taking care of your body. It's the only place you have to live."). And what is critical is that whatever one does, one needs to be balancing one's work and one's life—and having lesser stress and more so, being happy. Similar to swimming, jogging, riding, writing, or playing golf, balancing one's work and one's life as well as being happy is a matter of growing the habits; and indeed they can be learned and/or practised.

To this author, another key parallel of *silat* in relation to leadership is that the leader must indeed be mentally strong. Talib (2009, Introduction) spoke of himself having *silat* his companion and "making (him) mentally strong as (he) went through cancer." To be a leader, one too has to be psychologically strong and positive or indeed being tough and resilient.

Interestingly too, Talib (2009, Introduction) saw "*silat* as a vehicle for expression, growth and living". Energy motivates. And indeed *silat* can be a passion too; and by the same token, the art and skills of leadership can also be passionately and enthusiastically expressed, pursued, lived and enhanced. Jack Welch spoke of, "The world will belong to passionate, driven leaders—people who not only have enormous amount of energy but who can energize those whom they lead." (Crainer 2002, p. 50).

Islamic Values and Leadership

Do you love your Creator? Love your fellow-beings first. (Al-Suhrawardy et al. 1992, p. 102).

The teaching of Islam originates from the Holy Quran and it urges as well as inspires all Muslims to embrace and practise the values of faith, integrity, self-discipline, self-restraint, loving-kindness and giving; all Muslims are also encouraged to refrain from sinful acts and live their daily life in moderation. This also means that all Muslims must do the right things according to the guiding principles of Islam (from the Koranic perspective). Referring to the Prophet Muhammad's exemplary leadership paradigm, all Muslims must carry out two important roles as socially responsible individuals in any organizations (Family, company, society and nation) (Zaidi and Low 2014). To this author, it can be said that Islamic values are derived from these basic sources. And they can also be said to have been added on, over the years, by Islamic scholars and philosophers.

The Values of Faith, Discipline and Self-Restraint

In the concept of Islam, human beings are indebted to Allah for his best creation of human beings (95:4). Therefore, we are the servant of Allah. One in debt has the obligation to surrender to Allah and therefore, submission to Allah is a must for each human being. This led to the reason that performing daily prayers to Him is of paramount importance for the constant remembering of Allah. In Ibni Khaldun's Muqadimmah, the father advised his son to constantly seek for Allah's guidance. He said in his letter that, "In all your affairs, try to get in touch with Him, and you will always enjoy his favour". Prayers, as Allah said in Qur'an, "restrains from sins and evil". The father further advised his son to "let people come to you to pray together with you, and perform the prayers at the proper times and with all their rites, perform with the mention of Allah". This is an alignment (Tawhid/Iman) to the principle of Islam that, "there is only one God" and is also exemplified in the Islamic management ethics that a leader sets a good example to his fellow people to align and to abide to the rule of an organization (Ang et al. 2012, p. 213).

The Value of Integrity

"Those who earn an honest living are the beloved of God." (Al-Suhrawardy et al. 1992, p. 91). Islam indeed advocates the value of integrity.

And when hiring people and in building the human asset, this author, from his work experiences, sensitively understands that Islamic banks (or for that matter, any organisation) look for these three qualities: Integrity, Intelligence and Energy. And if anyone does not have the first (Integrity), the other two will kill him or her.

Integrity guarantees prosperity. Integrity is the strict requirement of Syariah. "The noblest of you in the sight of Allah is the best of you in conduct." The Quran, (49:13), (2.188)

The Value of Dignity

Related to the value of integrity is the value of dignity. It is thus safe to say that if one has no integrity, one would have no dignity.

In discussing Ibni Khaldun's Muqaddimah, Ang et al. (2012, p. 213) also highlighted that the father's caution to "his son not to succumb to deceitfulness and levity in any enterprise he engaged in and that his son should uphold the value of dignity. He said, 'Control you yourself and do not get angry. Prefer dignity and mildness'. This advice is valuable to our youth as anger is a serious disease and its impact is far reaching. The Prophet Muhammad prescribed a remedy for the person in a state of anger, instructing him to sit down or lie down until (s)he cools off."

The Values of Justice/Having a Just Society/Corporate Social Responsibility (CSR)/Charity and Compassion (Loving-Kindness and Giving)

In essence, CSR as a practice is not possible in an unjust society. In a just society, a person's superiority over another one will not be based on the incidence of one's birth. The Koran avows that one is superior only so far as one's behaviour is concerned:

> O mankind, indeed we have created you from male and female and made you peoples and tribes that you may know one another. Indeed, the most noble of you in the sight of Allah is the most righteous of you. Indeed, Allah is Knowing and Acquainted (49:13, also cited in Zaidi and Low 2014, p. 113).

It is worthy to note that the Koranic concept of society is based upon an individual-collective duality. First, there is the individual who has free agency to live and is solely responsible for his/her acts. According to the Koran,

> Nor can a bearer of burdens bear another's burden. If one heavily laden should call another to (bear) his load, not the least portion of it can be carried (by the other), even though he be nearly related. And whosoever purifies himself does so for the benefit of his own soul. (35:18). And whatever good you do, you shall not be denied the just reward of it. As for the unbelievers, their riches shall not avail them, neither their children against God; those are the inhabitants of the Fire, dwelling therein forever (3:115–16, also cited in Zaidi and Low 2014, p. 113).

But at the same time, the Koran accepts that a just society can be built only on the collective level. The nature of social composition is such that people do not live on their own; they are bound up with one another as social beings. This is spelt out in the following verse:

> The believers, men and women, are guardians of one another; they enjoin good and evil, perform the prayer, give alms, and obey God and His Prophet. (9:71). Whoever does a righteous deed, whether man or women, and has faith, we will give a good life; and we shall reward them according to the best of their actions (16:97, also cited in Zaidi and Low 2014, p. 113).

There thus should, overall, not be usury or exploitation ("The taker of usury and the giver of it, and the writer of its papers and the witness to it, are equal in crime." Al-Suhrawardy et al. 1992, p. 114), and in a just society, exploitation, deception, perjury, and all types of abuses are anathema. Gambling and intoxicants are also forbidden; they are considered as anti-social activities.

Note that giving and charity are basic to a system which wishes to reduce and ultimately get rid of deprivation. No society can prosper where the rich do not help the poor. This is why the Koran introduces the concept of zakat (alms) which is so imperative in Islam that a Muslim who does not give it to the need ceases to be one (Zaidi and Low 2014, p. 115).

All in all, there should be respect for human life. Next, taking care of the environment, humans must also be responsible for conservation. Note that both environment and humans are inseparably connected; the Koran declares that humans are God's vicegerents on earth.

And while creating wealth, it is also important that charity is practised. [But charity must be given in moderation. Excess in anything brings about personal and social problems.] Note that the accumulation of wealth can be dangerous; in fact, there is always a danger that instead of doing good; wealth will generate problems in society. Besides, wealth accumulation can mislead a person from the righteous path laid down by God.

Such a value of CSR is also based on charity. People who own any business or enterprise are encouraged to build a viable society. The Koran wants people to be socially responsible. The Koran understands business activities in ethical terms. This is so because CSR is meaningful only if a business operates in accordance with religious-moral dictates. In one of the verses about the relationship between business and religious moral activities, the Koran says,

> By men whom neither traffic nor merchandise can divert from the Remembrance of Allah, nor from regular Prayer, nor from the practice of regular charity: Their (only) fear is for the Day when hearts and eyes will be transformed (in a world wholly new) (24: 37, also cited in Zaidi and Low 2014, p. 121).

The Koran is all-inclusive: It takes in its fold every aspect of human activity. Business in its widest sense is also subject to Koranic injunction. It is important to note that the centrality of a just society, viable environment, and charitable human existence form the perfect background against which such values of social justice/a just society and CSR can be meaningfully practised. This is why, the Koran requires people—including corporate areas which consist of people—to be involved and be especially socially responsible. All in all, it can be seen that the Koranic view of CSR and such Islamic values can bring about people and business to prosper only in an orderly society. The attendant key beliefs and values of compassion and charity/charitable welfare can bring about caring and being cared for as well as giving/making peace and bringing about prosperity in society.

As for the value of compassion and loving-kindness as well as giving, the Prophet Mohammad said these:

61. When the child (of Zainab) was brought to Muhammad, dying; its body trembling and moving; the eyes of the Apostle of God shed many tears. And S'ad said, . . . O Messenger of God! What is this weeping and shedding of tears?" Muhammad replied, "This is an expression of the tenderness and compassion, which the Lord hath put into the hearts of His servants; the Lord doth not have compassion on and commiserate with His servants, except such as are tender and full of feeling." (Al-Suhrawardy et al. 1992, p. 60–61)

248. He who helpeth his fellow-creature in the hour of need, and he who helpeth the oppressed, him will God help in the Day of Travail.

249. What actions are most excellent? To gladden the heart of a human being, to feed the hungry, to help the afflicted, to lighten the sorrow of the sorrowful, and to remove the wrongs of the injured.

250. Who is the most favoured of God? He from whom the greatest good cometh to His creatures.

251. All God's creatures are His family; and he is the most beloved of God who doeth most good to God's creatures.

252. Whoever is kind to His creatures, God is kind to him; therefore be kind to man on earth, whether good or bad; and being kind to the bad, is to withhold him from badness, thus in Heaven you will be treated kindly (Al-Suhrawardy et al. 1992, pp. 89–90).

Besides, with regard to authority, the Islamic leader "to show kindness to his subjects as Allah has been benevolent to him. In his letter, (the father) said to his son that, "You should know that royal authority belongs to Allah. . ." In order to carrying out his duties, his son has to let his intention be with God and that his certainty of Him is sincere. With a compassionate heart, his son has to perform his duty for the interest of his people according to the guiding principle of Allah. In the business world, the executives are hired by the corporation to run the business and whatever the decisions they made are for the interests of the owner (the shareholders and investors). The highest authority is the business owner. The interests of the most business owners are to maximize profit for them, and in most cases; the employees' welfares are not considered and are neglected. For example, low pay, poor living standards, child labour and others are very common in many large corporations. However, in the Islamic management ethics/values context, all human beings are held responsible to do good deeds for the God Almighty pleasure and not the business owners (Ang et al. 2012, p. 216).

The Value of Foresight

In Islam, the value of foresight is upheld; and leaders must treasure this value. This value of foresight is evidenced in Ibni Khaldun's Muqadimmah (Ang et al. 2012, p. 214); here, the father advised his son that:

before making his decision on any task, it is worthwhile for him to consider the outcome of the result. If he foresaw that the result would be healthy and sound, then it would be wise to proceed with the project. If not, further consultation with people of great insight, knowledge, and experience about the matter was necessary. (It is felt that) in any decision making in business, it is worthwhile to have a wider view of the subject matter and to have an appropriate risk management of the project before implementing it.

The Value of Learning

In Islam, learning is treasured. "The acquisition of knowledge is a duty incumbent on every Muslim, male and female." (Al-Suhrawardy et al. 1992, p. 94).

According to Al-Suhrawardy et al. (1992, p. 92), the Prophet Mohammad spoke of:

> The Messenger of God was asked, "What is the greatest vice of man?" He said, "You must not ask me about vice, but ask about virtue;" and he repeated this three times, after which he said, "Know ye! The worst of men is a bad learned man, and a good learned man is the best."

Interestingly, it is also stated that, "He dieth not who giveth life to learning" (Al-Suhrawardy et al. 1992, p. 92). "And whoever is given knowledge is given indeed abundant wealth." The Quran (2:269) states that, "Allah will exalt those of you who believe and those of you who are given knowledge to high degree". "And say, Oh My Lord! Increase me in knowledge..." The Quran (20:114).

The Value of Service

The value of service is also upheld in Islam. It is said that, "Do you love your Creator? Love your fellow-beings first." (Al-Suhrawardy et al. 1992, p. 102).

> Verily it is a good act to meet your brother with an open countenance, and to pour water from your own water-bag into his vessel. (Al-Suhrawardy et al. 1992, p. 59).

The Value of Continuous Improvement

Here, the value of continuous improvement can be interpreted as being embraced by Islam; after all, one must "seek knowledge from the cradle to the grave." (Al-Suhrawardy et al. 1992, p. 93), and also "be persistent in good actions." (Al-Suhrawardy et al. 1992, p. 84).

In Ibni Khaldun's Muqadimmah, Ang et al. (2012, p. 214, bold, the author's words) stated that, "it is very important (his son **or for that matter any Muslim**) "to consult jurists frequently" and "learn from men of experience and intelligence who are understanding and wise." It is further encouraged to "sit down often with scholars and seek their advice and company"... The father advised his son to consider noble people who are advanced in age and who have sincere intentions to be his adviser. He also stressed that, 'Select them for your service and be benevolent toward them.'"

The Value of Coaching/Mentoring and Relating With One's People

There is also this value of coaching and mentoring.

As advised by the father to his son in Ibni Khaldin's Muqadimmah, Ang et al. (2012, p. 217) indicated that an Islamic leader should "spend fruitful time with (one's) officials who served (them) in the office as well as those who served (one) at (one's) residence. . . ."Lend your ear and your eye, your mind and your intellect, to the things of that sort he presents to you. Go over it again and think it over." In the business world, the leader should have patience to listen to his employees so that the difficulties faced by the subordinates can be discussed and hopefully solved together.

Furthermore, with all the information (one) gathers from (one's) subordinates, a true leader is likely to be able to reason, judge and perceive. At the end of the day, a leader would empower (one's) subordinates to do a good job while at the same time to maintain a fair amount of supervision."

Islamic leaders need to be kind and helpful to their people or subjects especially to the weak. They should maintain close contact with good, righteous and honest people and also keep in touch with the blood relatives. It is very important for a leader to be humbled, allowing people to see him (her) so that people could see his (her) friendliness and "smiling countenance" (Ang et al. 2012, p. 217).

The Value of Humility

Islam also embraces the value of humility, and Muslims maintain such a value. In the Sayings of the Prophet Mohammad, Al-Suhrawardy et al. (1992, p. 87) cited these as the key beliefs and the value of humility which Islamic leaders should be aware and follow:

234. Humility and courtesy are acts of piety.

235. Verily God instructs me to be humble and lowly and not proud; and that no one should oppress another.

236. A tribe must desist from boasting of their forefathers; if they will not leave off boasting, verily they will be more abominable near God, than a black beetle which rolleth forward filth by its nose; and verily God has removed from you pride and arrogance. There is no man but either a righteous Mu'min or a sinner; mankind are all the sons of Adam, and he was from earth.

237. Whoever is humble to men for God's sake, may God exalt his eminence.

The Value of Moderation

In terms of the value of moderation in Islam, frequent statements have been documented in both the Quran and the Sunnah of the Prophet; these encourage moderation in food and drink. "And eat and drink and waste not. Truly, Allah Loves not the wasteful" (7:31). This Ayat from Quran is comprehensive in its Islamic guidance about sustenance. God has allowed us to enjoy food and bounties of this life which at the same time He has forbidden waste and extravagance.

However, in today's world, mass production and mass customization of products for many centuries by man has resulted in over usage of earthly materials leading to an imbalance world ecosystem. The excessive carbon dioxide emission and the global warming result in the earth's "green-house effect" leading to the melting of the ice caps (North and South Poles) and even of Mount Everest as well as various disastrous phenomena such as the Fukushima nuclear disaster in recent time. Take another example, in 2004 Tsunami, recent earthquakes in many countries namely China, Indonesia and Taiwan; Typhoons (happenings in South East Asia region) and Hurricane (in many other places such as New Orleans) (Ang et al. 2012, p. 214). These occurrences, to the author's mind, are the results of human greed and over exploitation of earth's resources. Hence, moderation can be said to be the key success factor to prevent human sufferings and for the future generation to attain happiness in this life and thereafter.

The Value of Work and That of Working Hard

A Muslim should work hard too. According to Al-Suhrawardy et al. (1992, p. 91–92), the Prophet Mohammad declared,

260. Pray to God morning and evening, and employ the day in your avocations.
261. He who neither worketh for himself, nor for others, will not receive the reward of God.
262. Whoso is able and fit and doth not work for himself, or for others, God is not gracious to him.
263. Those who earn an honest living are the beloved of God.
264. God is gracious to him that earneth his living by his own labour, and not by begging.
265. Whoever desireth the world and its riches, in a lawful manner, in order to withhold himself from begging, and for a livelihood for his family, and for being kind to his neighbour, will come to God with his face bright as the full moon on the fourteenth night of the lunar month. 91
266. Give the labourer his wage before his perspiration be dry.

In Ibni Khaldun's Muqadimmah, Ang et al. (2012, p. 216) wrote that:

In daily activities, it is very interesting to see that the father encourages his son to, "always ask your lord whether you should do a particular thing. Finish the work you have to do today and do not postpone it until tomorrow." The father said that accumulation of many days' undone work would eventually "make you ill". We agree wholeheartedly on this fatherly advice for this behaviour would help one to reduce work stress that is very common in this modern day, and completing work each day would contribute to the well-being of an individual as well as the good performance of an organization.

Section Concluding Remarks

At this point of the section, in concluding, it is apt and best to quote Ang et al. (2012, p. 217), that is, "Islamic leadership encourages leaders to practice the value of faith, integrity, dignity, self-discipline, self-restraint, loving-kindness and giving; leaders are also encouraged to refrain from sinful acts and live life in moderation. Ang et al. (2012, p. 217) then went on to "describe a benevolent father who is a good role model for his son in advising him to do the right things according to the guiding principles of Islam. Referring to the Prophet Muhammad's leadership paradigm, the father stressed very importantly the dual role that his son should adhere. They are: (1) how to be a good Muslim as a servant of Allah (A believer). (2) how to be a good leader as a Khalifah-Vicegerent for Allah (by applying the Islamic Management Ethics)".

Interestingly, whether as a Muslim or a Non-Muslim reflecting on the above values would positively help to facilitate, develop or enhance leadership ways and/ or (learning/ training/ coaching as well as mentoring and even service leadership) practices in their respective job(s) or organisation.

Chapter Conclusion

Like Singapore, Brunei is also politically stable. The Sultan as a father-leader is bringing about much growth in Brunei so that the Sultanate can attain a higher level of economic growth and achieve much progress. The port facilities at Muara are being further developed and improved upon while the development of the Sungei Liang Industrial Park (SPARK) are being initiated, planned and acted upon.

Interestingly, in the Singapore Case as argued by Low (2005), the Singapore Government provided the necessary infrastructure with a "politically stable" and "conducive environment for the growth of business". Singapore's success is bolstered by the Government's continuous efforts in laying down the required support, and infrastructure. Singapore has continued to be "the premier hub status in the Asia-Pacific"; in fact, it has won several accolades (Chin and Tongzon 1998, cited in Low 2005) including for "Singapore's Changi Airport … one of the best in the world" and in a business-traveller magazine survey, "the best for baggage retrieval …" (cited in Low 2005). With regard to the Singapore port—in spite of competition and cheaper port facilities' pricing with some players such as Evergreen and Maersk having moved from Singapore to neighbouring Johor Baru, Singapore is seen as "the best port in Asia and it is the world's busiest container

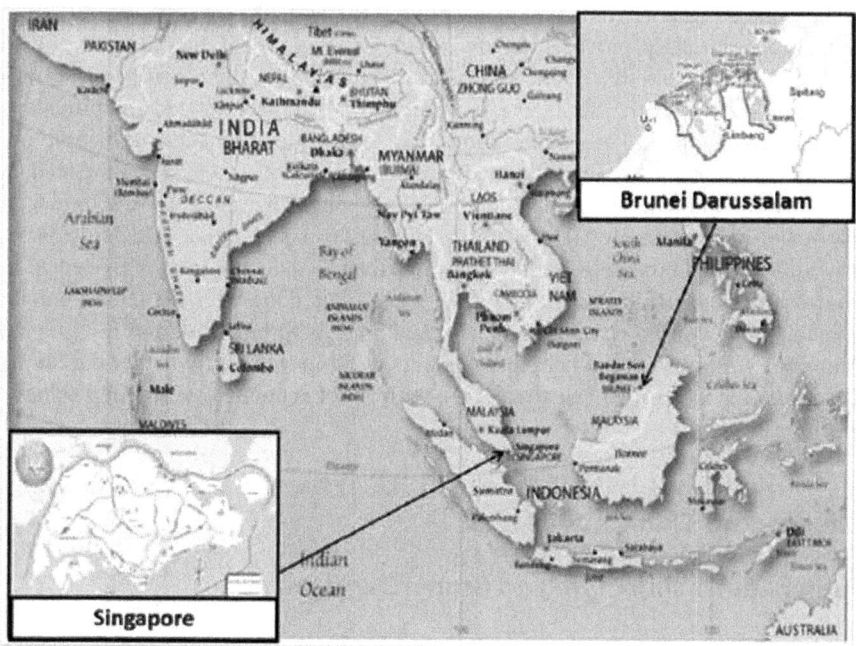

Fig. 10.2 Locations of Brunei Darussalam and Singapore

port" (Goh 2001). The World Competitiveness Yearbook 1999 ranked Singapore as the most attractive location in the world, apart from the USA, as a manufacturing hub (Institute for Management Development (IMD) 1999 cited in Low 2005). Additionally, Singaporean children today too are going to better schools than before (Fig. 10.2).

Like Singaporeans, Bruneians are also enjoying a high level of education; they enjoy free education and health services as provided by the Brunei Government. The Sultan's Scholarships are also given to Bruneian students who obtain commendable results in their 'A' levels or equivalent. Interestingly, the human development index (HDI) for Brunei Darussalam is 0.894 which gives the country a rank of 30th out of the 177 countries studied in the Human Development Report 2007/ 8 (Human Development Report 2008). The Health Ministry is also dedicated in "providing the best in terms of products and services to the country's citizens and residents" (Dewi 2007, cited in Low and Md Zain 2008).

Small businesses and entrepreneurship are encouraged, and His Majesty's Government is also laying the necessary infrastructure such as the building of more roads, highways, and fly-overs to facilitate business and economic growth. The size of the city Bandar Seri Bagawan is also to be expanded. Two new ferry terminals are built for both passengers and vehicles between Brunei and Labuan and Menumbok, East Malaysia (Zaini and Musdi 2008, p. 1).

Just like Singapore (its small size, roughly the size of Chicago with the same population, probably provides an overwhelming reason for the success of this Singapore model and this could be a possible attribute for the controlled development and success of the Singapore Government's paternalistic leadership model), Brunei is also small. The people know each other and it is said that people are usually connected with each other by blood ties and by other ways, and the leaders relate well with the people. Such being the case, one can argue that Brunei indeed has much space in the global economy as niche player with father leadership as the way of 'business' processes, and that can give the sultanate the competitive edge. In brief, father leadership has that edge; it gets things done with the leader's good relationships with the people. Father leadership is both high task and high touch. And what's more, with the people being united, all-in-the-family, under the Sultan as a father-leader, Brunei can attain a higher level of economic growth and achieve much progress.

Checkpoint: Think About It

Father Leadership in Negara Brunei Darussalam

1. What are the key cultural factors that support the practice of father leadership in Brunei Darussalam?
2. Let us review the national ideology of Brunei Darussalam.
3. What, to you, are the lessons of leadership derived from this chapter?
4. Which lessons or learning points would you subscribe or adopt for yourself?
5. How would you grow (the business of) your Organisation?

The World of Silat and Its Parallels to Leadership

1. What is *silat*?
2. What can be derived or applied from the world of silat, the Malay art of combat to making one's leadership successful?
3. In what ways, as a leader, can I serve and help others (the community/ society)?
4. In your view, what are the values espoused by silat warriors that can be applied to leadership?
5. Why should a leader be a passionate one?

Islamic Values and Leadership

1. Think of these Islamic Values; what are these values?
2. As a leader, how can one apply these Islamic values in one's leadership practices?
3. What are the benefits and advantages of applying and practising such values?

References

Abu Bakar, A. (2007, August 26). HRH visits water works dept. *The Brunei Times*, p. 1.

Abu Bakar, R., & Lakshmi, N. C. (2009). *Penghulu*s and village heads – Eyes and ears of the government. *The Brunei Times*, p. 5.

Al-Suhrawardy, Al-Mamun & Abdullah, A. S. (1992). *The sayings of Muhammad*. London: John Murray.

Andaya, B. W., & Andaya, L. Y. (2001). *A history of Malaysia* (2nd ed.). Honolulu: University of Hawaii Press.

Ang, S. L., Low, K. C. P., & Al-Harran, S. (2012, March). Islamic leadership lessons from the 9th century based on Ibn Khaldun's MUQADDIMAH. *Educational Research, 3*(3), 212–219.

Asia Inc. (2006, July/August). The way forward. *Asia Inc.*, No. 16, pp. 60–64.

Borneo, B. (2002, July 15). Spiritual way to peace. *Borneo Bulletin*, p. 1.

Chin, A., & Tongzon, J. (1998). Chapter 3: Maintaining Singapore as a major shipping and air transport hub. In T. M. Heng & T. K. Yam (Eds.), *Competitiveness of the Singapore economy, strategic perspective* (pp. 83–114). Singapore: Singapore University Press/World Scientific.

Clammer, J. (1998). *Race and state in independent Singapore 1965–1990*. UK: Ashgate.

Crainer, S. (2002). *Business ,the Jack Welch way*. India: Wiley.

Dewi, M. S. (2007, September 22). Brunei health expo to mark MoH's 100th year. *The Brunei Times*, p. 5.

DuBrin, A. J. (2007). *Fundamentals of organizational behavior*. Canada: Thomson South-Western.

Goh, T. W. (2001). *Today's Singapore*. Singapore: Rank Books.

Haji Abdul Aziz, U. (1992). *Melayu Islam Beraja Sebagai Falsafah Negara Brunei Darussalam. Esei-esei mengenai Negara Brunei Darussalam* (pp. 1–21). Akademi Pengajian Brunei: Brunei Darussalam.

Han, S. (2007, September 6). HRH: Adopt a healthy lifestyle. *The Brunei Times*, p. 1.

Human Development Report. (2008). *Country fact sheets – Brunei Darussalam*. Human Development Report 2007/2008. Retrieved August 15, 2008, from http://hrdstats.undp.org/countries/country_fact_sheets/cty_fs_BRN.html

Hussainmiya, B. A. (2006). *Brunei Darussalam: A nation at peace*. Retrieved October 2, 2007, from http://www.bsp.com.bn/PanagaClub/pnhs/History/BRUNEI%20DARUSSALAM.htm

Institute for Management Development (IMD). (1999). *The world competitiveness yearbook 1999*. Lausane: IMD.

Low, K. C. P. (2005). Father leadership: The Singapore case study. *Management Decision, 44*(1), 89–104.

Low, K. C. P. (2007, May). Islamic values, excellence & leadership (pp. 37–40). *Global CEO*, Institute of Chartered Financial Analyst India: ICFAI.

Low, K. C. P. (2008). Father leadership – The Malaysian perspective. *Leadership & Organizational Management Journal, 1*, 75–95. (http://www.franklinpublishing.net/leadership.html).

Low, K. C. P., & Md Zain, A. Y. (2008). *Creating the competitive edge, the father leadership way*. Paper presented in the International Conference on Business and Management, Universiti Brunei Darussalam, Brunei Darussalam, 8–9 January 2008.

Omar, D. P. H. M. (1996). The making of a national culture: Brunei's experience. In E. Thumboo (Ed.), *Cultures in ASEAN and the 21st century* (pp. 5–21). Singapore: Unipress/ASEAN-COCI.

Ong, J. (2007, July 12). HRH keeps in touch via working visits. *The Brunei Times*, p. 1.

Philips, A. A. B. (2002). *The best in Islaam according to Qur'aan and Sunnah*. India: Islamic Book Service.

Pike Place Fish Market. (2007). *Fish! Philosophy source*. Retrieved September 1, 2007, from http://www.pikeplacefish.com/philosophy/philosophy.htm

Sedyawati, E. (1996). The making and development of an Indonesian national culture. In E. Thumboo (Ed.), *Cultures in ASEAN and the 21st century* (pp. 54–60). Singapore: Unipress/ASEAN-COCI.

Talib, A. (2009). *Silat: A perspective on the Malay Martial Art*. Brunei: CreateSpace Independent Publishing Platform.

The Brunei Times. (2007, August 7). HM in Kampong Ayer – again. *The Brunei Times*, p. 1.

Waleed, P. D. M. (2008, February 15). HM gives Temburong folk reason to smile again. *The Brunei Times*. Retrieved March 21, 2008, from http://www.bt.com.bn/en/home_news/2008/02/15/hm_gives_temburong_folk_reason_to_smile_again

Wani Abdul, G. (2007, July 15). Happy 61st birthday your majesty. *The Brunei Times*, p. 1.

Wong, J. (2008, July/August). A modern ruler of an ancient legacy. *Muhibah, Inflight Magazine of Royal Brunei Airlines*, pp. 12–16.

Zaidi, A., & Low, K. C. P. (2014). Chapter 6: The Koranic discourse on corporate social responsibility. In K. C. P. Low, S. Idowu, & S. L. Ang (Eds.), *Corporate social responsibility in Asia - Practice and experience* (pp. 109–124). Heidelberg: Springer.

Zaini, Z., & Musdi, Z. (2008, May 4). New ferry terminal. *Borneo Bulletin*, pp. 1, 8.

Leadership in Singapore

Father Leadership in Singapore

The Roots and Support for Father Leadership

To forget one's ancestors is to be a brook without a source, a tree without root. (Chinese proverb)

The Singapore Government, having a tight grip on Singaporean politics, is also blessed with a civil bureaucracy that is "efficient" as well as having "considerable clout" (Gale 1999, pp. 2–3); Singapore has often been labelled as a nanny State (Tay 2001, p. 24) with the Government looming too large in too many sectors, of course, the Government's reasons being political stability. In Low (2002, 2009a) study, the value of governmental support and involvement is selected as one of the 12 Singaporean values. Such a value of governmental support and involvement is akin to the value of the benevolent father that is a common value, often resurfaced, if not widely practised in Asian societies.

In India, for example, there is the practice of "paternal authoritative-ness" of the leader (Brislin 1993, p. 275; Kumar and Saxena 1983; Sinha 1980). Paternal authority captures the expectations of concern and nurtures the belief that people or staff should be treated like the leader's family members. Desirable qualities in a leader are to be expert and knowledgeable—knowing what to do in a wide range of situations for the people's good. The leaders are obliged to not only ensure political stability but also to give good advice and offer help to the people. Similar results are reported by Yao (1987) study in the People's Republic of China (PR China) that endorses the concept of "paternal authoritative-ness"; there, the leaders need to be strong, effective and knowledgeable. The Chinese value system and working style is still dominated by a traditional value system.

The research reinforces Low (2002, 2009a) study where the value of Governmental support and involvement, getting 93.75% respondents' endorsement, and this can also be seen as endorsing Confucian beliefs. Lee Kuan Yew, Singapore's

© Springer International Publishing AG 2018
K.C.P. Low, *Leading Successfully in Asia*,
https://doi.org/10.1007/978-3-319-71347-2_11

first Premier, was the most prominent of the protagonists of Confucian values, perceiving the Confucian way of life and organizing society as correlated to Singapore's success. Here, in accord with Confucius, "unless the Government is in the hands of upright men, disaster would befall the country. By the way, in this respect, the PAP also believes the same thing." (Goh Chok Tong 1982 quoted in Bellows 1989, p. 216).

The Government, like a benevolent father, looks after the people's welfare (Zhang 1999, pp. 66–67). Here, the preferred management style is that of firm control and, at times, explicit direction, but essentially doing good for the society (Scarborough 1998) and the efficient political leadership together with the hard-working workforce has helped build Singapore (Tan 1989; Lu 1998). Here, one can also argue that although there have been much talk on raising the spirit of entrepreneurship in the Republic, it was again very much government-led and not led by some private bodies or personal initiatives. For example, even the national movement, the Action Community for Entrepreneurship (ACE) is a top-down initiative, with a public sector secretariat and led by a minister, no less (Long 2004).

Explicit direction is especially required when one analyses the applications of Hersey and Blanchard's "Situational theory of leadership" (Daft 2000, p. 515) as in the early years of a country's development—with the populace's prevailing low level of education (presumably, the followers' readiness can be taken as not able and not willing), a strong, telling leadership ("provide specific instructions and closely supervise performance") is necessary to lay the foundations for economic development and growth.

A case in point is that of Indonesia. Under President Suharto, Indonesia gradually recovered from the economic morass into which it had fallen under Sukarno. Until 1998, Suharto was the strongman who, during 32 years of his regime, directed the energies of the people, bringing political stability and prosperity to Indonesia. The turbulent and violent aftermath of Suharto's collapse—the ethnic conflicts, severe economic crisis and other problems, indeed so, dictate a strong, directing leadership to grow the nation's political stability and economic development. Today, 6 years after Suharto and three more presidents, Indonesia shows signs of progress; President Sukarnoputri then introduced direct presidential elections and the present President Susilo Bambang Yudhoyono was elected in the September Polls 2004, and now holding his second term of office. Thus, the "bapak" or father figure must be there. "The stability factor that has long been lacking in this country is now there," says Jochen Sauter, manager of the German Chamber of Commerce and Industry in Jakarta (http://www.taipeitimes.com/News/edit/archives/2003/05/21/2003052022).

With a multicultural population (77.8% Chinese; 14% Malays; 7.1% Indians; and the rest of the population, consisting of the Eurasians and others) (Singapore Census of Population 2000), the island-Republic of Singapore indeed needs a strong government and certainly, it cannot be denied that there are always potential "fault lines" along racial/ethnic lines that are usually human, emotional and fragile (Koh and Ooi 2002, p. 260). Just as few would have believed it after Suharto was pushed out when ethnic conflicts and naked violence exploded across the country, multi-racial Singaporeans certainly wants a good government too, one that is capable of being fatherly, fair and sensitive to their needs.

The Singapore Government does "provide the necessary infrastructure" with a "politically stable" and "conducive environment for the growth of business". Singapore's success is bolstered by the Government's continuous efforts in laying down the required support, and infrastructure. Singapore has continued to be "the premier hub status in the Asia-Pacific"; in fact, it has won several accolades (Chin and Tongzon 1998, pp. 83–114) including for "Singapore's Changi Airport . . . one of the best in the world" and in a business-traveller magazine survey, "the best for baggage retrieval . . ." (Tan 1992, p. 23). With regard to the Singapore port—in spite of competition and cheaper port facilities' pricing with some players such as Evergreen and Maersk having moved from Singapore to neighbouring Johor Baru, Singapore is seen as "the best port in Asia and it is the world's busiest container port" (Goh 2001).

The World Competitiveness Yearbook 1999 ranked Singapore as the most attractive location in the world, apart from the USA, as a manufacturing hub (Institute for Management Development (IMD) 1999).

Singaporean children today too are going to better schools than before. The Singapore Government sanctioned the use of Central Provident Funds (CPF) savings for tertiary education in 1989 (Low 2002, 2009a).

In 1998, Richard Hu, Minister for Finance, announced off-budget measures for education involving a total of S$282 million, including S$22 million for improvements in polytechnic CAD-CAM facilities, S$22 million for Nanyang Technological University's computer upgrading programme, and S$30 million for new IT equipment for secondary schools still under construction (Hu 1998; Davie 1999, p. 1, both cited in Low 2002). The Singapore Government invests in university education, seeking to make local universities "world-class" and "best in the region"; and "with Singapore's ambition to be the knowledge center of the region, it is only natural to emphasise research and development" (Cham 1998, pp. 35–40). Here, the Government's provision of education and political stability is all the more positively associated to this value of Governmental support and involvement. A strong Confucian undertone exists; paternalism exists alongside the "confidence of the people in the ruler" Lin (1938/1994), and being an orderly society is seen as a top Asian value (Low 2002, 2009a; Bjerke 1999, p. 148; Naisbitt 1994, p. 73).

With such Governmental efforts, Singaporeans are satisfied with the delivery of the goods; this mutual relation was a distinguishing feature of Confucian political ideology (Sie 1997, p. 69; Zhang 1999), and parallels the study of Kau et al. (1998) of Singaporeans' happiness level "with the way the Government runs the country". As well, the Singapore business community/public can rely on a "Public Service which is determined to outdo itself in serving them" (Lim 1998, p. 131); the study confirms Low (1998) study—a Government-made Singapore, creating a unique brand for Singapore, also ensures the nation's economic and political viability and survival.

True, one can also argue that Singapore's small size, roughly the size of Chicago with the same population, probably provides an overwhelming reason for the success of this Singapore model and this could be a possible attribute for the controlled development and success of the Singapore Government's paternalistic leadership model. Singaporeans are also hardworking. Perhaps too, "success has many fathers", as an old Asian saying goes but indeed, father leadership has helped to build the Singapore brand. And one cannot deny that thus far, the vision and the efficient civil service, subsumed under the father-leadership provided by the Government that has contributed to sustain Singapore's economy and her citizenry.

The Problems and Prospects of the Father Leadership Way

Father leadership is not without its problems. It can also raise problems in the South-East Asian and the Bangladeshi context; more so, when leaders adopt a paternalistic leadership style, certain strategies and practices may not be healthy. These can include patronage, nepotism, favouritism, cronyism, cliques and political manipulation (Westwood 1992, pp. 138–139).

Assuming that such problems do not exist in Singapore, Haley and Low (1998) pointed out that Governmental policies have produced great economic successes but, paradoxically, the Government's ideology and action, and even its undoubted success, entail apparent failure. This study confirms (Low 2002, 2009a) study, most focus group members, 80%, cited Singaporeans being less entrepreneurial (these were referred to 25 times) and this could be further explained by Haley and Low (1998)'s analysis that as Singapore ever more successfully achieves the ruling People Action Party's (PAP's) goal of effective nationhood, it becomes more deeply enmeshed within the global capitalist system. As Singapore becomes more technocratic, its citizens appear to lose the creativity and entrepreneurship it needs to prosper in a rapidly-changing, global context (Low 2004; Haley 1998).

The litmus test for Singapore to make advancements in entrepreneurship in this father leadership environment is when the people make their own initiatives. When the teenagers grow into adults, they take their own responsibilities. Role-modelling the Government-link Companies (GLCs), Singaporeans can capitalise on the Singapore brand name while tapping what the Singapore government has done well for them such as providing good roads, infrastructures and telecommunications; they can then make more overseas business ventures.

As an analogy, the Government is the father, driving the Singapore family car, and has steered it well in the past, with the passengers being happy to trust the driver-father's good sense to go in the right direction. Times are changing, however, and the driver-father is starting to see that he must attend to the wishes of the family-member passengers and try to involve them in selecting the direction and choosing the routes.

Yet Singapore society is very much like a working adult who still lives at home with his or her parents. Mother still cooks for him and her and father pays the mortgage. Since independence, almost everything has been taken care of by the

Singapore Government; the Singapore Government has, in fact, done very well in terms of looking after Singaporeans in terms of housing through Housing and Development Board (HDB) and Singaporeans' future through their Central Provident Funds (CPF). This form of governance/management has worked well with the majority. However, several critics have raised the issue that this may create Singaporeans' over-dependence on the government. One recent study on whether Singaporeans are ready for retirement, Low and Or (2004) highlights that it is "perhaps natural for the people to take things for granted; and these include freedom and financial security with nurturing parents and a fatherly government". Thus, independence and dependence sit uneasily together.

Besides, when having the father leadership way, it is both necessary and good to highlight here that even in the context of a broadly well-managed and highly successful economy though "unabashedly authoritarian government" (Haley 1998, p. 346), there exists a strong need to also cast a critical eye on public policies. Ngiam Tong Dow, a former civil servant and now chairman of the Housing and Development Board, had voiced this out, indicating that there can be several policy missteps in areas such as education, transport, public finance, exchange rate policy, land pricing and housing (Khanna 2004, p. 14). Nonetheless, the Singapore Government does attempt to recreate Singapore, getting inputs for the political, social and cultural aspects of the nation's survival or even its greater prosperity (www.remakingsingapore.gov.sg/).

Recently, the government as the father is applying more the selling style: explain decisions and supply opportunities for clarifications and occasionally, the participating style: "share ideas and facilitate in decision making", since the citizens are better educated which in a way, denotes being "able" but "unwilling" in terms of follower readiness in the Hersey and Blanchard's Situational Leadership context (Daft 2000, pp. 515–516). One such example is that of the Singapore Government's pro-baby measures, selling to Singaporeans that it wants to address the baby-shortage problem and encourage more singles to marry; the new Prime Minister Lee Hsien Loong highlighted this during the 2004 National Day Rally (Chia 2004; The Straits Times, 25 August 2004a).

When compared to the Malaysians, Singaporeans are almost the same; however, Malaysia's paternalism differs from the Singapore culture in that the former has its roots in the Malay or Bumiputra (sons-of-the-soil) culture's respect for the elders, seniority, the values of a hierarchical society and, in part, the Muslim faith (Asma 1996; Hofstede 1980/1984; Renwick and Witham 1997). According to the Malay adat (customs), age and leadership is valued; the older person is respected; one respects one's parents (Norazit 1998).

The Malaysian leadership style under its former Prime Minister, Dr. Mahathir Mohamad, can also be assessed as practising father-leadership. In Dr. Mohamad's view, Asian leaders need to assume and assert true leadership, seize the initiatives in terms of ideas and thoughts and get their people's respect. He viewed that some countries "suffer from too much democracy", with too many political parties; and even if good leaders were elected, they cannot finish their work or produce results within a short time (Today's Manager 2004/2005, p. 18). It appears that the West or some may suspect that governments are not democratic because the government party remains in power for so long. However, he argued that if the people choose the same party and the same leader, then it is the people's democratic right to do so as long as proper elections were held. He also cited some undemocratic leaders in the past such as China's Deng Xiaoping who have dragged their countries and people kicking and screaming into the modern world (Today's Manager 2004/2005).

In the USA, an antagonistic relationship between the Government and private business exists (Enderle 1995, p. 100) and the Americans would consider Government as an intrusion, interfering in their privacy. But this stands in contrast to the Singapore situation, where the Government takes care of its citizens through the Central Provident Funds. Public housing, home ownership, "dividend-paying" or subsidies such as the CPF Housing Grant launched in 1994 given to encourage married children to live with their parents (Low 1998) all testify to the fatherly, benevolent care accorded to the people by the Government. By contrast, Hongkongers never had the same sort of nurturing. What Westerners may regard as an interference in the private lives of citizens (Jose and Doran 1997), the Singapore Government, very much-Confucianism-influenced, like any concerned father takes care and even gets its single daughters match-made through the Social Development Unit (SDU). The initials: SDU, the joke goes, stands for single, desperate and ugly; the government tries to match using speed dating and Chinese zodiac dates. Its web site, www.lovebyte.org.sg, offers dates via cell-phone text messaging, and information on the baby bonuses (Nakashima 2004, p. A13).

It seems that nowhere in the world except in Singapore where the Government—like a father—shapes population policies based on the belief that graduates produce better babies (in 1983, the Singapore Government announced a graduate mothers scheme that granted privileges to children of graduate mothers. Less-educated, low-income mothers under 30 years of age given $10,000 if they themselves sterilised after their first or second child) (www.scwo.org.sg/resource/mile_sgwomen.html). The government, presently, is taking several measures to encourage higher birth-rates. Medisave from the Central Provident Funds can now be used for pre-delivery and delivery expenses incurred for all Singapore children born or after 1 August 2004 and for expenses incurred on procedures aiding conception, such as In-Vitro Fertilisation (The Straits Times 2004b).

Now, we turn to corporate leadership and management; Chinese management can be seen as very much similar to Japanese management. The Japanese also believe and practise *oyabun* or "father" leadership (Hanada and Yoshikawa 1991). The corporate leader is committed like a father to look after his staff's welfare; his staff on the other hand are committed and remained loyal to him. With mutual commitment and loyalty, the *wa* (harmony) spirit is fostered, thus ensuring industrial peace. Both the manager and his staff behave like a father and his children in one happy family.

Indonesian companies also practise father leadership way. Indonesian workers, generally obedient, tend to expect employers to provide transportation and refreshments such as a constant supply of drinking water (Low 2000, 2005a). In staff training, coaching and mentoring becomes critical. The manager is like a father looking after the children's interest and needs. *Sumonggo dawuh* is practised. *Sumonggo dawuh* can be interpreted as the way in which a staff acknowledges his supervisor as an example to follow (Low 2000, 2005a, p. 32).

Where Singapore companies are concerned, it can be further argued that they have one trait that stands out as different from the direct American companies' hiring and firing ways, and almost like the Japanese companies in their father *oyabun* leadership *kacho* (the employers/management takes care of their employees with reciprocal relationships) (Hanada and Yoshikawa 1991, p. 39, 40; Keeley 2001, pp. 45–46; Hodgetts and Luthans 1997; March 1996; Mitsuyuki 1985). In Singapore companies, there is this particular feeling trait or "*kum cheng*" (Hokkien dialect) (*Ganqing*—Mandarin) (relationship-based with a sense of mutual loyalty) value that exists. Singapore companies show care and concern for their employees and they want their people to feel concerned and care for the company (Adler 1997, p. 52; Low 2000, 2009a).

Coining the term "Singapore's Confucian heritage cultural model", Low (2000, 2009a) argues that like benevolent fathers, the corporate leaders or managers, use more saliva than drinking tea—meaning talking, coaching and taking personal interest in the employees' welfare. So, the business is run based more on good relationships, and employees are treated like all in the family situation; leaders also view their enterprises as an extension or part of their traditional families (Adler 1997, p. 52; Siew 1987; Chong 1987; Lee 1996; Sheh 2001). Informality and intimacy exists—with everyone undertaking a variety of activities to meet daily performance demands (Siew 1987; Bond 1991; Chan and Chiang 1994, pp. 55–56; Lasserre and Schutte 1995, p. 105; Low 2000, 2001, pp. 98–99, 2009a). Here, it only implies that within such a corporate culture, good conduct is stressed, and that leaders and members are expected to be both reliable and trustworthy to one another.

True, some critics may also point out that the Singapore model does not work effectively outside Singapore especially in People Republic of China: PRC. The "neo-authoritarian Singapore" in an alien environment (authoritarian PRC) overlooks competition to the Singapore government. Singapore has met harsh reality, and the Singaporean industrial parks are no more profitable or well managed (Tessensohn 2001; Law 1996). They may also cite the recent China Aviation Oil (Singapore) Corp's collapse (Presek 2004). However, let's not get carried away; "many observers think China aspires to become a giant Singapore—a place that embraces free markets, yet with a stern guiding government hand" (Presek 2004, p. 24), a tribute to the Singapore father leadership model. Haley (1998) speaks of Chinese cadres, taking inspiration from Singapore's high-growth with strong governmental hand in development and its exacting standards, have been writing blueprints for environmental and building regulation and land-use planning.) In fact, a side-argument here, some even believe that the USA, with its ever-growing amounts of debts, can be overtaken by China as the world's dominant economic power, and they may be right (Presek 2004).

Next, although one may perhaps argue that all Asians are not the same and each Asian country may offer different reasons and rationales for their unique brands of paternalism or Confucianism (Haley et al. 1998, 2004), in Asia, the argument that "father still knows best" appears to have some cultural acceptance in several Asian countries. Again, where the Americans would consider Government as an intrusion, disturbing their private affairs, this is not so in the Asian context. Take Vietnam for example, small businesses have boomed since the government passed a new law making it easier to set them up. Vietnam has become one of the fastest-growing countries in Asia (The Economist 2004).

Another recent example is that in Japan, a few terrified private citizens returned home after an awful captivity ordeal in Iraq. However, they were not warmly received. Why did they ignore the government's advice against going to Iraq and then get captured by kidnappers? Are they taking matters into their own hands? The Japanese government not only refused to negotiate with the kidnappers who eventually released the captives after intervention by Muslim clerics but also billed them at least US$21,700 towards the cost of bringing them home safely (Plate 2004). These individualistic citizens were disobedient to their father.

Basically, the father cares, disciplines yet administers the dosage accordingly and to the mutual benefits of all concerned; here, trust is the key. Trust needs to be built between the leaders and the followers. The leader, the authority figure must, in the first instance, be evidently competent, and he needs to be there through the thick and thin. Besides, fathering families may at times require fathers to give the bitter medicine, take an unpopular measure or sometimes an even painful, non quick-fix approach; and that the children will just have to understand, learn and adjust. And at times, talking with each other—or using more saliva than drinking tea—helps.

Lee Kuan Yew and His Leadership Ways

Introduction

Lee Kuan Yew was born on September 16, 1923. A lawyer by training, Lee Kuan Yew and his government-team led Singapore from a third to a first world country; Singapore's success is now well known. The island-Republic has often been ranked as having the most efficient port, airport, airline and civil service in the world (Mahbubani 2004; Low 2002, 2008a, 2009b).

Section's Aim and Objectives

The aim and objective of the section is to fundamentally examine the key leadership ways of Singapore's first Prime Minister Lee Kuan Yew. His communication style and ways are also examined. And at the same time, whatever that are good for business leaders to follow or emulate are also indicated.

The Father of Modern Singapore

> Make happy those who are near, and those who are far will come. (Chinese proverb; also attributed to Confucius)

The Founding Father of the prosperous city-state, Singapore's first Prime Minister Lee Kuan Yew (Christian name, Harry), served as the Senior Minister (1990–2004) when Goh Chok Tong was the Prime Minister and currently he serves as the Minister Mentor when Lee Hsien Loong, Lee's eldest son leads the Singapore Government in August 2004.

Stepping down on 28 November 1990, and handing over the prime ministership to Goh Chok Tong, Lee Kuan Yew was the world's longest ever serving Prime Minister. Now, Lee, the former Minister Mentor is senior adviser to the Government of Singapore Investment Corporation (GIC).

The sprucing and greening of Singapore with trees all over the island has also made the island-Republic a "First World oasis in a Third World region" and besides, this green trump card has helped to woo investors (Lee cited in Oon, 7 May 2009, p. A8). Going green thus makes good business sense; it is felt that going green helps reduce pollution as well as cut business costs. Other than setting up the necessary infra-structure and port facilities, the cleaning of dirty and smelly Singapore as in Singapore River and Kallang River is a good example of the priorities and many challenges Singapore faced upon gaining independence in 1965. The people of Singapore too, through education, campaigns and the government's various efforts, are also becoming eco-conscious, at least they get more empathetic or better appreciate nature and the environment.

The Key Skills, Qualities and Characteristics

> Live as if you were to die tomorrow. Learn as if you were to live forever. (Mahatma Gandhi)

The various key skills, qualities and traits that the 88 year-old Lee Kuan Yew has, over the years shown from his not-in-power days (pre-colonial days) to his Minister Mentor position (when he died), can in fact, be emulated by businesses and business leaders. These key leadership skills and qualities that are critical to building nations, to this practitioner-academician, are wanting to be in charge, wanting to make it realised, being proactive and besides, being a good communicator, relating well with the people or the grassroots. This is what former British Prime Minister, Margaret Thatcher (cited in McCarthy 1999, p. 89) spoke of him, "In office, I analyzed every speech of his. He had a way of penetrating the fog of propaganda and expressing with unique clarity the issues of our times and the way to tackle them."

Overall, one can categorise that Lee is said to possess these characteristics:

Displaying a High Locus of Control

The old horse in the stable still yearns to run 1000 miles. (Chinese proverb)

As evident in most leaders, Lee Kuan Yew displayed a high locus of control. Leaders with high locus of control normally believe that their actions determine what happens to them (Low 2011a). And in other words, they believe that they are the masters of their own fate (Daft 2008) or captains of their own ships, marshaling whatever the outside forces and making their own luck. Lee's high locus of control can be seen in one of his National Day speeches, he spoke of "even from my sick bed, even if you are going to lower me into the grave and I feel something is going wrong, I will get up." (Lee 1988; National Day Rally). One Singapore observer told this author that, "for Lee Kuan Yew, 'nothing is free' for Singapore; and Singaporeans just have to survive; be resilient and find ways and means to make it."

After Singapore's expulsion from Malaysia and its Caesarean birth in 1965, Lee was able to put the island-Republic onto an industrial growth path. Singapore today is a developed country according to the International Monetary Fund (IMF) and the World Bank (WB). The city-state, located at southern tip of the Malay Peninsula and south of Malaysia, is one of the original Asian Tigers: Hong Kong, Taiwan, South Korea and Singapore. And these were done in spite of the obstacles such as high unemployment in the 1960s, the British withdrawal in the 1970s and other obstacles.

Being in charge is good. Being an internal made the Singapore's leader very much of a planner with great foresight and vision as well as wanting to make things happen. He delivered the results—got independence, the island's progress and business growth. And Lee had also succeeded in ensuring a good succession.

Getting It All Geared and Well-Planned, Preparation and Planning Is So Essential

If you are *planning* for a year, sow rice; if you are *planning* for a decade, plant trees; if you are *planning* for a lifetime, educate people. (Chinese proverb)

If one knows the enemy and knows oneself, one needs not fear the result of a hundred or a thousand battles. If one knows oneself but not the enemy, for every victory gained, one will also suffer a defeat. If one knows neither the enemy nor oneself, one will succumb in every battle... These are the words of ancient Chinese philosopher and military strategist, Sun Tzu. And it is this author's perception that this is very much successfully practiced by Lee Kuan Yew.

Lee Kuan Yew was indeed a man with a vision. Yet to him, Sun Tzu's tenet of knowing oneself and one's audience (citizens, neighbouring countries and foreign powers), and that was overall so essential and critical.

In 1965, with Singapore unexpectedly independent, ejected from Malaysia, and having to rely on its own limited resources, Lee set about planning the island-

Republic's economic development with impressive single-mindedness. He also knew that economic growth was the best fighting method against the communism threat then; the people wanted economic progress and employment. He established the Economic Development Board, which set out to attract both foreign investment and any necessary outside expertise. The Board itself was staffed with experts in every necessary field. Lee employed the Dutch economist, Dr. Albert Winsemius, to help develop the country's national economic strategy. Singapore had traditionally relied on entrepot trade and the middleman role. The plan then was to transform Singapore from an entrepot economy to an industrialized manufacturing base within 10 years. And the rest is history with the island-Republic moving into its later phases of industrialization, further advancing its status of a high-tech industrialized country in the 1990s. Today, Singapore is attracting foreign talents to shore or supplement her manpower strengths, boosting her productivity.

Being far-sighted and a "master planner" who "virtually invented the place", turning Singapore into a "prosperous high-tech enclave" (Time 1999), Lee Kuan Yew had also planned the leadership transition well. Even from the start, Lee ensured a clean, effective and efficient government should run the island-Republic. [Although the one-party-ruled city-state has been criticized for lack of transparency in some areas, such as press freedom and secrecy in the financial industry, Singapore was ranked joint first—with Denmark and New Zealand—in Transparency International's 2010 Corruption Perceptions Index, topping the list of the world's least corrupt countries (Reuters 2010 cited in *Borneo Bulletin* 2010).] Preparations were made even as early as in the 1970s. In the 1980s, Goh and his younger colleagues started to assume key cabinet positions; and prior to this, all the old guards or the first-generation leaders, including Goh Keng Swee, Toh Chin Chye and S. Rajaratnam, retired. This was the first leadership transition since independence in 1965.

Being a Strategic Thinker

Better a diamond with a flaw than a pebble without one. (Chinese proverb)

Always think far ahead... And see or take long term perspectives. Lee Kuan Yew and his government-team led Singapore from a third to a first world country; Singapore's success is in fact well known. The island-Republic has often been ranked as having the most efficient port, airport, airline and civil service in the world (Mahbubani 2004; Low 2002, 2008a, 2009b). Tourism in the island-Republic can be said to be "a very well organized industry not only because of its infrastructure, but also its safety, cleanliness and efficiency of the whole system" (Travel and tourism info 2007). The island-Republic's tourist promotion slogan is "Uniquely Singapore".

It is interesting to observe that Singapore wants to maintain its position as unique, and in this sense, there was much strategic thinking on the part of Lee and the Singapore leaders. Here, Low (2009b) has argued that strategic maintenance has become critical and part of the Singapore's national traits or values. What the infrastructure rich, efficient city-state excels in is giving a great first impression... the tree-lined expressway from Changi Airport to the city centre is "one of the most beautiful drives to and from any airport, anywhere in the world." said an urban design commentator, Tyler Brule (Oon 2008, p. A34). The luxuriant greenery that Singapore the Garden City enjoys today is not by accident but rather it has been strategically planned; this strategic maintenance and management, in fact, took some 40 years of strong political will and the sweat and toil of many to sustain the effort. And the growing of a garden city is overall seen as a competitive factor in attracting investors and tourists alike to the island-republic (National Parks Singapore 2008; also in Low 2009b).

Perhaps influenced by the Minister Mentor, one Singapore Company that has ensured the strategic maintenance of Singapore's transport and infrastructural systems is Singapore Mass Rapid Transit (SMRT) which is a modern, air-conditioned passenger train service with stations all over the island. Exemplifying continuous effort and growth, this Singapore Company has also made many milestones since its incorporation in 1987. Among its many achievements and just to cite a few examples, SMRT, in 1999, opened the Bukit Panjang Light Railway Transit (LRT) system, and in 2002, opened the Changi Airport Station for passenger services. Last year, SMRT also acquired a 40 % equity interest in Shenzhen Zona Transportation Group Co. Ltd, a leading road transport company in Shenzhen, People's Republic of China (SMRT: 2009a, cited in Low 2009b).

In business, it is often good to have strategic maintenance as it is part of the process of continuous improvement, updating and sharpening the saw. Singapore Airlines updates its fleet often and has good safety records, and overall, that's critical in attracting and getting customers.

Being Proactive

Fighting a hundred battles and winning every one of them. (Chinese saying)

Orang yang menunggu perigi itu, bilakah ia mati dahaga?: One who sits by the well will never go thirsty. So too would one who mixes with the learned or the rich will never be wanting of knowledge or wealth. (Malay proverb)

Generally-speaking, one can immediately read Lee Kuan Yew as a proactive leader. At the time of writing, this author was fortunate enough to receive the input of several of Lee Kuan Yew's overseas admirers, and they expressed these: "A make-things-happen leader... and he is one who is learning, self-cultivating, communicates well, persuades or influences others and shares his ideas... and is highly likely to make things happen!"

Knowing the importance of effective law enforcement and rigorous administrative system, Lee set the model of creating a corruption-free society which is so vital for effective government, action and enforcement. Good corporate governance is the order of the day, and Lee gets the people's buy-in and motivation of what-is-good-for-business-and-the-nation and the value of corrupt-free efficiency.

And under his leadership, the Government has also been overall proactive in developing high standards of public health and a quality environment with clean air, land, water, as well as a control on noise pollution. In 1968, *Singapore: Garden City to Model Green City*, a clean and green city was acknowledged as the goal of the government. And it can be said that Lee's policy was consistent in succeeding years in creating a Garden City with a clean and green environment.

Lee gets things done; in fact, at 87 years of age, he is "always physically vigorous, (and) he combats the decline of age with a regime of exercises and an hour-by-hour daily schedule of meetings, speeches and conferences both in Singapore and overseas". He once spoke of himself as, "If I rest, I'll slide downhill fast." (Lee Kuan Yew, cited in Mydans 2010, p. 29).

Being Firm and Disciplined Yet Caring

As vicious as the tigers, they don't eat their own cubs. No parents should ever mistreat their children. (Chinese proverb).

Lee Kuan Yew, because he led the island-nation to higher economic growth, with good planning and with tight social control, is one of the most influential leaders in Asia, if not, the world. To Singaporeans, it appears nothing wrong with having strong discipline as long as for resource-poor Singapore, economic growth and prosperity comes with it. To be fair, Lee in fact adopts a caring, fatherly approach when leading. Here, father leadership can be said to be very much in practice (Low 2006), and as the Chinese saying goes, "vicious as a tiger can be, he never eats his own cubs".

Lee's care and concern for the resource-scarce island-Republic is also shown by the organization, the setting up of systems and a series of processes in place to build the capacity and ability of the people. Lee in 2008 said, "So they (Singaporeans) exert themselves, and that is why we are here. But once we are here, we keep on building the capabilities, we build the infrastructure so that your brain, your fingers and your organisations can lift your people up to a higher level." (Lee 2008 cited in The Brunei Times 2008).

Wielding Much Influence, Influencing Is So Critical

Walk with me. (Chinese saying)

A lawyer by training, Lee's opinions carried much weight with the public, even during Goh's Prime Ministership. His communication style was to back his speeches with facts and figures. Maier and Kourdi (2010, pp. 143–144) highlight that:

> His ability to use facts and information was recognized as first class. For example, speaking in New Dehli, at the age of 82, on the subject of an Asian renaissance, Lee marshalled a wealth of facts and data to support his central argument that India and China were leading an Asian renaissance and beginning to fulfil their potential. He explained how Singapore had fulfilled its own potential and how expectations could be beaten.

Sharing his analysis, Lee took time to explain his views and reasons. (Maier and Kourdi 2010).

In this regard, the late Lee Kuan Yew, as Singapore's founding father, has a great influence in Singapore and, in particular, in moulding Singaporeans. Singaporeans have been drilled to appreciate the benefits of multiculturalism and political stability; the reasons given by the government or Lee himself have been ample and rational (Low 2002, 2009b). In Low's (2002, 2009b) studies, he has, in fact, argued that one of the island-Republic's core values is that of rationalism. Logical analysis and sequential planning are adopted as the preferred processes for approaching new situations. If rationality is part of culture, then one would anticipate that decisions would be made from the perspective of an objective analyst, not motivated by subjective or personal concerns. Besides, being a small island-Republic, Singapore subscribes to and relies on the rule of the law to ensure its survival. This rule of the law also seems preferred and at work in the Pedra Banca or Pulau Batu Putih—Singapore versus Malaysia case. In the same vein, going by the principle of non-interference in the internal affairs of other States and rationalism, Singapore stood against the US intervention in Grenada as much as it opposed the Soviet intervention in Afghanistan and the Vietnamese intervention in Cambodia (Low 2002, 2009b). And what more, in business, there is a tendency for Singaporeans to be rational and level-headed, preferring to talk and sort things out (Low 2010), and besides, they want or tend to make the meetings harmonious and productive which is a key Confucian value (Scarborough 1998, cited in Low 2002, 2009b).

Taking some pains to explain issues, Lee also communicated clearly and simply. And easily establishing his rapport with his audience, he connects with them by stressing on shared experiences. His listeners are normally able to relate to him through shared experiences.

Indeed, walking the talk is important for a leader since the leader who takes action or makes things happen is likely to be trusted by the employees or people, even business customers and associates would trust such as leader. A make-things-happened leader, who is learning and self-cultivating, communicates well, persuades or influences others and shares his ideas is likely to make things happen; and these are what business leaders should emulate (Fig. 11.1).

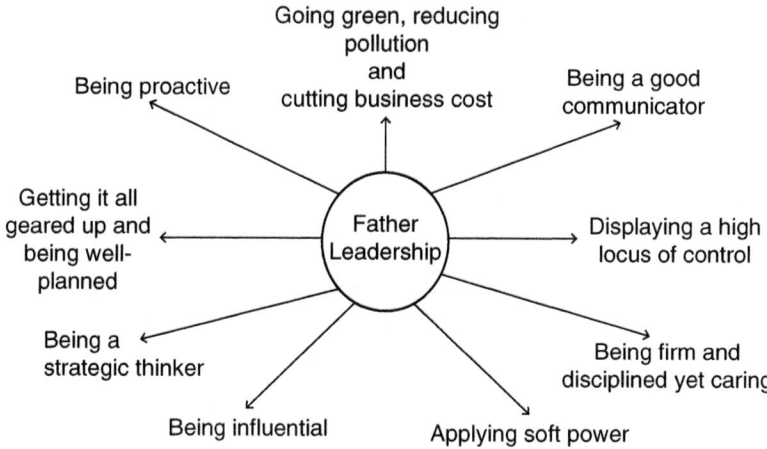

Low, K. C. P. (2011)'Lee Kuan Yew and His Key Leadership Ways', *Business Journal for Entrepreneurs*, Volume 2011 Issue 2, p. 50 - 62.
Low, K. C. P. (2006) 'Father leadership: the Singapore case study; *Management Decision,* Vol. 44 No. 1, 2006, p. 89-104.

Fig. 11.1 Characteristics of father leadership in Singapore

Applying Soft Power

Trust is an important tool of applying soft power. As Lee himself once said, the Singapore leadership's "greatest asset was the trust and confidence of the people", "the other valuable asset"—"hardworking, thrifty, eager to learn" (Lee 2000, p. 24). Having fought well against the communists, the Malay ultras, Lee was careful to take full advantage of a few assets such as a natural harbour sited in a strategic position astride one of the busiest sea lanes of the world.

Over the years, more so as Minister Mentor, Lee Kuan Yew can be said to be more of a selling, persuading leader as compared to his earlier Prime Minister days. This is particularly evident in his book, "Hard Truth" which was published in 2011; it is smartly, even wisely handled more in the form of questions and answers or interviews rather than straight lectures from Lee. And that is more appealing with readers having a sense of satisfaction as if having their questions answered.

These recent several years before his death in 23 March 2015 , Lee was more patient, and he plays more of an advisory role to his Cabinet members.

Lee Kuan Yew's Role and Appreciating the Context in Which Singapore Is In

When we see persons of worth, we should think of equalling them; when we see persons of a contrary character, we should turn inwards and examine ourselves. (Chinese proverb, also attributed to Confucius)

Lee Kuan Yew was indeed seen as "a giant among men" by Singapore Ministers when he died on 23 March 2015 (Today 2015). Deputy Prime Minister and Finance Minister Tharman Shanmugaratnam said: "We have lost Lee Kuan Yew, but Singapore will live on and better still, because of Mr Lee Kuan Yew. The foundations that he built up are the foundations for the future—everything, education, housing ownership, multiracialism, tripatism, clean government—everything that was Lee Kuan Yew is what will hold us for the future." (Today 2015).

Singapore, ranked as Southeast Asia's safest country to do business by France-based global credit insurer Coface, is set to be the world's fastest growing economy in 2010, as it rebounds spectacularly from the financial crisis (2008/2009) (Reuters 2010 cited in *Borneo Bulletin* 2010).

Internally, the Singapore's society is a multi-racial, multi-religious and multi-cultural society yet, say whatever security there may be, the potential fault-lines for racial or religious tensions and strife are all the time there. What more, religious tensions in neighbouring Malaysia could spill-over to the City-state. Singapore's future leaders need to grapple with these issues to ensure modern Singapore's political peace as well as economic growth and prosperity.

Lee Kuan Yew, having laid the necessary infrastructure and cultural value foundations as well as having affected a good leadership transfer, should be appreciated and his efforts and contributions in leading Singapore should be cherished when one bears in mind the island-Republic's situation in which she was and currently is in. It is worthy to note that Singapore, being small, is often subjected to being bullied by countries bigger than her or even by her neighbours. Singapore-bashing, in many regional countries, is a sure-fire way to win political capital. And relations with Indonesia, Malaysia and Thailand in particular are often difficult or tricky, and are further complicated by Singapore's serious investment in regional economies and its reliance on neighbours for some key resources.

Section Conclusion

Singapore ranked 17th on the World Bank's 2009 list in terms of the GDP per capita. The United States ranked 6th while Japan ranked 14th (Wikipedia 2010). It is remarkable what planning and strong preparations can attain.

In any case, it can be said that Singaporeans really appreciate peace and political stability. And true, the people are a hardworking lot, educated, rational, ever willing to work even harder (not wanting to lose what their forefathers and they have built on), and with a strong sense of unity, but it can still be assessed that Lee was overall a thinker and a good planner who has brought the island-Republic to where it is today. And such key qualities of Lee Kuan Yew are essential for any business leaders to emulate, learn and apply when doing business; there is certainly a need for business leaders to be proactive, strategic in thinking, pro-planning, learning, making it happens while having the determination as well as the concept of hardiness, if not, surviving in any given setting.

The Peranakans, Values and Leadership in Singapore

The idea to write this leadership cum anthropology section goes back to the year 1998 when the author, during his Ph.D. studies, then realised that there were clearly not many Peranakans left. "Peranakan culture has started to disappear in Malaysia and Singapore." (http://thehistoryofmalacca.blogspot.sg/2013/07/culture-of-peranakan-of-baba-andnyonya.html; Chia 1980). Even in terms of education, Chinese Singaporeans have to opt and learn Mandarin Chinese as second language; Singapore categorizes the Peranakans as ethnically Chinese, so they receive formal instruction in Mandarin Chinese as a second language (in accordance with the "Mother Tongue Policy") instead of Malay. And then again in 2008, a Singaporean television drama series The Little Nyonya was aired in Singapore, and was in Mandarin. Of interest, the Chinese community can afford to ease up on the use of dialect(s), but Singapore Prime Minister Lee Hsien Loong (cited in Ong 2014: 1) in the Speak Mandarin Campaign, highlighted that it would not be practical to do so, and there is a need to 'stick to Mandarin' "to maintain good standards" and to unite the Chinese.

That being the case, the Baba patois ["a Malay patois with Chinese words and phrases of the Hokkien dialect" (Chia 1980: 9) (Hokkien is a Southern Chinese dialect)] would, it seems, soon be lost and not be remembered; further, without a written language, any culture would slowly die off and eventually disappeared.

Section Objectives

It is the key intention, aim and objectives of this section to examine various cultural features and even common Peranakan proverbs or sayings and apply them to Peranakan leadership qualities, style and ways in Singapore. Note that the Peranakans "are fond of quotations (or sayings)", and most of them are understandably in Baba Malay (Chia 1980: 50). This section is derived mostly from Low's (2014) study which was also based on the researcher's interviews with a small group of Peranakans' professionals and his cultural background and his impressions as well as perceptions of the Peranakan leadership in Singapore as they and the author see it.

This section is apt after all, the Baba culture right now is being disintegrated, even back in 1980, Chia (1980: viii) then wrote, "I did not marry a Nyonya and my children speak only a little and faulty Baba Malay, the patois first Babas spoke. It is a corrupt form of the Malay language which includes words and phrases of the Hokkien dialect".

Leaders ordinarily influence their people (Achua and Lussier 2010; Maxwell 1993). And they are guided by the values they hold; "values are significant because they subconsciously shape our behavior on a dayto-day basis. People find it hard to go against their values." (Price and Price 2013: 59; Low 2008c). "It's (also) not hard to make decisions when you know what your values are." (Roy Disney, cited in Price and Price 2013: 59).

A value, an element of a culture, is a core belief (of a group of people or a community) and what one (members) strongly believe(s) in (Low 2002, Low 2009a; italics author's). Of significance, a value is comparable to the seed without which one cannot have any fruit; a value leads to 'signpost' (author's word: marker) or guiding feeling, thinking and action or behavior. Values are principles, standards, or qualities one considers worthwhile or desirable (http://www. providentplan.com/2036/the-importance-of-values/). To paraphrase the words of Marcus Aurelius (cited in Peale 1993: 58; the Roman leader who lived from AD 121 to 180), "Our life is what our thoughts make of it"—one can thus say—our leading ways and/or behaviors are what our values make of them.

Who Are the Straits-Chinese or the Peranakans?

Peranakan Chinese and Baba-Nyonya are terms used for the descendants of the fifteenth through seventeenth century Chinese immigrants to the Indonesian archipelago and British Malaya (now Peninsular Malaysia and Singapore) (West 2009: 657). Yeap (1975: 14), however, spoke of "Malacca (or Melaka)... as the nucleus of this unique ethnic group, for the Chinese had arrived as early as fifteenth century. Branches of the group had spread to Singapore and Penang. They were the offsprings of early Chinese immigrants, mostly Hokkiens who looked upon the Peranakans as the upper class of 'blue blood', since they were socially and economically established". Members of the Peranakan community in Malacca, Malaysia address themselves as the Nyonyas and the Babas (Chia 1980; Yeap 1975). Nyonyas is the term for the women and Babas for the men. Peranakan is a Malay word that means "born locally" (The Peranakan Resource Library 2003a), applying particularly to the ethnic Chinese populations of the British Straits Settlements of Malaya and the Dutch-controlled island of Java and other locations, who have adopted Nusantara customs—partially or in full—to be fairly assimilated into the local communities. Many were the elites of Singapore, more loyal to the British or anglophile than to China. Most have lived for generations along the straits of Malacca: Penang, Malacca and Singapore, "The Straits Settlement" as well as Sumatra/Java; and most have a lineage where intermarriages with the local Malays have occurred.

In the early days, most of the Peranakan men were seafarers who traded between the ports of southern China and those of Southeast Asia. In the eighteenth and nineteenth centuries, the Babas were involved in opium, nutmeg and liquor cargoes, cultivation of pepper and Gambier (an extract of the Uncaria plant native to Indonesia that is used in tanning and dying and as an anti-inflammatory Chinese medicinal herb), tin mining, commodity trading and property development. In the early 1900s, many Peranakans invested in rubber plantations. Most became very rich and spared no expense in housing, furnishings, dress, schooling, ceremonies, recreation and houses of worship (primarily Buddhist). (Hilary 2014).

Western Education, Peranakan Upbringing, Their Leaders, and Their Leadership Qualities, Style(s) and Ways

True, there might and may be lazy, lacking ambitions or irresponsible Peranakans around, but upholding certain values, the Babas are quintessentially taught to be, among other things, hard-working; and they should not take the credit or belittle the work of others. Chia (1980: 52) wrote that "the Babas do not believe in heavy bones" and they 'don't eat the drops of someone's sweat!' or 'jangan makan titik perloh orang' a Baba may admonish you. Shame on you for exploiting the labour of others!"

Additionally, brought up in a "fine or polite" ("halus"; Chia 1980: 23) cultural setting and through child-rearing practices, the Peranakans are taught to uphold the value of high integrity ("lien" as in the Confucian teachings) and to avoid being of "loose conduct" or "getek" (Chia 1980: 47).

The late Dr. Toh Chin Chye (a Peranakan and Singapore's Deputy Prime Minister, 5 June 1965–2 August 1968), for example, insisted that his grandchildren "should be sincere, and above all, it is important to be upright in our dealings with others" (Channel News Asia 2010).

The Peranakans prefer to be "berat mulot" or heavy mouth instead of indulging in gossiping and spreading rumors (Chia 1980). They must simply not have leaky mouths or "mulot bocho", from which will flow secrets (Chia 1980: 52). Each person—any Baba or Nyonya—must also not "buat sial" or "buat suay" (bring or do ill-luck; "suay": bad luck in Hokkien) (Chia 1980: 47), and in essence, they are taught to bring honor to the family.

Interestingly, most non-Peranakan Chinese in nineteenth-century Singapore continued welcoming plans to return to China: statistics from 1881 up to the 1960s show not only a continuous stream of Chinese immigration but also return emigration (Kwok 2000: 200). Where the Peranakans were concerned, however, while the early Chinese may have returned regularly to China to ship more goods, and the sons of the wealthier ones (a minority) to receive education. Lim (1917: 876), they always returned to the Straits; in fact, the Peranakans considered Malacca and Singapore their home.

Many Peranakans sent their children to English schools (Yeap 1975) instead to China and this gave them "the opportunity of learning the language which both the Baba trader and the Baba worker needed if they were to succeed in their respective fields" (Chia 1980: 71). (As leaders), most of the Straits Chinese served as compradores of banks, the East India Company and big mercantile companies or

Kapitan China where they acted as intermediaries between the Chinese community and the British (Okto 2014; Hilary 2014; http://scooponsingapore.blogspot.sg/2012/02/peranakan-culture-in-singapore.html); they were what is today called business development managers (Okto 2014).

Some prominent Peranakan leaders include Tan Tock Seng (1798–1850) and Dr. Lim Boon Keng (1869–1957) (Singapore Tatler 1992) who had also a road named after him. Others include: From rags to riches, Tan Tock Seng was well-known for contributing money to build a hospital called Tan Tock Seng Hospital as he saw many poor and sick people; he simply wanted to care for them. After Tan's death in 1850, his son Tan Kim Ching carried on the family support for the hospital which continues as one of Singapore's most prominent medical centers. (http://singaporepioneers.blogspot.sg/). Lim Nee Soon (1879–1936), Tan Kim Ching (Tan Tock Seng's eldest son) (1829–1892), and Seah Eu Chin (1805–1883) and Gan Eng Seng (1844–1899) were some of the wealthy businessmen who had earned the respect of the British authorities for their wealth, their command of English and political loyalty.

It is worthy to note that in the nineteenth and early twentieth century Singapore, outspoken and eloquent in the English language, these leaders indeed helped the British to maintain law and order while promoting social harmony (The Peranakan Resource Library 2003b). Take Tan Kim Seng, a wealthy Straits Chinese merchant and a philanthropist for example, in 1857, donated S$13,000 towards the improvement of the town's water supply (Singapore Infopedia 2004) and this donation helped in the building of Singapore's first impounding reservoir (National Parks Board 2014). And interestingly so, although he had little education, Gan Eng Seng realized the value of education as he prospered and became wealthy; his dream to build a school for the poor (which taught both English and Chinese, probably Cantonese or Hokkien, as Mandarin was not commonly used in Southeast Asia then) was fulfilled in 1885 when he built the Anglo-Chinese Free School for boys in some shop-houses in Telok Ayer Street (not related to the Anglo-Chinese School founded a year later by Bishop W.F. Oldham). In 1923, in Gan's honor, the school was renamed to Gan Eng Seng School (GESS) (GESSOSA 2006; Song 1984).

In present-day Singapore, the late Singapore President Wee Kim Wee (1915–2005) himself was also a Baba or a Peranakan who in his younger days was a passionate journalist. He was also a diplomat for many years as well as the Chancellor of NTU from 1991 to 1993 (The Peranakan Association 2012a). Wee Kim Wee was also noted to be humble (The Peranakan Association 2012a). Kind and big-hearted, Wee donated half a million Singapore dollars (in royalties received from his autobiography, Glimpses and Reflections and other donations) to eight charities in Singapore. (http://singaporepioneers.blogspot.sg/). Other Baba leaders include "Lee Kuan Yew, Toh Chin Chye and Goh Keng Swee... publicly described as English-educated Babas, (who) worked tirelessly to remove the separate political identity of the Baba... All Chinese children are learning Mandarin at school. Emphasis is being placed on Chinese identity as a merit." (The Peranakan Association 2011a). Note that Lee Kuan Yew (Minister Mentor), Dr. Goh Keng Swee, Toh Chin Chye and S. Rajaratnam are generally considered as the founding fathers of modern Singapore; they contributed much, helping to lead Singapore during the Republic's formative years.

Applying Father Leadership

Like the Penang's Baba counterpart (Yeap 1975), "the family is very important to us all" "(And) it is quite a characteristic (of Peranakan leadership) that the father-leader cares and shows concern." "Being paternalistic, wanting to care for their followers (employees)—who are seen as family members especially in family run businesses" (several interviewees' inputs).

Perhaps this 'applying father leadership' by the Peranakans can truly be said to be an Asian, if not in particular, a Singaporean characteristic especially of the political setting. Minister Mentor Lee Kuan Yew, the father of Modern Singapore has indeed left the running of Singapore to his younger PAP colleagues; and the Confucian influence (as argued by Low 2006, 2008c, 2013), the times and/or the environment—are now changing or evolving. A benevolent leadership style, caring for one's employees, is adopted. One interviewee spoke of, "My ah kong (grandpa) was very considerate to his workers, but my granduncle (kukong) was autocratic, but benevolent."

Practicing Family-Oriented Leadership Way

"The family is very important to us all, to the Peranakans. All of us come together when there are gatherings, praying sessions and celebrations", one interviewee intimated to this researcher. These are further affirmed by Chia's (1980: 44), "The Chinese's love of kinship extending to relatives related through marriage is also inherent in the Babas". "Peranakan leaders are warm, friendly and personable" (several interviewees' inputs).

And interestingly, several other interviewees also spoke of the family-oriented style of leadership in which the "leaders showed care and concern for the followers" (several interviewees' inputs), and it also engendered the "all-in-the-family feelings" (the words used by, at least, five of the interviewees) among the employees in the company. Here again, as a young child, the authors often heard another popular saying , that is, "tetak ayer, tetak darah, tak bolih putus", literally translated as one cannot chop up water or blood; like water, one cannot cut off blood ties. Or more or less, similar to Chia's (1980: 74) point of the Babas' "blood is thicker than water". Chia (1980: 26) also highlighted that "the force behind family love manifested itself clearly in those days as it was common to find married children who lived by themselves paying their parents weekend visits", and such familial bonds really "bound families, kindred and friends together in those days before the Second World War".

This reflects the all-in-the-family feeling that exists or pervades among the Peranakans, and that, in a way, can be said as familial leadership as exemplified among the Peranakans when they run family businesses or as depicted by Chinese businesses ala the Towkay corporate culture (Low 2002, 2009a).

Accommodating

One interviewee expressed (in Low's 2014 study) that, "Yes, I have fantastic family friends that are 'Peranakans.' My understanding of them is that... (due to) the merging of two worlds: the 'finesse' soft, respectful, clean, accommodating... polished culture of the Chinese and the friendliness, co-operative-ness of the kampong style Malays". [The Malays are considered as gentle, hospitable and cooperative; often, they are very polite or "berbudi" (Abdullah 1996.)]

"Being refined is considered as good". "They were or are gentle people and they would, in most instances, be accommodating and attend to the needs of their people (customers, and those they come into contact)." (several interviewees' inputs). These coincide with what Chia (1980: 83) highlighted, that is, the Babas "generated a prominent identity for themselves, bearing in mind the respect they held and the understanding and appreciation they had for the culture of other races, and even fusing some of those cultures with their own".

Respecting the Old

This is related to the Confucian concept and practice of filial piety ("xiao"). Yeap (1975: 140) indicated that "ancestral worship... was an important occasion for the family... (they, family members and servants) woke up early, as four o'clock to prepare the food that was to be offered to the departed ancestors. There were no less than ten varieties of dishes..." The Babas might have also merged such values or borrowed them from the Malays. As in most Asian culture, the Malays indeed have this respect for the old (Abdullah 1996). In the past ancestral worship was practiced by the Peranakans though it "is fast disappearing today and most Babas are now Christians" (Chia 1980: 22).

"Most Peranakans hormat (respect) the old or seniors and address them well and I guess these all apply to the Peranakan leaders." "They treat the older workers well and ageism is thus non-existent" (several interviewees' inputs).

Being Compassionate

Closely connected to respecting the old or seniors, the Peranakan leaders are "kind-hearted" and "often show... care and concern for the people or the poor." (several interviewees' inputs). One interviewee emphasized that, "(the roles and contributions of) Tan Tock Seng, Tan Kim Seng and the other Chinese pioneers" of Singapore; they were driven to meet the needs of the society and community they served.

Indeed Low (2014) reckoned that indeed many plus points exist in having such a caring or compassionate leadership. While ego-driven 'leaders', on one hand, have a harder time to keep their staff; they may also even refuse to see their staff's potential and a lot of that potential goes untapped, Menter (2003: 182–183) wrote that "caring leaders", on the other hand, "respect their staff and are often rewarded with the kind performance and loyalty money can't buy".

Interestingly, during the funeral service of the late Dr. Toh Chin Chye, his eldest grandson, then 15-year-old Matthew Ng (cited in Channel News Asia 2010), spoke of "his grandfather or 'Kong Kong' being caring and how his grandfather always reminded him and his siblings to study hard and to uphold certain values"; "family members remember Dr. Toh as caring person".

There are always the Baba leaders' "gentle ways of 'never mind, sharing and caring'", "relationship (guanxi) is stressed, and sharing and exchanges are valued" (several interviewees' inputs). These, to the author, can be conceivably analyzed as being attributed to the Peranakans' key values, strongly influenced by Confucianism ("ren ai") and Buddhism and/ or even Christianity (Low 2008c, 2013; Ueda 2013) and combined with the Malays' gentleness and values (Abdullah 1996) of strong hospitality, and kindness which indeed emphasize care and compassion for one's fellow beings.

Planning and Having a Prepared Style of Running Things

A Baba let alone a leader must not have "mulot gatal" or itchy mouth to say or commit something without thinking things over carefully, and regrets later what he has said (Chia 1980: 52).

In Low's (2014) study, several interviewees indicated these: "I respect Peranakan Singaporean leaders—for example, the late Goh Keng Swee who died in 2010. He was the Second Deputy Prime Minister and also Ministers for Education, Defence and Finance... he had a good mind, sharp and systematic... a good economist... he was a good planner." Goh was a key member of the PAP's Central Executive Committee, and later became its vice-chairman (The Straits Times 2010). Goh's contributions to Singapore were "wide, deep and incisive. Among the most notable were the creation of Jurong as an industrial hub, the formation of the Singapore Armed Forces (SAF), the Economic Development Board (EDB), the Monetary Authority of Singapore (MAS), and the Government Investment Corporation (GIC). All these key pillars of Singapore's success bear the imprint of Dr. Goh." (http://www.nlb.gov.sg/blogs/highbrowseonline/general/dr-goh-keng-swee-passes-1918-2010/#sthash.oWUfLJMU.dpuf). Dr. Goh indeed built up the foundations of the Singapore Armed Forces (SAF) which was based on a concept of a combination of conscription and a professional military on the Israeli Army model (Asiaone News 2010). And Kwa (2010: 6) wrote that Dr. Goh "will (indeed) be remembered more as a backroom strategist, planning Singapore's long political futures to complement the economic growth he was planning".

Generally speaking, "with no last-hour rush", the Peranakans "want(ed) to be systematic... ada kepala ada buntut" (literally translated as 'having both head and tail' or in Hokkien, it is 'Oo tow oo buay'"). Perhaps influenced by the British or Western ways, they disliked disorganisation, and "the Peranakan leadership seemed to be of the planning sort or organized" (several interviewees' inputs). They disliked or avoided panicking, choosing rather to be prepared, systematic and planned well. Here, often as a child, I heard the common admonitions by my parents that one needed to be better prepared. The author's mother often urged, "Bikin kerja jangan kalang kabut. Buat kerja mesti ada kepala ada buntut. Selalu bersiap-siap" literally means, one must not do a rush job; be systematic. Always be prepared; plan well. She often urged me not to get caught, unprepared and panicked; "jangan kalang kabut macham ayam hilang anak" (don't go helter-skelter).

Living Gentlemanly/Ladylike

A person must not be "jahat" (evil) or cruel. (Chia 1980). "Their socialization or child-rearing at home enables character-building." (several interviewees' inputs). "The Babas' conversation is always halus (fine or polite)." (Chia 1980: 23). They spoke, for example, of going to the toilet to pass motion as going to "the bank". (Chia 1980).

And in the Baba culture, children are taught to be polite and "greet everyone they met. ...If they did not know who was who, they were to ask their elders for guidance. To be branded as tak tau teriak orang or 'ignoring to greet others' was a slight to the family." (Chia 1980: 26). The Peranakan Association (2012b), in fact, added that, "The Babas have managed to maintain the refined nineteenth century customs and traditions of the Hokkien Chinese. (Also, mentioned in http://scooponsingapore.blogspot.sg/2012/02/peranakan-culture-in-singapore.html) (Many of these practices no longer survive in China or in local Hokkien communities.)"

By the same token, "leaders must be polite and gentle", "tak kasar" (translated: not crude). "The Peranakans often spoke of good upbringing and children are raised to be refined or 'halus'" (several interviewees' inputs). Here, the author reckons that this is perhaps the influence of Chinese, that is, Confucianism, a person must be a gentleperson ("jun zi"), practicing "ren" (humanism) and upholding his or her integrity (Low 2008c).

Besides, being English educated, and learning from the English, the Babas were or can be considered as strongly influenced by "the sense of fair play" (Chia 1980: 74).

Being Humble

"We learnt in our childhood to emulate the humble rice paddy", highlighted one interviewee. These aptly fit with Low's (2010: 90) "unlike the long grass (lallang) the paddy, though bent low, is loaded with rice grains......don't brag, be quiet. But make your own achievements, and let your results and how good you are, speak for themselves." "Jadi orang, jangan jadi sombong" (translated, as a person, one should not be proud or arrogant) expressed another interviewee.

The late Wee Kim Wee, a Peranakan, is said to have led and shown an "inspiring leadership, humility and humanity during his tenure as President of Singapore" (The Peranakan Association 2012a). "The Peranakans are taught or went through socialization to be humble. . . as leaders, they are not boastful or show-off." (several interviewees' inputs). This can, in part, be attributed to the Peranakans' subscription to Chinese Buddhism.

[Overall, the Peranakans subscribed to Chinese beliefs: Taoism, Confucianism and Chinese Buddhism (Chia 1980: 19), and they celebrated the Lunar New Year and the Lantern Festival; http://thehistoryofmalacca.blogspot.sg/2013/07/culture-of-peranakan-of-baba-and-nyonya.html]; after all, Buddhism undeniably encourages people to cooperate and live in harmony through eliminating their egos (Ueda 2013).

Besides, it should be noted that the Peranakan culture is really enriched by its adoption of some Malay songs, proverbs, poems or "pantuns" (Chia 1980). "Pantuns" significantly show the terseness and wit of sayings while affording pleasurable insight into precepts and shrewd observations of the Malay race (Hamilton 1987) and truly that of the Baba-Nyonyas too. And interestingly too, humility can also be seen in the Dondang Sayang which "is popular among the people, especially the Peranakan Babas and Nonyas", and Hudi (2002) wrote that the old Malay music genre "reflects courtesy and humility, characteristics of the Malays"; and indeed the Babas and Nyonyas "(acquire) the merging of two worlds: . . .the Chinese and... . . .the Malays". (one interviewee's inputs).

Being of Positive Frame of Mind

Although Chia (1980: 50) referred to the fact that "most Babas are fatalists", this author would differ and maintain that overall they, in fact, had and have a high sense of optimism. Here, optimism is defined as "a positive, upbeat attitude toward the world that sets you up for success in school, relationships, career, and life in general. It enables you to overcome life's difficulties – to bounce back and thrive. (MacDonald 2004: 14). Chia (2003) himself offered a good positive saying when he talked about "Kalu tak ah kledek, makan lah ubi kayu!" (If there is no sweet potato, then satisfy yourself with tapioca!). Indeed the Baba leaders ordinarily look at the bright side of things; and that they "were optimistic". "They prefer to look forward, letting bygones be bygones or what they most times call, 'buang keroh ambil jernih'". (several interviewees' inputs).

The late President Wee Kim Wee, for example, was noted to be "a courageous man who took his illness in stride (he was then having prostate cancer). His emails described his declining health in an extremely matter-of-fact way, without any self-pity or despondency. He last wrote to me on April Fool's Day last year, a month before his passing, enquiring when my brother's binjai tree would fruit again, as he had not had buah binjay for some time" (Lee Kip Lee 2006, President of The Peranakan Association Singapore till 2010 cited, in The Peranakan Association 2012a).

To add, the author, of Straits Chinese (Peranakan) descent/ background and as a young child and teenager, often heard his late grandmother, late uncles, aunts and even his widow mother (she became a widow at the age of 35, the author was then 8 years old; and his widow mother single-handedly raised her three young children) spoke of "Buang keroh ambil jernih". These are literally translated as scooping or throwing away the scum while retaining the clear soup—particularly so when boiling beef stock, reflecting the optimism or forward-looking that exists among the Peranakans. And that too can indeed be said to be attributed to one of the style/ ways of the Peranakan leadership.

Being Multi-cultural

Interestingly, the late President Wee Kim Wee was once cited (in The Peranakan Association 2012a) as saying, "Not many people realise that Peranakans have acted as a bridge to bring about understanding and harmony over more than a century and we are still continuing to do that job today." The Peranakan Resource Library (2003b) in fact stated that many of these leaders had helped to promote law and order as well as social harmony even back in the days of British Singapore.

"English-educated, the Babas were multicultural, and as leaders, they know English, and have had knowledge of Chinese people and the Malay people as well as their language". These coincide with what Chia (1980: 27) indicated of the Babas, "(their) most conspicuous characteristic… is their multicultural influence".

It is also said that the Peranakans "tolerate the beliefs (religions) of others. The Baba is willing to take part in others' religious events. The Baba is willing to offer coconut milk in the Hindu festival or to join in the Novena processions of the Catholics or to find spiritual guidance from the datok mediums with the understanding that they have the best of everything. In other words, the Baba's outlook is not negative as far as others' practices are concerned" (Baba Cedric Tan 2001 cited in The Peranakan Association 2011b).

Being Friendly, Warm-Hearted and Relationship-Centered

Price and Price's (2013: 137) study indicated that good and successful leaders are warm, affable and friendly. Baba leaders are "friendly", "warm" and "relationship-centered"; "Peranakan leaders dealt with their people, customers and others in a personable way" and "relationship (guanxi) is stressed". (several interviewees' inputs). And this point, in fact, reaffirms and bolsters the Peranakans' practice of family-oriented leadership as discussed above.

Fig. 11.2 Key characteristics of the Peranakan leadership (based on the various values and cultural practices) as examined above in Low's (2014) study

"Warm-hearted people" (several interviewees' inputs), the Peranakans socialized and at parties, they "joget" (danced) while parleying in "pantuns" (poems) (Tan 2004). They would find or seize every opportunity and occasion to celebrate (Tan 2004; Chia 1980). Chia (1980: 48) spoke of the Nyonyas referring to such a person as celebrating "Tahon Baru Monyet" or "The Monkey's New Year"; and he is then having a fine time ("Apa lagi, dia seh jit lah!") (Fig. 11.2).

Section Conclusion

Low's (2014) study has thus given us a snapshot of the Peranakans and their leadership in Singapore. Much has been learnt of the style(s) and interesting ways of the leadership of the Peranakans or the Baba-Nyonyas in Singapore. But of course because of modernization and influence of other cultures within and without multicultural Singapore, their ways are indeed ever changing.

And it can also be truly said though sad that the Baba culture is "fast disappearing with each generation. . . a minority race which keeps dwindling cannot hope to survive." (Chia 1980: 193). Indeed not many people speak the faulty Baba Malay, the patois first Baba-Nyonyas spoke. "There are very few monolingual Peranakans left—and they are very old—and fewer than 5000 people in Singapore now speak the language at all." (Journal of Thoughts 2009). One interviewee spoke of "(the Peranakans let alone the Peranakan leadership style and ways are) kind of fading away. All because of the new lifestyles of this modern times." And he continued that, "In reference to leadership. . . that is a huge question mark, as the traditional days and behavior of the old versus the new, is definitely no more the same... (besides), Singapore for example has made it very tough for the commoners to survive, due to the high cost of living, and the competitiveness (of businesses). The gentle ways of 'never mind, sharing and caring' is just not possible, as one has to be rough and tough in the present rat race."

Singapore Incorporated Leaders

> Only as high as I reach can I grow, only as far as I seek can I go, only as deep as I look can I see, only as much as I dream can I be. (Karen Ravn)

Singapore Incorporated leaders include Sim Kee Boon (Civil Service, Keppel and Civil Aviation, now retired), J.Y.M. Pillai, G.E. Bogaars, Ms Ho Ching (Temasek Holdings). Singapore Incorporated, according to Low and Theyagu (2003, p. 98) are "led by tough men and women with bold entrepreneurial visions." Keppel, for example, is no longer just one of the world's foremost rig-builders but has developed into a one-stop banking and financial service centre with its own bank and securities houses. Keppel has indeed shown that Singapore's local corporation can excel and achieve world-class status. "Airport ace" Mr. Sim Kee Boon ("aim for only the best") "is the man behind the success that is (Singapore's) Changi International Airport. His eye for detail has helped Mr. Sim Kee Boon make Changi International Airport a world-class one." Mr. Sim Kee Boon. Sim himself has this to say: "I spend a lot of time walking around the airport. But I do this without telling anyone, so that they cannot arrange anything." He says with a note of pride: "Other airports have a jaded look after about 20 years, but ours still looks very fresh" (*Sunday Times*, Sunday Plus, 12 September 1999, cited in Low and Theyagu 2003, pp. 98–99).

"Cannot" is Greek to Mr Sim Kee Boon. His favourite line is quoted to be "Don't give me 1001 reasons why it cannot be done, just give me one good reason how it can be done" (*Sunday Times*, Sunday Plus, 12 September 1999, cited in Low and Theyagu 2003, pp. 98–99).

Reflecting one of Singapore's core values, i.e. human capital value (Low 2002, 2009a, 2011b), the common thread underlying the Singapore Inc. and Singapore Unlimited corporate leaders' thinking is the belief that people are the company's greatest asset, the willingness to learn from others, the determination to run the show ourselves as well as resilience.

Interestingly, the majority of these Singapore Inc. leaders hailed from the Civil Service. Attributing the *Kathakalli* metaphor, a 'mechanical' South Indian dance, to the Singapore Civil Service (Low 2002, 2005b, 2008b, 2009a, 2011b) argues that the rationality element is its core, and that this core contributes, in fact, to good governance, with efficiency and effectiveness. Meritocracy is thus practiced, and besides, qualified, trained public employees make administrative decisions according to sets of written and rational rules. Rationality can also be taken as being clearly aware of the organisational goal(s). The civil servants "are aware of the goals, and (they) systematically pursue them". It also involves systematically assessing the various means to attain the goal, weighing the pros and cons of each means, and then selecting the most appropriate or reasonable means (Low 2008b, p. 116). The Singapore Civil Service is overall seen as being efficient and productive, getting things done (Leong 2000, p. 21) and having to avoid "throwing money at problems" (Quah 1994, pp. 152–185). Singapore leaders believe in investing in training and in growing their staff (Low 2002, 2009a, 2011b). Like the political leaders, they also normally train and groom their staff accordingly. Identified individuals with good potential or high-flyers are normally coached and/or mentored by the top Singapore Inc. leaders or even by the political leaders. Overall, they take their cues from the political leaders and the civil bureaucracy.

With the core values of hard work, achievement-oriented and thrift, these Singapore Inc. leaders have led Singapore's very own multi-national corporations (MNCs) in proactively building a modern Singapore and in venturing overseas; they help to grow the island-Republic's external wing. Fast transforming Singapore Inc. to becoming Singapore Unlimited, these Singapore leaders, in part, subscribe to networking and partnering while looking for like-minded partners overseas, who are financially strong and able to contribute significantly to joint projects.

Singapore Business Leaders

> Talk too much and arrive nowhere is the same as climbing a tree to catch a fish. (Chinese proverb)

Most of Singapore business people (including leaders) go for business and the bottom line. (interviewees' input).

Next, "Singapore business leaders, especially from the small and medium enterprises (SMEs), are normally parental in most ways and they show much care and concern for their employees" (interviewees' input). And these coincide with the studies of Low (2002, 2005b, 2009a, 2011a).

Mirroring Singapore's national culture, the *Confucian heritage cultural model* (Low 2002, 2009a), the business leaders or managers, like benevolent fathers, use more saliva than drinking tea. They normally talk, coach and take personal interest in the employees' welfare. Informality and intimacy exists—with everyone undertaking a variety of activities to meet daily performance demands (Low 2001: pp. 98–99; Siew, cited in Low 2002, 2009a, 2011a).

Learning is very much encouraged, and employees of Singapore organisations are normally sent for training courses and workshops, both in-house and externally organised.

And in what has been referred to as the modernising culture or the bumboat (boats with motorised engines), leaders of these SMEs are also interested in modernising, and so they would apply automation and technology to update and upgrade. Many also engage professionals. And they have usually made their offices more modern, congenial and comfortable, and most include libraries and even research rooms.

Most of such leaders would promote teamwork or a sense of unity, and motivate their staff accordingly in "all-in-the-family way"; some have even paid holidays or long breaks for their staff during Chinese New Year seasons and other festivals.

Checkpoint: Think About It

Father Leadership in Singapore

Read and review each section in this chapter:

1. What is father leadership?
2. What are the roots and support of father leadership in Singapore?
3. What are the typical or key characteristics of father leadership?
4. What are the benefits of father leadership?
5. What are the downsides of father leadership?
6. What are the problems and prospects of father leadership?
7. What are your views on father leadership?
8. Can we also apply father leadership to small business and project management? If so, why and how? If not, why and how?

Lee Kuan Yew and His Leadership Ways

- Displaying a high locus of control
- Getting it all geared and well-planned, preparation and planning is so essential
- Being a strategic thinker
- Being proactive
- Being firm and disciplined yet caring
- Wielding much influence, influencing is so critical
- Applying soft power

In terms of leadership ways, what are the points in which you would like to emulate or incorporate?

The Peranakans, Values and Leadership in Singapore

- Applying father leadership
- Practicing family-oriented leadership way
- Accommodating
- Respecting the old
- Being compassionate

- Planning and having a prepared style of running things
- Living gentlemanly/ ladylike
- Being humble
- Being of positive frame of mind
- Being multi-cultural
- Being friendly, warm-hearted and relationship-centered

Singapore Incorporated Leaders

In terms of leadership ways, what are the points in which you would like to follow or emulate?

Ask yourself these questions:

- What are the learning points here?
- How would you do differently?
- What can you adopt, adapt or modify and incorporate as part of your leadership ways?

Singapore Business Leaders

Ask yourself these questions:

- What are the key lessons here for you?
- How would you do differently?
- What can you adopt, adapt or modify and incorporate as part of your leadership ways?

References

Abdullah, A. (1996). *Going glocal*. Malaysian Institute of Management: Malaysia.

Achua, C. F., & Lussier, R. N. (2010). *Effective leadership*. South-Western Cengage Learning: Canada.

Adler, N. (1997). *International dimensions of organizational behavior*. Cincinnati, OH: South-Western College Publishing, ITPC. www.remakingsingapore.gov.sg/.

Asiaone News. (2010). Goh Keng Swee's Major Contributions. *Asiaone News*. Accessed July 22, 2014 from http://news.asiaone.com/News/AsiaOne+News/Singapore/Story/A1Story20100514-216195.html

Asma, A. (1996). *Going glocal*. Kuala Lumpur: Malaysian Institute of Management.

Bellows, T. J. (1989). Bridging tradition and modernisation: The Singapore bureaucracy. In T. Hung-Chao (Ed.), *Confucianism and economic development: An oriental alternative?* (pp. 195–223). Washington, DC: The Institute for Values in Public Policy.

Bjerke, B. (1999). *Business leadership and culture*. Aldershot: Edward Elgar.

Bond, M. H. (1991). *Beyond the Chinese face: Insights from psychology*. Hong Kong: Oxford University Press.

Borneo Bulletin. (2010). Key political risks to watch in Singapore. *Borneo Bulletin*, 2 December 2010, p. 33.

Brislin, R. (1993). *Understanding culture's influence on behavior*. San Diego, CA: Harcourt Brace and Company.

Cham, T. S. (1998). Making a world class university (I). *Commentary, 15*, 35–40.

Chan, K. B., & Chiang, S. N. C. (1994). *Stepping out: The making of Chinese entrepreneurs*. Singapore: Centre for Advanced Studies, National University of Singapore and Prentice-Hall.

Channel News Asia. (2010). Family members remember Dr. Toh as Caring Person. *Channel News Asia*. Accessed July 20, 2014.

Chia, F. (1980). *The Babas*. Times Book International: Singapore.

Chia, F. (2003). *Chakapan Tersilap – Misquoted Baba Sayings*. Singapore: The Peranakan Association. Accessed July 24, 2014 from http://www.peranakan.org.sg/2011/07/chakapan_tersilap-misquoted_babasayings/

Chia, S. A. (2004). Raising junior is easier now. *The Straits Times*, 26 August.

Chin, A., & Tongzon, J. (1998). Chapter 3: Maintaining Singapore as a major shipping and air transport hub. In M. H. Toh & K. Y. Tan (Eds.), *Competitiveness of the Singapore economy, strategic perspective* (pp. 83–114). Singapore: Singapore University Press/World Scientific.

Chong, L. C. (1987). History and managerial culture in Singapore: 'Pragmatism' and 'Openness' and 'Paternalism'. *Asia Pacific Journal of Management, 4*(3), 133–134.

Daft, R. (2000). *Management* (5th ed.). Hillsdale, IL: The Dryden Press.

Daft, R. L. (2008). *The leadership experience*. Mason, OH: South-Western Cengage Learning.

Davie, S. (1999). S$4.4 billion to be spent to upgrade, rebuild schools. *The Straits Times*, 12 May, p. 1.

Enderle, G. (1995). An outsider's view of the East Asian miracle: Lessons and questions. In S. Stewart & G. Donleavy (Eds.), *Whose business values?* Hong Kong: Hong Kong University Press.

Gale, B. (1999). Evaluating Singapore's national institutions. *Political and Economic Risk Consultancy Ltd – Library*, 28 July, PERC.

GESSOSA: Gan Eng Seng School Old Students' Association. (2006). *The pictorial history of Gan Eng Seng School*. Singapore: Stamford Press.

Goh, T. (2001). *Today's Singapore*. Singapore: Rank Books.

Haley, U. C. V. (1998). Virtual Singapore: Shaping international competitive environments through business-government partnerships. *Journal of Organizational Change Management, 11*(4), 338–356.

Haley, U. C. V., & Low, L. (1998). Crafted culture: Governmental sculpting of modern Singapore and effects on business environments. *Journal of Organizational Change Management, 11*(6), 530–553.

Haley, G. T., Tan, C. T., & Haley, U. C. V. (1998). *New Asian emperors: The overseas Chinese, their strategies and competitive advantages*. Oxford: Butterworth-Heinemann.

Haley, G. T., Haley, U. C. V., & Tan, C. T. (2004). *The Chinese Tao of business: The logic of successful business strategy*. New York: Wiley.

Hamilton, A. W. (1987). *Malay proverbs*. Times Book International: Singapore.

Hanada, M., & Yoshikawa, A. (1991). Shop-floor approach to management in Japan. In J. Putti (Ed.), *Management Asian context* (pp. 36–60). Singapore: McGraw-Hill.

Hilary. (2014). *Peranakan culture in Singapore*. Accessed June 26, 2014 from Blogspot: http://scooponsingapore.blogspot.sg/2012/02/peranakan-culture-in-singapore.html. Accessed July 1, 2014 from http://singaporepioneers.blogspot.sg/. Accessed July 16, 2014 from http://scooponsingapore.blogspot.sg/2012/02/peranakan-culture-in-singapore.html. Accessed July 8, 2014 from http://thehistoryofmalacca.blogspot.sg/2013/07/culture-of-peranakan-of-baba-and-nyonya.html. Accessed July 22, 2014 from http://www.nlb.gov.sg/blogs/highbrowseonline/general/dr-goh-keng-swee-passes-19182010/#sthash.oWUfLJMU.dpuf. Accessed July 18, 2014 from http://www.providentplan.com/2036/the-importance-of-values/

Hodgetts, R. M., & Luthans, F. (1997). *International management*. Singapore: McGraw-Hill.

Hofstede, G. (1980/1984). *Culture's consequences: International differences in work-related values*. Newbury Park, CA: Sage.

Hu, R. (1998). *Off-budget measures*. 1 August, Singapore Parliament.

Hudi, K. (2002). Dondang sayang is a form of royal entertainment. *Berita Harian*, 1 June 2002. (Translated by Abdullah, A.). Accessed July 2, 2014 from http://www.srimahligai.com/articles/article_ds.htm

Institute for Management Development (IMD). (1999). *The world competitiveness yearbook*. Lausane: IMD.

Jose, J., & Doran, C. (1997). Marriage and marginalisation in Singaporean politics. *Journal of Contemporary Asia, 27*(4), 475–488.

Journal of Thoughts. (2009). Peranakans and the Chinese Peranakans, 27 June, 2009, *Journal of Thoughts*. Accessed July 17 2014 from http://ivorylink.blogspot.sg/2009/06/peranakans-and-chinese-peranakans.html

Kau, A. K., Tan, S. J., & Wirtz, J. (1998). *Seven faces of Singaporeans: Their values, aspirations and lifestyles*. Singapore: Prentice-Hall.

Keeley, T. D. (2001). *International human resource management in Japanese firms*. Basingstoke: Palgrave.

Khanna, V. (2004). Commentary/analysis: 'good to cast a critical eye on public policies. *The Straits Times*, 20 January, p. 14.

Koh, G., & Ooi, G. L. (2002). Singapore a home, a nation? In *South-East Asian Affairs 2002* (pp. 255–281). Singapore: Institute of Southeast Asian Studies.

Kumar, U., & Saxena, S. (1983). Interpersonal construct system and work styles of Indian managers. In J. Deregowski, S. Dziurawiec, & R. Annis (Eds.), *Expiscations in cross-cultural psychology* (pp. 356–370). Lisse: Swets and Zeitlinger.

Kwa, C. G. (2010). Remembering Dr Goh Keng Swee. *Biblioasia, 6*(3), 4–9.

Kwok, K. W. (2000). Singapore. In L. Pan (Ed.), *The encyclopedia of the Chinese overseas* (pp. 200–217). Chinese Heritage Centre: Singapore.

Lasserre, P., & Schutte, H. (1995). *Strategies for Asia Pacific*. London: Macmillan Press.

Law, S. L. (1996). *Lion and dragon*. Accessed from Accessed February 1, Asiaweek.com, www.asiaweek.com/asiaweek/96/0621/biz1.html

Lee, K. Y. (1988). *1988 National Day Rally*. Singapore.

Lee, J. (1996). Culture and management – A study of small Chinese family businesses in Singapore. *Journal of Small Business Management, 34*, 63.

Lee, K. Y. (2000). *From third world to first*. Singapore: Times Media Pte. Ltd. & The Straits Times Press.

Leong, H. K. (2000). *The politics of policy-making in Singapore*. Singapore: Oxford University Press.

Lim, B. K. (1917). The Chinese in Malaya. In W. Feldwisk (Ed.), *Present days' impressions of the Far East and prominent and progressive Chinese at home and abroad: The history, people, commerce, industries and resources of China, Hong Kong, Indo-China, Malaya and Netherlands India*. London: Globe Encyclopedia Co..

Lim, S. G. (1998). PS21: Gearing up the public service for the 21st century. In M. Arun & T. Y. Lee (Eds.), *Singapore re-engineering success* (pp. 124–131). Singapore: Institute of Policy Studies/Oxford University Press.

Lin, Y. T. (1938/1994). *The wisdom of Confucius*. New York: Random House.

Long, S. (2004). Acid test is when we stop taking cue from government. *The Straits Times*, 14 March.

Low, L. (1998). *The political economy of a city-state: Government-made Singapore*. Singapore: Oxford University Press.

Low, K. C. P. (2000). Staff management in an Indonesian customer contact environment. *CCWORLD*. Available at: www.ccworldnet.com. 15 July.

Low, K. C. P. (2001). *The power of relationships*. Singapore: BusinesscrAFT™ Consultancy.

Low, K. C. P. (2002). *Corporate culture and values: Perceptions of corporate leaders of co-operatives in Singapore.* Unpublished PhD dissertation, International Graduate School of Management, University of South Australia, Adelaide, Australia.

Low, K. C. P. (2004). Cultural barriers to entrepreneurship – A Singapore perspective. In *International conference on operations and quantitative management*, October (pp. 25–27, 5th edn). Seoul: Hanyang University.

Low, K. C. P. (2005a). Capitalising on flexibility. *Today's Manager.* December 2004/January 2005, pp. 30–32.

Low, K. C. P. (2005b). Towards a framework and typologies of Singapore corporate cultures. *Management Development Journal of Singapore, 13*(1), 46–75.

Low, K. C. P. (2006). Father leadership – The Singapore case study. *Management Decision, 44*(2), 89–104. Emerald Insight (www.emeraldinsight.com/0262-1711.htm).

Low, K. C. P. (2008a). How to win big in place marketing battlefield – Formula one night race, the Singapore perspective. *Business Journal for Entrepreneurs, 2008*(4), 115–125.

Low, K. C. P. (2008b). The Singapore civil service bureaucracy And the *Kathakalli* corporate culture – The analogy revisited. *Leadership and Organizational Management Journal, 2008* (4), 108–133.

Low, K. C. P. (2008c). Value-based leadership: 'Leading, the Confucian way'. *Leadership and Organizational Management Journal, 2008*(3), 32–41.

Low, K. C. P. (2009a). *Corporate culture and values: Perception of corporate leaders of co-operatives in Singapore.* Germany: VDM-Verlag.

Low, K. C. P. (2009b). Strategic maintenance and leadership excellence in place marketing – The Singapore perspective. *Business Journal for Entrepreneurs, 2009*(3), 125–143.

Low, K. C. P. (2010). *Successfully negotiating in Asia.* Heidelberg, Germany: Springer.

Low, K. C. P. (2011a). Types of Singapore corporate culture. *Business Journal for Entrepreneurs, 2011*(2), 11–49.

Low, K. C. P. (2011b). Lee Kuan Yew and his key leadership ways. *Business Journal for Entrepreneurs, 2011*(2), 50–62.

Low, K. C. P. (2013). Leading Successfully in Asia. Heidelberg, Germany: Springer.

Low, K. C. P. (2014). Leadership, Values and the Peranakans. *International Journal of Business and Social Sciences, 5*(9), 132–143.

Low, K. C. P., & Or, K. H. F. (2004). Are Singaporeans ready for their retirement? *Management Journal Development of Singapore, 12*(1), 39–55.

Low, K. C. P., & Theyagu, D. (2003). *Developing true leadership potential.* Singapore: The Publishing Consultant.

Lu, D. (1998). Do values matter to development? Reflections on the role of confucianism in Singapore's public policies. In H. Lim & R. Singh (Eds.), *Values and development: A multidisciplinary approach with some comparative studies* (pp. 209–222). Singapore: Centre for Advanced Studies, Faculty of Arts and Social Sciences, National University of Singapore.

MacDonald, L. (2004). *Learn to be an optimist.* San Francisco, CA: Chronical Books LLC.

Mahbubani, K. (2004). Bridging the divide: The Singapore experience. In *Can Asians think?* (pp. 239–245). Singapore: Marshall Cavendish International (Asia).

Maier, S., & Kourdi, J. (2010). *The 100.* Singapore: Marshall Cavendish Business.

March, R. (1996). *Reading the Japanese mind.* Tokyo: Kodensha International.

Maxwell, J. C. (1993). *Developing the leader within you.* Nashville, TN: Thomas Nelson.

McCarthy, T. (1999). Lee Kuan Yew. *Time 100,* 23–30 Aug 1999, pp. 88–89.

Menter, M. (2003). *The Office Sutras.* Canada: Red Wheel.

Mitsuyuki, M. (1985). *Management and society.* Singapore: Singapore Institute of Management/ Federal Publications.

Mydans, S. (2010). If I rest, I'll slide downhill fast. *The Sunday Times,* 12 Sep 2010, p. 29.

Naisbitt, J. (1994). *Global paradox.* Sydney: Allen & Unwin.

Nakashima, E. (2004). With birthrate falling, Singapore targets 'lifestyle impotency'. *Washington Post Foreign Service,* 11 September, p. A13.

National Parks Board. (2014). *MacRitchie Reservoir*. National Parks Board. Accessed July 10, 2014 from http://nparks.eventshub.sg/fms/fms_wb_Resource.aspx?ResourceGroupID=45

National Parks Singapore. (2008). *Singapore the Garden City National Parks Singapore*. Accessed March 16, 2010 from http://www.nparks.gov.sg/cms/index.php?option=com_news&task=view&id=108&Itemid=50

Norazit, S. (1998). Malay political leadership: Going back to the roots. In H. Lim & R. Singh (Eds.), *Values and development: A multidisciplinary approach with some comparative studies* (pp. 115–120). Singapore: NUS.

Okto. (2014). 'History From the Hills', *Okto Channel*, 10 pm, 25 June 2014, Starhub.

Ong, A. (2014). Room for Dialect, but Stick with Mandarin. *The Sunday Times*, 6 July 2104, p. 1.

Oon, C. (2008). Lover of cities seeks extra oomph in Singapore, Review/Insight. *The Straits Times*, 24 October 2008, p. A34.

Oon, C. (2009). Singapore's green trump card. *The Straits Times*, 7 May 2009, p. A8.

Peale, N. V. (1993). *My Favourite Quotations, A Mandarin paperback*, Great Britain.

Plate, T. (2004). In Asia, father still knows best. *The Straits Times*, 28 April.

Presek, W. Jr. (2004). M.M. Lee's contrarian outlook for the US. *The Straits Times*, 8 December, p. 24.

Price, A., & Price, D. (2013). *Leadership: A practical guide*. Allen & Unwin Pty: St Leonards, NSW.

Quah, J. S. T. (1994). Improving the efficiency and productivity of the Singapore civil service, Chapter 7. In J. P. Burns (Ed.), *Asian civil service systems: Improving efficiency and productivity* (pp. 152–185). Singapore: Times Academic Press.

Renwick, G., & Witham, W. J. (1997). *Managing in Malaysia: Cultural insights and guidelines for Americans*. Yarmouth, ME: Intercultural Press.

Scarborough, J. (1998). Comparing Chinese and Western cultural roots: Why 'East is East and...'. *Business Horizons, 40*(6), 15.

Sheh, S. W. (2001). Chinese cultural values and their implications to Chinese management. In *Singapore management review* (2nd edn, Vol. 23(2), pp. 75–83).

Sie, K. H. B. (1997). *Singapore: A modern Asian city-state: Relationship between cultural and economic development*. Nimegen/Jakarta: Catholic University.

Siew, K. L. (1987). *A Chinese conception of management – An interpretive approach*. PhD dissertation, Graduate School of the University of Massachusetts, Boston

Singapore Census of Population. (2000). *Singapore census of population 2000*. Singapore: Department of Statistics, Ministry of Trade and Industry.

Singapore Infopedia. (2004). *MacRitchie Reservoir*. Singapore Infopedia. Accessed July 11, 2014 from http://eresources.nlb.gov.sg/infopedia/articles/SIP_159_2004-12-27.html

Singapore Tatler. (1992). *Singapore days of old: A special commemorative history of Singapore*. The 10th anniversary of Singapore Tatler, Singapore Tatler, Illustrated Magazine Publications, Hong Kong, p. 101.

Sinha, J. (1980). *The nurturant task master*. New Delhi: Sage.

Song, O. S. (1984). *One hundred years' history of the Chinese in Singapore* (pp. 273–274). Singapore: Oxford University Press.

Tan, C. H. (1989). Confucianism and nation-building in Singapore. In *Working paper series no. 89-28*, Faculty of Business Administration, National University of Singapore, Singapore.

Tan, C. H. (1992). Public sector management: Past achievement and future challenge. In L. Low & T. M. Heng (Eds.), *Public policies in Singapore* (pp. 12–29). Singapore: Times Academic Press.

Tan, G. S. (2004). *Gateway to Peranakan Food Culture*. Asiapac Books Pte: Singapore.

Tay, S. (2001). Commentary/analysis: What do Singaporeans want? Nanny states and markets. *The Straits Times*, 7 April, p. 24.

Tessensohn, J. (2001). *Suzhou adventure – Why not make it multi-billion high industrial theme park?* Accessed February 5 from www.geocities.com/newsintercom2001/sef97/snobbery.html

The Brunei Times. (2008). Lee Kuan Yew on Brunei's next level of growth. *The Brunei Times*, Tuesday, 15 January 2008. Accessed Feb 1, 2010 from http://www.bt.com.bn/en/home_news/2008/01/15/lee_kuan_yew_on_bruneis_next_level_of_growth

The Peranakan Association. (2011a). *The Chinese Peranakan Heritage in Singapore*. The Peranakan Association, Singapore. Accessed July 20, 2014 from http://www.peranakan.org.sg/2011/06/the-chinese-peranakan-heritage-insingapore/7/. October 26, 2012. Singapore: The Peranakan Association. Accessed June 30, 2014 from http://www.peranakan.org.sg/2012/10/let-us-support-ntus-wee-kim-wee-legacy-fund/

The Peranakan Association. (2011b). *What makes a Peranakan?* The Peranakan Association, Singapore. Accessed July 18, 2014 from http://www.peranakan.org.sg/2011/07/what-makes-a-peranakan/2/

The Peranakan Association. (2012a). *Let us support NTU's Wee Kim Wee Legacy Fund*

The Peranakan Association. (2012b). *Culture*. The Peranakan Association, Singapore. Accessed July 15, 2014 from http://www.peranakan.org.sg/culture/

The Peranakan Resource Library. (2003a). *In-depth research and analysis on Peranakan culture*. Accessed June 26, 2014 from http://peranakan.web1000.com/page8.htm

The Peranakan Resource Library. (2003b). *Peranakan political activities*. Accessed June 30, 2014 from http://peranakan.hostoi.com/Archives-Personalities.htm

(The) Economist. (2004). Vietnam's economy: The good pupil. *The Economist*, 8 May, p. 27.

(The) Straits Times. (2004a). *The Straits Times*, 25 August.

(The) Straits Times (2004b). *The Straits Times*, 22 May.

(The) Straits Times. (2010) From civil servant to PAP stalwart. *The Straits Times*, 15 May 2010, p. D2.

Time. (1999). Lee Kuan Yew. *Time*, 23–30 August 1999.

Today. (2015). Mr. Lee a giant among men: Ministers. *Today*, 5 April 2017, p. 9.

Today's Manager. (2004/2005). The need for strong Asian leaders. *Today's Manager*, December/January, pp. 17–18.

Travel & Tourism Info. (2007). *Singapore tourism – Travel and tourism guide*. Travel and tourism info.com. Accessed June 19, 2009 from http://www.travelandtourisminfo.com/Singapore/Singapore-Travel.asp

Ueda, N. (2013). *The Dalai Lama on What Matters Most*. Canada: Hampton Book Publishing Company.

West, B. A. (2009). *Encyclopedia of the peoples of Asia and Oceania*. New York: Facts On File.

Westwood, R. I. (1992). *Organisational behaviour: South East Asian perspectives*. Longman Group (Far East) Ltd: Hong Kong.

Wikipedia. (2010). List of countries by GDP (nominal) per capita. *Wikipedia*. Accessed October 8, 2010 from http://en.wikipedia.org/wiki/List_of_countries_by_GDP_(nominal)_per_capita

Yao, E. L. (1987). Cultivating Guan-Xi (personal relationships) with Chinese partners. *Business Marketing, 72*(1), 62.

Yeap, J. K. (1975). *The Patriarch*. Malaysia/ Singapore: Times.

Zhang, W.-B. (1999). *Confucianism and modernization*. New York: St Martin's Press.

Women and Mother Leadership

12

Mother Leadership

Of all rights of women, the greatest is to be a mother. (Lin Yu-tang)

Introduction

Courage is like a muscle. We strengthen it with use. (Ruth Gordon)

Mothers are ordinarily kind, caring and nurturing to their children. Motherhood and looking after the children and family is an important task. Mothers have, in fact, shown critical acts of leadership at home as they rear their children, but "49% of working women are mothers who together contribute $476 billion a year to their households" (referring to the United States situation, Jamie 2007). In short, motherhood, a helpful experience, builds leadership skills.

Aim and Objectives

This section examines leading, the mother way. The aim and objectives of the section are to identify what mother or maternal leadership is, assess what such leadership entails, its style and ways as well as to examine the benefits and the downsides of such a leadership style.

What Is Mother Leadership?

Go women! Go all out! (Patrick Kim Cheng Low)

© Springer International Publishing AG 2018
K.C.P. Low, *Leading Successfully in Asia*,
https://doi.org/10.1007/978-3-319-71347-2_12

Just as a leader should be proactive, a parent should also not be passive or non-involved. "Thou shalt not be a passive parent!" (Young 2004). Proactive, mother seems to lead best, and the leadership style is that of being "gentle" (respondents' inputs), nurturing, showing care and concern, as well as being soft (feeling, empathetic, kind, warm) yet getting things done. In some societies and cultures, women, in fact, play a key role, and this is more evident in certain matriarchal or matrilineal societies such as the Minangkabaus of Sumatra (Sorensen 1993, p. 100; Lebar 1972), Iroquois of North America and the Lovedu of Africa.

In Low's (2008a) paper when discussing father leadership, he raises the issue of:

> It seems that critics and/or European and North American readers would probably find the actual term and the explanation of organisational practice of father leadership to be gender-biased. That is, that the wholesale use of the male gender term appears to preclude women who may have these characteristics (and perhaps raises the question 'is there a term such as 'mother leadership' which can be characterised in the same way?). To respond to this, the author has these to say: the term 'father leadership' is used to refer to both male and female leadership and more so, it reflects paternal or maternal leadership.

True, paternal or maternal authority captures the expectations of concern and nurtures the belief that people or staff should be treated like the leader's family members (Low and Mohd Zain 2008). However, this author wishes to note that the style of mother leadership is perhaps different from that of father leadership (Low 2006a, b, 2007, 2008a, b, c). From the outset, it should be highlighted the former prefers or stresses on "nurturing" and "caring" while the latter is "protective", "directive" and "telling". Women have the soft touch to everything. "More people-oriented", they are "particularly more sensitive to people around them, and that becomes their advantage because being more sensitive, women leaders become more aware of employees' needs" (68.18% or 30 respondents' including 7 male respondents' inputs gave this view).

Next, it can be said that father leaders tend to "think" while mother leaders are more inclined to "feel". In the section "The Traits and Characteristics of Mother Leadership", the traits and characteristics of mother leadership will be further examined.

Grzelakowski (2005) has highlighted why motherhood transforms good leaders into great leaders. There is more to life than just work. People who eat, sleep and dream about their work do not make the best leaders. And maternal mothers, who could see things from other perspectives and angles, would make better leaders. Grzelakowski (2005) has pointed out that like politicians or Hollywood stars, business executives have become so driven by their own agendas and goals, they have or tend to lost sight of larger organizational needs. Here, it is best to quote her:

> Many times, though, the impulse is to do something more socially or culturally valuable than furthering corporate goals. You want to do something for people who really need the knowledge or services that you can provide.

You should seize the opportunity to involve yourself in a giving way over a sustained period of time. Serving those in need rather than your organization creates an effect similar to that of becoming a mother. In both cases, your perspective shifts. As a leader, you become better able to place events in perspective and avoid the overreactions and permanent-crisis mentality that often comes with top jobs in big companies.

Interestingly, "executives who are dual-centric—who give equal weight to work and personal life—feel more successful at work, are less stressed, and have an easier time managing the demands of their work and personal/family lives." "Women who are dual-centric (as opposed to women who are only focused on work) have advanced to higher reporting levels and feel more successful in their home lives" (Galinsky 2003, cited in Grzelakowski 2005, p. 38).

Perhaps what needs to be argued or highlighted is that not all mothers or motherhood automatically makes women better leaders, rather being motherhood helps, and it is also dependent on the process of individual's being aware and that individual overall learns. And even at that, whether the individual does well also depends on intra-personal learning. Generally speaking, most women also become more aware, perhaps as Grzelakowski (2005, p. 67) has pointed out, "less inhibited when they are pregnant. It starts in the doctor's office. Then, once you start to show, people react to you differently. They offer you their seats, open doors, and become more caring toward you... 'People do view you differently.'" One becomes more aware. Then, it triggers knowing and perhaps more unknowing learning in women that leads them to be leaders or at least grows some essential leadership skills.

The Traits and Characteristics of Mother Leadership

Heaven lieth at the feet of Mothers. (Prophet Mohammad)

The cock crows but it's the hen that delivers the goods. (Anonymous)

The interview surveys were conducted among 44 respondents: 23 females (16 married and 7 singles) and 21 males (13 married and 8 singles), all Asians living in Southeast Asia. Based on literature review, and respondents' inputs, the characteristics of mother leadership can be analysed as follows:

Nurturing, Caring and Showing Concern

Women are learning that they can be tender and giving as well as being strong and powerful. (Lee Bryce, *The Influential Woman*)

As Mother Teresa once said, "The biggest disease today is not leprosy or tuberculosis, but rather the feeling being unwanted, uncared for, and deserted by everybody" (Mother Teresa, cited in Maxwell 2001, p. 51). Mother leadership is nurturing, and because of this trait, all the more, it becomes very appropriate for mankind in today's world. Besides, "true leader stand tall. True leaders care" (Low and Theyagu 2003, p. 19).

"Like father leadership, the mother leader relates, and her concern for the people in an organisation is strong" (respondents' inputs; 100%). "The leader must establish good relationships with others" (DuBrin 2007, p. 235), and this aspect is well aided in mother leadership as one of the latter's traits is that of nurturing, caring and showing concern of the people. Nurturing is an umbrella term for the qualities that often emerge after women have babies. Specifically, these qualities include empathy, sensitivity, caring, warmth, and patience. From the pregnancy experience, mothers can also emerge soft and caring. Mothers with children tend to be more balanced, having other things in their life, considering other people's feelings and showing care. Grzelakowski (2005) has argued that when a mother is taking care of an infant, she no longer feels awkward or phony to respond to how another individual is feeling; and more critically, empathy becomes a very natural reaction. In a 2006 Mother's Day (United States) survey by the professional women's networking organization WorldWit, it was uncovered that 69% would rather work for a mother than a non-mother, and only 2% prefer a non-mother. The respondents viewed "mothers have patience and listening skills, and understand when others encounter family demands" (Jones 2006).

Interestingly, most executive women learned early in their careers that, just as there is no crying in baseball, there is no crying in the office. Typically, a tough male boss conveys that crying or any similar emotional display signals weakness. As a result, women learn not only how to shut off the tears but how to avoid turning red, acting frustrated, or speaking out of turn. This isn't all bad; learning to control emotional outbursts aided them become more effective leaders. Simultaneously, however, it de-sensitise them and in response to this early career lesson, some went too far in an emotionless direction, adopting an overly stoic style and lacking the warmth and passion that characterizes powerful leaders. Pregnancy then, according to Grzelakowski (2005, p. 65), "triggers women to soften their hard stance, to a certain extent forcing a happy medium between crying and being stone-faced". Yes, pregnant mothers do cry yet one can argue that as a leader, people will better appreciate that one has a full range of emotions, and that one is confident enough to express them in the work environment.

According to DuBrin (2007, p. 235), emotional intelligence (EQ) is major contributor to leadership effectiveness, and interestingly, based on Ellison's (2005) work, EQ appears to be the clearest category in which mothers benefit. One of the biggest brain boosts for mothers is the ability to see the world through someone else's eyes. In so many relationships, if one does not agree with a person, one can simply walk away. But one cannot walk away from one's child. At least, not if one wants to be a good parent. Instead, one has to stretch one's mind, be sensitive enough, to understand the child's point of view. That helps to raise a mother leader's emotional intelligence (Fig. 12.1).

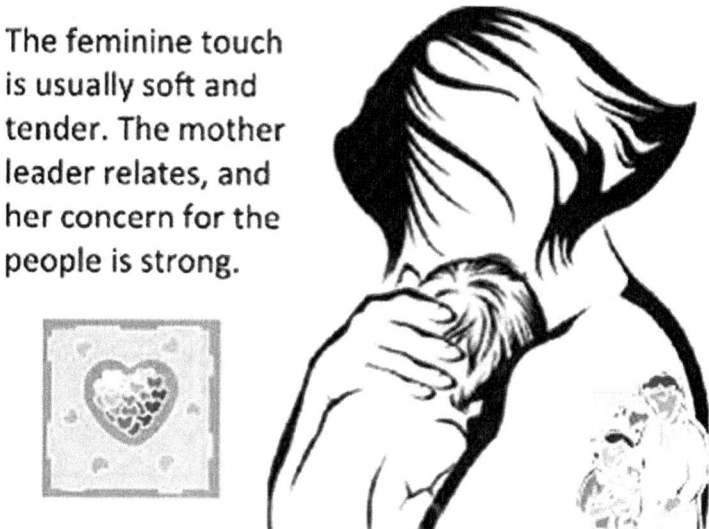

The feminine touch is usually soft and tender. The mother leader relates, and her concern for the people is strong.

Fig. 12.1 Mother leadership, normally people-centred, is nurturing and caring

Being Humane

> When women exercise their individual power, there is a ripple effect that helps us all. (Nita M. Lowey)

Grzelakowski (2005, p. 4) has highlighted that pregnancy brought out warmth in women for after all it also made them to "be incredibly concerned for their unborn child, avoiding behaviours that might put that child at risk". And in Grzelakowski's (2005, p. 67) study, several women commented that strangers would come up and touch their stomach. Although their personal space was invaded, these women understood those gestures were empathetic and welcomed the world's new way of seeing them. "Co-workers were often making a fuss by throwing showers or taking bets on the baby's birth date, sex, and weight." "Co-workers often pamper pregnant mothers and mothers show more kindness to their fellow employees." (respondents' inputs). All that affectionate attention encouraged or drew women to respond in kind. Beyond their attention, care and affection, they felt their children kicking and saw ultrasounds of their curled-up little bodies with thumbs stuck in their mouths. Indeed, if all that does not make one being humane, nothing will.

"Babies promote humaneness" (Grzelakowski 2005, p. 72). Children—their innocence, simplicity and honesty—ordinarily soften one as a person. And "human-ness in a leader is a great attribute" (Friedman 1992, pp. 61–62).

More critically from the trenches come these revealing and insightful pointers of mother leadership:

> My female supervisor is a nice and kind hearted person. She guides me in a 'spoon feeding' way although knowing that I should be treated in a more adult way. But her intention was to

ensure that I really understand and know how to do my given tasks. She's very lenient and flexible. She would use the nicest way to ask me to do my task, She always say, 'please help me do this'. . . I don't feel being force to do my task and I'm always willingly and motivated to perform the tasks given. I really feel cared for.

True some of you may say it depends on individual females, I feel that such (mother leader's) qualities should and can also be practised by all, even male leaders, leaders need to show niceties, much kindness. . . attention or be plainly humane.

Perhaps, at this point, readers need to reflect. . . feel. . . and how many of us would agree the undeniable gentle touch of motherly love felt in our tender youth. Does this not make us feel and understand the need to be gentle, humane, and give warmth and love to others? If so, should it not that motherly love be emulated by leaders towards their people?

Feeling

To be somebody, a woman does not have to be more like a man, but has to be more of a woman. (Sally E. Shaywitz)

Mother leaders tend to favour being feeling-oriented. Based on Myers-Briggs Type Indicator (MBTI) research, 75% of women are more likely to report as feeling types (Cooper 2008). In other words, they prefer to be more subjective and values based (Hirsh and Kummerow 1989). What mother leaders—as feelers—do is that they make decisions in a subjective, attached way. "My female supervisors maintain peace and harmony; they value the quiet and peaceful ways of doing things. They base their decisions in terms of ensuring harmonious relationships" (Respondents' inputs). These coincide with the feeling ways, that is, they decide the right thing to do by putting themselves in other people's shoes, seeking to maintain harmony.

"Mother leaders would want to have a connection with others" (Respondents' inputs), and perhaps, some may also add with 'everyone' and 'everything'. Feeling mother leaders include people in their visions of their world. Responsive to their followers' needs, they would mentor, coach and guide them yet they do not like conflicts.

Ms. Ho Ching, the wife of Singapore's Prime Minister and the then outgoing chief of the Temasek Corporation has been cited as the Singapore example of a mother leader. The labour movement has conferred Ms Ho Ching 2009's top labour (May Day) award for her support of the unions' work, safeguarding workers' interests and showing concern for them; she "engages the union leaders and cares for the workers" (Koh 2009, p. A4).

Being Cool and Calm

The strength of women comes from the fact that psychology cannot explain us. Men can be analysed, women . . .merely adored. (Oscar Wilde, *The Ideal Husband*)

People with clenched fists cannot shake hands. (Indira Gandhi)

Childhood emergencies show mothers that they cannot control every situation. There is no way to prevent bee stings, ear infections, and other maladies and mishaps. As painful as it is to see your child suffering, mothers also realise that sometimes all they can do is be cool, emotionally supportive and call the doctor.

Executive mothers who are used to being in control recognise that, at times, all they can do is comfort and wait (Grzelakowski 2005). They recognise that remaining calm, assessing the situation, and taking action only if things get worse is often the best course of action. As unpleasant as it is to hear your child screaming, you can't go rushing off to the emergency room every time they get a scrape or a fever. Every time your child spills ketchup on or dirty the newly cleaned (usually white) carpet, you can't scream and threaten in the belief such a display will stop it from happening again. These emergencies force mothers to face their need to control; mothers recognise that managing trouble, problems or chaos does not automatically mean taking immediate action.

In a world where change occurs at a fast pace, sometimes the best response to problems at work is to remain calm. "Mothers tend to wise up, learning how to be cool and calm, taking in the information, and then making the right decision(s)" (respondents' input).

Experiencing a Boost in Motivation and Being Resilient

Man may work from sun to sun, but women's work is never done. (Anonymous)

Pregnancy and the childbirth process tend to make the women stronger and resilient (Grzelakowski 2005). Ellison (2005) speaks of mothers experiencing a boost in motivation, fearlessness, and the ability to multitask while coping with stress. Additionally, there's also exciting new research suggesting that oxytocin—a hormone important to labour and breast-feeding—improves mothers' capacity for learning and memory which in this author's view, would certainly increase a mother leader's resilience.

We should note that executive life has also become incredibly frantic. Unexpected crises often disrupt carefully planned daily agendas. As downsizing, restructuring, global competition and technology breakthroughs change traditional practices, our business pace accelerates. More than ever, leaders need to function effectively in confusing, fast-paced cultures. Mothers become skilled at getting things done even when the household is in chaos. Toddlers too are adept at throwing things up for grabs. Fussy and messy eaters, they ask why constantly, whine, cry, move constantly and at times, throw temper tantrums. Their mobility too is a shock for mothers used to a relatively stationary child. Suddenly, they're wandering off, climbing or endangering fragile objects as well as themselves. The period between a child's first steps and the start of school days can be wild and unpredictable; women become adept, creative and "strong" (interviewees' input) at handling child-related surprises/crises and unpredictable events that make a mishmash of plans. And that, anecdotal evidence, the writer's observations/experience, and he would also be very sure that most mothers' experiences would support the above; overall, they can be considered as building or growing resilience in mother leaders.

Applying Team-Playing Skills

Each time, any or one of us gets successful, we all gain. (Patrick Kim Cheng Low)

As new members of the family are added on, "mothers (also) become natural team players or that they are forced to apply team-playing skills" (several married respondents' inputs). Similar to the Chinese proverb "though a mother give birth to nine sons, all nine will be different", the mother must relate well with her children each with different skills and each differently during the various phrases and stages of their lives.

The teens are the times that try parents' souls, and mothers emerge from these trials with a variety of new skills and traits: receptivity, boundary-setting (norms creation), open-mindedness, bargaining, negotiation, and influencing through others (Grzelakowski 2005). One female mother respondent expressed that, "like in the team, mothers have to be open to their growing-up teens' ideas, concerns and criticisms; they have to read signals, get cues, listen, accommodate, absorb or factor in their teens' views and ways."

As in team leading and playing, mothers also acquire hard-won wisdom during their child(ren)'s teenage years, and it helps them to team-lead wisely. Besides, mothers have to upkeep or pull the family together, handling the fathers, the off-springs and the in-laws (bearing in mind, the traditional mother-in-law and daughter-in-law's disagreements or discords are common in most families).

Harnessing the Yin: Capitalizing Women's Strengths

Every girl should use what Mother Nature gave her before Father Time takes it away. (Laurence J. Peter)

Interestingly, all respondents highlighted to the writer that "mother leadership does not necessarily mean a mother, but in fact, any women can adopt this leadership style" (Respondents' inputs). So, the time has come for the world to tap the power of *Yin* . . .

The late chairman Mao Zedong's "women hold up half the sky" is similar to Lao Tzu's Yin-Yang harmony; Lao Tzu speaks of:

All things have their backs to the female
and stand facing the male.
When male and female combine,
all things achieve harmony.

And at this point of our world's history, to this author, more women are needed, with their strengths and potentials tapped. When more women are employed or engaged, more rainbow colours are added by combining the views of both men and women. *TIME* magazine 24 March 2008 speaks of one of the 10 ideas that are changing the world and that is women's work—tapping the female entrepreneurial spirit can pay big dividends; accordingly, empowered women can bring about much economic growth (Walt 2008, p. 42). Besides, in terms of making decisions, women leaders are said to be more flexible than their male counterparts (Lowen 2011). Again, a woman leader is said to be open to learn new things, thus making her open to new experiences; she is not afraid to take risks and bring new procedures and innovations to improve the organisation's management (Lowen 2011).

As in the wisdom of the *Tao*, the *Yin* of the *Yin-Yang* needs to be harnessed. According to the *Worldwide Guide to Women in Leadership*, in 2009, Monaco became the last country in the world to have its first female member of government. Interestingly, in 1999, Sweden became the first country to have more female ministers than male: 11 women and 9 men and in 2007 the Finish government had 60% women (Christensen 2009).

In line with Low's (2009) argument, granted that one prefers not to discuss women in leadership, one can also see the logic or dare I say have the 'feel' and 'intuition' of the applications of *Yin* and *Yang* for the goodness or betterment of our world. One can also argue as such: To cite Capra (1983), he rightly draws us into a deeper reflection on the distinctions between *Yin* and *Yang* energy ["The rational and the intuitive are complementary modes of functioning of the human mind. Rational thinking is linear, focused and analytic. It belongs to the realm of the intellect, whose function it is to discriminate, measure and categorize. Thus rational knowledge tends to be fragmented. Intuitive knowledge, on the other hand, is based on a direct, non-intellectual experience of reality arising in an expanded state of awareness. It tends to be synthesizing, holistic, and nonlinear" (Capra 1983, p. 38).]. Capra's (1983) perspective is that for the past three centuries, our culture has consistently favoured the *Yang* over the *Yin* energies, and that our economic, social and political structures reflect and reinforce this imbalance. Here we should heed the advice couched in the Chinese proverb of "the frog and the sky". There's an argument between a bird which stopped to drink at a well and a frog therein. They were arguing about how the sky looked like. Each, referring to where they were, had a different view. The frog's vision was of course very limited and narrow. This proverb refers to somebody who has a very narrow-minded and insulated view of what (s)he sees or thinks.

Here, applying the Chinese saying that goes, "There's more to knowing than just being correct", and it is critical, a Taoist viewpoint, to encourage people to think about things in the right way. So imagine this: That those of us living on earth today who have roots in western historical traditions, have grown up within this economic, social, and political culture, and this, in fact, suggests that core beliefs include:

- Rational thinking is of greater value than intuition (*and feelings*),
- Competition is superior to cooperation,
- Science is to be trusted more than religion (*or spirituality*),
- Initiative is superior to responsiveness

are embedded in our own basic assumptions (Capra 1983, p. 39, *italics mine*). And it does nudge humankind to move to expanded awareness that our culture is tilted, not to say, way out of balance! Thus, [though critics may claim that these may be stretching it a bit too far,] mother leadership through the *Yin-Yang* applications can lead us to more balanced, holistic applications of the two opposites set of perspectives, and perhaps go beyond the opposites.

United States of America's President George W. Bush often referred to his US Secretary of State, Ms Condoleezza Rice (a professor, diplomat, author, and national security expert) for advice while present President Obama may also discuss issues with his Secretary of State, Hillary Clinton. And all these show that women or mother leadership is very much needed in organisations to give the feminine perspective as well as a balanced point of view. "The best ways... are to integrate both men's and women's viewpoints to find solutions" (respondents' inputs).

The Downsides and Benefits of Mother Leadership

"Emotions and being nurturing energise" (Respondents' inputs), and being emotionally involved is a key towards mother leadership, yet it can also lead to a problem, that is—the leader is being too emotional. This can perhaps blind them from seeing situations and handling things objectively. Women leaders should, in most ways, pay close attention to their feelings or empathetic nature so as to display and ensure a high EQ propriety in most situations.

Another downside of mother leadership as highlighted by respondents includes the fact that such a leader tends to be "too soft and may be taken advantage by the followers". But then one can also argue that there's nothing wrong of being soft, the followers sooner or in time would learn not to take advantage of such a leader; "she or he's too good or in fact, too kind, too nice to be taken advantage of."

In spite of the downsides identified, many benefits of practicing mother leadership exist. To paraphrase John Maxwell's words: the people or the followers normally do not care how much the leaders know until they know how much they care. And mother leadership is a caring leadership way, and being people-oriented, those actions are authentic, and appeal to the people. Besides, those who use this style run things with their hearts. What's appealing is that such a leader does not necessarily have to be coercive and exercise positional power to lead the organization or people.

Besides, most if not all women would be a natural in displaying or exercising such qualities such as nurturing and caring. The other benefits of such a leadership include "the quiet, gentleness and softness of such leadership style which creates a harmonious air, adding a cosy feeling within the organisation". Mother leadership also "balances the loud, 'hard' and aggressive nature of male leaders". "The people are happy; they stay motivated." Additionally, such a leader sets the example, and "nothing beats the actions of a leader. That puts dignity and charisma to the leadership holder" (Respondents' inputs). Interestingly, all the respondents accepted mother leadership in some ways or the other, and these include the unmarried female and single and married male respondents.

Limitations and Benefits of the Study

One of the limitations of the study is that it is not written to further the divide or distinguish between working or non-working mothers. Besides, the section is made not to claim that mothers are smarter than women who are not mothers. However, what it is saying is that being feminine or qualities of mother leadership are appealing, and leaders should emulate or incorporate such qualities in their leadership repertoire.

There is a caveat here; this is an exploratory study and more, in fact, needs to be done to find the support of such a leadership style and ways even among mothers, and single women as well as male leaders. Nonetheless, the paper however relevantly argues that motherhood can contribute or grow the leadership skills in women. And like Grzelakowski's (2005) study, it points out to further study particularly in Asia where women have been increasingly appointed to higher positions. And whether in Asia, where family and collectivist values are emphasized, mother leadership would have a niche in leading people effectively and persuasively.

Section Conclusion

> We need 4 hugs a day for survival. We need 8 hugs a day for maintenance.We need 12 hugs a day for growth. (Virginia Satir)

Today's young employees need or expect care, concern and compassion. They would then produce better output, both in quality and in quantity. When they were born, their parents cared for them, showing much affection, some even put signs in their cars warning other drivers: *Prince (Baby/Princess) on Board*. Even after their early childhood years, they were showered with tender, loving care. Fathers, teachers, and coaches showed them a lot more compassion than previous generations experienced. Consequently, they take it that parental figures at work will exhibit kindness and nurturing qualities. Companies are beginning to realize that leaders with character, care and compassion will win the hearts and minds not only of today's employees but also, tomorrow's best and brightest people. That's why, now and in the future, the teams led by the most mothers win. And perhaps more so in Asia, where family and collectivist values are emphasised, maternal leadership would all the more be encouraged.

The Glass Ceiling

> I can't change my sex. But you can change your policy. (Helen Kirkpatrick)

> Everything that irritates us about others can lead us to an understanding of ourselves. (Carl Jung)

Increasingly more women today are working in Asia. In Japan, in recent years, because of its ageing population, there have been more calls by the government for more (married) women to return to the workforce.

However, women in Asia, not to mention working women, face many barriers; a woman is often considered and/or treated as if she is less capable than her male counterpart. And this is due to sheer prejudice and/or discrimination. Women are assumed to be weak leaders, nature is also against them. They face menstruation, childbirth and suffer pre and postnatal blues.

A woman, if she puts her family photograph on her office desk, words will have it as if she is not working, just thinking about the family. And well, when a man does it, it is alright, he is the breadwinner; he cares for his family.

During office hours, a man, going to the restroom, is answering nature's call. But when a woman goes to the restroom, she is taken to be attending to her makeup, doing facials or some damage control. A man having lunch with his male supervisor, he is networking, but if a woman is having lunch with her male supervisor, words would have it or questions would be posed: "Are they having an affair?"

There is also much stereotyping of males and females. Women are said to be more emotional or feeling-oriented, and they cannot hold top positions or positions that requires clear thinking or objectivity. Men, on the other hand, are generally taken to be more rational, they are traditionally seen as thinking-oriented and hence they are assumed to be 'better' leaders.

Then again, at times, we may not be kind to our kind. We prefer to assist, support or mentor the other or opposite gender. From the author's work experiences and observations, men rather than women prefer to coach the women-folks. And in the multinational context, Western males prefer to coach or mentor Asian females than their own kind. Perhaps they are just based on observations, but certainly studies or research can be made in this area.

True Asia has been known for the unfairness in gender treatment and equality; it appears that more women in Asia are coming into power than any other region in the world. Looking at countries like India, Pakistan, Sri-Lanka as well as Israel, where regional cultures, traditions and religion are strongly practised, the women face much discrimination throughout their whole life, and this includes all sorts of abuses and hostile setting in which they function.

The Way Forward

Women are always beautiful. (Ville Valo)

Men, their rights and nothing more: Women, their rights and nothing less. (Susan B. Anthony, 1820–1906)

Through the historic Silk Road, the two worlds were connected. Similarly, through the employment of women and women leadership, the world can enjoy a higher level of growth and prosperity as well as societal progress.

Asian women can move up or to lead through these strategies or ways, and they are by:

Adopting the Human Capital Approach

Knowledge is power. (English proverb)

The human capital approach is one of the best ways for women to move up; women in Asia are increasingly updating and upgrading themselves through further education and training. Women can substantially build their ability and core competences through further studies and job training.

Adopting Win-Win Relationships

To control your cow, give it a bigger pasture. (Suzuki Roshi, Zen Master)

Asian women (though Low 2006c, p. 57 speaks of Singaporean women) could also win their spouses over, turning them to family-friendly men. They can, in fact, promote positive emotions among their husbands, focusing on thoughts that lead to positive emotions. Here, they can support or frame proposals in ways that appeal to the other party, tune in to what they might be thinking and feeling. They can play to the belief in fairness and equity as well as focusing on potential or mutual gains and benefits such as minimising family expenses. Women can be persuasive and most successful if they take into account the other party's or, in this case, their husbands' perspectives. As Low (2001, pp. 77–79; also cited in Low 2006c, p. 57) highlighted, win-win relationships can be attained (no matter how heated the debates are), when couples talk to each other, respecting each other's turf and both really realizing mutual benefit(s) together. Not unlike in business, through trust and shared goals (Tan and Lim 2004), spouses can indeed develop (long-term) win-win relationships.

Promoting and Self-Marketing

The best is yet to be. (Robert Browning)

As argued by Low (2008b, c), certain child-rearing practices needs to be overhauled or changed. Girls' power is to be promoted, and parents can also raise their girls—in Asian or, for example, Islamic ways—as strong individuals. In Brunei, one local writer has expressed that parents need to encourage their daughters to be "bolder" and not be "meek". "Father(s) should have... asked (the) daughter to have the first choice when (distributing candies or gifts) because that was what the Prophet Muhammad (peace be upon him) would have done." The

Prophet taught Muslims that when they had gifts, they should first give them to their daughters (Soekanto 2007, cited in Low 2008b, c). Indeed, girls who are raised in a family or household where her needs and preferences are respected would grow up to be empowered, self-respected, confident and achieving ladies.

"Such confident women know that they are equal to their brothers as long as they are bewaring of Allah S.W.T." (Soekanto 2007, cited in Low 2008b, c, p. 6). Woman is equal to man in the eyes of God (Al-Quran, *As Saffat* (37), p. 153, cited in Ide 1996, p. 7) and in Islamic context, the religion stresses on equality of treatment of sons and daughters. There are many *Hadiths* that stress on the importance of taking good care of the women-folks.

Asian women can thus promote and self-market themselves. They can promote themselves and women's roles through women's associations and clubs with prominent women figures including woman Ministers and/or Members of Parliaments (MPs) as their patronesses, benefactors *and sponsors* (Low 2006c, p. 59, *italics author's*).

As mentioned by Low (2008b, c), the media people and journalists—particularly women can also be a promoting and self-marketing force to bring about greater advancement and participation of women. They themselves have to change the stereotypes (Rosli 2007, cited in Low 2008b, c). Additionally, to break the artificial barriers or glass ceilings, women who are successful in their respective careers can also help, becoming mentors to their fellow female colleagues. The former can help to coach and teach the latter the ropes and skills to improve themselves and move up the corporate ladder.

Networking and Building Connections

Kill two birds with one stone. (English proverb)

They need to network and build their connections. (Low 2006c)

Not only in tapping overseas networks with other Asians and other nationalities, Asian women can also help each other succeed, that is, networking among the girls' cliques.

Like the men, they can also rely on their old schoolgirls' network, associations and contacts. They can network when sent for company training and talks. They can gather to a pub after work or "enjoy sporting activities together" (respondents' inputs) and talk what the boys normally talk about. Such cliques will help each other when promotion time comes.

Coaching, Guiding and Mentoring

A candle loses nothing by lighting another candle. (Buddhist proverb)

Asian women can also help each other—coach and guide among themselves. Women in top positions can help to mentor their juniors so as to assist them to advance in their respective career paths.

It is fascinating to note that building support systems, with each other, among women helps; it enables the sharing of competencies without competition and the sharing of feelings and needs with sincerity (Carr-Ruffino 1997, cited in Low 2006c, p. 59).

Applying Soft Power

Use power to curb power. (Chinese proverb)

Low (2006c) has also argued that women can also apply soft power to move up the leader. Singapore woman entrepreneur, Theresa Chew-Tan also has something to add: "Human relations skills are most important. . . accommodate and be patient" (Siu 2000, cited in Low 2006c, p. 58). Overall then, "recognizing, accepting and expressing feelings" and "respecting feelings as an essential part of life" is feminine strengths women can apply and grow (Carr-Ruffino 1997, cited in Low 2006c, p. 58).

Promoting Entrepreneurial Skills

He profits most who serves best. (Arthur F. Sheldon)

As highlighted by Low (2006c, p. 59), Asian women can be entrepreneurs and advance themselves.

Interestingly, Leonie Still has argued that self-employment supplies the opportunity for women to advance "outside conventional organizational careers" (Still 1993, p. 54) and therefore dodge or avoid the obstacles that often stand in their path. Here, it is worth stressing that such an action is not a reaction or that women are seeking refuge from discriminations, but rather it must be seen as a pro-active step, a career development planning. And this should be applauded.

Having Role Models to Emulate

We can be wise from goodness and good from wisdom. (Marie Von Ebner-Eshenbach)

This author also strongly advocates the twin ideas of leading or senior professional women serving as role models as well as taking the responsibilities of mentoring their female juniors.

Successful women corporate leaders and entrepreneurs as well as women professionals can also be role models for women to follow, emulate or be simply inspired by.

Asian women can do like what Singapore women do (Low 2006c, p. 60), that is, Singaporean women can look up to, for example, Raffles Holdings' chief executive Jennie Chua who is also Singapore's first Cornell trustee member. Cornell is the largest in the Ivy league group of elite United States universities, with about 18,500 students from 125 countries. Cornell trustees elect the university's top leadership, advise on educational policy and academic programs and oversee financial operations. Sri Mulyani Indrawati, the well-known Indonesian Economist is another woman role model whom Indonesian or Asian women can seek to emulate. Prof. Chan Heng Chee, the intelligent and successful Singapore Ambassador to the United States, can also be another role model for Singapore and/or Asian women to emulate.

Some Examples in the Various Asian Countries

Next, like in the West, many excellent examples of women leaders also exist in Asia, and they serve as inspiration or role models who can enthuse and move present female youth. And they, the names are by no means exhaustive, but just to name a few, these include:

Bangladesh

Sheikh Hasina A Bangladeshi politician and current Prime Minister of Bangladesh, Ms Hasina has been the President of the Awami League, a major political party, since 1981. She is the eldest of five children of Sheikh Mujibur Rahman, the founding father (and first president) of Bangladesh and widow of a reputed nuclear scientist, MA. M. A. Wazed Miah. Sheikh Hasina's party defeated the BNP-led Four-Party Alliance in the 2008 parliamentary elections, thus assuring her of the post of prime minister. Sheikh Hasina has once before held the office, from 1996 to 2001. The Awami League won 146 seats in the 1996 parliamentary elections. The support of the Jatiya Party and a few independent candidates were enough for the 150+ seats needed for the required majority. Hasina took the oath as Prime minister of Bangladesh. She vowed to create a *Government of National Unity*. Prime Minister Hasina is a member of the Council of Women World Leaders, an International network of current and former women presidents and prime ministers, whose mission is to mobilize women leaders globally for collective action on issues of critical importance to women's development.

Brunei Darussalam

Princess Masna Bolkiah Born in 1948, Princess Masna Bolkiah is the sister of His Majesty Sultan Haji Hassanal Bolkiah, the head of state of Brunei Darussalam. She graduated from Universiti Brunei Darussalam with a first degree and a Masters. In 1995, she was appointed as the Ambassador-at-Large at the Ministry of Foreign Affairs where she led a number of delegations abroad both as Acting Minister of Foreign Affairs as well as Ambassador-at-large. She is also active in other areas including being the Patron for the Girl Guides Association as well as being Commander of the Women's Police Corps.

Hajah Hayati Hj Mohd Salleh Hajah Hayati is Brunei's first woman Attorney General, and this is a considerable promotion for her who was also the first local woman High Court Judge. Justice Datin Paduka Hajah Hayati obtained her early education from SMRIF, STPRI and SOAS College in Bandar Seri Begawan. She went on to pursue her 'A' Levels at Exeter College of Further Education, UK under a Brunei Government Scholarship in 1974 and thereafter graduated with a Bachelor of Arts (Law) Degree in 1979. In 1980, she qualified as a Barrister-At-Law of Lincolns Inn. She began her legal career with the Attorney General's Chambers as a Deputy Public Prosecutor and Legal Counsel. Later, she was transferred to the State Judiciary Department as a Magistrate, and subsequently as Chief Magistrate/Deputy Chief Registrar of the Supreme Court, Chief Registrar/Intermediate Court Judge and Judicial Commissioner of the Supreme Court. On 1 January 2001, she was appointed by His Majesty as a High Court Judge, the first woman to be honoured with such appointment. On July 15, 1999, she was awarded The Most Honourable Order of the Crown of Brunei, Second Class (DPMB) which carries the title Datin Paduka by His Majesty. Apart from her judicial duties, she is a member of various committees including The Law Revision Committee, The National Education Council and a member of the 'Badan Perencana Kemajuan Jangka Panjang' the body responsible for formulating Brunei Darussalam's long term development and for monitoring its implementation. She is also Chairman of the Working Committee on Legal Profession Act.

Datin Hajah Adina bte Othman Awarded the Brunei Woman Leader in the Civil Society accolade in July 2009, Datin Hajah Adina has made a mark in history by becoming the first woman Deputy Minister (the Deputy Minister of Culture, Youth and Sports) in the Sultanate since the implementation of a ministerial system of government in Brunei in 1984. She had served the Brunei government for 32 years before she retired. Having led the Community Development Department during her successful career, Datin Hajah Adina is known for her strong stance behind women and children rights, and voicing out the importance of community and family values. To Datin Hajah Adina, the role of women in Brunei Darussalam is important as women play a major part in contributing not only towards their families but also to the country's development. She felt that her challenge ahead is not merely to improve and increase the participation of women but rather to increase the participation of both men and women together, in equity and in unison for the nation. She also see the challenge ahead in the development of young

Bruneians with positive mind set, dynamism, self-confidence and high moral values which is vital for the survival of our nation. Many see her appointment as an inspiration to Bruneian women athletes to strive harder and improve their performances.

China (People's Republic of China)

Consort Yang Yuhuan, often known as **Yáng Guìfēi**, was one of the four beauties of ancient China. She was a daughter of a nobleman in the little village and when she 16 years old, her father sent her to the palace to be a wife of the 16 years old prince who is ranked no. 18 amongst the princes. After she got into the palace, her beautiful appearance attracted the Emperor; the Emperor fell in love with her immediately and accommodated her into his palace. She became the beloved consort of Emperor Xuanzong of Tang Dynasty. At that time Emperor Xuanzong was 56 years old and Yáng Guìfēi was 22 years old. Yáng Guìfēi was not only beautiful but she was also very clever, learned fast and talented in music and dancing. The sound of music played by Yáng Guìfēiwould delighted the emperor and brought him into day-dreaming. The smile of Yáng Guìfēi was enough to enchant and encapture the emperor. The emperor loved her more than anything in the world; he even built her a natural warm spring pool which she could take a bath at spring time. From an ordinary girl, Yáng Guìfēi became the favourite concubine of the Emperor and gradually her family's members gained the high position in the government; Yang's family gained enormous power in the Tang Court. Because of her example, people in Tang Dynasty preferred to have daughters than sons. Most people hoped that their daughters could also have the luck to be the favorite concubine of the Emperor one day. During the Anshi Rebellion, as Emperor Xuanzong was fleeing from the capital Chang'an to Chengdu, she was killed because people were not happy with the powerful and corrupt members of Yang's family who were then running the country.

    Ching-Tsae The mother of Confucius, her son owed much to her wise counsels; and at her death, Confucius honoured her with 3 years of mourning, first preparing a burial mound with revival of all ancient rites, under which his father's remains were also entombed.

    Chang-shih As Mencius' mother, she changed her residence three times out of her concern for Mencius. At first, they lived near a cemetery, and the young Mencius amused himself with acting the various scenes which he witnessed at the tombs. "This", said his mother, "is no place for my son", and she moved to a house in the marketplace. But the change was no improvement. The boy took to playing the part of a salesman, boasting about his wares, and exchanging light chaff and banter with customers. His mother sought a new house, and found one at last close by a public school. There her child's attention was caught by the various exercises in correct manners by which the scholars were taught, and he endeavoured to imitate them. The mother was satisfied. "This," she said, "is the proper place for my son." Mencius' mother was a woman of very superior character, and that her son's subsequent distinction was in a great decree owing to her influence and training.

Holly Chang A Chinese-American social entrepreneur based in Beijing with 10 years of large-scale project management experience in both the US and China, Holly previously worked as a plant engineer, is managing fast-tracked projects with budgets up to $1.3 billion at the international operations headquarters: HQ for UPS. In 2007, she invested her life savings to establish The Golden Bridges Foundation and has since worked with over 100 non-profit organizations in Beijing, empowering non-profit leaders to become powerful agents of social change. Ms. Chang concurrently holds the position of vice president of International Relations at the China Foundation Centre, a new initiative that advances transparency and professionalism in philanthropy in China. Ms. Chang holds a B.Sc. in Civil Engineering, a B.S. in Psychology and a M.B.A. with a thesis on the China market.

Angela Leong On Kei Director, SJM Holdings, Hong Kong and Macau. A Macau entrepreneur and a member of the Legislative Council of Macau, she is the fourth wife of casino king, Stanley Ho. She is widely expected to take control of Hong Kong-listed SJM's 16 casinos, 4 slot parlours and Macau's Grand Lisboa Hotel. Now 47; grew up poor in Guangdong, became Macau dancer and casino worker before meeting Ho. Holds posts and stakes in both SJM Holdings and unlisted parent STDM.

Wu Yi, also known as China's Iron Lady, graduated from Lanzhou Women's Middle School in 1956. She went on to study at the Beijing Petroleum Institute, where she majored in oil refinery engineering and graduated in 1962. She was part of only a handful of women who studied there at that time. Wu joined the Communist Party the same year she graduated, and worked as a technician at the Lanzhou Oil Refinery. In 1965, she became a technician at the Ministry of Petroleum Industry, Production and Technology Department. Two years later, she worked at the Beijing Dongfang Hong Refinery where she went from technician to deputy director. From 1983 to 1988, she was deputy general manager of the Yanshan Petrochemical Corporation, also serving as the company's Communist Party Secretary. In 1987, she was an alternate member of the central committee of the 13th Communist Party Congress. Wu was elected deputy mayor of Beijing in 1988. A year into her tenure, as protests in Tiananmen Square got bloody, she persuaded coal workers to continue working after some of their co-workers were killed in the protest. From 1991 to 1998, she served at high levels in the Ministry of Foreign Economic Relations, then headed the Ministry of International Trade and Economic Cooperation. She was critical in negotiations for China's entry into the World Trade Organization and gained an esteemed reputation among colleagues and her foreign counterparts for her forthrightness, charm, and deft negotiation skills. While her government career rose, so did her stature in the Chinese Communist Party. She was a member of the 14th (1992–1997) and 15th (1997–2002) Communist Party Congress central committee, and a member of the central committee's politburo in the 16th Party Congress (2002–2007), a position only three other women had held before. The politburo is the Party's second highest governing power. In 2003, she was appointed Vice Premier of China's State Council, making her the most powerful woman in China. Her last role as Vice Premier was to better China's product-safety enforcement apparatus following lead contamination in Chinese exports. In late 2007, she announced her retirement, and joked in a speech to colleagues that she hoped they would totally forget her. She also urged her colleagues to always remain transparent and to remain financially clean. She served out her term in March 2008. Wu is highly regarded in China and in the world. She's known as the "Iron Lady" of China for her tough negotiation skills, but has also been praised for her compassion and honesty. *Forbes* Magazine named her the second most powerful woman in the world three times. Throughout her career, she excelled in the traditionally male-dominated petroleum industry and in public office. The five-foot-tall Wu never married, and lives with her niece in an apartment near the Forbidden City. She is reported to love Russian literature and fishing.

Hongkong

Carrie Lam is the Chief Executive of Hong Kong, and she was appointed since 1 July 2017.

Coming from a working-class background, Carrie Lam joined the civil service in 1980 after graduating from the University of Hong Kong (BBC News 2017). Although seen as Beijing's proxy, not popular with Hong Kongers and out of touch with ordinary people, the lifelong civil servant Carrie Lam has a name for being an efficient and pragmatic administrator. Carrie Lam becomes Hong Kong's first female leader and its fourth since British colonial control ended in 1997 (CBC News 2017).

"A mother of two adult sons, Lam is known as a tough and effective enforcer." (Rappler.com 2017). In 2007, Carrie Lam in person faced off with protesters over the demolition of a historic pier built during Hong Kong's colonial days under British rule. The landmark was ultimately destroyed (Rappler.com 2017).

In an interview (June 2017) with Chinese state news agency Xinhua, Lam expressed that the government should imbue the young generation with a sense of Chinese national identity. The government will "strictly enforce the law" against any acts advocating Hong Kong independence, she told Xinhua (Rappler.com 2017).

India

Indira Gandhi The daughter of Jawaharlal Nehru, she was India's first prime minister and played a significant role in Indian politics for nearly 30 years. The president of the National Congress Party (1959) and minister of information and broadcasting (1964), Indira became India's first female prime minister in 1966. In 1975, faced with domestic unrest and accusations of violating election laws, Gandhi declared a state of national emergency, suspending civil liberties and arresting thousands of political dissidents. She was defeated in the 1977 elections, but made a spectacular comeback 3 years later, and served as prime minister until her 1984 assassination by Sikh conspirators.

Mother Teresa A Catholic nun of Albanian ethnicity and an Indian citizen, Mother Teresa founded the Missionaries of Charity in Calcutta, India in 1950. For over 45 years, she ministered the poor, sick, orphaned, and the dying while guiding the Missionaries of Charity's expansion, first throughout India and then in other countries. Following her death, she was beatified by Pope John Paul II and given the title "Blessed Teresa of Calcutta".

Sonia Gandhi Born in 1946 and an Italian by birth, Sonia is the widow, daughter-in-law and granddaughter-in-law of Indian Prime Ministers. In 1964, she studied English at the Bell Education Trust's language school in the city of Cambridge. She worked at a Greek restaurant as a waitress to make ends meet and while working there she met her future husband, Rajiv Gandhi. Sonia married Rajiv Gandhi in 1968, following which she moved into the house of her mother-in-law and then the prime minister, Indira Gandhi. After Rajiv Gandhi's assassination in 1991, she was invited by the Indian Congress Party to take over the Congress but Sonia refused and stayed away from politics. Sonia Gandhi finally entered politics, becoming the leader of India's Congress Party in 1998 "The strange and inspiring story of the Italian woman who became India's dominant force" (*Time* 2008, p. 38). Sonia Gandhi became a member of India's most well-known political family in 1968 when she married Rajiv Gandhi, son of former Prime Minister Indira Gandhi. In 2004, Sonia Gandhi shocked the nation when she was elected prime minister but rejected the post fearing the question of her nationality would tear apart the country the Gandhi family had sacrificed so much for.

Indonesia

Sri Mulyani Indrawati is an Indonesian economist. Having obtained her degree from Universitas Indonesia in 1986, Sri Mulyani received her master and doctorate in economics from the University of Illinois at Urbana-Champaign in 1992. In 2001, Mulyani left for Atlanta, Georgia, to serve as a consultant with the US Aid Agency (USAID) for programs to strengthen Indonesia's autonomy. Sri Mulyani was selected as Indonesian Finance Minister in 2005 by President Susilo Bambang Yudhoyono. As Indonesian finance minister from 2005 to 2010, Sri Mulyani has fought against government corruption, created tax incentives and simplified investment laws. In August 2008, Mulyani was ranked by *Forbes* Magazine as the 23rd most powerful woman in the world and the most powerful woman in Indonesia. She is also known as a tough reformist and has largely been credited with strengthening Indonesia's economy, increasing investments and steering Southeast Asia's largest economy through the 2007–2010 financial crisis. On May 5, 2010, Mulyani was appointed as one of three Managing Directors of the World Bank Group, overseeing

74 nations in Latin America, Caribbean, East Asia and Pacific, Middle East and North Africa.

Japan

Akiko Amano Director, Sohke Hanabi Kagiya, Japan. She runs Kagiya which her family has operated for three centuries. She is the 15th proprietor of Sohke Hanabi Kagiya Co., one of the nation's most prestigious fireworks companies with a history dating from the Edo period (1603–1867). She runs the business as Tokyo fireworks maker and show producer with Intricate displays light up Japanese skies every summer. At 38, she was the first Japanese woman to become a judo judge at the Olympics.

Malaysia

Marina binti Mahathir The daughter and eldest child of the fourth Prime Minister of Malaysia, Tun Mahathir Mohammad. Graduated from the University if Sussex. Marina is well known as a leader in many non-governmental organizations, and these include the Malaysian AIDS Foundation. She is currently an active socio-political blogger, and writes a bi-weekly column in *The Star*. Marina has called for an end to discrimination based on sexual orientation. Married to an Indonesian professional photographer, Tara Sosrowardoyo, Marina has three children.

    Michelle Yeoh Choo-Kheng A Hong Kong-based Malaysian actress, Michelle Yeo is well known for performing her own stunts in the action films that brought her to fame in the early 1990s. She was born in Ipoh, Malaysia and was keen on dance from an early age, beginning ballet at the age of four. At the age of 15, she moved with her parents to England, where she was enrolled in a boarding school. Yeoh later studied at the Royal Academy of Dance in London, majoring in ballet. However, a spinal injury prevented her from becoming a professional ballet dancer, and she transferred her attention to choreography and other arts. She later received a B.A. degree in Creative Arts with a minor in Drama. On 19 April 2001, Yeoh was awarded the Darjah Datuk Paduka Mahkota Perak (DPMP), which carries the title Dato by Sultan Azlan Shah, the Sultan of Perak, her home state, in recognition of the fame she brought to the state. The award was given in conjunction with the Sultan's 73rd birthday celebrations. Yeoh is also a supporter and ambassador of the Save China's Tigers project committed to protect the endangered South China Tiger.

    Tan Sri Rafidah binti Abdul Aziz, dubbed as Malaysia's Iron Lady. Rafidah became a senator at the age of 30 and served as the International Trade and Industry Minister from 1987 to 2008. She was one of the longest serving cabinet ministers in the Government until she was dropped from cabinet in March 2008.

    During her term as minister, Rafidah was given the nickname "Iron Lady" because of her exterior sternness or aggressiveness. She has a good communication skill and did display a high locus of control and self-efficacy. She was well-known to be a non-nonsense woman with her basic principle being, "I'm working for my country and its people, and I won't compromise my country's interest for anything" (Kok 2010).

Myanmar

Aung Sun Suu Kyi Aung San Suu Kyi is the third child and only daughter of Aung San, considered to be the father of modern-day Burma. Having been put under house arrest for a number of times, Suu Kyi is the leader of the struggle for human rights and democracy in Myanmar. She has been the inspirational leader of attempts to restore democracy to her country.

Although she was prohibited from becoming the President due to a clause in the constitution—her late husband and children are foreign citizens—she accepted the newly created role of State Counsellor (since April 2016), a role similar to a Prime Minister or a head of government. Aung San Suu Kyi has gained international acclaim, having received many honours. (She was the Leader of the Opposition from 2 May 2012 to 29 January 2016.)

In the 1990 general election, Aung San Suu Kyi's National League for Democracy party won 59% of the national votes and 81% (392 of 485) of the seats in Parliament. She had, however, already been detained under house arrest before the elections. She remained under house arrest in Burma for almost 15 of the 21 years from 20 July 1989 until her release on 13 November 2010. Primarily in response to her detention, Aung San Suu Kyi received the Rafto Prize and the Sakharov Prize for Freedom of Thought in 1990 and the Nobel Peace Prize in 1991. In 1992, she was awarded the Jawaharlal Nehru Award for International Understanding by the government of India and the International Simon Bolivar Prize from the government of Venezuela. In 2007, the Government of Canada made her an honorary citizen of that country, one of only five people ever to receive the honor.

Pakistan

Benazir Bhutto was born in Karachi. The late Ms. Bhutto studied politics at Harvard and international law at Oxford before returning to Pakistan, where she led the then-opposition Pakistan People's Party during a decade of political upheaval. Arrested nine times, Bhutto spent nearly 6 years under detention before becoming Pakistan's prime minister in 1988, the first woman to head an Islamic government. Bhutto championed democracy, education, and health reform for the poor, and pledged to end discrimination against women.

Philippines

Corazon Aquino President of the Philippines from 1986 to 1992, the late Corazon Aquino was the wife of Benigno S. Aquino, Jr. who had been leader of the opposition against the Marcos administration until his assassination in 1983. Assuming leadership of the opposition, she ran against Marcos in 1985 and after much non-violent 'strategic planning', people power and contesting of ballot results, won and forced him from office.

   Maria Gloria Macapagal-Arroyo Born in 5 April 1947, Gloria Arroyo was the President of the Philippines from 2001 to 2010. She was the country's second female president (after Corazon Aquino), and the daughter of former President Diosdado Macapagal. She was a former professor of economics at Ateneo De Manila University when the current President of Philippines, Benigno Aquino III, was one of her students. She entered the government service in 1987, serving as assistant secretary and undersecretary of the Department of Trade and Industry upon the invitation of President Corazón Aquino. Despite the obstacles and various charges of impropriety directed at those close to her, Gloria Arroyo was elected to a full 6-year presidential term in May 2004. She made international headlines in July after a Filipino driver was kidnapped by militant rebels in war-torn Iraq. In defiance of the United States government's requests, Gloria Arroyo honoured the rebels' demands to pull all Filipino troops out of the country.

   Victoria P. Garchitorena Considered as one of the pillars of the Philippines' non-governmental organization sector, Victoria was the founding chair of the League of Corporate Foundations, Philippines Council for NGO Certification, Philippines Association for Volunteer Efforts, Metro South Cooperative Bank, and the Makati NGO Network. She is/has been Chair or Trustee of the following: Justice Cecilia Munoz Palma Foundation, Pinoy ME, Ramon Magsaysay Awards Foundation, EDSA People Power Commission, AIM Alumni Association, Mendiola Consortium, Ateneo de Manila University, De La Salle University, College of the Holy Spirit, International Center for Innovation, Transformation and Excellence in Government, Management Association of the Philippines, among others. She was also a Board Member of the United States-based Council on Foundations and is a Senior Adviser of the World Bank's Asia-Pacific Advisory Council Against Corruption. Ms. Garchitorena has also served as the Senior Consultant of the Office of the President of the Philippines, the Head of the Presidential Management Staff, and Secretary to the Cabinet. She is a Managing Director of Ayala Corporation and President of Ayala Foundation, Inc. and Ayala Foundation, USA.

Singapore

Claire Chiang Born in 1951, social activist, entrepreneur and author Claire Chiang lived in a shop-house along Race Course Road in Little India, a home which she shared with 11 other Hainanese family members. She was the youngest and only daughter of five boys. Her father worked as an accountant while her mother did various odd jobs. She never had a bed to herself until she reached adulthood, having to share her room with two other brothers and her paternal grandmother. Through this, however, she grew closer to her paternal grandmother who, along with her mother, influenced her early ideas on feminism and womanhood. Several interesting careers in academia and business marked Chiang's life. She was a research sociologist and a sociology tutor at tertiary level, with her research skills culminating in the publication of the award-winning book, *Stepping out: The making of Chinese entrepreneurs* (1993), which was subsequently made into a Chinese drama serial in 1999. She is executive director of the Banyan Tree Gallery, a company that she conceptualised. Her business acumen led her to break the long-standing tradition of an all-male Singapore Chinese Chamber of Commerce & Industry (SCCI) in 1995 by becoming one of the first two women to be admitted to it. Despite her achievements, she has remained down-to-earth and is an active advocate for women's rights, family life and the disadvantaged in society.

Halimah binti Yacob Born 23 August 1954, Halimah, the Singaporean politician is currently the President of Singapore. A former member of the country's governing People's Action Party (PAP), Halimah Yacob was the ninth Speaker of Parliament (first woman speaker, CNA 2017), from January 2013 to August 2017. She was a Member of Parliament (MP) representing Jurong Group Representation Constituency between 2001 and 2015, and Marsiling-Yew Tee Group Representation Constituency between 2015 and 2017.

On 7 August 2017, she resigned from her positions as Speaker and MP, and from her membership in the PAP, to stand as a candidate for the 2017 Singapore presidential election. On 13 September 2017, she was declared President-elect in a walkover, as no other presidential hopeful was issued the Certificate of Eligibility; she was then sworn in the following day, becoming the first female president in the island-Republic's history.

Ho Ching The wife of the Prime Minister of Singapore, Lee Hsien Loong, has played a significant role in the Singapore Business and Investment sector; she is the CEO of Temasek Holdings which holds over USD 100 billion in assets owned by Singapore's Ministry of Finance. Ms. Ho Ching graduated from the National University of Singapore and also holds a MSc from Stanford University, USA. In 1987, she joined the Singapore Technologies group as Deputy Director of Engineering, and became its President and Chief Executive Officer before retiring in 2001. She later joined Temasek Holdings in May 2002. She is also an Honorary Fellow of the Institution of Engineers, Singapore.

Kwa Geok Choo was a Singaporean most widely known as the wife of Singapore's former Minister Mentor and former Prime Minister Lee Kuan Yew and was one of the partners in the Law firm, Lee & Lee. The late Kwa was also the mother of current Prime Minister Lee Hsien Loong. She was a former pupil of Methodist Girls' School and read law at Girton College, Cambridge University, where she was a Queen's Scholar from Malaya. During the formation of the Peoples' Action Party (PAP), Kwa helped in drafting the Constitution of the PAP. She provided legal advice to the NTUC and she was also a principal drafter of the Singapore Labor Foundation Act. When Singapore separated from the Malaysian Federation, Kwa drafted the clauses in the Separation Agreement for the guaranteeing of the water agreement between the State of Johor and Singapore. This guarantee was done via a constitutional amendment to the Federation of Malaysia's Constitution.

Dato Dr. Jannie Tay is executive vice-chairman of watch retailer, The Hour Glass Ltd. She got into the watch retailing business by, as it were, marrying into it; her father-in-law was in the business. Soon after joining the family in the 1960s, Jannie joined the family as a salesgirl despite her degree in pharmacology. In 1979, she co-founded the business and has guided its growth from a single retail operation to a network of 23 luxury boutiques in Australia, Hong Kong, Japan, Malaysia, Singapore, Thailand and Indonesia. Among her many achievements, Dato Dr. Tay is the first female president of both the Singapore Retailers Association and the ASEAN Business Forum. She had won several awards for devoting a great deal of her time in many charity projects with The Community Chest of Singapore. She was appointed the Patron of Yuhua Community Service Centre in 1983. Dato Dr. Tay also held several positions in various women's organisations and is noted for her dedicated work related to women's issue.

Sri Lanka

Sirimavo Ratwatte Dias Bandaranaike A Sri Lankan politician and the world's first female head of government, Mrs Bandaranaike served as the Prime Minister of Ceylon and Sri Lanka three times, 1960–1965, 1970–1977 and 1994–2000, and was a long-time leader of the Sri Lanka Freedom Party. The widow of a previous Sri Lankan prime minister, Solomon Bandaranaike, Sirimavo Bandaranaike was the mother of Sri Lanka's third President Chandrika Kumaratunga and Anura Bandaranaike, former speaker and cabinet minister. She was born to a prominent Radala family, who were descended from Ratwatte Dissawa, Dissawa of Matale, a signatory on behalf of the Singhalese to the Kandyan Convention of 1815. The eldest of six, with four brothers and one sister, Mrs. Bandaranaike was educated at St Bridget's Convent, Colombo, but was a practising Buddhist.

Taiwan

Nadia Chen Born and grew up in Taiwan, Nadia works at The Bank of New York Mellon Taipei Branch (BK) as a client executive for almost 3 years. Her main responsibilities include: promoting a wide array of the bank's group products and services mainly to institutional clients (banks, pension funds, insurance companies, securities houses, asset management companies and corporate); and maintaining and managing senior level relationships with clients and government entities. Prior to working for BK, Ms. Chen worked for German's second largest bank, Commerzbank Taipei Representative Office, as the Chief Representative for almost

5 years. Her main responsibilities covered developing business and client relationships in Taiwan. In Ms. Chen's over 20-year banking career, she has had the chance to work with different colleagues from different countries under different cultures. She enjoys the challenge of meeting new people and learning from them. She is a sponsor to World Vision Taiwan and has sponsored over ten children in under development countries in the past 25 years. She is a lifetime member of YWCA Taiwan.

Thailand

Yingluck Shinawatra A Thai politician and frontrunner of the Pheu Thai Party. Yingluck was the Prime Minister-designate of Thailand following the 3 July 2011 general election. Born in Chiang Mai, Yingluck Shinawatra earned a bachelor's degree from Chiang Mai University and a Master's degree from Kentucky State University, both in public administration. She became an executive in the businesses founded by her elder brother, Thaksin Shinawatra, former Prime Minister of Thailand and later she became the president of property developer SC Asset and managing director of Advanced Info Service. In May 2011, the Pheu Thai Party, which maintained close ties to Thaksin, nominated Yingluck as their candidate for Prime Minister in the 2011 general election. Preliminary election results indicated that Pheu Thai won a landslide victory 265 out of 500-seat House of Representatives of Thailand, making it only the second time in Thai political history that a single party won a parliamentary majority. Yingluck Shinawatra was then (in 2013) became Thailand's first female Prime Minister.

Checkpoint: Think About It

Women and Mother Leadership

Mother Leadership
Let us reflect and think about it.

1. What are the arguments for mother leadership?
2. What are the traits and characteristics of mother leadership?
3. What qualities of mother leadership do you find attractive? And why? If not, examine the reasons against it?
4. What are the benefits and advantages of mother leadership?
5. What are the downsides of mother leadership?

The Glass Ceiling

1. What do you think are the strengths of women leadership?

2. What are some of the common stereotypes of males and females in your country?
3. What do you think are the obstacles to women leadership?
4. How would you remove these obstacles?
5. Suggest more ways to remove them?

The Way Forward

1. Are you helping yourself by:
   (a) Adopting the human capital approach?
   (b) Adopting win-win relationships?
   (c) Promoting and self-marketing?
   (d) Networking and building connections?
   (e) Coaching, guiding and mentoring?
   (f) Applying soft power?
   (g) Promoting entrepreneurial skills?
   (h) Having role models to emulate?
2. Suggest ways in which you can promote win-win relationships with your spouse (others/colleagues/supervisors/employees)?
3. What are the various strategies or ways in which women can move up the corporate ladder?
4. State the various women leaders in Asia and explain what makes them famous, well-known or popular.
5. Identify your role models to emulate. And state the reasons for your choice.
6. Identify a mentor and work out areas (ways) to learn from her (him).
7. Identify a mentee and work out areas (ways) to guide her (him).
8. Identify a coach and work out ways to learn from her (him).
9. Identify a coachee and work out ways to coach or teach her (him).
10. Suggest ways to expand your contacts/connections and expand your network?

References

BBC News. (2017). Carrie Lam: Hong Kong's new leader faces an uphill battle, *BBC News*, 26 March 2017. Accessed August 2, 2017 from http://www.bbc.com/news/world-asia-china-39385262

Capra, F. (1983). *The turning point: Science, society, and the rising culture*. New York: Bantam Books.

CBC News. (2017). *Carrie Lam, Beijing's pick, chosen as Hong Kong's leader – Chief executive-elect had support of Chinese leadership in Beijing*. Accessed August 1, 2017 from www.cbc.ca

Christensen, M. K. I. (2009). *Worldwide guide to women in leadership*. Accessed April 7, 2009 from http://www.guide2womenleaders.com/

CNA – Channel News Asia (2017). Singapore's first female Speaker of Parliament. *Channel News Asia*. Accessed January 9, 2013.

Cooper, S. (2008). *Women, leadership and personality: Insights from the Myers-briggs type indicator*. ArticlesBase.com, 25 September 2008. Accessed April 25, 2009 from http://www.

articlesbase.com/business-articles/women-leadership-and-personality-insights-form-the-myersbriggs-type-indicator-578640.html

DuBrin, A. J. (2007). *Fundamentals of organizational behavior*. Canada: Thomson South-Western.

Ellison, K. (2005). *The mommy brain: How motherhood makes us smarter*. New York: Basic Books.

Friedman, M. B. (1992). *The leadership myth*. Pittsburgh, PA: Dorrance Publishing.

Grzelakowski, M. (2005). *Mother leads best*. Chicago: Dearborn Trade Publishing, A Kaplan Professional Company.

Hirsh, S., & Kummerow, J. (1989). *Life types*. New York: Warner Books.

Ide, A. F. (1996). *The Qur'an on woman, marriage, birth control and divorce*. Las Colinas, TX: Tnagelwuld Press.

Jamie, W. (2007). *Time for mother leadership*. Momsrising.com, 9 April 2007. Accessed April 20, 2009 from http://www.momsrising.org/node/485

Jones, D. (2006, May 24). Do moms make better managers? *USA Today*. Accessed April 22, 2009 from http://www.usatoday.com/money/companies/management/2006-05-11-women-leaders-usat_x.htm

Koh, K. B. (2009, April 30). Outgoing temasek chief Ho Ching gets top award. *The Straits Times*, 30 April 2009, p. A4.

Kok, C. (2010, November 20). *Up Close with Rafidah Aziz*. Retrieved 21 Aug 2011, from The Star Online: http://biz.thestar.com.my/news/story.asp?file=/2010/11/20/business/7457738&sec=business

Lebar, F. M. (1972). *Ethnic groups of insular South East Asia* (Vol. 1). New Haven, CT: Human Relations Area Files Press.

Low, K. C. P. (2001). *The power of relationships*. Singapore: BusinesscrAFT™ Consultancy.

Low, K. C. P. (2006a). Father leadership—The Singapore case study. *Management Decision, 44* (2), 89–104.

Low, K. C. P. (2006b). Father leadership in project management: A Kazakhstan case study. *GITAM Journal of Management*, July–December 2006 issue, GITAM, India, pp. 12–20.

Low, K. C. P. (2006c). The participation of women as a national value: A study in Singapore. *The Icfaian Journal of Management Research, V*(1), 49–63. The Institute of Chartered Financial Analyst India: ICFAI University Press.

Low, K. C. P. (2007). Father leadership and small business management: The Singapore case study. *i-manager's Journal on Management, 1*(3), 5–13. December 2006–February 2007.

Low, K. C. P. (2008a). Father leadership with special reference to Negara Brunei Darussalam. *E-Leader 2008 conference, Chinese American Scholars Association: CASA*, Krakow, Poland, 9–11 June 2008. Accessed April 25, 2009 from http://www.g-casa.com/PDF/Krakow%202008/krakow%20papers%20pdf/paper%20database%20krakow/Cheng.pdf

Low, K. C. P. (2008b). Father leadership – The Malaysian perspective. *Leadership and Organizational Management Journal, 2008*(1), 75–95. Franklin Publishing (http://www.franklinpublishing.net/leadership.html).

Low, K. C. P. (2008c). Women and human capital—Creating the competitive edge in transitional economies with special reference to Brunei Darussalam. *The International Conference on Business and Management*. Brunei Darussalam: Universiti Brunei Darussalam, 8–9 Jan 2008.

Low, K. C. P., & Mohd. Zain, A. Y. (2008). Creating the competitive edge, The father leadership way. *International conference on business and management*, Universiti Brunei Darussalam Brunei Darussalam, 8–9 Jan 2008.

Low, K. C. P., & Theyagu, D. (2003). *Developing true leadership potential*. Singapore: Booksmith Consultancy.

Lowen, L. (2011). Qualities of women leaders; the unique leadership characteristics of Women. About.com. *Women's Issues*. Retrieved from http://womensissues.about.com/od/intheworkplace/a/WomenLeaders.htm

Maxwell, J. C. (2001). *Power of influence*. Malaysia: Advantage Quest Publications.

Rappler.com. (2017). *Hong Kong's new leader, Carrie Lam*, 1 July 2017. www.rappler.com. Accessed August 3, 2017 from http://www.rappler.com/world/regions/asia-pacific/174415-hong-kong-carrie-lam-profile

Sorensen, C. W. (1993). Asian families. In G. Evans (Ed.), *Asia's cultural mosaic*. Prentice Hall: Singapore.

Still, L. V. (1993). *Where to from here? The managerial woman in transition*. Sydney: Business and Professional Publishing.

Tan, J. S., & Lim, E. N. K. (2004). *Strategies for effective cross-cultural negotiation*. Singapore: McGraw-Hill.

Walt, V. (2008, March 24). #9 Women's work. Tapping the female entrepreneurial spirit can pay big dividends. *TIME, 171*(11), 42.

Young, E. (2004). *The 10 commandments of parenting*. Chicago, IL: Moody Publishers.

Leadership and the Twelve Chinese Zodiac Animals

13

Introduction

Everything has beauty, 'but not everyone sees it'. (Confucius)

There is much wisdom (here the wisdom lies from observations and drawing parallels) here, and this chapter has a refreshing approach to the study of leadership and it reflects biomimicry or what man can learn from nature. And in this case, what leaders and even ordinary people can learn much about leadership from nature, particularly so from animals. In this chapter, we will discuss the various Chinese zodiac animal signs and highlight the leadership equivalents and its relevance.

Indeed leadership matters. And there is a great need for better leaders (Low and Theyagu 2003; Beam 2004). Certainly if one wants to be successful, should one develop one's leadership skills?

Leadership skills are a skill set that can be possessed both in humans and in animals. Animals can be good examples of leaders for they lead their groups by influencing, showing examples, guiding and constantly communicating with their followers. They have the aim and goal for their followers to follow. For example, animals that travel in groups, when making migratory or movement decisions, often depends on social interactions among their own group members. This is important since they need to have good communicating skills; they transfer information and/or show action. This is done by signaling to one another or making noises which can only be understood by their own species. Information that is transferred is crucial as in many cases, very few of them have enough information, such as knowledge about the location of a food source, or of a migration route, and therefore in a group there is always a leader that knows all the information and thus guides its followers in the right direction. This leader is the one that takes responsibility of the safety of its followers (caring them) and in turn, the followers are dependent on their leader.

To this author, leadership involves using the **5Hs**: the **H**ead, the **H**eart, the **H**elicopter vision (having the eyes and foresight), the **H**ands and **H**indsight. The leader should make full use of his or her head—conceptual or analytical skills and social or interpersonal skills.

In terms of "helicopter vision" or using the eyes, perhaps we can borrow from Low and Ang (2010) in which they use the animal metaphor of an eagle; they argue that:

> With a superior mind, the leader can come up with a vision or a dream, and that vision should be communicated to the people. And how true, creating a vision for the people, the leader's dreams can help create a better world for the people. They continued,
>
> One leadership lesson drawn from the eagle is that of vision. It is said that the eagle soars or flies high when it is hunting. From the way of the eagle, the leader can learn the need to have a high vantage point, giving vision to the people. The leader should have a vision and see the big picture. And vision, having it is a necessity, serves as a guide or even as a beacon and a guiding light to the people.

The "heart" next basically means the leader should have the heart, relating and caring for the people (s)he leads. This is similar to what Lao Tzu, *Tao de ching*, verse 70, has said, "If you want to know me, look inside your heart." Lao-tzu (2008)

By "using the hands", we take it to mean that the leader should lead by the example, actions that the leader not only speaks of but perform. The leader lends a hand to assist people. The leader also needs to be hands-on or practical. Leader can learn much from hindsight, reflecting on actions done and taking action, amending or bettering things and promoting better understanding among people. Leaders also learn from errors and failures while improving things and harmonising relationships, and it is an ever going process.

As in Aesop's fables where lessons are learnt from stories told, here, leadership lessons are learnt from the nature and habits of animals, the Chinese zodiac animals. The purpose and objectives of this chapter is to indicate and draw parallels, and highlight the leadership lessons and its applications from nature with special reference to the Chinese zodiac animals, and where necessary, such interpretations are seen from the Chinese angle.

The Animals

The Chinese animal signs are a 12-year cycle used for dating the years. The Chinese animal signs represent a cyclical concept of time, rather than the Western linear concept of time. The Chinese lunar calendar is based on the cycles of the moon, and is constructed in a different fashion than the Western solar calendar. Based on the Chinese lunar calendar, the beginning of the year normally falls somewhere between late January and early February.

The Chinese zodiac animal signs also represent 12 different types of personalities. The zodiac traditionally begins with the sign of the Rat, and though there are many stories about the origins of the Chinese Zodiac—these are outside the ambit of this chapter and book. It is also not the intention of the chapter to provide personalities or horoscope readings of those born under these Chinese animal signs, hence the years in which each of these animal signs occur are intentionally omitted. [Note that though helpful to the Chinese, these animal signs also serve a useful social function. They help to find out people's ages, and instead of asking directly how old a person is, people often ask what his or her animal sign is. This would locate that person's age within a cycle of 12 years, and with a bit of common sense, we can deduce the exact age. More often, though, people ask for animal signs not to compute a person's exact numerical age, but to simply know who is older among one's group of friends and acquaintances.]

The following are the 12 zodiac signs in order and their characteristics.

1. Rat
2. Ox or Bull or Cow
3. Tiger
4. Rabbit (or Cat in Vietnam)
5. Dragon
6. Snake
7. Horse
8. Ram or Goat
9. Monkey
10. Rooster or Cock
11. Dog
12. Pig

The Rat

Look before you leap.
  Money grows in the tree of patience. (Proverbs)

Most times, people tend to attribute a number of nasty things or negative qualities to animals, and the rat is one of such animals. In the West, "Rats!", for example, is used as a substitute for various vulgar interjections in the English language.

On the positive side, the rat is said to be a nibbler, it eats bit and bit. And in that aspect, when applied to leadership, it means bit by bit, little by little, the work gets done, and the results produced.

To the Chinese, the rat also represents prudence and savings. Savings and prudence is critical to bringing about economic growth, development and prosperity to societies. And leaders should not be extravagant in spending the organisational or national resources and finances.

Rats, when they are specially bred, have also been known to be kept as pets. Tamed rats are generally friendly and can be taught to perform selected behaviours. In India, rats are traditionally recognised as the vehicle of Lord Ganesh and a rat's statue is always found in a temple of Ganesh. In the North Western Indian city of Deshnoke, the rats at the Karni Mata Temple are held to be destined for reincarnations Sandhus (Hindu holy men). The attending priests feed milk and grain to the rats, of which the pilgrims also partake. Eating food that has been touched by rats is in fact regarded a blessing from god.

The Ox or the Bull

> Though this may sound very much like a cliché, it's useful and relevant—the more you work, the luckier you get! (Patrick Kim Cheng Low)

The ox or the bull is attributed to be a hardworking animal; it tilts the land, preparing for the farmers to grow their crops and have bountiful harvests. The ox, to this author, represents a hardworking leader, preparing the ground for the work to be done. To emulate the positive qualities of the ox, leaders also need to plough up the ground for change and innovation. The ox is needed; no farmer sows seeds into hard, unbroken ground. Leaders have to prepare the way for change, creativity and innovation; complacency can be a great enemy to change than fear. As organisations get bigger, more paperwork prevails, people tend to get more risk-averse, and they cease to be enterprising.

The bull or the ox also represents the strong character and determination of the leader. (S)he perseveres and achieves what (s)he wants. Old-fashioned managerial command and control ways need to give way to real leadership and creative ways. The leader needs to set for change and innovation, enlivening and growing the organisation with the spirit of enterprise, mind growth and innovation.

Note that in the Chinese character, there is no distinction between the bull and the cow. The female counterpart of the Ox or the cow supplies dairy products, particularly milk and that supplies nourishments; so also, the leader directs and nourishes the people with his vision, direction and insights when leading the entire organisation or community.

Interestingly, perhaps we can also apply this Ox analogy to training and growth for new hires and recruits. Leaders can deploy such a way or technique to get your new hires trained. The Chinese used to apply this, when it comes to farming, they make full use of the trained ox (or buffalo) to 'guide' the new or untrained ox. They simply yoke the new ox with one already trained, one that knew how to work and had been around for awhile, and allow the seasoned ox to guide and teach the newcomer. After a while, the newcomer realise that the simple and best thing to do is to follow the trained ox, to go with the plan. In a few weeks, both oxen had the same training agenda. If you want to guide your new hires or recruits, find willing oxen (trainers, coaches and mentors) within your company; get them to guide and coach the recruits. It is simple, quick and it works.

The Tiger

> Without courage, wisdom bears no fruit. (Baltasar Gracian)

Here, it can be taken that a leader also needs to be a risk taker. (S)he should take some risks and venture. And interestingly, this brings to mind a Chinese saying that goes, "if you do not enter the tiger's den, how can you get his cub?"

As pointed out by Low and Ang (2010), having powerfully built shoulders and legs, the tiger, the largest of the four big cats of the *panthera* family, is also seen by the Chinese as courageous as well as upholding justice. It protects the weak. Being seen as the King of the Beasts in East Asian cultures, paintings of tiger(s) are normally put in the house to ward off evil spirits.

There is another Chinese proverb that goes, "there are times when even the tiger sleeps." Here, it is taken that even a leader makes a mistake, yet, as a leader, it would be more big-hearted for him or her to admit rather than to deny it. One would then learn from the mistake, adopting an overall continuous improvement or *kaizen* attitude.

We can also look at the tiger from the martial arts perspective. Here, Shaolin Tiger style of martial arts is said to be full of strength and power, and such a style requires strong body, tough arm-work and quick legwork. The Tiger style martial artists would often go for the opponents' throat. Shaolin Tiger martial artist style is tough and resilient, often forging ahead, defending and attacking with much power and vigour. Leaders can learn from the Shaolin martial arts Tiger style and deploys this strategy, that is, (when two tigers fight), there are fiercely no retreat and no surrender; it is a fight to the end. As such this makes it almost impossible for two Tigers to have a fight. As an old Chinese saying goes; "when two tigers fight, one is lost, and one will be severely hurt". Indeed when two tigers have a fight, the result will be disastrous even for the winning tiger. There is also another Chinese saying that goes, "Two tigers cannot live on one mountain."

The Rabbit (or The Cat in Vietnam)

A real friend is one who walks in when the rest of the world walks out. (Walter Winchell)

The rabbit has long ears and powerful hind legs which enable then to run quite well. The rabbit is a quiet, gentle and timid creature.

Such a leader, as represented by the rabbit sign, can be said to be a good listener, listening well to his or her followers. Leaders often care for and love to help or serve others. And this means that they are often servant leaders, having their people's needs and interests in their minds and hearts.

Sensitive, and a real friend, (s)he is an empathetic listener. Such a leader relates well with the people, and his or her ears are always on the ground.

Living in the wild, rabbits or hares are also smart; they have many holes and easily escaped from being captured by having more than one hole. This is strategic; leaders can also have many ways and styles so as to be flexible in influencing and persuading their people; they have an armoury of weapons so that they can pursue and attain their goals.

The Dragon

Where so ever you go, go with all your heart. (Confucius)

The dragon is a mythical animal. Low (2009, 2010a) uses the analogy of the Chinese dragon to exemplify critical strategic leadership ways. To the Chinese, the dragon is a divine mythical creature, signifies power, greatness, benevolence, goodness and blessings. The dragon is also a symbol of the Yellow emperor, and hence is an auspicious sign.

Among other things, in emulating and following the way of the dragon, the strategic leader thus leads with example and integrity (Low 2009, 2010b); (s)he leads justly and with compassion. Relying on the wisdom of the old, humaneness, the *Tao* of the ancient emperors (now practiced by strategic leaders) is put forth; this still has great relevance in an age of rapid changes, and hence its appeal. When you lead, lead with all your heart, and win your people's hearts. Positive and harmonious relationships are emphasised, with the country (the world) and its citizens enjoying the 'Big Peace'.

The Snake

All things must pass. (English proverb)

One of the twelve celestial animals of the Chinese Zodiac in the Chinese calendar, the snake in Christianity, the serpent has been seen as Satan's representative. It is seen as sly plotting, as in the description in Genesis, Chap. 3 of a snake in the Garden of Eden, tempting Eve. Saint Patrick is reputed to have expelled all snakes from Ireland while Christianizing the country in the fifth century, thus explaining the absence of snakes there (Low and Ang 2010).

Snakes such as pythons are said to have swallowed dogs or even huge animals such as buffaloes; this is because of their flexible jaws which can open up to accommodate the size of their preys. Here, we can liken this to the confidence and ambitions of a leader. The leader is usually big-hearted and magnanimous, wanting to move the people towards the vision he or she envisages (Low and Ang 2010).

Snakes also shed off or change their skins often; here, leaders need to lead change by being fluid in accepting and managing change (Fig. 13.1). Creating a sense of urgency, they motivate their people Ito accept and implement the change. Leaders lead change well. Leaders celebrate successes, no matter how little; and they also get their people to see the benefits of the change (Hayes 2007). This is to keep the change momentum going while moving towards realising the change.

When applying the Shaolin Snake martial arts style to leadership I take it that the leader needs to act fast. The Shaolin Snake style, to this author, is to hold and grab or capture the opponent, the right strike is critical. It can be said to be a style of power without violence, speed without haste and knowledge without dominance.

Fig. 13.1 Snakes also shed off their skins often; here, that analogy is that leaders lead change by being flexible in accepting and bringing about change

Essentially, leaders then should make the right strike, taking quick (timely) and right or good decisions.

The Horse

So long a man is angry he cannot be in the right. (Chinese proverb)

In the Western tradition, there is always a wild horse in us and one in which we, as a person or leader needs to tame or put it under control. That wild horse can be our emotions and feelings. The leader should be emotionally stable, and in fact, possess high emotional quotient (EQ). Here, in the Chinese context, the leader should have "the uncontaminated heart" (清靜心) [purity of heart, care for his or her people] and the clarity of mind [to set goals and get the tasks or job done].

In fact, the Chinese phrase, "馬到功成" meaning "immediate success" is commonly used in Chinese paintings and Chinese calligraphy, and most often used as gifts for Chinese businesspeople to display at their new offices or residences. To most Chinese business people, hanging a big painting of eight running, sturdy horses with an inscription of "八駿馬圖", meaning, "eight handsome running horses" is taken as good luck. Here, it is believed that business would flourish similar to a team of strong horses, running purposefully in unison (Fig. 13.2). Besides, the number eight in Chinese can also sound and mean "prosperity", hence the number of horses in the painting.

It is worthy to note that horses also have a great sense of balance, in part due to their ability to feel their footing and in part due to the highly developed proprioceptive abilities (that is, the unconscious sense of where the body and limbs are at all times) (Thomas 1998). In this aspect, leaders need to be high in self-monitoring, with a good sense of balance and flexibility, mixing with all kinds of people. Having a good sense of balance and a wide area of interests, a leader would not be too rigid,

Fig. 13.2 Shows eight horses, running purposefully in unison, signifying prosperity. To the Chinese, a horse also represents vigour and vitality

lop-sided and easily stressed. Low self-monitoring, with limited options open, can often act inflexibly or be inflexible (DuBrin 2007), and people who are flexible and skilled in networking and mixing with different and groups of people usually score high on the self-monitoring factor.

As a sign, horses, to the Chinese, are overall seen as active and hence, leaders should be proactive, and they get things done.

The Ram or the Goat

When the going gets tough, the tough get going. (American saying)

When domesticated, the goat is a useful animal; it supplies milk to man.

In the wild, just as a mountain goat can agilely climb up and down the mountain slopes, overcoming obstacles, the leader, unafraid of hardships, also skilfully avoids or minimises any obstacles encountered.

Rams and goats are hardy animals. Like the saying, "every path has its puddle", all leaders would face some forms of problems or difficulties, and likewise, leaders need to be resilient. Just as an African saying goes, 'A smooth sea does not make a skilful sailor', leaders must positively translate problems into challenges, transforming them into their strengths, and weathering through the event(s) as well as building their characters.

Solving corporate problems well, a good leader also leads the organisation through any crises, overcoming whatever obstacles faced. (S)he makes smart decisions.

The Monkey

Creativity is thinking new things. Innovation is doing new things. (Theodore Levitt)

The monkey is seen as active, often swinging from tree to tree; and it can be taken that similar to the monkey, leaders should be responsive. They should be quick in taking actions.

Low and Ang (2010) relevantly point out the Chinese saying that 'even monkeys at times fall from the trees'. Leaders also make mistakes, and it is good that leaders learn from these mistakes. Additionally, they need to allow their people to learn from mistakes while building and growing their organisations into learning organisations.

A prominent divine entity in Hinduism, the monkey can be said to bestow longevity. In Buddhism, the monkey is an early incarnation of Buddha but may also represent trickery and ugliness. The Chinese Buddhist, the "mind monkey" metaphor refers to the unsettled, restless state of human mind. The *Mizaru* or three wise monkeys are revered in Japanese folklore. To the Chinese, the monkey is normally seen as clever. Some species of monkeys, for example, the capuchin monkeys, can be trained to be monkey helpers, assisting quadriplegics and other people with severe spinal cord injuries or mobility impairments. After being socialised in a human home as infants, the monkeys undergo extensive training before being placed with a quadriplegic. Around the house, the monkeys assist by doing tasks including microwaving food, washing the quadriplegic's face and opening drink bottles.

It is worthy to note that several countries, including the United States and France, have used monkeys as part of their space exploration programmes.

Here, as leaders, we need to be creative and cleverly push for innovation. We need to think also in terms of leadership for smart innovations, encouraging team creativity and ensuring real commitment from the top for organisational innovation and growth. While cutting down bureaucratic red-tape and paperwork, the innovative leader should know how to harvest ideas, ranging from brainstorming, suggestion schemes to quality circles, team creativity and coaching as well as training and education.

"The Pilgrimage to the West", one of the greatest novels in the Chinese Literature written by (吳承恩) Wu Cheng-en (1500–1582) in the Ming Dynasty, occupying an important place in World Mythology. Here, the Monkey God or Sun Wu Kong is depicted as a brave, courageous, diligent hero who is afraid of nothing not even the Jade Emperor or Yama, the underworld king (C.C. Low & Associates 1975). He is a radical leader who thinks differently from other people; he uses his wonder magic iron cudgel to fight demons and kings. From here, we can liken this to a leader who is brave and courageous and set a role model example to his team. Besides, to stand out and carve a competitive edge, a leader perhaps needs to be different and even creative.

Drawing from the Hindu texts and wisdom, Low (2010b, pp. 140–141) highlights that we can infer the negotiation ways of the Monkey God (also known as Hanuman), and can emulate the qualities of Hanuman in the negotiation process. He attributes to the Monkey God as having, among other key traits, these qualities:

> Hanuman as Lord Rama's emissary and negotiator is an ideal negotiator. A good negotiator should indeed be perceptive, tactful, cool-headed, ethical and humble. He should also have a complete command of the situation. . . The character of Hanuman indeed teaches us of the unlimited power that lies untapped within each one of us.

As leaders, it is critical to remember "the unlimited power that lies untapped within each one of us" (Low 2010b, p. 140) as this boosts our confidence, self-esteem and self-efficacy, and thus enhance our ways to get things done and accomplish our goals.

In martial arts, the Shaolin Monkey style can be said to be unusual and effective, the monkey kung fu fighter would emulate the slyness and trickiness of the monkey and hence gain an upper hand over his(her) opponents. The monkey style also involves a lot of bluffing (tricks) as well as being devilish and unpredictable. And when we apply this idea to leadership, it is to be noted that leaders need to be MAD: Make A Difference. Leaders need to differentiate themselves to create and build their brand.

The Rooster

> Communication is not only the essence of being human, but also a vital property of life.
> (John A. Piece)

If the art of communication is the language of leadership, leaders, in most ways, should emulate the ways of the rooster or cock, the male chicken.

The rooster crows at the beginning of the day. The female chicken is a hen. Roosters will occasionally make a patterned series of clucks to attract hens to a food source the same way as a mother hen does for her chicks.

Such a leader can be seen as (s)he capitalises, highlights and showcases the organisation's strengths, positive aspects and events as publicity and promotion tools to raise its profile and image.

It can also be taken that such a leader, like the rooster, is a good communicator. Using whatever media, tools such as corporate videos, and/or in face to face interactions, the leader communicates well; (s)he touches base with the people.

The Dog

In the sweetness of friendship let there be laughter, for in the dew of little things the heart finds its morning and is refreshed. (Kahlil Gibran)

The dog, human's best friend, is said to be a loyal animal. The loyalty of the followers and the leaders' loyalty to their followers are one of the critical factors for leadership success in organisations. A true team leader would, in most ways, stick with his or her people through thick and thin no matter what. Here, I would also take it that leaders have to a key role to play, persuading, bringing or gathering their followers rather quickly into the fold or in-group to up their loyalty, and motivate them, making them happy—more so, talents need to be retained as well as nurtured. Leaders need to ensure that their employees feel less and less of being an out-group. Feeling or gaining the feeling of being members of the out-group would lead employees to feel dissatisfied, unmotivated, and subsequently quit.

Dogs have lived and worked with humans in many and varied roles. They have also been bred for herding livestock, hunting (for example, pointers and hounds), rodent control, guarding, helping fishermen with nets, and pulling loads, in addition to their roles as companions.

Customs dogs help to sniff drugs and prohibited drugs in luggage and customs controls. Service dogs such as guide dogs, utility dogs, assistance dogs, hearing dogs, and psychological therapy dogs also provide assistance to individuals with physical or mental disabilities such as visually impaired or blind. Interestingly, some dogs owned by epileptics have been shown to alert their handler when the handler shows signs of an impending seizure, sometimes well in advance of onset, allowing the owner to seek safety, medication, or medical care.

To this author, it only shows that leaders can play a variety of roles such as being figurehead, playing the unifying role, the teambuilding role, the championing of a cause or value(s) role, the nurturing role, the coordinating role and many other roles.

Leaders also need to be versatile; and they often do a number and varieties of tasks and in one go. In short, multi-skilled, leaders, at most times, have to multitask to get their goals accomplished.

The Pig

The benevolent man is attracted to benevolence because he feels at home in it. The wise man is attracted to benevolence because he finds it to his advantage. (Confucius)

The pig is not as dirty as commonly seen though it has been often wrongly taken as "dirty pig". In spite of their reputation for greed and gluttony, they are generally social and intelligent animals.

Overall, the pig, to this author, represents the knowledge, skills, reserves and/or the pool of resources that the leader has or needs to have in order to work things out when leading the organisation.

Pigs that are allowed to forage may be watched by swineherds. Indeed because of their foraging abilities and excellent sense of smell, pigs in France and other European countries are used to find truffles. Likewise, leaders should have a good sense of justice, showing concern and caring for the people; they should have the vital people touch.

In the legend Journey to the West, the famous Piggy (Chu Bajie) is often seen as rough, uncultivated, and at times, stubborn. At times, Piggy appears to have also forgotten the purpose of the journey and this creates trouble for Monkey God or Sun Wu Kong. He is also able to create different magical transformations. And on the whole, Piggy's key strength is his obedience to the Master, Monk Tang San Zang, and also, he's kind and a great help in the Journey, from China to India, to gather the Buddhist scriptures or the Sutras.

Chapter Conclusion

Here, what I am emphasising are several good features and habits of the animals without denying that bad habits and behaviour do exist or prevail—just as in human beings. However, to stress on these bad behaviours would be indulging in negative thinking, hence the emphasis on such positive attributes. Similarly, anyone can make mistakes but more critically, we need to learn from them, and in this case, more specifically, we are learning from these good features and behaviours.

Learning from the positive attributes of the zodiac animals examined above, the key success factors for good leaders are having vision, being active, strong and resilient, guiding yet flexible while being compassionate and caring. They also lead change. Using these positive attributes, the leaders can grow themselves and perform effectively; and the organisation and the people they lead also benefit and grow.

Checkpoint: Think About It

Leadership and the Twelve Chinese Zodiac Animals

Review the following key points and when you have finished the quiz, check your answers with a close friend or a mentor.

1. What key leadership lessons can you derive from each of these Chinese zodiac animal signs?
   Rat
   Ox
   Tiger
   Rabbit (or Cat in Vietnam)
   Dragon
   Snake
   Horse

Ram or Goat
Monkey
Rooster
Dog
Pig

2. Are you friendly and approachable as a leader? What can you do more?
3. As a leader, what are the benefits of being passionate? Are you leading passionately? Are you leading with your heart? What can you do more?
4. Are you winning your people's hearts? What can you do more to win the hearts of your people?
5. Are you communicating enough to your people? How can you communicate further with your people?
6. Are you listening enough to your people?
7. Are you people smart? Are you people-centred? What can you do more?
8. Are you being creative enough?
9. Think of the ways in which you, as a leader, can be more creative?
10. Are you being persuasive enough?
11. Think of the ways in which you, as a leader, can be more persuasive to your people?
12. Choose one of the Chinese zodiac animal signs and search for leadership qualities you wish to cultivate for this year, and another animal sign, a different one, for the next year. Have an action plan on the qualities you wish to grow.

References

Beam, H. H. (2004). Why smart executives fail. *Academy of Management, 18*(2), 157–158.

C.C. Low & Associates. (Trans.) (1975). Pictorial stories of Chinese classical legend. In *The adventure of the Monkey God* (Vol. 1). Singapore: Canfonian Pte. Ltd.

DuBrin, A. J. (2007). *The fundamentals of organizational behavior*. Canada: Thomson South-Western.

Hayes, J. (2007). *The theory and practice of change management* (2nd ed.). New York: Palgrave Macmillan.

Lao-tzu. (2008). *Tao te Ching* (From a translation by S. Mitchell). Accessed May 22, 2008 from http://acc6.its.brooklyn.cuny.edu/~phalsall/texts/taote-v3.html

Low, K. C. P. (2009). The way of the dragon: Some strategic leadership ways. *Leadership and Organizational Management Journal, 2009*(2), 40–59.

Low, K. C. P. (2010a). *Successfully negotiating in Asia*. Heidelberg: Springer.

Low, K. C. P. (2010b). *Applying strategic leadership, the way of the dragon?* In e-Leader, Chinese American Scholars' Association: CASA conference, Singapore, 4–6 Jan 2010.

Low, K. C. P., & Ang, S.-L. (2010). *Leadership lessons from the animal kingdom?* In e-Leader, Chinese American Scholars' Association: CASA Conference, Singapore, 4–6 Jan 2010.

Low, K. C. P., & Theyagu, D. (2003). *Developing true leadership potential*. Singapore: The Publishing Consultant.

Thomas, H. S. (1998, October 17). True horse sense. *Thoroughbred Times*, Thoroughbred Times Company. Accessed December 7, 2009 from http://www.thoroughbredtimes.com/horse-health/1998/October/17/True-horse-sense.aspx

Leadership and Change

14

Change

Arrow goes forward only after pulling it backward, bullet goes forward only after pressing the trigger backward, every human being will get happy only after facing the changes (difficulties) in their life path; so don't be afraid to face your changes (difficulties), they will push you forward. (Author Unknown)

Before talking about leading change, it is good to examine ourselves.

What, to us, is change?

Most of us feel uncomfortable with change. In fact, most of us do not like change. We are creatures of comfort. Yes, we do not want to be inconvenienced.

Perhaps, all this while we have not thought of it, then it's time and it is now good to reflect on it, jotting down our thinking of change. What is your notion or idea of change? What is your attitude towards change? Do you like change(s)? What attitude should you adopt if you want to cope well with change? How would you implement the change?

Weak Leaders and Leading Change

When the moon is not full, the stars shine more brightly. (African proverb)
Those in a hurry do not arrive. (Zen wisdom)

It is good to note that weak or bad (incompetents/non) leaders (referred to as Tsunami leaders by Low and Teo 2015) are not capable of leading, managing and implementing and/or progressing change. And at times, the onus of change can be irresponsibly thrown onto the shoulders of the lieutenant(s) of these Tsunami leaders—be they competent or otherwise.

What is worse is that when these weak leaders implement change, the implementation of change is not done in a good and/or transparent way; "it is haphazardly

© Springer International Publishing AG 2018
K.C.P. Low, *Leading Successfully in Asia*,
https://doi.org/10.1007/978-3-319-71347-2_14

done with little transparency" (several interviewees' inputs) and what more, there is lack of regard to the employees' confidence and security (Low and Teo 2015).

Change is made with no or little people touch; organisational stability and growth are also affected. Instead there is much organizational disruption and destruction, and employees' morale suffers too (Low and Teo 2015, p. 36).

Interestingly too, Low and Teo (2015, pp. 39–40) added that during the change implementation, often the policies or procedures are ill-prepared or poorly planned and thought through. Yet they are implemented and in a rush. Often a rush job, these too bring about many surprises and/or unpleasantness or damage to the people and they are caught with their pants down. Many a times, the people are either poorly informed or not informed at all. They just have to take instructions and they are indeed not empowered to make any decisions.

In such hurry situations, with little information available and with short notices, a lack of ownership occurs, and this may even endanger the implementation, let alone acceptance, of such changes. This also reinforces the above pointer on subordinates not giving much support to the leaders. To avoid shocking policies, organisations and businesses—amidst much paperwork—need to implement change control policies to minimize the unintended creation of flawed operations or procedures (Carnall 2007, cited in Low and Teo 2015, p. 40). These are not done by weak leaders; the policy would need to be brought up-to-date periodically to reflect the organsation's current needs. [Change control policies cover much ground especially in top management levels simply because the impact will be throughout organisations. For example, a thorough change control policies should address issues of managing human resource vital asset for the organisation. A procedure for updating the policy and propagating the new revisions also needs to be covered in the policy. The policy should also have a schedule for periodic reviews built into (Honadle 1981, cited in Low and Teo 2015, p. 40)].

With the above in mind, what then can successful, let alone leaders do when leading change?

What Do Leaders Need to Do When Leading Change?

To change and to change for the better are two different things. (Unknown)

Leaders need to encourage and in fact actively promote change. They constantly and gently remind the people that change is good or beneficial. They remind their people that change is good because change keeps us on our toes, and not to be complacent. We need to change for the better, and move towards excellence.

Don't just instruct change or give change commands. Leaders need to allay fears of uncertainties faced by their people whenever change occurs. They need to encourage or persuade their people to change.

Preparing their people for change, leaders should listen to their people, get their input and discuss the issues with them. During the change process, leaders should also encourage their people to express their feelings, and this serves as a catharsis. And they move on.

To reduce the fears, uncertainties and anxieties of change in their people, leaders need to instead show the advantages and benefits (what's in store) and the positive aspects of change to them. To initiate and promote change, leaders also need to reduce the perceived risks that come with change.

Leaders must facilitate the process of change too. They can time or schedule the change process; they can plan or have a series of programmes and action steps. They should give the people the necessary monies or budgets as well as the needed resources such as manpower, equipment and materials to effect the change.

If need be, leaders can also coach or train their people to prepare them for the change. Training will equip the people with the necessary skills set and mental frame to meet with the challenges of change.

And appointing change agents to champion the cause(s) and the change process; leaders should also motivate these champions. These change champions and agents can indeed set examples or be role models for others to follow or emulate them.

Celebrate the little successes of change with the people, and this will motivate or inspire them to greater or newer heights of change.

Tao and Leading Change

> The person who spends today wishing he'd done differently yesterday will do the same tomorrow. (Unknown)

We lead change by accepting change and floating by [we then can be in harmony or do well]. Be supple and flexible, we'll do well.

Ordinarily, it is difficult to change. We are creatures of habit. Routine offers us the feelings of stability and security. We prefer our usual ways; not liking changes, they cause inconvenience to us.

When change happens, we resist change.

It is proposed that by following the tenets highlighted by Lao Tzu's *Tao Teh Ching* (the "Book of Meaning and Life"), one can manage change well in one's life. Here, those tenets and wisdom are examined.

Introduction

> Everything flows, nothing stays still. (Heraclitus)

Much of the wisdom of Taoism is gleaned from Lao Tzu's *Tao Teh Ching*, the "Book of Meaning and Life". Taoism philosophy is a holistic philosophy that emphasises the inter-relationships and interactions of every entity and everything in the universe.

Section Purpose and Objectives

The purpose and objectives of the section are to illustrate the critical importance of the practice of Tao, and show its influence on leading and managing change. To the Tao practitioner, when subscribing to and applying Tao, one is not bothered by change; it is natural and should be accepted as part and parcel of life.

Tao cannot be described; Tao is ineffable. In fact, to describe Tao Itself is un-Tao, words are outside Tao and therefore things outside Tao cannot describe or be attributed to what's inside Tao. Words, belonging to this-worldly, cannot be used to describe the other-worldly.

To the Taoists, change is important.

Move! There is a need for movement. There is a need to change and be as flexible as water. "The highest form of goodness is like water." (Verse 8, *Tao Teh Ching*, Lao Tzu, cited in Wu 1990, p. 10). Water is flexible. We are to be like water, be adaptable, "water knows how to benefit all things without striking with them." (Verse 8, *Tao Teh Ching*, Lao Tzu, cited in Wu 1990, p. 10).

Life's a Rhythm

He who rejects change is the architect of decay. The only institution which rejects progress is the cemetery. (Harold Wilson)

Accept change. Accept change is a constant in our lives and in the universe.

To be the unchanging, let the changing change (Grigg 1994b, p. 123).

Life is in rhythm, there are ups and downs. There's always yin and yang. Life is a long, continuous line of cycles. All nature has a rhythm to it. On earth, in autumn, the most welcoming sights are the green leaves turning gold, and the yellow school buses turning into our streets. Winter comes, and then spring is in the air. Youths are seen playing in the parks. In summer, leaves are green, and trees bear fruits. The earth, the sun, the moon and the planets all travel together with a rhythm. Rhythm is important in music; it must have rhythm to be successful. When our body has a rhythm, we become much stronger and healthier.

In commerce and business, companies are formed and they also grow, undergoing the process of waxing and waning. To grow they need to embrace, accept change; otherwise, they will decline.

Accept change with enthusiasm and change things. Ralph Waldo Emerson said it well, "Nothing great is ever achieved without enthusiasm." With each of us, there lies this spirit of enthusiasm, waiting to be ignited, and good leaders trigger this fire of enthusiasm in people. Once employees and companies accept change, they would gain the edge of being innovative and/or grow. To innovate means to introduce or bring in something new. Innovation is a form of change (though change is a wider concept than innovation and all changes are not necessarily innovations), but indeed, companies and employees must overcome the resistance to change.

Embrace change. Change happens all the time. What one holds as a basic truth today may be outdated tomorrow. Consequently, one will never be successful if one sticks to rigid patterns of thought and let 10 years pass as though they were a single day.

What will follow is a series of ways in which one can lead and manage change:

Meditate

Meditation brings wisdom, lack of meditation leaves ignorance. Know well what leads you forward and what hold you back, and choose the path leads to wisdom. (The Buddha)

How does one cope with change?

Chuang Tzu once said this, "To the mind that is still, the whole universe surrenders."

We meditate to get constancy, and to add regularity. And stable our lives in the universe of change. When we talk about meditation, we are not referring to thinking about our problems; that is thought. In meditation, we attempt to clear our minds.

Our minds are always working. Just relax and allow or give the mind the opportunity to work freely, and our minds too can be creative.

It is often good to have a time or a routine to meditate. Meditation can assist to regulate one's life so that daily living does not create pressures. At times, if one has the time and one should spare such a time, one can take a morning walk. Usually, if there are beautiful trees or a park in one's neighborhood, they can give one a good feeling.

Be Detached

He who stays where he has found his true home endures long. (Lao Tzu, *Tao de ching*, verse 33)

Be unattached; be free.

Do not be attached to the past.

Do not be attached to the future.

Attachment hurts, it causes sufferings and problems.

Just be detached. Do not attach ourselves to anything. When we are detached we have no expectations, anything goes and come what may.

Accept Change

Nothing in this world is permanent. (German proverb)

One does not react with force. (A Taoist tenet and contributions to martial arts such as *Taichi* and *Aikido*)

Change happens. Accept change. Allow change to happen.

Absorb change and melt or merge with change; breathe in change. Change is the basic principle of nature. In trade and business, customers' needs, requirements and tastes change. Technology changes too. When we accept change, we don't become complacent or take things for granted.

Accept all possibilities. There's no limit to what can happen or change.

A snake has to shed its old skin to allow growth and change to occur. "They keep moving the cheese." (Johnson 1998). Resistance is futile. Going against the grain does not serve any purpose.

In our lives, we should "smell the cheese often so you know when it is getting old." (Johnson 1998). We need to get out of our comfort zone. And accept the change as a challenge (Low 2001).

This point can perhaps be better understood when seen from the perspective of the eagles' renewal process. When eagles are 30 years old, they go through a process of renewal. Finding a secret or hidden place high in the mountains, the old eagle with curved beak begins to claw at its face, and tear out the old feathers that by now become less airborne. As a result, it bleeds badly. But this is necessary for the eagle in order to revitalise or renew its strengths. If the eagle did not do this, it would not be able to live to its normal 40 years (Ozirney 2009). It is thus vital for the eagle to undergo the change and the challenging process to strengthen and be rejuvenated (Low and Ang 2010). We simply need to accept the change (challenging) process, learn and grow. It's part of life and living.

Accept Certainty, Accept Uncertainty

> If you're in bad situation, don't worry it'll change. If you're in a good situation, don't worry it'll change. (John A. Simone, Jr.)

Tao is everything yet it is nothing. Tao is certain; Tao is uncertain. There is the Yin, and there is the Yang.

Life is breathing in. Death is breathing out. Each time we breathe in, we live or are alive and each time, we breathe out, we are dead. We change.

Life is change. "Move with the cheese" (Johnson 1998). And not only that, the Tao proponent even stabilizes change. (S)he meditates. Accept change as a rhythm and meditation as constancy and regularity. And that settles it!

Then again, life is uncertain. Accept uncertainty. And now we are adding certainty to uncertainty!

In life and as a leader, the moment we give up certainty, learning begins Grigg (1994a). Be absolutely sure and certain, we'll never learn. (Low 2011). When we are raw, we are in the process of ripening—we learn but when we think we are ripe, we rot! We think we are ripe, we stop learning, we don't learn!

Go with the Flow

> Life belongs to the living, and he who lives must be prepared for changes. (Goethe)

There must be a flow Cite Heider (1994). There should not be a blockade or a choke. Blood is life; it should be well circulated within the body. Blood must flow, life must go on.

Air must flow, air must be circulated. Money is given, received, and exchanged. Buildings are built, renovated and demolished. Anything, everything on earth must come and go. What comes must go.

Roses grow from buds and the seedling matures and flowers. The roses wither, and the rose plant dies. And the dead plant provides fertiliser for the growth of a new rose plant.

And this will also pass.

One does not resent change, but understands and accepts it. One does not resent life but enjoys it.

Contrary to Johnson (1998)'s anticipate change as one gets ready for the cheese to move on. Here, in Taoism, it is advised to go with the flow; be with nature. Be natural. Rain drops, they go downwards and they do not go upwards. Once one accepts change, one does not anticipate as anticipation only brings anxieties, fears and unnecessary worries—what may come? (Is it something bad? Is it something dangerous?) How do we know? Who knows? Who cares? Just float or go with the flow, and there is no anticipation.

Going with the flow also means accepting the outcome, whether it is good, bad or ugly. Or whatever it may be. One just does without any expectations or even thinking of what the outcome may be.

This author also holds the view that as we go with the flow, no one can go back and make a brand new start, but each and every one of us can start from now and make a brand new end. And interestingly, every end or exit is an entry somewhere else.

Appreciate the Present

Z stands for zest for life. It is to appreciate life in all its vitality and exuberance. (Deepak Chopra)

Have a zest for the present.

When one's attention is in the present moment, one is in the presence of the Tao and Tao is present in one.

One is where one is. Take oneself to the present. Appreciate the present. Simply know and be aware of the present, of what you are doing.

The presence of Tao is everywhere, and one has only to consciously know and embrace it your awareness and attention.

Be Supple

When we are no longer able to change a situation, we are challenged to change ourselves. (Victor Frankl)

He who rejects change is the architect of decay. The only human institution which rejects progress is the cemetery. (Harold Wilson)

And be flexible enough. When we willingly accept change, we are like babies whose bodies are supple. When we accept change, that's life and living! We then become disciples of life and living.

When we refuse to change or are inflexible to change, we get clumsy to change, we are courting hardships and death. When death comes, our body is inflexible and rigid. Clearly, we would want to avoid death or rigidity in our lives.

Realise the Energy (*ki or chi*) (That Comes with Each Change)

Happiness is the absence of the striving for happiness. (Chuang Tzu)
    Life is about chi, when we have chi, we become enthusiastic, we will act and change will take place. (Patrick Kim Cheng Low)

There's no point in resisting.

Harmonise instead. Harmonise the interaction of all the elements or forces.

Realise that with each change comes a high level of energy (*chi* or *ki*), embrace change and tap the energy well.

Realise the power with the change. In terms of power, "feel powerful! When you feel weak, you will lose. Feel powerful and be powerful, you will be powerful!" (Low 2010a).

Seek the Permanent

A thing of beauty is a joy forever. (English proverb)

To paraphrase a Zen saying, perhaps we can say this: To follow the path, look to the master (Absolute Reality), follow the master (Absolute Reality), walk with the master (Absolute Reality), see through the master (Absolute Reality), become the master (Absolute Reality). In other words, merge with the Absolute Reality.

Or to be less esoteric and more concrete, anchor ourselves in the Absolute Reality, the Universe or God, rely on God. Don't follow in the footsteps of the sages, but seek what they sought (Low 2011).

Anchor ourselves in the spirit and in spirituality; and what is internal or inside us. After all, our spirit or some may call our soul lives.

Section Conclusion

Overall, one should note that "desire that has no desire is the Way" (Loy 1990, p. 33) to coping with and leading change. Pursuing allure and riches, we only find clouds and smoke. Profit, gain and repute are obstacles to pupils of the Way; come what may, we simply move. Everything in the heart should be as one, that is, emptiness.

Life is change, get out of the comfort zone, understand, absorb and accept change. Meditate and have stability in place in the sea of changes. We appreciate the present, then learn and improve ourselves while living the fullest and most importantly, we need to secure ourselves in the spirit and in spirituality; that is not temporal but permanent.

Leading Change, the Way of Confucius

Introduction

> The world hates change, yet it is the only thing that has brought progress. (Charles F. Kettering)

Understanding change and leading change are the key themes of leadership and management today. Here, we look at leading change from the Confucian perspective. Note that Confucius himself changed jobs and travelled from county to county, advising various rulers.

This aim and objectives of the section are to examine leading change as derived from the teachings of Confucius. These are accordingly based on the author's interpretations of the Master's teachings as well as his dialogues and interviews with several Confucian or Chinese respondents in Brunei Darussalam, Malaysia and Singapore. The Confucian perspective on leading change includes these features, and they are as follows:

Having No Attachment

> Be awake. (The Buddha)

If you find yourself resisting change, ask yourself why? Are you being attached to an existing way?

For Confucius, there should be no attachment, things come and go. Adapting to the ever-changing present is essential for success in the unpredictable future.

Here, non-attachment as well as learning and self-cultivation help. As long as we live we learn, it is a never-ending process.

Looking at Rites and Rituals

> Celebrate what you want to see more of. (Tom Peters)

These are aimed at disciplining oneself as well as giving one the necessary stability. Routines are not at all entirely bad; they are necessary to give one a sense of security too.

Though in some ways one can grow one's attachment to a particular ritual or practice, rituals are simply practical or pragmatic. They, to this author, also remind us of our unchanging values or key principles which we adhere to—things changed and/or may change, but not our core values.

Interestingly, Confucius said that individuals have the internal ability to develop moral standards and abide by them, and that rule by man is more effective than rule by law. Such a belief diminishes the importance of regulation by rules. (Sun 2008, p. 121)

Changing Naturally

> When you pass through, no one can pin you down, no one can call you ack. (Ying-An)

It is certainly good to take things naturally. And we need to keep reminding ourselves that change is natural.

> While standing by a river, the Master said, 'What passes away is, perhaps, like this. Day and night it never lets up.' (*Confucius—The Analects*, Chap. IX, verse 17) (Lau 1979, p. 98).

One Chinese respondent spoke of "As the world is changing so rapidly, we must learn, keep on changing, and be keen to apply new knowledge; otherwise, we'll be obsolete in no time."

People live with change constantly in a lifetime; everyone goes through personal transformation from infancy to teenager, young adult to middle age and finally old age. But what is critical is that each learns and self-cultivates oneself for the better (striving to be a gentle-person, *junzi*).

The Master pointed out, "It is these things that cause me concern: failure to cultivate virtue, failure to go more deeply into what I have learned, inability, when I am told what is right, to move to where it is, and inability to reform myself when I have defects." (*Confucius—The Analects*, Book VII: 3, Lau 1979: 86).

There are always ups and downs, and one changes (and for the better).

Remembering and Avoiding Complacency

> Change yourself and your fortune will change. (Portuguese saying)

> Do not be like cold rice! (Or lukewarm in one's approach) Most people like warm rice; it's better and nicer to eat warm rice. (Patrick Kim Cheng Low)

We need to be prudent. Confucians also value being cautious or prudent.

Note that success normally carries a hidden risk; we need to be careful since we can also get complacent. And we need to avoid this and embrace change willingly. Here, we can say that the Confucian leaders are also achievement-orientated.

"If my children are not so good to take over by business, I'll prudently or in fact, smartly hire professionals. . . . . .to better my business", said one respondent to this author.

Treating People Humanely and Compassionately

> People before products. (Matsushita Konosuke)

> To put the world right in order, we must first put the nation in order; to put the nation in order, we must first put the family in order; to put the family in order, we must first cultivate our personal life; we must first set our hearts right. (Confucius)

Fig. 14.1 People are gems, they are uncut diamonds. For Confucian leaders, they get their hearts right first; they show their care and look at the human side of change

Like Gandhi, though these were said more than 2000 years ago, Confucius urged people that the change starts with oneself, that is, us! Be the change that we want to be. Indeed this is a good way, and this aspect is very positive.

For Confucius, human beings are important. A modern-day Confucian such as the late Matsushita Konosuke believed that "people are diamonds in the rough" (PHP Institute Inc. 1994, p. 54).

We really need to get our hearts right first. We should look at the human side of change. Do not implement change for the sake of change. Be prudent. Adopt gradual change; this is a wise move; after all, gradual change is easier to be accepted and implemented (Fig. 14.1).

Applying the Golden Rule and Being Empathetic

> The Golden Rule is of no use to you whatever unless you realise it is your move. (Frank Crane)

Applying the Golden Rule and being empathetic (Low 2010b, c), the Confucian leader listens and helps his or her people to cope with and tide over the change.

The Confucian leader practises *"Shu"* or reciprocity. And a person attempting to live by this rule or value treats all people with consideration. She does not impose on others what she herself does not desire. Be nice to others when effecting change. "Therefore, in an organization or nation where everybody is considerate, treating each other and the environment well, there would be less conflict in all dealings *and change"*. (Low 2010b, p. 56, *italics mine*).

The Confucian leader really assists others. Working in a team fashion, (s)he is helpful and relates well with his or her people; he shows much warm and compassionate.

Learning

One should learn and be trained, becoming "little dragons" (Patrick Kim Cheng Low 2010d, p. 16)

Learn to think continentally. (Alexander Hamilton)

It is said that most people rust out than wear out—this is when they do little learning. Several respondents expressed that "we learn" and "we cannot take it that that this company would operate in a stable state". Besides, "overtime, internal and external circumstances and setting keep on changing, and that is why we need to learn and improve or be innovative in our business."

Confucius stressed on learning. The Master pointed out, "Quietly to store up knowledge in my mind, to learn without flagging, to teach without growing weary, these present me with no difficulties." (*Confucius—The Analects*, Book VII: 2, Lau 1979, p. 86).

"Learning prevents one from being narrow-minded" (Low 2009a, b, 2010b, p. 18), and instead be more open to ideas and change. This is the beauty of it as we (individually, groups and organisations) learn; there is much generative learning. Individual learning as well as team learning is encouraged, and everyone grows. Organisations become organic or organismic (biological) organisations; they are alive and respond well to a changing environment. Becoming learning organisations and being flexible, such organisations can better cope with the competition and change.

It is worthy to note that at each stage of our life, we learn to cope with change. Learn from others. We should seek out people who welcome change, and become their friends and allies. In business, we "should learn and continuously keep on improving the service" (Low 2010a, p. 58), this is part of the change for the better process.

Correcting Mistakes

Not to correct the mistake one has made is to err indeed. (Confucius, cited in Zhou 2005, p. 78)

Low (2010a) has also argued that for Confucius, changes need to be made to correct one's mistakes and the change should be responsive, and not reactive. For the Master, "one should never be afraid of correcting mistakes one has made". Service excellence (change) thus also needs to instituted; and indeed be done well; it should be planned and not be reactive. One has to plan.

The Master said, "To attack a task from the wrong end can do nothing but harm." (*Confucius—The Analects*, Book II: 16, Lau 1979, cited in Low 2010a, p. 59). And "not to correct the mistake one has made is to err indeed." (Zhou 2005, p. 78). Here, in initiating or implementing change, business owners, managers and leaders need to plan and have service recovery programmes, handling and rectifying customer complaints as well as correcting service breakdowns.

Giving Training

Learning colours a man more than the deepest dye. (Chinese proverb) (Also cited in Low 2005, p. 9)

As said, Confucius encouraged learning. To lead change, leaders need to educate their people; leaders care for their people and they guide, train and/or coach them to cope with change.

Low (2005, p. 65) has also highlighted the need to encourage participation in training and change; he cites a Spanish proverb, "more things grow in the garden than the garden grows". Ask your people for suggestions while weaving ideas together and involving them in the training and the change process.

Benchmarking

We cannot change anything until we accept it. Condemnation does not liberate, it oppresses. (Carl Jung)

The hindering behaviour to change is perhaps when we have no reference points to compare, contrast or benchmark. For organisations, benchmarking should be adopted. Benchmarking is a reference or position from which measurements may be made. And this is necessary to avoid or prevent us from getting complacent or obsolete as well as to continuously improve ourselves and change for the better.

The Master once said, "Even when walking in the company of two other men, I am bound to be able to learn from them. The good points of the one I copy; the bad points of the other I correct in myself." (*Confucius—The Analects*, VII verse 22) (Lau 1979, p. 88).

In *The Great Learning,* Confucius noted that:

Illustrious virtue; to renovate the people; and to rest in the highest excellence. Su et al. (1998, p. 6).

In other words, to attain the ultimate in learning, one must start from knowing the point at which to rest. The object of pursuit is then determined. With that being determined, a "calm unperturbedness" (as cited from Confucius in *The Great Learning*) may then be achieved. From that calmness, tranquil repose can then be achieved. In that repose, there may be careful deliberation (decision-making) and that deliberation will be followed by the attainment of the desired end.

Section Conclusion

Learning is good, embrace learning. Change is good, embrace change. Learning to cope with change, we improve ourselves.

It is good here to reinstate what Low (2010b, p. 60) has pointed out, and to paraphrase it ultimately, the Confucian principles and values are intended to be put into practice. And without practice and actions, they are useless. What more, better performance comes hand in hand with practice, service improvements and more change actions.

Agreeably, a leader who thus leads change require to demonstrate and to set a good example that (s)he can change him(herself) or otherwise it is very hard for him or her to influence or persuade his or her team (company) to change.

Checkpoint: Think About It

Read and review each section in this chapter.

Review these key points and when you have finished the quiz, check your answers. Check also with your close friends or associates.

Change

1. What is your notion or idea of change?
2. What is your attitude towards change?
3. Do you like changes? How do you find change?
4. What attitude should you adopt if you want to cope well with change?
5. How open are you to change?
6. How are you to cope with change?
7. Do you understand the issues involved in the change? How well do you learn and understand the issues involved in the change? How well are you to cope with the change?
8. How equipped are you to meet the change? How well are you to meet the change?
9. How well are you to meet the challenges?
10. How driven are you to effect the change?
11. Identify people and ask yourself: Who can champion your change process?
12. How well can you get support from those around you?

Weak Leaders and Leading Change

1. What weak leaders do when leading change?
2. What are the bad ways of weak leaders when leading change?
3. What should the things I need to avoid when leading change?

What Do Leaders Need to Do When Leading Change?

1. What should I do when leading change?
2. How can I prepare for change? What should I do to prepare for change?
3. What should the things I need to do when leading change?

4. What are the resources I need to effect the change?

Tao and Leading Change

1. What are your views to change?
2. What should leaders do to lead change?
3. How do you respond to change?
4. What are your people's views of change?
5. How your people respond to change?
6. How can you lead change?
7. Look through these points in terms of Tao and leading change, do you
   - Meditate?
   - Practise detachment?
   - Accept change?
   - Accept certainty, Accept uncertainty?
   - Go with the flow?
   - Feel and appreciate the present?
   - Become supple?
   - Realise or tap the energy (*ki*) (that comes with each change)?
   - Seek the permanent?
8. How do you move your people from status quo to change?
9. How do you motivate your people to change?
10. How do you motivate your people to excel?

Leading Change, the Way of Confucius

1. Review these key points and when you have finished the quiz, check your answers. Check also with your close friends or associates. To lead change—the Confucius' way, do I apply the following?
   - Having no attachment
   - Looking at rites and rituals
   - Changing naturally
   - Remembering and avoiding complacency
   - Treating people humanely and compassionately
   - Learning
   - Correcting mistakes
   - Giving training
   - Benchmarking
2. Write down the key lessons you gain from this section "Leading Change, the Way of Confucius".

   _____

   _____

   _____

3. Write down or list any change you would like and plan for them.

   _____

   _____

   _____

4. List what you would like to learn or improve upon.

   _____

   _____

   _____

5. What can you learn from others (here, please specify the "others")?
6. How can you learn from them?
7. Write down what you would like to be able to do in the future.

   _____

   _____

   _____

8. Write down what skills you would like to have in the future.

   _____

   _____

   _____

9. What are the ways in which your (unit/department) organisation can cope with change?
10. Who can champion the change initiative(s) and process?

Self-Esteem Booster Activities/Exercises

1. Each morning the minute when you get up, repeat to yourself at least three times: "The only person you can change is you."

Also, visualise your change or switch. See yourself happily adopting the change.

References

Grigg, R. (1994a). *The Tao of being*. Singapore: S.S. Mubaruk & Brothers Pte. Ltd.

Grigg, R. (1994b). *The Tao of relationships*. Singapore: S.S. Mubaruk & Brothers Pte. Ltd.

Heider, J. (1994). *The Tao of leadership*. Singapore: S.S. Mubaruk & Brothers Pte. Ltd.

Johnson, S. (1998). *Who moved my cheese?* New York: Putnam Adult.

Lau, D. C. (1979). *Confucius – The Analects (Lun Yu)*. London: Penguin Group.

Low, K. C. P. (2001). *The power of relationships*. Singapore: BusinesscrAFT Consultancy.

Low, K. C. P. (2005). *Training success: Understanding the learning and training essentials*. India: The ICFAI University Press.

Low, K. C. P. (2009a). The way of the dragon: Some strategic leadership ways. *Leadership and Organizational Management Journal, 2009*(2), 40–59.

Low, K. C. P. (2009b). Leading globally – What makes a successful global leader in today's turbulent times?. In *e-Leader conference*. CASA: Chinese American Scholars Association, Tallinn, Estonia, 8–10 June 2009. Accessed September 5, 2009 from http://www.g-casa.com/conferences/tallinn/pdf%20papers/Low.pdf

Low, K. C. P. (2010a). *Successfully negotiating in Asia.* Heidelberg: Springer.

Low, K. C. P. (2010b). Values make a leader, the Confucian perspective. *Insights to a Changing World, 2010*(2), 13–28.

Low, K. C. P. (2010c). Confucius, customer service and serve excellence. *Conflict Resolution and Negotiation, 2010*(4), 53–61.

Low, K. C. P. (2010d). Applying strategic leadership, the way of the dragon. In *e-Leader Conference.* Chinese American Scholars' Association: CASA, 4–6 January 2010, Singapore.

Low, K. C. P. (2011). Confucius, the value of benevolence and what's in it for humanity? *Conflict Resolution and Negotiation Journal, 2011*(1), 32–43.

Low, K. C. P., & Ang, S. L. (2010). Leadership lessons from the animal kingdom?. In *e-Leader Chinese American Scholars' Association: CASA Conference.* 4–6 January 2010, Singapore.

Low, K. C. P., & Teo, T. C. (2015). Tsunami leaders and their style(s) and ways. *International Journal of Business and Social Science, 6*(9), 31–46.

Loy, C.-Y. (1990). *The book of the heart: Embracing the Tao.* Boston: Shambala.

Ozirney, L. (2009). *Eagles.* Women Ministries, Baptist general conference of Canada. Accessed September 12, 2009 from http://www.bgc.ca/index.php?option=com_content&task=view&id=139&Itemid=198

PHP Institute, Inc. (1994). *Matsushita Konosuke (1894–1989): His life & his legacy.* Japan: PHP Institute, Inc..

Su, D. S., Yang, Z., & Hulpke, J. F. (1998). A management culture revolution for the new century?. *Journal of Applied Management Studies*, June edition [Online]. Available: http://www.proquest.wni.com/PQdweb.htm

Sun, C. T. L. (2008). *Themes in Chinese psychology.* Singapore: Cengage Learning.

Wu, J. C. H. (1990). *Lao Tzu: Tao Teh Ching.* Boston/London: Shambala Publications Inc..

Zhou, K. (2005). *A basic Confucius* (1st ed.). China: Long River Press.

The *Shinkansen* (Japanese Bullet Train) Effect

Leadership and Team Lessons

From the outset, it should be stressed that greater emphasis should be made on collective rather than individual leadership If individual leadership is stressed, then leadership development has become and develop to a point of being too individually focused and/or even elitist. There is a transition occurring from the old paradigm in which leadership resided in a person or role, to a new one in which leadership is a collective process that is spread throughout networks or groups of people. The question will change from, "Who are the leaders?" to "What conditions or situations do all of us need for leadership to grow or succeed in the group?" How do we spread leadership capacity throughout the organisation and democratise leadership?

Interestingly, in the Asian context, *wayang* (Malay for a theatrical performance employing puppets or human dancers) or Chinese opera is an open-air theatre performance that includes a wide range of art forms such as song, mime, dance, acrobatics and even martial arts. Chinese opera performance or *getai* are common during the Hungry Ghosts Festivals (Seventh Lunar Month periods). These were and are still common in China (it is said that Beijing Opera is the quintessence of China) and especially in the South East Asian countries such as in Malaysia and Singapore—indeed these groups or troupe members have learnt (or are forced to learn) to be team players and practice teambuilding.

And indeed so when teambuilding is applied in the monasteries and nunneries, monks and nuns respectively carry out their various duties in teamwork or synergized ways, they function well. Living and working with mutual respect, people are happy, in harmony and with concord.

In most organisational work, teambuilding and team success lead to organisational success. And in sales, team success brings about sales success—successful teamselling (Low and Ibrayeva 2006).

In this section, what are thus being examined are the leadership and team lessons and insights drawn from *Shinkansen*, the Japanese bullet train, and in essence, the paper, using a variety of wise sayings and proverbs, demonstrates the relevance of team leadership cum effective teamwork to organisations and businesses. Basically, if we can apply the *Shinkansen* effect which is so much needed, the future of an organisation would most certainly be better.

Introduction

Talent wins games, but teamwork and intelligence wins championships. (Michael Jordan)

Section's Purpose and Objectives

The purpose and objectives of the section are to draw team leadership cum team lessons and insights from *Shinkansen* or even the *Harmony Express*, the Chinese equivalent, and assess what is relevant to organisations and businesses.

It was the Japanese who invented the famous bullet train that stunned the world with its unmatched speed. Indeed the Japanese bullet train system has been long credited with being the world's first purpose-built high-speed railway, and the model and inspiration for all other similar type systems running today. The reputation it has earned for safety, speed and punctuality is unsurpassed. [Wholly Chinese-built, though using technology from Siemens and Kawasaki, the Harmony Express is faster than Japan's *Shinkansen* bullet trains and France's TGVs (Train à Grande Vitesse, meaning high-speed train)—*The Telegraph* 2010.]

In terms of safety, it is said that there has never been a death on the bullet train system since its inception in 1964, other than that caused by deliberate passenger misadventure. There has never been a serious accident, let alone a fatality, to any of the three billion passengers who have so far used the *Shinkansen* lines (Semmens 1995).

As for speed, the *Shinkansen* holds the present world records for the fastest average speed between two station stops—261.8 kilometres per hour (km/h) between Hiroshima and Kokura (192.0 km in 44 min), and the fastest average speed between starting and terminating stations—242.5 km/h between Shin-Osaka and Hakata (553.7 km in 2 h 17 min). These records are from the 500 series *Nozomi* trains running at a maximum speed of 300 km/h between Shin-Osaka and Hakata, which commenced in March 1997. A magnetic levitation test vehicle has also clocked the fastest manned run at 531 km/h.

With regard to punctuality, the Japanese bullet trains arrive at their destination punctually One record shows that in 1 year, the total time that ALL bullets trains were late by was 12 s! (http://www.geocities.com/Tokyo/island/2589/nmt/bullet.html)

The bullet train's secret lies in that each car has its own small engine, and the total force of these motors produces a final speed that is faster, more efficient, and nearly instantaneous. The synergised effect of these engines all moving the train in unison is called the *Shinkansen* effect. Imagine or picture an organisation as a huge train, with its motors and cars. Each unit of an organisation is to ensure that all or the entire organisation attains *Shinkansen*, the sense of smart teamwork that creates better service. *Shinkansen*—becomes the feeling of all for one and one for all. *Shinkansen* or team success as what the author would attribute to—this effort that lends value to our work and imagination to our service. Basically, if we can apply the *Shinkansen* effect which is so much needed, the future of an organisation would most certainly be better.

The *Shinkansen* Effect on Team Leadership and Teamwork

Coming together is a beginning, staying together is progress, and working together is success. (Henry Ford)

Using the *Shinkansen* metaphor and applications (as in Low 2011a), the author is putting up the case of the effects and benefits of effective team leadership cum teamwork. Accordingly, the future is team leadership cum smart teamwork. The world is becoming increasingly diversified, and smart teamwork, despite their individual differences, capitalise on their common goal and common ground that supply the thread that defines and enables them to work as a team, and at that, even more so successfully.

To demonstrate the fundamentals of teamwork, this author would like to indicate what Low (2003, p. 1) has highlighted; he uses an analogy on organisational structures when there is essentially little or no collaboration and teamwork. Such organisational structure precisely happen when there is wedge between an organisation's lead and the led and when little or no team spirit. To quote:

An organisation is like a tree full of monkeys—all on different levels, some climbing up.
The monkeys at the top look down and see a tree full of smiling faces.
The monkeys at the bottom look up and see nothing but 'ass holes'.
All the while, the monkeys at the top will get the fruits first, and most of the time, they will eventually produce SHIT for all the monkeys below. And all the time, that is what the monkeys below will get.

Low (2003, p. 2) further indicates that such thing happens, there is much lack of trust. On one hand, the managers get all the credits for the work done. On the other hand, the organisation's employees feel exploited and de-motivated. The managers also do not communicate much with their subordinates; and team spirit is really needed in any organisation.

Moving from Goodness to Greatness

If two men unite, their money will buy gold. (Chinese proverb)

TEAM: Together Even Achieves More; after all—as a Zen Japanese saying goes, "The moon shows in every pool; in every pool the one moon" (Low 2010a, p. 8).

A Chinese proverb goes as follows, "a single tree makes no forest; one string makes no music." It's really teamwork for the greater good. Interestingly, Wells et al. (2010) speak of the ant colonies operating through organised co-operation and task-sharing. Work together marvellously, ants even capture prey that is bigger than they are, and they can call up extra workers when an abundant food source is discovered; and they can defend a colony by fending off invaders.

Practical case evidence also suggests that teams typically outperform individuals when the tasks being done require multiple skills, judgment and experience (Macmillan 2001). There's a clear need to use strengths in numbers—"Spices are nice. Spiced rice is thrice nice." And like a maestro, team leader will play to their strengths to create a melodious symphony (Low 2003, p. 21).

Like *Shinkansen* in which each car has its own small engine (also read as its own strengths), winning teams can be powerful or cutting edge with superior outputs and high relationships when their team leaders know and play up to their people's strengths. It's the basic business insight that inspired Collins' (2001) *Good to Great* book, and this idea also applies to team success and the way team leaders lead. It is far more effective to build on one's people strengths than to worry too much about their weaknesses. Such an idea and insight can also be very motivating to the people one motivates. Of course, the leader really needs to know his (her) people's strengths so that (s)he can help them to express even more. [Note that Clifton and Nelson (1992) also argued that time and energy spent trying to improve a weakness could far more productively be focused on maximising a particular strength. Each of us needs to "manage" weakness, not try to "overcome" them, because it is our strengths which we can best contribute to the world, and that will bring us our greatest satisfaction.]

Interestingly, Fisher et al. (1995) offered this useful pointer—team leaders should assume the best about people for team success. When team leaders assume that the people they work with are lazy, mean or stupid, it becomes very counter-productive. This is because, among other things, such assumptions cause people to want to defend their viewpoints and fight to win for their side of the argument. This makes it difficult to sit down and work things out or improve things together. As team leaders, we thus need to change the way we think about work and about others. In other words, as opposed to McGregor's (1960, 2006) Theory X, the latter's Theory Y is embraced—akin to one of Matsushita's leadership tenets, that is, a leader must trust his staff to get the best out of them (Matsushita 1991). And what more, effective team leaders need to assume that problem(s) is caused by good people who are trying their best they could with the information, systems and skills they had at the time. Then, team leaders work to better information, systems and skills. More specifically, they need to focus on creating good real-time information systems; without them, teams can't make good decisions.

Boosting the 1 + 1 = 5 (Synergy)

To beat a tiger, one must have a brothers help. (Chinese proverb)

In Malay-Muslim majority countries such as Malaysia and Brunei, the Malays are said to be united and cooperative. A Malay proverb goes as such, *kuat berdiri pohon kerana akarnya, kuat akar kerana tanah*. In English, it means, 'the strength of the trunk derives from the roots, the strength of the roots derives from the earth'; a country or an organisation is strong as a result of its prominent leader, who in turn, is strong because the followers (subordinates) are united. They synergise well and the work gets done.

In the same way as the Chinese saying goes, "one cannot clap with one hand", none of us is as smart as all of us; and without teamwork, there is no synergy.

Henry Ford's quote is also ever relevant; he once said, "Coming together is a beginning. Keeping together is progress. Working together is success." Through team success, superior outputs and high productivity are attained. As Low (2003, p. 10) has argued, teams and allow its members to "get a better perspective on the whole task and a better understanding of ways to make improvement." And because of synergy, the team can and will outperform a group of individuals. Interestingly, teamwork thus divides the task, with different team members having different tea roles, and doubles the success.

What more, with team and "action-centred leadership", the job or task gets done, the relationships get going—team members are happy, and the individuals grow and develop themselves, being coached and trained by the team leader. Adair (1998) sees "action-centred leadership" as a process of meeting all three of these essential needs: the task (the needs relating to achieving the goal), the team (the needs relating to building and maintaining the group) and the individual (the needs of the follower(s)).

Enhancing Successful Leadership, Team Roles and Shared Leadership

Help your brother's boat across, and your own will reach the shore. (Hindu proverb)

Leaders are fundamental to teams since they set the vision and bring the team together. Strong leaders also protect their teams.

It is almost impossible to reach one's goals alone. We need people, roles and relationships. And we need teams. Team members, when given their respective roles and responsibilities, do and execute their tasks can produce wonderful output or get good results. And when a team goal is achieved, there is a payoff for all the team members. Achievement is shared, rewards are distributed, every one wins.

Michael Jordan once said that "talent wins games, but teamwork and intelligence wins championships." Teamwork is so essential. "Usually personal motives would be pushed aside to allow the team motives to succeed. With teamwork, there is increased ability and desire to improve" (Low 2003, p. 12). Now and in the future, team effectiveness is the key to successful leadership as well as management.

Shared leadership should also be encouraged and practiced. Like each powered *Shinkansen* carriage, each team member holds the potential or seed for greatness, and into that greatness they will become when empowered or allowed to. Be a team leader, not a boss. There is also a need to rotate team leadership among team members.

Effecting Increased Communications

The more high-tech the world gets, the more 'cold' it is and, the more we need the soft human touch. (Low 2001, p. 13)

Team members get comfortable and relate well with each other. Status within the team is removed, if not minimised, akin to the Russian proverb, "after the game, the king and the pawn are kept in the same box". And other barriers are also removed. There is better coordination, and team(s) result(s) in increased communications within the organisation, with the left hand now knowing what the right hand is doing.

Hallam and Campbell's (1992) research indicated that high levels of communications were often associated with effective teams. The authors believed this level of communication helped team members to stay focused on the mission and to take advantage of the skills, knowledge and resources available to the team. High levels of communication too helped to reduce or minimise interpersonal conflicts on the team which often drained energy needed for team success and effectiveness. The current authors believe that high levels of communication lead to high-touch and better relationships.

Increased communications indeed promote better relationships among the team members. Many people who are involved in teams intimated these to this author, "they like working in teams, and enjoy the relationships with team members. The nice or sweet thing about teamwork is that you always have others on your side"; "we support each other, and all of us feel good and we can overcome whatever obstacles" (interviewees' input).

Growing Holistic Thinking

Even a sheet of paper has two sides. (Japanese proverb)
    A fog cannot be dispelled by a fan. (Japanese saying)

Narrow thinking can be myopic and stuffy, it can, in fact, lead to bad decisions being made; it should thus be avoided.

On the other hand, holistic or big picture thinking results in better decision-making; not just a portion, part of the picture or a tree, but the whole picture—the entire forest—is seen.

Being Organic

Virtue is not knowing but doing. (Japanese)

With keen learning, open-mindedness and practical creativity stressed (Low, 2005), teams can indeed be organic (not mechanistic). Teams are organic, and being organic has its key advantages and benefits. "Teams learn and grow. They are dynamic. They lead to continuous improvement. No one knows the job, tasks and goals better than a team" (Low 2003, p. 12).

There is also a shift from individually-led mindset to a participative mind growth. Empowering leadership involves the continual process of creating expanded competence and giving away responsibility. With this, it means leadership exists at every level of the organisation (Low 2003, p. 62).

With much open-mindedness that prevails, team culture is very much in practice in organic organisations. In such organisations, hierarchies are also discouraged while horizontal communication is promoted and paperwork minimized. In contrast with mechanistic organisations which stresses on centralisation and bureaucratic procedures, organic organisations emphasise decentralisation and empowerment. Besides, staff creativity, initiative and team learning are also encouraged, and the people tend to be entrepreneurial and forward-looking (Daft 1998; Cummings and Worley 2001, 2009). In rejuvenating organisations (Organisational Life Cycle: OLC—see Fig. 7.2), teams can also be used to introduce much creativity, life and growth; self-directing teams can serve as a tool to rejuvenate organisations especially when they get old, with too much administration, bureaucratic procedures, paperwork and red-tape as well as slower decisions made. Many prevailing hierarchies and rigidity as well as mechanistic ways of the mature organisation can be got rid of; and smart team small is beautiful and simple ways can then replace them.

Having Improved Morale and Greater Job Satisfaction

It is better to be the head of a chicken than the rear of an ox. (Japanese proverb)

"The history of company success is the history of staff empowerment, involvement and ownership" (Low 2000, 2006, p. 77). And self-directing or empowered teams allow for greater involvement, learning, personal growth and ownership.

Team members learn and grow and team learning is encouraged. As a leader, one lets one's people see one is learning. One also lets the people know that one is a work in progress (Chandler 2009). All these make the team members happy, enjoying an improved morale (Low 2003). Team members ordinarily also enjoy higher self-esteem and increased job satisfaction. Teams, when self-directed or empowered like the powered engine of each *Shinkansen* carriage, thus own their success, and overall, team members are motivated and have a strong sense of fulfilment.

Having a Higher Level of Creativity and Better Problem Resolutions

Two heads are better than one. (English saying)

Teams can be creative, and new product development (NPD) reaped. By bringing together people with a variety of experiences and backgrounds, cross-functional teams increase the creative capacity of an organisation. Studies (for example, Maggin 2004; Parker 2003; Low 2003) have repeatedly shown that the quality of ideas/decisions and the level of creativity emerging from teams are substantially better than from average individuals working alone. A great team, in fact, produces fast, creative, smart, decisive, consistent results. The point is no one can go it alone. People really need to get together to share ideas to achieve a common goal.

Teams such as Quality Circles (QCs) can be tapped to solve problems. Through empowered teams, employees are creatively involved in brainstorming, streamlining work processes and coming out with good or wise solutions as well as product and/or service ideas to work on. Teams can even be innovative, coming out with new and improved products and services for the company's customers.

Creating Greater Customer Satisfaction, Higher Sales and Increased Market Share

Beginning is easy, continuing, hard. (Japanese proverb)

Empowered teams can focus their resources and better satisfy their customers (Low 2000, 2002, 2006; Parker 2003). Units and departments operating in silos, separated from one another, are no good for customer excellence and service recovery (Low 2000, 2002, 2006). Yes, staff in one department may say, "It's not my department! Please refer to the Marketing side"; however, as far as the customer is concerned it doesn't matter which department is responsible, the buck must stop at the Company. And (s)he is indeed dealing with the Company. In many companies such as 3Ms, teamwork should be carried out to attend to the customers, satisfying their needs and requirements. For example, when a new product is to be out, employees in all the local branches are team-briefed so that there is much coordination, and everyone within the team/company is in the know so as to better attend to the customers should there be any enquiries.

Organisations that develop strategies, organisations and human resources based on teambuilding and teamwork will reap countless benefits. In the first instance, it is easier for organisation to implement or carry out the strategies since everyone within the organisation sings the same tune, and from the same song sheet; they understand one another (Low 2003).

Bringing About Greater Business Success

If brothers disagree, the bystander takes advantage. (Chinese proverb)

Low (2003) speaks of the world is changing, companies aplenty and competition goes intense. There are now increasingly strong global competitors. Predators would try to seize the most attractive opportunities. Technology is changing. New products and services are produced and sold. In such a challenging environment, we will find ourselves working with our colleagues, looking at new ways to cooperate, work together and finding the competitive edge. We can also add that a successful team beats with one heart; they are of one mind, sharing the same core values and getting things done in winning ways. Teams are the path to business success and excellence. Only those organisations that have skilful leaders committed to team-work can look into the future with more confidence.

Overall, while the business part is being fulfilled, that is only one part of the equation and the other part, a critical part too is the relationships—as Anthony Robbins puts it, "The quality of your life is the quality of your relationships". The support, people joys, connections and relationships that are so vital to life and human spirit, and that keep us going. It adds purpose and meaning to our lives, sharing key moments of our lives with people who matter. And that, whatever it takes employers and team leaders need to build teams into, growing teams as "families", being supportive to one another as well as life-giving and harmonious living.

Section Concluding Remarks

Go to the people
Learn from them
Love them
Start with what they know
Build on what they have
But of the best leaders
When their task is accomplished
Their work is done
The people will say:
'We have done it ourselves.' (Old Chinese proverb—of Taoist origin)
Teamwork is the fuel that allows common people to attain uncommon results. (Unknown)

It is appropriate to conclude with a quote from Vince Lombardi, a football coach (1913–1970) who once said that, "Individual commitment to a group effort—that is what makes a team work, a company work, a society work, a civilisation work." The future is in the team, teams can be flexible. The future is organisational growth, and that future lies in teams.

Yes, do believe in teams. Even the ants are good in teamwork. There is wisdom and much to learn from the ants (Low 2011b), and their colonies in terms of teamwork and fostering the team spirit among human beings. Yes, do believe in the wisdom of teams. Be team-wise. Certainly there is no better way to address a lack of conviction about teams than by seeing teams in action.

Tao and Team-Building

In this section, the philosophy of Taoism is discussed in relation to how as a leader, one can team-lead, foster relationships with others and practise teambuilding, the *Tao* way. Though coming from various ethnic or racial groups, human beings are ALL ONE (We are all from the one and same source). And all the more cooperation, collaboration and teamwork should be practiced.

Introduction

The Philosophy of Taoism

Much of Taoism wisdom is gleaned from Lao Tzu's *Tao de ching*, the "Book of Meaning and Life" and/or *I Ching* ("Book of Changes"), written some 2500 years ago. Lao Tzu describes the sage, embodying the teachings of the Tao or the Way, as one who places himself behind others in an attitude of humbleness, and thus finds himself ahead. Because they are selfless or without ego, they can succeed in all things.

Tao is said to be ineffable; Tao is non-describable. In fact, to describe Tao Itself is un-Tao, things or words are outside Tao and therefore things outside Tao cannot be described or be attributed to what's inside Tao.

> From of old there are not lacking things that have attained Oneness. The sky attained Oneness and became clear. The earth attained Oneness and became calm. The spirits attained Oneness and became charged with mystical powers; the fountains attained Oneness and became full. The ten thousand creatures attained Oneness ad became reproductive.......All of them are what they are by virtue of Oneness. If the sky were not clear, it would be likely to fall to pieces. If the earth were not calm, it would be likely to burst into bits. If the spirits were not charged with mystical powers, they would be likely cease from being; if the fountains were not full, they would be likely to dry up. If the ten thousand creatures were not reproductive, they would be likely to come to extinction... (Verse 39, *Tao Teh Ching*, Lao Tzu cited in Wu 1990, pp. 58–60).

We are ALL ONE. And all the more teamwork should be practiced.

In Taoism, *Chi* or *ki* (energy) is the life force; all things without *chi* are dead. *Chi* is what gives things life.

Breathing and meditation teach the Tao practitioner to be one with the *chi* of the Universe and to give respect to all the Creator's creatures. When inhaling accordingly, we are drawing in the *chi* to our one point. The *chi* unites with our body to give us strength. And when exhaling, we should feel our own *chi* pour forth from our one point and reach towards the heavens. It is said that this sharing of life energy unites us with the universe.

The air that we breathe is so critically important; it is a gift of love from the universe. We should always be grateful and appreciative of the air we breathe. So also we should learn to appreciate everything in the universe. Through breathing and meditation, it is believed, that we share part of the infinite universe in which all things are united.

Section's Purpose and Objectives

The aim and objectives of this section are to examine good team-leading, the various ways to foster relationships with others (high touch) as well as to practice teambuilding, applying the way of the *Tao*.

The Tao (Yin-Yang) of Relationships: A Balancing of Individual and Team

A cloth is not woven from a single thread. (Chinese proverb)

The individual is in harmony with the team, and the team is harmony with the other teams or organisation as a whole. There is a good balance between the team and other teams or organisation.

Within the team, the wise leader is like water. The leader is not domineering. The Tao leader, as a facilitator, assists and makes things possible. The leader does not push. And the group does not resist. (S)he is aware and applies "in action, timing is everything" (Heider 1994, p. 13).

Lao Tzu says:

Overfill a bowl
And it will spill.
Sharpen a blade too much
And it will lose its sharpness.
Accumulate riches
And you will not be able to safeguard them.
Just complete the tasks before you.
Then withdraw when your work is done.
This is the way of Heaven.

The Tao leader, as an example setter, trusts and be trusted. Speaking quietly and simply, (s)he coaches. Personable, gentle and nurturing, the Tao leader settles for good work and allows others to have the floor.

This author would agree with what one Taoism practitioner had expressed to him; accordingly, he highlighted that "in a team where a leader embraces or works in the way of the Tao, one would not blindly force one's staff to do things that (s)he is not capable of. It basically means that the leader have already studied and understood capability of one's staff beforehand, and one would confidently arrange tasks or a project that (s)he can contribute well to the team, fully using his or her potential."

Forging the bonds between team members, the Tao leader learns to lead:

- Without force or coercion.
- By tapping the potentials of his or her people.
- In a nourishing way; (s)he grows his or her people.
- Without being possessive.
- By being helpful yet without taking credit.

Embrace and Enhance Cooperation and Collaboration

When spiders unite, they can tie up a lion. (An Ethiopian proverb)

One can't throw mud without getting a little on oneself. The reverse is to love and care. . . . . . .learn to love and care. The way of the Tao (Low 2009a, 2009b) is to be compassionate, cooperate and collaborate.

When it comes to working together and team playing, each team member needs to adopt this compassionate stance: Blame yourself as you would blame others; excuse others as you would excuse yourself. And here, the practical questions, as team members, we need to ask include: Do team members listen to each other? At team meetings, do we consider or ignore each other's input? And at work sessions, do we build on the ideas of others? What can team members do promote trust and collaborations?

As an old Chinese saying goes, "The more you sweat in peace time, the less you bleed during war." And of course, every member of the team should put in some efforts to listen to each other, and avoid conflict or disharmony. Fundamentally, team members need to embrace that we are born to cooperate and collaborate, and that teamwork is good; it helps much. Human beings are here, in business and the world, to cooperate and collaborate. It is said that this is human, and this is natural. Tap what is natural for even "without words, without even understanding, lovers find each other" (Grigg 1994a, p. 61; Grigg 1994b).

True, when children are born they hold on to things and that give them a feeling of security. Toddlers are often reluctant to let go of their blankets, bottles and other possessions. They may reuse to share; sharing is something they will learn later, and as parents this is one of the things they need to teach their children. Life is about giving and taking and seriously this author has not seen any successful person who keeps; keeps and keeps. It is very important for human beings to learn to give and share.

It is good to have a cooperative or collaborative atmosphere, building the common ground and generating win-win outcomes for all parties involved (Low 2010b). And the Tao leader indeed downplays the differences and builds the common ground. He links and builds bridges between and among people, individuals within the team.

And indeed people must subscribe that synergy is good. Synergy increases team's efficiency and effectiveness. The work gets done and the people are happy; both the tasks and the relationship factor are taken care of Low (2003).

Adopt an Overall Win-Win Posture and Spirit

One finger can lift a pebble. (Unknown)

Everyone wins when we are in it together, and team work/spirit is applied. This seems pretty obvious, but it is little practiced. It is really the attitude, action and practice that count. Everyone tries. Everyone needs to work at winning together.

How can we adopt or achieve this win-win posture? One way is to use the image of water. Lao Tzu tells us that the supreme virtue is to be like water. Water, he says, benefits all things, yet never contends or competes.

Indeed this brings to mind what is akin to the Chinese proverb that speaks of: "By scrambling for something, both parties look bad; by giving up something, both parties win."

Encourage Equality and Rotate Team Roles

Though a month be a unit, its days are many. (Pashto proverb)

The ox works on the strength of the grass, and the plough on the ox's neck. (Pashto proverb)

After the game of chess, the King, the Queen and the pawns go into the box together. Besides, no matter how high the majestic throne a person sits on, she still sits on his bottom.

The Tao leader practices rotational leadership. Everyone in the team gets the opportunity to play different roles. Everyone has the chance to lead and be led. And as pointed out by Low (2003, pp. 35–40), the team leadership role and several other team roles (for example, supporter, balancer, information giver, recording, coordinating; harmonising) may be used by team members to grow an effective team.

Keep It Simple: Stick to the Vision

There is no more sure tie between friends than when they are united in their objects and wishes. (Cicero)

A leader embracing, seeking or in the path of the Tao would be able to explain and influence the team where one is leading them to. The team members would trust the leader, be convinced and committed to the vision and goals that are laid down by their leader. (Several respondents input)

Perhaps, of Taoism origin, one Chinese proverb says "never do anything that you can do sitting or anything sitting that you can do lying down". As one of Lao Tzu's three treasures is simplicity, the team leader keeps the teamwork simple, sticking to the team's vision. The team's vision ties everyone together within the team, and as one.

If the leader gets too busy, it's the time for the leader has come to return to selfless silence. And leader stays focused of the team's vision and goals.

If the team gets too busy, it's the time for the team has come to return to selfless silence; they ought to go for retreat and take stock of themselves. Have open discussions, and stay focused of the team's vision and its goals.

If there are any conflicts among team members, team members should return to reflections or selfless silence. Instead of squabbling, they need to reflect or see how they can be of help to each other, be team meaningful and stay focused of the team's vision and goals.

Strike a Balance

The miracle is not to fly in the air, or to walk on the water, but to walk on the earth. (Chinese proverb)

The team leader is to seek a balancing of individual and team. There should be a Yin-Yang balance.

Note that too loud and we are not heard. Too bright, and we are not seen.

The Tao leader does not interfere much. (S)he lets the group functions without much interference. The Tao leader does not insists that things come out a certain way.

It is noteworthy that the wise leader does not intervene unnecessarily. His or her presence is felt, but often the group runs itself.

Heider (1994, p. 33) highlights that:

Lesser leaders do a lot, say a lot, have followers and form cliques or cults. Even worse ones use fear to move the group and force to overcome resistance. Only the most dreadful leaders have had bad reputations.

The team should not simply stress on the work, the tasks to be done. It should not be all work; relationships matter too. Strike a balance or be high on both tasks and touch.

The team can also have a balance of good *Yin* and *Yang* activities. Yang activities are of a more outward nature. They include team sports, karaoke and white-rafting. Yin activities are those that lead the team inward, such as meditation, contemplation, walking, reading, or listening to music. By participating in both types of activities, the team is able to balance itself, both internally and externally, thereby achieving harmony in the lives of members within the team.

Facilitate and Make Easy the Teamwork

> Three smiles form a matrimonial connection. A smile can bind a couple, and thus a smile can also impact one's destiny. (Chinese saying)

Using the analogy of being a midwife, Heider (1994, p. 33) points out that the leaders role is to facilitate, helping the process, "do(ing) good without show or fuss".

Keep the members informed. And be willing to share information with them.

Do not intrude. Do not control. "If you must take the lead, lead so that the mother (*team*) is helped, yet still free and in charge." (Heider 1994, p. 33, *italics mine*).

When the baby is born (the team work done and the team's mission accomplished), the mother (the team members) will rightly say, "We did it ourselves!"

Be Without Greed

> A man's greed is like a snake that wants to swallow an elephant. (Chinese proverb)

There is a Chinese saying that goes, "A greedy eagle will rip off its own legs." Greed is self-interest, ego, desire and attachment, one wants to possess and own. And greed is not good.

> The Tao leader is not greedy, selfish or demanding and shares credit with the team members (Heider 1994, p. 149).

If every team member chips in and contributes well, things really get done. And it is, in fact, amazing how much people get things done if they do not worry about who get the credit.

The team will not do well or prosper if the leader gets the lion share of the credit for the team's good work that has been done. The team members will rebel or resist if the leader has strict controls; (s)he needs to ensure that the credits are shared by all the team members, and they get them!

Team members or in fact, all of us should just do the work and get the job done; and that is all. In this regard, this Chinese proverb is apt:

When the sun rises, I go to work.

When the sun goes down, I take my rest. I dig the well from which I drink. I farm the soil which yields my food. I share creation. Kings can do no more.

Be in Harmony

If there is light in the soul

There will be beauty in the person. If there is beauty in the person, there will be harmony in the house. If there is harmony in the house, there will be order in the nation. If there is order in the nation, there will be peace in the world. (Chinese Taoism-inspired proverb)

The Chinese normally prize harmony above all things. A large part of Chinese literature is based on the idea of harmony (Towler 2002).

In Chinese landscape painting, the individual is usually a small dot or speck in the midst of huge mountains piercing through the clouds and rivers, reflecting the fact that the individual blends or harmonises with the environment and setting. Individuals are thus understood to be a small part of the larger universe, hence reminding us of the importance of teamwork, the bigger picture and the Tao.

Just like a family in harmony, a team in harmony will prosper in everything.

In Taoism, a sage is a person who is in total harmony with their world—the world around them as well as the world within them. And team spirit is an essential tool or way to harmonise with others, and the world around us.

By adhering with the words of Lao-tzu, all of us can find a path of personal harmony that will support us in times of conflict:

Yield and become whole.
Bend and one will become straight.
Empty oneself and one will become filled.
Though one grows old
One will be renewed.

It is worthy to note that maintaining one's inner harmony is really more important than one's outer harmony. It is when one depends on outside circumstances for one's inner harmony that one often finds oneself in conflict or in trouble.

One sees things as they really are; one lets go. And by becoming a person with inner harmony and peace, one will bring that sense of harmony and peace to everyone one comes into contact with. This reinforces the team spirit and the joy in working together.

Boost Team Creativity

First attain skill; creativity comes later. (Chinese proverb)

Those who sing always find the song. (Swedish proverb)

Give team incentives and reward team work as well as tap team creativity; the Tao leader needs to boost the *chi* or *ki* (energy) of the team. (S)he should tap the diversity of the team, team members who have different skills, experiences and backgrounds.

Remember two heads are always better than one, and of course the more the merrier! Yes, make team creativity a commonplace and a habit, part and parcel of the teams ways to resolving work problems or coming with better solutions. Team creativity is so vital for the growth of organisations, the organisations get more entrepreneurial. Yes, have fun too. And energise the team by encouraging humour and creativity.

'Many hands make light work', as the Chinese saying goes. The Tao leader should also encourage broad thinking, viewing things or issues from a number of perspectives. (S)he lets many people contribute. Certainly, let a thousand flowers bloom; encourage different perspectives. Promote brainstorming, and let it be one of the team norms or even values; and every member of the team believes in and practices brainstorming, creativity and team synergy.

On the other hand, the leader should also be aware that teams also need outside views or perspectives to prevent group-think; teams need outside or third parties' opinions to give new perspectives. Teams also need a wisp of fresh air coming into the room; otherwise, it's going to one real stuffy room!

Section Conclusion

Through the Tao way, the team leader can indeed forge a greater sense of unity; (s)he creates and leads a winning and effective team, and what more, the team leader has motivated team members with him or her.

Checkpoint: Think About It

Team Leadership and Teambuilding

Review these key points and when you have finished the quiz, check your answers. Check also with your close friends or associates.

Team Leadership and Teambuilding

1. Distinguish a group from a team. What is your notion or idea of a team?
2. What is your attitude towards team leadership/teambuilding?
3. Do you like (promote) teamwork?

4. Do you rotate the team leadership roles among team members?
5. As a team leader, do you ensure that there is the Tao (Yin-Yang) of relationships—a balancing of individual and team?

The Shinkansen (Japanese Bullet Train) Effect

Leadership and Team Lessons

1. Check and review, suggest on the various ways in which as a leader, you could be:
   - Moving from goodness to greatness
   - Boosting the $1 + 1 = 5$ (Synergy)
   - Enhancing successful leadership, team roles and shared leadership
   - Effecting increased communications
   - Growing holistic thinking
   - Being organic
   - Having improved morale and greater job satisfaction
   - Having a higher level of creativity and better problem resolutions
   - Creating greater customer satisfaction, higher sales and increased market share
   - Bringing about greater business success

Tao and Team-Building

1. Look through these points in terms of Tao and team-building, do you:
   - Embrace and enhance cooperation and collaboration?
   - Adopt an overall win-win posture and spirit?
   - Encourage equality and rotate team roles?
   - Keep it simple—stick to the vision?
   - Strike a balance?
   - Facilitate and make easy the teamwork?
   - Be without greed?
   - Be in harmony?
   - Boost team creativity?

Self-Esteem Booster Activities/Exercises

1. Each morning the minute when you get up, repeat to yourself at least three times: "I am a good team leader."

   Also, visualise yourself as such. See yourself happily adopting the team leader role.

References

Adair, J. (1998). *Action-centred leadership*. London: Ashgate Publishing Limited.

Chandler, S. (2009). *100 ways to motivate others*. Singapore: McGraw-Hill.

Clifton, D. O., & Nelson, P. (1992). *Soar with your strengths*. New York: Dell.

Collins, J. (2001). *Good to great*. New York: HarperBusiness.

Cummings, T. G., & Worley, C. G. (2001). *Organization development and change* (7th ed.). Cincinnati, OH: South-Western College.

Cummings, T. G., & Worley, C. G. (2009). *Organization development and change* (8th ed.). Mason, OH: Thomson South-Western.

Daft, R. (1998). *Organization theory and design* (6th ed.). Mason, OH: International Thomson.

Fisher, K., Rayner, S., Belgard, W., et al. (1995). *Tips for teams*. New York: McGraw-Hill.

Grigg, R. (1994a). *The Tao of being*. Singapore: S.S. Mubaruk & Brothers.

Grigg, R. (1994b). *The Tao of relationships*. Singapore: S.S. Mubaruk & Brothers.

Hallam, G. I., & Campbell, D. P. (1992). Selecting team members? Start with a theory of team effectiveness. *Seventh annual meeting of the society of industrial organizational psychologists*, May 1992, Montreal, Canada.

Heider, J. (1994). *The Tao of leadership*. Singapore: S.S. Mubaruk & Brothers.

Low, K. C. P. (2000). *Strategic customer management*. Singapore: BusinesscrAFT™ Consultancy.

Low, K. C. P. (2001). *The power of relationships*. Singapore: BusinesscrAFT™ Consultancy.

Low, K. C. P. (2002). *Strategic customer management*. Singapore: BusinesscrAFT™ Consultancy.

Low, K. C. P. (2003). *Team success*. Singapore: BusinesscrAFT™ Consultancy and Humber Lincoln Resources.

Low, K. C. P. (2005, April–May). Putting learning and creative thinking into practice – The Tao way. *Today's Manager*, pp. 48–49.

Low, K. C. P. (2006). *Strategic customer management* (3rd ed.). Almaty, Kazakhstan: Caspian Publishing House.

Low, K. C. P. (2009a). The way of the dragon: Some strategic leadership ways. *Leadership and Organizational Management Journal, 2009*(2), 40–59.

Low, K. C. P. (2009b). Leading globally – What makes a successful global leader in today's turbulent times? *e-Leader conference*, Tallinn, Estonia: CASA: Chinese American Scholars Association, 8–10 June 2009. Accessed September 5, 2009 from http://www.g-casa.com/conferences/tallinn/pdf%20papers/Low.pdf

Low, K. C. P. (2010a). Zen and leadership – Growing one's leadership excellence. *Insights to a Changing World, 2010*(1), 1–10.

Low, K. C. P. (2010b). *Successfully negotiating in Asia*. Heidelberg: Springer.

Low, K. C. P. (2011a). Learning teamwork and other lessons from the ants. *Business Journal for Entrepreneurs, 2011*(1), 101–116.

Low, K. C. P. (2011b). Leadership and team lessons from *Shinkansen*, the Japanese Bullet Train. *Global Education Journal, 2011*(2), 181–195.

Low, K. C. P., & Ibrayeva, E. (2006). *Sales success: Up our sales*. Almaty, Kazakhstan: I.P. Lukyanova.

Macmillan, P. (2001). *The performance factor: Unlocking the secrets of teamwork*. Nashville, TN: Broadman & Holman.

Maggin, M. (2004). *Making teams work*. New York: McGraw-Hill.

Matsushita, K. (1991). *Velvet glove, iron fist*. Japan: PHP Institute.

McGregor, D. (1960, 2006). *The human side of enterprise* (p. 2006). New York: McGraw-Hill.

Parker, G. M. (2003). *Cross-functional teams*. San Francisco: Jossey-Bass.

Semmens, P. (1995, March). Shinkansen practice and performance. *Japan Railway and Transport Review*, pp. 38–39.

The Telegraph. (2010). China steams ahead with world's fastest train. *The Telegraph*. Accessed December 7, 2010 from http://www.telegraph.co.uk/news/worldnews/asia/china/7230137/China-steams-ahead-with-worlds-fastest-train.html

Towler, S. (2002). *CHI energy of harmony*. China: MQ Publications.

http://www.geocities.com/Tokyo/island/2589/nmt/bullet.html. Accessed 17 Nov 2008.

Wells, S., Bailey, E, Keller, L. L., Kim, C. P., & Ang, S.-L. (2010). *What animals can teach us about leadership*, 30 Oct 2010. Accessed December 16, 2010 from http://guamanimalsinneed.blogspot.com/2010/10/what-animals-can-teach-us-about.html

Wu, J. C. H. (1990). *Lao Tzu: Tao Teh Ching*. Boston & London: Shambala Publications.

Resilience and Leadership in Asia

16

Being Resilient

No strength within, no respect without. (Indian proverb)
  When bad things happen to me, I have learnt to keep the lesson but throw away the event. (Patrick Kim Cheng Low)

Before talking about resilience, there is a need to define adversity since resilience is the ability to overcome adversity. Adversity is a condition characterised by misfortunate, serious difficulty, drawback or perhaps a disaster. Medical doctors have to grapple with the fact that some of their patients died on them. Academicians face with rejections for their articles from journal editors and reviewers while sales people face their customers' or prospects' repeated rejections of their products as well as loss of market share. And indeed adversity can come in any form, shape or size, ranging from a life-threatening illness, a divorce to a business failure. It never rains, but pours and adversity can come to a person or leader in one go!

There's this common saying that, "If there's no pain, there's no gain." So by the way of pain, we grow. The learning in adversity can, in fact, be taken as deeper than learning in good times. The late Matsushita founder, Matsushita Konosuke (1984, p. 92) once referred to resilience as "troubles and dilemmas", routine in business as, good teachers. Failures help us to achieve wisdom, and defeat supplies a valuable fund of experience to draw from later on, "giving useful insights into ourselves and our circumstances. From it, we can grow and progress".

Adger (2000) has indicated that the concept of resilience can be expanded to include vulnerability. Vulnerability, which encompasses disruption to livelihoods and a loss of security, can be observed at different scales and in a wide range of phenomena. Adger (2000) states that resilience enables one to cope with stress and can be a loose opposite for vulnerability, therefore resilience can be observed in the same way as vulnerability—how one instead overturns the table to one's favour, if not advantage?

For our purpose and intent, to be resilient can be basically taken as to be strong or tough. To be resilient is also to have the staying power and to persevere. It is the power to prevail, the power to go on despite the odds. You can get the defeat and pain to eat you, you get down further or you can fight, and fight you CAN!

A resilient (*uruthi*—in Tamil) leader is being able to withstand the hardships and sufferings. Problems may emerge yet they are seen as challenges and opportunities to grow. When one loses a big deal, one learns from one's mistake(s), steadfastly believes and acts to gain other customers and win other contracts. One builds the market share by looking at other potential customers and markets while effecting good service recovery and excellence.

If you want a well, keep digging in one place. Implicitly having that far-sighted view, persistence involves setting a goal, committing to a course of action, making the necessary sacrifices, overcoming hindrances, setbacks and even criticisms—all the while up-keeping your motivation, energy and faith in oneself. One persists or perseveres, develops a good staying power, and is determined to succeed, one is like to succeed. One should not give up at the sight of the first obstacle or difficulty. Proverbially speaking, one should not be "a monk for just 3 days" as eloquently put in the Japanese proverb.

And in fact, one remains and continues in the task or venture. One, being emotionally strong, confidently tries to do whatever it takes to make a turnaround. And succeed. Overall such die-hard efforts do not stop; one overcomes obstacles, continues and moves on.

The CORE Qualities

What appears to be a genius is often nothing more than 'the art of taking pains'. (Claude Hopkins)
    Fire is the test of gold; adversity of strong men. (Seneca)

To be resilient and to overcome adversity, as a leader, one needs to develop one's CORE qualities (Stoltz 1998).

The **C** here represents control, how much in control does one perceives to have. To what extent one can influence the situation. The more control one perceives to have, all the more one feels cool and calm or less stressed. For example, "I should be exercising often, I know I should, and I feel very much in control; I'll organise my time and have time slots for regular exercises during the week." This will make me more resilient.

Next, the **O**, here it means accepting the ownership, that is, to what extent one owns and is accountable to play some role in improving or making the situation better. For example, "If I own the situation, I hold myself responsible to improve the situation, then I will get out or grow out of this unfortunate situation."

The **R** refers to the reach, that is, how far does the fallout of the situation reach into other areas of one's work or life? A weak person or a less tough leader tends to blow up or catastrophise, allowing a setback in one area to extend or bleed to other, unrelated areas and become destructive. For example, "My girlfriend left me, no ladies would ever love me; I'll never get married; and I take it that I'll be a bachelor for life!" Here, one should take the opposite view and instead take it that, "Well, my girlfriend has left me, I have to accept the fact, start anew... move on and meet more people. And let new relationships develop and grow."

The **E** in the CORE qualities here is endurance (How long will this adversity endure?). Looking beyond even seeing enormous difficulties is an essential skill for maintaining hope. Tough people and leaders have the uncanny ability to see past the most never-ending difficulties and upkeep much hope and optimism. Tough people do not quit. Less tough people tend to see adversity as dragging on indefinitely, if not permanently.

Boosting Endurance and Being Resilient

The nose of the bulldog is slanted backwards so he can continue to breathe without letting go. (Winston Churchill)

"Hendakkan buah si-manggis, hutan, masak ranun tergantung tinggi." [English equivalent: Like anticipating the ripened mangosteen, suspended high in the forest. Although the fruit or object is difficult to obtain, with sufficient effort, it may be ultimately obtained.] (Malay proverb)

While the Americans seem to stress highly on one's ability and competence or even talent as the key to success, the Chinese stress more on work ethic; they take industry and diligence one step further—to endurance. To the Chinese, this must happen or at least be understood—"In prosperity, think of adversity; in adversity never think of prosperity". The Chinese in fact see *chiku nailao* as much more important and honourable. *Chi ku nai lao* refers to being enduring and hardy, or literally translated, meaning eating bitterness and enduring labour. [In the Hokkien dialect, it is *chia ko nai law*.]

To be enduring and resilient, one needs to be able to:

Say No to Negativity

I must endure the presence of two or three caterpillars if I wish to become acquainted with the butterflies. It seems that they are very beautiful. (Antoine de Saint-Exupéry, *The Little Prince*)

"'N' stands for saying no to negativity", as Deepak Chopra advises.

Negativity is like a cancerous growth, it wipes out everything. It makes everything ugly, dark and bleak. It's a dark, dark, dark universe.

Instead, make sunshine. Your life, make it as bright—even in its darkest moment—as you want it to be.

Remember that the Chinese believe in a common saying, that is, "all things at first appear difficult".

Also, in whatever one does, one needs to cultivate a generous or giving spirit. One who gives has more. Say no to negativity; say no to nothing to share; there is plenty for all, plenty to share. Reframe our minds and response with the perception that we have plenty, and we'll be strong or even grow stronger.

Not to Ignore the Negatives

Learning is not child's play, we cannot learn without pain. (Aristotle)

A well-fed man, when offered food, will say nice dishes are no good. Bill gates once said that, "Success is a lousy teacher. They seduce people into thinking they can't lose."

When we are exposed to too many good things, we may take things for granted. However, when we face hardships, inconvenience and/or adversities, we should not ignore the negatives.

Rather than ignoring the negatives, resilient leaders address them in a realistic way, and solve problems. Here, one is not afraid to make mistakes. One learns from failures. For Confucius, being resilient is being wise for a wise person, when erred, would reform. To a wise man, to make a mistake and not reform is indeed abysmal folly.

Welcome disagreements or opposing viewpoints from your rank and file, your people; it's difficult though. In fact, it may even irritate you. However, as a Russian saying goes, mere friends will agree with you, but real friends will argue. Speaking candidly, real friends will give you different perspectives and insights.

Negatives, in fact, need to be put into the right context; they are challenges to be tackled and overcome. Perhaps, it's all a matter of "no pain, no gain".

The seed of weakness or badness is in any great event as in 'the yin in the yang' of all things. And there's a seed of greatness in any bad event ('the yang in the yin'). As such, we need to heed the advices in these Chinese saying, "In the days of affluence, always think of poverty: do not let want come upon you, and make you remember with regret the time of plenty." (And not to adopt the attitude and posture of "let us get drunk today while we have wine; the sorrows of to-morrow may be borne to-morrow.") In failure, there is a seed of success if one learns from it; and in being successful, there is a seed of downturn or failure if one gets complacent. The two (yin-yang) must be seen as one. One leads to the other, in oneness of things as in the *Tao*.

See the Positive Aspects

Always bear in mind that your own resolution to succeed is more important than any other thing. (Abraham Lincoln)
The reverse side also has the reverse side. (Zen saying)

Low and Theyagu (2003, p. 47) highlight that "a little stress is a good thing". It spurs one to action. You have to be able to cope with stress. You can cope with stress once you understand your needs fully. Only by understanding your needs will you be better able to understand the needs of your people. Stress, from a leader's perspective, comes about because of a lack of knowledge of the tasks at hand or a lack of the power of control. Your inability to control stress would also mean your inability to lead the group. So take charge of your life and control the crises that arise in your life. Not easily discouraged, a leader must instead boldly seize opportunities, and turn them around. (S)he should be an optimist, seeing the positive aspects.

True, we cannot totally control or prevent a misfortune from happening to us. Yet in the same way, as one Chinese proverb goes, "You cannot prevent the birds of sadness from passing over your head, but you can prevent their making a nest in your hair". Yes, look for the lessons adversity teaches. Seneca, the Roman playwright once said, "The good things which belong to prosperity are to be wished, but the good things to adversity are to be admired."

In the garden, one looks at the green leaves and the beautiful flowers and not at the dropped flowers or dried, brown leaves on the ground. One looks at the bright stars, and not the dark sky, and one appreciates the beauty of the brilliant, shining stars.

Over-reactions can sometimes lead to serious or bigger trouble. Serious trouble can be better handled by being calm and cool. Avoid over reaction in anger and in grief. One instead dances on the carpet as it is moved from under one's feet. Both positive and passionate, a successful leader talks and stresses on what's working well, and attempts to find ways to fix what isn't. (S)he moves on to produce better results.

As one looks at the positive aspects too, one avoids over-reaction on one's part, and one does not burn the barn to get rid or kill the rats. One thus restrains over-reaction, make sane decisions and take appropriate and thought-out actions.

Overall, cherish the positive points. Just to share with you and you can use it too, I always like this particular Indian proverb which I often use to helpfully remind myself: "Do not blame God for having created the tiger, but thank him for not having given it wings."

Be Prudent

> When prosperity comes, do not use all of it. (Chinese proverb; also attributed as one of Confucius's sayings.)
> Dig a well before you are thirsty. (Chinese proverb)

Save and be prudent. Be prepared for the raining days.

It is good and wise to save and be prudent by recycling, reusing and/or reducing (not wasting) our uses of resources and things. We need to conserve our resources and energy. After all, as the Chinese proverb goes, "Don't waste good iron for nails or good men for soldiers?"

A case in point is that of dam management as embraced and practised by the late Matsushita Konosuke. Believing in savings and holding the umbrella, he was ever ready for the rainy days. This accounted for his building up and growing of Matsushita Group's financial strengths.

Be Green

> The king was ill and called a wise one in for advice, who told him to be healed he must look on the color green. The king ordered lakhs and lakhs of money to be spent painting the entire kingdom. The wise one returned and said to him Would it not have been better to put on green glasses? (Sri Sathya Sai Baba)

One Chinese proverb speaks of the pine staying green in winter... wisdom in hardship. To be sustainable enables one to be resilient too.

To be green helps one to be sustainable. To be green is also to be prudent. As a Chinese proverb goes, "Do not use a lot when a little will do"; such a green way and attitude helps one to save, and one reduces one's consumption. One can also re-use or recycle things. And one minimizes waste—waste not, want not.

For individuals and businesses, being green helps to cut costs and be lean. Yes, a little done, a little effort goes a long way, and it builds the business and the individual.

Be Creative

> Creativity is allowing yourself to make mistakes. Art is knowing which ones to keep. (Scott Adams)

When one is positive, one tends to be more creative, and thinks out of the box in which case, one then adapts. One does not feel depressed or totally bogged down by the issue. One takes and sees a different perspective. And one can also think in many different ways.

Being positive, a resilient leader is also a creative person, thinking laterally. (S) he comes up or facilitates the growth of a variety of ideas and solutions to resolve the problem at hand.

Yes, overall, be daring to try out new things.

Be Open: There's Always a Way!

> There's always a way—if you're committed. (Anthony Robbins)

I 'd always like what Jane Austen once said, "There will be little rubs and disappointments everywhere, and we are all apt to expect too much; but then, if one scheme of happiness fails, human nature turns to another; if the first calculation is wrong, we make a second better: we find comfort somewhere."

There is always a way, and if one thinks like that, then there are at all times a way out.

No matter how one will get out! One will overcome whatever obstacles or hindrances.

There is always a route to achieving things and to getting things done if one is committed to it. Commitment is so powerful. It creates the will for one. And when one is committed, one gets the necessary power, one is duly empowered, and that gives us the strengths. Remember that life works to the degree that one tells one's mind to it. Commitment builds in us the resilience too. A committed soldier fights willingly and he fights even to death!

The Way of the Warrior

Man never made any material as resilient as the human spirit. (Bernard Williams)

The Japanese have often been cited as being tough, the Samurai way. And for Kazakhstan, it is the way of the Golden Warrior (Man) (Zolotoi Chelovek, in Russian) (Low 2017).

To worry, on one hand, is to immobilize oneself (a leader); besides, worrying is negative; and it is not worth or helpful doing so.

On the other hand, to be resilient, one is a warrior and not a worrier. To be a warrior is to be proactive and productive.

The Soviet times had been hard, and the land of the Great Steppes had been neglected yet the Kazakhs/ Kazakhstanis prodded on. It was determined to achieve its independence; and it received its independence in 1991. After the Soviet era, there were many abandoned cities (Russian: *zabroshennyye goroda*) yet economic development, growth and progress was affected, and since 1991, the country has made much progress. When the Soviet Union collapsed, government did not have funds to support some of these small cities. People of these cities were left all by themselves. There's no drinking water; water and electricity supplies were stopped. And the people had to leave these forsaken cities and move. Yet many people survived; some people were lucky to find their place in Almaty and other cities; and they continued with their lives, working doing odd jobs or as junkyard traders to make ends meet. The author understands that presently Chilik near to Almaty was once an abandoned city, but after 20 years or so, it has improved with better facilities and new buildings. More people are returning or coming to Chilik. The same also applies to Zhanatas (meaning "New Stones" in Kazakh) near Shymkent (which means "City Made from Stones" in Kazakh); it has grown or sprouted again.

And in modern times, through Baikonur, the Republic of Kazakhstan "(made its) much-needed first step into space, a step dictated by history itself", making its way to the stars (Nazarbayev 2008, p. 276). Traditionally, modern Kazakhstan has the Golden Warrior (Man) (Zolotoi Chelovek, in Russian) as its symbol and icon (Kazakhworld.com 2017).

Clearly, one does not get stalled or immobilized by a problem and/ or an obstacle. One takes action, a concrete or proactive step to move on; one has the resolution and courage to move on. "Every Kazakhstani should have a sense of his own worth and take responsibility for his actions and life." And drawing parallels to the Republic and Kazakhstanis, citing the great Abai, Nazarbayev (2008, p. 329) spoke of "If you want to be rich, learn a trade" and citing Kazakh sayings, he spoke of "Try to master seven languages and know seven sciences"; thus, learning, education and action are important to the Republic's economic growth and its modern development and progress.

Besides, Kazakh Wisdom has it that as a nomad, one needs to make full use of whatever that is given, especially so in a hardy and tough setting. Indeed so, "one key way to be a warrior is to proactively plan, to plan forward and always be prepared". In this aspect, , like a ship's anchor, the Government has often played a crucial pro-active role as can be seen from President Nursultan Nazarbayev's determination to get independence for Kazakhstan in the pre-independence days as well as in the Vision 2030/Business Strategy Vision 2050. The Government through President Nursultan Nazarbayev has created "a solid pathway for the people of Kazakhstan to foster forward their dream of becoming one of the greatest nations of the world" (Noor 2013).

Be Adaptable

By a long journey, we know a horse's strength, so the length of days shows a man's heart. (Chinese proverb)

To be tough, one needs to be adaptable or flexible enough; one adjusts oneself to new or changed circumstances. This, in essence, is similar to the Indian saying, "If you live in the river, you should make friends with the crocodile."

One should be adaptable, possessing what one Japanese corporate leader the late Matsushita Konosuke called "the untrapped mind", that is, the ability to see things with free and open mind. One would then have the quality of "ready adaptability", and to illustrate the concept, Matsushita chose the legendary confrontational example between the twelfth century warlord, Minamoto no Yoshitsune and the formidable Benkei, who afterwards became Yoshitsune's faithful servant (Matsushita 1994a, b, p. 62).

In contemporary terms, Matsushita saw "the untrapped mind" as changing one's view readily if necessary, and to deal with new situations effectively without sticking rigidly to just one point of view. Matsushita expressed these, "Flowing water does not fuss and fret when it meets an obstacle in its path, but moves around it and goes merrily on its way. You should always meet difficulties with the same ready versatility, smoothly shifting your course when necessary" (Matsushita 1994a, b, p. 63; Low and Theyagu 2003).

Learn from Nature

No snowflake ever falls in the wrong place. (Zen quote)

In *Tao de ching*, Lao-Tzu speaks of:

Express yourself completely, then keep quiet. Be like the forces of nature: when it blows, there is only wind; when it rains, there is only rain; when the clouds pass, the sun shines through. If you open yourself to the Tao, you are at one with the Tao and you can embody it completely. If you open yourself to insight, you are at one with insight and you can use it completely. If you open yourself to loss, you are at one with loss and you can accept it completely. Open yourself to the Tao, then trust your natural responses; and everything will fall into place.
    Look and learn from nature.

Take a look at the willow tree—unlike the oak tree, it is not rigid. The willow tree is flexible. Look at cacti in the desert; they are resilient too.

Next, look at the bamboo, it is so resilient. When strong winds blow, the bamboos bend. The various parts of the bamboo can be used by men for a variety of purposes and have many uses. Bamboos can be made into poles, traps, cages and houses; and its leaves can be weaved into baskets or made into fans. The young shoots of the bamboo can also be eaten.

In Asia, coconut trees are also resilient; when the winds blow, they bend. Like the bamboo, coconut trees supply people with many uses, ranging from food (coconut milk, brown sugar, coconut water), alcoholic drinks (toddy from the coconut flowers) to packaging materials (coconut husks) and roofing materials (coconut leaves).

The point to note here is that as leaders, we should be versatile and be multi-skilled. Indeed we would not run out of jobs or employment when we are multi-skilled. And more so, when we are ever willing to learn, and improve ourselves.

Yet another example from nature is that of clay. Clay, a type of soil, is a resilient natural material; it can be hardened when dried or fried. Hence, they are used to be made into pots and bricks and tiles or building materials.

In its original or natural form, the hardness of the clay is seen as a property or its ability to retain water as water is trapped in the clay's mineral structure. This property is significant in various areas, such as in farming. Clay indeed provides fertility for the cultivation of wet rice that is very important for the paddy plants which need water throughout their growing season, in several parts of Asia, for example, in Indonesia, Malaysia, the Philippines and in Thailand as well as Myanmar and Vietnam.

The hardness of clay reflects its strengths. Regardless of climatic changes, the clay would maintain its characteristic hardiness and being tough. In dry period, the

Fig. 16.1 Look at the resilient bamboo. When strong winds blow, the bamboos bend. The various parts of the bamboo are also used by humans for a variety of purposes and have many uses

soil maintains its toughness from being degraded by the hot weather, thus, supplies the water it retains to plants. During wet season, more water from the rain is retained; as such that it maintains a water reserve. Thus, with this ability, plants can grow normally as the supply of water is adequate for the plants' cellular respiration. The same should also be applied to the handling and dealing with crisis. We can learn from the hardness of the clay that leaders need to be strong and tough. Being tough means that they need to have the right mind and right attitude. Positive-minded and being able to think outside the box, leaders should be courageous, determined, flexible, motivated (enthusiastic) and persistent (Fig. 16.1).

Visualise Success

> You are the hero of your life. (Matsushita Konosuke)

Think success. Visualise success. Imagine success.

Visualisation is powerful.

See yourself strong ad resilient.

Ever wonder how Chinese art and paintings are created?

Western art are normally representative while traditional Chinese paintings, consisting so strokes and lines, can be imaginative and leave to the mind to conjure images. Chinese paintings can indeed be very beautiful. A few strokes or lines can purposefully depict the intended objects.

Ordinarily, the traditional artist would take a long walk, looking at the landscape and scenery and at times, meditating for hours. Then he would go to his chamber, and would lock himself, and there, he would imagine and draw or paint from his mind's eye. What the mind's eye sees is more creative than the physical sightings. He would then imagine the landscape(s) seen and paint accordingly.

In the same way, we can visualise success and become successful. The mind's eye is so powerful! We don't give up. We don't quit. We imagine success, keep on imaging success. What is imagined (steadily and slowly) becomes a reality.

Have a Good Sense of Humour

If you can laugh at your own weaknesses, you can move forward Comedy breaks down walls... (Goldie Hawn)

When misfortune or bad things happen to us, we can either cry or at least attempt to laugh it off to relieve or ease ourselves.

Laughter's the best medicine.

Laugh, it helps. In life, it's good to be serious, but not all the time, we must also have the funny bone. To the Japanese, as their common saying goes, "Time spent laughing is time spent with gods".

(Feeling Low Energy?) Get Energy and Recharged!

Fall seven times, stand up eight. (Japanese proverb)

Heard of power breakfast, now, turn to power naps. Get recharged! A 10–20 min nap is great for refuelling. Many of the busiest high achievers are good in taking naps at odd places in order to refuel themselves during a long work day

Next, there is nothing like spending some time during the day outdoors to refresh one's energy, and give one a renewed outlook on life. Spend a day at a beach, and if one can't do that, spend a few hours in the park. Let the energy of nature to make one feels calmer and fitter.

In *Tai-chi, Tai-chi* Masters speak of the *ki*, and the need for us to replenish or recharge the *ki*. When one goes to nature, seeing a beautiful mountainous landscape, doing a nature walk or walking along the beach, one can absorb the *ki* of the place or what I would term "the natural goodness", that good refreshing feeling.

If the above sounds metaphysical, then for the realists, I would suggest that one should surround oneself with high energy mentors—learn from them what they do to keep up their energy or be with enthusiastic friends; these then are the things that one can do to energise, facing life and moving on.

Oh, yes, another thing—never be half-hearted. Half heartedness in things, an unsteady spirit is a hindrance in one's study and pursuits of "*ki*" (Tao). Full-heartedness, willpower—determined effort in practice—this is the key to be fully charged or energized.

Have the Clarity of Mind

Clarity of the mind leads to total insight. (Patrick Kim Cheng Low)
   Perseverance is strength. (Japanese proverb)

Pace yourself for inner peace and go forward, and get out from the crisis.

Here, meditation helps. One meditates to achieve this. And this is, of course, not a one-off process, but rather an ongoing process.

Indeed, there is always a solution to any problem no matter how big or serious it is. When one faces an adverse situation, to this author, one needs to meditate to have the clarity of mind. The reason being, when one meditates, one develops and grows one's clarity of mind; at which stage one then sees the positive aspects while appreciating the negatives and seeing the latter rather realistically. One then sees the whole issue or the entire picture in totality. When one is attached, one would not see the negatives in a realistic manner, and one feels overwhelmed or even panicked as if the negatives are overshadowing whatever few positives that stands.

When one meditates, one develops very little or no sense of attachment. And without any sense of attachment, unfazed and being cool and composed, one can then know which direction to go or proceed.

Besides, as one meditates, one raises one's consciousness, and as Lao Tzu's once said, "The key to growth is the introduction of higher dimensions of consciousness into our awareness."

Human beings are made for far better and greater things to gain and accomplish, and so, whatever, problems and hardships can be surmounted, and we grow.

It is worthy to note that meditation overall helps one to grow one's patience and perseverance; one becomes more disciplined and detached when evaluating things or events. Ta Mo, the founder of the Shaolin Martial Arts, for example, encouraged and taught the monks to meditate in isolated caves or facing the temple walls in solitude so as to be disciplined while growing their personal mastery and resilience.

As one meditates, one attains the no-classification and oneness of everything (oneness with the Universe), freeing one's thinking and attaining, so to speak, the untrapped mind. The untrapped mind helps—it is linked with free mind, and no classifications. In that state, it can be taken that one can then learn more and better and see greater and more possibilities.

Get Help from Family or Close Friends

A harmonious family forebodes prosperity. (Chinese saying)

Ask around. There are many people who are willing to help—if only one ask.

Get whatever help you can get; yes, get help from your family or close friends. True, one may want to be independent yet we can seek the help of our family members and close friends if we really need their help. And besides, treat it only as the final resort.

Yes, sometimes help from a community helps a lot. Let me explain. There is an Iban, a branch of the tribal Dayak people living in the island of formerly British Borneo or now, Kalimantan, saying that goes, "Agi idup agi ngelaban", when translated means, as long as one lives, one will continue to fight, seek challenges, strive to achieve and go all-out for improvements and overall success. Historically, the Ibans were renowned for practicing headhunting and tribal/territorial expansion; presently, the Iban population is concentrated in Sarawak, Brunei and the West Kalimantan region of Indonesia. Living in long houses or *rumah panjang*, they hunted foods in groups and cultivated rice in the cleared hill areas; and the Ibans are also well-known for their rice wine (better known as *tuak*, the wine is also made from rice alternatives such as sugarcane, ginger and corn) which is used to serve guests. Most of the activities such as hunting and fishing were done in groups, normally, in groups of a few families with leader(s). In the past, hunting in groups and engaging in team activities enabled the Ibans' better survival. These days, though the Ibans consist of different faiths, they do help each other during *gawais* or festivals such as the rice harvesting festival on 1 June. Friendly, the Ibans indeed believe in helping and having fun together.

We have been conditioned from young from the many movies we watched and the many novels we read, there are always these romantic visuals we all have of a rugged individual, the toughie relying on his or her own stubborn strength. That, my dear friends, is only a romantic fantasy. There is no reason to do everything yourself. Besides, we can rely on our technical-who, and get help. The tenacity of the team adds strength, additional skills and hands and in fact, multiplies the individual's tenacity.

Go Bit by Bit, Inch Your Way Through... and Still Make It!

Know the masculine. Keep to the feminine... Know the white, keep to the black... hence, a great tailor does little cutting. (Lao-Tzu, *Tao de ching*, verse 28)

A Chinese proverb reads, "The man who removes a mountain begins by carrying away small stones". And a Zen saying indicates that, "Nature does not hurry yet everything is accomplished." That's how resilient leaders get successful. They are also patient.

Rome was not built in a single day!

Even in ordinary living, what more than to say when facing obstacles, little things can create or lead to big results. That's how tough leaders work.

Strong and tough leaders are indeed persevering. In my youth, I learnt a useful Malay saying that goes, *Belakang parang jika diasah nescaya tajam juga akhirnya*, translated meaning, even the back of a chopper, if honed, is sure to get sharpened. The saying can keep one motivated to carry on, being strong and resilience. After all, even a fool, if sufficiently schooled, will eventually not be dense, and in fact can be smart.

Drip by drip, even water, over time, cuts solid rocks. And rapids and waterfalls are formed.

A Doctor of Philosophy (Ph.D.)—a terminal degree, for example, seems to be an insurmountable, if not a difficult task more so, after we have left college a long time ago. At first, one would think one would never have made it. The efforts and work involved seem as if light years ahead from one's Master's degree; indeed it is a long, arduous journey. Indeed the thesis will be written and new knowledge uncovered; but the Ph.D. candidate must be strong and persists. In research work, much groundwork and digging is done; bit by bit, the researcher asks around, surveys and interviews and gathers information. The researcher patiently seeks to uncover things and ultimately, when the data is amassed, it is analysed, and Voila! With facts and figures assembled and things put together, telling trends emerge. And of course, before the final thesis done, there would be many amendments and numerous editing, and the Ph.D. candidate would undoubtedly face several roadblocks or even dead-ends, but (s)he needs to steer, finding ways to get out, and purposefully proceeds.

So it's critical that one persistently finds one's way around, and if one can't find a way, one makes one—no matter how small that way is. And from that small way, one inches one way out and forward.

Perhaps even in building our strengths, one can go bit by bit, inch by inch. One can do kind acts every day; and grow our kindness and overall grow our character. In this regard, the Buddha speaks of "A jug fills drop by drop."

Have Staying Power

> Don't imagine 'Impossibles'. (Matsushita Konosuke)
> If you keep hitting it, even the ammi will move. (Ammi is a large grind stone usually not moved from its position) (Tamil proverb)

Every Olympic athlete, leader and every human being has an inclination at times at the first or slightest sign of frustration to throw the towel, and call it quit. At times, we may just want to turn on the Quit or Resign switch. However, we need to throw away that switch. Instead...

Press on.
Never give up. Never quit.

Note that time helps, time also heals; and is a cure-all. Time really heals all wounds.
Do not give up, just give it more time. It is interesting to watch how children get
   what they want. And you'll see the natural, built-in persistence.
So, on our part, we need to be patient. Persist.
Keep going. There's always better and best. Move on.
Tough people keep going when the going gets tough.

Perhaps, here it is good to see examples. Japanese corporate leader Soichiro
Honda (1906–1991) can be said to be a very determined and persistent leader. Once
Honda set a goal, he was a leader "who would not tolerate the idea that something
was impossible without first putting in a decent effort" (Honda, cited in Low and
Theyagu 2003, p. 95). Interestingly, Ibuka, Sony's Chairman once remarked that
the high performance work principles of Soichiro Honda indeed embodied the spirit
of "persuasive engineering"; one gets the idea, researches it and translates it to the
farthest extent. This, in fact, speaks volume of a leader's determination and staying
power. Soichiro Honda's staying power or always better and best can be supremely
seen in that he wanted that the best and the strongest cars were produced.

Napoleon Hill once wrote, "Persistence is to the character of man as carbon is to
steel." Indeed another quality that seems to be indispensable to leadership success is
the staying power of the person. Come high waters, thunder and lightning or
drought, the leader's hard drive and determination ensures his or her overcoming
every storm of his or her life. The leader also sees the world in terms of inevitable
success, making it a better place to live and moving towards wonderful and greater
accomplishments for others as well.

Believe in Yourself

Whether you think you can or whether you think you can't, you're right. (Henry Ford)

Golda Meir, the Israeli Prime Minister once said this, "Trust yourself. Create the
kind of self that you will be happy to live with all your life. Make the most of
yourself by fanning the tiny, inner sparks of possibility into flames of achievement."

Yes, trust yourself and be confident. And persist.
Be very confident. And persist.
The more one persists, the more one believes in oneself.
When one believes in oneself, others will, too.

This is the Western way, but perhaps to put in the Eastern fashion, we can apply
Chu's (1992) Thick Face: The Thick Face person has the ability to put self doubt
aside. (S)he refuses to accept the limitations that others have tried to impose and,
more importantly, (s)he does not accept any of the limitations that we commonly
impose on ourselves. The world has a tendency to accept our own judgment of
ourselves.

By his (her) absolute self-confidence, the Thick Face person instills confidence in others. They see him (her) as successful and allow him (her) the latitude to succeed. [A Thick Face need not be assertive or aggressive. (S)he may be humble and submissive. Thick Face is the ability to adopt whatever manner the situation calls for without regard for what other people think.]

This brings to mind the idea of self-efficacy—the individual believes that (s)he is able to do the job. The higher the self-efficacy, the more confidence one has in one's ability to succeed in the job. Self-efficacy is a personality trait of most leaders; in difficult situations, people with high self efficacy are less likely to give up, instead they try harder to master the challenge or overcome the problem. People with low self-efficacy are more likely to lessen their effort or simply give up altogether.

Build the Ballast, Getting Help from the Beyond

The eyes of the Universe are upon me. If I should fall, the Universe will help me get up. (Patrick Kim Cheng Low)
   When the Lord closes a door, somewhere He opens a window. (Maria, *The Sound of Music*, the Movie)

One good example is that of Mahatma Gandhi. In a 1914 tribute to Gandhi, Professor Gilbert Murray of Oxford wrote, "Be careful in dealing with a man who cares nothing for sensual pleasures, nothing for comfort or praise or promotion, but simply determined to do what he believes to be right. He is dangerous and uncomfortable enemy because his body which you can always conquer gives you so little purchase over his soul."

Indeed when one has the necessary ballast, and that ballast can be a set of core values or convictions that one strongly believes in or steadfastly holds onto. That core values can also be some religious or spiritual values. And the latter strengthens the individuals. One keeps knocking again even though one just had the door slammed in one's face.

Life itself is the Universe's gift to us. Life is beautiful. Life is a prayer. Life is abundance. There is indeed much abundance. Deepak Chopra once wrote, "Affluence, unbounded-ness, and abundance are our natural states. We just need to restore the memory of what we already know".

Life is also all possibilities.

There is also an attraction of all-goodness to one. Remember what Jesus was doing, he performed the miracle of two fish and five loaves of bread; he multiplied the food and fed the multitude. "They all ate, and were satisfied, and the disciples picked up twelve basketfuls of broken pieces that were left over" (Matthew 14: 20).

By all means, do seek resources from the Universe to meet the maelstrom of needs round us.

In building one's strengths and growing one's resilience, the Chinese in Taiwan and even a number of Indonesians, Thais, Vietnamese and others in various Asian countries commonly pray and invoke the help of Guan Yin, known as the Goddess of Mercy in the West. Guan Yin, the Heart of Compassion is also said to be the patron saint of those who need help and withstand the hardships to become tough and renewed.

One image of Guan Yin that is believed to have the power of handling or banishing difficulty or misfortune is that of the Blue-throat Guan Yin. This Tantric Buddhist form of Guan Yin is compared to the Indian God Shiva who drank poison extracted from the sea of milk after it was churned, and whose throat remained blue thereafter (Koh 2004, p. 35).

Another image of Guan Yin is that of the One-leaf Guan Yin; here the Bodhisattva is shown standing or seated on a lotus leaf floating in the ocean. It is said that "if those who are tossed about in deep and treacherous waters call Avakitesvara's name (Guan Yin), they will quickly reach the shallows."

Section Conclusion

> I was taught very early that I would have to depend entirely upon myself; that my future lay in my own hands. (Darius Ogden Mills)

Overall, it can be taken that resilience can and should be taught and/or learned, and this is similar to what has been said by a Chinese Malaysian business leader, Tan Sri Dato' Dr. Lim Kok Wing (cited in Khoo 2001, p. 126), "My children have not gone through hardship. They are nice kids, kind and very trusting. But they have never had to fend for themselves. Are they well prepared for the world? No they are not. Suffering hardship is one way of learning. I suppose the young could be taught about helping others and to be helped by others, not to be greedy, dishonest or selfish, but to be giving, tolerant and to accept others as they are."

Buddha, Buddhism and Being Resilient

Introduction

> By your own efforts, waken yourself, watch yourself, and live joyfully. Follow the truth of the way. Reflect upon it. Make it your own. Live it. It will always sustain you. (The Dhammapada)

Buddha and Buddhism teach us to be resilient. Every day in our lives, there is a need to actively avoid bad thoughts. "'Look how he abused me and beat me, how he throw me down and robbed me.' Live with such thoughts and you live with hate. . . Abandon such thoughts, live in love." (*The Dhammapada* translated by Thomas Byrom, cited by Kornfield and Fronsdal 1991; Low 2010a). Bad thoughts are negative and they generate negative energies, and they can, in fact, cause conflicts and unhappy events or pain and sufferings for ourselves and others.

Yet every morning, when we wake up, we have 24 brand new hours to live. What a precious gift! (Thich 1992). We must choose the right attitude. We have the ability and capability to live in a way that these 24 h will bring peace, joy and happiness to ourselves and others. When we choose the right attitude, we live and live right.

In this section, it is hoped to show that Buddhism teaches us to be resilient. Because Buddhism upholds and advances positive thinking, and that positive thinking and attitude in itself helps in building one's resilience.

The Path

> The ultimate authority must always rest with the individual's own reason and critical analysis. (The Dalai Lama)

The Buddha points the vision or beautiful path to all of us, but it is left for us to wisely follow that self-reliant path to obtain our purification. "To depend on others for salvation is negative, but to depend on oneself is positive," Dependence on others means a surrender of one's effort. And blessings, without one's efforts, are not possible to come. Blessings must come from within (The Dalai Lama 1998), and that will free us form misery and to supply us with happiness and the cause of happiness.

Being Self-Reliant and Tough

> It is under the greatest adversity that there exists the greatest potential for doing good, both for oneself and others. (The Dalai Lama)

It was Buddha who sought to find solutions for people to get happiness, in fact, the ultimate happiness. Buddha taught the concept and applications of *anatta* (Pali) (non-self or soullessness); it was he who educated the ego-centric world the noble ideal of selfless service. Do not attach to the "I" or "mine"; that clinging to them as if they were "what I am", or were "mine", gives rise to unhappiness. Serve and extend service to assist others. Serve to bring happiness to others. It was the Buddha who revolted against the degrading caste system and taught equality of mankind and gave equal opportunities for all to distinguish themselves in every walk of life.

Make others happy first and foremost. Being motivated to bring happiness to others, *The Way of the Bodhisattva* (cited in The Dalai Lama 2007, p. 146) is made noticeable and etched in this well-known verse:

> Whatever happiness there is in this world
>> All comes from desiring others to be happy.
>> And whatever suffering there is in this world
>> All comes from desiring oneself to be happy.

The Buddha lives in hell and that is resilience for it is said that the Buddha lives or is reborn (as a Bodhisattva) so as to help all sentient beings; and all sentient beings are the Buddha's buddhas or saviors.

The Buddha affirmed that the gates of success and prosperity were open to all in every condition of life, high or low, saint or criminal, who would care to turn a new leaf and aspire to perfection. Buddhism is also proactive; it moves us to action (Low 2010a). The Buddhist practitioner has to be awake, (s)he has to be alert. (S)he is clear, mindful and (s)he watches. The Buddhist practitioner has to be awake, (s)he has to be alert. (S)he is clear and (s)he watches (Low 2010b, c). And (s)he then practices compassionate, otherwise, just remaining as an idea, compassion is of little value (The Dalai Lama 2001). The task of a person, according to the Dalai Lama (1998) is to help others, and the basic question is better relations; better relations among human beings—and whatever that can contribute to that—and here, one can figure it out, that is, to obtain happiness for one and all.

It is said that "Buddhism rests on the pivot of sorrow. But it does not thereby follow that Buddhism is pessimistic" (Thera 2009, 1933), and as said, "One would be justified in calling the Buddha a pessimist if He had only enunciated the Truth of suffering without suggesting a means to put an end to it." Instead, The Buddha perceived the universality of sorrow and did prescribe a universal remedy for this common sickness of humanity. According to the Buddha, the highest conceivable happiness for any person is Nirvana or *Nibbiina* (literally, become extinguished. *Nibbiina* constitutes the highest and ultimate goal of all Buddhist aspirations; Low 2010d, e) which is the total destruction of pain and suffering.

It can also be argued that instead of trying to rationalize suffering, Buddhism takes suffering head-on as given and part of life, and then positively seeks the cause to eradicate it. And this presents beautiful answers. For the Buddha and in Buddhism, suffering exists as long as there is craving. It can be eliminated by treading the Noble Eightfold Path and (striving to) attaining Nirvana or *Nibbiina*.

Living in the World of *Anicca*

Even royal chariots, well-embellished, get run down, and so does the body succumb to old age. But the Dhamma of the good doesn't succumb to old age: the good let the civilized know. (Dhammapada, 11, translated by Thanissaro Bhikkhu)

Human beings are living in a transient world or what the Buddhists call *anicca*, and being positive helps us immensely to do well in this temporary world. Indeed as the Dalai Lama once said and to paraphrase him, people who die young serve as masters of disguises in teaching us impermanence, and indeed how positive this is!

In this contemporary world, where our frenzied pursuit of pleasure and comfort leaves us 'like children playing in a house on fire, refusing to let go of our toys'. Khema (1991) prompts us joy comes from understanding that the senses only doom us to be sorry and dissatisfaction and that, everything being impermanent; in essence, 'there is nothing to hang on to, nothing to worry about, nowhere to go...'

One should be proactive (Low 2010a, b, c), and in fact motivated. One should not be lazy. Instead one should realize that laziness and idleness—not doing what we are supposed to do, can lead to one's downfall. Be diligent and break the hold of hurtful fixations (Master Hsing Yun 2001) and we become strong. Passiveness, lethargy and laziness will stop one's progress in one's spiritual practice. One can be deceived by three types of laziness: the laziness of indolence, which is the wish to procrastinate, the laziness of inferiority, which is distrusting or suspecting one's capabilities and the laziness that is attachment to negative actions or putting great effort into non virtue (The Dalai Lama 1998). By contrast, when we become more aware of the transient world, we become more positive and active, and work hard towards our goal.

Acquiring Higher Awareness, We Can Transform Ourselves

> For as long as space endures, and for as long as living beings remain, until then may I, too, abide to dispel the misery of the world. (The Dalai Lama)

Determined to attain higher awareness, one self-reflects. Seeing things rightly, one is to also adopt the practice of thinking rightly, and having the wisdom. Everyone is to solve his or her own problem. One can receive advices from others, but in the end, one has to solve the problem on one's own.

And yes, we can transform ourselves. And how superb is! What can we do? Prior to renouncing cyclic existence and becoming strong, one must first positively acknowledge and accept that we shall all inevitably die. Human beings are born with the seed of their own death. From the moment of birth, we are approaching this inevitable or predictable demise. Then we should also ponder that the time of our death is uncertain. Death does not wait for us to tidy up our lives; it just strikes unannounced. At the time of our death, friends and family, the treasured possessions we have so meticulously collected throughout our lives, are of no value. Not even this valued body, the vehicle of this lifetime, is of any use. Such thoughts help us reduce our preoccupation with the concerns of our present lives (The Dalai Lama 2001).

Yet it is critical that we realize the great value of human existence, the vital possibility and the potential that our brief lives provide us. It is only as humans that we have this precious opportunity of implementing changes in our lives... and becoming tougher, for the better.

All of us can grab the opportunity to practice loving others. A positive attitude to adopt is to adopt a compassionate attitude, and this helps. This is that the Dalai Lama (2008, p. 38) has highlighted:

> A compassionate attitude helps you communicate easily with fellow human beings and other central beings. As a result, you make more genuine friends; the atmosphere is more positive, which gives you inner ballast. This inner strength helps you voluntarily concern yourself with others, instead of just thinking about your own self.

Of importance, he further adds that scientific research has demonstrated that those individuals who often use words such as *me, I*, and *mine* face a greater risk of a heart attack. If a person always thinks of him(her)self, that person's thinking becomes very narrow; even a small problem appears very big and unbearable. Bertrand Russell gives us his vision of a better and wiser human being, one who chooses the perspective of the 'not-self' with which to view the world. Should we start from the 'not-Self', and work through its greatness the boundaries of the Self are enlarged (Russell 2007, 1912). When people think of others, their minds expand, and within that large space, even big personal problems may appear small or insignificant. This makes all the difference, and in that sense we become hardy.

Being Aware of Situations Creating Negativity

Be awake (The Dalai Lama)

Reflect.
Purify one's thought tape. Have good thoughts, build within and build our inner strengths (Okawa 2005). The mind is an interesting, powerful machine, and it can be tapped to one's benefits.

And one should be aware of situations creating negativity and these include being arrogant, looking down on others, criticizing others without rendering help or support, working in isolation away from others, high fear of change, destructive conflicts including tit-for-tat, win-lose situations, low self-esteem, poor job fits and many other negative situations. To this author, one good technique is to side-step or steer away from negative thinking. This finds support in what Okawa (2002) has argued, that is, if one's mind is filled with useless thoughts, just as if it were full of mental junk, it must be said that one is leading an empty life. On the other hand, if one's mind is full of beautiful thoughts, it can be said that one is leading a wonderful life.

Assume positive thinking, and meditate upon positive ways to overcome the issues. Recite, if we can, mantras so that we have beautiful thoughts. Focus then on the strengths of others as well as the ways to bring happiness or help to others. Focus on the win-win ways in which others and we gain.

Watching, Observing and Taking Note of Positive Influences

Joy and sorrow exist only in the mind. (Japanese Buddhist proverb)

Buddha taught these, "Not to do any evil, to cultivate good, and to purify one's mind."

It is vital to lead our lives responsibly and meaningfully. And as the Dalai Lama (2001, p. 40) has highlighted, "We must avoid the influences of bad companions, unsavory friends who can lead us astray. It isn't always easy to judge others, but we can see that certain lifestyles lead to less righteous ways. A kind and gentle person can easily become influenced by dubious friends to follow a less moral path. We must be careful to avoid such negative influences and must cultivate loyal friends who help make our human existence spiritually meaningful and purposeful."

Even when bad things happen to us, when we adopt a positive paradigm, we see the world bearable. Something that is unfortunate may even prove to be a blessing in disguise. Rough seas make skilled sailors, and a person must learn to sail in all winds. When we are positive, there's more sun-shine than rain and gloomy skies. And what more, the sun often shines brighter after a downpour.

One needs to prepare to endure, to continue to practice. One needs to anticipate the many obstacles that one is bound to face along the path and, as the Dalai Lama (1998, p. 325) has indicated, that "the key to a successful practice is never to lose...determination. Such a resolute approach is very important. The story of the Buddha's personal life is the story of someone who attained full enlightenment through hard work and unwavering dedication".

Having Ideals

Be a lamp unto yourself. (Buddha)

All of us need stars as a guide to navigate in the dark night. We all need ideals or morals. Ideals are generated by having a positive mind. Ideals, supplying the standards, move or galvanize us to actions. Like the stars, positive thinking brightens our darkest moments and gives us something to move forward.

Ideals are important in one's life, with ideals, in spite of the odds, we move and we make progress. Without ideals, we cannot move, let alone make progress.

(In Spite of the Odds,) Being Motivated, and Moving on

Encountering sufferings will definitely contribute to the elevation of your spiritual practice, provided you are able to transform calamity and misfortune into the path. (The Dalai Lama)

Positive and of the right thought, should one want to improve oneself, the only thing one can do is to make the maximum effort to refine and purify one's own thoughts. One also develops the motivation, determination and stamina in moving towards one's goal. This also coincides with Stoltz's (1997) notion of Adversity Quotient: AQ; here, he speaks of the resilient individual, being a climber, in spite of the odds, strives to attain the goal (see also Lim 1999).

Coping with One's Environment

The creatures that inhabit this earth-be they human beings or animals-are here to contribute, each in its own particular way, to the beauty and prosperity of the world. (The Dalai Lama)

There is a Buddhist saying that goes, "All know the Way, but few actually walk it". And how true, one needs to be resilient to be a practicing Buddhist.

There is a Japanese saying that goes, "in even a cat the Buddha-nature exists". One of the key precepts of the Buddhist Ethics/Buddhism is to refrain from killing or non-injury to all creatures, big and small. In showing love and compassion, a Buddhist should minimize the amount of killing everyday, even the killing of the lowest form of living things such as mosquitoes and ants. By doing so, a Buddhist would not incur, or better still, reduce his or her karma. And devoted Buddhists would go to the extreme of clearing the way when walking along the path with long soft brushes on every step so that there are no tiny living creatures that may be trampled upon. It is also another Buddhist belief that every living thing, be it to the smallest creature has its element or potential of Buddhahood similar to human beings, and each and every one of them should not be hurt or worse be killed. In order to practice this precept, one requires a resilient character to do so for one should not eat meat. Imagine when one is with friends in a business circle for a dinner, this would require a resilient character to refrain and avoid eating any 'killing' food.

Interestingly, one interviewee expressed to this researcher these: "An active Buddhist living in a meat-eating environment (such as family and friends who prefers taking meat during meals) would have to take much trouble of arranging or preparing for oneself vegetarian food all. Very often tempted yet one may not like to be seen as the odd one; and one tends to avoid any social events such as dinner party or wedding banquet. In this way, one might miss the opportunity of meeting good to friends whom one have not seen for while, or miss an opportunity of improving one's friendship with some important business partners. Refraining from all these functions just because of one's beliefs in Buddhism (vegetarianism) may lead one to change one's mind in terms of not practicing as what a practicing Buddhist should do". And these can be implicitly assessed as it takes a resilient character to stick to as well as to be motivated with one's ideals such as resorting to vegetarianism while holding onto to the Buddhist faith and beliefs. Besides, "to continue to be resilient, a practicing Buddhist should also take special care in selecting and taking vegetarian food for adequate or sufficient nutrients to maintain a healthy body" (several interviewees' input).

Having the Positive Thinking's Edge

There is nothing so disobedient as an undisciplined mind, and there is nothing so obedient as a disciplined mind. (Buddha)

When we meditate, we examine ourselves. When we meditate, we become still, calm and peaceful. We become mindful.

Meditation assists us to reflect if we are living a purposeful life; if not, we can change it for the better. Meditation in fact helps or leads us to positive thinking. Positive thinking keeps us motivated. We think about good things and we think, and keep thinking of making others happy through service.

We reap what we have sown. And when we are positive, we create positive results.

Human beings are responsible for their own actions, happiness and misery. They build their own hells. They can create their own heavens (Thera 2009, 1933). Human beings are indeed the architects and builders of our own fate. In short, they are their own karma.

Positive thinking also helps us to be self-reliant. Simply by ourselves, we grow. If we think positively and we think that we need to become patient, then we learn to be tolerant. We make effort to see the good and beautiful of others.

We are motivated. By ourselves, we learn to avoid evil or wrong doings. By ourselves, we endure pain. By ourselves, crease from wrong. By ourselves, we seek happiness and by ourselves, we seek to make others happy. No one but ourselves should walk the Path which Buddha merely shows the way.

When we are positive minded, we are at peace. We look at the good side, and we overcome any craving or desires. We are detached from our desires. We eliminate our desires. And because we are detached, we do not feel pain or suffer.

Section Conclusion

> Your worst enemy cannot harm you as much as your own unguarded thoughts. (Buddha)

When we are thinking positively, we would be telling ourselves to be: generous, helpful; independent, well-disciplined, resolute and be diligent till we attain our goal. We become loving and compassionate to others, one and all. We create happiness for others as well as for ourselves.

Being Resilient, the Confucian Way

Introduction

"Being resilient" is defined by the Oxford English Dictionary as rising readily again after being depressed, hence buoyant or resolute (http://dictionary.oed.com/cgi/entry/00204038, cited in Low 2002, 2009; also cited in Low 2007). We will thus define "to be resilient" as to be able to perform or remain stable to (continue to) function in the face of trouble, disruption or difficulty.

The Chinese has a saying that goes, "When one falls, one picks oneself up again." One should not stop, in spite of the obstacles. And one just goes on, and keeps going. Tough people last, and in spite drawbacks or obstacles, they keep on going. And according to Confucius (551 B.C.–479 B.C.), adversity indeed has its good effects, beneficial results and consequences. For Confucius, a person's greatest glory lies not in never falling, but in rising each time (s)he falls.

Confucius was a Chinese thinker and social philosopher, whose teachings and philosophy have deeply influenced Chinese, Korean, Japanese and Vietnamese as well as, to some extent, Singaporean (Low 2002, 2005, 2009) thought and life. His philosophy stressed on personal and governmental morality, correctness of social relationships, justice and sincerity. The purpose and objective of the section is to relate Confucius' teachings and various aspects of Confucianism that relate to and support the idea and concept of being resilience in the person/leader as well as ensuring resilience or more specifically, continuity in business.

One cannot be a real leader unless one is resilient; "a king (*leader*) can't become a real ruler, without encountering difficulties" (Zhou 2005, p. 169, *italics mine*). Mencius, the disciple of Confucius' grandson maintained that, "There is goodness out of adversity" (Chew 2000, p. 43). Tired, poverty, hunger, hardship and frustration will stir a man's mind, toughen his character and make good his defects.

Learning Helps, Continuous Learning Benefits

As a person and a leader, one needs to be open and broad-minded [Low (2010a) stresses on this further and applies this to customer service and excellence]. This parallel can be seen when Mencius spoke of Confucius that is, when Confucius ascended the Eastern Mountain, he realized how small the state of Lu was. When he ascended Mount Tai, he saw how small the empire was. . . (Mencius says 2009). A leader needs to be broad-minded, to learn and grow.

For Confucius, a person or a leader who thinks him(her)self wise cannot hear any advice, and he does not learn or cannot improve him(her)self. However, learning prevents one from being narrow-minded. Learning also helps build one's resilience. And for Confucius, it is very important for individuals to learn, and keep on learning. Here, Matsushita (1994a, b), a Confucian and the late founder of the Matsushita Electric Company (now Panasonic) speaks of the un-trapped mind. We can take it that the Confucian idea of never afraid or ashamed of asking questions (Zhou 2005) here is applied, and this broadens one's thinking and horizons.

It is definitely wise to learn, and it is wisdom when one is aware of what one knows, and when one does not, one acknowledges one's ignorance. One learns from one's mistakes, and embarks on the path to improvement. Confucius said that if one finds a good man, emulate his example and if one finds a bad man, search for his mistakes or fault so as to learn. And for Confucius, more critically, if one makes a mistake and does not learn from it, one is actually making a double mistake, if not a serious one.

Interestingly, the resilient leader also learns, correcting him(her)self; (s)he strengthens and grows. In *The Analects*, Confucius presents himself as a "transmitter who invented nothing" (Wikipedia 2007). He put the greatest emphasis on the importance of study or learning, highlighting that:

Not to correct the mistake one made is to err indeed (Zhou 2005, p. 79).
Never be afraid of correcting mistakes one has made (Zhou 2005, p. 80).

For Confucius, it is good to review the old and deducing the new [and one who does these becomes a teacher]. To this researcher, overall, this means that the leader learns; benchmarks, learns and improves. Here, it can also be said that there's a touch of *kaizen* (continuous improvement); continuous improvement indeed builds and enhances resilience in a leader.

Concluding that Singapore has the *Confucian Heritage* national culture (Low 2002, 2009), Low (2007) highlights that Singaporeans value learning. And the typical Singapore Company grows, and could cope well with changes in the external environment. These also indicated that the island-nation's small and medium enterprises (SMEs), including family-run companies, could also learn to cultivate winning values such as being prudent, hardworking and resilient so that they can really turn into SMEs: small (strong), and mighty enterprises (Low 2002; 2009). Besides, with public sector support, Singaporean workers learn and they upgrade (Lee 2000a, b); the Confucian value of learning is there and they are motivated; these overall contribute to the nation's embracing the value of learning and human capital, making Singaporeans resilient.

Positive Thinking Pays

The gentleman is to have no evil or negative thoughts. Positive in thinking and outlook, he becomes strong and resilient. And what more, the more man meditates upon good thoughts, the better will be his world and the world at large.

What not only a Confucian but a person thinks is so important. A person's mind is indeed influenced by the setting or the surroundings the person is in. Such a thinking can indeed be argued as Confucian as in the case of Mencius who enjoyed the lessons of his kind mother; she thrice changed her residence on his account. When they lived near a cemetery, Mencius diverted himself with acting the various mourning scenes which he witnessed at the tombs; and when finally staying near a public school, it became the proper place for Mencius as the child was taken with the various exercises of the politeness which the scholars were taught, and he endeavored to imitate. (Legge 1970, pp. 16–17, also cited in Low 2016, p. 14). One needs to be positive and thinks positively so that one can then also act in a positive way.

For Confucius, "the mind of the gentleman(*lady*) (*junzi*) progresses upwards; the vulgar mind progresses downwards" (Chew 2000, p. 22, *italics mine*). When one looks inwards, one would improve oneself, and become strong and tough. Confucius said, "A gentleman (*junzi*) blames himself while a common man blames others" (Lin 1994, p. 181). This, to the author, means that the Confucian leader is more of an internal than an external; the leader is the Captain of his(her) ship and (s)he is the master (mistress) of his(her) destiny.

Detached and un-trapped by power, position and wealth, the positive Confucian steadfastly serves and makes good the given situation. Business can survive and continue to exist. That service attitude can help the person to be more influential or persuasive, attracting customers and prospects. (S)he willingly serves. "A gentleman (*lady*) is (*also*) conscious only in the knowledge of others' comfort; the mean is conscious only of his (*her*) own comfort" (Chew 2000, p. 2, *italics mine*).

Besides, the Confucian leader does more than (s)he cannot bear. Or (s)he has something that (s)he cannot bear. Mencius commented that everyone has something that he cannot allow or stomach. To extend such distaste to what he can bear is benevolence. Everyone has something that (s)he refuses to do; and to enlarge such dislike to what (s)he is willing to do is righteousness. To this author, to broaden such aversion to such obstacles to what he is willing to do is to be positive, indeed having that inner strength and resilience.

Assistance to Others Builds One's Character and Resilience

Resilient leaders are also benevolent. The gentleman (lady) (*jen*) is not only kind and benevolent to one's parents and family members, those within the family and those outside the family and friends, but also to other people. The gentleman (lady) is a source of affection and kindness to all.

A man is ailing if he makes no progress in virtue, learns nothing or leaves no bad habits and corrects no mistakes. But as one learns, one betters oneself; one makes progress in one's virtue, and as one betters oneself, is it not that one indirectly improving one's family, one's country, and ultimately the world?

When profits are made, the Confucian business would return some to the community in the form of help and assistance to others. Care for others and social responsibility is thus 'built-in'. For Confucius, not only during normal times but also during a crisis, a good leader helps others especially the needy. (S)he does strive to make the rich more rich (Chew 2000).

Integrity and Character Wins Business and Customers

Being morally good is good for business and winning customers.

Confucius expressed, "The power of the spiritual forces in the Universe—how active it is everywhere! Invisible to the eyes, and impalpable to the senses, it is inherent in all things, and nothing can escape its operation" (Lin 1994, p. 109).

Although business is not the primary concern, but once the baseline is settled [one's integrity and character is established, there is much trust (*xin*) and], business and profits would (naturally) be in place. A case in point that can be seen in practice is that of Singapore's Choon Keng Tang or better known as C.K. Tang, honesty and diligence were the guiding principles of the pastor's son who built a commercial edifice. He believed that "in business, one must not cheat people", and he earned much trust of others (Tang, cited in Lee 2000, p. 42). In the late 1970s, C.K. Tang expanded his business, and in 1992, the Tang Complex, a 33-floor deluxe hotel and shopping complex was built along Singapore's popular tourist area and high street, Orchard Road.

"A gentleman(lady) (junzi) understands what is moral; a base man (lady) understands what is advantageous or profitable" (Confucius cited in Chew 2000, p. 9; italics mine). Interestingly, for Confucius, virtue is never alone; a good man (lady) is sure to attract other good men (ladies). Virtue also inspires respect of others. Confucius also highly stressed on integrity, business associates and people in general would often want to do business with a business person of character and integrity. When one has the character, high integrity and good example, one shines like the North Polar Star, and thus able to attract other people including one's business associates and customers.

Mencius once expressed that, "A great carpenter teaches his apprentice to use squares and compasses. The man, who wants to cultivate himself, must also have squares and compasses for his conduct in his business and in living" (Lin 1994, p. 290, italics mine). When one is not greedy, and being virtuous as well as having "a sensitive heart which cannot bear to see suffering in others" (Mencius cited in Chew 2000, p. 36), other people's trust on one is being built; there is also trust between business partners and associates, and goodwill spreads. And a virtuous business person, being credible, thus succeeds.

Build the Customers' (People's) Trust (*Xin*)

When leading (ruling) the country, it is critical that the leaders have the support and trust of the people. For the Confucian adherents, trust (*xin*) is very important when doing business (ruling the country). The leaders should not be resting on one's laurels or be complacent; otherwise they will lose the support and trust of the customers (people).

Confucian, the late Matsushita Konosuke, the founder of Matsushita Electric Company, now Panasonic, for example, believed in building the customers' trust. Customers' trust, with quality Company's delivery of good and services, can help to grow the Company, its markets and overall business.

Merchants normally work hard to create a respected name for their shops or companies; they seek to sell goods whose quality lived up to that name. Confucian in his ways, for Matsushita Konosuke, no matter how old and esteemed its name may be, a business today would receive no quarter if it shows incompetence or inadequacy in its performance, and it would eventually go under. Matsushita (1994a, b) highlighted that the Company or one should not be resting on one's laurels but keep on improving after establishing the reputation—and that will assure the Company of continued success.

Proactiveness Ensures Business Survival, If Not Growth

We can safely assert that Confucianism promotes pro-activeness. The business owner is daring yet (s)he "exercises judgment in the course being daring" (Chew 2000, p. 10). (S)he is "slow to speak but prompt to act" (Chew 2000, p. 10).

Being kind and benevolent, one also serves and extends help to others. There is much customer service and care.

Much warmth is generated. The Confucian leader is always willing to help others (taken as customers) no matter how difficult the problem others are facing with. (S)he would listen patiently to the customer's problem and would make suggestions and ways for him or her to solve the problem. The leader is constantly by the customer's side guiding him or her to achieve the customer's goals or needs. (S)he is considerate and always help to ease the customer's way when facing any difficulty (*The Analects*, Chap. 7 verse 38).

Perseverance Is a Boon

Citing Matsushita Konosuke as an example of a Confucian Japanese entrepreneur-leader, Low (2016, p. 17) spoke of:

(him, (being) thrown into poverty at a young age of four. . . The late Konosuke Matsushita was and is a role model who has inspired many; he struggled with the early deaths of family members, an apprenticeship which demanded sixteen-hour days at age nine, all the problems related to starting a business with neither money nor connections, the death of his only son, the Great Depression, the horror of World War 2 in Japan and more. Yet despite grounded by these hardships, Konosuke Matsushita grew to be a splendidly successful entrepreneur (Kotter 1997, cited in Low 2016, p. 17). The Master once said, "The gentleman is generous without its costing him anything, works others hard without their complaining. . ." (The Analects, XX verse 2 (Lau 1979: 159–160; also cited in Low 2016, p. 17).".

Interestingly too, Yeung and Tung's 1996 PRC study (cited in Low 2009, 2002) has also found that a relationship exists between certain Confucian values (such as perseverance) and firm performance. (A leader's) perseverance and industriousness lead logically to focus, working towards the company goals that enhance company profitability, adding to corporate success. Indeed, the value of resilience can be considered as the people's or followers' vitality and their drive and, indeed, the latter has made countries such as Germany, Japan and South Korea (Isaak 1997) economically successful.

Be Bold and Have the Necessary Determination

Resilient leaders should not seek to act or decide on things to make themselves popular, but rather seek to do things no matter how unpleasant they may be, but what that may be the long-term good for the people and the organization as a whole.

The Confucian leader is bold. "Act resolutely, and both heaven and hell will respect you" (Matsushita, cited in PHP 1991, p. 39). When one, as a leader, makes up one's mind to do something, one must have the resolute and determination to carry it out.

Additionally, as Confucius puts it, "One who has his arms broken three times may become a good doctor" (Zhou 2005, p. 170). Confucius has further pointed out that:

> ...a king can't become a real ruler without encountering difficulties; and soldiers can't become crack troops without suffering setbacks (Zhou 2005, p. 171).

To best cite a practical example, this researcher would highlight these: With the *Confucian Heritage* culture (Low 2002, 2005, 2006a, 2009), Singapore's ejection from Malaysia in 1965, its caesarean national birth and the influence of other factors as highlighted by Low (2007), Singapore/Singaporeans are said to possess resilience. Most or older workers, who have lost their jobs, persevere in finding jobs, and being flexible being open to options in their job search. In times of recession and unemployment, they search for opportunities to keep afloat. They to some extent also welcome foreign talents while facing some competition to their jobs and means of survival; overall, they bravely face the issues and forge on. Perhaps, this could be interpreted as Confucian leadership of the ordinary people in their everyday lives. They, in fact, subscribe very much to the Chinese saying of "not be afraid of going slow, but be very much afraid of standing still" (Low 2007, p. 142; also cited in Low 2008).

Thriftiness and Prudence Adds to the Leader's Resilient Qualities

Being thrifty and prudent are Confucian qualities, and what Matsushita (1994) refers to as dam management—it is in fact a useful practice for enterprises (nations) whose aim is long term stability and development. Prudence also aptly adds to the resilience of the leaders and Singapore's economic strengths (Low 2006b, 2008).

The Singapore Government (Singaporeans are under forced prudence?) can also be said to be prudent in their Central Provident Fund policies as well as maintaining the island-Republic's national reserves. Dr. Goh Keng Swee (Singapore's former Deputy Prime Minister and Finance Minister/Education Minister February 1979 to May 1980 and from June 1981 to December 1984) was one of the key men who helped to make Singapore what it is today; as one of the Singapore's Old Guards who can, in some ways, be said to be Confucian (and who recently passed away), Dr Goh was known for his values of "thriftiness, perseverance, courage and diligence" (Chiam See Tong, cited in *The Sunday Times* 2010, p. 6).

Proper Procedures (*Li*: Rituals) and Transparency Helps and Builds Transparency

With a strong value of governmental support and involvement, the Singapore Government builds road and provides the necessary infrastructure (Low 2002, 2009). Certainly, paternalism also exists alongside the "confidence of the people in the ruler" (Lin 1998 cited in Low 2002, 2009), and being an orderly society is seen as a top Asian value (Bjerke 1999 and Naisbitt 1995 cited in Low 2002, 2009).

For a Confucian, rites and rituals help to build discipline and establish stability as well as a sense of orderliness. It is good to have proper and systematic procedures, and that helps, and in the Singapore case, it leads to an effective and efficient civil service [recruited and hiring talents in a meritocratic manner], contributing to greater transparency and good governance of the island-Republic. With an "efficient and honest civil service that promptly attended to the needs of its citizens" (Ganesan 2002 cited in Low 2002, 2009), Singapore everything was on the table with clear rules (Thurow 1996, p. viii, Schein 1996, p. 169). There is also little or no corruption. And all these contribute to the island-nation's business and economic-resilience.

Section Conclusion

Overall, as argued by Low (2016), the Confucian's key concepts and values discussed, that is, in terms of character, integrity, learning, positive thinking, continuous improvement; trust (xin), diligence and prudence—are still relevant in today's world; and holding key leadership lessons and hallmarks of success, they truly facilitate and contribute to building and growing one's leadership resilience and toughness, if not, leadership excellence. Yu Dan (2010: 10) interestingly highlighted that, "The truths that Confucius gives us are always the easiest of truths"; and to paraphrase her, Confucius' teachings tell us all how we can live or lead the kind of happy (resilient or tough) leadership life that our spirit needs.

Checkpoint: Think About It

Resilience and Leadership in Asia
Being Resilient
The CORE Qualities
Boosting Endurance and Being Resilient
1. When faced with an adverse situation, do you:
   - Say No to negativity?
   - Ignore the negatives? (Suppose you try not to ignore the negatives)
   - See the positive aspects (Are you seizing any opportunity?)
   - Save? Are you prepared for the rainy days?
   - Try to be creative?

- Adopt/ adapt to 'be open—There's always a way!'?
- Adopt the way of the warrior?
- Attempt to be adaptable?
- Learn from nature?
- Visualise success?
- Have a good sense of humour?
- Get energy and recharged?
- Have the clarity of mind?
- Get help from family or close friends?
- Go bit by bit, inch your way through... and still make it?
- Have staying power?
- Move on, attempting and attaining the better and the best?
- Believe in yourself?
- Build the ballast, getting help from the beyond?

2. What are the lessons that can be learnt from adversity (a particular adverse event)?
3. What are the ways in which you limit yourself?
4. What are your assets that make you strong?
5. What steps can you take to develop your strengths?
6. When faced with a problem (adversity), are you still putting forth the total effort, or have you grown callous or insensitive (care less)?
7. Are you stopping on the one-yard line? Are you finishing your commitments? (Give up now and you'll never find the ballast or inner strength you have.)
8. Are you running to win or merely seek to survive?
9. What are your dreams and hopes that you wish to achieve?
10. Are you denying yourself things (resources) which would help you doing your best?
11. Are you keeping your spirits up, passionate about the things you are currently doing? Are you turning them to the challenges?
12. What steps can you take to make (a) your job and (b) your organization more meaningful?
13. When going through a bad time, think about others who have gone through adversity and made it out the other side. Find out the ways which have made them make it out the other side. What can you adopt or adapt to suit you?
14. When you're going through a bad time, think about your blessings.
15. Are you creative enough? Are you coming up with various solutions to resolve the problem(s)?

Buddha, Buddhism and Being Resilient
1. Reflect and relate each of the following to your leadership ways:
- The Path
- Being self-reliant and tough
- Living in the world of Anicca
- Acquiring higher awareness, we can transform ourselves
- Being aware of situations creating negativity
- Watching, observing and taking note of positive influences

- Having ideals
- (In spite of the odds,) being motivated, and moving on
- Coping with one's environment
- Having the positive thinking's edge

Being Resilient, the Confucian Way

Reflect and relate each of the following to your leadership ways:

- Learning helps, continuous learning benefits
- Positive thinking pays
- Assistance to others builds one's character and resilience
- Integrity and character wins business and customers
- Build the customers' (people's) tust (xin)
- Proactive-ness ensures business survival, if not growth
- Perseverance is a boon
- Be bold and have the necessary determination
- Thriftiness and prudence adds to the leader's resilient qualities
- Proper procedures (li—rituals) and transparency helps and builds transparency

2. What can you learn from the section: 'Buddha, Buddhism and Being Resilient'? In what ways can you make yourself more resilient?
3. What can you learn from the section: 'Resilience, the Confucian Way'? In what other ways can you make yourself more resilient?
4. What can you learn or gather from this chapter about Resilience and China?
5. What can you gather from this chapter about Resilience and India?
6. What can you gather from this chapter about Resilience and Japan?
7. What can you gather from this chapter about Resilience and Kazakhstan?
8. What can you gather from this chapter about Resilience and Singapore?
9. What can you gather from this chapter about Change and Resilience?
10. How does thinking positively help one to be a better leader? Or to be a resilient leader?

References

Adger, W. N. (2000). Social and ecological resilience: Are they related? *Progress in Human Geography, 24*(3), 347–364.

Chew Kheng Hoe, P. (2000). *A gentleman's code*. Singapore: Graham Brash.

Chu, C.-N. (1992). *Thick face, black heart*. Beavertown: AMC Publishing.

Isaak, R. (1997). Making 'economic miracles': Explaining extraordinary national economic achievement. *American Economist, 41*(1), 59–69.

Kazakhworld.com. (2017). The Golden Warrior: A Kazakh icon of independence, prosperity and heritage. Accessed April 5/September 2, 2017 from http://kazakhworld.com/the-golden-warrior-a-kazakh-icon-of-independence-prosperity-and-heritage/

Khema, A. (1991). *When the iron eagle flies*. London: Penguin.

Khoo, C. (Ed.). (2001). *Malaysia savvy*. Malaysia: PHP International Singapore Pte. Ltd. and Malaysia Institute of Management.

Koh, K. K. (2004). *Guan Yin, heart of compassion*. Singapore: Asiapac Books.

Kornfield, J., & Fronsdal, G. (Eds.). (1991). *Teachings of the Buddha*. Boston & London: Shambhala.

Lao-tzu *Tao te Ching* (From a translation by S. Mitchell). Accessed May 22, 2008., from http://acc6.its.brooklyn.cuny.edu/~phalsall/texts/taote-v3.html

Lau, D. C. (1979). *Confucius: The Analects – Lun Yu*. England: Penguin Books.

Lee, B. Y. (2000a). Lifelong learning a must in the new economy, speech at Mendaki's CREST Gold Collar Worker Award, 2 Sept 2000, *Speeches 2000*. Ministry of Information and The Arts, pp. 46–50.

Lee, P. (2000b, September 4). Salesperson every shopper knew. *The Straits Times*, p. 42.

Legge, J. (1970). *The works of Mencius*. London: Constable and Company.

Lim, S. (1999). *Peak conquerors*. Singapore: Research Communication International.

Lin, Y. (1994). *The wisdom of Confucius*. New York: The Modern Library.

Low, K. C. P. (2002). *Corporate culture and values: Perception of corporate leaders of co-operatives in Singapore*. Unpublished PhD thesis, The University of South Australia, Adelaide.

Low, K. C. P. (2005). Towards a framework & typologies of Singapore corporate cultures. *Management Development Journal of Singapore, 13*(1), 46–75.

Low, K. C. P. (2006a). Father leadership – The Singapore case study. *Management Decision, 44* (2), 89–104.

Low, K. C. P. (2006b). Crisis management – Can core values be considered as a built-in safety net? The Singapore case. *Insights to a Changing World, 2006*(3), 133–150.

Low, K. C. P. (2007). The cultural value of resilience – The Singapore case study. *Cross-cultural Management: An International Journal, 14*(2), 136–149.

Low, K. C. P. (2008). Value-based leadership: Leading, the Confucian way. *Leadership & Organizational Management Journal, 2008*(3), 32–41.

Low, K. C. P. (2009). *Corporate culture and values: Perceptions of corporate leaders of co-operatives in Singapore*. London: VDM-Verlag.

Low, K. C. P. (2010a). Leading, the Buddhist proactive way (Vietnam). GLOBALTRADE.net. http://www.globaltrade.net/folder/topic/content/Vietnam/Business%20Environment/3135. html

Low, K. C. P. (2010b). Leading the Buddha way. *Insights to a Changing World Journal (since 1992), 2010*(1), 23–33.

Low, K. C. P. (2010c). Proactive leading, the Buddhist way (Thailand). GLOBALTRADE.net. http://www.globaltrade.net/folder/topic/content/Thailand/Living/3134.html

Low, K. C. P. (2010d). Confucius, customer service and service excellence. *Conflict Resolution & Negotiation Journal, 2010*(4), 53–61.

Low, K. C. P. (2010e). Buddhism and positive thinking – What's in store for us? GLOBALTRADE.net. http://www.globaltrade.net/folder/topic/content/Thailand/Living/3394.html

Low, K. C. P. (2016). Creating resilient leaders with reference to the teachings of old master Confucius. *International Journal of Business and Social Science, 7*(7), 12–21.

Low, K.C. P. (2017). Leading and managing the value of resilience, the Kazakhstan Way. 5th National Conference of the Partners of PMI Kazakhstan Potential Chapter (Almaty), 30 May 2017, Turan University, Almaty, Kazakhstan.

Low, K. C. P., & Theyagu, D. (2003). *Developing true leadership potential*. Singapore: The Publishing Consultant.

Master, H. Y. (2001). *Buddhism pure and simple*. New York: Weatherhill.

Matsushita, K. (1984). *Not for bread alone*. New York: PHP Institute of America.

Matsushita, K. (1994a). *Matsushita Konosuke (1894–1989): His life and his legacy*. Japan: PHP Institute.

Matsushita, K. (1994b). *Not for bread alone*. New York: Berkley Books.

Mencius says. (2009). *Mencius says*. Malaysia: Zi Publications Sdn Bhd.

Nazarbayev, N. (Bulter, J.; translator). (2008). *The Kazakhstan way*. London: Stacey International.

Noor, M. A. (2013). Vision 2050: Nazarbayev's visionary approach for future. www.astanatimes. com. Accessed September 16, 2017, from http://astanatimes.com/2013/09/vision-2050-nazarbayevs-visionary-approach-for-future/

Okawa, R. (2002). *The essence of Buddha*. London: Time Warner Books.

Okawa, R. (2005). *10 principles of universal wisdom*. Malaysia: Jaico Publishing House.

PHP Institute. (1991). *Velvet glove, iron fist and 101 other dimensions of leadership*. Japan: PHP Institute.

Russell, B. (2007, 1912). *The problems of philosophy*. New York: Cosimo.

Schein, E. H. (1996). *Strategic pragmatism, the culture of Singapore's Economic Development Board*. Cambridge: Massachusetts Institute of Technology.

Stoltz, P. G. (1997). *Adversity quotient: Turning obstacles to opportunities*. New York: Wiley.

Stoltz, P. (1998). *Adversity quotient: Turning obstacles into opportunities*. New York: Wiley.

The Dalai Lama. (1998). *The path to tranquility – Daily wisdom*. New York: The Penguin Group.

The Dalai Lama. (2001). *An open heart, practicing compassion in everyday life*. London: Hodder & Stoughton.

The Dalai Lama. (2007). *Mind in comfort and ease*. New York: Wisdom Publications.

The Dalai Lama, & Mehrotra, R. (2008). *The Dalai Lama on happiness, life, living and much more*. New York: Hay House.

The Sunday Times. (2010, May 16). Remembering Goh Keng Swee. *The Sunday Times*, p. 6.

Thera, N. (2009, 1933). *Buddhism in a nutshell*. Sri Lanka: Buddhist Cultural Centre.

Thich, N. N. (1992). *Peace is every step*. New York: Bantam Books.

Thurow, L. (1996). Foreword. In E. H. Schein (Ed.), *Strategic pragmatism, the culture of Singapore's Economic Development Board*. Cambridge: Massachusetts Institute of Technology.

Wikipedia. (2007). Confucius. *Wikipedia*. Accessed June 6, 2007, from http://en.wikipedia.org/wiki/Confucius

Yu, D. (2010). *Confucius from the heart*. England: Pan Books.

Zhou, K. (2005). *A basic Confucius* (1st ed.). Hong Kong: Long River Press.

http://www.globaltrade.net/folder/topic/content/Vietnam/Business%20Environment/3135.html

Using Soft Power

17

What Is Soft Power?

Soft power (Nye 1991) can be defined as the ability to obtain what one wants through co-option and attraction, the carrot way. The author will elaborate in the later section.

To understand soft power better perhaps we should discuss hard power first. Soft power is the reverse or opposite of 'hard power'. 'Hard power' uses coercion and payment (fines and penalties) or essentially, applies the big stick. Leaders make a big mistake when they get bossy. Successful leadership is not about instructing, using force or bossing around; it is a sure sign of insecurity when the leader pushes the point that (s)he is the boss.

All of us are so used to using the stick ("Just whack'em!") and applying hard power; after all, as Andre Gide once said, "One does not discover new lands without consenting to lose sight of the shore for a very long time"; it will indeed, for some of us, take some time to get used to applying soft rather than hard power.

[These days, we have or can get more and more information at hand through internet, surfing and handphones; besides, more choices (satellite television has a variety of channels and shows) and more options are available and unlike in the past where leaders, let alone managers have monopoly or much control over information. Hence, leaders have to apply more and more of soft power in order to be persuasive.]

The Chinese have this saying that goes, "A paper tiger cannot bear close scrutiny"; this means that that a threat is or can be frightening only from a distance, but it is not effective when viewed closely. In short, threats and similar ways of hard power are in actuality not only unattractive, but also ineffective in persuading others (Low 2010b).

© Springer International Publishing AG 2018
K.C.P. Low, *Leading Successfully in Asia*,
https://doi.org/10.1007/978-3-319-71347-2_17

Applying Soft Power, the Confucius' Way

A little explanation is necessary here. As stated in Low (2010b), lately (in the past several years), the ancient Confucian philosophy has been interpreted as a justification for China's authoritarian government control that "emphasizes social stability through rule of virtue rather than rule of law" (Gordon 2009). However, this is not true or applicable as it is merely seen from the political perspective. [Officials have insisted the Confucius Institutes are not about spreading soft power (The Useless Tree 2010a).] Critics has pointed out that the Chinese Communist Party once reviled the philosophy, but is now promoting it through Confucian slogans and the more than 300 Confucius Institutes that have been set up throughout the world. They highlighted that the Confucian revival is purely a Government conspiracy. But whatever the political designs are, to say such a thing is to overlook or ignore the relevance, strengths and benefits of the Confucian philosophy, akin to confining oneself to psychic-prison thinking. Perhaps we should not close our minds, instead let us find out and know more of this Confucian soft power. It is also not authoritarian as ordinarily stereotyped by most US media. Confucian soft power is basically about promoting fellowships as well as love, and driving fear out of the work place (organization/nation). And this is appealing. But they are to be put into practice!

From the outset, it should be stressed that Confucian soft power is basically, so to speak, neutral. It is indeed the action and practices that count. Let me explain further, take meritocracy, for example, it was not new to the Chinese since Confucian scholars, having done well in the State examinations, would be accorded official positions in the Chinese bureaucracy—they became the Mandarins, ruling ancient China. Confucius does stand for a meritocracy of sorts. Confucian modernizers would say that there's full inclusion and participation of women in public life and this is completely consistent with Confucian principles (although the past uses of Confucianism in China were powerfully patriarchal); modern Confucian meritocracy includes women (The Useless Tree 2010b; Low 2002a, 2009a). However, one of the things that are quite noticeable about China's public administration in recent years is corruption, officials using their public offices for personal gain. Chairman's Mao grandson Mao Xinyu, 40, was appointed as China's youngest ever major-general in July 2010; it seemed that revolutionary heritage had triumphed over martial prowess. Mao Xinyu then confirmed that nepotism did play its part in his promotion, acknowledging to a popular Chinese website that his family background was "definitely a factor" in the decision to add a second star to his epaulettes (The Useless Tree 2010b). Thus to reinstate the concepts and ideas of Confucian soft power are neutral though when applied, it can be used, and history has shown, in the good or bad sense, and indeed the action and practices that count. And ultimately, a leader should bear in mind that what's critical is that the soft power must (not be abused instead) benefit the masses or people not the minority or worse the chosen few so that indeed it stays soft or attractive.

Having said all these, let us next examine the Confucian ways of using soft power.

Confucian Ways and Applications of Using Soft Power

Strength does lie in might, force or wealth, instead strengths and power lies in attraction and in the following ways. And Confucian soft power can be attained by:

Being Virtuous

It is worthy to note to begin with that the idea of attracting or persuading others as a source of power goes or dates back to ancient Chinese philosophers such as Confucius and Lao-Tzu in the seventh century B.C. For example, Lao-Tzu speaks of having or building up virtue, and one then master all. Confucius too spoke of being benevolent (*ren*). The Master also said, "Virtue never stands alone. It is bound to have neighbours" (*The Analects*, IV verse 25) Lau (1979) and Legge (2008).

A person's virtues are attractive to others around him. For Confucius, the political leaders need to desire the good themselves and the ordinary citizens will be good. "The virtue of the gentleman is like wind; the virtue of the small man is like grass. Let the wind blow over the grass and it is sure to bend" (*The Analects*, XII verse 19).

A virtuous or kind leader is well respected and influential, and thus, (s)he gains much gravity or respect and trust from his (her) life followers. Or better still, powerlessness is also another source of soft power, the powerful or others would want to assist or lend a hand to those without power (Low 2010a). Perhaps, they may also take pity and help.

Leading by Example

The example of a leader is like a ringing church bell that calls people to come forth.

"If the stick is crooked, the shadow cannot be straight," observes Low (2000, 2002a, 2006a, p. 139) and leaders must set the example, though he was speaking in the context of building service excellence in organizations. Low (2008a, p. 33) has highlighted that, "the leadership message Confucius impresses on us is that: As leaders, we need to act and behave as gentlemen (*junzi*)." It is the role of the leaders to guide by virtue (*The Analects*, II verse 3). True leaders stand out; people observe the actions of the leader, 'monkeys see and monkeys do' (Low and Theyagu 2003, p. 35). Becoming a role model is one of the most effective ways in which leader can encourage his followers to achieve the goals set.

For Confucius, to this author's mind, life is a pure flame; and each of us live by an invisible sun within ourselves. A Confucian leader maintains his or her character and integrity (*lien*), and indeed when people feel that the leader has enough gravity in one's doings, then they will axiomatically or obviously respect the leader.

Being Trustworthy

Soft power is about building the people's trust of the leader. The Master once said, 'Make it your guiding principle to do your best for others and to be trustworthy in what you say' (*The Analects*, IX verse 25).

True leaders gain their followers' trust (Low and Theyagu 2003). For Confucius, one has to build trust (*xin*) and lead by example; people are always watching their leaders, and a leader's behaviour and actions need to match what (s)he advocates. To grow trust as a leader, the Confucian leader sets the standards, "using oneself as a measure to gauge others" (*The Analects*, IV verse 15). "The Master said, 'If one sets strict standards for oneself and makes allowances for others when making demands on them, one will stay clear of ill will'", and thus reliability, leading to trust which is built upon, and it is expanded (*The Analects*, XV verse 15).

And what more, the leader grows the people's trust (*xin*) of his or her character and integrity (*lien*) with dedication and commitment.

Being Approachable and Friendly

Of clear conscience, the gentleman(lady) is relaxed (*The Analects*, XII verse 4). And unlike a petty person, (s)he is not anxious and thus deals well with people. Relaxed, "likeable" (respondents' input) and personable, the Confucian leader is approachable and friendly, and such a leader is influential; people like such a leader.

Where government (a group of leaders) is concerned, it is also about government's establishing their rapport with peoples and building goodwill as well as their deepening of their friendships and relationships with them. Even in this modern age of info-communications and high-tech, Government leaders should thus not be aloof or distant, uninterested, let alone, be uncaring. The personal touch should be there.

Sharing the Same Values, Fostering a Sense of Unity

This is turning the soft stuff into advantage. Culture can be a tremendous competitive edge and it is not easily replicable (Taylor 2004; Barker and Coy 2004). However, most organisations are not investing, growing in culture or promoting certain core values at the level that will differentiate them from their rivals.

It is worthy to note that the Confucian leader studies people. For Confucius, a leader can understand a person by observing what (s)he does, how (s)he arrives at his (her) present position and how (s)he feels about it. Then, there is a need to ask whether there is anything about the person (s)he does not understand (*The Analects*, Chap. II verse 10). It is very important to work with good people and lead them. Working with petty people, those not sharing the higher ideals of virtue, benevolence and learning are not encouraged in the Confucian way. Confucius also expressed that "while the gentleman cherishes virtue, the petty man cherishes his native place; while the gentleman cherishes the law, the petty man cherishes his self interests."

To further explain, when referring to the same core values, it is good to know that the Chinese character for heart [心] (*Hanyu Pinyin: xin*) symbolizes the biological organ heart itself and is used in the Chinese language to express the human feelings and the characteristic of an individual or a group. This shows the common intent and purpose (among members of a team) necessary to attain synergy. And when the leader shares the same values and the common convictions with the people, the people and the leader are of one mind and one heart. And of like-minds, it is easier to work out together and attain whatever goal(s) set. Confucianism stresses on this sense of unity, and this value, in fact, becomes an edge, encouraging people to work hard and together overcome hardships and whatever obstacles faced.

In Asia, government leaders are doing this by stressing on shared or common Asian values to their constituents, and these values include integrity, family togetherness, relationship-building and other Confucian and/ or Asian values. Sharing the same core values with people make people feel that they, in fact, share a common goal or destiny with the government or their leaders (Low 2008b). And other things being equal, this can also ensure the success of government initiatives and project implementations.

Empowering the People

Related to the foregoing sense of unity is this soft power way of sharing power or empowering others. When the leader delegates or empowers his or her people, (s)he shares power with the people. And by giving power to people, they are kept active, involved, motivated and striving; synergy emerges. And with synergy, the equation is $1 + 1 + 1 = 5$ (not 3). Much strength of the people is put into use; and these result in the following equation: Strength + strength + strength = synergy.

Cooperating and Collaborating

"Within the four seas, all men are brothers." Cooperating and collaborating is yet another source of soft power. How true, a single tree cannot make a forest, and a single beam cannot support a big house. In same way, leaders when they are collaborative, they can get the support of the people. And one good way to get collaboration and cooperation from the people is by educating them. When governing a country, Confucius stressed on the importance of giving them economic growth, alleviating poverty as well as equipping them with the necessary education. And as in the case of Singapore with its *Confucian Heritage* national culture, after setting up the necessary foundations—good government and political stability (Low 2002b, 2009a), the government then, using various schemes and incentives (Bhasin and Low 2002), seeks to attract foreign talents. [For Confucius, "distant subjects" or foreigners will come when they are attracted by good and stable government (*The Analects*, XVI verse 1)].

Besides, when leaders foster cooperation, good teamwork and a sense of unity, they get things done. Together even achieve more (Low 2003). What is good for the hive now becomes good for the bee; and with the hive's prosperity, every bees gain.

In the small business situation, the father leader/small business-owner collaborates with his "family members" in a purposeful team fashion, "rubbing shoulders and doing something together also gives the opportunity to share. There is joint purpose, sharing the same dreams and bringing the relationship to a higher plane. There is also synergy" (Low 2001, p. 101, 2005, 2007). Employees' successes are celebrated and with effective team leadership, teamwork is fostered and higher performance attained (Zimmerer and Scarborough 2006, cited in Low 2007).

Standing for Values, Moral Courage and What a Leader Stands For

The gentleman (lady) stands tall, and understands what is right and ethical (*The Analects*, IV verse 16).

The hallmark of true leadership is really standing for one's values, moral courage and what one stands for. Low and Theyagu (2003, p. 14) have highlighted that "by the leader's values, moral courage and what he stands for, people know if he is committed". One should not be caught in a situation where one is seen less than honest and candid. If one is caught in a compromising situation, one misplaces the people's or the followers' trust. Essentially it boils down to who one is and what one stands for. People usually admire who one is and what one stand for. And in the Confucian sense, one needs to be a gentleman (lady) (*jen*), and be kind and benevolent to one's people. When the people trust the leader's values, they are likely to follow the leader.

Educating the People

Confucius stressed a lot on learning and education; he brought education to the masses (*The Analects*, XVI verse 9, I verse 14; VII verse 7). The people are educated; they learn and are motivated.

Here, the author wishes to highlight the case of Singapore, a City-state with the *Confucian Heritage* national culture (Low 2002b, 2009a). The public, people of all ages, young and old, are educated on the uses and benefits of e-government. The Singapore government has built up a national information technology (IT) culture that involved a massive public education campaign and this is one of the factors that accounts for the success of its e-government. School children are educated not only to be open to IT, but also to be IT-savvy, the students use computers and laptops, and were exposed to the use and benefits of computers, IT and technology as a whole. And to this author, this helps to bring about the vital soft people power—the platform and vital increasing awareness, acceptance and appreciation of Infocomm-Communications Technology (ICT) and successful e-government implementation. The plan also called for the involvement of schools, businesses, community centres, the mass media and other grassroots organizations to create awareness and promote IT education and literacy (IDA 2006).

Additionally, various campaigns were held annually to raise public awareness of the e-lifestyle. These campaigns in Singapore stress on the 4Es—e-Learning, e-Entertainment, e-Communications and e-Transactions—to provide Singaporeans five strong reasons why they have got to be connected to information communication technology (Rahman et al. 2011; Low 2008b). To stir citizens from being aware to adopting an e-lifestyle, a series of thematic online fairs are also planned to boost consumer confidence in online services such as shopping for groceries, purchasing travel packages and banking online.

Being Charming and Engaging

Soft power is also about the ability to influence the people's preference, likings and acceptance through appeal and attraction. The leader charms by winning the people over; presenting convincing arguments and giving much information to engage them. When the leader informs the people, they are involved. Confucius said, 'Artful words will ruin one's (the leader's) virtue" (*The Analects*, XV verse 27); clear transparency is required and that also supplies the way to good governance of organizations (nations). And as Low and Theyagu (2003) indicate nothing is ever gained by hiding necessary information from people who need to know. And inform people and they are engaged.

What should also be practiced which Confucius stressed is that of getting input or feedback from the grassroots (*The Analects*, Chap. V verse 15; Chap. VIII verse 5). And the benefits of this will certainly be that of helping leaders to carry out the right policies, ensuring that they are, with the people's input, well-thought while in the drawing-board stage. And more importantly, the leaders can understand and work to meet the people's needs.

Being Ever Encouraging

Another form of soft power is that of being increasingly encouraging. What more, if the leader is encouraging, it really makes him or her likeable.

Confucius encouraged learning, and he would not want to refuse any student who would want to learn something from him (*The Analects*, VII verse 7). Eager to learn (*The Analects*, I verse 14), the Confucian leader also encourages people to learn. Self-cultivating (*The Analects*, XII verse 24), (s)he also encourages others to mend and self-cultivate themselves.

Fig. 17.1 Depiction of an
inspiring leader who is not
only encouraging, but who is
also humble and patient. No
one likes a proud or an
arrogant person

Being Humble

The petty and the arrogant leader is not liked, if not, loathed.

On the other hand, humility is power. And when the leader is humble, (s)he
becomes pleasant and persuasive. One of the four things that Confucius refused to
have anything to do with is that of being egotistical (*The Analects*, IX verse 4). The
Confucian leader is quiet, "loath to speak… (fearing or) shameful if their person
failed to keep up with their words" (*The Analects*, IV verse 22), and achieving or
hardworking. When the silent achiever speaks, people listen (Fig. 17.1).

One respondent highlighted these:

Confucian leader is never seen to be arrogant for (s)he studies extensively, sets
standards and regulates him(her)self with the rites. This also makes him (her) a
reliable person, trusted and a leader who is depended upon when the followers are
in need of the leader's help.

The Master said, 'The gentleman is at ease without being arrogant; the small
man is arrogant without being at ease' (*The Analects*, XIII verse 26). A good leader
does not boast or brag; indeed a good general does not blow his own trumpet.
Besides, to Confucius, it is rare, indeed, for a man with cunning words and a
flattering face to be a gentleman (*The Analects*, I verse 3).

In public, setting the paradigm, Confucius was meek and seemed to be tongue-
tied. In the ancestral temple and at court, though fluent, he did not speak lightly (*The
Analects*, X verse 1). The Confucian leader should thus be cautious in speech (*The
Analects*, I verse 14). And that is more persuasive.

Being Patient

Patience is wisdom in waiting, and applying wisdom is power, soft power. On the surface it appears timid and weak, but this is power and it can grow. "Sparing of speech but trustworthy in what he says" (*The Analects*, I verse 6), when a leader listens, he shows he is patient. And when a leader is patient with the people or person(s) concerned, he is often showing care and concern. And the people feels cared for and many appreciate such a gesture.

One may also add that for Confucius, the lack of self-restraint or being impatient in small matters will bring ruin to great plans (*The Analects*, XV verse 27). Hence, to be successful in project management too, the leader should study the feasibility before embarking on it; and during the project, there is a need for good coordination as well as patiently attending to details. Patient, the leader should also be willing to teach or coach the people.

Being Caring

Success is in serving and caring too, and that is a variant of soft power. The Master said, ". . .do your best for others" (*The Analects*, IX verse 25), and when the leaders care, they attract the people; akin to applying the power of nice (Low 2001).

In the case of Singapore, Low (2006b) has highlighted that the Government, like a benevolent father, looks after the people's welfare. Here, the preferred management style is that of firm control and, at times, explicit direction, but essentially doing good for the society and the efficient political leadership together with the hardworking workforce has helped build Singapore. Singapore government has done well; they showed they have cared for the population and businesses by providing good roads, infrastructures and telecommunications as well as a clean and green environment. Whatever the grouses or complaints of the population aside, the Singapore Government did facilitate much economic growth and progress of the island-Republic as well as the welfare and well-being of the local populace. They have also ensured strategic maintenance of the facilities while effecting good place marketing of the City-state (Low 2009b); all these give them the vital soft power.

Returning or Paying Back to the Community

According to Confucius, if one is directed by profit in one's actions, one will invite much ill will (*The Analects*, IV verse 12). For Confucius, power and success does not lie in making profits, but rather in giving or returning back to the community. Returning to the community gives success, soft power to the business givers as the business owners or companies fulfil their corporate social responsibility (CSR). Businesses can return to the community by giving donations or building community hospitals, and the people are helped or attended to.

In multicultural Singapore case, early Chinese settlers worked hard to accumulate wealth and at the same time contributed to the society in which they lived by building schools, hospitals and bridges (Lee and Low 2009; Low 2002a, 2009a). The same can be said of pioneer Chinese Singaporeans such as Tan Tock Seng (1798–1850), Tan Kim Seng (1805–1864), Aw Boon Haw (1893–1957), Lee Kong Chian (1893–1970), and Tan Kah Kee (1873–1961), to name a few. "If you make money from society, you must try your best to give something back to society" (Lien and Kraar 1994, cited in Low 2002a, 2009a).

And in Chinese-minority Brunei Darussalam society, the Chinese also do likewise. It was reported, for example, that Lim Teck Hoo Holdings Sdn Bhd. (LTH) donated in the form of scholarships to eight schools to help provide quality education for the less unfortunate students in the schools (Noor 2010, p. B3).

Section Conclusion

In contrast to hard power, soft power, like the carrot, is certainly more appealing and attractive to the people. And it is the honey, not vinegar, that attracts the ants, and the followers feel connected to the leaders. The concept of soft power as seen through the Confucian visor is fine paradigms of good attraction, particularly so of the leaders' caring for the people; the key issue lies in its action and sincere practices, and they should not be abused—manipulated by the leaders for their self-interest advantages in which case they will not be considered as a leader in the Confucian sense. They will then be petty people.

Applying Soft Power, the Lao Tzu (the Tao)'s Way

In this section, will examine the various sources, ways and applications of soft power through the visor of Taoism, namely, that of the teachings of the founder of Chinese Taoism (also spelled "Daoism"), Lao Tzu (*Hanyu Pinyin*: Lao Zi). These ways and applications—interpreted and given a modern twist, to mention just a few, include being simple, humble, other-centred and giving power to others as well as empowering or allowing people to own—and these, in fact, give power to the giver and leader.

Seemingly abstract, Lao Tzu focused on how human being perceived in a 'nature' setting, and work hand-in-hand with the surrounding setting or environment. Lao Tzu encouraged human beings to understand nature and live with nature. His meaning of nature as a whole consists of Heaven, Earth and Man. As Heaven contains emptiness, space and energy or *Chi*, he propounded the theory of *yin* and *yang* for the understanding the way of heaven (not solid or empty) and the theory of soft and hard for understanding of the way of the Earth (solid). Based on these theories which was written in the *Tao de ching* and when a person understand the ways of how nature works, (s)he through self-cultivation would attain virtue. Virtue indeed means thinking and doing what is right, and avoiding what is wrong and it also means a good quality or way of living and behaving as human towards nature. One Taoism proponent whom this researcher spoke to agreed with this, and he maintained that *"Tao de ching* or Lao Tzu in direct translation means 'The teaching of the path of life to attain virtue.' Therefore in a nutshell, *Tao* is based on the teachings of Lao Tzu, it is, in fact, all about human beings living in a natural way and he propounded *wu wei (action through inaction)"* Overall, as human beings, we just live and we need "to act according to the natural way without any human desires".

Tao is power; Tao is valued (Chap. 62 verse 1, *Tao de ching*). Soft power is an appeal, indirect persuasion or attraction. Being a virtuous person itself is power; it gives indirect but abundant power to the bearer of virtues.

The Tao nurtures by not forcing. But by not dominating, the Master (leader) leads. Lao Tzu prefers to do nothing; by "doing nothing", here it really means "not overdoing", the latter defeats the purpose.

Soft power can be defined as power based on intangible or indirect influences such as an organization's (nation's) culture, core values, and philosophy or beliefs. Yet in the Lao Tzu's sense, it is essentially about self-cultivation, growing one's virtues, and practicing one's values based on virtues.

The West by conquest, hard power and domination of their cultures, has in a way also used soft power, more so, not forgetting the fact that history and records are at most times dictated by the victors. It should also be borne in mind that Eastern or Asian ideas, during the colonial masters' time, have not been given much prominence for fear of triggering the spirit of self-determination and nationalism.

And having said these, let us next examine one by one the sources and applications of soft power in the sections that follow:

Applying Neum Pactum ('My Word Is My Bond' or 'My Word Is My Honour!')

The teeth have dropped or died; but the tongue remains. The hard ones [teeth] died, but the soft one [the tongue] lives; the soft power is more potent than the hard power. That's the Tao.

My word is my honour should be applied. One's words and promises should be acted upon. One's virtues need to be put into practice.

For Lao Tzu, light promising makes one lose or diminish one's credibility, and thinking things easy leads to difficulty.

In Chap. 58, *Tao de ching*, it is said that when one tries to make people happy, and one lays the groundwork for misery. When one tries to make people moral, one lays the groundwork for vice. The Master says that one should be content to serve as an example and not to impose his or her will. One is pointed, but doesn't pierce. One is straightforward, but supple, and radiant, but easy on the eyes.

Being Simple

To be simple is to be powerful. One can easily deal with matters using understanding. It is as easy as using sunlight to melt ice. Simplicity helps in building one's leadership as well as organizational growth (Low 2009c). Nature is simple yet powerful. Leaders, just be simple, and simply do good and do what is right for your people.

Simplicity, the first of Lao Tzu's three treasures, is often appreciated (Chap. 67 verse 2, *Tao de ching*). To be simple in communicating with others is to be better understood and there is no gap or barrier between the leader and the led. The people feel at ease.

In Mitchell's (1995) version of Chap. 57 of *Tao de ching*, Lao Tzu said, "The more prohibitions you have, the less virtuous people will be. The more weapons you have, the less secure people will be. The more subsidies you have, the less self-reliant people will be."

Therefore the Master says: I let go of the law, and people become honest. I let go of economics, and people become prosperous. I let go of religion, and people become serene. I let go of all desire for the common good, and the good becomes common as grass." In essence, "I am without desire, and the people of themselves are simple" (Fung 1948, pp. 102–103).

Being in Harmony with Nature Is Power

It is good to move along with nature. Lao Tzu says, "Something undifferentiated was born before heaven and earth; still and silent, standing alone and unchanging, going through cycles unending, able to be mother to the world" (*Tao de ching*, Chap. 25 verse 1) (Cleary 1993).

Uniting with the Tao, it makes sense to be green. It is good to be saving energy while harmonizing with nature and all, not to be polluting or dirtying one's environment and not to be ailing Mother Earth.

For the business, it is good instead not to waste, but to take care and safeguard the environment; it indeed gives power to the business. It is being responsible; the business is subscribing to Corporate Social Responsibility (CSR). Nature is simple and to get along with Nature is power. Nature does not over-do, over-destroy or kill, it instead maintains a balance. Following men do not over-fish or over-do things (Low and Ang 2011).

Another thing about nature is that it needs to evolve. Nature and time are allies; things have to evolve. Take the case of the national dress or costume of the island-Republic of Singapore, this writer remembers that in the 1980s, there were much talk and discussions of such a creation, but it was so rigidly synthetic or artificial. Many combinations of the various ethnic groups' dresses were incorporated, a hotchpotch of traditional Chinese *cheong-sum*, Indian *saris*, *longi*, Malay *baju kurung* and *sarung kebaya*, but they looked ridiculously stiff and did not get the popular support or acceptance of the people. It just needs time to evolve; nature does nothing yet it accomplishes. Given some time, Singapore would have its own national costume, and it, as it evolves, would be widely and naturally accepted by Singaporeans.

Being Humble Helps to Acquire Power

"He who knows does not show off his learning" (Lao Zi says 2009, p. 184). The sage or a wise leader knows oneself, but does not show off oneself. There is no need for one especially a leader to boast and sing ones' own praises.

Generally speaking, one would, in fact, be more forgiving to a humble leader than an arrogant one, should they both make mistakes.

When a great person makes a mistake, (s)he realizes it. Having realized it, (s)he admits it. Having admitted it, (s)he corrects it. (S)he considers those who point out his or her faults as his or her most benevolent teachers (Chap. 61 verse 2, *Tao de ching*). Here, we take it that if a leader makes mistakes, (s)he can simply apologize for it, but there are leaders who do not apologize for their mistakes, and this can be a serious fault, definitely not an attraction. Leaders can certainly endear themselves to people by becoming more modest and caring persons.

Interestingly, one Lao Tzu's soft power advocate expressed these, "A humble leader would attract people since (s)he would be very approachable and in times of trouble or when his followers have problem(s), they would convey it to the leader soon. On the contrary, a proud leader may make the followers feel small in front of him or her, and even if there's a small problem, none of the followers would dare to speak up or relate to such a leader. If it's difficult to approach or talk to a leader, then this would cause trouble or even aggravate the problem(s) as the time goes by; small problems would grow and become big troubles. And even worse, when such a thing happens, the leader would not be aware of the situation, and that could spell badly, if not catastrophic, for the group or company."

Being Patient Is Good

Patience (the second of Lao Tzu's three treasures, Chap. 67 verse 2, *Tao de ching*) is a virtue and strength. Being patient reflects one's care and concern for others; one is essentially being other-centred, having the time as well as putting effort to care and tend to others.

When it comes to disengaging people, there is also a need for patience, and leaders need to investigate and be quite careful. They need to understand their people's perspectives and allow them to express and explain things, seeing their viewpoints rather than simply fire them and have them instantaneously replaced. Such an act shows lack of patience, not to mention, imprudence, and besides, it may have a spill-over effect of de-motivating the rest of the troops. Here, a gradual process of replacements with due notices given should instead be practiced; faces are also saved. That is how talents or virtues in people are motivated and managed.

Patience, a charismatic leadership commodity, bears fruits, and such a quality in leaders is often liked or admired by the followers. Being patient overall reflects one's sensitivity to people as well as being other centred, which leads us to the next point.

Being Other-Centred

Compassion, the third of Lao Tzu's three treasures, is indeed valued (Chap. 67 verse 2, *Tao de ching*). And with a servant leadership attitude, the leader gives more of him(her)self to others (Low 2009c). As stated in Chap. 81 verse 2, *Tao de ching*:

The sage does not accumulate (for himself). The more that he expends for others, the more does he possess of his own; the more that he gives to others, the more does he have himself.

When a person is fascinated by others, their life experience and their work, others simply find the person irresistibly attractive. Others get attracted to the person, and the person is able to raise his or her influence. And we see charisma, personal magnetism or power at work.

Lao Tzu said, "Know a person in the perspective of a person; know a family in the perspective of a family" (Lao Zi says 2009, p. 154). This, to the author, denotes that the leader is other-centred, focusing and connecting to others. All is one and one is all.

To extend the argument further, according to Lao Tzu, the sage has no unchanging personal will; he considers the people's will as his own. The same also applies to a successful leader. (S)he thinks of his or her followers and their needs and interests. The leader thus makes the mind of the people his or her mind.

Allowing People to Own

For Lao Tzu, to give birth to all things but not to take possession of them is allow them to own. When people have the ownership, they are united with the leader and they feel motivated as well.

The Singapore Government, for example, since the island-Republic's independence in 1965, has allowed affordable land ownership and the purchase of housing (Housing and Development Board: HDB) units makes Singaporeans feel having a stake in the City-state. National Service (NS) among its male citizens reaching the age of 18 also serves to bind their loyalties to motherland Republic of Singapore.

Empowering Others Is Giving Power to Oneself

"He does not merely rely on his own eyes, therefore he is wise and penetrating" (Lao Zi says 2009, p. 10). Besides, accordingly, to hold and fill is not as good as to give up. To give up is also to allow others to be virtuous or practice their virtues.

Here, one can take it that Lao Tzu subscribes to empowering others. For Lao Tzu, sharing power, one becomes even more powerful. Others enjoy a sense of belonging, feeling empowered and connected to the leader. Thus, sharing power with others is actually giving power to oneself. In that sense it is very democratic.

Gone are the days where command and control way is the way. It is the people or employees who now decides and by doing this, they gain much job satisfaction. Soft power, giving power to others also includes giving people choices and the power to choose. A case in point that was reported in Singapore newspapers is that of the Development Bank of Singapore (DBS Bank). DBS Bank's employees in the past hesitated to ask for transfers but that was before Mr. Koh Boon Hwee joined the bank's board in 2005. These days, it is fine for employees to ask their supervisors for new assignments within the bank, and the Bank's employee engagement manual is applied. With this, the bank also gains instead of losing their good staff to other banks or companies (The Sunday Times 2010, p. 41)

Applying the Power of Pause

Similar to what has been mentioned by Low (2010a, b), one should often rely and practice on the power of pause. One can then reflect if one is taking the right course of actions. When influencing others, during the post-negotiation stage, one should have a post-mortem to review or check one's actions.

A pause or a break is good; it is line with nature and is thus in the flow of things—fast, slow, speed, sluggishness and breaks. Besides, in Lao Tzu's words, "The greatest skill seems to be clumsy. The greatest eloquence seems to stammer" (Lao Zi says 2009, p. 22). A stammer is a pause. A pause in a speech, when used appropriately and well-timed, can draw the audience's attention to the speaker and his or her emphasis.

Another thing is that a pause is to still things. If one does not pause, how can one understand others? Besides, if one does not pause or still oneself, how can one look within and understand oneself?

Subscribing to Peace and Non-Violence

Being friendly is power. Subscribing to peace (Chap. 31, verse 2, *Tao de ching*) and non-violence is often admirable, and such a leader is magnanimous; others are attracted to him or her. Gentleness is preferred (Chap. 67 verse 4, *Tao de ching*).

Take the case of newly-freed democracy icon Aung San Suu Kyi, she called for a "non-violent revolution" in Myanmar as she knuckled down to the task of rebuilding her weakened opposition movement. She expressed that, "I don't want to see the military falling. I want to see the military rising to dignified heights of professionalism and true patriotism" (The Brunei Times 2010, pp. 1–2). She thus basically expressed the need for the greater good and overall peace and harmony in Myanmar.

It is better to trade and do business than to quarrel, fight or have disharmony. Peace makes wealth, and it leads to economic growth, progress and prosperity. This writer likes the case of India and China, setting aside or sidestepping thorny issues yet hailing their cooperation and ties with each other. In December 2010, both signed a series of agreements and set USD132 billion trade target—they agree that the world was big for both of them. Bilateral trade has grown from almost nothing just a decade ago to USD60 billion a year now (The Straits Times 2010a, p. 1). Now that is power for both China and India.

Bearing Full Responsibility Is Indeed Graciousness, If Not Soft Power

> He who bears the humiliation of the whole state can be the lord of the country. He who bears the disaster of the whole state can be the king of all under Heaven.

Here, one can perhaps cite the resignation of the South Korean Minister of Defence as an example and very much in the spirit of Taoism and soft power. In the face of North Korea's attack and artillery barrage on South Korea and in the light of South Korea's weak military response, the Seoul Minister Kim Tae Young accepted the responsibility and accordingly resigned (The Straits Times 2010b, p. 1).

Using the Heart

At this point, it is good that we note Carl Gustav Jung's words, that is, "we should not pretend to understand the world only by the intellect; we apprehend it just as much by feeling. Therefore, the judgment of the intellect is, at best, only the half of truth, as must, if it be honest, also come an understanding of its inadequacy." As the case maybe, this author suggests that we can also know the world, and realize its power by opening our hearts.

Yes, know the Tao by opening one's heart (*xin*). Be humane. Be benevolent (*ren*). Be people-oriented.

Apply the power of the HEART. To apply one's feelings is power; one indeed needs to apply one's feelings to understand things and human beings. Apply love, and one understands the Universe.

"My teachings are easy to understand and easy to put into practice. Yet your intellect will never grasp them, and if you try to practice them, you'll fail" (Chap. 70 verse 1, *Tao de ching*).

"If you want to know me, look inside your heart" (Chap. 70 verse 3, *Tao de ching*). [In the Western tradition, God is love and love is God; similarly, so to know *Tao*, know one's heart.]

Being Flexible

Lao Tzu has highlighted that all living growth is pliant until death grips it. Thus persons who have hardened or stiff are relations of death, and persons who stay soft are relations of life.

Rituals are dead when without the spirit essence. Flexibility is life and power. The Way is only a guide; it is not a fixed path. Many can attain or be virtuous, but it is critical that they make attempts and be flexible.

"Men are born soft and supple; dead, they are stiff and hard. Plats are born tender and pliant; dead, they are brittle and dry." (Chap. 76 verse 1, *Tao de ching*).

"There is a time for being ahead, a time for being behind; a time for being in motion, a time for being at rest; a time for being vigorous, a time for being exhausted; a time for being safe, a time for being in danger" (Chap. 29 verse 3, *Tao de ching*). When leading, different situations in life call for different approaches and ways. At times especially in a crisis situation, one commands and at times, one consults and gathers the views of one's followers. And at other times, being patient and other ways are applied.

Nothing on earth is as soft and yielding as water, "the supreme good" (Chap. 8 verse 1, *Tao de ching*). Leaders need to be like water and be flexible. "The highest good is like water." "The softest thing under Heaven is able to run in and out of the hardest" (Lao Zi says 2009, p. 133).

Section Conclusion

In short, "the Tao is like a well: used but never used up. It is like the eternal void: filled with infinite possibilities. It is hidden but always present. I don't know who gave birth to it. It is older than God" (Chap. 4 verses 1 and 2, *Tao de ching*). When tapping on Tao, needless to say, its power and influence is limitless. However, before we can tap the power of Tao, we need to really self-cultivate ourselves and be virtuous; ultimately when we actually get power, we, duly responsible, can then act responsibly—similar to the character Peter Parker's (*Spiderman*, the movie) famous line "Whatever life holds in store for me, I will never forget these words: 'With great power comes great responsibility.'".

Applying Soft Power, the Chuang Tzu (Zhuang Zi)'s Way

Here, in this section, the practitioner-academician examines the various sources, ways and applications of soft power through the visor of Taoism, namely, that of the teachings of Chinese Taoist philosopher, Chuang Tzu (*Hanyu Pinyin*: Zhuang Zi), a disciple of Lao Tzu (*Hanyu Pinyin*: Lao Zi), a modern touch is also added.

Section Introduction

In a typical traditional Chinese fashion, the suffix 'Zi' (Tzu) is accorded to wise men. They have had their many walks and journeys; they also have more experiences, having read more books, experienced more happiness and having gone through or endured greater sufferings. Besides, an old horse knows its way around. That in itself is power; so when they speak, they speak with much authority, similar to the Chinese saying that "when an old dog barks, he gives counsel".

Who Is Chuang Tzu (Zhuang Zi)?

Chuang Tzu (*Hanyu Pinyin*: Zhuang Zi) (Chuang Chou, ca, 360 BC), along with Lao Tzu (*Hanyu Pinyin*: Zhuang Zi), is a defining figure in Chinese Taoism.

Section's Aim and Objectives

In Taoism, the person of supreme virtue is the sage who follows in the footsteps of the Tao. And it is critical for a person especially a leader to be virtuous. This section seeks to demonstrate the sources, uses and ways of soft power as wisely seen and practiced from the perspective of the teachings of Chinese Taoist philosopher, Chuang Tzu (Zhuang Zi), Lao Tzu's (Lao Zi) famous disciple; they are also given a modern touch or twist.

Soft power is simple and natural. There is no force; what is natural and not synthetic is good. As Chuang Tzu once said that the long is not to be regarded too much and the short is not to be considered too little. Thus, short as the legs are, the duck will come to difficulties if we stretch them out. Long as the legs are, the crane will come into misery if we cut them short. What is natural is thus good. Although some authors attribute anarchism to what Chuang Tzu is referring to, but to this author, it is not anarchism but rather the people should be not over-controlled or forced. When leading people, the leader should instead ensure that the likes, potentials and strengths of the individuals match and fit with the tasks and overall job function of the individual job holders. And that they do what they like and like what they do, and being happy, their productivity would then go up.

We will next examine the sources and applications of soft power, one by one, in the following sections.

Gaining the People's Trust and Support

A leader, to have more than enough power, should be trustworthy. The leader is dependent on the people and their support like fish is to water.

Political leaders should fulfil their electoral promises after the elections when they assumed into power. There should not be gaps between what have been previously promised and the actions or what have been delivered.

When the leader wages a war, (s)he can destroy a state without losing the support of the people. He can grant favours on all the things in the world without being himself a true lover of the people.

Being of Character and High Integrity

It is important for a person to be virtuous. Chuang Tzu asked, "If you are virtuous and do not think so, where would you go without being loved?" (Zhuang Zi says 2009, p. 163).

The character and integrity of a person attracts others to him or her; they build much respect for the bearer. Interestingly, "respect is so crucial to a leader's standing because no matter how difficult the task is, if the leader wants the followers to do, they would do willingly and promptly. They would certainly listen to the leader......without respect in the first place, they would not listen, let alone be willing to perform the task" (several respondents' input). A virtuous person, although having physical defects, is always admired and respected; and such a person gains the support of the people.

Indeed so one who shares one's virtue with others is wise and one who shares one's talents with others is called a worthy person.

For Chuang Tzu, as much as a dog is not considered as a good dog if it barks well, a person is not considered as wise person merely because (s)he speaks well. This, to the author, means that a person must have the virtue and the integrity. A leader's words should carry weight only when one is honest and is of good character; otherwise, one speaks but one's words are empty or are taken lightly; the leader's speech and words are of no value to the audience.

Integrity is power; it is the intrinsic quality of a person that matters most.

Encouraging Self-Cultivation

We need to grow our virtues. We need to find out more and learn about doing good, and be virtuous. The fungi that sprout in the morning and die before evening do not know the wavering of night and day.

It can be taken that for Chuang Tzu, the leader is a person who grows and develops him(her)self. That will gain the people's admiration and attraction for the leader. The leader who "persists in cultivating his (her) mind [*(s)he will*] will not feel ashamed for his (her) humble and low position" (Zhuang Zi says 2009, p. 191, *italics author's*).

Fulfilling the Needs of the Followers

Doing a favour for people with the objective of receiving rewards is not a favour at all. Even traders and merchants hold such conducts in contempt.

Chuang Tzu once spoke of, "the tiger is of different species from man, yet is gentle to its keeper because the keeper complies with its disposition." The tiger gets vicious or ferocious when it is irritated or provoked (Zhuang Zi says 2009, p. 59).

Leaders who know and seek to satisfy the needs of their followers are likely to succeed than those who seek to fulfil or satisfy their self-interests or individual needs. Needless to say, the former attracts followers.

Serving and Caring

Being helpful is charming. To serve is to care; and what more, serving and caring is all the more very pleasing and appealing. True critics may argue that caring and cooperation works only if others cooperate; however, when one party offers good service while showing much cooperation and cares, others may find it hard to resist. Others are pulled or attracted by one's service as well as one's caring nature and actions. "Men endowed with Tao become humane when all the individual traits are manifested in them" (Zhuang Zi says 2009, p. 99). Caring is also another form of soft power.

A good example of individuals who showed much care and compassion is the late Mother Teresa of Calcutta, an exemplary model who showed the world that a genuine love for others opens the door to knowing and being with the Tao or God in the Christian sense.

Companies and various organisations can also use caring and human touch as strengths to enhance its services and businesses. Hospitals in Singapore such as Tan Tock Seng Hospital (TTSH), for example, supply facilities and provide preventive care to the sports community while helping to drive the island-Republic's agenda of nurturing healthy, resilient people. The increasing participation of people in sports, the growth of sports medicine industry as well as provisions of free clinic and health information/consultations can build, if not raise, the soft power of these institutions.

Being Humble: Humility Is Greatness

Quiet, the leader needs not boast or brag, after all, there is no need to exaggerate to make one looks good or great.

For Chuang Tzu, the swans are white despite they do not bathe themselves daily and the crows are black though they do not dye themselves everyday. As intrinsic simplicity of black and white is not to be wrangled over, so the extrinsic glory of fame and name is not to be embellished or overstated (Zhuang Zi says 2009).

It is helpful for the leader to be humble; being humble means a leader can understand or empathise with the delights, pains and needs of the people and that they are as important as the leaders, even though they don't feel so. When we are humble, we can laugh at our self-importance and at times, even, set it aside. We can see our own faults and the strengths of others, and we recognize how much we have been given, unearned. It is said that humility allows us to be more aware of our personal limitations and broadly-speaking, the limitations of humanity.

Being Cool, Calm and Composed

Being cool and calm exudes power to a person, making him or her looks tranquil and steady. If one is detached, then one can think more objectively without any desire. When one has no desire or worldly concerns, one owns nothing in possession and fame yet one is cool. One is indeed gentle and actually thinks well and straight.

A leader will not crave for property and wealth and will not strive for fame and position. This leads to accomplishing without overdoing things. For all of us too, having no desires creates contentment and satisfaction, the cure against modern disease of materialism, overachievement and stress.

One will play with skill when one makes a gamble with tiles; one will play with worry and care when one makes a bet with a silver buckle; one will lose one's wits when he makes a bet with gold. One's skill is the same, but one's anxiety grows with the increasing value of one's bet. Consideration of external things always unsettles or disturbs people internally.

This is better illustrated when we examine what Chuang Tzu said. When we go around telling each other, I do this, I do that—but how do we know this "I" really has any "I" to it? One dreams that one is a bird and soars up into the sky; one dreams that one is a fish and dive down in the pool. But now, when one tells another about it, the other party does not know whether the telling party is awake or dreaming. Just be content to go along... and forget about change and then one can enter the mysterious oneness of Heaven.

Being Flexible

Like water, the leader is flexible. When a leader is flexible, (s)he can adjust, adapt and work well with the grassroots. (S)he can also, in fact, get along well and work with anyone from any levels of the society. And this really makes a good leader, connecting with people and helping them.

Enduring: Endurance Gives Patience and Power to a Person

Brightness originates from darkness. When one faces and goes through hardships and sufferings, one learns, endures and improves oneself; that attracts others to the person. Patience also brings out the gentleness of the person, and one's perseverance and determination becomes the source of the admiration of others, and this personal power can be built upon by the bearer.

Setting the Precedent, Then Letting Things Fall into Place

Once a precedent is set or a model established, things get done in a similar fashion. Besides, it becomes a fait accompli. It has been done and for that simple reason, it should just be accepted. Chuang Tzu spoke of, "a path is formed because we walk on it; a thing has a name because we call it so" (Zhuang Zi says 2009, p. 27).

One Chinese saying goes, "Not the cry, but the flight of the wild duck, leads the flock to fly and follow" and this shows that an example of the leader is very influential. For Chuang Tzu, since there is no dust on a mirror, it is bright while a dusty mirror is not bright; the leader's shining example, clearly seen by all, will be subscribed and followed by the followers. Besides, Chuang Tzu highlighted that perfect men in the past saw to it that they had Tao in themselves before they passed it on to others.

Building Goodwill and Preferring Peace, Harmony and Non-Violence

The Dalai Lama is an outstanding example of promoting goodwill and peace; in spite of Tibet's being subjugated by China, he promotes goodwill and specifically encourages Tibetans to support peace and love their Chinese brothers—and in this regard, he is much admired. This is soft power in practice.

This is soft power in action. It should be borne in mind that promoting happiness, being the voice of a peacemaker, reconciling and resolving conflicts makes others and one happy, and thus we will then have a happy leader leading his or her flock. To be in harmony with people is called "human joy". Even at the personal level, when one's friends or family members are upset or unhappy with one another, one would feel their air of overall despair and unhappiness. One should then really make an attempt to be the voice of peace, reason and reconciliation.

Goodwill is built, and peace is well-liked and harmony is valued; and the leaders give peace and political stability to the citizenry.

Promoting Cooperation and Collaboration (Oneness in All Things)

Cooperate with others; we cooperate and collaborate with others in one synergistic whole. The pragmatic aspects in business here is that we need to network and build or expand our connections. When Chinese clan associations network, they will grow their connections, contacts, contracts and trade. In fact, Overseas Chinese should tap their trade associations to network, introduce newcomers and expand, if not, break into the Chinese market and increase business with China. Or the Indians should do likewise, tapping their Indian diasporias to network and increase business and trade with India.

Cooperation begets cooperation. According to Chuang Tzu, it was essential that we transcend all the dualities of existence. Observing Nature at work and the way in which it brings together these polar opposites points the way to the Tao where all dualities or differences are resolved into unity; the universe is the unity or agreement of all things. If one recognizes one's identity with this unity, then the parts of one's body mean no more to one than so much dirt, and death and life, end and beginning, disturb one's tranquillity no more than the alternation of day and night.

Besides, the wise person has the sun and the moon by her side. She takes hold the universe under her arm. She blends everything into a harmonious whole, casts aside whatever is confused or obscured, and considers the lowly as honourable. While the people toil, she seems to be foolish and non-discriminative. She blends the disparities of 10,000 years into a single, complete purity. All things are blended like this and mutually involve each other.

Applying the Strength of a Pause, Being Still

During negotiations, pauses are necessary. A pause is a break; it strengthens one as one is able to gain strength, recuperate or simply rest (Low 2010a). Same also as in going through in our lives, we need pauses or reflection periods, taking stock before moving forward.

For Chuang Tzu, men only use still water as a mirror; they do not use running water as a mirror.

Only things that are still in themselves can still other things. Most people find it difficult to change, their habits die hard; and a true leader does not change others by force. Only when one can make change, then one can make others change.

In applying the power of the pause, one is also applying the power of example. Only when knows of oneself, then one can know of others.

Only when one is patient, then one can make others patient. One needs to demonstrate or show a model. Only when one shows an example of oneself, then one can get others to do it.

Understanding the World and Applying Its True Meaning Is Power

Material wealth and all the riches are not power. For Chuang Tzu, life ("The life of a man between Heaven and Earth is as brief as the passage of a horse through a crevice in the wall"; Zhuang Zi says 2009, pp. 108–109) is brief and transitory and that the pursuit of wealth and personal aggrandizement were vain follies, which distracted from seeing and understanding the world, contemplating and finding its meaning.

Leaders can contribute, donate, volunteer and do what they can to the multitude; these in fact give leaders power and influence. Giving and making others feel good, and they feel good in themselves. Giving and sharing happiness, the leaders themselves receive happiness.

Section Conclusion

Like a powerful magnet, soft power attracts, exerting a pull towards the leader. If soft power is practised, then there is in a way no need to take care of the business and then the latter will take care of itself in the same way as a baby learns to speak; it learns to speak without learned teachers since it lives among people who can speak.

Checkpoint: Think About It

Using Soft Power

What Is Soft Power?

1. How do you define soft power?

Applying Soft Power, the Confucius' Way
Review these key points and when you have finished the quiz, check your answers. Check also with your close friends or associates.

2. To raise my soft power or influence—the Confucius' way, do I apply the following?
   • Being virtuous
   • Leading by example
   • Being trustworthy
   • Being approachable and friendly
   • Sharing the same values, fostering a sense of unity
   • Empowering the people
   • Cooperating and collaborating
   • Standing for values, moral courage and what a leader stands for
   • Educating the people
   • Being charming and engaging
   • Being ever encouraging
   • Being humble
   • Being patient
   • Being caring
   • Returning or paying back to the community

Applying Soft Power, the Lao Tzu (the Tao)'s Way

3. To raise my soft power or influence—the Lao Tzu's way, do I apply the following?
   - Applying *neum pactum* ('My Word Is My Bond' Or 'My word Is My Honour!')
   - Being simple
   - Being in harmony with nature is power
   - Being humble helps to acquire power
   - Being patient is good
   - Being other-centred
   - Allowing people to own
   - Empowering others is giving power to oneself
   - Applying the power of Pause
   - Subscribing to peace and non-violence
   - Bearing full responsibility is indeed graciousness, if not soft power
   - Using the heart
   - Being flexible
4. What other ways, Lao Tzu's, can I apply to raise my soft power?

Applying Soft Power, the Chuang Tzu (Zhuang Zi)'s Way

1. To raise my soft power or influence—the Chuang Tzu's way, do I apply the following?
   - Gaining the people's trust and support
   - Being of character and high integrity
   - Encouraging self-cultivation
   - Fulfilling the needs of the followers
   - Serving and caring
   - Being humble. humility is greatness
   - Being cool, calm and composed
   - Being flexible
   - Enduring. endurance gives patience and power to a person
   - Setting the precedent, then letting things fall into place
   - Building goodwill and preferring peace, harmony and non-violence
   - Promoting cooperation and collaboration (oneness in all things)
   - Applying the strength of a pause, being still

Self-Esteem Booster Activities/Exercises

1. Each morning the minute when you get up, repeat to yourself at least three times:

"I am applying soft power."
Also, visualise yourself as such. See yourself happily applying soft power.

References

Barker, C., & Coy, R. (Eds.). (2004). *The power of culture – Driving today's organisation*. New South Wales: McGraw-Hill.

Bhasin, B. B., & Low, K. C. P. (2002). The fight for global talent: New directions, new competitors. *Career Development International, 7*(2), 109–114.

Cleary, T. (1993). *The essential Tao*. New York: HarperOne.

Fung, Y.-L. (1948). *A short history of Chinese philosophy*. New York: The Free Press.

Gordon, B. (2009, July 21). China's Confucian soft power. *UTNE Reader*. Accessed November 12, 2010, from http://www.utne.com/Spirituality/Chinas-Confucian-Soft-Power.aspx

IDA: Infocomm Development Authority of Singapore. (2006). *The great campaign*. Singapore: IDA.

Lao Zi says. (2009). *Zhuang Zi says*. Malaysia: Zi Publications.

Lau, D. C. (1979). *Confucius – The Analects*. London: The Penguin Group.

Lee, K. K. S., & Low, K. C. P. (2009). The role of Chinese clan associations for Singapore's economic development. *Business Journal for Entrepreneurs, 2009*(1), 49–58.

Legge, J. (translator). (2008). (From a 1891 edition) *Lao Tse, The Tao te ching*. The Floating Press.

Lien, Y. C., & Kraar, L. (1994). *From Chinese villager to Singapore Tycoon: My life story*. Singapore: Times Publishing International.

Low, K. C. P. (2000). *Strategic customer management*. Singapore: BusinesscrAFT™ Consultancy.

Low, K. C. P. (2001). *The power of relationships*. Singapore: BusinesscrAFT™ Consultancy.

Low, K. C. P. (2002a). *Strategic customer management* (2nd ed.). Singapore: BusinesscrAFT™ Consultancy.

Low, K. C. P. (2002b). *Corporate culture and values: Perceptions of corporate leaders of co-operatives in Singapore*. Unpublished PhD thesis, The University of South Australia.

Low, K. C. P. (2003). *Team success*. Singapore: BusinesscrAFT Consultancy and Humber Lincoln Resources.

Low, K. C. P. (2005). Towards a framework & typologies of Singapore corporate cultures. *Management Development Journal of Singapore, 13*(1), 46–75.

Low, K. C. P. (2006a). *Strategic customer management* (3rd ed.). Almaty, Kazakhstan: Caspian Publishing House.

Low, K. C. P. (2006b). Father leadership – The Singapore case study. *Management Decision, 44* (2), 89–104.

Low, K. C. P. (2007). Father leadership and small business management: The Singapore case study, i-manager's. *Journal on Management*. December 2006–February 2007, 5–13.

Low, K. C. P. (2008a). Value-based leadership: Leading, the Confucian way. *Leadership and Organizational Management Journal, 2008*(3), 32–41.

Low, K. C. P. (2008b). Core values that can propel e-government to be successfully implemented in Negara Brunei Darussalam. *Insights to a Changing World Journal, 2008*(4), 106–120.

Low, K. C. P. (2009a). *Corporate culture and values: Perceptions of corporate leaders of co-operatives in Singapore*. London: VDM-Verlag.

Low, K. C. P. (2009b). Strategic maintenance & leadership excellence in place marketing – The Singapore perspective. *Business Journal for Entrepreneurs, 2009*(3), 125–143.

Low, K. C. P. (2009c). Lao Tzu's three treasures, leadership & organizational growth. *Leadership and Organizational Management Journal, 2009*(3), 27–36.

Low, K. C. P. (2010a). *Successfully negotiating in Asia*. Heidelberg: Springer.

Low, K. C. P. (2010b). Applying soft power, the Confucian way. *Conflict Resolution and Negotiation, 2010*(4), 37–46.

Low, K. C. P., & Ang, S. L. (2011). Taoism and corporate social responsibility (CSR). In S. O. Idowu (Ed.), *Encyclopedia of corporate social responsibility*. Heidelberg: Springer.

Low, K. C. P., & Theyagu, D. (2003). *Developing true leadership potential*. Singapore: The Publishing Consultant.

Mitchell, S. (1995). *Tao Te Ching written by Lao Tzu*. Accessed May 22, 2007, from http://acc6. its.brooklyn.cuny.edu/~phalsall/texts/taote-v3.html

Noor, A. (2010, November 20). LTH donates to 8 schools. *The Brunei Times*, p. B3.

Nye, J. S., Jr. (1991). *Bound to lead: The changing nature of American power*. New York: Basic Books.

Rahman, M. H., Low, K. C. P., Almunawar, M. N., Mohiddin, F., & Ang, S.-L. (2011). E-Government policy implementation in Brunei: Lessons learnt from Singapore, from e-government to e-governance: Winning people's trust. In A. Manohan & M. Holzer (Eds.), *E-governance and civic engagement: Factors and determinants of e-democracy*. New York: IGI Global.

Taylor, C. (2004). Chapter 1: The power of culture: Turning the soft stuff into business advantage. In C. Barker & R. Coy (Eds.), *The power of culture – Driving today's organisation*. Australia: McGraw-Hill.

The Brunei Times. (2010, November 16). Suu Kyi calls for non-violent revolution. *The Brunei Times*, pp. 1–2.

The Straits Times. (2010a, December 17). India, China hail ties, sidestep thorny issues. *The Straits Times*, p. 1.

The Straits Times. (2010b, November 26). Seoul minister quits amid criticism. *The Straits Times*, p. 1.

The Sunday Times. (2010, November 28). Getting the job done the HP way. *The Sunday Times*, p. 41.

The Useless Tree. (2010a, May 26). *Confucius: Soft power symbol or historical failure?*. The useless tree: Ancient Chinese thought in modern American life. Accessed November 7, 2010, from http://uselesstree.typepad.com/useless_tree/2010/05/confucius-soft-power-symbol-or-historical-failure.html

The Useless Tree. (2010b, September 24). *More on Confucian soft power*. The useless tree: Ancient Chinese thought in modern American life. Accessed November 7, 2010, from http://uselesstree.typepad.com/useless_tree/2010/09/more-on-confucian-soft-power.html

Zhuang Zi says. (2009). *Zhuang Zi says*. Malaysia: Zi Publications.

Zimmerer, T. W., & Scarborough, N. M. (2006). *Essentials of entrepreneurship and small business management*. Upper Saddle River: Pearson-Prentice-Hall.

Food for Thoughts and Actions: From Baby Steps to Bold Charges

18

Keep Moving

> I always like to try for the best. (Lien Ying Chow, cited in Low and Theyagu 2003, p. 100)
> Cause something to happen. (Paul 'Bear' Bryant)

A person is Heaven and Earth in a miniature, as the Chinese saying goes.
Do act and be proactive.

As leaders, we need to increase our potential. Keep on growing. We decide; we are the masters of our own fate and destiny. Keep on learning. We need to increase our talents, what we are each given and born with.

The author ardently hopes that you have done your Checkpoint, Activities and Exercises at the end of each Chapter. Search and explore for yourself leadership opportunities. Turn gaps and situations into opportunities to learn, grow, recreate and innovate.

Renewing the Mind

> The God of heaven will give us success. We his servants will start rebuilding. (Nehemiah 2:20)

All of us need to be awakened—seeing bigger pitctures, moving away from being just a pedestrian.

We need to ask ourselves: Are you doing things perfunctorily? Are you doing things routinely? Do you do things or receive instructions from the headquarters mindlessly or at least, with little thinking? Do you simply follow the instructions of your CEO/senor management or the precedures and processes of the organization with much thinking or reflections?

Are we adopting mind growth?

Reflect on this Zen Koan, "A free mind. A free Universe."

© Springer International Publishing AG 2018
K.C.P. Low, *Leading Successfully in Asia*,
https://doi.org/10.1007/978-3-319-71347-2_18

As a wise Maori saying goes, "Turn your face to the sun and the shadows fall behind you." And as in the Old Testament case, in the destruction of Sodom and Gomorrah, Lot's wife turned into a pillar of salt as she looked back. Let us move forward by reflectively ask: Which of the chapter(s) in the book that you wish to re-read?

Are there any other (further) insight(s) that you have picked?

Choose an area you need to work on.

Perhaps you want to work out and incorporate certain leadership points as part of your daily (weekly, fortnightly, monthly, quarterly, yearly) action points, values or habits?

What challenges do you see and wish to take?

What about your leadership style? And what are your leadership ways? Am I gentle? Are my leadership style and ways marked by a sincere consideration of people? Do you need to find more about your leadership way(s), to check with your close friends and loved ones?

Are you able to look beyond your personal or corporate goals and see other, deeper, things at work? Do remember the value of advisers and good counsel. Remember what's indicated in the Book of Proverbs: "Plans fail for lack of counsel, but with many advisers, they succeed." (Proverbs 15:22).

Which leader(s)—national and/or corporate—that you wish to find out more about? What are their strengths? Which of these leaders you wish to emulate? What do they stand for?

What Is Your Vision?

Where there is no vision, the people perish. (Proverbs 29: 18)
    You don't look out there for God, something in the sky, you look in you. (Alan Watts)

Is it big enough? Is it bold enough?

What is your vision?

Have you consciously come up with a vision? Yes, have a vision, a sort of dream and a broad big picture. Have a view from the top and have a high concept, the headwater for your priorities and goals.

Pause, think and reflect: As a leader, what are you going to be?

What Is Your Mission?

Our thoughts are most important. All that we are is the result of what we have thought. (The Buddha)

Next, what about mission? Have a mission; this mission is to be something that is more specific than the vision. What will be your mission as a leader?

What Is Your Personal Slogan?

Thought is action in rehearsal. (Sigmund Freud)

At this point, if you do not have one, I would like you, as a leader, to come up with your own personal slogan. A slogan is a memorable motto or phrase repetitively expressing an idea, and it adds a purpose and meaning for you.

Such a personal slogan should be short and catchy, and it would be your war-cry to get things accomplished and results produced. Very much like companies' slogans (for example, Nike: "Just do it!" Kit Kat: "Have break, have a Kit Kat!"), personal slogans too should be motivating, if not inspiring.

Your personal slogan or mantra incorporates and embeds your own values, convictions and/or what you stand by for; it moves you to action.

What Are the Set of Values You Hold?

One who does not remember where he comes from will not reach his destination. (Filipino proverb)
The tragedy of life is not death but what we let die inside of us while we live. (Native Amercian saying)

What are the things that are close or dear to your heart? What are your key beliefs? What are your convictions? Have you identified your set of core values? If not, work out a set of core values which will help you; they serve as your operating principles and guidelines.

What Are Your Priorities and Goal(s)?

The future depends on what we do today. (Mahatma Gandhi)

If we do not change our direction, we are likely to end up where we are headed. (Chinese proverb)

Set priorities and goal(s) for yourself. And these goals are plucked from your values which support your vision and mission. These goals would move you (organisation) to action.

To the author, the priorities and goals can, in a way, be a sort of purpose for the organisation. Successful leaders create their own purpose and that of the organisation. And according to Llopis (2013, cited in Low and Teo 2015, p. 41), they create a purpose—not just profits—for the organisation.

What Are Your Action Plan(s)?

A good plan implemented today is better than a perfect plan implemented tomorrow. (George S. Patton)

Personal action is your pathway to success, even if it is a little bit at a time! (Catherine Pulsifer)

Without action, nothing gets done. So now that you have your vision, mission, values and goals, what are your action plans?

What actions are you going to initiate?

What actions are you going to take?

What old habits are you going to eliminate?

What bad habits or ways are you going to get rid off?

Enhance, Empower, Extend and Expand

Enhance, Extend and Expand. (Jack Welch)

We have much in abundance and we create the affluence. We should feel abundance, and create that reality too.

Then, we lend a hand to others (Fig. 18.1).

We empower ourselves to achieve. And we attain greater things. As we empower ourselves, so also we should empower others. This author very much subscribe to what Bill Gates' beliefs that, "as we look into the next century, leaders will be those who empower others". Bill Gates is not running a business that allows him to achieve technological superpower even he is able to. He is, in fact, running a business for others to be able to control, manipulate or better still reap technology. It is by this same concept that people would want Bill gates' services and this can be applied in the leadership context.

We lead to allow others to lead.

Have you ever thought of giving more time toward improving others instead of criticising them? Try it! Do it!

Do the same for yourself too.

As you pitch in and do what you can and what is needed for the team, you also get your team ("many hands make light work") going on your action plan(s).

Involve others. Let others grow too. You need the support of your peers and colleagues to realise your action plans. Others can also assist you in your action plans, so network, connect, engage and involve others.

As we climb ladders and mountains, conquering peaks, we also make the climbing easy for others.

Allow other people to realise their potentials too.

We will next discuss what I believe as an important in leadership and living... the need to reflect or take stock...

Reflecting...

Fig. 18.1 There is the need to plan ahead while kicking off bad habit(s). Are you breaking useless habits and starting anew? What such habits are you going to get rid of?

What We, As Leaders, Should Think?

Stop, Look and Go. (Traffic Lights)

In this final section, I wish to highlight the importance of leaders' taking stock of their actions and events to better or improve their leadership ways, and in most ways, this paper serves as a checklist or more importantly, as a leadership audit sheet.

Introduction

There is a need to remind ourselves that activities and events can, in most time, lead us to mere doing and action, and if that is so, this leads us to little thinking and reflection. No matter how busy we are, there is a need to allocate sometime to reflect.

Section Aims and Objectives

Confucius once said that one should excel and not just living a good life, but also one should live a full life. It is good to be introspective, and reflect upon our actions with the view to improve on things. For Confucius, when a leader is popular, it is necessary to check or inquire why people dislike him (her). When (s)he is popular, it is also necessary to inquire why people like him.

The purpose of this section is thus to float ideas on what leaders should focus on, think about and reflect upon. As leaders, as things or events unfold, they need to have an overview of things yet knowing what possible outcome(s) they wish to accomplish out of these events and also the effects or consequences of these actions.

Leaders Should Be Thinking About. . .

Being Open and Effecting Mind Growth

> Great minds discuss ideas. Average minds discuss events. Small minds discuss people.
> (Eleanor Roosevelt)

In their study's findings, Low and Teo (2015, p. 36) spoke of Tsunami or bad leaders "having wrong perceptions about the real situations—especially at the frontline, seeing issues in their own narrow or ostrich perspective(s) and consequently; create confusion leading to chaotic situations; have poor levels of achievement"

So we need to ask ourselves these:

Are we open enough? Are we open to new ideas? Are we open to new or fresh perspectives?

This is not only for themselves but also for their followers. Leaders should welcome and encourage fresh ideas, and be able to see things from the various perspectives and angles. This is to enable leaders to make right and good decisions for their organisations and people.

Knowing the Goals (Where Are We Leading Our People to?)

Do you know where you are heading? Do you know where you are leading your (organisation) people?

If this is so, leaders can then align their people's goals (needs) to that of the organisation's (nation's). Then leaders can sell better to their people. They can also highlight the core benefits of attaining these goals, thus motivating their people further (Low and Ang 2010).

Creating Sustainable Development

Indeed, this is a critical point. How can leaders create and sustain development for their countries and companies or organisations? How can they grow and ensure the success of their organisations?

Are you (your organisation) being green?

Can your Company (Organisation) sustain itself?

Do you network enough and increase contacts to helping your business grow or nation develop?

Carrying Their People Along with Them

An old dying patient, having the presence of her children, was telling these to Alexander 'Alex' Michael Karev: 'People are better than no people'. (Grey's Anatomy, an Amercian Medial drama series, Season 5 Episode 19)

Be with your people, and let your people be with you.

And often ask yourself: Are your people with you? Are you carrying your people along with you?

Leaders should be able to influence and persuade their people, getting them to follow the leaders in the pursuit of their organisation's (nation's) goals.

Leaders need to seriously think about how they can be more persuasive and convincing to their followers. So ask...

How persuasive are you? How can you make yourself more persuasive?

Learning and Cultivating Core Values

Values (shared beliefs) make up our character, conviction and integrity. Decide the values for yourself and what you would stand for.

Remember values are clock builder. Values are lasting, and indeed critical in building clocks (Collins and Porras 1997, cited in Low 2006a). Normally, (visionary) leaders, whose ideas live on long after they are gone, build strong companies or institutions.

More critically, leading or managing a crisis can be seen as a test of the quality, strengths and stamina of leaders as much as it is a test of their skill and expertise. Companies or nations that cope well with crises have put their houses in order. They know what their values are and have a well-articulated purpose or mission that permeates the organisation. They know what they stand for. Crises can strengthen these organisations, even as they undermine—or destroy—those that do not know what they stand for (Low 2006a, 2010).

Ask...

What are some of the values you stand for?

What are some of these values for our people (children) to imbibe? Are these values essential and complete?

Can these values enable or sustain our growth?

Being Aware of Intergenerational Gaps, Problems and Issues

These workforces everywhere is getting more and more diverse. We are diverse not only in culture but also in terms of age; there is a number of multiple generations working side by side in organizations. Note here generations is consisted of a group or collection of persons born within a particular shared life span (birth years) who experienced the same world events, which shifts them together and bonds them through time.

All of us gets older and as we gets older, we should be aware of intergenerational gaps, issues and/or conflicts. We may be different from those born in different eras, let alone, we can even, at time,s be very different from those in our own age group.

Ordinarily so, people born in different times may have different interests and needs. Each multigenerational work group possesses their own uniqueness, values, morals, and mindsets and/or mind growth with regard to their work (styles, ways and habits) and organisation, based on the individual's/group's life encounters.

It is said that diverse views on concerns like employment standards, the ability to lead, and the right to command could create disagreements, instensification, and confusion if not handled properly.

The problem of leading a multigenerational workforce comes from conflict or tension brought on due to a lack of understanding of employees" generational differences and the leadership skills needed to lead multiple generations.

Empathy, magnanimity, high-mindedness, patience and perseverance are qualities that need to be employed when dealing with such intergenerational gaps, issues and problems. Leaders indeed need to own a number of intelligences such as social intelligence and other types of intelligences; they need to learn, apply, update and grow. Owning emotional intelligence is also a skill that allows individual leaders to manage themselves and their relationships with different people and groups. Individual understanding of the power of emotions and mastering the ability to control and express emotions could boost both the leader's and the organisation's effectiveness. At this point, it is worthy to highlight that leaders too need to be flexible as well as deploying different leadership styles and ways such as servant leadership and other style/ways to deal with intergenerational issues, conflicts and/or problems.

To nurture a positive intergenerational environment, a leader can consider several of these strategies:

Cherish individual strengths: Discard the stereotypes that come with labeling groups of people. In its place, treasure and maximise the potential of each member of your team by empathising and appreciating his (her) background/experiences, skills and goals.

Give training: It's not enough to simply assemble an intergenerational team and expect it to work flawlessly and seamlessly. Provide awareness training and allow employees to learn about their differences, as well as their similarities.

Generate partnerships and collaborations: Establish mentoring partnerships among the generations. For example, team a tech-savvy Millennial (generation born between 1980 and 2000) with a baby boomer (the generation born between 1946 and 1964) who appreciates technology but needs some hands-on training.

Be flexible (as mentioned above): Acknowledge and, where and when possible, accommodate various work styles. That may include offering flexible hours and work-from-home options. It might also involve catering to different food and drink preferences in the company cafeteria, or providing wireless connections for employees' personal mobile devices or charging stations for their electric vehicles.

(Continuously) Asking "Am I Caring Enough for My People?"

Kindness should become the natural way of life, not the exception. (The Buddha)

Leaders need to check on this as, sometimes, ego may slip in. And leader (s) forget the very reason for existence of their leadership, and the causes of the people.

The late S.R. Nathan (1924–2016), the former elected president of Singapore, was a caring leader. And making himself like the common man, he was a people-orientated leader, and "a social worker at heart"; he was always caring for the ordinary folks. (The Straits Times 2016, p. A8).

Are you training your people? Are you growing your people? Are you tapping your people potential? Are you tapping the synergy of your people? Have you considered the team dynamics of your people?

Do you give back to your community too? Citing Confucius, Low (2008) speaks of if a gentleman were to go and live among uncivilized peoples, then how could these peoples be crude? His very character, integrity and actions will help change them for the better. A gentleman(lady)-leader must do something for the community too.

Being Strong, Tough and Resilient

The spirit, the will to win, and the will to excel are the things that endure. These qualities are so much more important than the evnts that occur. (Vince Lombardi)
    I will go anywhere as long as it's forward. (David Livingston)

Ever see and/or play with the Japanese Daruma doll? It bounces and stands upright back when thrown. And the Japanese has this saying, "Nana karobi yaoki", meaning in English: "Fall down seven times, get up eight." Japan's Daruma doll reminds us to never, ever give up on our dreams and what you want to do; we must persist and be resilient. So...

Are you resilient enough? Are you well prepared to shoulder and soldier on in time (s) of crisis? Is your organization (nation) well-equipped to meet these challenges (crisis)?

Leaders need the grit and resilience to succeed, and you have it.

Successful leaders have little room for negative thinking in their minds.

Do look at your past acoomplishments and successes. Do a mental survey. Re-affirm your pool of resources, skills and strengths and confidence; you're able and capable of resolving the issue(s)—you've indeed the necessary resources and assets.

It is said that nothing does more good or help than upkeeping a positive outlook and regularly expressing gratitude. These two actions have been shown to decrease anxiety, reduce symptoms of illness, and improve the quality of one's sleep. True, one needs not only to be optimistic, but also to say a great deal of "thank yous", showing gratitude. Interestingly, a person, according to Kopans (2016), can increase the effect of these activities by keeping a record of one's positive interactions, events, and memories. Maintain a simple list of things you're grateful for or are looking forward to in a paper notebook, or enter them into a spreadsheet. Even digital gratitude journals exist in which one can download and use. But one needs to find a regular time—say, first thing in the morning or at the end of the workday—to check and add to these records. Studies have shown that doing so builds a leader's/one's resilience.

Though this saying comes from an anynonmous source, but overall, it's often said,"The best way to escape from a problem is to solve it". So choose your tools and aids, deal with the issue(s) and move on.

Move forward. And do what you can do about it.

It's useful here to remember what Richard Exley once said, that is, "Failing doesn't make you a failure. Giving up, accepting your failure, refusing to try again, does!"

Yes, ignite. And just do it!

Capitalising on Opportunities

Oh, this is the joy of the rose: that it blows. And goes. (Willa Cather, 1873–1947 from *The Rose Time*)

When things are good and even the economy is doing well, these are the best times for leaders to reflect and think about creating opportunities for organisational growth and/or business expansion.

To this author, leaders should also breathe well and, in fact, be in no hurry, reflecting, meditating upon their actions and taking breathing spaces at regular intervals with the view to take stock of things.

Doing What They Say and Taking Action

You are what you do, habits make you as a person and leader (Tracy 2005). And examples are critical (Low 2002a, b, 2005, 2006a, b, 2009; Low and Theyagu

2003). It is monkeys see, monkeys do! People are looking at the leaders' action(s); and the latter send a green light or a red light to follow or emulate the leaders.

Are you the example? Are you setting the example? Are you the role model? Are you being the light or guide to your people?

Balancing Work with Other Spheres of Life

"Just living is not enough," said the butterfly, "one must have sunshine, freedom and a little flower." (Hans Christian Andersen)

Having the right balance is important as it, in fact, leads one to having little or no stress. A leader needs to relax too. So ask. . .

Are we lop-sided? Are you having the right balance in carrying out your leadership role? Is there a right balance between work and personal spheres?

Are you just taking care of the job or the tasks at hand? What about the people content of your tasks as a leader? Are you also taking care of the soft aspects, the people side of things? Are you taking care of your human side too?

Are you taking care of your family and relationships with your loved ones too?

One's loved ones are also important in one's life. But are we also doing something for them? Do you show enough care for them too?

Also, are we having any other interests and pursuits? What are the other hobbies that we can creatively pursue and occupy our time?

Section Conclusion

The above can be used as a checklist or an audit for leaders to consciously and systematically think about.

Chapter Conclusion

Do not lose hold of your dreams or aspirations. For if you do, you may still exist but you have ceased to live.(Henry David Thoreau)

Your body is the harp of your soul. And it is yours to bring forth sweet music from it or confused sounds. (Khalil Gibran)

March on. Do not tarry. To go forward is to move toward perfection. March on, and fear not the thorns, or the sharp stones on life's path. (Kahlil Gibran)

Each of us has a Buddha potential, a spark of divinity. Lao Tzu expressed as such, "At the centre of your being, you have the answer; you know who you are and you know what you want."

Just as Rumi has said, "Let the waters settle you will see stars and moon mirrored in your Being", so also, allow our Universe-given potential to be triggered, and grow while expanding or crystallising our leadership actions and achievements.

Orison Swett Marden once said, "A strong, successful man is not the victim of his environment. He creates favourable conditions. His own inherent force and energy compel things to turn out as he desires." Each of us is our own destiny, and we own and create that destiny. We can indeed go forth and multiply...

Checkpoint: Think About It

1. Pick your role model(s). Reflecting on them, who could you be tomorrow? And why? Give substantial reasons.
2. Look into these key points.
   - What bad habits do you wish to get rid of?
   - What is your vision?
   - What is your mission?
   - What is your personal slogan?
   - What are the set of values you hold?
   - What are the core values of your Company?
   - What are your priorities and goal(s)?
   - What are your action plan(s)?
   - How are you, as a leader, enhancing, empowering, extending and expanding?
3. Are you effecting a mind growth for yourself? And if so, in what ways are you doing it?
4. What new topic(s) or field(s) that you wish to learn? When are you going to start this learning? Are you doing anything about it now?
5. Are you aware of inetrgeenrational gaps, issues and problems (conflicts) that exist among your people? What are you going to do about it? What approaches and ways are you taking to deal with these iussues and/or problems?
6. Are you taking care of the sustainable development of your Organisation? If so, in what ways are you doing it?
7. Are you simply taking care of the job or the tasks at hand? As a leader, what about the people content of your tasks as a leader? Are you also taking care of the soft aspects, the people side of things? Are you also taking care of your human side?
8. Are you with your people? Do you carry them along with you?
9. Are you investing in your people?
10. Are you resilient enough?
11. Think of ways in whuch one can toughen oneself: How can you strengthen your resilience?
12. Think and think hard: What opportuntiies are there? Are you capitalising on the opportunities available to you?
13. Are you doing what you say and are taking actions? Are you setting an example?
14. Are you balancing work with other spheres in your life?
15. How do you relax? List the various ways in which you relax or take things easy.

16. How are you taking care of your family and relationships with your loved ones?

Activities and Exercises

1. What is the most important one thing you would do or improve upon in your life and how could you do this in an excellent fashion?
2. Create an ideal future vision for your Company and your career. If your situation were perfect 3–5 years from now, what would you envisage it; in other words, what would it look like?
3. What is your greatest strength in your business, and how could you organise your time so that you are doing more of it?
4. What other strengths in your business do you have? Think of ways to soar your strengths.
5. What is your greatest weakness in your business, and how could you defend or compensate for it?

References

Kopans, D. (2016). How to evaluate, manage and strengthen your resilience, 14 June 2016. *Harvard Business Review*. Accessed September 1, 2016, from https://hbr.org/2016/06/how-to-evaluate-manage-and-strengthen-your-resilience?cm_mmc=email-_-newsletter-_-management_tip-_-tip_date&referral=00203&utm_source=newsletter_management_tip&utm_medium=email&utm_campaign=tip_date

Low, K. C. P. (2002a). *Strategic customer management*. Singapore: BusinesscrAFT™ Consultancy.

Low, K. C. P. (2002b). *Corporate culture and values: Perception of corporate leaders of co-operatives in Singapore*. PhD thesis, The University of South Australia, Adelaide.

Low, K. C. P. (2005). Towards a framework & typologies of Singapore corporate cultures. *Management Development Journal of Singapore, 13*(1), 46–75.

Low, K. C. P. (2006a). Crisis management – Can core values be considered as a built-in safety net? The Singapore case. *Insights to a Changing World, 2006*(3), 133–150.

Low, K. C. P. (2006b). *Strategic customer management*. Kazakhstan: Caspian Publishing House.

Low, K. C. P. (2008). Value-based leadership: Leading, the Confucian way. *Leadership and Organizational Management Journal, 2008*(3), 32–41.

Low, K. C. P. (2009). *Corporate culture and values: Perceptions of corporate leaders of co-operatives in Singapore*. London: VDM-Verlag.

Low, K. C. P., & Ang, S. L. (2010). Reflecting… What we, as leaders, should think?. *GLOBALTRADE.net*. http://www.globaltrade.net/miniportal/country/Singapore.html

Low, K. C. P., & Teo, T. C. (2015). Tsunami leaders and their style(s) and ways. *International Journal of Business and Social Science, 6*(9), 31–46.

Low, K. C. P., & Theyagu, D. (2003). *Developing true leadership potential*. Singapore: The Publishing Consultant.

The Straits Times. (2016). S.R. Nathan 1924–2016. *The Straits Times*, 25 August 2016, A8–A9.

Tracy, B. (2005). *Million dollar habits*. Singapore: McGraw-Hill.

The Future: Going Further, Doing More, Going Stronger

19

Introduction

Success has a simple formula: do your best, and people may like it. (Sam Ewing)

When you dance, your purpose is not to get to a certain place on the floor.It's to enjoy each step along the way. (Wayne Dyer)

How can leaders go further? How can they make progress? How can they be stronger?

Leaders must be responsible. They must act or work out for the good of their people or followers. Leaders should meet and satisfy the needs of their people and followers. They need to get prepared for what lies ahead.

Note that "great minds have purposes, others have wishes" (Washington Irving).

And yes, always be preparing, always preparing, always thinking and always going for. . .

The next goal, the next step. . .

Moving from Being Just a Leader to Being a Leadership Titan

Success comes from knowing that you did your best to become the best that you are capable of becoming. (John Wooden)

You may occasionally give out—but never give up. (Mary Crowley)

Many a time, I wanted to stop talking and find out what I really believed. (Walter Lippmann 1889–1974)

A silent killer, complacency or smugness kills.

It is like barnacles growing on the surfaces of the sides and the bottom of the boat, these barnacles, not only adding weight, but also slowing the boat. And they make the boat moves in a less streamlined and sleek way. Complacency is harmful

© Springer International Publishing AG 2018
K.C.P. Low, *Leading Successfully in Asia*,
https://doi.org/10.1007/978-3-319-71347-2_19

or antithesis to (leadership) growth; it's harmful to learning; leaders must not take their success for granted.

Complacency almost always comes from a sense of victory long after the success that created it is spent. Complacency becomes the silent killer when it slips to collapse and loss.

Some (non)leaders may get complacent and (start to) play games, putting on charades while showing that they are working hard. These mama-dramas or papa-dramas even dramatise the errors of others and/or their people. Hardly producing or producing little, they too belittle and deride the efforts of others to aggrandise or glorify their works.

Worse, some leaders get complacent, and instead of rewarding their people, they simply resort to using the stick and apply force. Bloated with power and thinking that might makes right, these leaders just bark orders and issue instructions. And what's worse, simply scold, they simply whack and punish their people while simultaneously demotivating and demoralising them.

Then again, some leaders are also not grateful for what their people have done or helped them. (For a leader (let alone, any person) to be resilient and succeed, optimism is not enough, but one also has to say a lot of "thank you", showing one's gratitude to others; Kopans 2016). Complacent leaders may also take their people for granted; some carry with them the attitude or malaise that "after all, they are employees; these people, my staff are paid for their jobs". Some leaders may lead and do their task(s) with fits of temper as if their people owe them a living; these leaders even adopt an inspection or headquarter attitude. And that they are there to inspect and with arms folded, without being hands-on or lifting a finger, demand answers, and at most times, want such information or data impatiently from their staff. Non-empathetic, these leaders too emphasised the task(s) at hand rather than being people-centred or concerned. Very rarely do they ask themselves: "How are their people affected by their (impatient/non-empathetic?) action(s) or (cold or impersonal?) behaviour(s)?"

Some leaders became conceited and overconfident leading to destruction; leaders should indeed avoid or shun complacency. Leaders need to make progress. And they need to ask and be aware of the various ways to avoid getting complacent; and only then can they move to being a good, if not a great leader.

Yes, they can rest or take a break, but not resting or camping for a long time. They must soon be on the go. And act. Learn and act. They should move from having a blocked mind-set ("I stereotype others"; "I retain my bias and prejudice")/ fixed mind-set ("I'm smart enough"; "I know a lot. . . . . .there's no need for me to learn further") to mind growth ("Keeping an open mind, I benchmark and learn from others"), keep on learning and growing. They should also move from being negative (e.g. "I CAN'T"; "I'm bound to FAIL") to being positive (e.g. "I CAN and I WILL"; I CAN SUCCEED). [This brings to mind John Wooden's words, that is, positively speaking, "never let what you cannot do interfere with what you can do."]

Successful leaders do not find excuses in outside factors or hide behind the cover of management and day-to-day tasks (which unfortunately can become the focus of leaders when they lose singlemindedness or become complacent).

Leaders must take charge.

They must recharge their batteries. Leaders need to GO FURTHER. Yes, they pause. And they go. They stop, look, recharge and GO.

Tobin (2013) spoke of these: "Successful people are extremely driven. They do not work a 9–5 day and often go for long periods of time without what most people would call "work/life balance." This is necessary for life at the top. But in order to avoid complacency you must build in time for rest, relaxation, hobbies, reflection and quality time with family and friends. This is what gives you the energy to continue to compete, innovate and succeed. Otherwise you become the proverbial hamster in the wheel. The wheel (or the hamster) ultimately breaks down."

As the Buddha once said, "Sit quietly and listen to the voice of your mind. Do you like the words it speaks", so too at periodic intervals, leaders should ask themselves: what are the ways in which their mind is telling them? Are they getting complacent? Or are they getting over confidence? And also, what are the ways in which they could avoid complacency? To avoid complacency or smugness, do they listen to their people? In what ways can they listen to their people?

Do leaders embrace change well?

Here, it is good to quote these: "Complacency is akin to something called rustout. Rustout is more common in America than in other developed countries and it's actually even scarier than 'burnout' because, while burnout can wear down your body, rustout can wipe out your soul and spirit." (https://www.pickthebrain. com/blog/complacency-how-to-avoid-the-silent-killer/#bAXQ2RyiQc86vH1b.99)

Interestingly, 'rustout' is the slow loss or death that follows when leaders and/or even ordinary folks stop making the choices that keep life alive. It's "the feeling of numbness that comes from taking the safe way, never accepting new challenges, continually surrendering to the day-to-day routine. 'Rustout' means we are no longer growing, but at best, are simply maintaining. It implies that we have traded the sensation of life for the security of a paycheck ... Rustout is the opposite of burnout. Burnout is overdoing ... rustout is underbeing." (https://www. pickthebrain.com/blog/complacency-how-to-avoid-the-silent-killer/ #bAXQ2RyiQc86vH1b.99)

What's worse, there are, at most times, no major alarms or warning signs. Nothing seems wrong or broken, and it is said that complacency is also highly harmful because it is immune to or excused from change and innovation; it fails to recognise either new opportunities or would-be hazards. In fast-moving environments of risk, uncertainty, and the unknown, history books show us that such a thinking or way is the perfect recipe for failure or ruin.

Are leaders getting used to the routine? They must stop giving in to day-to-day routines. They need to also ask: Are they getting to be (un)comfortable with change?

Leaders need to ask, "What are the ways in which you can become a leadership titan?" "Are you accepting new challenges?" "Are you taking risks?"

To ward off complacency, it is always wise to have healthy competition. All of us love competition; it keeps us sharp and running. Leaders need to create ways to help themselves (teams) or their people to compete against themselves or the goals they surpassed last year. The leader can also define an outside rival/Company as the source of his or her energy, focus and effort.

They also need to ask themselves: "What are the key values that (would) put them in a strong or stable position?"

From time to time, leaders should ask themselves: "What aspects of leadership can they improve in themselves?" or "In what ways can they, as leaders become excellent?"

Saving, Sustaining and Growing Organisations

One is born, one dies; the land increases. (African proverb)

It is also interesting to note that leaders should not be short-sighted (myopic) or succumbed to short-term thinking. Indeed the said quality is one of the key traits of a weak, incompetent leader or even a non-leader (Low and Teo 2015). Tsunami leaders are not strategic (Low and Teo 2015, p. 39).

Successful leaders think ahead (Low and Teo 2015). And make their organisation successful and sustainable. They need to build resilient business.

Corporate social responsibility (CSR) is used by long-term thinking leaders to fulfill social obligations and to create opportunities for new business through strengthened community involvement. However, it is sure that there is a need for CSR activities to go beyond single philanthropic gestures and pursue long-term partnerships with non-profit organisations that create greater value while minimising risk in society.

Leaders too must indeed ensure and safeguard, if not enhance, the future and potentials of the generations to come; they must save, if not grow organisations from greed and corruption, and care for the people while fulfilling their vision, mission and values. Indeed leaders should be leading businesses with honesty and a high sense of integrity.

Rightly so, they should also grow the potentials of everyone including the physically and mentally challenged while providing them with the necessary care and amenities.

To substantially grow or sustain the organisation/company, a vital need exists to link the human resources section/department with the Company's vision, mission and values or key beliefs.

Successful leaders must prudently cut costs such as that of their companies' operations yet make their organisations strong and sustainable. They need to continuously search, find and act on the various ways not only to prevent themselves from sliding down, but also on whatever more ways to make their organisations sustainable, if not preventing them, from sliding down.

Cultivating a Garden of Greatness

Truth emerges from the clash of adverse ideas. (John Stuart Mill)

Make friends with your shower: If inspired to sing, maybe the song has an idea in it for you. (Albert Einstein)

How do leaders get stronger? How do leaders go further?

First, leaders must welcome ideas when cultivating a garden of greatness. They should be unlocking and growing creativity and innovation in organisations (countries) they lead and in individuals therein.

Second, it should be noted that creativity is not all about hard work, it can be fun too. Leaders can love themselves, their creativity, work, play and have fun as well as enjoying their gifts to the world. They need to be willing to understand and pay attention to their creativity, unlocking as well as nurturing it. Successful leaders need to appreciate the pleasing qualities of being creative while enjoying the excitement, pleasure, hope and joy. They also know and have favourite ways to be creative, and they too explore many other ways to be creative and innovative.

Yes, do laugh at yourself. Laugh and have fun with others. Note that laughter is wonderfully cathartic on the creative front. And note too that successful leaders also translate their pleasures and enjoyment of being creative and having fun to their people. Do cherish those colleagues and friends you laugh with. It is good to recreate the natural delight of giggling you loved as a child. Can you really manufacture laughter?

Third, in creating an idea-friendly setting, leaders need to make their people creative, and always look for the second right answers or solutions to any problem (s). Here, they should also encourage their people to be creative by having, for example, brainstorming sessions.

Leaders can also encourage their people to take a what-if (hypothetical) position or view(s) so as to generate (new) ideas. They can also encourage or hearten their people to take an opposite (Yang-Yang) view or position to get fresh ideas. They should encourage their people to use different shoes or wear different hats, taking different (fresh) perspectives. They can also encourage their people to take the contrarian (being different) approach to view issues and problems. They should encourage the use of analogies and metaphors. Leaders should truly foster openness to new ideas within the organisation as well as in any individual.

Besides, effective leaders should also look at various ways to improve their Companies/products and their product packaging; they also need to look at various ways to better serve, service and satisfy their customers.

Successful leaders too really need to reassure their people to make a try and attempt. It is okay to fail or not be successful as long as one learns. Leaders too need to reduce the penalties for failure. It is said that if failure is not taking place, so is innovation; the latter is also not happening.

Good leaders too need to ensure that the penalties or punishments for failure are lower or not greater than the penalties for doing nothing.

And they should give more office time for thinking while reducing the time to putting out fires or being reactive. Leaders need to ask themselves and answer honestly whether they are being more reactive or more responsive. They then need to think of ways to be more responsive while nurturing a garden of greatness.

Leaders also need to let their people know that they are objective, and that they are not personal. True, leaders may argue or disagree, but they should also let their people know or impress on them that just because they disagree or argue strongly it does not mean that they dislike the person(s) involved—it just means that they disagree with him (her/them). They should also thank them for their viewpoint (s) expressed. This is good as it would encourage the people to speak out and express.

Bringing About Learning Organisations

A thoughtless life is truly an evil life. (The Dhammapada)

It is apt to cite what Jeffrey Gitomer once said, "People who are cocky and arrogant say, 'I know that' and move along. People who confident and positive ask themselves, 'How good am I at that?' and seek to improve."

When the status quo is preferred or that learning is of no concern, importance or a priority, complacency can then set in.

Successful leaders must create learning organisations out of their organisations/companies. Authentic learning must really exist. The whole organisation/company should be "a learning organisation" (Senge 1990) with its organisational members] being professional learners. Also, learning from mistakes and growing with reflective teaching and good teaching practices.

Organisational/faculty members must be engaged in deep, broad study of learning (in their domain or discipline) and really understand what works and what does not. They ask: What makes learners most motivated (or their learning most successful)? Where are the challenges (or struggles) faced by learners, and why? What can the school do about it? [Thus, the meaning of professionalism and the inside people being professional learners is the ability to addressing and attending to these questions.]

In terms of human resources development (HRD), a special mention here since after all, this is the author's field, leaders need to get feedback. Leaders, leading schools, institutions and the academia/training departments, can ensure and/or implement peer evaluations or reviews. Here, peer evaluation is a process of collegial feedback on quality of teaching (this term is interchangeable with training). As a purposeful process of gathering information and evidence about the effectiveness of teaching processes and the educational environment while having constructive critical scrutiny, peer evaluation usually starts with people identifying what areas they would like feedback on, and works best where the process is reciprocal between peers. A key part of peer evaluation is peer review of current practice often based on peer observation of teaching interactions. It should always be viewed as an opportunity (collaborative, coaching, friendly and in a sharing mode) not a threat for both parties.

Effecting Instructional Leadership

A little rain each day will fill the rivers to overflowing. (African proverb)

In HRD too, instructional leadership should be realised; here, it is generally defined as the management of curriculum and instruction by the Training Head/ Director. This term appeared as a result of research associated with the effective school movement/management of the 1980s, which revealed that the key to running successful schools lies in the principals' role. The concepts of the framework are based on five core beliefs.

They drive our work in school leadership here at the Centre for Educational Leadership.

1. Instructional leadership is learning-focused, learning for both students and adults, and learning which is measured by improvement in instruction and in the quality of student learning.
2. Instructional leadership must reside with a team of leaders of which the principal serves as the "leader of leaders".
3. A culture of public practice and reflective practice is essential for effective instructional leadership and the improvement of instructional practice.
4. Instructional leadership addresses the cultural, linguistic, socioeconomic and learning diversity in the school community.
5. Instructional leadership focuses upon the effective management of resources and of people—recruiting, hiring, developing, evaluating—particularly in changing environments.

Guaranteeing Gaia

The fool is thirsty in the midst of water. (African proverb)

In essence, the Gaia hypothesis/theory or Gaia principle, suggests that organisms interact with their inorganic surroundings on mother earth to form a synergistic self-regulating, complex system that helps to keep and perpetuate the conditions for life on earth.

Leaders must the safeguard the future of the generations to come. The earth is indeed our heritage. The skies are our roof and the earth is our ground; it's our home. And all of us need to be socially responsible; we need to take care of nature. Leaders in particular should be socially responsible; they need to take care of nature.

These days we know that there is some wrong in the air, in the skies, in the sea and in the lands that we live. Plastic and rubbish are found in manatees, dolphins and other sea creatures' stomachs and our seas are polluted. Forests, jungles and trees are exploited. All of us especially leaders who set the example must be careful with the resources they use. Leaders when leading our organisations need to reduce or conserve, reuse and recycle the resources employed.

Of significance, it is strongly felt that long-termism and being universe-friendly must be embraced and practised by leaders. Though *Star Trek* is a fictional account, Low and Low (2015, p. 274) aptly pointed out the leadership lessons for the future, and to quote:

> Long-termism needs to be embraced by all of us; one must indeed think long-term. In In Star Trek, the Prime Directive is a universal rule for all Federation explorers that stipulates that they must not interfere with the natural development of any of the planets or peoples they face. In the cases where this rule is tested by circumstances it is never disregarded or circumvented. Interestingly, another, less noticeable, guiding principle is the complete lack of racial, gender or any other kind of bias or discrimination. This is unstated as a Value because it has become a universal principle of Gene Roddenberry's vision of the future of the human race (Warner 2012, cited in Low and Low 2015, p. 274).
>
> Akin to the fact that we owe much to our next generations so that they can inherit a clean and green Earth/nature, the leadership of Star Trek embraces the paramount value of being green or earth-friendly, as well as respecting and being kind to nature and our universe. And that is the legacy (we owe to ourselves and our children and children's children) that we need to uphold and live on. Interestingly, the authors interpret this as being epitomized by these conversations between Captain Jean Luc Picard and Riker (Star Trek: The Next Generation 2014, cited in Low and Low 2015, p. 274):
>
> > Picard: What we leave behind is as important as how we've lived. After all, Number One, we're only mortal. Riker: Speak for yourself, sir. I plan to live forever.
>
> Humankind indeed needs to plan well to ensure Earth's greenness. Indeed we need to do our act, contribute and when it comes to being green and should the environment is going to be saved, we must truly believe that each of us will have to take the leadership role and be the home base—undeniably let it begin with ME.

Being Self-control and Disciplined and Encouraging Sustainable Development

> Little by little grows the bananas. (African proverb)

Leaders need to self-control and disciplined as well as encouraging and enhancing sustainable development. And indeed this is for the future of the world.

Interestingly as Tom Peters once said, "There is no such thing as a minor lapse of integrity". Indeed leaders need to be in charge of themselves. And truly in reading and understanding the lives of great people or leaders, one would find that the very "first victory they won was over themselves... Self-discipline with all of them came first." (Harry S. Truman). And as leaders, they know that there are often distractions and track diversions or even temptations. However, they need to be self-disciplined, upholding the value of integrity as well as thinking about ecology and the environment.

Political leaders should grow their countries, developing beautiful cities or cities with good design, with good infra-structure and ensuring economic growth while keeping the ecological balance or taste. And for the citizenry, jobs and employment are to be adequately provided for. Besides, with the poor, the sick and the old well-taken care of, the national budgets should be wisely channelled to primarily make people enjoy a better quality of living, indeed improving their overall well-being.

Most of the present leaders will be dead before Earth suffers the full consequences of acid rain, global warming, ozone depletion and widespread desertification as well as species loss. All of us have a common future. And sustainable development needs to be embraced and even enhanced. Rather than overexploiting resources, leaders should be sculpturing beauty, upping well-being and creating happiness for their people. And these they must do (satisfactorily) than selfishly lining their own pockets and perks as well as living lavishly.

Dwight Eisenhower once said that, "The supreme quality for a leader is unquestionably integrity. Without it no real success is possible." Societies and leaders should act right. And nations and businesses want to stand tall (Low and Low 2015, p. 275). Leaders need to be, in one way, not greedy—but rather help the needy while staying non-corrupt. And in another way, leaders need to be circumspect in using resources; they should not be extravagant. They should not waste resources. Want not and waste not; they put demands on themselves to be careful and prudent. They do not waste or overspend resources, but use and apply them judiciously and sensibly. They should thus, overall, be moving towards sustainable development, and this is about meeting or getting the needs of the present without compromising or undermining the ability of the future generations to meet their own needs.

Building Relationships

Life is to be in relations. (Lao-Tzu)

The gem of communication (relationship-building) is be found in one's immediate experience or setting, in the fire-fly rather than the star. (Kim Cheng Patrick Low.)

How do leaders get more persuasive? How do leaders get greater support?

Leaders need to create and build relationships; they need to invest in creating and growing relationships. They need to bridge the gaps between various generations, baby boomers and others. At the end of the day, leaders need to have their people's and followers' trust of them.

Leaders should not be divorced or detached from their people and followers. Leaders should not be desk-bound, but be with the people; they should be on the ground, talking, listening and understanding their people and followers with the latter, over time, trusting the leaders increasingly.

These days, technology: Internet, Instagram, Facebook and/or the use of the hand-phone has become so common and in fact the centrepiece of our lives. And messaging and game playing become usual, normal and everyday even in family dinners, get-togethers and company gatherings. One really needs to get out into the REAL world, CONNECTING, INTERACTING and RELATING with PEOPLE. One needs to truly feel the pulse, understanding people at first hand too.

Interestingly, Low and Low (2015, p. 278) underscored this point when they cited: Armin Shimerman, the actor who played Quark in Star Trek Deep Space Nine; Shimerman attractively pointed out the importance of relationships even off-stage, he spoke of his continued connections or liaisons with fellow actors: "Some of the Star Trek people, like Rene (Auberjonois) and Michael Dorn and a number of others, I talk to and see on a regular basis because we all live in L.A. But a lot of friends and colleagues live around the country, and some are around the world. So I don't get to see them very often. So, to be able to reconnect with people who were very important in my life, at these conventions, that's really delightful." (StarTrek.com Staff 2010, cited in Low and Low 2015, p. 278).

Price and Price (2013, pp. 74–80) underlined the critical importance of leaders in terms of inspiring their people by connecting with them through, among other things, learning their names, praising them for their efforts or performance, showing that they noticed when their people weren't around and demonstrating concern when their people aren't their normal selves. Great leaders also make everyone feel like they are the most important person. In their research, Price and Price (2013, p. 137) testified that successful leaders were also warm and outgoing; they "enjoy working with other people. 90% of the participants rated this behaviour as very important to successful leadership".

A good inspiration, to this author, comes from the late S.R. Nathan, the second elected President of Singapore in office from 1999 to 2011, and was the longest-serving elected President the Republic to-date has. He was "a very warm person", "always interested in people" and was "a very caring person". (Channel News Asia 2016; Channel 5 2016; The Straits Times 2016a, A4–A6). He reached out to people of different faith and community groups in multiracial Singapore; the late S.R. Nathan's also "remembered for efforts to foster multiracialism and inter-religious harmony" (The Straits Times 2016a, A5).

It is also truly laudable to note that leaders should not be exclusive; non-successful leaders or in fact, non-leaders are ordinarily cut off from their people. Without good rapport or deep connections with their people, often they cannot relate well with or understand their people. It is praiseworthy to note that people are indeed happy when they realise their inter-connectedness with others (Lonely Planet 2011: 125; cited in Low and Low 2015, p. 278), particularly so, with their leaders. And that they feel very happy, if not glad when their leaders care. Indeed all of us need to show that we care for (our) people.

Besides, Schlacter (2013) spoke of (leaders should) "always be listening". The best leaders are always listening to those they are working with. Successful leaders apply this to gain specific insight(s), gather feedback, or even to find a solution or answers. Listening skills bestow strong leaders as people who not only care about business, but also people and their concerns.

Powering the Future

No yesterday, not tomorrow, and no today. (Sheng T'san)

Care enough for a result, and you will almost certainly attain it. (William James)

Leaders need to be both creative and innovative.

And connected to saving Gaia is the concern for conserving the world's energy. As the world's energy demand rises in tandem with population growth and advances in technology, we need to find new sources of energy, that is to say, humankind needs to have more energy while reducing the carbon dioxide/gas emissions or the greenhouse effect.

There is also certainly a need to explore or look for the water, solar, wind, recycling (rubbish?) powered or other forms of power revolution or transformation.

Leaders too can explore and/or search for ways to trigger or begin a cheaper battery revolution.

Facing Issues and/or Problems with the Yes Attitude

Every day is a good day. (Yun-Men)

An ill-directed mind will cause greater harm to a person than his enemy. (The Buddha)

How do leaders get more things done or implemented?

Yes, a leader's tasks are never easy. Life itself has many issues and problems. And leaders too face many issues and problems; and they have to resolve them.

Do note that "It's not the snow, the rain, the thunder or lightning, the competition, the Country, the Government, the Chief Executive Officer (CEO), the Company, the spouse, the job or the kids—it's YOU! And it always has been." Get your thinking RIGHT and be POSITIVE.

Negativity or negative thinking is like a thief, it steals happiness from you. Negativity is like a robber; it robs you of achieving things and goals. Negative thinking can certainly suck one of one's self-confidence, and/or it can also make one feel down or retreat to one's shell. Such thinking is definitely not helpful.

As such, leaders need to be positive minded while surmounting and overcoming these tribulations and challenges. Positive thinking can be useful as they give the thinker helpful tips and pointers to move on; they prompt and provoke the thinker to go forward. Avoiding negative thinking, leaders need to remain clear-minded and focused with a positive mind growth. This positive mind growth is the YES attitude.

Keep on believing and believe that better things lie ahead.

A problem becomes a challenge. And with a positive attitude or mind growth leaders strive and thrive with challenges. With a positive mind growth, leaders lead with a smile; they serve with a smile.

It has been said that no medicine can cure a pessimist while no poison can harm or kill an optimist; great mind growth or attitude creates great altitude. And really such a mind growth or attitude makes things easier and challenges easily overcome.

Leaders must think that along these lines:

"I CAN"

"I CAN DO it!"

"I FEEL GOOD about myself."

"I am the best."

"Today is my best day."

"I CAN OVERCOME whatever challenges!"

Having a YES Attitude is like feeling on top of the world, and such leaders can move on and accomplish things. Note that a leader's strength is not what (s)he has, but more so, what and how (s)he positively uses or applies to overcome the situation (s) (s)he faces. (S)he makes good of the situation that (s)he's being thrown into.

Setting the Sights Further

We are still masters of our fate. We are still captains of our souls. (Winston Churchill)

Act as if what you do makes a difference. It does. (William James)

How do leaders go even further?

Leading without planning is akin to a moth darting into a flame. Leaders must plan, they must continue to plan. Plan they must! One must always plan well before one starts and/or further one's journey. One needs to always remember the Carpenter's and Tailor's rules, that is, measure twice, but cut once.

And with a positive mind growth, one can be bold enough, and one can indeed set one's sights further. How can one set one's sights further? One can further provide products of highest quality, a comprehensive management and a good human capital management.

Carving a name across the country, if not the world, leaders should be building their Company (Country) and product brands, bringing and adding value to customers. As a leader, how then can one build one's brands?

It is also good to be different. And yes, one should play up one's (Company's/ Country's) differentiation factor(s). So, how different one (the Company's/ Country's) can be? How unique can one be?

As a leader (of the Company's/Country's) one should also do out-of-the-box thinking. One can think of ways to do one's out-of-the-box leadership. How then can one do one's out-of-the-box thinking? One can think of ways to transform one's people lives.

Besides, as a leader, one can also do such things as: How can one do one's out-of-the-box sales and marketing? How can one do one's out-of-the-box logistic management? How can one do one's out-of-the-box human capital management?

Creating Leadership Circles

Great leaders are almost always great simplifiers, who can cut through argument, debate and doubt, to offer a solution everybody can understand. (Colin Powell)

Truth often suffers more by the heat of its defenders than the arguments of its opposers. (William Penn)

When leaders require ground-breaking or innovative ideas to grow their company, they often turn to their direct reports for guidance. But this group or team, by design, embodies the present operating units and functions, which frequently have a status quo to protect or defend.

So when leaders need creative thinking, attempt forming a leadership circle, a diverse, ad hoc team of 15–18 people from all over the company who can work together for about 6 months. The circle should focus on the future, NOT the past, and beneficial debate(s) should be encouraged. Within the circle, each member should hold equal status and should not feel that (s)he is being expected to represent the viewpoint of marketing, accounting, human resources, shipping, or whatever their home department is (Pistrui 2016). Vitally so, whatever ideas come out of a leadership circle should be run in the same way they were generated: They should be rigorously and systematically argued, debated and explored.

Being Entrepreneurial

There is no education like adversity. (Benjamin Disreali)

(Leaders who are) entrepreneurial... may also espouse and even uphold certain values that really make them entrepreneurs. To be more entrepreneurial is thus to be capitalising on key resource availability, idea/opportunity-seeking, making one's "life more challenging or gratifying" (Gold 2008, cited in Low and Sajnani 2015, p. 31), making more money... "get(ting) the most satisfaction" and being more business-minded while growing the business (e.g. Andrew Carnegie) and venturing into commercial activities both locally and overseas. When one subscribes to such a way of thinking, one would prepare to take risk and set up business(es) to gain or reap profits, invest or be an industrialist rather than just opting for regular or steady employment whether in governments or in multinational corporations (MNCs). To be more entrepreneurial too is to be enterprisingly creative, adopting Gold's (2008, Chap. 1, cited in Low and Sajnani, p. 31) "wonderful madness" or being innovative in running one's business (e.g. Thomas J. Watson Sr.); entrepreneurs may also be resourceful in cutting costs and flexibly finding avenues to boost profits. (Low and Sajnani 2015, p. 31)

To move away from complacency, leaders truly need to be (more) entrepreneurial, daring and be willing to take (more) risks. Perhaps this is best put forth by the Prime Minister of the Republic of Singapore, Lee Hsien Loong (in his National Day Rally on 21 August 2016), and true, he was referring to the need for Singaporeans to be (more) entrepreneurial or risk being left behind. But this author would urge leaders to remember not to be complacent; after all, as Lee said, "Things are changing fast, old models are coming thick and fast and we are having to adjust and to keep up. Because of technology and globalisation, the disruption (*to businesses, products, product lifecycles, employment and jobs*) will happen over and over again, relentlessly." [Lee Hsien Loong, (*italics author's*) cited in The Straits Times 2016b, p. A6]

Here, Low and Sajnani (2015) highlighted that to be entrepreneurial, one needs to be a PHD person, and that is, one needs to be **P**oor, **H**ungry and **D**esperate. What they argued is that in rich or developed countries when the people are comfortable, having secured jobs or employment, this can really serve as obstacles to being entrepreneurial. They "choose the easy way out" instead of being entrepreneurial. "This can be in the form of owning properties and collecting rents instead of being in business. Some even just farm out licences." (several interviewees' inputs, cited in Low and Sajnani 2015, p. 35). The research study was done in Brunei Darussalam, and the researchers spoke to various people across the society including long-time seven expatriates and foreigners (employers and employees) residing in the Sultanate and many opined that "most businesses such as operating mini-marts, convenience stores, tailoring or dress making and retail outlets and even including contract work and supplies, and other various small businesses are in fact straight forward business". "... yet these businesses were then mostly operated on the "Ali Baba" mode with the people lending their names to the business registration and become sleeping partners." (Note Ali Baba is a business practice in Malaysia—and/or even in Indonesia and Brunei, where a Malay company obtains a contract from the government-sponsored affirmative action system for the Bumiputera (the Malaysian New Economic Policy under Ketuanan Melayu) and subcontracts it to an ethnically Chinese-owned company. (Pak 2011, cited in Low and Sajnani 2015, p. 35). The "Ali" refers to the Malay while the term: "Baba" refers to the Chinese from the Baba-Nyonya of Straits Chinese people.) Several interviewees further indicated or posed these questions, that is, "if they cannot handle such simple businesses to gain experiences, one would then wonder how can be able to handle bigger business management?" "Why can't the leaders/people, 'the qualified business degree holders' or tradespeople managed these businesses by themselves; these business can indeed possibly or high likely to bring about an income that is better than being in employment." A few expatriates also pointed out that, "it is not the question of eliminating the foreign business people in the country, but more towards, having the leaders/people being able to "manage" and build up their business experiences from the ground level up." Here, the researchers indicated the strong need for actual experiences or experiential learning; all entrepreneurs must have certain degree of real-life managing experiences of handling certain or in fact, any situation(s) which can essentially happen if they themselves were involved in the business itself.

There is a true need to be daring, dare to try, feel or 'test the waters' and to know or at least sense exactly what is truly needed in the reality of a business setting. The latter is vital; after all, theories are mere guidelines or tips, but it's experience that really counts.

To be entrepreneurial, the people must have PHDs. Low and Sajnani (2015, p. 35–36) explained that PHD means that the people are **Poor, Hungry**, starving, and in most ways, **Desperate** or often **Daring**, Dare to try and being as such would boost them to be entrepreneurial. To quote:

> The people, when they are poor—they would surely search for ways to get fed, or survive. They would certainly not want to remain or continue to be poor; they would want to improve and break away from the status quo. Being poor can thus lead them to search for ways to do business and be entrepreneurial. Based on the researchers' observations and travel experiences, they noticed that in Vietnam and Kampuchea, the poor children were resilient; they creatively made model airplanes, cut from thrown-away Cola-Cola cans and toy dragon-flies carved from bamboos. The people really need to be hungry or at least feel a bit of hunger; if people are too secured and comfortable, they would not want to get out of their comfort zone. Conversely, it would be difficult for them to embrace change from safe and steady employment to business and entrepreneurship with uncertain incomes or profits. Only when people are lacking, famished or even a little bit hungry, they've to survive, then, they just have to get up, and they got to, and surely be proactively entrepreneurial. Take the case of India, for example, the spirit of enterprise is much rife. Entrepreneurship helps to reduce poverty while growing the numbers of middle class people within the country; and occasional slum-dog millionaires emerged, being bred in poverty-stricken areas of increasingly prosperous Indian cities such as Mumbai. More and more, everyday individuals with a bit of money, hungry yet with a blob of resourcefulness and abundance of ambition, they feel emboldened to turn to businesses or be entrepreneurs (Gupte 2004, cited in Low and Sajnani 2015). When these successful businesspersons emerge, their examples and cases can be highlighted and publicized; etched in the minds of the young, these role models can be emulated by them. The people also needs to desperate, and that makes them to wanting to get out from the situation.

The present author strongly believes then that leaders may not be poor, but they must be equally motivated and driven to make money, be rich or wealthy; they are not self-satisfied and certainly they do not wish to revert to being poor, suffer or be labelled as a non-leader.

To paraphrase Low and Sajnani (2015, p. 39), one can sum up this pointer that leaders need to be have PHDs: Businesses, together with new products and innovation, will be increasingly crucial to a country's economy. If leaders change the way they think—getting out of their comfort zone and not being self-satisfied but proactive, being global or internationalised, having more role models and family businesses, with more private sector initiative while having more success stories and with the critical mass, surely, the entrepreneurial mind growth in leadership will take shape, be moulded and leaders will even steadily grow from strength to strength.

Tapping the Passion

Live with intention. Walk to the edge. Listen hard. Practice wellness. Play with abandon.
Laugh. Choose with no regret. Appreciate your friends. Continue to learn. Do what
you love.
Live as if this is all there is. (Mary Anne Radmacher)

I like this—what I once came across; Johnny Carson once said, "Never continue in a job you don't enjoy. If you're happy in what you're doing, you'll like yourself, you'll have inner peace. And if you have that, along with physical health, you will have had more success than you could possibly have imagined.'

Note that passion creates energy, eagerness and enthusiasm, and it can also be electrifying. But when passion fades or it no longer exists in us, we can get complacent, slide down and/or get into trouble. However, interestingly, leaders can truly energise and grow their organisations by doing and working more of what they really love. And they can further excite others of their love and interests.

So what does one like and love? What does one really love? Can one tap on one's passion to grow one's Company (Country)?

What more, leaders can also do (more) to find out and tap their people's passion to align with the companies' (countries') vision, mission and values, and further grow their companies (countries). In essence, leaders can tap their (and/or their people's) passion to be differentiator and a game changer while creating a competitive edge for themselves and their companies (organisations/countries)?

Recognising Diamonds in the Rough and Valuing the Talent in People

Anticipate the good so that you may enjoy it. (African saying)

You are beautiful because of your possessions. (African proverb)

Low and Low (2015, pp. 279–280) spoke of the successful leaders' characteristic focus on people. Ray (2009, cited in Low and Low 2015, p. 279) showed that, "Their crews were not mere tools to be used to accomplish a mission, but unique individuals, each with a contribution to make."

Jack Welch cited in Crainer (2002, p. 23) spoke of investing in people and leaders should value people as "the idea flow from the human spirit is absolutely unlimited".

Here, leaders need to polish or refine the ability to recognise creativity and/or talent and not to dismiss people due to preconceptions. In the episode, "Ensign Ro" (Star Trek The Next Generation 2014), a new crewmember was assigned to the ship, with initial displeasure among the crew members due to reports of her actions made during previous assignments. However, when crisis developed and Ro went to Captain Picard to ask for help, Picard made the decision to go ahead in trusting

Ensign Ro due to his own personal experience with her, and not based on reports that he had read.

His trust of her came from his own judgment of her abilities and motives, and not based on negative reports or rumours that he had received. Although wary of any deception, the problem at hand was too great for Captain Picard to dismiss her concerns, and a necessary working relationship was formed. The abilities and potential that Captain Picard saw in Ensign Ro was a determining factor in having her on board the ship in the end, as his own time working with her gave him an insight to her motives and convictions.

Undeniably, there is a need to look past people's weaknesses. In "Hollow Pursuits" (Star Trek The Next Generation 2014), the authors see Barclay's lack of confidence impeded him in carrying out his job, but his talent and insights were very useful to the crew. Geordie La Forge, the chief engineer, made the effort to reach out to him despite his personal feelings, and found out more about Barclay, which became crucial in solving the problem at hand (Low and Low 2015).

Marching Forward with Servant Leadership

Let a poor man live wisely. Let a rich man live wisely. (The Buddha)
Use your strength to help the weak, not humiliate the poor. (The Buddha)

Another critical pointer to avoid complacency is that leaders should remember that they are around to serve rather than (expect) to be served. Jack Welch cited in Crainer (2002) spoke of "Think Service" (Do not expect lest there are utter disappointments.) Leaders are there not because to boost their egos. Ego is indeed a short word but it can offend a bigger issue or thing (a bigger or a longer word) which is called relationships.

Leaders can really get complacent when they care more for themselves or serve their interests better. Chief in the minds of successful leaders is the thinking or priority that they must truly serve their constituents and their people well. [All of us or servant leaders have moral duty to one another and as leaders, we have to serve and lead.] And these they may, at times, do even to the point of making their own (self) sacrifices or in some sense, inconvenienced. Here, a strong service orientation exists or put it in another way, the leaders have a strong desire to help others, rather than the desire to achieve power and control over others.

This, to the author, is very much in line with the essence or spirit of servant leadership.

Interestingly, in Taoism and in nature, it is said that the clouds do not exact compensation from grasses for the value of the rain; trees are not indebted to sun for its abundant warmth. Sun, moon and the earth's mountains are free to the eye.

So too, humankind should be free to each other, helping, receiving and giving; after all as in nature and in a typically green way, giving is a gift of itself and receiving is a type of giving.

Seek and serve, fear not of being rejected, just sit down with people and understand what they are doing and how you can be of help and of benefit to them; listen to them. This is critical in your professional life as in your personal life. When you meet a person, seek out what's critical to that person, what (s)he does and his (her) goals are. Then think of you can serve that person.

Overall, all of us are to serve, share, cooperate and collaborate, and all of us, in spite of everything, are to exist in harmony.

Chapter Conclusion

> When you rise in the morning, give thanks for the light, for your life, for your strength. Give thanks for your food and for the joy of living. If you see no reason to give thanks, the fault lies in yourself. (Tecumseh)

> Do what you can, with what you have, where you are. (Theodore Roosevelt)

As a leader, it is important, to summarise Parry (2001), to ask oneself, "How is this leadership phenomenon manifested in the situation (culture or society/country) to achieve the desired outcomes?"

And overall then, leaders should not be complacent and quite the opposite of being complacent, they must indeed be responsible, caring for and serving their constituents and attending to their respective needs. They are attuned to what their people want. Yes, yet, what more, they put it efforts and strive to achieve even greater heights. Successful leaders always value their people and relationships while factoring in the bigger picture, embracing long-termism, corporate social responsibility (CSR) and being green as well as being earth (universe)-friendly.

Dealing with the mounting competition, withstanding the pressures, fighting fatigue and pushing to the next higher (goal or) level, successful leadership requires much energy (*ki* or *chi*), stamina and resilience

Finally and it's worth repeating here that all of us, not only leaders must realise that success is not a destination, but it's a journey. And all of us—bearing in mind that complacency's the enemy of success—need to pace ourselves accordingly—staying motivated, open, positively driven or mentally strong; being entrepreneurial and staying in charge.

Checkpoint: Think About It

The Future: Going Further, Doing More, Going Stronger

Read and review each section in this chapter.

Answer the questions below.

Review these key points and when you have finished the quiz, check your answers. Check also with your close friends or associates.

Moving from Being Just a Leader to Being a Leadership Titan

1. In what ways can you, as a leader, move to becoming a leadership titan?
2. In what ways can you, as a leader, avoid complacency?
3. In what ways can I avoid getting over-confidence?
4. Are you optimistic? In what ways can you be optimistic?
5. Do you show gratitude to your people?
6. In what ways can you show gratitude to your people?
7. In what ways can I listen to my people/others?
8. Are you getting uncomfortable with change(s)? If so, why? If not, why not?
9. Are you accepting new challenges?
10. Are you taking risks?
11. In what ways do you, as a leader, encourage healthy competition?
12. Do you encourage your teams to compete against themselves?
13. What key value(s) would put you in a steadfast position?
14. What aspects of leadership can you improve in yourself?
15. What are the ways in which you can become a good, if not a great leader? Or in what ways can I, as a leader, excel?

Saving, Sustaining and Growing Organisations

1. In what ways are you, as a leader, will be driving your future?
2. What is your notion or idea of value?
3. What are your Company's/organisation's vision?
4. What are your Company's/organisation's mission?
5. What are your Company's/organisation's values?
6. What is your vision?
7. What is your mission?
8. What are your values?
9. In what ways do your values match or fit with the company's?
10. In what ways can I help to attain or grow my Company's/organisation's vision and mission?
11. What are the ways in which you, as a leader, can prevent yourself from sliding down?
12. What are the ways in which you, as a leader, can prevent your Organisation from sliding down?

Cultivating a Garden of Greatness

1. As a leader, do you appreciate your gifts of creativity?
2. Do you seek to understand and nurture your creativity? In what ways do you seek to understand and nurture your creativity?
3. How can you, as a leader, have fun while being creative?
4. How do you feel when you apply your favourite ways to be creative? How do you express your fun and/or enjoyment?
5. How or in what ways can you, as a leader, translate or transfer your enjoyment and fun of creativity to your people?
6. How or in what ways can you inject creativity and fun to your people?
7. As a leader, do you welcome ideas?
8. How do you welcome ideas from your people?

9. Do you cultivate a garden of greatness?
10. Are you unlocking and growing creativity and innovation within your organisation?
11. In what ways are you growing creativity and innovation within your organisation?
12. Do you encourage your people to do brainstorming?
13. In what ways can you encourage your people to take an opposite (Yang-Yang) view or position to get fresh ideas?
14. Do you encourage your people to take a what-if (hypothetical) position or view (s)?
15. In what ways can you encourage your people to take different (fresh) perspectives?
16. In what ways can you encourage your people to use or apply metaphors and analogies?
17. In what ways can you improve your Company/its products and product packaging?
18. What are the ways that you can do to better serve, service and satisfy your customers?
19. Do you encourage attempts or make tries though they may fail?
20. How do you assess yourself? Are you being more reactive or more responsive?
21. Do you have lesser penalties for failures than penalties for doing nothing?
22. How do you encourage openness?
23. Are you being objective? In what ways you as a leader can be objective?
24. Do you take things personally when you disagree or argue with your people?
25. How do you let them know that you are simply disagreeing or arguing strongly with them and that it does not mean that you dislike the person(s) involved—it just means that they disagree with him (her/them)?

Brining About Learning Organisations
1. As a leader, do you believe in learning?
2. Do you uphold the value of learning?
3. In what ways do you practice the value of learning?
4. In what ways do the Company/organisation practice the value of learning?
5. As a leader, do you believe in learning organisation (LO)?
6. Do you coach others?
7. Do you mentor (advise) others?
8. Do you create a learning organisation culture?

Effecting Instructional Leadership
1. Do you create instructional leadership?
2. In what ways can you create instructional leadership?
3. Do you give feedback to people (others)?
4. Do you get feedback from your people (others)?
5. In what ways do you get feedback from people (others)?

Guaranteeing Gaia
1. How are you in terms of being socially responsible?
2. Do you uphold the value of corporate social responsibility?

3. In what ways can you reduce, reuse and recycle my resources?
4. In what ways can you reduce, reuse and recycle my Company's/organisation's resources?
5. How are you in terms of building or developing your Company's/organisation's corporate social responsibility (CSR)?

Being Self-control and Disciplined and Encouraging Sustainable Development
1. How self-disciplined are you?
2. How much emphasis do you place on the tasks and outcome(s) to be achieved?

Building Relationships
1. How much emphasis do you place on the relationships and the people I know?
2. In what ways am I bridging the gaps between the various generations (e.g. Baby boomers, Generation X, Generation Y, etc.)?
3. In what ways can you, as a leader, create and build trust among my people of me?
4. How are you when it comes to initiating or creating relationships?
5. Identify the ways in which you, as a leader, can initiate or create good relationships with your people?
6. In your own views, how are you when it comes to building relationships?
7. Are you communicating enough to the people around you? How can you communicate further with them?
8. In what ways can you improve or enhance your relationships with your people and followers?
9. Do you care for your people? Do you really care for your people?
10. In what ways do you, as a leader, show that you care for your people?

Powering the Future
1. How do you want to power your future?
2. What would you plan for?
3. What are the ways that you can get from water power?
4. What are the ways that you can get from solar power?
5. What are the ways that you can get from wind power?
6. What are the ways that you can get from recycling (rubbish?) power?
7. What are the ways that you can get from cheaper battery revolution?
8. What are the ways in which you can get from other (alternative) sources of power?

Facing Issues and/or Problems with the Yes Attitude
1. Reflect on negativity or negative thinking. Think of its pluses and minuses.
2. Reflect on positive thinking. Think of its pluses and minuses.
3. Do you have a positive mind growth?
4. In what ways can you grow your positive mind growth?
5. How can one do one's out-of-the-box leadership?

Setting the Sights Further
1. Are you setting your sights further? If so what are they?
2. How can you build your brands?
3. How can you bring and add value to your customers?
4. What services can your Company/you give to your customers?

5. How different can you be? How unique can you be?
6. How can your Country (Company/you) do out-of-the-box thinking?
7. How can your Country (Company/you) do out-of-the-box sales and marketing?
8. How can your Country (Company/you) do out-of-the-box human capital management?
9. How can your Country (Company/you) transform the lives of your people and followers?
10. How can your Country (Company/you) do your out-of-the-box logistics management?

Creating Leadership Circles
1. Have you created leadership circle(s)?
2. How do you form leadership circle(s)?
3. How do you grow ideas in the leadership circles?
4. How do you generate arguments in the leadership circles?
5. How do you handle ideas created by the leadership circles?

Being Entrepreneurial
1. Are you being entrepreneurial? Are you entrepreneurial enough?
2. What are the ways in which you, as a leader, can be (more) entrepreneurial?
3. Are you poor enough to be entrepreneurial?
4. If so, what are the ways in which you can overcome your poverty?
5. Are you motivated enough to be driven to be rich or be wealthy, at least not to suffer or be in a state of poverty or deprivation?
6. In what ways can you, as a leader, become rich or be wealthy?
7. Are you hungry enough to be entrepreneurial?
8. In what ways can you, as a leader, overcome your being not hungry or satisfied?
9. Are you desperate enough to be entrepreneurial?
10. In what ways can you, as a leader, overcome your being desperate?

Tapping the Passion
1. What is your passion? What is your key love?
2. How can you grow your passion (and interests)?
3. Is there any fit or match of your passion with the Company's vision, mission and values?
4. Can you tap on your passion to grow your Country (Company)?
5. In what ways or how can you further tap your passion to further excites others?
6. In what ways can your Company/organisation benefit from your passion?
7. Do you know your (key) people's passion?
8. What are your people's (key) passion(s)?
9. Can your passion (your people's) passion be a game changer (creating an edge for your company)? If so, in what ways can you, as a leader, tap them?
10. In what ways or how can you tap your people's passion to grow them (your Company/organisation)?

Recognising Diamonds in the Rough and Valuing the Talent in People
1. Do you value your people and their talents?
2. Do you really know your people?
3. What talent(s) do your people have? What talent(s) do they really have?

Servant Leadership
1. How can you, as a leader, be a servant leader?
2. In what ways can you best serve your people?
3. How or in what ways can you give to your constituents/people?

References

Accessed August 16, 2016., from https://www.pickthebrain.com/blog/complacency-how-to-avoid-the-silent-killer/#bAXQ2RyiQc86vH1b.99

Channel 5. (2016). *News* 9.00 pm., Channel 5, 23 August 2016, Singapore.

Channel News Asia: CNA. (2016) *News*, 23 August 2016, Singapore.

Crainer, S. (2002). *Business ,the Jack Welch way*. India: Wiley.

Kopans, D. (2016). How to evaluate, manage and strengthen your resilience, 14 June 2016. *Harvard Business Review*. Accessed September 1, 2016, from https://hbr.org/2016/06/how-to-evaluate-manage-and-strengthen-your-resilience?cm_mmc=email-_-newsletter-_-manage ment_tip-_-tip_date&referral=00203&utm_source=newsletter_management_tip&utm_ medium=email&utm_campaign=tip_date

Low, T. W. D., & Low, K. C. P. (2015). What leadership lessons can we glean from Star Trek? *International Journal of Business and Social Science, 6*(2), 273–283.

Low, K. C. P., & Sajnani, M. N. (2015). Who wants to become an entrepreneur in Brunei Darussalam? *International Journal of Business and Social Science, 6*(7), 30–40.

Low, K. C. P., & Teo, T. C. (2015). Tsunami leaders and their style(s) and ways. *International Journal of Business and Social Science, 6*(9), 31–46.

Parry, K. W. (2001). Conclusions, implications and a leader profile. In K. W. Parry (Ed.), *Leadership in the Antipodes: Findings, implications and a leader profile* (pp. 225–241). Wellington, New Zealand: Institute of Policy Studies and the Centre for the Study of Leadership.

Pistrui, J. (2016). To create the future, create a leadership circle. *Harvard Business Review*, 23 June 2016. Accessed September 6, 2016, from https://hbr.org/2016/06/to-seize-the-future-create-a-leadership-circle?cm_mmc=email-_-newsletter-_-management_tip-_-tip_date& referral=00203&utm_source=newsletter_management_tip&utm_medium=email&utm_ campaign=tip_date

Price, A., & Price, D. (2013). *Leadership – A practical guide*. London: Icon Books.

Schlacter, B. (2013). The 10 Commandments of good leadership, 1 April 2013. comerecommended.com. Accessed July 26, 2014, from http://comerecommended.com/the-10-commandments-of-good-leadership/

Senge, P. (1990). *1990, The Fifth Discipline: The art and practice of the learning organization*. New York: Doubleday.

The Straits Times. (2016a). SR Nathan, 1924–2016. *The Straits Times*, 24 August 2016, A4–A6.

The Straits Times. (2016b). National Rally 2016. *The Straits Times*, 23 August 2016, Singapore, p. A16.

Tobin, M. (2013). *5 Steps to avoid complacency*. The Tobin Company. Accessed August 16, 2016, from http://thetobincompany.com/5-steps-to-avoid-complacency/

Index

© Springer International Publishing AG 2018
K.C.P. Low, *Leading Successfully in Asia*,
https://doi.org/10.1007/978-3-319-71347-2

Printed by Books on Demand, Germany